EXCAVATIONS AT HARAPPA

EXCAVATIONS AT HARAPPA

BEING AN ACCOUNT OF ARCHAEOLOGICAL EXCAVATIONS AT HARAPPA CARRIED OUT BETWEEN THE YEARS 1920-21 AND 1933-34

BY

MADHO SARUP VATS, M.A.,

Deputy Director-General of Archaeology in India

In two volumes with plans and plates

Volume I. —Text
Volume II.—139 Plates

GYAN

Published by

Gyan Publishing House
5, Ansari Road
Daryaganj, New Delhi-110002
Phone: 011-47034999, 9811692060
E-mail: books@gyanbooks.com

Distribution Network
gyanbooks.com
India, USA, Canada, UK, Australia, France

ISBN : 978-81-212-2792-6 (HB)
First Published, 1940

2nd Impression 2021

Printed at: Gyan Press, Delhi.

Excavations At Harappa
Author: Madho Sarup Vats

EXCAVATIONS AT HARAPPĀ

BEING AN ACCOUNT OF ARCHÆOLOGICAL EXCAVATIONS AT HARAPPĀ CARRIED OUT BETWEEN THE YEARS 1920-21 AND 1933-34

BY

MADHO SARUP VATS, M.A.,

Deputy Director-General of Archæology in India

In two volumes with plans and plates

Volume I.—Text
Volume II.—139 Plates

PUBLISHED BY MANAGER OF PUBLICATIONS, DELHI
PRINTED BY MANAGER, GOVERNMENT OF INDIA PRESS, CALCUTTA
1940

List of Agents in India from whom Government of India Publications are available.

(a) PROVINCIAL GOVERNMENT BOOK DEPOTS.

ASSAM :—Superintendent, Assam Secretariat Press, Shillong.

BIHAR :—Superintendent, Government Printing, P. O. Gulzarbagh, Patna.

BOMBAY :—Superintendent, Government Printing and Stationery, Queen's Road, Bombay.

CENTRAL PROVINCES :—Superintendent, Government Printing, Central Provinces, Nagpur.

MADRAS :—Superintendent, Government Press, Mount Road, Madras.

NORTH-WEST FRONTIER PROVINCE :—Manager, Government Printing and Stationery, Peshawar.

ORISSA :—Press Officer, Secretariat, Cuttack.

PUNJAB :—Superintendent, Government Printing, Punjab, Lahore.

SIND :—Manager, Sind Government Book Depot and Record Office, Karachi (Sadar).

UNITED PROVINCES :—Superintendent, Printing and Stationery, U. P., Allahabad.

(b) PRIVATE BOOKSELLERS.

Advani & Co., The Mall, Cawnpore.
Aero Stores, Karachi.*
Army Musketry Stores, Moga (Punjab).†
Banthiya & Co., Ltd., Station Road, Ajmer.
Bengal Flying Club, Dum Dum Cantt.*
Bhawnani & Sons, New Delhi.
Bombay Book Depot, Charni Road, Girgaon, Bombay.
Book Company, Calcutta.
Booklover's Resort, Taikad, Trivandrum, South India.
British Book Depot, Lucknow.
British Book Depot, Risalpore.
British Stationery Mart, Booksellers, Peshawar Cantt.
Buckingham & Co., Booksellers and Stationers, Greenwood Street, Sialkot City.
Burma Book Club, Ltd., Rangoon.
Cambridge Book Co., Booksellers, New Dak Bungalow Road, Patna.
Chandrakant Chimanlal Vora, Ahmedabad.
Chatterjee & Co., 3, Bacharam Chatterjee Lane, Calcutta.
Chinoy & Sons, Booksellers, etc., Dhantoli, Nagpur, C. P.
Chukervertty, Chatterjee & Co., Ltd., 13, College Square, Calcutta.
Das Gupta & Co., 54/3, College Street, Calcutta.
Dastane Brothers, Home Service, 456, Raviwar Peth, Poona 2.
Delhi and U. P. Flying Club, Ltd., Delhi.*
Deshmukh Book Depot, Station Road, Sholapur.
English Book Depot, Ferozepore.
English Bookstall, Karachi.
English Book Depot, Taj Road, Agra.
English Book Store, Abbottabad, N.-W. F. P.
Faqir Chand Marwah, Peshawar Cantonment.
Higginbothams, Madras.
Hindu Library, 137-F, Balaram De Street, Calcutta.
H. L. College of Commerce, Co-operative Stores, Ltd., Ahmedabad.
Hyderabad Book Depot, Chaderghat, Hyderabad (Deccan).
Ideal Book Depot, Rajpur Road, Dehra Dun and Bombay Bazar, Meerut.
Imperial Book Depot and Press, near Jama Masjid, (Machhliwalan), Delhi.
Imperial Publishing Coy., Lahore.
Indian Army Book Depot, Dayalbagh, Agra.
Indian Army Book Depot, Daryaganj, Delhi.
Indian School Supply Depot, Central Avenue, South, P. O. Dharamtala, Calcutta.
International Book Service, Poona 4.
Jaina & Bros., Mori Gate Delhi, and Connaught Place, New Delhi, Messrs. J. M.
Joshi, News Agent, Devgad Baria *via* Piplod, Bombay, Mr. V. G.
Kamala Book Depot, 15, College Square, Calcutta.
Kansil & Co., 9, Commercial Buildings, The Mall, Lahore, Messrs. N. C.
Karnataka Sahitya Mandir, Dharwar (S. India).
Keale & Co., 65, Britto Road, Karachi (Sadar).
Kitabistan, 17-A, City Road, Allahabad.
Krishnaswami & Co., Teppakulam P. O., Trichinopoly Fort, Messrs. S.
Lahiri & Co., Ltd., Calcutta, Messrs. S. K.
London Book Co. (India), Arbab Road, Peshawar, Murree, Nowshera, and Rawalpindi.
Lyall Book Depot, Lyallpore.
Malhotra & Co., Post Box No. 94, Lahore, Messrs. U. P.
Mathur & Co., Messrs. B. S., Chatur-Vilas, Paota, Civil Lines, Jodhpur (Rajputana).
Minerva Book Shop, Anarkali Street, Lahore.
Modern Book Depot, Bazar Road, Sialkot Cantt.
Mohanlal Dossabhai Shah, Rajkot.
Mohan News Agency, Kotah (Rajputana).
National Welfare Publicity Ltd., Mangalore.
New Book Co., "Kitab Mahal", 192, Hornby Road, Bombay.
Newman & Co., Ltd., Calcutta, Messrs. W.
Oxford Book and Stationery Company, Delhi, Lahore, Simla, Meerut and Calcutta.
Parikh & Co., Baroda, Messrs. B.
Pioneer Book Supply Co., 20, Shib Narayan Das Lane, Calcutta and 219, Cloth Market, Delhi.
Popular Book Depot, Grant Road, Bombay.
Punjab Religious Book Society, Lahore.
Punjab Sanskrit Book Depot, Lahore.
Raghunath Prasad & Sons, Patna City.
Rama Krishna & Sons, Booksellers, Anarkali, Lahore.
Ram Krishna Bros., Opposite Bishrambag, Poona City.
Ramesh Book Depot and Stationery Mart, Kashmere Gate, Delhi.
Ray & Sons, 43, K. & L. Edwardes Road, Rawalpindi, Murree and Peshawar, Messrs. J.
Reliance Stores, Booksellers, Princess Street, Karachi.
Roy Chowdhury & Co., 72, Harrison Road, Calcutta, Messrs. N. M.
Saraswati Book Depot, 15, Lady Hardinge Road, New Delhi.
Sarcar & Sons, 15, College Square, Calcutta, Messrs. M. C.
Sharada Mandir, Ltd., Nai Sarak, Delhi.
Standard Book Depot, Cawnpore.
Standard Book Depot, Lahore, Delhi and Simla.
Standard Bookstall, Karachi.
Standard Bookstall, Quetta.
Standard Law Book Society, 79/1, Harrison Road, Calcutta.
Subhan, Book-Seller and Publisher, Bilaspur C. P., Mr. M. A.
Swaminatha Sivam & Co., Puddukotah, Messrs. P. N.
Tanawada & Sons, Booksellers, Sangli.
Tara & Sons, Razmak (India), Messrs. B. S.
Taraporevala Sons & Co., Bombay, Messrs. D. B.
Thacker & Co., Ltd., Bombay.
Thacker, Spink & Co. (1933), Ltd., Calcutta.
Tripathi & Co., Booksellers, Princess Street, Kalbadevi Road, Bombay, Messrs. N. M.
Uberoy, J. C., Journalist, Printer and Publisher, Jaycee House, Alexandra Road, Ambala.
University Book Agency, Kacheri Road, Lahore.
Upper India Publishing House, Ltd., Literature Palace, Ammuddaula Park, Lucknow.
Varadachary & Co., Madras, Messrs. P.
Venkatasubban, A., Law Bookseller, Vellore.
Wheeler & Co., Allahabad, Calcutta and Bombay Messrs. A. H.
Young Man & Co. (Regd.), Egerton Road, Delhi.

* Agents for publications on Aviation only.
† Agent for Army Publications only.

PREFACE.

THE excavations at Harappā described in this Volume were carried out between the years 1920-21 and 1933-34. Being one of the two best known and important sites of the Indus Valley Culture, large scale work was undertaken here by the Archæological Department and the excavations have contributed not a little to our knowledge of the prehistoric civilization of India. On account of the close relation and mutual dependence of the discoveries made at Harappā and Mohenjo-daro, this monograph has been planned as a complement to the three monumental volumes on *Mohenjo-daro and the Indus Civilization* edited by Sir John Marshall and the two volumes of *Further Excavations at Mohenjo-daro* by Dr. E. J. H. Mackay. The arrangement of Chapters and Plates follows the former work as far as possible. In *Mohenjo-daro and the Indus Civilization*, Sir John Marshall has most ably dealt with the Art, Religion, Disposal of the Dead, Extent and the Age and Authors of the Indus Civilization mainly on the basis of the discoveries made at the above two sites, while Dr. Mackay has fully described and illustrated numerous finds, mostly identical with those of Harappā—notably Plain and Painted Pottery—and other experts have written on the Indus Script, System of Weights, Minerals and Metals, etc. To that extent, not only has it been possible for me to avoid much needless duplication and to curtail my own work, but what is more, I have derived infinite help and guidance from their masterly handling of so many difficult problems for which I am greatly beholden to them all. To Sir John Marshall I owe a very special and infinite debt of gratitude not only for the thorough guidance and inspiration I received from his great work and the instructions given by him from time to time both in the conduct of excavations and for the preparation of these volumes, but also for the very great trouble he generously undertook (at the sacrifice of much valuable time when he was fully occupied with several pressing works of his own) in preliminarily editing my work, in course of which he made numerous corrections and many valuable suggestions which I have gratefully incorporated.

With the plan and scope thus somewhat defined, I have generally refrained in this monograph from covering common ground as regards various types of finds already described and illustrated in *Mohenjo-daro and the Indus Civilization*, though a little overlapping of such material could not be avoided altogether if the individuality of the site was to be maintained. Happily, Harappā has its own distinct contributions to make to the Proto-Indian Civilization in the shape of the Cemetery with its highly interesting and fascinating pottery much of which is painted and the miniature amulet seals and sealings of an amazing variety of shapes associated with strata of the Middle and Early Periods (Pl. LXXXIV), the like of which are not known elsewhere. These discoveries help us in tracing this civilization forwards and backwards from the time it flourished at Mohenjo-daro.

In making plans of the Cemetery, each burial pot (howsoever small) or earth-burial was plotted with the utmost care: the sections were drawn to the scale of one foot to an inch by means of a dumpy level to allow of groups or individual pots being shown with scientific accuracy exactly in the manner they were found. The whole of Chapter VI, illustrated by 26 Plates (Nos. XLIII-LXVIII), has been devoted to the Cemetery and besides the plans and sections, and photographic views of the two strata of burials and of the contents of burial pots, the types of burial pottery have been illustrated both by means of photographs and drawings, thus bringing out the peculiarities of the highly interesting paintings and the obvious differences between them and the designs painted on household pottery from the city sites (Chapter VII). Inscribed or stamped pottery, again, has been illustrated in 4 Plates (Nos. CI-CIV) as it is much more common here than at Mohenjo-daro. The best buildings, so far discovered in the excavations at Harappā, are those of the Middle Period, which include the Great Granary, one or two better class houses, some neat pavements, wells and two large public drains of rectangular section. The art of Harappā is similar to what is found at Mohenjo-daro, but the Harappā torso of a nude male figure in red sandstone and the statuette of a dancer in grey stone (illustrated in Plates LXXX and LXXXI) perhaps mark the acme of perfection that was seldom attained by the ancients until Greek times. In contrast with these, the statuary at Mohenjo-daro is remarkably poor, even crude. But if Harappā, by its size and importance, may thus be regarded as one of the twin centres of the Indus Valley Civilization, such buildings as it possessed have mostly been swept away by brick diggings carried on for more than three quarters of a century until the site was declared protected in 1920. So few are the structural remains left that for carrying on work and recording finds and other facts, I was compelled to stick on till the end to the system of squares referred to at pp. 8 and 9.

In order to show the extent of this civilization, I have added at the end of this volume very brief notices of two other contemporary sites discovered by me, namely, Chak Purbāne Syāl which lies on the deserted bed of the Beas some 13 miles south-east of Harappā and Koṭla Nihang Khān near Rupar in the Ambala district between the Sutlej and Jamna. To the already known prehistoric sites in Balūchistān, Sindh, Derājāt districts and the Punjāb I should add my latest discovery of a site at Rangpur[1] village in the Limbdi State of Kāthiāwād near the gulf of Cambay. Besides other things, I found that the pottery of this site bore a family likeness to that of the Indus sites and striking resemblances to paintings on the Harappā burial pottery.

The circumstances in which the writing of this monograph was begun were far from propitious. The crippling blows of the retrenchment axe of 1931 brought some special disabilities. The old Hindu and Buddhist Monuments, Northern

[1] *A. S. R.* 1934-35, pp. 34-38, pls. XII-XV.

Circle, Lahore, as Superintendent of which I did most of the excavation work was abolished in 1931 and its Panjab portion amalgamated with the Frontier Circle, to which I was attached *pro tem.* for taking detailed notes and getting together the illustrative Plates. Most of the latter work was accomplished in the years 1932 and 1933 through the very generous help and co-operation of Mr. J. F. Blakiston, then Superintendent of the Frontier Circle, who very kindly placed his Draftsmen and Photographer at my disposal. Without this help, for which I am greatly indebted to him, my work could hardly have taken shape. Early in 1933, I had to take over the charge of the Frontier Circle on Mr. Blakiston's temporary appointment as Director General and subsequent departure on long leave. Retrenchment thus affected the production of this work particularly badly, inasmuch as, instead of being placed on special duty for writing this monograph as originally proposed by Sir John Marshall, I was transferred to Poona in January 1934, as Superintendent of the Western Circle. The manuscript was actually prepared at Poona during the next three years, far away from the scene of my labours and in the midst of heavy duties of the Circle. The magnitude of the task demanded far more concentrated effort than I have been able to devote, but in the circumstances detailed here, I have done my best and must crave the reader's indulgence for my failings of which I am only too conscious.

In the completion of this work, my grateful thanks are due to Khan Bahadur Mohammad Sana Ullah, M.Sc., F.C.S., Archæological Chemist in India, for contributing a very valuable account in Part I, Chapter XIV of "The Sources, Composition and Technique of Copper and its Alloys", for his note on a Harappā linear measure and many analyses of metal and other objects; to Mr. E. A. Wraight, A.R.S.M., M.I.M.M., F.I.C., Metallurgical Inspector, Indian Stores Department, for his "Report of the Metallography of two Ancient Bronze Specimens"; to Mr. H. C. Beck, F.S.A., for his illuminating and highly interesting "Report on Selected Beads from Harappā" (Chapter XV, Part I) each of which has greatly enhanced the value of this work; and last, but not the least, to Rao Bahadur K. N. Dikshit, M.A., F.R.A.S.B., Director General of Archæology in India, who very kindly read through more than half of the proof and made several valuable suggestions, and to Mr. Q. M. Moneer, Superintendent of the Western Circle, for going through my manuscript.

Due to the difficulties briefly referred to above, this work has been deprived of the valuable contribution of Dr. Baini Prasad, Director, Zoological Survey of India, on "The Animal Remains from Harappā" which has already been published as Memoir No. 51 of the Archæological Survey of India and of Dr. B. S. Guha's contribution on the human remains which is not yet ready. I am, however, much indebted to the former for the identification of certain shells and to the latter for his laborious work on the skeletal remains in the Cemetery H and Area G and for all the craniological information contained in this volume; to the Director, Geological Survey of India and Mr. A. L. Coulson of his Department for the determination of certain stones; to Sir Bryce Burt, formerly Agricultural Expert of the Imperial Council of Agricultural Research, to Rai Sahib

Jaichand Luthra, Associate Professor of Botany at the Punjab Agricultural College, Lyallpur and to the Director, Royal Botanic Gardens, Kew, Surrey, for the identification of certain cereals; to Mr. V. Narayanaswami of the Royal Botanic Gardens, Sibpur, Calcutta, for the identification of several varieties of charcoal, and all authors referred to in the bibliography for the great help I have derived from their works.

My best thanks are also due to Pandit K. N. Sastri, Excavation Assistant, for much help in preliminary work; to Mr. Sadhu Ram, Assistant Surveyor, and Messrs. U. C. Chopra, N. K. Bose and S. S. Sarkar for careful work on the skeletal remains; to Messrs. Jata Shankar, Abdus Salam and S. P. Date, Draftsmen, for the preparation of drawings and the Sign Manual; to Messrs. Mangat Rai Mehta and J. P. Joglekar, Photographers, for the photographic plates and to Messrs. Ishwar Dass Mehta and R. D. Gupta, my Clerk and Stenographer respectively, for much laborious typing of the manuscript.

I am also greatly indebted to Messrs. D. D. Majumdar and R. A. Halfhide, Deputy Controllers of the Printing and Stationery Department, India, for their very sympathetic and helpful attitude in pushing the publication through the Government of India Press, Calcutta.

TABLE OF CONTENTS.

PAGES.

CHAPTER I.

THE COUNTRY, CLIMATE, SYSTEM OF SQUARES, STORY OF EXCAVATIONS, ETC.

CHAPTER II.

MOUND F.

PAGES.

CHAPTER III.

MOUND AB.

CHAPTER IV.

AREA J.

CHAPTER V.

AREA G.

PAGES.

CHAPTER VI.

AREA H: THE PREHISTORIC CEMETERY.

CHAPTER VII.

PAINTED POTSHERDS FROM VARIOUS MOUNDS AND THEIR CLASSIFICATION.

CHAPTER VIII.

HOUSEHOLD POTTERY JARS AND POST-CREMATION URNS FROM THE MOUNDS TOGETHER WITH TABULATION OF THE LATTERS CONTENTS.

CHAPTER IX.

PLAIN AND PAINTED POTTERY.

CHAPTER X.

HUMAN AND ANIMAL FIGURINES.

CHAPTER XI.

STONE AND FAIENCE VESSELS AND UNGUENT VASES.

CHAPTER XII.

SEALS AND SEAL IMPRESSION WITH TABULATION.

CHAPTER XIII.

HOUSEHOLD OBJECTS, TOOLS AND IMPLEMENTS.

CHAPTER XIV.

PART I.—THE SOURCES, COMPOSITION AND TECHNIQUE OF COPPER AND ITS ALL ALLOYS.

By KHAN BAHADUR MOHAMMAD SANA ULLAH, M.Sc., F.C.S.,
Archæological Chemist in India.

PAGES.

PART II.—COPPER, BRONZE AND SILVER UTENSILS AND OTHER METAL OBJECTS.

By the Author.

CHAPTER XV.

PART I.—REPORT ON SELECTED BEADS FROM HARAPPĀ.

By MR. H. C. BECK, F.S.A.

PART II.—PERSONAL ORNAMENTS.

By the Author.

CHAPTER XVI.

Playthings and Games.

CHAPTER XVII.

Ivory, Shell, Faience and other Objects of Technical Interest.

PAGES.

CHAPTER XVIII.

FURNACES IN TRENCH IV, MOUND F.

CHAPTER XIX.

CHAK PŪRBĀNE SYĀL AND KOṬLA NIHANG KHĀN.

TEXT ILLUSTRATIONS.

BOOKS CITED.

ALOYS SPRENGER.—*El Masudi's Historical Encyclopædia* entitled "Meadows of Gold and Mines of Gems", Vol. I, 1841.

Annual Report of the Archæological Survey of India, 1908-09, 1920-21, 1923-24, 1924-25, 1926-27, 1927-28, 1928-29, and 1934-35.

Archæologia, Vol. LXXVII.

BECK, H. C.—"Beads from Nineveh", *Antiquity*. December, 1931.

„ "Etched Carnelian Beads", *Antiquaries' Journal*, Vol. XIII.

„ "Etched Carnelians", *Antiquaries' Journal*, Vol. XIII.

„ "Note on certain Agate Beads", *Antiquaries' Journal*, 1930. Vol. X, No. 2.

Cambridge Ancient History, Plates Vol.

CUNNINGHAM, A.—*Ancient Geography of India* edited by S. N. Majumdar. 1924.

„ *Archæological Survey of India Report*, Vol. V.

CURZON, LORD G. N.—*Persia and the Persian Question*. 2 Vols. 1892.

DESCH, C. H.—*Report of the British Association for the Advancement of Science*, 1928-31.

Encyclopædia Britannica. Vols. 15 & 18. 14th edition.

Encyclopædia of Religion and Ethics, Vol. 4.

FRANKFORT, H.—"Sumerians, Semites, and the origin of Copper-working", *Antiquaries' Journal*, April. 1928, VIII.

Gazetteer of the District of Montgomery. 1883-84.

GORDON CHILDE.—*New Light on the Most Ancient East*.

GREGG, J. L.—*Arsenical and Argentiferous Copper*.

GRIFFITH, R. T. H.—*Hymns of the Rigveda*, Third Edition. 2 Vols. 1920.

„ *Hymns of the Atharva-Veda*, Second Edition. 2 Vols. 1916.

Indian Antiquary, Vols. XXXIV and XXXVI.

Journal Royal Anthropological Institute, Vol. XXXVI.

KEITH, A. B.—*Religion and Philosophy of the Veda and Upanishads*. 2 Vols. 1925.

KING, L. W.—*A History of Sumer and Akkad*.

LANGDON, S.—*Excavations at Kish*, Vol. I. 1924.

LA TOUCHE, T. H. D.—*A bibliography of Indian Geology and Physical Geography*. Part II. 1918.

LAW, E. F.—*Alloys*.

LUCAS, A.—*Ancient Egyptian Materials*. 1926.

LYDEKKER, R.—*Game Animals of India, Burma, Malaya and Tibet*. 1907.

MACKAY, E. J. H.—*Further Excavations at Mohenjo-Daro*, Vols. I—II. 1938.

MARSHALL, SIR JOHN.—*Mohenjo-daro and the Indus Civilization*, Vols. I—III. 1931.

Memoirs of the Archæological Survey of India.

NILSSON, M. P.—*The Minoan-Mycenæan Religion*, 1927.

PEAKE, H.—"Copper Mountain of Megan" *Antiquity*, Dec. 1928.

PETRIE, SIR FLINDERS.—*Arts and Crafts of Ancient Egypt*.

„ *Objects of Daily Use*. 1927.

„ *Tools and Weapons*. 1917.

PENDLEBURY, JOHN.—*Tell El-Amarna*. 1935.

PUMPELLY, R.—*Explorations in Turkestan*, Vol. I. 1908.

REA, A.—*Catalogue of Prehistoric Antiquities*, Adichanallur and Perumbair. 1915.

RICKARD, T. A.—*Man and Metals.*

ROY, S. C.—"*Distribution and Nature of Asur Sites in Chota Nagpur.*" J. B. & O. R. S. Sept. 1920.

SMITH, V. A.—*The Early History of India.* 4th Ed. 1924.

WOOLLEY, SIR LEONARD.—*The Sumerians.*

" *Ur Excavations*, Vol. II.

" *Ur of the Chaldes.*

" *Digging up the Past.*

ABBREVIATIONS.

A. S. R.	Annual Reports of the Archæological Survey of India.
B. S.	Below surface.
C. A. H.	Cambridge Ancient History.
Chap.	Chapter.
Cir.	Circa.
C. S. R.	Archæological Survey of India Reports by A. Cunningham.
Dg.	Designation.
Diag.	Diagonal.
Diam.	Diameter.
Edn.	Edition.
E. R. E.	Encyclopædia of Religion and Ethics.
Ff.	Following.
Fig.	Figure.
Ft.	Foot or feet.
Ht.	Height.
In.	Inch or inches.
L.	Length.
Mem. A. S. I.	Memoirs of the Archæological Survey of India.
M. I. C.	Mohenjo-daro and the Indus Civilisation.
P.	Page.
Pl.	Plate.
Pp.	Pages.
Sq.	Square.
Th.	Thickness.
Vol.	Volume.
W.	Width.

EXCAVATIONS AT HARAPPĀ

CHAPTER I.

The Country, Climate and Rivers, System of Squares, Story of Excavations, etc.

Natural fertility of the district round Harappā.

THERE was a time when the tract of country comprising the present District of Montgomery must have been far more fertile than it is at present. That was when the Rāvi[1] comprised two streams instead of one, which (confluencing at Harappā) ran parallel to each other at distances of four and eight miles respectively to the south of its present bed. At that time, the Beās bisecting the whole district, as indicated by its deserted ancient bed, also flowed in a tortuous way skirted by the great Dhāyā[2] ridge; and the Sutlej alone ran along its south-east border. Moreover, the valley which lay between the ancient bed of the Beās and the present Sutlej was then irrigated by two other streams, *viz.*, the Sohāg north and south and the Pārā distributary.[3] Thus, we may then visualise the waters of these meandering rivers perennially supplying more than ample means of irrigation and inundating the country at the time of annual floods during which they deposited the rich alluvium for which the Rāvi with its tributary the Deg,[4] which joins it at Ghaṭṭā Phaknī Hithār near Sayyadwālā, are regarded as specially valuable. No doubt, too, the Rāvi, the Beās, and the Sutlej served as dependable waterways for frequent and easy communication by the people living on their banks, otherwise it is unlikely that large cities like Harappā would have sprung up on their banks. The uniformity of their culture as revealed by the excavations at Mohenjo-daro and Harappā in " houses, drains, bricks, pottery, weapons, household utensils, ornaments, seals ",[5] etc., is so complete that essential similarity of life in the two cities and constant mutual

---

[1] Both of them having dried are now termed *Sukhrāvās*.

[2] This is described as follows in the *Montgomery District Gazetteer* at pp. 1 and 2 " Almost in the middle of the district, in the Bāri Doāb a ridge of high land runs from north-east to south-west, the whole length of the district. This ridge is often called the Dhāyā, though the term is more properly applied to the slope to the top of the ridge from the low lands at its foot. This slope is generally gradual, and in places, especially on the northern or Rāvi side of the ridge, almost imperceptible. The slope on the southern, or Sutlej side, is more marked, and towards the Lahore border it becomes very abrupt, and is cut into deep chasms by the rain-water running down into the valley beneath. The edge of the high bank here bears a remarkable resemblance to the right bank of the Beās (*Sic.* Sutlej as the Beās does not touch anywhere near Phillour) as seen at Phillour. The average breadth of this ridge is about ten miles. The country slopes down from the top of it to the rivers, the slope to the Sutlej opposite Montgomery being about 40 feet, and to the Rāvi half that." Regarding the ancient courses of the Rāvi and Beās on either side of the Dhāyā ridge see p. 2 of the Gazetteer.

[3] The above river system is shown in Survey of India maps drawn to a scale of 1 inch to four miles and is described in the *Montgomery District Gazetteer*, pp. 2 *ff.* See also V. A. Smith, *The Early History of India*, Fourth Edition, pp. 40-41.

[4] *District Gazetteer*, p. 5.

[5] *M. I. C.*, p. 91.

Places connected by land and water.

intercourse between them may be taken for granted. The finds of *śaṅkh*, coral, and mussel shells presuppose communication with the sea; steatite, copper and lead with Rājpūtāna; agate, agate-jasper, carnelian, onyx and chalcedony with Kāthiāwād and Rājpīpla; green earth with Balūchistān; gold with South India and Afghānistān, the Faranjāl mine in the latter being a possible source of silver also; hæmatite and red ochre with Hormuz and other islands in the Persian Gulf; while nearer sources for alabaster would have been the Salt Range and for slate the Kāṅgra and Gurgāon Districts of the Panjāb.[1] It may thus be assumed that there must have been frequent communication mainly by the rivers, but overland as well, with many contemporary towns and sites in Sind, Rājpūtāna, and perhaps also with a number of places in Balūchistān where numerous prehistoric sites have been discovered due west of the Lārkāna District in Sind and the Derājāt Districts in the Panjāb. Presumably, numerous contemporary sites must also have existed between the Bāri Doāb and the Sind Sāgar Doāb which will doubtless be discovered[2] when systematic exploration comes to be undertaken in those districts, and with which it would be natural to suppose that Harappā had frequent communication.

Situation and means of access.

In this well watered district on the north bank of the great Dhāyā ridge, stands Harappā at the confluence of the two *Sukhrāvās*.[3] Its exact situation is in north latitude 30° 38′, east longitude 72° 52′, that is to say, some four miles north-east-north of Harappā Road, a station on the North Western Railway with which it is connected by a *kachchā* service road, and 15 miles west-south-west of Montgomery town, the District headquarters. From the latter, it can be reached along the canal bank road except for the last two miles which are traversed by the service road referred to above.

Extent of mounds as estimated by Burnes and Cunningham.

The mounds at Harappā are a prominent landmark in the countryside visible long distances away. They were visited by Masson in 1826, by Burnes five years later, and by General Cunningham twice in 1853 and 1856. Burnes estimated the extent of the ruins as "about three miles in circumference, which", says Cunningham, "is one-half too much, as the actual ruined mound forms an irregular square of only half a mile on each side or two miles in circuit. But this comprises only the remains of the walled town, to which we may fairly add the suburbs, or fields now covered with the broken bricks or other remains, which would bring the size of the old town quite up to Burnes's estimate."[4] Cunningham published a plan of the mounds together with an account of what he saw in 1853 and again in 1856 in his Annual Report for 1872-73.[5] "On the north, the west and the south", says he, "there is a continuous line of mounds about 3,500 feet in length, but on the east side, which is only 2,000 feet in length, there is a complete gap of 800 feet, for which I am unable to account. The whole circuit of ruins is, therefore, about 12,500 feet or nearly 2½ miles. The

[1] For sources of the above minerals and metals see *M. I. C.*, Chap. XXXII.

[2] In 1937 five prehistoric sites have been discovered in the Shaikhupura district, viz., Asrur and Kala Shah Kaku by Dr. C. L. Fābri and Mian Ali Sahib, Khaira Khazana and Momanpura Tibba by Mr. H. L. Srivastava.

[3] A local term meaning dry bed of the Rāvi.

[4] Cunningham, *Ancient Geography of India*, 1924 Edition, p. 242.

[5] *C. S. R.*, Vol. V. pp. 105-108.

highest mound is on the north-west, which is 60 feet above the fields. On the south-west and south the mounds range from 40 to 50 feet in height, and on the north side towards the old bed of the Rāvi, from 25 feet to 30 feet." Cunningham traced the remains of flights of steps on both the eastern and western faces of the high mound at the north-west, as well as the basement of a large square building. This part has been designated on his plan as AB. None of these structures is traceable now, though the tomb of Naugazā and the ruined Id-gāh are still to be seen on the eastern slope of the mound. Cunningham also saw on the south face of the southern mound, designated E[1] on his plan, the traces of a large square building with rooms on four sides surrounding a courtyard, the walls of which were said to be very massive.

Buildings noticed by Cunningham.

According to him the remains at Harappā had more than sufficed to furnish brick ballast for about 100 miles of the Lahore-Multān Railway. Since then brick-digging has been carried on with equal vigour by the people as a ready means of livelihood, for, it is patent that the town of Harappā, which shelters about 5,000 souls, as well as some neighbouring *Chaks* (colonies) mainly owe their burnt brick houses to these ruins. The mounds were declared protected under the Ancient Monuments Preservation Act (VII) of 1904 only in January, 1920, and it was not till 1919 that the first brick kiln for manufacturing bricks was started here. Regarding the spoliation of the mounds Cunningham says "I made several excavations at Harappā, but the whole surface had been so completely cleared out by the railway contractors that I found very little worth preserving". Working on Mound D, I myeself picked up an iron fish-plate and a few bolts of the light railway mentioned by General Cunningham. After eleven years work by the Archæological Department, it is all too apparent that General Cunningham was justified in what he said; and from the time of his visit in 1856 till the protection of the mounds in 1919, under the Ancient Monuments Preservation Act, the depredations, referred to by him, went on to an ever increasing extent. The little that has actually survived is a perpetual puzzle which at every step baffles the excavator. Only once in a while can one hope to find anything more than a complete room, let alone houses, streets and such elaborate complexes as are to be seen at Mohenjo-daro.

Mounds freely used for ballast and modern buildings.

As far as is known, the ruins of Harappā are the most extensive of all old sites in the Montgomery District. From the *Sukhrāvā*, the mounds extend southwards roughly in a parallelogram of which the circuit is nearly two and a half miles—a circuit very near to Cunningham's estimate (Pl. I). Together with the low-lying tumuli, however, *viz.*, Area G to the south-east, the cultivated fields to the east of the *Thānā* mound, and to the south-west of Mounds AB and D, the Cemetery H, and the low oval tumulus which forms the westward continuation of Mound F, the circuit is over $3\frac{1}{2}$ miles, but it is not possible now to determine the exact extent of the ruins. What Cunningham calls a gap of 800 feet on the east side is in reality the low-lying section between the mounds occupied by the *Thānā* and the modern town of Harappā. Like the valley formed between the latter and Mound F and that enclosed within the parallelogram of the mounds,

Full extent of ruins not yet determined.

[1] To avoid confusion Cunningham's nomenclature has been adopted on the plan of Harappā, Pl. I.

Present condition of the mounds.

it was once an inhabited part of the city, generally older than the settlements higher up the mounds. The latter have shrunk not a little, while the low lying tumuli, now mostly converted into smiling fields by irrigation from the Lower Bāri Doāb Canal, have either been totally swept away or become so worn that there is now little to distiuguish them from the surrounding fields except the tiny bits of potsherds and brickbats with which their surface is strewn.

Owing to excessive saltpetre in the Dhāyā plateau the soil sustains little besides the evergreen *farash* (*Tamarix orjentalis*), *karil* (*Capparis aphya*), *wan* (*Vitex negundo*), *jand* (*Prosopis Spicigera*), *ber* (*Zizyphus Jujube*) and some coarse wild grasses, including the *sarr* (*Saccharum munja*) which is particularly useful in providing reeds for thatched roofs and bark for making ropes. The trees mentioned above grow as well on the mounds as they do over the rest of the plateau.

Climate and rainfall.

Regarding the present day climate I quote the following from the *District Gazetteer of Montgomery*[1] "From May to the middle of October the heat during the day is intense, but the nights are fairly cool. Towards the end of August the mornings become a little fresh and about the middle of September a change in temperature after sunset may be noticed. A breeze, often changing into a strong wind, blows usually at night during the hot weather. Dust-storms are not uncommon. Hail-storms are very rare. The rains set in generally about the end of June. The fall is, on the average, greatest in August. The rains, as a rule, cease in this month. In November it never rains. About the end of the year a couple of showers may be expected, and again in March. During the four months from November to February, inclusive, the days are not hot and the nights are cold with frequent frost." The average rainfall during the last ten years in the Montgomery *Tehsil* is ten inches only, but in 1932 the rainfall was as low as 4·52 in. and in 1931, 15·38 in.[2] The present aridity of climate and general aspect of the country round Harappā is very much the same as at Mohenjo-daro. And in the prehistoric period, with which we are concerned here, the similarity between the two would appear to have been no less striking inasmuch as both appear to have been far more fertile and to have had a substantially heavier rainfall then than now.[3] Let me point out to a few specific features in support. Firstly, from the earliest level or the VIIIth stratum in Mound F, the use of burnt brick was as common here as at Mohenjo-daro, though from the VIth stratum onwards till the latest occupation on the site sun-dried brick is found to have been used side by side with burnt brick. Secondly, with a favourable river system described above there must also have been good forests and sufficient vegetation to induce a larger rainfall than at present. And, thirdly, the animals depicted on the Harappā and Mohenjo-daro seals, as already pointed out by Sir John Marshall,[4] are commonly found in a damp,

Internal evidence of higher rainfall in the prehistoric period.

---

[1] P. 15.

[2] I am indebted for this information to the Director General of Observatories, Poona.

[3] For the natural fertility and more abundant rainfall at Mohenjo-daro during the prehistoric times see *M. I. C.*, Chap. I.

[4] *M. I. C.*, p. 2.

jungly country.[1] The cumulative effect of this evidence tends to show that during the prehistoric period the rainfall at Harappā was materially in excess of what it is now, and consequently the climate may be supposed to have undergone a substantial change. "Muslim writers up to the close of the fourteenth[2] century A. D. frequently allude to the rainy seasons in the Multān Province, which is now well within the dry zone, though it occasionally feels the force of cyclonic storms travelling westward from the head of the Bay."[3] Moreover, Sind and the Panjāb were reputed the richest and the most populous of all the *Satrapies*[4] of the Achaemenid Empire, and the same picture is drawn of the country round Kamāliā and Shorkot by the historians of Alexander the Great who fought some memorable battles[5] with the Malloi on the confluence of the Hydraōtes (Rāvi) with the Asekinēs (Chināb) including the Hydaspes (Jihlam). Thus, we have reason to picture the present Montgomery District as at least fairly well wooded in the prehistoric period with plenty of cultivation and pasturage—a tract of country which would be singularly well fitted for focussing a big population in a large city like Harappā. We may also reasonably assume that the Beās, when it flowed across the Montgomery District along the great Dhāyā ridge, was, like the Rāvi, mostly a beneficent river.

Historical evidence.

The following picture of the life[6] that was lead by the Indus peoples of the 3rd and 4th millenia B. C. who were in possession of a highly developed culture, in which no vestige of Indo-Āryan influence is to be found, is drawn by Sir John Marshall and is based on the discoveries made at Mohenjo-daro and Harappā. "Like the rest of Western Asia, the Indus Country is still in the Chalcolithic Age—that age in which arms and utensils of stone continue to be used side by

Life of the Indus peoples.

[1] *Cf.* Dr. Baini Prashad, *Mem. A.S.I.*, No. 51, p. 31, where he remarks that "The find (from Trench VI, Mound F) of an almost complete right shoulder girdle of rhinoceros at Harappā considered with the records detailed above indicates that the distribution of this species in the earlier times was much more extensive in the Punjāb and that probably there were marshy forest areas in the neighbourhood of Harappā where the rhinoceros was found". Marshes in the river valleys in the area corresponding to the present district of Montgomery are referred to in connection with Alexander's campaign against the formidable tribe of the Malloi. *Cf.* V. A. Smith, *The Early History of India*, Fourth Edn., p. 100.

[2] A'l Masūdi of Baghdād who visited the Indus Valley in 915 A. D. in his famous work "*The Meadows of gold* (942 *A. D.*)" has left a glowing account of Mutlān which he describes as the greatest of the countries in the neighbourhood of which were 1,00,000 villages and estates, which fact testifies to the fertility of the region during the early period of Muhammadan occupation. *Cf.* Aloys Sprenger's English Translation of El-Masudi's *Historical Encyclopaedia* entitled "*Meadows of gold and Mines of gems*", Vol. I, p. 384, Edn. 1841.

[3] *M. I. C.*, p. 4.

[4] *Ibid.*, p. 6; see also V. A. Smith, *op. cit.*, p. 40.

[5] In order to offer strenuous resistance to the invasion of Alexander, the confederacy of the gallant Malloi, the Oxydrakai and other independent tribes raised a large force comprising "80,000 or 90,000 fully equipped infantry, 10,000 cavalry, and from 700 to 900 chariots". But before the Oxydrakai could come to the aid of the Malloi, Alexander with a flying column at his disposal completely surprised the latter and swept down upon them, while they were working unarmed in fields, and extinguished their military power. In their flight they were pursued in the marshes on the ford of the Hydraōtes (Rāvi) which was defended by 50,000 men and in a small fortified town near the boundary of the Jhang and Montgomery districts 80 or 90 miles to the north-east of Multān. Mustering of such heavy forces, and subsequent submission of the Malloi and the Oxydrakai to Alexander who received from the latter "presents which are said to have included 1,030 four-horsed chariots, 1,000 bucklers of native manufacture, 100 talents of steel, great store of 'linen' goods, a quantity of tortoise-shells, the skins of large lizards, with tame lions and tigers, in addition to a contingent of 300 horsemen" testify to the great prosperity of the region between the Chināb and Beās. *Cf.* V. A. Smith, *op. cit.*, pp. 98-102.

[6] *M. I. C.*, Preface, pp. v and vi.

side with those of copper or bronze. Their society is organized in cities; their wealth derived mainly from agriculture and trade, which appears to have extended far and wide in all directions. They cultivate wheat and barley as well as the date-plam. They have domesticated the humped zebu, buffalo, and short horned bull, besides the sheep, pig, dog, elephant, and camel; but the cat[1] and probably the horse[2] are unknown to them. For transport they have wheeled vehicles, to which oxen doubtless were yoked. They are skilful metal workers, with a plentiful supply of gold, silver, and copper. Lead, too, and tin are in use, but the latter only as an alloy in the making of bronze. With spinning and weaving they are thoroughly conversant. Their weapons of war and of the chase are the bow and arrow, spear, axe, dagger, and mace. The sword they have not yet evolved; nor is there any evidence of defensive body armour. Among their other implements, hatchets, sickles, saws, chisels, and razors are made of both copper and bronze; knives and celts sometimes of these metals, sometimes of chert or other hard stones. For the crushing of grain they have the muller and saddle-quern but not the circular grindstone. Their domestic vessles are commonly of earthenware turned on the wheel and not infrequently painted with encaustic designs; more rarely they are of copper, bronze, or silver. The ornaments of the rich are made of the precious metals or of copper, sometimes overlaid with gold, of faience, ivory, carnelian, and other stones; for the poor, they are usually of shell or terracotta. Figurines and toys, for which there is a wide vogue, are of terracotta, and shell and faience are freely used, as they are in Sumer and the West generally, not only for personal ornaments but for inlay work and other purposes. With the invention of writing the Indus peoples are also familiar, and employ for this purpose a form of script which, though peculiar to India, is evidently analogous to other contemporary scripts of Western Asia and the Nearer East."

Food. Besides the cultivation of wheat, barley, and date-palm, evidence of which has also been found at Mohenjo-daro, the inhabitants of Harappā cultivated peas and sesamum too. Nevertheless, for their food they were not dependent entirely on agriculture, for it is notorious that there is hardly a place at Harappā[3] where bones are not upturned by the spade. Moreover, the numerous sling balls of clay, the copper fish hooks, the arrow-heads, the flaying knives, constitute sufficient proof, if proof were needed, of the extent to which the inhabitants of Harappā depended for their food on birds and beasts and fish. Among the animal remains from Harappā Dr. Baini Prashad[4] has identified several fragments of hyoplastron, hypoplastron and xiphiplastron species of turtle which were caught for food and found at depths varying from 5 ft. to 13 ft. 6 in. in Mound F.

[1] An example of a terracotta quadruped, which looks like a cat, has been discovered at Harappā and is figured in Pl. LXXIX, 58. Bones of cat from Harappā have also been identified by Dr. Baini Prashad, *vide Mem. A.S.I.*, No. 51, pp. 7-8 and 15-17 (Pl. II, figs. 2 and 2a). Dr. Prashad concludes that "The Harappā Cat appears to be the first representative of the Domestic Cat, the remains of which have so far been unearthed any where in India. I, therefore, following Hilzheimer and Pocock have adopted for it the name *Felis ocreata* Gmelin, race *domestica* Brisson".

[2] The remains of ass, though not of horse, have also been found at Harappā, *vide* Dr. Prashad, *op. cit.*, p. 8.

[3] At Mohenjo-daro bones are not so ubiquitous.

[4] *Mem. A.S.I.*, No. 51, pp. 14-15.

Change in the river system in Montgomery District.

The southward recession of the Beās, which now joins the Sutlej above Ferozepur, must have had a very destructive effect on what is now known as the Beās *bār*.[1] For not only did it cease to irrigate the country south of the Dhāyā ridge, but, on the contrary, when combined with the mighty Sutlej began to be productive of great havoc. It is stated in the Gazetteer that "The course of the river[2] is tolerably straight. But it is very changeable. It is impossible to say where it may be any one year. Whole villages,—indeed clusters of villages,—are one week on the right bank, the next on the left." The recession of the Beās was seemingly the direct cause of the destruction of the prehistoric site at Chak Pūrbāne Syāl[3] which stands at the south end of the Bahlolwala minor[4] at the opposite edge of the Dhāyā ridge from where Harappā is not more than 12 miles.

Change in the course of the Rāvi and destruction of Harappā.

Similarly, the destruction of Harappā is apparently due mainly to the change in the course of the Rāvi which now flows some six miles north. There was nothing to sustain a flourishing city like Harappā after the river had shifted far away, for it must be remembered that the Dhāyā plateau on which the ancient ruins stand was entirely uncultivated before the construction of the Lower Bāri Doāb Canal which now bisects it. The soil of the plateau is generally inferior and saline, at places remarkably so, though with the present plentiful supply of water much of the land has been brought under cultivation.

Danger from floods.

That during the prehistoric period, despite the beneficent river system with an equitable distribution of water in the area which now corresponds to the Montgomery District, and despite also the extremely tortuous and consequently much longer and less destructive course of the ancient Rāvi, the site was not infrequently exposed to floods is proved by the solid masses of sun-dried brick filling at the foot and on the sides of almost all the mounds. From such low levels as the southern foot of Mound D (contour line 545 ft.) the filling is found to rise 15 ft. along the northern edge of Mound AB (contour line 560 ft., Pl. II, *a* and *d*, and Pl. XXXVI, *e*). Such filling is also quite common in the lower parts of Mound D and in the valley between it and Mound AB. As the level of the ruins gradually rose it was put in higher and higher. Laborious work like this is not likely to have been carried out, unless there was a very real danger from floods, the more so as most of the buildings, exposed, are not such as to have justified costly plinths or artificial terraces. Thus, it was probably on account of the ever present danger of floods that what now appear to be large gaps on the east and north sides of the valley enclosed by the mounds, were, in reality, among the oldest[5] parts of the site to be occupied, and were gradually abandoned in favour of the higher mounds to which the population was obliged to shift.

---

[1] This is a Panjābi term denoting an uncultivated tract of land.

[2] Before entering the Montgomery district the Beās has already merged into the Sutlej. See *Montgomery District Gazetteer*, p. 3.

[3] For its description see Chapter XIX *infra*.

[4] This term is used by the Irrigation Department for a watercourse of lesser capacity than a distributary.

[5] In course of digging for foundations of modern houses ancient remains have actually been brought to light in what Cunningham calls a gap of 800 ft. on the east side, and from Extension I of Trench VI, Mound F, p. 206 *infra* (Pl. XXVI) it is clear that below the cultivated fields there are the regular remains of ancient houses.

Configuration of mounds.

As already stated, the principal mounds form a rough parallelogram. Those designated AB, E, and the one occupied by the present town are higher and larger than Mounds F, D and the *Thānā* Mound.[1] The contours[2] of the town mound and of Mounds F and D do not follow each other so quickly as those of the remaining three. On the other hand, the Cemetery H and Area G, lying as they do almost on the level of surrounding fields, are hardly noticeable. How these various parts were inter-connected, one with the other, is difficult to say since up till now excavations have been confined, principally to Mound F, and to parts of Mound AB, Areas J, G, and the Cemetery H. Nevertheless, it may be inferred that, when the valley was occupied by a continuous series of buildings there must have existed a public thoroughfare aligued, perhaps as at present, from east to west, and another one taking off from it and going south from between the *Thānā* and Mound E towards Area G. At present, however, this is nothing more than a surmise. With the shrinkage and successive occupation of the mounds the level of the ancient thoroughfares has also risen. For instance, the level of the Workmen's Quarters in the southern part of Trench IV in Mound F is lower than that of the present thoroughfare which passes along their south border, but it is possible that it might be lying on some building contemporary with the Workmen's Quarters beneath which, again, there are the remains of four earlier strata.

Alignment of ancient thoroughfares.

Site plan.

The plan of the ancient site of Harappā, which appears on Pl. I, has been drawn on a scale of 500 ft. to an inch. The contours on it indicate a vertical rise of five feet in level and their values have been co-ordinated with sea-level as recorded at the bridge over the Lower Bāri Doāb Canal which flows half way between the site and the Harappā Road railway station.

The discoveries which had already been made by the Archæological Department at Nāl, Mohenjo-daro, Taxila, Nālanda and other sites had fortunately roused such wide spread interest that Sir John Marshall—then Director General of Archæology in India—had little difficulty in 1925 in persuading Government to grant more liberal funds for exploration. Accordingly, in 1926-27 it became possible to construct at Harappā a small building consisting of two rooms for antiquities, one workroom and a room for the Superintendent, and to this was subsequently added another large room at the back also. This supplied a long felt want and enabled all antiquities to be housed locally, but unfortunately financial stringency soon followed and stood in the way of providing appropriate showcases for exhibiting many of the important finds.

System of squaring.

To co-ordinate the entire site and to locate accurately the finds and scattered bits of surviving buildings, a comprehensive system of squaring has been found absolutely necessary. For this purpose the whole site has been divided into squares measuring one hundred feet each way, those running west to east being named A, B, C, etc., and similarly those going from north to south, 1, 2, 3, and so on. Each of these major squares has been divided, again, into twentyfive smaller squares whose numbers have been given on the plans as far

---

[1] This is so called because the *Thānā* or modern Police Station stands on it.

[2] The contour lines indicate a vertical rise of every five feet.

as possible near the centre. As the larger squares run from north to south and from west to east it has been found convenient to number them at the south-east corner and in order to distinguish them from their own sub-squares, the boundaries of the larger ones have been drawn in bolder lines. Their nomenclature is simple. Thus, for example, squares resulting from the intersection of the one hundred feet divisions H & 13, J & 19, etc., are designated in the plans as H 13, J 19, etc., and similarly the ninth sub-squares of the above larger squares are designated as H 13/9, J 19/9, etc. Letters of the alphabet, being limited in number, are, where necessary, duplicated as AA, AB, AC, and so forth.

Stratification.

The number of strata varies considerably in different mounds which are not all contemporary with each other. In the present state of our knowledge their dating can hardly be definite. At best it must be rough and provisional, with a fair margin for error when accounting for the upper and lower limits of the culture[1] at Harappā as revealed up till now. On the basis of the evidence regarding the chronology of Mohenjo-daro, which has been so ably discussed by Sir John Marshall,[2] I tabulate below the tentative and comparative age of Mounds F, AB, Areas J and G, and of the Cemetery H.

Comparative chronology.

Period.		Strata.	Date.
Mound F	Late I	Ist to IIIrd	Circa 2750 B.C. to 3050 B.C.
	Late II		
	Late III		
	Intermediate I	IVth to VIIth	Circa 3050 B.C. to 3500 B.C.
	Intermediate II		
	Intermediate III		
	Intermediate IV		
	Early I	VIIIth	First half of the 4th Millennium B.C.
Mound AB	Late I	Ist to IVth	Contemporary with the Late Period in Mound F, but the Ist stratum is possibly later still.
	Late II		
	Late III		
	Late IV		
	Intermediate I	Vth and VIth	Before Circa 3050 B.C.
	Intermediate II		

[1] In this accounting the Gupta stratum, which is confined to the highest but only a small portion of Mound AB, has been left out. See pp. 137-38 *infra*.

[2] *M. I. C.*, pp. 9-10 and 103-07.

Period.		Strata.	Date.
Area J	Late I	Ist and IInd	Circa 2850 to 3050 B.C.
	Late II		
	Intermediate I	IIIrd and IVth	Before Circa 3050 B.C.
	Intermediate II		
Area G	Late I	Ist and IInd	Circa 2700 B.C. to 2800 B.C.
	Late II		
	Intermediate I	IIIrd	Circa 3250 B.C.
Cemetery H	Late I	Ist and IInd	Circa 2000 B.C. to 2500 B.C. (Approximate upper and lower limits between which the two strata may be supposed to have existed at any time. A difference of about 50 years between them should be ample.)
	Late II		

Reasons for above dating. *Mound F*, so far as the buildings and antiquities of every kind (including the seals) are concerned, is contemporary with the Late and Intermediate Periods of Mohenjo-daro, but from the IVth stratum downwards it contains an increasing proportion of tiny seals and sealings of an archaic type which are peculiar to Harappā and the like of which have not been found hitherto at Mohenjo-daro. From the IVth stratum downwards, therefore, this mound may be said to be earlier than Mohenjo-daro.

Mound AB. Strata II to IV are contemporary with the Late Period in Mound F, but the Ist is possibly a bit later. Below the IVth stratum the tiny seals and sealings begin to appear and accordingly the Vth and VIth strata may be assigned to the latter part of the Intermediate Period in Mound F.

Area G. The first two strata, to judge from the more developed types of pottery as seen in Pls. XLI, *b*, XLII, *a*, and LXX, 5-6, 8-12, 14, 16-17, 20, 22-24, and 35-36, appear to be contemporary with the corresponding strata in Mound AB. While some of the pottery found with the multiple burial No. G-289 and the groups of pottery Nos. G15 and G130 forms, as it were, a kind of bridge[1] between the pottery from the Cemetery H and that of the Late Period from Mounds F and AB, most of the other finds are absolutely indistinguishable from antiquities of the Late Period in the above two mounds. The line of demarcation is, therefore, not clearly marked. Between Strata II and III, however, there seems to have been a wide gulf of time, since in the latter stratum tiny seals of archaic type begin to be suddenly met with.

The Cemetery H shows only two strata of occupation which are evidently later than the Late Period of the mounds, but how much later, it is difficult to

[1] *Cf.* Pl. LXX, 10, 14, 16 and 20.

say. The lateness of the Cemetery is demonstrated by the well-developed forms of pottery found with burials of Strata I and II (Pls. LX and LXI), the more so as sherds of similar vessels were found overlying the latest strata of several mounds and also by the distinctly different character of the paintings which mark an abrupt break from the paintings on the non-cemetery types of pottery recovered from the mounds. I do not, however, think that pottery from the Cemetery H is likely to be later than Circa 2000 B.C.

Story of excavations.

The site of Harappā has long been known to Archæologists as the find-place of a certain class of seals engraved for the most part with the effigy of a unicorn and bearing inscriptions in an unknown pictographic script. Over three quarters of a century ago, some specimens of these seals were obtained by Sir Alexander Cunningham when he visited Harappā. An account of the site, a few seals and other antiquities were published by him in his *Annual Report* for 1875[1]. Other specimens were subsequently acquired by the British Museum and published by Dr. J. F. Fleet in the *Journal of the Royal Asiatic Society* for 1912.[2] It was, however, not till the winter of 1920-21 that the excavation of the site was begun by Rai Bahadur Daya Ram Sahni at the instance of Sir John Marshall, then Director General of Archæology in India. Even before coming out to India, as far back as 1901, and again in 1906, when he went home to England, Sir John had interested himself in the British Museum seals from Harappā and had set his heart on excavating the site; and it was under his instructions that Rai Bahadur Daya Ram Sahni acquired Mounds F and AB, and began excavations on both of them in January, 1921 and subsequently continued them during the winter seasons of 1923-24 and 1924-25. His excavations, though necessarily limited for want of time and funds, were enough to demonstrate conclusively that the remains at Harappā, including the inscribed seals, were referable to the Chalcolithic Age and contemporary with the pre-historic site of Mohenjo-daro the excavation of which was taken up in 1922.

Excavation by Rai Bahadur Daya Ram Sahni.

His work in Mound F was confined to the north-west portion, where he excavated the diagonal Trench A which revealed the existence of two remarkable series of parallel walls forming a part of what has been provisionally identified as the Great Granary, as well as Trenches Af and Ae. In Mound AB he excavated the large Trench B to the west of the tomb of Naugazā and four pits in the southern half of the same mound designated Pits I, II, III and IV on the site plan (Pl. I). The first two of these have since merged in the extension which I made round them later. Accounts of these excavations have been published by the Rai Bahadur in the *Archæological Survey Reports* for the years 1920-21, 1923-24 and 1924-25.

Extent of his diggings.

Excavations of Mr. M. S. Vats.

From 1926-27 to 1933-34 it has been my privilege to work here successively for eight years; for the first five on a larger scale than before, thanks to the more liberal grants then available, and for the remaining three under exceptional handicaps due to shortage of funds and the consequent lack of trained assistants. During this period, I have excavated not only in the two mounds

[1] *C. S. R.*, Vol. V. pp. 105-08.
[2] Pp. 699-701.

referred to above but also in Area J which includes Mound D, as well as further south in the Cemetery H, and Area G. All the excavations carried out up to that date are shown in red on the site plan (Pl. I). Owing to his many duties as Director General of Archæology in India, it has not, unfortunately, been possible for the Rai Bahadur to contribute an account of his diggings to this monograph, and it has therefore fallen to me to describe here the excavations carried out by him and myself.

Nature of remains.

Early use of burnt brick.

The aspect of the ruins, so far brought to light, is in general so hopelessly mutilated that in 95 per cent of cases it is impossible to draw even a tentative plan of what the houses once looked like, much less to reconstruct their façades, or the layout of streets, drainage systems, and the like. Nevertheless, it is obvious that from the earliest times onwards most of the people of Harappā lived in houses made of burnt brick, the usual size[1] of which is 11 by 5·5 by 2·5 to 3 in.

Mud and mud brick houses.

Mixed construction.

Side by side with burnt brick middle class houses of the Intermediate Period dwellings of the poor were made of mud and mud brick, *e.g.*, Houses 1-4 in Trench I, Mound D (Pl. XXXVIII, *b*). Sometimes in the better class houses mud bricks were used in alternate courses along with burnt brick masonry (Pl. XXVII, *d*). Mud brick[2] was also used for raising solid terraces to guard against the danger of floods (Pl. XXXVI, *e*). Where used in masonry it was always well moulded, and once the walls were plastered over with mud and straw, no distinction would be possible between the two.

Foundations.

The foundations varied greatly in quality. In the better class buildings of the Intermediate Period they were carried to a greater depth, and placed, as often as not, on a thick bed of well burnt clay nodules, which are more common at Harappā than at Mohenjo-daro, and sometimes on a well rammed bed of clay. During the Late Period, however, most of the foundations of numerous fragmentary walls seem to have been laid on any kind of slipshod débris, possibly as a majority of them had nothing more than a thatched roof to support. Indeed, this is exemplified by the Late III dwellings in the Extension of Pits I and II in Mound AB where a considerable quantity of charcoal of pinewood rafters, bamboos and reeds was brought to light.

Mortars.

Generally, mud alone was used as mortar, but sometimes gypsum appears to have been employed for pointing. Instances of such use of gypsum are the brick-on-edge pavement of Stratum III in Trench VI (Pl. XXVII, *b*), the series

---

[1] As at Mohenjo-daro, the size of burnt bricks continued to be the same from the earliest to the latest occupation. It cannot, therefore, be taken as a criterion for the dating of buildings of any particular period. Occasionally, bricks of the following sizes are also found in strata of the Periods against which they are shown below:—

Early Period	No complete bricks available.
Intermediate and Late Periods .	1. 9·5×4·5 to 5×2 to 2·5 in.
	2. 10×3·75 to 5·25×1·75 to 2·5 in.
	3. 10·5×5 to 5·5×2 to 2·75 in.
	4. 10·75×5·25 to 5·75×2·25 to 2·75 in.
	5. 11×5 to 5·5×2 to 2·75 in.
	6. 11·5×5·5×2 to 2·75 in.
Late Period	7. 11·25×5·5×2·5 in.

[2] At Mohenjo-daro mud brick was used only for filling or raising terraces, but not for building purposes.

of circular platforms in Trenches IV and V in Mound F (Pl. XII, *c*), the large public drain in the Extension of Pits I and II in Mound AB (Pl. XXXII, *c*), etc.

Floors. Floors were made either of mud, or of bricks laid flat[1] or on edge,[2] but almost invariably bathrooms were paved with well. rubbed bricks with very fine joints. Pavements were usually bordered with bricks laid on edge—either on their longer or their shorter sides.

No windows to speak of have survived at Harappā, nor could any be expected up to the height of the dados, which is all that remains of the walls in the few houses left to us. Probably for a similar reason, not much of corbelling has been found on this site.

Stairways. Only three stairways have been discovered so far. Two of them are in the central aisle of the Great Granary (Pl. IV, *a*), and the third one at the north-east corner of House 1 in Trench VI, each with no more than a few steps. Their risers are high and the treads narrow.

Drains. Surface drains made of burnt bricks were as much a feature of Harappā as of Mohenjo-daro. They are of several kinds, that is to say, either covered with flat-bricks[3] as illustrated in *M. I. C.*, Pl. LXXVII, 4, or with a gabled roof (Pl. XXXII, *b*) as in No. 9 in the same plate, or perfectly open. Those of the latter type are either small channels or big public drains[4] meant for the drainage of particular areas. One irregular drain of the Late Period found in the Extension of Pits I and II is circular and covered with brick-on-edge.[5] Most notable among them, however, are the two public drains[6] of Strata IV and V which bisect the Extension of Pits I and II in Mound AB. Both of them are sloped down towards the valley on the east and follow the same alignment one above the other. **Dustbins.** Alongside the drains the dustbins,[7] which, of course, were sunk below the ground level and always paved, were built at convenient points in the streets. They were used for throwing in the sweepings of houses and like the **Refuse water pits.** refuse water pits lined with jars,[8] which were meant for the storage of used up water from the baths or kitchens. were cleaned by the street scavenger—an example of the extent to which conservancy matters engaged the attention of the civic authorities. No rubbish chutes or vertical drains made of terracotta pipes have yet been found at Harappā.

Wells. Compared with Mohenjo-daro, wells are rare at Harappā. Altogether only six[9] examples, situated at long distances from each other, have been found,

---

[1] An excellent example of this is found in Stratum V, Trench I, Mound F (Pl. XXI, *d*).

[2] As example of this may be cited the floor with jar stands of Stratum III, Trench VI, Mound F (Pl. XXVII, *b*).

[3] *E.g.*, Pl. XXXV, squares R 28/20 and R 28/3.

[4] *E.g.*, Pl. XXXII, *c*.

[5] Pl. XXXI, squares Q 23/20 and 25.

[6] *See* pp. 155-56 *infra*.

[7] *E.g.* the two bins to the east of House I in Trench VI, Mound F. One of them is seen in Pl. XXVIII, *a*.

[8] Two of these belonging to different strata are seen in Pl. XXXIII, *a*.

[9] Of these, one is situated on the open terrace of House 1 in Trench VI, Mound F, one in Trench Ae, two more in Trenches IV and V in the same mound, a double well in the Trench at the Southern Edge of Mound AB, and the last in Trench II, Area G.

Their sizes and scarcity.

and without exception[1] they were all public wells. Their diameter ranges from 1 ft. 10 in. to 7 ft. Those in Mound F (diam. 1 ft. 10 in. to 2 ft. 9 in.) are so small that two people cannot draw water from them at one and the same time. On the other hand, the diameter of the other two wells, which are situated far away from the ancient Râvi, is much larger. From this it appears probable that people living close to the river used well-water only for cooking and drinking, their other requirements being met with river water. On the other hand, people living far from the riverside had to depend on well-water for all and sundry purposes, and therefore larger wells, which could be simultaneously used by at least two persons, were a necessity. It may also be noted that, except in the inner ring of the well in the Trench at the Southern Edge of Mound AB,

Wedge-shaped bricks.

wedge-shaped bricks,[2] which in that case appear to have been specially moulded, are not used anywhere. Sometimes wells appear to have been used also as

Piau.

public *piau* or free stalls for water. For instance, the three large jars beside the well in Trench V, Mound F (Pl. XVI, *d*), were apparently meant for the storage of drinking water for the wayfarers.

Two classes of buildings.

The buildings, so far uncovered at Harappā, may be divided into two classes, *viz.*, (1) dwelling houses, and (2) public buildings among which may be included the Great Granary and the rows of circular brick-on-edge platforms which are confined to a portion of Trenches IV and V only.

House 1 of Trench VI, Mound F.

To give some idea of an ordinary upper-class house at Harappā, I give an oblique projection of House 1 in the IVth stratum of Trench VI (Pl. XV, *b*). With a frontage of over 100 ft. on the east this house has quite a palatial appearance, but its depth cannot be determined at present as it is partly broken and partly buried underneath the western edge of the trench. Its plan is carefully designed so as to separate the female apartments from the rest of the house. Standing on its open terrace to the south-east is a well 2 ft. 9 in. in diameter which is conveniently situated both for the inmates and neighbours. To north, opposite the well, is the porter's lodge No. 7 behind which starts the Z-shaped gallery No. 6 communicating first with room No. 5 and then with closet No. 4 which gave access to the female apartments Nos. 3 and 2. On the west, opposite the well and porter's lodge rooms Nos. 9 and 11, which open on the terrace mentioned above, could be conveniently used as guest-rooms. Behind these, room No. 10 and others, which are no longer traceable, could well have been used by the inmates themselves. Between rooms Nos. 9 and 10 on the south and room No. 1 on the north is the large courtyard No. 8 connected with gallery No. 6 on the one hand and the women's room No. 3 on the other. It may be observed that all the doorways of this building are fairly small. From the later pavement in room No. 5 and two walls in room No. 3, this house, or at any rate, a part of it, appears to have been renovated with the IIIrd stratum. For fuller details the reader is referred to pp. 131-32 *infra*.

---

[1] The well on the terrace of House 1 in Trench VI, Mound F apparently belonged to the house, but as it stands besides a lane to the east presumably the neighbours, too, were allowed to use it.

[2] At Mohenjo-daro, however, the bricks used in the construction of wells are almost invariably wedge-shaped. *Cf. M. I. C.*, p. 269.

Circular platforms.

Among structures made seemingly for public use may be mentioned first a scheme of twelve circular platforms running in a double row along the southern edge of Trench V with indications of two more in the eastward extension of Trench IV and three others in the northern part of Trench IV (Pl. XI). All of them stand in open public places, are of the same size, and, with the exception of P15, are equidistant from each other. The longer distances between platforms P5 and P6 and between the corresponding ones in the opposite row are apparently due to the previous existence of an older well which continued to be used as a public *chhabīl* in the Late III Period when these platforms came into existence. They are made only of single courses of brick-on-edge laid in concentric rings, but their purpose is not apparent.

The Great Granary.

The most remarkable and the largest building at Harappā is the Great Granary (Pl. VI) which has been laid bare in the north-west quarter of Mound F. It belongs to the Intermediate II Period and consists of two precisely similar blocks opposite each other with an aisle 23 ft. wide between them (Pl. IV, *a*). Each block comprises six halls (marked I I', II II', III III', etc. on the plan) alternating regularly with five corridors which open only on the outside (marked AA', BB', CC', etc., Pl. III). Every one of these halls is partitioned into four narrow divisions by means of three equidistant, full-length walls which terminate in broader piers at both ends. Excepting the piers, which are invariably made of burnt brick, the remaining portion of these partition walls is made sometimes of burnt brick, but more usually of mixed construction, that is to say of burnt and sundried bricks and has survived but little. Sometime later, the air passages formed by partitioning the halls had to be narrowed down at the far end of each block by making at a higher level a series of rectangular, battered additions which were pierced with triangular holes in order to maintain the free circulation of air through the original passages. A peculiar feature of this complex is that along both ends of the central aisle there is a common foundation wall, 3 ft. 6 in. wide, which runs underneath the entire length of the two blocks without any corresponding walls at the opposite ends. Round the two blocks again there is a battered retaining wall which does not run along the whole perimeter. Apparently, it was hidden from view. This extraordinary complex, which measures 168 ft. from north to south by 135 ft. from east to west, was obviously a public building of great importance for the whole city. In trying to reconstruct this it must be remembered that by building piers at the opposite ends of the dividing walls in the halls, the width of the slits was narrowed down to 1 ft. 6 in. only and this made their spanning quite easy by corbelling or timbering. It is also notorious that at both ends the piers have bulged out laterally on account of great pressure from above. We may thus suppose, not without reason, that with these piers and the longer sides of corridors as foundations, large halls, each measuring about 52 by 17 ft., were reared on them. These halls had no doubt timbered floors which, as shown in the oblique projection, rested on walls of mixed construction. Access to them could be had direct from the corridors which were probably sloped up to the entrance of the hall

[1] For its detailed description see pp. 16-22 *infra*.

or from the aisle side as shown in the part restoration of the Granary (Pl. VI). When there was no currency and taxes had to be paid in kind the public treasury must have taken the form of great store houses which are known from other countries as well, such as the long and narrow store houses attached to the Minoan Palaces at Cnossus and Phæstus in Crete. In this connection Sir John Marshall writes to me that " In some of the Roman Forts in England and Germany there are structures remarkably like the Great Granary at Harappā with the same long narrow galleries and the same small apertures at the bottom of the end walls—intended to allow the circulation of air under the floors, to prevent the grain becoming mildewed. The resemblance of one of these granaries, which I visited on the Roman Wall this summer, to the Harappā Granary was very striking."[1]

Cemetery H.

An important discovery, which may be mentioned here in passing, is the prehistoric Cemetery H which lies in low ground to the south of Mounds D and E. As only a part of it has been excavated it is not possible to define its limits. Nevertheless, enough has been done to show the kinds of burials that might be expected from an extended excavation of this area.

Earth and pot-burials.

Clearly, it reveals two ways of disposal of the dead, one earlier and the other later. The earlier burials relegated to Stratum II in the plan (Pls. XLIII and XLVIII) are found not infrequently buried under those of Stratum I. By how much vertical distance the earlier ones were actually separated from the later burials is best seen in the sections of the Cemetery (Pls. XLIV and XLIX). The former, consisting of dead bodies, entire or fractional, which were generally accompanied by some funerary pottery or grave furniture, being found consigned to earth (by digging pits) have been called Earth-burials. Similarly, the later burials have been designated Pot-burials, as the urns comprising Stratum I contain merely the remains of one or more dead bodies to the extent they have survived exposure to birds and beasts of prey. A detailed description of the Cemetery is given in Chapter VI.

[1] The letter is dated January, 1933.

CHAPTER II.

Mound F.

Situation and configuration of the mound.

Mound F, where work has been continued during all the eleven years and which claims nearly half of the excavations on this site, stands on the south bank of the *Sukhrāvā*,[1] a dry bed of the Rāvi, and is the northernmost of the western line of mounds. It is roughly rectangular in shape, measuring approximately 970 ft. from east to west and 780 ft. from north to south. At the highest point, it rises to a little more than 550 ft. above the mean sea-level as co-ordinated with the bridge over the lower Bāri Doāb canal on the road to Harappā Railway Station, or about 30 ft. above the level of the dry river bed (Pl. I). Almost bisecting the mound from north to south, there is a broad, raised belt ranging in height from 540 to 545 ft. from which the surface slopes down to 530 ft. on the east, to 535 ft. on the north-west, while in the south-west portion of the mound the ground level is more or less the same as that of the central belt. Six large trenches have been sunk in this mound, *viz.*, three to the west and three to the east of the central belt. The former comprise the Great Granary Area (Trench II) with one small Trench Ae to its south-west and two Trenches Af and Ai to its south, all occupying the north-west quarter of this mound and Trenches IV and V in the south-west quarter. The other three trenches, namely I, III and VI, lie in the eastern part across the central belt. In the following account of explorations in this mound I shall describe each one of these trenches in the above order.

Traces of brick-diggers, pits and trenches.

Like the high Mound AB adjoining it on the south, this mound had suffered much from brick-diggers, but in this case the holes left by their operations had become mostly filled up and the mound presented the appearance of being untouched. The lowest of such holes was traced at a depth of 16 ft. in Trench I. From the remains so far uncovered it appears that Harappā lacked the opulence of Mohenjo-daro and never had many imposing buildings. Such buildings, however, as it did possess, have either been swept away almost entirely or mutilated beyond recognition by promiscuous and extensive brick-digging carried on from time immemorial. But if the structural remains on the whole, are disappointing, happily, this is not the case with portable finds. In this respect, apart from its interesting ruins, Mound F has proved exceptionally fertile and has more than repaid the labour expended on its excavation.

Paucity of buildings.

The Great Granary Area.

In January 1921, Rai Bahadur Daya Ram Sahni sank in the north-western part of this mound the diagonal Trench A, 16 ft. wide and 500 ft. long from south-east to north-west, starting from the centre of the mound and reaching

[1] Literally dry Rāvi.

Discovery of the Great Granary. almost to its north-western end (Pl. I). In the course of his operations here he succeeded in tracing out, in 1923-24, a little more than the southern half of the Eastern Block of the Great Granary and a small part of the Western Block also. In describing the portion uncovered by him the Rai Bahadur observed, that "The most important architectural discovery (Pl. XXIV, *c*) of the year was made about the centre of this mound which, though only partially exposed, already embraces an area of 106 feet from east to west by 120 feet from north to south. The purpose and character of this building are shrouded in mystery, but it may be hoped that further exploration will supply the explanation. I was led to the examination of this portion of the site by the existence of two solidly built walls, running parallel to each other without any party walls, which had been brought to light here in the preceding year, but the exact meaning of which could not be ascertained. With these walls as a starting point the excavation was taken in hand and great was my surprise when the operations continued to reveal, in quick succession at narrow intervals, wall after wall, until I had a series of fourteen of them, all running parallel to each other and of the same length, *viz.*, 51 ft. 9 in. All of them terminated on the west on

Identical plan of both blocks. an open corridor 24[1] feet wide beyond which stretched a similar set of walls in precise correlation with those in the opposite series. So far only six of the walls have been found on the west but there seems no doubt that when the excavation is continued, each of the walls in the eastern row will be found to have its counterpart on the other side".[2] That the Western Block was an exact counterpart of the Eastern one became at once apparent from the plan which I was able to trace out completely in the years 1926-27 and 1928-29 (Pls. III and VI). Taken individually, each block covers an area of 150[3] ft. from north to south by 56 ft. from east to west and is connected with the other by means of an aisle or passage 23 ft. wide between them (Pl. IV, *a*). The Western Block, at any rate, so far as the five corridors and the two extreme end walls are concerned, is, on the whole, much better preserved, and has considerably helped me in clearing the eastern and western ends of the other block, and in preserving the several shapeless bits of intermediate walls which, as originally constructed, were doubtless linked with the end piers. As, in a large nnmber of cases, these walls are preserved only in patches and are of mixed construction, that is to say of burnt and sun-dried bricks and occasionally (in small sections) of rammed mud also, there was a real danger of their being mistaken for débris. Thanks, however, to the plan of the Great Granary becoming clear at an early stage it was possible to unearth whatever remained of it without much difficulty.

The Western Block.

Plan of the Western Block. Now I shall first describe the Western Block in detail, so that its mutilated counterpart on the east may be followed with ease. It consists of six halls, each

[1] The actual width is 23 ft. and not 24.

[2] *A. S. R.* for 1924-25, p. 76.

[3] With the rectangular battered additions at the outer ends the length is 159 ft. and with the retaining wall and common foundation wall 170 ft.

measuring 51 ft. 9 in. long by 17 ft. 6 in.[1] wide, designated I, II, III, etc., on the plan and of five corridors between them, of similar length but 5 ft. 6 in. wide, which are marked *a, b, c,* etc. Each of the halls, which Sir John Marshall was the first to recognise as granaries, is regularly partitioned into four narrow divisions by means of three equidistant walls. These were evidently intended for the foundations of the granary floor, which was no doubt of timber—the interspaces between them serving as so many air passages just as they did in Roman and other granaries to prevent the grain or stores, for which the halls appear to have been intended, getting sweated or mildewed. A conjectural restoration showing how the stores would be brought into the granaries is given in the isometric projection and part restoration on Pl. VI. The outer walls of the halls are 1 ft. 6 in. wide, and, together with the piers, rise only to a height of 3 ft. 10 in. above their foundation. A glance at this restoration will also show that all the air passages on the west were later narrowed down by making a series of small battered additions with triangular holes, each measuring 4 ft. long by 2 ft. 9 in. wide, which are nowhere bonded with the main building, and the foundations of which are higher by 1 ft. 4 in. than those of the latter. The corridors however, in order to retain the ramps, had to be closed on the east or aisle side by strong walls of a uniform thickness of 3 ft. 9 in. and left open on the west for the admission of the carriers bringing in the stores (Pl. IV, *b*). A remarkable feature of this block is, that there is a broad and well preserved wall which runs underneath its entire eastern edge for a length of about 170 ft. from north to south, and with this are bonded one and all of the closing walls of the corridors and that part of the piers which rests on it. But it has no counterpart along the opposite side of this block. This may be conveniently called the common foundation wall. It has slightly sunk from the corridor *e* southwards. It may also be added that the outer ends of the extreme end walls of this block are strengthened by the addition of solid buttresses of masonry which are much more substantial on the south. The buttress at the eastern extremity of the northern end wall, together with the wall itself, is broken away.

The Eastern Block.

Exact similarity of the Eastern Block.

Coming now to the Eastern Block we find that the foundations of the halls together with the partition walls, corridors and additions with air holes on the east, whether taken individually or collectively, exactly correspond to similar features in the Western Block (Pl. IV, *b*). Although, unfortunately, all the closing walls of the corridors in this block have disappeared, there can be no doubt as to their former existence. Indeed, this is evidenced by the jagged western end of the northern wall of corridor *d'* which is irregularly serrated towards the south owing to the breaking away of the closing wall at this point. Moreover, just as in the Western Block, there was a common foundation wall going underneath the west end of this block also, but of this only traces have survived. A part

[1] This works out as the average width which on actual measurement is found to vary between 17 ft. 3 in. and 17 ft. 7 in.

of it is indicated in the panoramic view (Pl. IV, *a*) by two men standing to the left of the survey tent which is seen pitched in the central aisle. The masonry buttresses, which we should have expected at the ends of the extreme north wall of this block, are no longer there. One of them, however, has been traced at the eastern end of the extreme south wall, of which the other end, being buried below a thick wall of the Intermediate I Period, cannot be reached without demolishing it.

Later reconstruction of the Eastern Block.

Here, it is necessary to point out that immediately over the original partition walls of Hall VI′ was built, at a later date, another similar set of four walls[1] running parallel to each other. The alignment of these walls does not exactly coincide with those of the original hall which I have excavated below this set and shown in dotted lines on the plan. It is to this later construction that the next two walls on the south, as well as the thick and higher walls which rise from the corridors *a′*, *b′*, *c′*, and *d′*, as also the upper part of the middle intervening wall of Hall III′, and of the walls immediately to the south of the corridors *c′* and *d′* belong. Most of them can be seen rising up from the Eastern Block in the panoramic view (Pl. IV, *a*), and in the further of the two blocks in Pl. IV, *b*. To this same restoration must also be attributed the pavement which was put in over and between the eastern piers of the original Hall VI′, but in order to show the piers clearly I have refrained from showing this pavement on the plan.

The battered retaining wall.

All along the south of the two blocks there is a battered retaining wall which, including the breaks shown on the plan by a dotted line, has been traced for a length of 129 ft. At both ends it is found to turn northwards. From the south-east corner it extends only for a length of 5 ft., while at the opposite end it extends, with two breaks, to 50 ft. On the east it was picked up again for a length of 18 ft. against the corridor *b′* and a portion of the Hall III′ (Pl. V, *b*, foreground and background of the deep and narrow trench). Being only a retaining wall, it has no inner face, and at the best preserved portion stands to a maximum height of 3 ft. 7 in. in eighteen receding and stepped courses where it has a maximum slope of 1 ft. 10 in. (Pl. V, *d*). Its top is coterminus with the foundation of the Great Granary, so that, whatever may have been the floor level of the latter, the retaining wall must always have been completely buried and hidden from view. It is also worthy of note that, except at the places already mentioned, where its ends are finished, the retaining wall could not be found any where else, although deep and narrow trenches were sunk to trace it out. Hence, it appears that for two-thirds of the perimeter of this granary it was not evidently regarded as necessary. The reason for this may be that throughout the south and parts of the east and west sides, where it has been traced, the vertical cuttings showed large masses of loose rubbish consisting chiefly of terracotta nodules and ashes which made the ground insecure and necessitated the construction of this retaining wall. On the other hand, over the rest of the perimeter the ground was hard and compact and free from nodules, so that the retaining wall could be dispensed with.

Built in sections only.

[1] Unlike the walls below, these are made throughout of burnt brick masonry.

In the central aisle there are several rectangular patches of brick-on-edge pavements, some piers against the walls of the two blocks, and two small flights of steps, one abutting against Hall VI' of the Eastern Block (Pl. IV, *a*, yonder steps in the aisle), and the other against Hall V of the Western Block (Pl. VI). All these, except perhaps the floor at the foot of the latter steps, which appears to be earlier, were part and parcel of the Great Granary. But an innovation was made later. Along the far end of each block was built a series of rectangular battered additions which were pierced with triangular air holes in order to maintain intact the original arrangement for the circulation of air, though this was inevitably restricted since the original apertures were now considerably reduced. These and the probable purpose of the steps and low pylons in the central aisle are shown in the isometric projection on Pl. VI.

Pavements, steps, and piers in the central aisle and their relative date.

Later air holes.

Like all other buildings of the various strata, this amazing complex is composed of well burnt bricks of fine texture which are laid throughout in good tenacious mud. The bricks measure 11 by 5¼ by 2½ to 3 in., of which the chief interest lies in the scientific proportion of two widths to the length—a size which makes for good structural bonding. In both blocks, the infilling was of rammed mud, extraordinarily hard and compact, but while in the corridors the clay was quite pure, in the halls it was mixed with brickbats no doubt from the débris of the underground partition walls. A few potsherds were also found in the air passages between the piers, which had probably found their way there from the later strata above.

Size of bricks used.

Rammed mud infilling.

A constructional feature common to both the blocks, which has some bearing on their proposed identification as granaries is, that uniformly for a length of 7 ft. at both ends, the walls of the halls were intentionally made 4½[1] in. thicker than the remaining portion, thus suggesting that the superstructure along both ends was exceptionally heavy, and this inference is borne out by the bulged out appearance of the end piers evidently due to pressure from above.

A constructional feature.

If the restoration proposed on Pl. VI be correct, it is not unlikely that the central aisle itself was originally roofed over. On this supposition it is easy to explain the presence of the special foundation wall on either side of the aisle which would be needed for the extra weight of the roof. Sir John Marshall, who was the first to recognise the true purpose of these granaries, has pointed out to me the close analogy between them and the granaries (horrea) attached to many Roman Forts in ancient Britain, notably to those of Housesteads, Pen-y-darren, Birrens and Ambleside. Such granaries were usually provisioned with a year's supplies in case of siege. "They took the form", says Prof. Haverfield, "of oblong halls or barns, long and narrow, with unusually thick walls strengthened by external buttresses. Inside, the floors were raised two or three feet above the adjacent ground level. Beneath the floor was a shallow basement, not unlike a hypocaust basement, but wholly devoid of furnace or other means of heating, and elaborately ventilated by slender apertures in the outer walls, which admitted through draughts and obviated all risks of damp and

Possible purpose of the common foundation walls.

[1] 4½ in. is the mean, the extra thickness at these points varies between 3 to 6 or 7 in. As the walls have bulged out the exact measurements, which were presumably uniform, are not obtainable now.

dry-rot. Pilæ of brick or lower sleeper walls of stone supported these floors. Above the floors, the buildings were large open halls, in which presumably the grain was stored, probably in wooden partitions. Often two such halls stood side by side, close together—a device which ensured ample space without requiring unduly wide spans of roof; sometimes a row of columns down the middle of the hall helped to support the roof. The dimensions of these structures in Britain show some uniformity. The widths vary, mostly, between 20 and 25 feet. The lengths differ more widely; a few halls seem to have been over 100 feet long; others are barely half". Thus the floor-space differs greatly. In the granary of Rough Castle it is only 115 square yards; at Pen-y-darren, 180 square yards; at Housesteads, 266 square yards; at Birrens, 532 square yards; and at Newstead, 711 square yards.

Not a residential building.

A fact worth noticing in connection with the excavation of these granaries was the complete dearth of those small finds which are met with in such large numbers among the residential buildings. Indeed, the only objects that merit notice at all were three large and broken earthenware jars Nos. 10232 *a-c*, of which two are napiform and one carrot-shaped.[1] These were found lying together near the south end of the central aisle in front of the flight of steps attached to the Eastern Block. Close to them lay a tiny rectangular steatite seal inscribed on one side only (No. 2702, Pl. XCVI, 467). Being found considerably above the level of the pavements these objects may be dated to the Intermediate I Period. A round mace-head (No. 3614) of yellow Jaisalmer stone (Pl. LXXXIII, 16) from one of the western air passages of Hall III of the Western Block appears to have found its way down from an upper stratum.

The diagonal Trench A.

The diagonal Trench A.

To revert to the long Trench A. Rai Bahadur Daya Ram Sahni made there two finds of value. Not far from its south-east end in square J 9/20 he found in association with Stratum II a unicorn seal (No. A214) showing inscription in the upper field and the usual animal with incense-burner below his neck in the remaining ground (Pl. LXXXVIII, 85). But a much more interesting find that he made in this trench, was the wonderful torso of a dancer (No. Ab959, Pl. LXXXI, *a-d*), made of dark grey stone, which was recovered in the Intermediate I level where it lay touching the western end of the thick later wall abutting on the south of Hall VI[1] of the Eastern Block. This statuette measures 3·9 in. high and its lower right leg as well as the left, up to and inclusive of a part of the thigh, is broken. From the excellent sketch illustrating its dancing pose as reconstructed by Sir John Marshall[2] it appears that the right leg was planted on the ground and the left drawn high in front, both arms being thrown out to left. The arms and unusually bulky head of this figure were fixed in separately as in the male torso of red stone statuette[3] described elsewhere in this chapter in the account of Trench V. For this purpose, the arms below the

Grey stone statuette of a dancer.

[1] *Cf. M. I. C.*, Pl. LXXXV, 3.

[2] *M. I. C.*, p. 46, Fig. 1.

[3] See pp. 74-76 *infra*.

shoulders were cut almost horizontally and the neck obliquely, and at each of these points a hole was drilled for the attachment of the separate parts. There is also a deep hole for the insertion of the *membrum virile*, a cluster of seven holes in the hind part of the neck, and one sidewise in the left thigh. The breasts, with the nipples separately fixed in with cement, are very low and suggest a male figure. I quote the following interesting remarks regarding its identification by Sir John Marshall,[1] who described it for the first time. "Although its contours are soft and effiminate, the figure is that of a male, and it seems likely that it was ithyphallic, since the *membrum virile* was made in a separate piece. I infer, too, from the abnormal thickness of the neck, that the dancer was three-headed or at any rate three-faced, and I conjecture that he may represent the youthful Śiva Naṭeśa. On the other hand, it is possible that the head was that of an animal. Whatever it may have been, no parallel to this statuette is to be found among Indian sculptures of the historic period." This and the red stone statuette referred to above are incomparably superior to the crude human statuary found at Mohenjo-daro. To the matter of their date I shall refer in connection with the other statuette. From the same level, but near the north-western extension of this trench, was found a copper nail-cutter (No. A608, Pl. CXXV, 39).

Extensions Ab, Aa, Ad and Ae.

Finds from the Extension Ab.

In order to trace some more walls of the two blocks of the Great Granary Mr. Sahni made a few stray extensions about the centre of Trench A both towards the east and west. In the former direction, that part which lies to the north of corridor *é* was termed Ab, and the one to the south as Aa, while the two small westward extensions were termed Ac and Ad. In the area Ab, close to the statuette of the dancer and in the same stratum, he found a plano-convex, rectangular steatite seal (No. Ab922, Pl. XCII, 275), and an excellent representation of a terracotta ant-eater (No. Ab923, Pl. LXXVIII, 26). Scattered over the remaining part of this extension he found from Stratum I an inscribed pointed ivory rod (No. Ab62, Pl. XCIX, 643), and in association with Stratum II a cuboid chert weight[2] (A616), a rectangular cake of red ochre (No. Ab104), a plano-convex rectangular steatite seal (No. Ab130, Pl. XCII, 269), half of a square faience sealing (No. Ab44, Pl. XCV, 394) inscribed with a double square, a tiny rectangular faience sealing (No. Ab473) inscribed on both sides (Pl. C, 672), a pierced vase-shaped pottery cage (No. Ab554) showing one bird coming out from an aperture and another perched on the side (Pl. CXX, 22), a pear-shaped, flat-bottomed pottery vase with horizontal flutes (No. Ab268, ht. 4¼ in., Pl. LXXI, 17, and Pl. LXX, 42), and a painted potsherd (No. Ab207), which shows a peacock and a hen facing each other, part of another quadruped, etc. (Pl. LXVIII, 54). From the IIIrd stratum were recovered a rectangular, plano-convex steatite seal (No. Ab553, Pl. XCII, 274), two faience sealings of which No. Ab707 is lentoid and inscribed on both sides (Pl. XCV, 380), and No. Ab269

---

[1] *Op. cit.*, p. 46.

[2] Size 1·63 × 1·63 × 1·13 in.

rectangular but semi-round in section, having pictograms on one side and an acacia tree enclosed in a platform on the other (similar to No. 328 in Pl. XCIII), a faience chessman-shaped object holed on the underside (Ab867), and a red stone cylinder (ht. 1 5/16 in.) with a deep hole at the top and shallow socket at bottom (Ab349). In the IVth stratum was recovered a square, bossed faience sealing (Ab43) with double triangles in fields on either side of the diagonal line (Pl. XCV, 400).

From the Extension Aa. In the extension Aa were found in Stratum II a broken unicorn seal (Ab102, Pl. LXXXVI, 27), and a large spoon of shell[1] (Aa167, l. 7½ in.), the largest so far found at Harappā or Mohenjo-daro. Further down, in the following stratum, were recovered a fragmentary unicorn seal (Aa30) showing part of the animal, with the incense-burner and only one surviving pictogram, as well as a corner piece of another steatite seal (No. Aa31).

An interesting chessman-shaped object from the Extension Ad. From the extension Ad, Mr. Sahni found an interesting chessman-shaped terracotta *liṅgam* (Ad2, Pl. CXVII, 29) which is 4·5 in. high and 2·2 in. in diameter at the base. For fixation, it is pierced on the underside with a hole 1·8 in. deep, and there is another hole at the top 0·75 in. deep.

Extension at the north-western end of Trench A.

Fragmentary remains. Westward along the north-western end of Trench A Mr. Sahni made another extension. It is 90 ft. long from east to west and averages 55 ft. in width. It was excavated to a depth of 4 ft. 6 in. only and revealed several fragmentary walls and broken pavements of the IInd stratum between 2 ft. to 3 ft. 3 in. below the surface, and a few walls of the IIIrd stratum at a depth of 4 ft. 6 in. The mound having fallen here 7 to 10 ft. as compared with the opposite end of the trench, walls of the 1st stratum, except one or two little fragments along the higher northern edge, have altogether disappeared.

Finds of Stratum II. Scattered about in this extension and in association with Stratum II were found a unicorn seal (No. A263, Pl. LXXXVI, 21), an excellent pair of heart-shaped bangles (A182) of blue faience with deep indentation on the outside (Pl. CXXXVIII, 2 and 3), a polished biconical weight (A333) of hornblende (3·65 in. long), half of a plano-convex, rectangular seal (A341, similar to No. 629 in Pl. XCIX) of faience in which material this shape is rare, and a round terracotta sealing (No. A233, Pl. C, 657). Along the eastern half of the southern edge of this extension were found a squat bi-convex pottery vase (A406, ht. 2·13 in., Pl. LXXXII, 9) which contained six assorted miniature vases ranging in height from 0·5 to 0·65 in. (Pl. CXXXIX, 53-55 and 61-63), and the painted neck of an oval jar (A442) similar in shape and painting to the well preserved jar found by Mr. K. N. Dikshit[2] at Mohenjo-daro.

Stratum III. Parallel to and at a distance of about 20 ft. from the northern edge of this extension is a fairly thick, though fragmentary, wall of the IIIrd stratum which extends for about 80 ft. from east to west. Only two broken party-walls on the

---

[1] This is illustrated in *A. S. R.* for 1924-25, Pl. XXVII, *e*.

[2] *A. S. R.* for 1924-25, Pl. XXIII.

south, of which one is thicker than the other, appear to be connected with it. Between this wall and the southern edge of this extension were found a faience sealing (No. A816, Pl. XCV, 397) inscribed with a *svastika*, a unicorn seal (No. A336, Pl. LXXXVIII, 105), three stone beads including one of banded agate (A307), a small chert weight[1] (A67), fifteen oval tablets[2] of alabaster (A525) ranging in size from 2·25 by 1·9 to 4·2 by 3·1 in. (Pl. CXVII, 52 and 55), and a well executed, jugate terracotta tiger-head (A815) springing from a holed base (Pl. LXXIX, 88). Each of the tigers has two holes on its head, possibly for fixing horns.[3] The conception of this chimera creature is paralleled in the representation of the triple, interlaced tigers on seal 386[4] from Mohenjo-daro. Close to the alabaster tablets mentioned above was found a well preserved copper blade-axe (A784) with tapering sides. It is 3·75 in. long, 2 in. wide and is inscribed with the figure of a bat on one side. **A jugate tiger-head.**

Extent of the Granary Area. A large area has been excavated on all sides of the Great Granary described above. The whole of it, measuring 230 ft. square together with Trench A[5] and its extension at the north-western end, has now been termed the Granary Area. The extensions on the west, south, east and north of the Great Granary, being disconnected with each other, are described below separately. In them, digging has rarely proceeded below the Vth stratum or Intermediate II level which, as represented by the Granary, is the best preserved of all. **Stratification.** The Ist stratum, coming close to the surface, is very fragmentary, and survives here and there only in a course or two, while the IInd, IIIrd and IVth strata, though better preserved than the Ist, are also fragmentary and do not, except for a couple of houses[6] of the IVth stratum, make an intelligible plan. The Granary being the largest and most important building at Harappā, rising, as it does, from a uniform depth, furnishes a convenient datum in terms of which I shall speak, where necessary, of the earlier and later strata, not only in this area, but also in the other parts of Mound F.

The Western Extension.

Its extent and original surface. The Western Extension measures 230 ft. from north to south by 40 ft. across. A reference to the site plan (Pl. I) will show that almost all the surface covered by this extension lay between the contour lines of 535 and 540 ft. From south to north there is a gradual decline of 6 to 7 ft. in the surface. **Stratum I.** Near its south end there is but one wall assignable to the Ist stratum, but that it originally existed over a larger area is proved, among others, by the following finds, which have been recovered from a level higher than that of the IInd stratum:—

1. Fragmentary unicorn seal, unfinished. Pl. LXXXVII, 60. Extant side 1¼ in. No. 5551; Square I 9/2; Depth 9 in. b.s.

---

[1] Size ·5 × ·43 × ·38 in.

[2] These might have been used as palettes.

[3] On the Mohenjo-daro seal No. 357 a horned tiger is being attacked by a composite monster, *cf.* Sir John Marshall, *op. cit.*, p. 67, Pl. XIII, 17.

[4] *Ibid.*, p. 67, Pl. CXII, 386.

[5] For economy of space the south-east end of this trench, being devoid of walls, has been left out from the plan.

[6] These are House 3 to the west of the Great Granary and House 4 to its east.

2. Bossed, fragmentary faience sealing showing a cross at the centre enclosed in a periphery and a square dot at each of the resulting corners; similar to No. 391 in Pl. XCV. $\frac{1}{4}$ in. sq. No. 5788; Square I 9/2; Depth 2 ft. b.s.
3. Tiny, rectangular, faience sealing with 3 pictograms on one side only. Pl. C, 655. Size $\frac{3}{8}\times\frac{5}{12}$ in. No. 5724; Square I 9/1; Depth 1 ft. 10 in. b.s.
4. Lozenge-shaped red stone object with concave bevelled edges for inlay. Diag. 1·2 in. No. 1939; Square I 9/7; Depth 1 ft. b.s.

An interesting *lingam*.

5. Tiny, conical steatite *lingam* holed at bottom and painted red to simulate carnelian. It is decorated with six oblique white bands meeting at the top and rising from the bends of a ring undulating upwards only. It is possible that this undulating band was intended to represent a ringstone or *yoni* round a bætylic phallus. Pl. CXVII, 35. Ht. $\frac{11}{16}$ in. No. 5795; Square I 9/1; Depth 2 ft. b.s.
6. Tapering hornblende pendent, grooved at the head. No. 5894; Square I 9/2; Depth 2 ft. 8 in. b.s.
7. Star-shaped nose-disc of paste. No. 5733; Square H 9/21; Depth 1 ft. 10 in. b.s.
8. Faience ear-button. No. 5114; Square I 9/3; Depth 1 ft. b.s.
9. Tiny faience owl with sockets for separate insertion of eyes and feet. Pl. LXXVIII, 5. L. $1\frac{1}{4}$ in. No. 5893; Square I 9/2, Depth 2 ft. 8 in. b.s.
10. Tiny barrel-shaped gold bead. No. 5725; Square I 9/1; Depth 1 ft. 10 in. b.s.
11. Mica pieces. No. 5792; Square I 9/2; Depth 1 ft. 6 in. b.s.
12. Two tiny pottery cones holed at bottom. No. 5732; Square I 9/3; Depth 1 ft. 10 in. b.s.

Stratum II.

The IInd stratum, which lies 1 ft. 8 in. to 4 ft. below the surface, is represented near the north end of this extension by some isolated walls, and in the southern portion by one wall and two corners. In the middle portion, however, there are the extremely fragmentary remains of House 1, consisting of one small room of feeble construction in squares H 8/25 and H 9/21, another room to its south, of which the walls exist on three sides only (though the southern one is not bonded), traces of a room to the north, and of another one to the east across a narrow passage. To the east of these rooms there are two fairly long walls in the same stratum which may once have formed part of the same house and marked its eastern limit.

Fragmentary remains of a house.

Remains and finds in the central portion.

To the south of the above-mentioned house are a small pavement in squares H 9/21 and H 9/22, the T-shaped remains of two rooms in square H 9/23, another wall along the eastern edge of this extension, and one or two isolated bits of walls. Scattered about in them were found a number of antiquities of which the most interesting ones comprise a unicorn seal (No. 3212) with 4 pictograms (Pl. LXXXIX. 108), a rectangular copper piece with 3 pictograms in relief (Pl. CXXV,

21) together with a pin of the same substance (No. 2165), one copper spear-head (No. 7389), part of a copper dish, with straight rim, 9 in. in diameter (No. 7282, Pl. CXXIV, 31), a small goblet-shaped faience vase (No. 7772c), a chessman-shaped faience object (No. 7077), a cubical stone weight[1] (No. 7110) broken, a squat, tapering, pottery tumbler painted green (No. 3762), a corn measure (No. 3154) with concave body (Pl. LXXII, 15), a small perforated vase (No. 7429), and two terracotta female figures. Of the latter, No. 675—a pregnant woman, possibly carrying bread—may be an ex-voto offering (Pl. LXXVI, 30), while the other is a bust (No. 7079) wearing a torque and high head-dress from under which the hair, twisted in coils, falls on the shoulders (Pl. LXXVII, 42).

Finds in the southern portion.

In the southern part of this extension were found a much blurred tetrahedron-shaped terracotta seal (No. 5796), a copper celt 4½ in. long and 2¾ in. broad at the cutting edge (No. 3290), a leaf-shaped copper spear-head (No. 3291) 8½ in. long with a vertical mid-rib,[2] which on the whole is of rare occurrence (Pl. CXXIV, 49), a long-barrel grey stone weight[3] (No. 7070, 1·2¾ in.), and a pottery whistling hen (No. 5897). In this section was also found at a depth of 4 ft. 6 in. in square H 9/23 a large, crushed earthenware jar (Pl. VII, a, along the left edge). In the lower half it contained some animal bones including a large antler, tiny bones—perhaps of birds, a small faience bead, and some pottery which comprised five entire and over a dozen broken goblets with pointed bases, one complete and one broken, medium-sized, cylindrical vase, sherds of some other vessels, fragments of two bangles, a tubular bead, a wheel, and a ram. In addition to the above objects, this jar also contained some bricks and brickbats, besides several long pieces of slag[4] in pencil-like formation.

An interesting post-cremation urn.

Stratum III.

The IIIrd stratum lies between 4 ft. 1 in. and 7 ft. below the surface. In connection with this were found, at the northern end, a flat, oblong steatite seal with 5 pictograms (No. 4965, Pl. XCII, 262), and a trough-shaped, miniature, faience vase (No. 2705, Pl. LXXXII, 15). The seal is peculiar in having at the back a holed knob, which is characteristic of the square seals. With the single exception of No. 1259 (Pl. XCII, 294), all other seals of this kind are plano-convex and bored across the centre thickness.[5]

A rare seal.

Two fragmentary houses.

In the middle portion of this extension are the remains of two extremely fragmentary houses. In the northern one of these are indications of a set of three rooms built, without bonding, against the extreme south wall of House 3 of the IVth stratum (*see* p. 28 *infra*). It is possible that the entire south part of this house was occupied by a courtyard of which no trace is left now. In this latter was found a tiny triangular faience sealing (No. 3855) showing pictograms in two lines on one face and a symbol resembling the Roman numeral VIII on the other (Pl. XCV, 386). The second house (No. 2), which stands

---

[1] Size ·5 × ·43 × ·38 in.

[2] Such a mid-rib or reinforcing seam also occurs on the copper knife blade from a Pre-Sargonic burial at Kish. *Cf.* S. Langdon, *Excavations at Kish*, p. 77, Pl. XVIII, No. 2.

[3] For weights of this type *see* pp. 361-62 *infra*.

[4] Slag has not so far been met with in any other jar.

[5] Oblong seals with a boss at the back are also rare at Mohenjo-daro. Cf. *M. I. C.*, p. 376. Also *cf.* p. 47, No. 14 *infra*.

immediately south of the former, is of equally poor construction, and even more fragmentary. On the east, it has a rectangular room measuring 19 by 10 ft., to the south of which is a fairly long east and west wall pierced by a doorway, but no useful guess can be made regarding its plan. Scattered about in this house were found two cylindrical pottery sealings (Nos. 7541 and 7591, Pl. XCIV, 339), each showing a crocodile (*Gavialis gangeticus*) on one side and three pictograms on the other, a faience ear-button (No. 7487), a large (fragmentary) earthenware lid with tapering sides and hollow knob rising from the centre (No. 7809), a terracotta ball-rattle (No. 7708), and an inscribed potsherd (No. 7865).

Several interesting finds from the southern section.

At the south-east end of this extension are the remains of three rooms. In one of these, in square I 9/5, were found two cubical chert weights (No. 7285[1] and 7542[2]), and a flat piece of ivory decorated with incised circles (No. 7701). In the remaining portion, up to the southern limit of the two houses mentioned above, were recovered a number of antiquities, of which three deserve special notice. The first (No. 7786) is an elephant seal (Pl. XCI, 227), from square I 9/4. The second from square H 9/25 is an oblong pottery sealing lentoid in section (No. 7483, Pl. XCIII, 318) with 3 pictograms on one side, and, on the other a standing figure wearing a three-plumed head-dress, posed between two posts, each crowned with a *pīpal* (*ficus religiosa*) leaf. His left arm appears to carry a number of bangles. Unfortunately, the sealing is blurred and the object in his right hand is not clear.[3] The third object is a polychrome pottery vase, 2¾ in. in height (No. 7788), shaped like a pomegranate (Pl. LXXI, 21). Its ground is painted white, but the scheme of decoration in red and green is worn past recognition. Among the other antiquities found in this section may be mentioned a copper chisel (No. 7430), a leaf-shaped copper spear-head in four pieces (No. 7658), a faience ear-button (No. 7775), three hollow semi-circular pottery terminals (Nos. 7615, 7662 and 7741), and a round pottery vase (ht. 3⅜ in.) painted with black bands (No. 1461).

Stratum IV.

A nearly complete house.

The only more or less complete house in this extension was discovered in the IVth stratum at a depth of 7 ft. below the surface. It stands immediately west of the store halls III and IV of the Great Granary (Pl. III), but its foundation is about 1 ft. 9 in. higher. From Pl. VII, *b*, it will appear that there are three rooms on the south numbered 1 to 3 on the plan, of which the middle or largest one is 11 ft. by 8 ft. 3 in. There is also a fair sized room No. 5 on the west side, but its northern part is broken. Between this and the corner room No. 3 is a narrow chamber No. 4. The north outer wall of this house, as well as a part of the east wall have disappeared. Since there is no indication of a doorway now, the floor level appears to have been pretty high, and this is also indicated by a 3 ft. high offset on the inner face of its extreme south wall. Obviously, the whole of the north-eastern part of this house was the courtyard No. 6 in which was found a square, bossed seal (No. 1692) engraved with the effigy of an elephant (Pl. XCI, 228). In room No. 1

---

[1] Size ·9 × ·9 × ·75 in.

[2] Broken. Size 2 × 2 × 1·5 in.

[3] Among the numerous sealings of faience and terracotta there is not one which is not more or less blurred.

was found a thin copper strip $6\frac{3}{4}$ in. long (No. 2825), and in room No. 3 a rectangular pottery sealing (No. 3801) showing four pictograms on one side, and on the other a humpless bull with incense-burner below his neck exactly similar to that associated with the unicorns, as well as a symbol resembling the Roman numeral VII (Pl. XCIII, 314). It is noteworthy that apart from its two horns, which are a little shorter, the animal is apparently the same as the unicorn which is so ubiquitous on seals[1] from Harappā and Mohenjo-daro. It may, therefore, be that the so-called unicorn is after all no other than the humpless ox shown in profile in such a way that only one horn would be visible. But, at present, there is no other evidence regarding the identity or otherwise of this animal with the so-called unicorn, and the above suggestion must not be regarded as anything more than a mere possibility.

Sealing with humpless bull.

Abutting on to the east outer wall of the above house is a paved sink, measuring 2 ft. 1 in. by 1 ft. 6 in. by 2 ft. 7 in., which was filled with drinking goblets and potsherds. In square I 9/6 was found at a depth of 7 ft. 2 in. a rectangular copper piece measuring $\frac{1}{16}$ by $\frac{7}{16}$ in.

Sink.

To trace the retaining wall along the Western Block of the Great Granary it became necessary to sink a deep and narrow trench immediately outside the line of buttresses, but the search, as already stated, proved futile. The digging was, however, rewarded by the following finds made in the Vth, VIth and VIIth strata :—

Finds of Strata V to VII.

Stratum V.—

1. Oval pottery cage pierced with five openings round the body and one through the roof where there is also a circular depression apparently caused by the breaking off of a seated bird. Pl. CXX, 26. Observe the differences between this cage and cage No. Ab554 (Pl. CXX, 22). Ht. 3 in.; diams. 4 and 3 in. No. 3826; Square I 7/10; Depth 9 ft. 10 in. b.s.
2. Hornblende pendent, grooved at the head. Ht. $1\frac{3}{8}$ in. No. 2970; Square I 8/7; Depth 11 ft. b.s.

Stratum VI.—

1. Tiny, rectangular steatite seal with 2 pictograms on one side, and a hill goat with horns curved backwards, facing left, on the other. Pl. XCVI, 429. Size $\frac{1}{2} \times \frac{3}{8}$ in. No. 10359; Square I 8/10; Depth 15 ft. 6 in. b.s.
2. Three-sided, prismoid faience sealing with faint inscriptions on each face. Pl. XCVIII, 600. L. $\frac{3}{16}$ in.; w. $\frac{4}{10}$ in. No. 10177; Square I 9/12; Depth 11 ft. 9 in. b.s.
3. Rectangular, faience sealing with 3 pictograms on one side, and a symbol resembling the Roman numeral VIII on the other. Pl. XCVIII, 607. Size $\frac{5}{16} \times \frac{3}{10}$ in. No. 10178; Square J 9/11; Depth 12 ft. 6 in. b.s.

Stratum VII.—

1. Fragment of a legged pottery stool with ribbed surface. Ht. $2\frac{1}{4}$ in.; existing side $4\frac{1}{8}$ in. No. 10109; Square I 7/10; Depth 17 ft. b.s.

[1] *Cf.* Sir John Marshall, *op. cit.*, pp. 68-69.

The Southern Extension.

Limits of the Southern Extension. By the Southern Extension is meant that part of the area to the south of the Great Granary which lies between the southern ends of the Eastern and Western Extensions. It is limited along the south edge by squares I 9/10 to J 9/15, and measures 120 ft. from east to west by 45 ft., across. The whole of it, lying between the contour lines of 540 and 545 ft., is higher than the Western Extension, and slopes down gradually from east to west.

Finds from Stratum I. In this the 1st stratum is indicated merely by finds which include a double convex, discoid alabaster mace-head (No. 6042) from the west end, half of a unicorn seal (No. 1244) from the middle (Pl. XC, 188), and a tiny conical gold boss (No. 5062) from the east end.

Stratum II. Walls of the IInd stratum are scarce and extremely fragmentary. Scattered about in the whole extension were found two fragmentary unicorn seals (No. 1650, Pl. XC, 204, and No. 2001); fragment of a now restored ivory cup (No. 1652) 2½ in. in diameter (Pl. CXIX, 2), a leaf-shaped copper spear-head 4½ in. long (No. 3353), a polished, biconical weight of hornblende (No. 1651, 1. 3·7 in., Pl. CXVII, 47), a shell disc (No. 5206) cut into the form of a circumscribed lozenge[1] for inlay (Pl. CXXXIX, 85), a double-convex discoid stone mace-head (No. 5203), a chessman-shaped faience object (No. 5304), and a flat bottomed, round terracotta rattle[2] (No. 5200, Pl. CXX, 34). In the eastern section scattered over 60 ft. in the adjoining squares I 9/20 to J 9/10 were found a long and slender faience ear pendent[3] with a holed conical knob at the upper end (No. 5207, Pl. CXXXIX, 40), a tiny jade pendent (No. 5257), a tapering cylindrical bead of faience with fine vertical fluting (No. 5497, Pl. CXXVIII, 17), and a unicorn seal (No. 5399, Pl. XCIX, 614).

Stratum III. The IIIrd stratum is also fragmentary and represented by a few bits of floors and some broken walls widely scattered about. Its construction is, however, better than that of the IInd. Most of the finds of this stratum came from the adjoining squares I 9/10, I 9/14 and I 9/15. They comprise a unicorn seal (No. 1697, Pl. LXXXVIII, 76), a rectangular and plano-convex steatite seal (No. 5436, Pl. XCII, 264), a cylindrical pottery sealing (No. 5498) inscribed on opposite faces (Pl. XCIV, 362), a rectangular faience sealing (No. 5388) inscribed on one side only (similar to No. 367*a* in Pl. XCVII), and a tiny, couchant, faience ram (No. 1693). From the central portion of this extension may be noticed the fragment of a plano-convex, rectangular steatite seal (No. 5389, Pl. XCII, 300), and two inscribed potsherds (Nos. 1460 and 5387, Pl. CIV, 59 and 82): and from the eastern, a square faience sealing (No. 271) inscribed with a *svastika* (Pl. XCV, 399), a double-holed rectangular steatite amulet (No. 5343) and a much rusted V-shaped copper arrow-tip (No. 6040). Over and across a wall of this stratum in square I 9/15, were found a number of animal bones which must be assigned to a time when buildings of this stratum had already fallen to ruins.

---

[1] Such patterns are quite common on painted pottery from the Indus Valley sites.

[2] & [3] These shapes are unique.

Remains and finds of Stratum IV. The little that remains of the IVth stratum is widely scattered; every bit of it is decidedly better and more substantial than the remains of the two uppermost strata, and also superior to many walls of Stratum III. Most of these walls are 3 ft. thick and one of them, in square J 9/10, is as much as 6 ft. thick. Constructed as they are over a raised part of the mound, where the surface is higher than at the Western Extension, their foundations stand 3 to 5 ft. higher than those of the contemporary house No. 3 on that side. The following finds of Stratum IV were found fairly evenly distributed over the whole of this extension :—

1. Unicorn seal with 8 pictograms. Pl. LXXXIX, 119. $\frac{13}{16}$ in. sq. No. 2281 ; Square I 9/13 ; Depth 8 ft. 6 in. b.s.
2. Unicorn seal with 7 pictograms. Pl. LXXXV, 12. $1\frac{1}{8}$ in. sq. No. 5880 ; Square J 9/10 ; Depth 8 ft. 8 in. b.s.
3. Unicorn seal, pictograms broken away. Pl. LXXXVII, 48. Side $1\frac{1}{4}$ in. No. 2097 ; Square J 9/9 ; Depth 10 ft. 3 in. b.s.
4. Unicorn seal, left side broken. Pl. XC, 189. 1 in. sq. No. 2700 ; Square J 9/14 ; Depth 11 ft. 5 in. b.s.
5. Unicorn seal with 5 pictograms, broken at the lower left corner. Pl. LXXXIX, 147. $\frac{11}{16}$ in. sq. No. 2961 ; Square J 9/14 ; Depth 12 ft. b.s.
6. Bossed seal showing a short humped bull (*Bos indicus*) feeding from a trough,[1] which has almost disappeared, and two pictograms in upper field. This seal is rare, as it shows a bull feeding from a trough which is always shown in front of such wild beasts as the Indian bisón, the rhinoceros, and the tiger which are not likely to have been domesticated. The elephant and the buffalo are sometimes shown feeding from it and sometimes not. Pl. XCI, 235. Side $\frac{7}{8}$ in. No. 2415 ; Square I 9/19 ; Depth 10 ft. 6 in. b.s.
7. Tiny, three-sided prism seal of steatite with 3 pictograms on one side, fish on the second, and 3 dotted circles on the third. Pl. XCVII, 575. L. $\frac{5}{16}$ in. No. 3534 ; Square I 9/24 ; Depth 10 ft. b.s.
8. Tiny, rectangular faience sealing showing on either face a well executed, regardant hill-goat, and in the remaining space an inscription, which, on one side, resembles the Roman numeral VIII. Pl. XCVIII, 601. Size $\frac{3}{8} \times \frac{5}{16}$ in. No. 2276 ; Square J 9/4 ; Depth 9 ft 6 in. b.s.
9. Tiny, faience sealing resembling the stone of a date-palm, inscribed on either side of the axial groove. Pl. XCV, 385. L. $\frac{3}{4}$ in. No. 2701 ; Square J 9/4 ; Depth 10 ft. b.s.
10. Thick, rectangular terracotta sealing with 5 pictograms on one side, and a well executed acacia tree enclosed by a railing on the other. Pl. XCIII, 325. The railing is quite clear and exceptionally interesting, as it was destined to become a very important motif of Buddhist religious architecture. Size $1 \times \frac{1}{2} \times \frac{3}{8}$ in. No. 5617 ; Square I 9/20 ; Depth 7 ft. 2 in. b.s.

---

[1] Sir John Marshall has suggested that the troughs were meant to symbolise food offerings to animals which were objects of worship. *Cf. M. I. C.*, pp. 70-1.

11. Cylindrical terracotta sealing with 3 pictograms on one side, and an acacia tree enclosed by a platform on the other. Pl. XCIII, 323. L. 1 in. No. 1991; Square I 9/24; Depth 8 ft. 6 in. b.s.
12. Long-barrel bead of carnelian broken at one end. No. 7850; Square I 9/14; Depth 10 ft. 6 in. b.s.
13. Two pottery dishes. Diam. 9 in. each. No. 5390; Square I 9/10; Depth 6 ft. 1 in. b.s.

In addition to the above-mentioned finds may be noticed from square I 9/2 a somewhat irregularly shaped, thin walled, oval jar (No. 3760) with short neck and everted rim[1] (Pl. VIII, *c*). It is 2 ft. high, 1 ft. 2 in. in diameter at the mouth, and the only one of this shape from Harappā. Its contents were similar to those of the large-sized post cremation urns.

Finds from Strata V and VI. In this extension, the Vth stratum was confined only to a width of 31 ft. along the south of the Western Block of the Great Granary where the excavation was carried down deeper. Not a single wall belonging to it was traced. In quest of the retaining wall, which was found broken,[2] the northern part of this lower portion was dug deeper to a depth of over 8 ft. below the foundation of the IVth stratum. Throughout this deeper excavation there was a very thick layer of terracotta nodules, potsherds and ashes, forming, as it were, a solid substratum over which walls of the IVth stratum were subsequently raised. Lying promiscuously in this enormous dump were a number of interesting antiquities which must obviously be relegated to a time earlier than the IVth stratum. They have been tentatively assigned to the Vth or VIth stratum according as they come up to or are below the foundation of the Great Granary. Among those of the Vth stratum are :—

1. Unicorn seal with 5 pictograms, incense-burner broken. Pl. LXXXIX, 139. $\frac{3}{4}$ in. sq. No. 2266; Square I 9/14; Depth 10 ft. b.s.
2. Unicorn seal with 3 pictograms surviving. Left half broken. Pl. LXXXIX, 144. $1\frac{1}{16}$ in. sq. No. 2367; Square I 9/19; Depth 10 ft. 3 in. b.s.
3. Fragment of a unicorn seal with 3 pictograms surviving. Lower half broken. Pl. XCIX, 620. L. $\frac{3}{4}$ in. No. 2960; Square I 9/23; Depth 12 ft. 9 in. b.s.
4. Unicorn seal with 4 pictograms. This is one of the smallest of square seals. Pl. LXXXIX, 161. $\frac{5}{16}$ in. sq. No. 2962; Square I 9/19; Depth 13 ft. 5 in. b.s.
5. Tiny, rectangular seal with 3 pictograms on one side, and 1 on the other. Pl. XCVI, 453. Size $\frac{1}{2}\times\frac{5}{16}$ in. No. 3484; Square I 9/24; Depth 10 ft. 6 in. b.s.
6. Tiny, rectangular seal with 4 pictograms on one side, and 3 on the other. Pl. XCVI, 454. Size $\frac{11}{16}\times\frac{5}{16}$ in. No. 2868; Square I 9/23; Depth 12 ft. b.s.

[1] For a similar jar *cf.* *M. I. C.*, Pl. LXXXV, 5.

[2] See p. 20 *supra*.

7. Fragment of a seal engraved with the figure of a composite monster now showing only an elephant's trunk and bovine forelegs. Pl. XCI, 247. L. 1 1/16 in. No. 2453; Square I 9/18; Depth 10 ft. 6 in. b.s.
8. Cylindrical faience sealing, lentoid in section, with a foliated twig[1] on opposite faces; similar to Nos. 705 and 706 in Pl. CI. L. 1/2 in. No. 2608; Square J 9/8; Depth 11 ft. 3 in. b.s.
9. Tiny, rectangular faience sealing with 3 pictograms on one side, and 1 on the other. Pl. XCIV, 347. Size 13/16 × 3/8 in. No. 2891; Square I 9/9; Depth 11 ft. 9 in. b.s.
10. Tiny, three-sided faience sealing showing on one side a bison grazing in a trough, 4 pictograms on the second, and a VII-like symbol on the third. Pl. XCIV, 342. L. 3/8 in. No. 8800; Square I 9/22; Depth 12 ft. b.s.
11. Hornblende pendent, grooved at the head. Ht. 1 1/8 in. No. 2849; Square I 9/23; Depth 12 ft. b.s.
12. Ear-ring of thin copper wire. Diam. 1 1/4 in. No. 2424; Square I 9/14; Depth 10 ft. b.s.
13. Copper razor of Irish pattern.[2] Pl. CXXV, 47. Size 4×2 1/8 in. No. 2892; Square I 9/23; Depth 12 ft. b.s.
14. Oval pottery vase with prominent neck. Ht. 8 1/4 in. No. 2912; Square I 9/13; Depth 12 ft. 8 in. b.s.
15. Two rough, carinated pottery vases marked with a cross in the concave upper portion. Ht. 3 1/4 in. No. 2919; Square J 9/14; Depth 13 ft. 8 in. b.s.

The following objects may be assigned to the VIth stratum:—

1. Unicorn seal with 4 pictograms. Incense-burner broken. Pl. LXXXIX, 110. 1 in. sq. No. 3482; Square I 9/24; Depth 16 ft. 4 in. b.s.
2. Tiny, rectangular seal with 3 pictograms on one side, and 1 on the other. Broken in several pieces; similar to No. 508 in Pl. XCVII. Size 9/16 × 5/16 in. No. 3678; Square I 9/8; Depth 12 ft. 6 in. b.s.
3. Tiny, rectangular faience sealing with 3 pictograms on one side, and 1 on the other. Pl. C, 692. Size 9/16 × 1/4 in. No. 3483; Square I 9/24; Depth 16 ft. 4 in. b.s.
4. Tiny, rectangular faience sealing with 4 pictograms on one side and 3 on the other. Pl. XCIV, 356. Size 3/4 × 5/16 in. No. 9015; Square J 9/3; Depth 13 ft. b.s.
5. Rectangular, plano-convex, terracotta sealing with 5 pictograms on one side. and 4 on the other. Pl. XCIV, 344. L. 1/2 in. No. 3581; Square I 9/24; Depth 15 ft. 6 in. b.s.
6. Thick, alabaster ring. Pl. LXXXIII, 23. Diam. 2 1/8 in. No. 3340; Square I 9/3; Depth 16 ft. 6 in. b.s.
7. Ear-ring of thin copper wire. Diam. 1 3/8 in. No. 3642; Square I 9/19; Depth 16 ft. b.s.

---

[1] This is illustrated in *A. S. R.* for 1926-27, Pl. XXI, *b*, 49.

[2] *Cf.* F. Petrie, *Tools and Weapons*, Pl. LX, 51-53; also *cf.* Sir John Marshall, *op. cit.*, Pl. CXXXVII, 5, and Pl. CXXXVIII, 12.

Find of animal bones in a packing of terracotta nodules.

Immediately outside the south-east corner of the retaining wall, where the mound has a marked slope, was found between 10 to 14 ft. below the surface a large quantity of animal bones, mixed up with nodules and ashes. All the bones were discoloured green, and most of them had become very hard. Two long bones (Nos. 2882 and 2596) and one horn had become extraordinarily hard. I have assigned the above antiquities to the Vth or VIth stratum only tentatively as the rubbish below the walls of the IVth stratum formed one unbroken mass and was found to continue still lower down, so that if, perchance, a deep pit had been filled up at this place prior to the construction of the IVth stratum, the depth of a given find would obviously not be an index to its age.

Finds from Trench A.

The portion of Trench A immediately south of this extension was deepened for a length of about 20 ft. In this, standing against a wall of the IIIrd stratum along the eastern edge of the trench, was discovered the crater-like store jar No. 299 which is 2 ft. 6 in. in height and 1 ft. 7 in. in diameter at the mouth. From top to bottom it was filled with loose, greenish and porous earth, which was probably the decomposed remains of some cereal. Opposite this, and partly buried below the other edge of the trench, were found together at a depth of 11 ft. 2 in. 27 crude, carinated pottery vases (Pl. LXXI, 42), 17 of which are scratched with a diagonal cross, several chert scrapers and a copper rod (No. 2535).

The Eastern Extension.

Its extent.

The extension along the east of the Great Granary is larger than any on the remaining three sides, being 230 ft. long from north to south and 46 ft. across. Throughout this area, the ground slopes towards the north and west, the surface at the south-east corner, *viz.*, 547 ft. above the sea-level, being the highest. From here, there is a fall of 6 to 7 ft. at the northern edge—sharp for the first one-third of the extension and gradual over the remaining two-thirds. The Ist

Stratum I.

stratum is represented only in the southern portion by one corner, which has since been demolished and two other walls in squares J 9/17 and J 9/23. As might have been expected, almost all finds of the Ist stratum have been recovered from the southern half. In the adjoining squares J 8/25 and J 9/21 was found a set of seven long oval vases (No. 4184) broken at the neck (Pl. VIII, *e*). Of these, five contained one or two medium-sized tumblers lying one over the other, and with one exception, each of them contained a like miniature vase. But in the central or fourth oval vase there were only three miniature vases overlapping one another, while the second from the right was quite empty. From the southern half of this extension the following antiquities may be mentioned :—

1. Unicorn seal, upper part with pictograms broken. Pl. LXXXVIII, 68. Side 1⅜ in. No. 4013 ; Square K 9/2 ; Depth 2 ft. 8 in. b.s.
2. Rectangular, plano-convex steatite seal with 4 pictograms. Pl. XCII, 268. Size 1¼×½ in. No. 4058 ; Square K 8/5 ; Depth 3 ft. b.s.
3. Cylindrical, faience sealing with 3 pictograms on one side, and a large acacia tree enclosed in a platform on the other ; similar to No. 327 in Pl. XCIII. L. 1⅜ in. No. 3333 ; Square K 9/5 ; Depth 1 ft. b.s.

4. Cylindrical, terracotta sealing with 11 pictograms on one side, and a crocodile on the other. Pl. XCIV, 336. L. 1¼ in. No. 4261; Square J 9/25; Depth 5 ft. 3 in. b.s.
5. Cubical chert weight. Wt. 1·85 gms.; size ·4×·4×·3 in. No. 3993; Square K 9/2; Depth 1 ft. 2 in. b.s.
6. Cubical chert weight. Wt. 29·5 gms.; size ·9×·9×·8 in. No. 3995; Square K 9/2; Depth 2 ft. 6 in. b.s.
7. Faience tetrahedron with a dotted circle on each face. Pl. CXX, 55. Side ⅞ in. No. 32; Square J 8/23; Depth 9 in. b.s.
8. Faience ball with linear decoration hatched in opposite directions in each quarter. Pl. CXX, 42. Diam. 1⅜ in. No. 53; Square J 9/21; Depth 2 ft. b.s.
9. Gadrooned bead of faience. Pl. CXXVIII, 10. Diam. ·6 in. No. 4412; Square K 9/5; Depth 7 ft. 4 in. b.s.
10. Tiny, copper boss. Diam. 1·25 in. No. 4321; Square J 9/24; Depth 5 ft. 3 in. b.s.
11. Globular pottery vase painted with a series of horizontal bands. Ht. 3¼ in. No. 3232; Square J 7/24; Depth 2 ft. b.s.
12. Globular pottery vase with fine red slip. Ht. 4 in. No. 4039; Square K 8/3; Depth 3 ft. b.s.
13. Terracotta female bust with the usual lunette-shaped head-dress behind the head, three flowers in the head-dress, and cup-like appendages at the ears below which are rough conical ornaments. Pl. LXXVII, 36. No. 4059; Square K 8/5; Depth 3 ft. b.s.

The only find of this stratum from the northern end is a round pottery vase (No. 3232).

Remains of Stratum II hopelessly mutilated.

In the southern half of this extension, where the surface was higher, walls of the IInd stratum appeared between 3 ft. 6 in. and 7 ft. below the surface, whereas in the remaining half their depth varied from 2 ft. 8 in. to 4 ft. 3 in. Scattered throughout this extension are numerous walls belonging to Stratum II, which in most cases are not more than a few feet in length. Altogether, they are so hopelessly mutilated that it is nowhere possible to obtain from them a connected plan (*cf.* higher walls mostly along the edge of the trench in Pl. VII, *c*). In the western one of two rooms in square K 8/5 was found a blurred, cylindrical terracotta sealing (No. 4309) bored lengthwise. It has an illegible inscription on one side, and a crocodile on the other (Pl. XCIV, 333). This is the only holed Cylinder found here which resembles those of Mesopotamia.[1]

Bored cylindrical sealing with crocodile.

Finds.

A large number of antiquities were recovered from this stratum, of which a list is given below. It may be noticed that these antiquities were fairly evenly distributed over 170 ft. from the southern edge of this extension, but the northern 60 ft. were quite devoid of them—

1. Unicorn seal with 4 pictograms. Pl. LXXXVIII, 88. Size $1\frac{1}{16}\times1\frac{1}{16}$ in.[2] No. 945; Square J 9/18; Depth 3 ft. 9 in. b.s.

[1] *Cf.* L. W. King, *History of Sumer and Akkad*, Figs. 53 and 55, pp. 174-75.

[2] This is exceptional in not being a perfect square.

2. Unicorn seal with 8 pictograms. Pl. LXXXVI, 23. 1½ in. sq. No. 180; Square J 8/25; Depth 4 ft. b.s.
3. Rectangular, plano-convex steatite seal with 2 pictograms. Unique among seals of this type in being holed lengthwise across the thickness. Pl. XCII, 286. Size $\frac{7}{16}$×½ in. No. 4276; Square K 8/2; Depth 5 ft. 4 in. b.s.
4. Right half of a rectangular, plano-convex steatite seal with 2 pictograms surviving. Pl. XCIX, 632. L. ⅜ in. No. 4588; Square K 9/5; Depth 8 ft. b.s.
5. Tiny, discoid seal with 3 pictograms on one side, and VIII-like symbol on the other. Pl. XCVII, 550. Diam. ⅜ in. No. 4269; Square K 9/2; Depth 5 ft. 9 in. b.s.
6. Rectangular faience sealing with 4 pictograms on one side, and VII-like symbol on the other. Pl. C, 679. Size ⅝×½ in. No. 4631; Square K 9/3; Depth 7 ft. 7 in. b.s.
7. Right half of an oblong faience sealing, lentoid in section, with two pictograms on each of the two sides; similar to No. 321 in Pl. XCIII. W. ½ in. No. 4411; Square K 9/4; Depth 6 ft. 8 in. b.s.
8. Cylindrical, terracotta sealing with 11 pictograms on one side, and crocodile on the other. Pl. XCIV, 325. L. 1$\frac{3}{16}$ in. No. 1201; Square J 9/19; Depth 4 ft. b.s.
9. Much blurred, oblong terracotta sealing, lentoid in section. On one side it had an acacia tree, of which only the trunk is now visible, and possibly pictograms on the other; similar to No. 328 in Pl. XCIII. Size 1$\frac{1}{16}$×$\frac{5}{16}$ in. No. 4181; Square K 9/2; Depth 5 ft. b.s.
10. Cylindrical, terracotta sealing with 11 blurred pictograms on one side, and crocodile on the other; similar to No. 334 in Pl. XCIV. L. 1⅛ in. No. 1123; Square J 9/19; Depth 5 ft. b.s.
11. Rectangular, plano-convex terracotta sealing distorted in firing and inscribed on one face only. Pl. XCIV, 366*a*. L. ⅞ in. No. 2759; Square J 10/16; Depth 6 ft. 7 in. b.s.
12. Large, cuboid chert core, proLably an unfinished weight. Pl. CXVIII, 12. Size 4×4×2¼ in. No. 1095; Square J 9/23; Depth 4 ft. b.s.
13. Barrel-shaped polished weight of hornblende. Pl. CXVII, 48. Wt. 130·2 gms.; 1·3⅝ in. No. 1094; Square J 9/23; Depth 4 ft. b.s.
14. Tapering steatite pendent, grooved at the head, unfinished. No. 4274; Square K 8/4; Depth 5 ft. 1 in. b.s.
15. Cuboid chert weight. Wt. 28 gms.; size ·9×·9×·75 in. No. 4192; Square K 9/3; Depth 5 ft. 2 in. b.s.
16. Chert weight with unusually small thickness. Broken. Wt. 11·99 gms.; size ·75×·75×·45 in. No. 4311; Square K 8/4; Depth 5 ft. 7 in. b.s.
17. Cuboid chert weight. Wt. 6·65 gms.; size ·55×·55×·45 in. No. 4783; Square J 9/25; Depth 8 ft. b.s.

18. Copper fish hook. Pl. CXXV, 8. L. $1\frac{11}{16}$ in. No. 1057; Square J 9/24; Depth 4 ft. 6 in. b.s.

19. Mica pieces. No. 4228; Square K 9/2; Depth 4 ft. 8 in. b.s.

20. Mica pieces. Nos. 4787 and 4890; Square J 9/25; Depth 8 ft. b.s.

21. Shell ball incised with a series of four double concentric circles round the body and one in each of the resulting opposite spaces. Similar ornamentation is also found on faience balls. Diam. $1\frac{1}{4}$ in. No. 4098; Square K 9/1; Depth 3 ft. 6 in. b.s.

22. Shell spoon. Pl. LXXXII, 4. Size $2\frac{3}{4}\times1\frac{3}{16}$ in. No. 156; Square J 8/25; Depth 4 ft. 6 in. b.s.

23. Fragment of a cylindrical and deeply undulating ring of shell. Pl. CXVII, 12. Ht. $1\frac{1}{16}$ in. No. 2607; Square J 9/24; Depth 4 ft. 6 in. b.s.

24. Shell ball, plain. Diam. $1\frac{1}{8}$ in. No. 4239; Square K 9/2; Depth 5 ft. 6 in. b.s.

25. Cylindrical bone baluster with cross hatched lines in three compartments. L. 1/78 in. No. 1101; Square J 9/23; Depth 4 ft. b.s.

26. Cylindrical ivory baluster, thicker than usual, divided into two compartments by three equidistant bands of cross-hatched lines at the ends and centre. Both compartments and the ends are decorated with incised circles. Pl. CXIX, 30. L. $1\frac{7}{8}$ in.; diam. $\frac{5}{8}$ in. No. 4528; Square J 9/25; Depth 7 ft. b.s.

27. Fragment of an ivory comb with concentric circle decoration. Pl. CXIX, 3. Originally it had a handle at the lower end as in comb No. 7038. No. 4530; Square J 9/25; Depth 7 ft. b.s.

Pottery objects—

28. Bi-convex vase with flat bottom, painted with a series of bands over the body. Pl. LXXI, 52. Ht. $3\frac{1}{16}$ in. No. 1093; Square J 9/24; Depth 4 ft. b.s.

29. Miniature vase with flat bottom and double convex body. Has traces of fine red glaze. Diam. $\frac{3}{4}$ in.; Ht. $\frac{1}{2}$ in. No. 4275; Square K 8/2; Depth 5 ft. 3 in. b.s.

30. Miniature round vase with flat bottom. Ht. $\frac{1}{4}$ in. No. 4268; Square K 9/2; Depth 5 ft. 9 in. b.s.

31. Oval vase with flat bottom, body deeply scored with a series of grooves. Ht. $6\frac{1}{4}$ in. No. 28; Square J 9/19; Depth 6 ft. b.s.

32. A small dish on a broad funnel-shaped stand (fragmentary). Ht. 4 in.; diam. of dish $5\frac{1}{4}$ in. No. 903; Square J 9/17; Depth 6 ft. 6 in. b.s.

33. Fragmentary spoon of black pottery shaped like those of shell. Its bottom is, however, flat. No. 4699; Square K 9/2; Depth 7 ft. 4 in. b.s.

34. Keeled bangle of vitreous texture and bright red colour (*cf.* similar bangles Nos. 8989 and 8990 from Trench V). Diam. $3\frac{5}{8}$ in. No. 4101; Square K 8/4; Depth 4 ft. b.s.

35. Toy offerings' dish with some vegetables or fruits on it. Ht. 1 3/10 in. No. 4124; Square K 8/4; Depth 4 ft. 2 in. b.s.

36. Standing figure of a mother suckling a baby. She has the usual lunette-shaped head-dress, wears a conical ornament like the modern *chauk* attached to a braid of hair, a torque and necklace. Pl. LXXVII, 31. Ht. 2⅜ in. No. 213; Square J 9/21; Depth 5 ft. b.s.

37. A toy hound carrying a hare in his mouth. Pl. LXXVIII, 48. L. 3 in. No. 4481; Square K 9/1; Depth 6 ft. b.s.

Stratum III.

Remains slightly better preserved than those of Stratum II.

The IIIrd stratum lies 7 ft. to 10 ft. 6 in. below the surface in the raised southern part, and at a depth of 4 ft. 4 in. to 8 ft. in the remaining portion. In point of construction, the remains of this stratum are as poor as those of the IInd, but are slightly better preserved. Near the northern end of the trench there is a complete room measuring 19 ft. by 7 ft. 10 in. lying mostly in Square J 8/16, in which was found a plano-convex, rectangular, steatite seal (No. 867, Pl. XCII, 273). Along its northern wall is a small drain covered by bricks laid flat. At this place, there are also two more incomplete rooms, probably belonging to the same house, *i.e.*, one to the north with a small pavement and the other to the south. In the southern section, in Squares K 9/3 and 4, and in what may have been the remains of two rooms, were found a copper spear-head (No. 5210) 5¼ in. long, an inscribed potsherd (No. 7180, Pl. CI, 711), an ivory chessman-shaped object (No. 4753), one small chert weight[1] (No. 5042), and the upper part of a vase-shaped pottery cage (No. 5043) with a bird seated on it (Pl. CXX, 23). A little to the north of the above room are two small pavements with brick edging in Square K 9/2. In the centre of the trench (Squares K 8/5 and J 8/25) is a 31 ft. long wall running east and west. Its eastern part is thicker than the western, but, all along, the inner or southern face is one. On either side of the main wall were found two unicorn seals (No. 272, Pl. LXXXIX, 137, and No. 474, Pl. LXXXVIII, 84). Close by in Square J 8/20 is the west wall of a room broken at both corners. In addition to these, there are a few corners and other broken bits with which nothing particular was associated.

Finds of Stratum III.

The following antiquities were found scattered in this stratum:—

1. Fragment of a small sized unicorn seal with only the head of the animal and incense-burner left. L. 1/2 in. No. 4640; Square K 8/4; Depth 7 ft. 4 in. b.s.

2. Flat and roughly rectangular, unfinished seal of grey steatite with 2 pictograms on either side. The piece having chipped off at several places in course of making was apparently rejected. Pl. XC, 222. L. 1⅝ in.; W. 1½ in. No. 1204; Square J 9/24; Depth 8 ft. b.s.

3. Tiny, rectangular steatite seal with 2 pictograms on one side, and 1 on the other. Pl. XCVI, 438. Size 11/16 × 5/16 in. No. 1282; Square J 9/19; Depth 7 ft. 3 in. b.s.

---

[1] Size ·9×·9×·8 in.

4. Right hand part of a tiny rectangular faience sealing with 2 pictograms surviving. It is inscribed on one side only; similar to No. 669 in Pl. C. L. $\frac{3}{8}$ in. No. 1010; Square J 8/22; Depth 8 ft. b.s.
5. Right hand part of a tiny amygdaloid steatite seal with pictograms on both sides; similar to No. 553 in Pl. XCVII. L. $\frac{7}{16}$ in. No. 4970; Square J 9/19; Depth 8 ft. b.s.
6. Oblong faience sealing, lentoid in section, with 5 pictograms on one side, and incense-burner on the other. Pl. XCIII, 320. L. $1\frac{3}{8}$ in. No. 4971; Square J 9/19; Depth 9 ft. b.s.
7. Bossed, faience sealing inscribed with a double line *svastika* and a short stroke in each of the resulting spaces. Pl. XCV, 397. $\frac{1}{2}$ in. sq. No. 5420; Square K 9/5; Depth 12 ft. 8 in. b.s.
8. Cylindrical terracotta sealing with crocodile (*Gavialis gangeticus*) on one side, and 11 pictograms on the other. Pl. XCIV, 336. L. $1\frac{1}{2}$ in. No. 4531; Square K 8/5; Depth 6 ft. 9 in. b.s.
9. Cylindrical terracotta sealing exactly similar to above, and obviously from the same mould. L. $1\frac{3}{8}$ in. No. 4532; Square K 8/5; Depth 6 ft. 9 in. b.s.
10. Discoid, terracotta sealing with the Indian bison (*Bos gaurus*) facing left and one pictogram in upper field. The blurred head of the animal appears to be somewhat bent down, possibly over a trough which is not now visible. This is one of the rare sealings where the animal faces left instead of right. Pl. XCIII, 311. Diam. 1 in. No. 1245; Square J 9/23; Depth 7 ft. 9 in. b.s.
11. Cylindrical, terracotta sealing with 11 pictograms on one side, and crocodile (*Gavialis gangeticus*) on the other; similar to No. 335 in Pl. XCIV. L. $1\frac{3}{16}$ in. No. 1236; Square J 9/24; Depth 8 ft. b.s.
12. Rectangular, terracotta sealing, distorted in firing. It has 4 pictograms on one face and a row of 3 incense-burners on the other, separated by four vertical rows of three circles each. Pl. XCIII, 322. L. $1\frac{3}{8}$ in. No. 2867; Square J 10/16; Depth 9 ft. 5 in. b.s.
13. Cylindrical terracotta sealing with crocodile on one side, and indistinct pictograms on the other; similar to No. 339 in Pl. XCIV. L. $1\frac{5}{16}$ in. No. 2866; Square J 10/16; Depth 9 ft. 5 in. b.s.
14. Chert core. L. 2 in. No. 440; Square J 8/20; Depth 4 ft. 10 in. b.s.
15. Flint ball, well polished. Pl. CXX, 38. Diam. $1\frac{3}{8}$ in. No. 929; Square J 8/22; Depth 5 ft. b.s.
16. Cubical chert weight. Wt. 56·0 gms.; size 1·1×1·1×1 in. No. 4540; Square K 8/3; Depth 6 ft. 3 in. b.s.
17. Oval, steatite bead, lentoid in section. Pl. CXXVIII, 38. L. 1 in. No. 4785; Square K 9/1; Depth 8 ft. 7 in. b.s.
18. Cubical chert weight. Wt. 13·6 gms.; size ·75×·75×·55 in. No. 4836; Square K 8/3; Depth 8 ft. 7 in. b.s.
19. Tiny barrel-shaped bead of jade. L. $\frac{1}{4}$ in. No. 4983; Square K 8/4; Depth 9 ft. 7 in. b.s.

20. Rectangular bead of translucent, banded, green stone, lentoid in section. L. ⅝ in. No. 5172; Square K 9/2; Depth 10 ft. b.s.

21. Miniature, faience goblet with pointed base, scored over the body. Pl. LXXXII, 17. Ht. 1¼ in. No. 4784; Square K 9/1; Depth 8 ft. 7 in. b.s.

22. Copper chisel. L. 1⅞ in. No. 5121; Square K 9/5; Depth 10 ft. 3 in. b.s.

23. Copper spear-head. L. 5$\frac{1}{10}$ in. No. 6097; Square K 9/4; Depth 11 ft. 10 in. b.s.

24. Mica pieces. No. 5287; Square K 9/1; Depth 9 ft. b.s.

25. Mica pieces. No. 5052; Square K 9/2; Depth 9 ft. 8 in. b.s.

26. Mica pieces. No. 5217; Square K 9/3; Depth 10 ft. 3 in. b.s.

Pottery objects—

27. Thick ware, red washed dish with broad, splayed lip and ring-base. It contained three pieces of bone and a fragment of a terracotta bangle. Diam. 1 ft. No. 4599; Square K 8/3; Depth 7 ft. 3 in. b.s.

28. Squat vase with ring-base, body decorated with rows of dots enclosed by black bands. Ht. 6 in.; diam. 3¼ in. No. 4590; Square K 9/4; Depth 7 ft. 5 in. b.s.

29. Round vase with broad open mouth 3½ in. in diameter. Ht. 3¾ in. No. 4755; Square K 8/3; Depth 7 ft. 6 in. b.s.

30. Jar-stand, fragmentary. Diam. 8$\frac{3}{10}$ in.; Ht. 4¼ in. No. 650; Square J 9/22; Depth 9 ft. b.s.

31. Carinated vase with concave upper portion, decorated with irregular chequered pattern. Ht. 2$\frac{15}{16}$ in. No. 655; Square J 9/22; Depth 9 ft. b.s.

32. Miniature, oval vase with pointed base, hand-made. Ht. 1½ in. No. 5171; Square K 9/3; Depth 10 ft. 3 in. b.s.

33. Large dish, fragmentary. Diam. 15¾ in. No. 3362; Square J 7/24; Depth 4 ft. 9 in. b.s.

34. Corn measure with splayed neck and flat bottom. Pl. LXXII, 16. Ht. 4 in. No. 273; Square J 8/24; Depth 5 ft. b.s.

35. Barrel-shaped, solid, pottery flesh rubber, square in section. L. 3¼ in. No. 930; Square J 8/22; Depth 5 ft. b.s.

36. Triangular device[1] with 5 holes along the lower edge and a larger one at the apex. Pl. LXXI,. 74. L. 3$\frac{11}{12}$ in.; Ht. 2 in. No. 217; Square J 8/20; Depth 8 ft. b.s.

37. Seated figure of a bearded man with clean shaven lip wearing a four-stringed necklace with clasps at the centre, and a loin cloth studded with conical bhsses.[2] His hair falls in large coils over the ears, and at the back. The figure is split vertically. It was originally seated on a stool which has broken off, leaving a mark on the

---

[1] This is probably a terminal of some sort. From the direction of the upper hole it could not have been used for suspending small bells from the neck of an animal.

[2] For somewhat similar bosses in gold *cf.* Pl. CXXXVII, 6 and 20.

underside. Pl. LXXVI, 12. Ht. 7 in. No. 1451; Square J 9/4; Depth 8 ft. 9 in. b.s.

38. Peacock with extended plumes. Pl. LXXVIII, 14. Ht. 2¾ in. No. 5040; Square K 9/2; Depth 9 ft. 8 in. b.s.

Remains of Stratum IV. The walls of the IVth stratum, though fragmentary, are comparatively better preserved and also better built than those of the Late Period. Over a length of about 50 ft. at the northern end covered by squares J 7/25, J 8/21 and J 8/22 remains of Strata II to V overlap and intersect each other so haphazardly that while little survives of the IInd and IIIrd strata, it has not been possible to get at the plan of earlier buildings. Among them, however, may be mentioned in square J 8/16 an L-shaped wall with a neat pilaster at the east end. It is over 22 ft. long and 2 ft. 3 in. thick. A part of it is encumbered by two bits of walls of Stratum III. In the above medley, and in connection with Stratum IV were found in square J 7/25 an exquisitely finished, fan-shaped, semi-circular faience pendent (No. 3537) with simple linear decoration at the centre and border (Pl. CXXXIX, 2), and a cylindrical terracotta sealing (No. 3608), bent in firing, showing an acacia tree on one side and an inscription on the other (similar to No. 323 in Pl. XCIII). From square J 7/19 came a fragmentary unicorn seal (No. 7680, Pl. XC, 168), and in square J 7/20, partly buried below a parti-wall of Stratum III, was discovered a large cylindrical, pottery trough (No. 3885, ht. 2 ft. 3 in.) decorated with black bands. Besides some bones, it contained an interesting terracotta female figure wearing a copper bangle on the right arm (Pl. LXXVII, 48), which is entire, another seated male figurine, an animal toy, a pottery basin 9½ in. in diameter (Pl. LXXII, 4), a goblet with pointed base, a cylindrical vase and another pottery object shaped like a horn. A little to the south-east in square J 8/21 was found a unicorn seal (No. 1055, Pl. LXXXVIII, 82).

A somewhat complete house. Next, towards the south, are the remains of house No. 4 of which the northern and a little of the eastern part are encumbered by walls of Strata II and III. It is 41 ft. 6 in. long from east to west by 25 ft. 9 in. broad and has rooms on three sides with a courtyard in the centre of the north side. On the south there are two small rooms: No. 1 measuring 8 ft. 8 in. by 5 ft. 2 in., and No. 2, 10 ft. 2 in. by 6 ft. 9 in. In the latter there is a *gharā* at the south-west corner embedded in a small pavement. Along the west of room No. 2 and the courtyard No. 4 is an oblong room No. 3, measuring 21 ft. 3 in. by 8 ft. 4 in. Its north wall, which is not bonded, is a little earlier and appears to have been raised higher at the same time as the other walls of this house. The west wall has all but perished. Of room No. 5 on the east, the width is 6 ft. 9 in., but the length can no longer be determined, though it would be reasonable to expect that it went only as far north as room No. 3. The courtyard No. 4 lying between Rooms 3 and 5 is 19 ft. 9 in. by 12 ft. 3 in. No antiquities were found in this house.

Going towards the south there is nothing to record in the next 40 ft., but after that, commencing from the last 8 ft. of Square J 8/24, were found, over a space of 55 by 20 ft., a number of interesting antiquities. As there are no

Terracotta sealing suggestive of human sacrifice.

buildings worth referring to in this area, I shall pause only to describe the finds. One of them, No. 649 (Pl. XCIII, 304) is an oblong terracotta sealing measuring $1\frac{11}{16}$ by $\frac{1}{2}$ in. which, on account of the scenes depicted on both sides, is more than usually interesting. To the right, on the obverse face, it shows a nude female figure upside down with legs wide apart, and "with a plant issuing from her womb".[1] Her arms are thrown slantingly downwards. In the centre is an inscription of 6 pictograms, and, at the extreme left, a pair of tigers[2] standing face to face. On the reverse side, to the left is a man armed with a shield in his left hand and a sickle-shaped weapon in his right, standing in a menacing attitude in front of a woman seated on the ground. Apparently, the man is threatening to behead the woman, whose hair is dishevelled, and arms raised in alarm. To the right, is repeated the same inscription as on the obverse face. Sir John Marshall is of opinion that the "scene is intended to portray a human sacrifice connected with the Earth Goddess depicted on the other side with whom we must also associate the two genii" whom he takes to be ministrants of the deity. "The two beasts on the Harappā sealing", says he, "are more interesting (Plate XII, 12) as they belong to a class of officiant animal genii, which have long been familiar in the Aegean area and to which most instructive parallels have recently been found by Mr. (now Sir) Woolley at Ur in Mesopotamia. On the Mohenjo-daro (sic. Harappā) sealing the two genii appear to be lions or tigers (probably the latter), but, whether they be real or imaginary creatures, there can be little doubt that they are meant to be taking part in some ritual ceremony, just like the pair of genii on the well known Vaphio gem, who are watering young palms with libation ewers, or those on the plaques of shell inlay from the King's grave at Ur, one of which, a dog, is carrying some sacrificial heads on an altar, while a lion holds two sacrificial vessels, and another dog is playing on a harp. That the conception of these animal genii arose independently in Greece, Mesopotamia, and India is hardly conceivable, but whether it originated in the East or West has yet to be determined".[3]

Other finds.

The following other antiquities were also recovered from this area :—

1. Unicorn seal inscribed with 5 pictograms. Pl. LXXXVI, 37. $1\frac{1}{4}$ in. sq. No. 5253; Square K 9/1; Depth 9 ft. 2 in. b.s.
2. Unicorn seal, with only 2 pictograms surviving. Pl. LXXXVII, 53. Side $1\frac{1}{16}$ in. No. 781; Square J 8/25; Depth 11 ft. b.s.
3. Steatite seal showing a life-like rhinoceros, with trough in front and 4 pictograms in upper field. The folds of his skin are shown in plate-like sections over the haunches and shoulders. Pl. XCI, 253. $1\frac{1}{4}$ in. sq. No. 5534; Square K 9/2; Depth 10 ft. 8 in. b.s.
4. Rectangular, plano-convex steatite seal on which all pictograms except the one at the extreme left have been erased. Pl. XCII, 301. Size $1\frac{1}{8}\times\frac{1}{8}$ in. No. 7787; Square K 9/2; Depth 12 ft. b.s.

---

[1] *Cf. M. I. C.*, p. 52.

[2] On one side of a bead seal from Phaestus are shown in a precisely similar way two demons facing each other. *Cf.* M. P. Nilsson, *The Minoan-Mycenaean Religion*, p. 326, Fig. 100.

[3] *M. I. C.*, p. 70. See also footnotes 1 and 2 on the same page.

5. Right upper fragment of a square seal with 7 pictograms. Pl. XCII, 263. L. 1⅓ in. No. 5254; Square K 9/1; Depth 9 ft. 2 in. b.s.
6. Bossed,[1] terracotta seal divided by diagonal lines into four triangular compartments, each showing a deep circumscribed hole. Pl. XCI, 257. 11/16 in. sq. No. 725; Square J 8/20; Depth 10 ft. b.s.
7. Discoid, faience sealing with 6 pictograms on one side, and 2 on the other. Pl. XCV, 372. Diam. 11/16 in. No. 726; Square J 8/24; Depth 9 ft. 6 in. b.s.
8. Rectangular, faience sealing with 5 pictograms on one side only. Pl. C, 654. Size 1¼×½ in. No. 4917; Square K 8/5; Depth 10 ft. 2 in. b.s.
9. Cylindrical, terracotta sealing showing crocodile on one side, and possibly 4 blurred pictograms on the other; similar to No. 339 in Pl. XCIV. L. 1 3/16 in. No. 7055; Square K 9/1: Depth 10 ft. 8 in. b.s.
10. Large, squat, chessman-shaped object of yellow Jaisalmer stone with a black band round the neck. Pl. CXVII, 32. Diam. at base 5½ in.; Ht. 3¼ in. No. 755; Square J 8/24; Depth 9 ft. b.s.
11. Cubical chert weight. Wt. 27·65 gms.; size ·9×·9×·75 in. No. 5531; Square K 9/2; Depth 11 ft. b.s.
12. Cubical chert weight. Wt. 28·37 gms.; size ·95×·95×·7 in. No. 5755; Square J 9/19; Depth 14 ft. 6 in. b.s.
13. Cubical chert weight. Wt. 27·3 gms.: size ·92×·92×·7 in. No. 5756; Square J 9/19; Depth 14 ft. 6 in. b.s.
14. Pottery vase with short neck, broad mouth, and flat bottom. It has a row of dotted circles at the neck, a broad frieze of hachured *pīpal* (*ficus religiosa*) leaves, cross hatched ornament over the body, and rows of dots and bands on the lower portion. Pl. LXIX, 6. The painting is faint. Ht. 6¼ in. No. 5797; Square J 9/24; Depth 14 ft. 6 in. b.s.
15. Long, barrel-shaped, hollow pottery flesh rubber, square in section. L. 7½ in. No. 819; Square J 8/24; Depth 10 ft. 6 in. b.s.

One seal and two sealings of mythological character.

The next 75 ft. to the south were quite unproductive except for a tapering pendent of hornblende (No. 5408), and a small terracotta basket (No. 5800) made in close imitation of basketry-work (Pl. CXX, 29). But from the following 35 ft. at the southern end, beginning with square J 9/23, were obtained several antiquities, of which three are particularly interesting. One of them, No. 5211, is a bossed steatite seal 1⅛ in. square (Pl. XCI, 249) showing 3 pictograms in the upper field, and, in the lower, a composite monster whose fore-part, consisting of the body, forelegs, head and horns, is bovine, while the face is human, the tusk and trunk those of an elephant, and the hind part, comprising the haunches, legs, and tail, that of a lion.[2] The other two are terracotta sealings (Nos. 2410

[1] The seal is very rough and so is the boss.

[2] For the sacred or divine nature of such therianthropic beasts and parallels from Mesopotamia *cf.* Sir John Marshall, *op. cit.*, p. 66.

and 2409), which are also of a mythological character. Of these, the former is 1¼ in. long by ½ in. wide and lentoid in section (Pl. XCIII, 307). On the obverse face it shows a deity wearing a kilt or short tunic and a three-pointed head-dress standing under an ornamental arch, which appears to be made of the bent bough of a *pīpal* (*ficus religiosa*) tree.[1] The lower ends of this bough are rounded up to form loops, each enclosing a star. The head of the deity is turned a little towards the right and on both arms he wears a number of armlets. The other side is inscribed with three pictograms. The second sealing (No. 2409) is a three-sided, tapering prism, 9/10 in. long and ¼ in. wide, with a pivotal hole at the bottom (Pl. XCIII, 305). On each of its three faces is a standing mythical figure with a shaped pictogram near the legs. Of the three figures, the right hand one appears to be feminine, but its head is altogether obliterated, while the arms and lower legs, which are probably not human, are also blurred. The left hand figure is human above the waist and bovine below, while the middle one, to judge from the massive hips, also appears to have animal legs. The first two figures appear to be holding a staff across the shoulder, which in the case of the left hand figure seems to have a transverse limb attached to the upper end.[2] It is a pity that all the figures are blurred and their forms are not clear, but, their therianthropic nature can hardly be doubted. Two more seals and one sealing described below were also found here:—

Other finds.

1. Unicorn seal with 6 pictograms which are repeated on the upper edge[3]. Pl. LXXXVIII, 75. 1 in. sq. No. 2540; Square J 9/23; Depth 12 ft. b.s.
2. Fragment of a tiny, rectangular steatite seal inscribed on both sides. Pl. XCVII, 566. W. 3 in. No. 6026; Square J 9/19; Depth 14 ft. 7 in. b.s.
3. Oblong, terracotta sealing, lentoid in section, with a number of vertical and horizontal scratches on both sides. L. 1¼ in. No. 2411; Square J 9/24; Depth 11 ft. 9 in. b.s.

A jar half full of triangular cakes.

In this area were also found an alabaster grindstone (No. 2412), 7½ in. long (Pl. CXVII, 50), a tapering pendent of hornblende (No. 5956), a solid copper bangle (No. 2147, Pl. CXXV, 2), a cog-wheel shaped paste nose-ring (No. 6027), two terracotta temple ornaments (Nos. 6028 and 6029), a rattling ball (No. 5959), a small carinated vase (No. 5922), and three household pottery jars of medium size. One of the latter, which lay in square J 9/24, was found to be half full of triangular terracotta cakes (Pl. VIII, *a*), its upper part being filled with fine percolated earth in which a bone was sticking.

At lower levels, which were attained only at the north and south ends of this extension and in the narrow trench[4] immediately outside the line of buttresses on the east of the Great Granary (Pl. V, *b*), were found a few objects referable

---

[1] For connection of this deity with tree-worship *cf.* Sir John Marshall, *op. cit.*, p. 63 ff. and footnote 2.

[2] Possibly it is intended for a plough (*hala*).

[3] This is the only bossed square seal from Harappā so inscribed. At Mohenjo-daro, however, there are two square seals without boss (L323; HR2240) which are inscribed on both faces, as well as on the edge, and a bossed seal is also similarly inscribed, *cf. M. I. C.*, pp. 372-73, and 206.

[4] This was sunk in quest of the retaining wall of the Great Granary and then filled up.

to the Vth stratum. At the northern end are the remains of two rooms, one of which has a couple of wall recesses. Here, in square J 7/19, was found a rectangular terracotta sealing (No. 3565) twisted in firing. It is $1\frac{1}{8}$ in. long and inscribed on one side only (Pl. XCIV, 365*a*). About the centre of the narrow trench mentioned above (square J 8/18) was found a flat-bottomed, globular vase (No. 1313) with splaying neck (Pl. LXXI, 50), and at its south end a tiny seal (No. 2703) inscribed on both faces (Pl. XCVI, 464). Let me also add that at the south-east corner of this trench, in square K 9/5, were found, at a depth of 15 ft., some hardened animal bones in a highly compressed layer of earth. **Stratum V.**

Deeper down in this same narrow trench was found, at the northern end and at a depth of 13 ft., a hexagonal faience sealing (No. 9059), $\frac{11}{16}$ in. long with 4 pictograms on one side, and an acacia tree and VII-like symbol on the other (Pl. XCIII, 324); and at the southern end, at a depth of 20 ft. 6 in. and 20 ft. 3 in. respectively, was found a three-sided prism (No. 10140, $1\frac{3}{8}$ in.), also of faience, showing a crocodile on one side, 3 pictograms on the second, and an VIII-like symbol on the third (similar to No. 641 in Pl. XCIX), together with a small, broken unicorn seal (No. 10170) only $\frac{7}{8}$ in. long (Pl. XC, 186). The above three antiquities may be assigned to the VIth or VIIth stratum. **Finds of Stratum VI or VII.**

The Northern Extension.

The large dump of spoil earth lying to the north of the Great Granary occupies the last inch of the acquired area, and there was no more than a space of fifteen feet for extension on this side. Here the surface is almost level, being just under 540 ft. above the mean sea-level. In this extension, along the north of the Great Granary is a wall of the IVth stratum, and close to it, at a higher level, a stout wall (5 ft. 3 in. thick) of the IIIrd, which, again, was encumbered by a haphazard room of the Ist stratum in square I 7/14 and 15 (Pl. IV, *b*, extreme left foreground). In this room was found a group of earthenware vessels, comprising several narrow-necked, medium-sized, round *gharās*, some large crushed jars, a few broken, long oval vases and basins (Pl. VIII, *b*). The peculiarity of this group, as of another to be mentioned below from Trench I (see p. 85 *infra*), is the flat bottom of most of the vessels as compared with the usually pointed or, more rarely, round bottom of larger wares. To the east of this room may be seen several fragments of walls of Strata I to IV. Here, too, connected with the Ist stratum, was found in square I 7/24 a group of pottery (Nos. 7338 to 7340 and 7360) consisting of several vases of different shapes, two lids, one sieve, a double-handled cup, and the horizontally fluted, hollow stem of an offerings' dish (Pl. VIII, *d*). **Only a few remains.** **A pottery group.** **Another pottery group.**

The following mentionable antiquities were recovered from the various strata in this extension :—

Stratum I—

1. Medium-sized, narrow-necked, round *gharā* with the lower part roughened by finger grooving.[1] Its narrow mouth and everted rim are in

[1] This grooving was obtained by passing fingers round the body of a jar while it was wet and being rotated on the wheel. There are many jars with similar patterning from the Cemetery H.

marked contrast with the broad mouth, and straight and short rim of *ghaṛās* with similar grooving from the Cemetery H. Ht. $13\frac{3}{4}$ in. No. 2822; Square J 7/10; Depth 2 ft. 6 in. b.s.

Stratum II—

2. Inscribed potsherd. Size $5\frac{1}{2}\times4\frac{1}{4}$ in. No. 3655; Square J 7; Depth 0 to 3 ft. b.s.

Stratum III—

3. Unicorn seal with 6 pictograms. Pl. LXXXVI, 17. $1\frac{1}{2}$ in. sq. No. 3545; Square I 7/24; Depth 6 ft. b.s.
4. Inscribed potsherd. Pl. CII, 3. Size $9\frac{3}{4}\times7$ in. No. 3656; Square J 7; Depth 3 to 6 ft. b.s.
5. Polished, hemispherical hollow cap of yellow Jaisalmer limestone pierced with a one inch square hole through the apex. The underside rim, $\frac{3}{4}$ in. wide, is finely finished and has three equidistant tube-drill holes for fixation to a lower member. Pl. LXXXIII, 13. Ht. $3\frac{7}{16}$ in.; diam. 7 in. No. 2438; Square I 7/10; Depth 5 ft. b.s.

Stratum VI—

6. Bossed, seal with the Brāhmanī bull (*Bos indicus*) bearing 3 pictograms. It is the smallest of its kind being only $\frac{11}{16}$ in. square. Pl. XCI, 233. No. 9080; Square J 7/9; Depth 17 ft. 2 in. b.s.
7. Tiny, rectangular seal with one pictogram on one side and incense-burner on the other. Pl. XCVI, 443. Size $\frac{13}{16}\times\frac{3}{8}$ in. No. 10069; Square I 7/24; Depth 17 ft. 5 in. b.s.
8. Cylindrical, faience sealing with a foliated twig[1] on both sides. Pl. CI, 706. L. $\frac{1}{2}$ in. No. 8965; Square I 7/20; Depth 11 ft. 8 in. b.s.

Later remains over the Great Granary. Standing over and between the two blocks of the Great Granary are several remains of later strata. Among them may be mentioned the foundations of three thick walls, and a few fragments of the IIIrd stratum standing over halls I, III, IV and VI of the Western Block, and a small fragment of the IInd stratum over hall V' of the Eastern Block. In addition to these, there are in the central aisle, a number of walls of Strata I to IV,[2] mostly standing alongside the Western Block, but they are too fragmentary to call for any remarks (Pl. IV, *b*). Scattered among them, and also at deeper levels, which were attained in the narrow trenches along the periphery of the Great Granary, were found the following objects in association with the several strata:—

Stratum I—

Stray finds of Strata I to VI.

1. Unicorn seal with 6 pictograms. Pl. LXXXV, 2. 2 in. sq. No. 1056; Square J 8/6; Depth 2 ft. 6 in. b.s.

---

[1] A similar sealing is illustrated in *A. S. R.* for 1926-27, Pl. XXI, *b*, 49.

[2] In order to give a clear plan of the Great Granary these later walls have been purposely left out.

2. Hemispherical, four chambered pottery object with a shallow socket on the underside for fixation. Pl. LXXII, 37. Ht. $4\frac{1}{8}$ in.; diam. $5\frac{1}{4}$ in. No. 1136; Square J 8/11; Depth 2 ft. 6 in. b.s.

Stratum II—

3. Faience cone with a deep hole at bottom. Ht. 1 in. No. 728; Square I 9/11; Depth 2 ft. 6 in. b.s.
4. Chessman-shaped object of shell. Ht. 1 in. No. 3302; Square I 7/25; Depth 4 ft. b.s.
5. Fine pottery top dish (of an offerings' dish) with painted rim. Diam. $10\frac{3}{4}$ in. No. 2447; Square J 7/10; Depth 3 ft. b.s.

Stratum III—

6. Fragment of a unicorn seal. No. 3476; Square I 7/25; Depth 7 ft. 2 in. b.s.
7. Unicorn seal with four pictograms surviving, left part broken. Pl. LXXXVII, 51. Side $1\frac{1}{4}$ in. No. 3644; Square I 8/16; Depth 8 ft. b.s.
8. Tiny, rectangular faience sealing showing a crocodile (*Gavialis gangeticus*) in a river represented by four fishes on one side, and 3 pictograms on the other. Pl. XCIV, 340. Size $\frac{13}{16} \times \frac{5}{16}$ in. No. 9041; Square I 8/17; Depth 8 ft. b.s.
9. Cylindrical, terracotta sealing showing a crocodile on one face. There is no trace of pictograms on the other side; similar to No. 334 in Pl. XCIV. L. $1\frac{3}{8}$ in. No. 1459; Square I 8/22; Depth 7 ft. 6 in. b.s.
10. Rectangular faience amulet with horizontal fluting pierced lengthwise with two holes through the raised flutes. The holes are, however, not in the centre. Pl. CXXXVIII, 43. Size $1\frac{3}{16} \times \frac{3}{4}$ in. No. 3847; Square I 8/10; Depth 4 ft. 9 in. b.s.
11. Chessman-shaped object of chalcedony. Ht. $\frac{13}{16}$ in. No. 1734; Square I 8/11; Depth 8 ft. b.s.
12. Copper celt with slightly tapering sides, edge dented at one place by use. L. $4\frac{7}{8}$ in.; w. at butt end $1\frac{7}{8}$ in.; w. across the cutting edge $2\frac{1}{4}$ in. No. 1410; Square I 8/11; Depth 6 ft. b.s.
13. Pottery basin with tapering sides. Pl. LXXII, 5. Diam. $12\frac{3}{8}$ in. No. 3886; Square I 7/25; Depth 7 ft. 9 in. b.s.

Stratum IV—

14. Rectangular, bossed steatite seal with 4 pictograms. This type is rare, as with the exception of seal No. 4965 (see p. 27 *supra*), all others of its kind are bossless and plano-convex in shape. Pl. XCII, 294. Size $\frac{15}{16} \times \frac{9}{16}$ in. No. 1259; Square I 8/14; Depth 7 ft. 2 in. b.s.
15. Bronze gouge (in two pieces) with a sharp semi-circular edge. It was probably used for cutting small strips of steatite or faience for making seals and sealings of tiny size. Pl. CXXV, 42. Another use of this instrument may have been for ribbing alabaster or other

stones, for example, *cf.* Pl. LXXXIII, 47-49 ,and 51-52. For so doing a great deal of force was required and for this reason mark the strong alabaster handle of a similar tool (Pl. CXXV, 41). L. 3⅛ in. No. 8802; Square J 9/2; Depth 12 ft. b.s.

16. Three rusted copper objects lumped together, *viz.*, a stilus, chisel and gouge. Of these, the stilus and gouge are illustrated in Pl. CXXV, 43 and 44. L. 2¾, 3⅜ and 2⅝ in., respectively. No. 8801; Square J 9/2; Depth 12 ft. b.s.

Stratum V—

17. Fragmentary steatite seal showing part of the body and horns of a buffalo (?) and 4 pictograms. Pl. XCI, 239. Side ¾ in. No. 3611; Square I 8/25; Depth 11 ft. 9 in. b.s.
18. Tiny, rectangular steatite seal inscribed on one face only. Pl. XCVI, 467. Size ⅜ × $\frac{5}{16}$ in. No. 2702; Square I 9/2; Depth 12 ft. b.s.
19. Spherical, limestone mace-head[1] with a deep socket on the underside. It would probably have required a leather thong to bind it firmly with a wooden stick. Pl. LXXXIII, 16. Diam. 1⅝ in. No. 3614; Square I 8/14; Depth 11 ft. 9 in. b.s.
20. Tiny, four-sided bar-shaped seal with 4 blurred pictograms on one face, and a row of 3 dotted circles on each of the remaining sides. Pl. XCVII, 541. L. ¾ in. No. 2981; Square I 7/15; Depth 15 ft. 8 in. b.s.

Stratum VI—

21. Tiny, three-sided prism seal of steatite with 3 pictograms on one face, crocodile on the second, and 4 dotted circles on the third; similar to No. 592 in Pl. XCVIII. L. $\frac{7}{16}$ in. No. 3341; Square I 9/23; Depth 16 ft. 6 in. b.s.

Trench Ae.

Its shape and dimensions and configuration of the surface.

About 25 ft. south-west of the Great Granary Area is an irregular, polygonal trench called Ae, sunk by Rai Bahadur Daya Ram Sahni, which measures 157 ft. on the longer axis from north to south by 55 ft. wide on the average (Pl. IX). Here the mound is low, as it lies between the contour lines of 540 and 545 ft., and the ground continually slopes down from south to north.

Stratum I.

Two floors with brick edging mistaken for sepulchre.

The 1st stratum was found just near the surface in the raised southern part of this trench. In referring to it, Mr. Sahni says "The uppermost stratum yielded, besides a number of fragmentary walls, a well preserved sepulchre[2] constructed with burnt bricks of the usual size and lying east to west (Plate XXIV, *a*) with probably another structure of the same kind adjoining it on the south side, but placed at right angles to it. The former structure consists of a horizontal platform of a single course of bricks laid flat and protected on three sides by bricks standing upright on the narrow edge. The roof was composed

[1] For a similar marble implement of slightly larger size from Anau *cf.* R. Pumpelly, *Explorations in Turkestan*, Vol. I, p. 167, Fig. 391.

[2] Square H 10/7.

of an inclined plane of a single course of bricks. Brick by brick the upper layer was removed to examine the contents of the structure which were found to consist of fine brick concrete and earth with a number of very small pieces of charred bone which, though too small to be identified, must undoubtedly have belonged to a cremated human body".[1] This structure, as will appear from Pl. X, *d*, is nothing more than a small brick-on-edge pavement of the usual type with a border of bricks standing on edge, and the second one to its south is another composed of bricks laid flat. No receptacle for bones was found in either of them. On the other hand, similar brick concrete mixed with numerous bits of charred and uncharred bones, both above and below the level of these floors, is still found at the same spot. My experience, based on much larger operations at this place, is that Harappā—specially in the later strata—is so full of bones that they come out in greater or lesser quantities, wherever the mounds are dug, due no doubt to the fact that the inhabitants depended a great deal on animal food, perhaps, to an even larger extent than did the people of Mohenjo-daro. The presence of fine brick concrete and earth would seem to indicate that the bone fragments, as at so many other places, were a part of the foundation concrete or débris and not confined merely to the above pavements. Perhaps, I may also add that in the large area which has since been excavated on this and other mounds at Harappā, not a single sepulchre has so far been met with. I shall deal with the subject of cremation and the probable form that it may have taken in Chapter VIII. **Bones in or under them, only a part of the débris.**

In the centre of the trench, in squares H 10/6 and 7, against the south face of an older wall were found, built close to each other without bonding, three walls of Stratum II which are now fragmentary. The west one of these is only half a brick thick, and apparently its pilaster was constructed as a support. Some other fragmentary walls of this stratum are found scattered about in this trench, and in association with them were found two post-cremation urns standing one over the other in square H 10/6, and another one in square H 10/8 filled in each case with the usual contents, *viz.*, small earthenware vessels, terracotta objects, etc. **Stratum II.**

The IIIrd stratum is represented in the northern portion by a small well 1 ft. 10 in. in diameter with brick-on-edge steening, by a fine pavement of chiselled and well-rubbed bricks, and by a drain which pours itself on the west into a 2 ft. 4 in. square paved sink for the storage of used up water (Pl. X, *b*). In the central portion may be noticed a fairly well built corner of a large room with a covered drain, another broken drain to its west, and, to its south, two more walls in squares H 10/7 and H 10/12. In the southern portion there is a covered drain in square H 10/3. **Stratum III.**

Scattered about in this trench were found the following objects belonging to Stratum III :— **Finds.**

1. Unicorn seal with four pictograms. Pl. LXXXV, 10. 1$\frac{1}{16}$ in. sq. No. Ae106; Square H 10/3; Depth 3 ft. 6 in. b.s.

[1] *A. S. R.* for 1924-25, p. 75.

2. Biconical bead of banded stone. L. 1½ in. No. Ae281; Square H 9/10; Depth 4 ft. 8 in. b.s.
3. Two cubical stone weights. Wts. 27·0 and 3·45 gms.; size 1×1×·55 and ·45×·45×·37 in. No. Ae155; Square H 10/6; Depth 5 ft. b.s.
4. Cubical chert weight. Damaged. Wt. 3·65 gms.; size ·48×·48×·43 in. No. Ae159; Square H 10/11; Depth 7 ft. b.s.
5. Small cone of shell. Ht. 11/16 in. No. Ae395; Depth 4 ft. b.s.
6. Large spoon of shell. Size 7½×6¼ in. No. Ae167; Square H 9/15; Depth 4 ft. b.s.
7. Handmade, spouted feeding pottery vase. Ht. 1⅝ in. No. Ae275; Depth 3 ft. b.s.
8. Terracotta cat[1] (?). Pl. LXXIX, 58. Ht. 1 1/16 in. No. Ae317; Depth 3 ft. 4 in. b.s.

Trenches Af and Ai.

Situation. In the centre of the western part of this mound Rai Bahadur Daya Ram Sahni dug two shallow trenches designated on the site plan as Af and Ai, which measure along the major axes 119 by 89 ft., and 100 by 30 ft. respectively (Pl. I). The whole of Ai and the greater part of Af lie between the contour lines of 545 and 550. Neither of them contains more than a few fragmentary brick remains

Configuration of the ground. assignable to the Ist and IInd strata.[2] In Trench Af, are two small paved circular structures resting on a thick substratum of burnt brick nodules (Pl. X, *a*, foreground). In describing one of them the Rai Bahadur says "Another little structure consists of a paved platform surrounded by a single course of brick laid on edge, which might have been a bathing platform as a large earthen jar was standing on one side of it. Underneath this platform was a mass of cremated human bones and, about 16′ from it, a large heap of ashes and charcoal with human bones, which undoubtedly represents the remains of several funeral pyres. This trench yielded a large number of stone mortars and pestles, which recall the practice of burying such objects with the dead in Mesopotamian sites".[3] Just such a mass of charcoal, ashes, bones, stones, and nodules was found by me in the southern part of Trench IV, which lies close by, but I have no doubt that it was nothing more than the rubbish which is so plentiful in all the raised parts of Mound F. In my view, it is highly improbable that cremation platforms or funeral pyres would have been made in the midst of dwelling houses all over the site. A small secluded crematorium by the river side, such as is found in most of our modern Indian towns, would have been much more likely.

Finds. The following antiquities were found scattered in Trench Af:—

1. Unicorn seal with 4 pictograms. Pl. LXXXVIII, 86. 11/16 in. sq. No. Af9; Depth 1 ft. b.s.

---

[1] One skull and a left humerus of cats have been identified from Harappā by Dr. B. Prashad, *cf. Mem. ASI.*, No. 51, pp. 15 ff.

[2] A plan of these trenches is unnecessary.

[3] *A. S. R.* for 1924-25, p. 77.

2. Fragment of a unicorn seal with only the front legs and part of the animal surviving. Pl. XC, 210. L. $\frac{3}{4}$ in. No. Af116; Depth 3 ft. b.s.
3. Small fragment of a rectangular, plano-convex steatite seal with part of a pictogram surviving. Pl. XC, 212. L. $\frac{5}{16}$ in. No. Af25; Depth 3 ft. b.s.
4. Tiny, rectangular steatite seal inscribed on both faces; similar to No. 490 in Pl. XCVI. Size $\frac{7}{16} \times \frac{1}{4}$ in. No. Ab24; Depth 4 ft. b.s.
5. Shield-shaped,[1] tiny steatite seal inscribed on both faces. Slightly broken. Pl. XCVII, 556. L. $\frac{3}{8}$ in. No. Af97; Depth 5 ft. 3 in. b.s.
6. Tiny, discoid steatite seal inscribed on both faces. Pl. XCVII, 549. Diam. $\frac{1}{3}$ in. No. Af113; Depth 5 ft. 8 in. b.s.
7. Fragment of a tiny, rectangular faience sealing. Pl. XCVIII, 608. L. $\frac{9}{16}$ in.; W. $\frac{3}{8}$ in. No. Af153; Depth 1 ft. 6 in. b.s.
8. Fragment of an oblong faience sealing inscribed on both sides, plano-convex in section; similar to No. 321 in Pl. XCIII. L. $\frac{1}{2}$ in. No. Af115; Depth 3 ft. b.s.
9. Rectangular faience sealing with a humped bull standing to left on one side, and 4 pictograms on the other. Pl. XCIII, 312. Size $1\frac{1}{16} \times \frac{5}{8}$ in. No. Af22; Depth 4 ft. b.s.
10. Fragment of a cylindrical terracotta sealing with crocodile on one side and pictograms on the other; similar to No. 335 in Pl. XCIV. L. 1 in. No. Af168; Depth 3 ft. b.s.
11. Cylindrical terracotta sealing, bent in firing, with crocodile (*Gavialis gangeticus*) on one side, and 11 pictograms on the other. Pl. XCIV, 335. L. $1\frac{1}{2}$ in. No. Af29; Depth 3 ft. 3 in. b.s.
12. Discoid, plano-convex steatite temple ornament relieved with four concentric circles and cable border. Pl. CXXXVIII, 34. Diam. $1\frac{3}{16}$ in. No. Af12; Depth 1 ft. b.s.
13. Fragment of a miniature steatite wavy ring with white glaze. Ht. $\frac{11}{16}$ in. No. Af10; Depth 1 ft. b.s.
14. A life-like, couchant rhinoceros in the round holed on the underside for fixation. It is made of steatite and has a thick coating of white glaze. Pl. LXXIX, 74. L. $1\frac{1}{10}$ in.; ht. $\frac{1}{2}$ in. No. Af66.
15. Miniature couchant faience ram. L. $1\frac{1}{10}$ in. No. Af40; Depth 1 ft. 6 in. b.s.

In the western part of this trench was found a well preserved, large napiform jar No. Af21 at a depth of 4 ft. It is 3 ft. $1\frac{1}{2}$ in. in height and 2 ft. 9 in. in diameter, and presumably had the usual contents of post-cremation urns.

In the adjoining Trench Ai, 5 ft. 6 in. below the surface, was found a stone *lingam*[2] (No. Ai40, Pl. X, *c*). It measures 11 in. high and $7\frac{5}{8}$ in. in diameter at

[1] In the Minoan Civilization a shield of this shape was a common ornamental motif, but that it was a cult object is disputed by M. P. Nilsson, see *op. cit.*, p. 353.

[2] Since then I have found two stone *lingams* of a larger size from Trenches III and IV in this mound. Both of them are smoothed all over.

the base and is rough all over. The following five objects were also recovered from this trench :—

1. Left upper quarter of a unicorn seal with only two pictograms, neck of the animal, and upper part of the incense-burner surviving. Pl. XC, 171. L. $\frac{11}{16}$ in. No. Ai16 ; Depth 2 ft. b.s.
2. Fragment of a unicorn seal with only the incense-burner, a little of the neck, and chest of the animal surviving. Pl. XC, 193. L. $\frac{11}{16}$ in. No. Ai139 ; Depth 4 ft. b.s.
3. Right side of a unicorn seal. Pl. LXXXIX, 150. Side $\frac{13}{16}$ in. No. Ai132 ; Depth 4 ft. b.s.
4. Cubical chert weight, edges chipped off. Wt. 129·0 gms. ; size 1·5×1·5×1·3 in. No. Ai161 ; Depth 7 ft. b.s.
5. Pedestalled, terracotta pigeon. Pl. LXXVIII, 8. Ht. 1¼ in. No. Ai133 ; Depth 4 ft. b.s.

Later, from the surface near this trench, I picked up a cubical terracotta die (No. 12415, 1¼ in. cube, Pl. CXX, 47) marked with the numbers 1 and 2 opposite, 3 and 4 opposite, and 5 and 6 opposite.

Trenches IV and V.

Locale. In the south-west part of this mound, where the surface is comparatively higher, were sunk two trenches named IV and V. The former runs from north to south close to the western edge of the mound, and the latter from east to west, joining Trench IV at right angles about 60 ft. from its northern end (Pl. XI). It appeared at first sight as if at this point the mound was intact, but, as elsewhere, this expectation has turned out untrue. On examination, these trenches were found to be full of deep accumulations of rubbish consisting of potsherds—seemingly more plentiful than anywhere else in this mound—nodules, ashes, and brickbats. Among potsherds, those of goblets with pointed bases preponderated.

Composition.

Stratification. Four strata of buildings have been brought to light in them. Of these, the first three are definitely late, and, at most places, follow each other in quick succession. so much so, that at a number of points it becomes really difficult to distinguish the one from the other. At some other places, walls of the Ist stratum stand immediately over those of the IInd, and of the IInd over those of the IIIrd. With a few exceptions, however, there is a more or less distinct interval between the IVth and the IIIrd stratum, and this distinction also holds good in the northern portion of Trench IV, where there is a sharp fall in the ground, as well as in the western part of Trench V.

Configuration of the ground and limits of various strata. To bring out more clearly the rise and fall of the surface in these trenches and in order to explain in an intelligible manner at what depth these strata actually occur, it will be convenient if I divide Trench IV into the Northern, Middle and Southern Sections, which are more or less equidistant, and Trench V, into the Eastern and Western Sections. Of the latter trench, the Western Section, which has a considerable bend along the southern edge, is about three-fifths of the whole. In the Northern Section of Trench IV, due to a marked fall of the surface, the Ist stratum is nowhere represented, the IInd goes down to about 4 ft. 6 in., the IIIrd to about 6 ft. 9 in., and the IVth to about 8 ft. 4 in. In the other two sections, all the four strata are present. In the middle one, which is the highest, the Ist stratum occupies some 3 ft. 4 in. below the surface, the IInd extends to 5 ft. 8 in., the IIIrd to 8 ft. 5 in., and the IVth to 9 ft. 9 in., while in the Southern Section the Ist statum extends to 2 ft. 8 in. only, the IInd to 4 ft. 5 in., the IIIrd to 8 ft. 9 in., and the IVth to 9 ft. 5 in. In Trench V, the Eastern Section is higher than the rest, and to this alone are confined a few bits of walls of the Ist stratum which goes down to a depth of 2 ft. 9 in. only. Here, the IInd stratum extends to 8 ft. below the surface, whereas in the Western Section it extends to 5 ft. 2 in. only. Again, in the Eastern Section, the IIIrd stratum extends to 10 ft. 2 in., and the IVth to about 11 ft., while in the Western Section, the lower limit of the IIIrd stratum is from 5 ft. 7 in. to 7 ft. 8 in., and of the IVth from 7 ft. 9 in. to 8 ft. 9 in. Here, let me state once again that the levels for the different strata, as given above, are merely tentative and approximate. For a depth of 4 ft. from the surface nothing was found in either of these trenches save a few miscellaneous objects and some interesting potsherds. Below that level the profusion of sherds began to diminish. The few bits of walls of the Ist stratum, wherever they occurred, were found entirely enveloped in rubbish. In the IInd stratum, the walls of Trench IV were rather thicker than those of Trench V, but, with a few exceptions in the Southern Section of Trench IV, they are nothing more than fragments. In the two following strata the remains are better preserved, comprising a number of circular brick-on-edge platforms in Stratum III, and over a dozen houses belonging to the Workmen's Quarters in Stratum IV. Of these, I shall have more to say presently.

Nature of remains.

Trench IV.

Remains of Strata I and II.

Trench IV is 337 ft. long from north to south by 192 ft. wide from east to west, except at the north where for a space of 67 ft. its width is 65 ft. only (Pl. XI). Like Trench V, it was excavated to an average depth of 9 ft. 5 in. The only structure in it worthy of mention in connection with Stratum I is a cylindrical furnace (No. Fm in square I 13/21), in which slag was freely met with. The following antiquities were recovered from Stratum I:—

Finds of Stratum I.

1. Rectangular, plano-convex steatite seal with 7 pictograms. Pl. XCII, 261. Size $1\frac{13}{16} \times \frac{7}{16}$ in. No. 8360; Square I 13/7; Depth 2 ft. b.s.
2. Tiny, steatite seal carved in the form of a couchant hare. It has a cross-shaped groove on the underside for fixation. Pl. XCV, 423. Size $\frac{7}{16} \times \frac{5}{16}$ in. No. 10409; Square I 11/15; Depth 6 in. b.s.
3. Miniature *lingam* of black stone. Ht. $\frac{3}{4}$ in. No. 8354; Square I 12/9; Depth 6 in. b.s.
4. Cubical chert weight. Pl. CXVIII, 21. Wt. 27·35 gms.; size ·9 × ·9 × ·73 in. No. 8197; Square I 13/10; Depth 1 ft. b.s.
5. Miniature, undulating stone ring. Diam. 3 in. No. 12241; Square I 13/15; Depth 2 ft. 6 in. b.s.

6. Fragment of a miniature, undulating soapstone ring glazed red to simulate carnelian and painted with dotted heart-shaped designs in white. Pl. CXVII, 17. L. $1\frac{1}{2}$ in. No. 11514; Square I 13/16; Depth 2 ft. 6 in. b.s.
7. Half of a miniature, trough-shaped, faience vase showing thread marks[1] inside. Pl. LXXXII, 15. Ht. $1\frac{1}{4}$ in.; diam. $1\frac{3}{4}$ in. No. 8380; Square I 12/8; Depth 9 in. b.s.
8. Faience ear-button. Diam. $\frac{7}{16}$ in. No. 10229; Square I 12/13; Depth 9 in. b.s.
9. Seated faience ram. L. $1\frac{1}{16}$ in. No. 11494; Square I 13/18; Depth 1 ft. b.s.
10. Pear-shaped faience vase with broad, horizontal rim. It is decorated with incised chevrons all over the body. Pl. LXXXII, 19. Ht. 2 in. No. 12226; Square I 13/19; Depth 1 ft. 6 in. b.s.
11. Faience ear-button with cable border. Diam. $\frac{11}{16}$ in. No. 10276; Square I 13/13; Depth 3 ft. b.s.
12. Sherd painted with a deer and stars. Its texture and painting are typical of burial pottery. Pl. LXVI, 45. L. $6\frac{1}{4}$ in. No. 8149; Square I 14/10; Depth 6 in. b.s.
13. Fairly well modelled pottery bull with eyes, ears, and nostrils indicated by shallow pittings. Pl. LXXIX, 59. L. $7\frac{3}{4}$ in. No. 11510; Square I 13/18; Depth 2 ft. 3 in. b.s.

Remains of Stratum II.

The IInd stratum is also very fragmentary, but it can still boast of two paved circular mangers lined with brick-on-edge (in squares I 12/11[2] and H 11/22), of two furnaces[3] (No. Fj in square I 13/13, Pl. XVII, *e*, and No. Fa in square H 14/25, Pl. XVII, *a* and *b*), of a thick wall in the Northern Section standing between the circular platforms P1 and P2, and of several walls between Lanes I and III in the Southern Section. Against the west wall of the corner in square I 14/1 and 2 was found a well preserved copper bangle (No. 7947) with ends overlapping to about the two-thirds of its diameter (Pl. CXXV, 60).

Finds.

Scattered over the whole trench were found the following objects from Stratum II :—

1. Bossed seal of black steatite bearing some pictograms. Unfinished and broken along the right side. Pl. XC, 224. W. 1 in. No. 10260; Square I 14/11; Depth 3 ft. b.s.
2. Unicorn seal with 8 pictograms. Pl. LXXXVIII, 81. $1\frac{3}{16}$ in. sq. No. 11942; Square I 14/20; Depth 4 ft. b.s.
3. Unicorn seal with 4 pictograms, damaged. Pl. LXXXIX, 121. $1\frac{1}{16}$ in. sq. No. 11559; Square I 13/23; Depth 4 ft. 11 in. b.s.
4. Tiny, rectangular steatite seal inscribed on both faces. One end broken. Pl. XCVI, 494. W. $\frac{5}{16}$ in. No. 10176; Square I 11/5; Depth 4 ft. 4 in. b.s.

---

[1] These marks are the survivals of a cloth ball wrapped round with thread and used as a core for moulding faience vases which were then put in fire. The core would thus burn leaving marks on the faience paste.

[2] This is illustrated in Pl. XVII, *e*.

[3] For a detailed description of these and other furnaces, see Chap. XVIII *infra*.

5. Tiny, faience sealing inscribed on both faces. One end broken. Pl. C, 667. W. $\frac{5}{12}$ in. No. 10137; Square I 11/10; Depth 3 ft. b.s.
6. Tiny, faience sealing shaped like the stone of a date palm, and inscribed on either side of the axial groove; similar to No. 385 in Pl. XCV. L. $\frac{11}{16}$ in. No. 12278; Square I 13/24; Depth 3 ft. 6 in. b.s.
7. Tiny, discoid faience sealing showing on the obverse a god wearing a helmet and a number of armlets. He is standing under a formalised *pīpal* arch. On the reverse is a *svastika* enclosed by a square, with an inscription along the border. Pl. XCIII, 317. Diam. $\frac{7}{16}$ in. No. 8716; Square I 13/7; Depth 5 ft. 6 in. b.s.
8. Ear-button of burnt steatite relieved at the centre with a four-pointed lozenge-in-circle, enclosed in leafy border. The knob is pierced transversely. At its centre is a hole for inlaying some coloured paste. Pl. CXXXIX, 12. Diam. $\frac{5}{8}$ in. No. 10269; Square I 14/13; Depth 3 ft. b.s.
9. Yellow Jaisalmer sandstone *lingam* with a fine continuous spiral groove over the body. Lower part broken. Pl. CXVII, 28. Ht. $4\frac{3}{4}$ in.; diam. at base $2\frac{3}{8}$ in. No. 11537; Square I 13/11; Depth 3 ft. 6 in. b.s.
10. Small tapering faience cylinder inscribed with a circle at top and bottom. L. $\frac{3}{8}$ in. No. 10172; Square I 11/10; Depth 2 ft. 9 in. b.s.
11. Shell cylinder with cross-shaped grooves at both ends. Ht. $\frac{11}{16}$ in.; diam. $\frac{5}{8}$ in. No. 10138; Square I 13/11; Depth 5 ft. 3 in. b.s.
12. Open-mouthed, globular pottery vase painted with black bands. Ht. $4\frac{1}{4}$ in. No. 8280; Square I 14/8; Depth 2 ft. 10 in. b.s.
13. Pottery corn-measure with concave sides and flat bottom. Ht. $2\frac{3}{4}$ in.; diam. $3\frac{3}{4}$ in. No. 10233; Square I 12/13; Depth 3 ft. 6 in. b.s.
14 Lower portion of a pottery standard dish painted with a tree, leafy, and scaly designs. Ht. $7\frac{1}{4}$ in.; diam. 8 in. No. 12324; Square I 13/21; Depth 4 ft. 6 in. b.s.
15. Terracotta male figure with a broad plait of hair which is doubled and tied with a fillet over the head. Pl. LXXVI, 16. Ht. 3 in. No. 8568; Square I 12/10; Depth 3 ft. 6 in. b.s.
16. Three inscribed potsherds. For example see Pl. CIII, 45. L. across $4\frac{1}{4}$ to 7 in. No. 10289; Square I 11; Depth 0 to 3 ft. b.s.
17. Two inscribed potsherds. L. across $4\frac{1}{2}$ and $4\frac{3}{4}$ in. No. 10353; Square I 12; Depth 0 to 3 ft. b.s.
18. Potsherd with two bird-headed human figures of whom the left hand one is carrying a stick across the shoulder. Pl. LXIX, 2. Cf. bird-headed figures on pot-burial No. 206b and sherd No. 11995 (Pl. LXII, 1, *a* and *b*, and Pl. LXIX, 18). Size $5\frac{3}{4}\times4$ in. No. 8890; Square I 12; Depth 0 to 3 ft. b.s.

Remains of Stratum III. Most of the walls of Stratum III, which are usually quite thick, occur in the Middle Section, those in the Northern and Southern Sections being comparatively few. In addition to them, this stratum can also boast of one circular paved manger lined inside with standing bricks (square I 12/5), the remains of a room (over the Deep Digging) in squares I 13/16 and 17, part of a cylindrical granary (square I 13/14), a number of circular brick-on-edge platforms,[1] and several furnaces.

Two bronze tools with tube holes.

This stratum was richer in minor antiquities than the upper two. Three things, which came from the southern portion of the trench, deserve special notice. Two of these were found between Lanes I and II over the place occupied by House 6. Of them, No. 12359 (square I 13/20) comprises two objects of cast bronze identical in shape, one being larger than the other in size (Pl. CXXII, 28 and 33, and Pl. CXXIV, 42-43). The larger one is 3¾ in. long and 1⅝ in. broad, and the smaller one 2⅜ in. long and 1 in. broad. On the inner side and across the centre both have a tubular hole through which was threaded a long nail, which in the case of the larger object had one end turned down and the other broken. On one side of this tubular hole are two short, straight, and tapering prongs rectangular in section, opposite which, again, are two curved lines pointing inwards, thus showing the direction in which the objects were used. As, except the tapering prongs, the objects are finished all over it appears as if that part alone was intended to be let into a double holed, wooden piece or handle. The nail threading the tube-hole being thinner than its receptacle could either be hooked on to grip a detachable handle independently from outside, as shown in the text illustration (fig. *a*), or could act as a pivot on which the objects could be hinged or turned about. In the latter case, they might have been door latches or catches of dentate wheels.

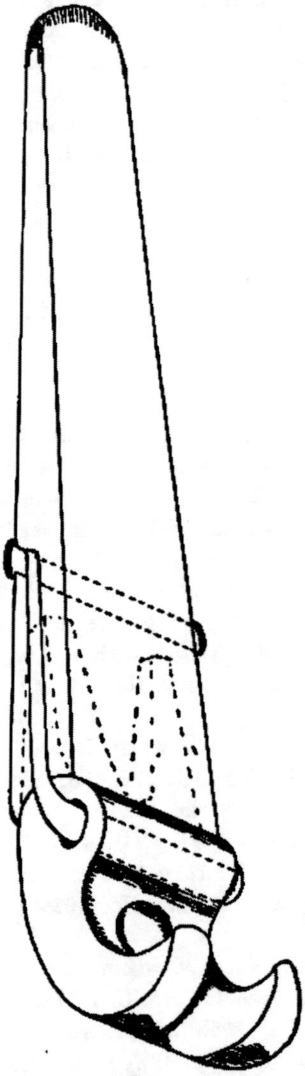

FIG. *a*.

Store jar No. 12414 with contents of stone and shell.

The second find was the crushed napiform jar No. 12414 found in square I 14/16 at a depth of 6 ft. 5 in. Its height was 2 ft. 4 in. and diameter at mouth 9 in. Filling the interior were numerous objects of stone and shell. Those of stone comprised a fragmentary unicorn seal (Pl. LXXXVII, 47), five squat, conical limestone *liṅgams*, 3½ to 6 in. in height, one large sandstone *liṅgam* (ht. 9½ in., diam. 5¾ in.), a quatrefoil alabaster flower cone, a large hone of grey sandstone

[1] See p. 74 *infra*.

stone (7½ by 2¾ in.), an oblong block of sandstone (7⅝ by 2½ by $\frac{9}{10}$ in.), four grindstones (two triangular and two rectangular in section), and a block of chalcedony (6½ by 4¼ by 5 in.). The shell details consisted of six larger and seven smaller pieces shaped like petals, and 25 other tiny pieces which are triangular, discoid, rectangular, lentoid, etc. (Pl. LXXXII, 42). Earth inside this jar was slightly greyish brown and contained about half an ounce of tiny delicate bones of some bird or reptile, bits of charcoal, and some potsherds.

About 30 ft. south of Lane II and in square I 14/10 was made the third find (No. 8592), between 6 ft. 9 in. and 7 ft. below the surface. It comprised numerous thin, disc beads of burnt steatite, one oval bead lentoid in section, three conical, and some assorted tiny beads of the same substance, numerous cylindrical beads of whitish, bluish and blackish faience, some miscellaneous beads, a tiny shell ball, rusted copper pieces, etc. **Lot of beads No. 8592.**

The following interesting antiquities of this stratum were found widely scattered over the whole trench:— **Other finds.**

1. Broken unicorn seal with 4 pictograms. Pl. LXXXVIII, 71. 1¼ in. sq. No. 10142; Square I 11/10; Depth 3 ft. 2 in. b.s.
2. Unicorn seal with 4 pictograms. Pl. LXXXIX, 133. $\frac{15}{16}$ in. sq. No. 11630; Square I 13/17; Depth 8 ft. 3 in. b.s.
3. Unicorn seal fragment. Pl. XC, 199. L. $\frac{15}{16}$ in. No. 11631; Square I 13/11; Depth 8 ft. 3 in. b.s.
4. Fragment of a tiny, rectangular steatite seal inscribed on both sides. Pl. CI, 700. L. ⅜ in. No. 11597; Square I 13/21; Depth 6 ft. 7 in. b.s.
5. Rectangular, faience sealing, plano-convex in section, inscribed on both sides. Pl. XCIV, 351. Size ⅝×$\frac{5}{16}$ in. No. 12377; Square I 14/22; Depth 6 ft. 8 in. b.s.
6. Limestone *lingam*, fragmentary. Ht. 5¾ in.; diam. 6¼ in. No. 12334; Square I 14/24; Depth 4 ft. 6 in. b.s.
7. Oblong slab with deep grooves, probably made by sharpening tools. Size 9¼×3 in. No. 12333; Square I 14/18; Depth 4 ft. 8 in. b.s.
8. Large, oval weight of granite. Wt. 26,535·60 gms.; ht. 11¼ in., diam. 10 in. No. 12368; Square I 14/21; Depth 4 ft. 10 in. b.s.
9. Polished, cubical chert weight intentionally roughened in the centre on all sides. Broken. Wt. 125·25 gms.; size 1⅝×1⅝×1½ in. No. 8680; Square I 14/7; Depth 8 ft. 2 in. b.s.
10. Tiny, conical faience boss with two pairs of holes at opposite sides of the rim and five blind holes between them. Diam. ⅜ in. No. 12335; Square I 14/18; Depth 4 ft. 8 in. b.s.
11. Frustum of a tiny faience cone inscribed with a circle at top and bottom. Pl. CXX, 49. Ht. ½ in. No. 10279; Square I 12/13; Depth 6 ft. b.s.
12. Knobbed faience lid resembling covers of silver vases from Mohenjo-daro. *Cf. M. I. C.*, Pl. CXLVIII, B. Diam. 2 in. No. 8565; Square I 14/6; Depth 7 ft. b.s.

13. A child's copper bangle with overlapping ends.[1] Pl. CXXV, 56. Diam. $1\frac{1}{4}$ in. No. 10272; Square I 12/2; Depth 4 ft. 6 in. b.s.
14. Cylindrical bone baluster with linear decoration. L. 2 in. No. 10293; Square I 12/11; Depth 5 ft. 6 in. b.s.
15. Smooth ivory bar, square in section and with two parallel grooves on one side. L. $2\frac{3}{16}$ in.; section $\frac{1}{2}$ in. sq. No. 10300; Square H 12/22; Depth 6 ft. b.s.

Pottery—

16. Narrow-mouthed, biconvex vase. Ht. 3 in.; diam. 4 in. No. 10273; Square I 12/2; Depth 4 ft. 6 in. b.s.
17. Narrow-necked bottle with double-convex body, painted with sets of black bands. Pl. LXXII, 32. Ht. 6 in.; diam. $7\frac{3}{8}$ in. No. 8430; Square I 14/8; Depth 5 ft. 2 in. b.s.
18. Tile, incised with cross-hatched pattern. Pl. LXXII, 26. Size $10\times8\frac{3}{4}\times1\frac{1}{4}$ in. No. 8100; Square I 12/2; Depth 5 ft. 10 in. b.s.
19. Toy in the form of two monkeys or squirrels climbing up the stump of a tree. Pl. LXXVIII, 33. Ht. $2\frac{1}{4}$ in. No. 11598; Square I 13/21; Depth 6 ft. 7 in. b.s.
20. Disc (lentoid in section), with three holes in the centre and a horizontal groove round the rim, for twining thread. Diam. $1\frac{7}{16}$ in. No. 12040; Square I 13/20; Depth 7 ft. 4 in. b.s.
21. Painted potsherd showing an ass (?), peacock, goat, grasshopper, etc. Observe the crudeness of the animal designs as compared with similar paintings on burial pottery. Pl. LXIX, 11. Size $5\frac{3}{8}\times3\frac{5}{8}$ in. No. 9023; Square I 12; Depth 3 to 6 ft. b.s.

Stratum IV.

The IVth stratum was found to be exceptionally interesting. In it were recovered not only a number of instructive antiquities, including a representative collection of jewellery, but also a well and fourteen Workmen's Quarters of peculiar design.

Northern Section.

At the northern end, there are a few bits of walls of burnt and sun-dried bricks, as well as of mud, and, at the centre is a broken platform of mud bricks close to which were found two large jars with open mouths and pointed bases.

Two earthenware jars of rare type.

Of these, No. 10312 resembles the typical drinking goblet (Pl. XVIII, *g*), and No. 10360, a large carinated *deg* (Pl. XVIII, *d*), both shapes being rare among the larger jars.

A large group of finds (No. 8650).

Close by, near the north-west corner of this trench was recovered a group of finds (No. 8650) of great interest, consisting of a large number of seals and sealings, besides numerous objects of stone, faience, gold, and copper, as well as other things. The most prolific spot was the left hand ground shown in Pl. XII, *d*. A list of the objects in this group, found in squares H 12/21 and I 12/1 between 4 to 7 ft. below the surface, is given below:—

Seals and sealings.

1. Bossed, steatite seal showing a bison grazing in a trough and 7 pictograms. Pl. XCI, 241. $1\frac{1}{16}$ in. sq. No. 8650*a*.
2. Nine tiny rectangular steatite seals with identical pictograms on both sides. Pl. XCVI, 433. Size $\frac{11}{16}\times\frac{7}{16}$ to $\frac{5}{8}\times\frac{1}{4}$ in. No. 8650*b*.

---

[1] *Cf.* similar bangle No. 7947 from Stratum II in this very trench, p. 54 *supra*.

3. Four tiny rectangular steatite seals with identical pictograms on both sides. Pl. XCVI, 448 and 452. Size $\frac{3}{8}\times\frac{1}{16}$ and $\frac{3}{8}\times\frac{3}{16}$ in. No. 8650*c*.
4. Tiny, four-sided, bar-shaped steatite seal inscribed with a fish on top, 2 pictograms on the left hand side, and 2 parallel grooves at bottom. Pl. XCVIII, 590. Size $\frac{3}{8}\times\frac{1}{4}$ in. No. 8650*e*.
5. Tiny, plano-convex, discoid seal with 2[1] pictograms on the plane face. Like others of its kind, it has bevelled edges and could well have been used as the bezel of a finger ring; similar to No. 414 in Pl. XCV. Diam. $\frac{5}{16}$ in. No. 8650*f*.
6. Discoid faience sealing with a rosette of seven *pīpal* (*ficus religiosa*) leaves on one side, and 3 pictograms on the other. Pl. C, 664. Diam. $\frac{7}{12}$ in. No. 8650*d*.
7. Oblong, plano-convex terracotta sealing broken at the right hand. To left, on the plane side, it shows a man attacking a tiger from a *machān*[2] set up against an acacia tree, this representation being identical with that of the seal illustrated in Pl. XCI, 248. The right hand part of the scene is missing. On the convex side, the scene is depicted vertically from top to bottom. In the centre of the upper field stands a man between two rampant animals, but, unfortunately, the heads of all the three figures are missing. The animals, to judge from their bodies and claws, are lions. In the lower field is an elephant, facing right, symbolic, perhaps, of a dense forest. Pl. XCIII, 308. This scene may be identified with the exploits of Eabani[3] or Enkidu who is represented in Sumerian legends as fighting with lions and bulls in forests. W. $\frac{3}{8}$ in. No. 8650*g*.
8. One gold bead and a tiny boss. No. 8650*h*.

Beads and pendents.

9. Two small cubical weights, one of white limestone and the other of grey stone with a white band. Wt. 26·3 and 4·3 gms.; size ·95×·95×·65 and ·55×·5×·35 in. No. 8650*i*.
10. Seven conical tapering pendents of steatite[4], each with a deep groove at the head. Ht. $\frac{3}{32}$ to $\frac{5}{8}$ in. No. 8650*j*.
11. Similar pendent of lapis lazuli[5]. Ht. $\frac{9}{16}$ in. No. 8650*k*.
12. Crescent-shaped, banded faience pendent. L. $\frac{11}{16}$ in. No. 8650*l*.
13. Barrel-shaped bead of burnt steatite, lentoid in section. It is drilled with shallow circular grooves for inlay in single, double, or trefoil formation.[6] Pl. CXXVIII, 15. L. $\frac{3}{4}$ in. No. 8650*n*.

---

[1] Seals of this shape are always of the same size and have the same two pictograms.

[2] Being but a side view the *machān* is represented only by a line. *Cf. M. I. C.*, Pl. CXI, 352, 353 and 355.

[3] Regarding the concept of this therianthropic deity or demon, cf. Sir John Marshall, *op. cit.*, p. 67, and Mohenjo-daro seals, 356-57. See also L. W. King, *History of Sumer and Akkad*, pp. 77 and 174, plate opposite p. 76 and figures 52 and 54.

[4] These pendents are usually better finished and commonly made of hornblende.

[5] Lapis lazuli is very rarely used and this pendent is the only one of this stone.

[6] For similar decoration at Mohenjo-daro, *cf. M. I. C.*, Pl. CXLVI, 49 and 53.

More finds from the same place. Forming part of the above lot were a small ring of thin lead wire, a V-shaped copper arrow-tip, two tiny copper bosses, four cylindrical and two round beads of copper and two copper ferules stuck together (Pl. CXXV, 9-11). With them was found a large collection of other beads comprising 28 of carnelian, 1 oblong bead of steatite, oval in section, numerous thin and discoid beads of the same substance, 12 of different shapes and stones, 5 of shell, 71 round ones of faience, and 3 others with fluted surface, 10 barrel-shaped beads of faience and paste, 99 cylindrical beads of faience and steatite, and 24 of different shapes in faience or paste. An ivory baluster, several chert cores and knives, some river shells, pieces of shell, a painted terracotta wheel, and a triangular cake completed the remainder of this find. Near this were also found in square I 11/15, at a depth of 5 ft. 7 in. two tiny rectangular steatite seals (No. 10928*a*, Pl. XCVI, 442 and Pl. XCVII, 523) one of which is badly broken. On account of their tiny size, the things mentioned above had to be collected with the greatest care necessitating the employment of knives and sieves continuously for three months. Subsequent to the recording of this lot the following eight seals and a cobbler's awl (?) (Pl. CXXV, 32) were also found from the same area :—

1. Unicorn seal with 3 ctograms. Pl. LXXXVIII, 94. $\frac{9}{16}$ in. sq. No. 10061 ; Square I 12/1 ; Depth 6 ft. b.s.
2. Tiny, rectangular seal inscribed on both sides. Pl. XCVII, 504. Size $\frac{1}{2}\times\frac{1}{4}$ in. No. 10059 ; Square I 12/1 ; Depth 6 ft. b.s.
3. Tiny, ovoid seal inscribed on both sides. Pl. XCVII, 544. Size $\frac{11}{16}\times\frac{5}{16}$ in. No. 10060 ; Square I 12/1 ; Depth 6 ft. b.s.
4. Tiny, four-sided, bar-shaped seal with two pictograms on one side, fish on the second, and two parallel grooves on the third.[1] Size $\frac{3}{8}\times\frac{3}{16}$ in. No. 10086 ; Square I 12/1 ; Depth 6 ft. b.s.
5. Tiny, rectangular seal (fragmentary) with pictograms on one side, and dotted circles on the other. Pl. XCVII, 538. W. $\frac{1}{3}$ in. No. 8154 ; Square I 12/1 ; Depth 7 ft. b.s.
6. Tiny, rectangular seal (fragmentary) with pictograms on one side and dotted circles on the other. Pl. XCVII, 505. W. $\frac{1}{3}$ in. No. 10226 ; Square I 12/1 ; Depth 7 ft. 2 in. b.s.
7. Rectangular faience sealing showing unicorn and incense-burner on one side, and 4 pictograms on the other. Unique in being of such tiny size. Pl. CI, 701. Size $\frac{3}{16}\times\frac{5}{32}$ in. No. 8150 ; Square I 12/1 ; Depth 6 ft. 5 in. b.s.
8. Rectangular, plano-convex terracotta sealing inscribed on both faces. The convex face shows impression left by a straw. Pl. XCIV, 352. Size $1\times\frac{5}{8}$ in. No. 10058 ; Square I 12/1 ; Depth 6 ft. b.s.
9. Thick, flattish copper bar, rectangular in section, thinning out towards the ends. Fragmentary. L. $9\frac{5}{8}$ in. No. 10204 ; Square I 12/1 ; Depth 5 ft. 6 in. b.s.

Middle Section. Near the northern end of the Middle Section were found two paved chambers (Sink 1 and Sink 2) of the IVth stratum in squares I 13/1 and I 12/10, neither of

[1] It is similar to seal No. 8650*e*, serial No. 4 on p. 59 *supra*.

which is provided with a doorway. It appears that originally they were used as some kind of store-chambers, but were later converted into rubbish bins. Of these, the second is 6 ft. 10 in. square, and paved with brick-on-edge. It is buttressed from without at the centre of each side by masonry props of one brick length, and stands to a maximum height of 6 ft. (Pl. XVI, *c*, centre foreground). In it were found a round, medium-sized vase with horizontal grooving, an open-mouthed *hāṇḍi*-shaped jar of medium size, a large crushed jar, and five goblets with pointed bases. The other, with a pavement of flat bricks, measures 4 ft. 10 in. by 3 ft. 10 in. internally and stands to a height of 5 ft. It was filled with potsherds of numerous varieties of vessels in which, as usual, there was a preponderance of goblets with pointed bases.

Two paved chambers.

Well and inlay objects from it.

To the south of chamber No. 1 in the adjoining square I 13/1 is a well, of which the diameter is only 2 ft. 8 in. With this is connected a broken pavement from which the ablution water was taken away by a drain going towards the west end of the mound. In the course of clearing the well were found lumped together, at a depth of 18 ft. below its existing top (which, by the way, is broken), several objects of copper, faience, and ivory (No. 10111). The copper pieces, five in number, are made of a thin sheet and are broader at the centre than at the ends (Pl. CXXIV, 41). None of them is entire. Sticking to them were found a number of objects of burnt steatite and faience, of which 10 are crescent-shaped, 2 fan-shaped, 2 roughly semi-circular, 2 rhomboidal, 7 triangular, 4 resembling the outline of a helmet, and a few miscellaneous bits (Pl. CXXXIX, 65-76, 82 and 83). All of them are finely fluted vertically and have chamferred edges for inlay. In several cases they have a keyhole or holes on the reverse or in the sides or in both. Mixed up with these were found an ivory rod, a baluster, and a tablet rounded at the upper end, which is holed.

East of chamber No. I were found a carrot-shaped jar[1] (No. 10054) with traces of black paint on it, and the lower part of a pottery trough with straight sides and flat bottom incised with interlacing circles[2] (No. 8240).

A circular platform.

In this section, close to the western edge of the trench and in square I 13/4, was found a circular platform made of a succession of seven rows of brick-on-edge, laid north and south, which diminish progressively on either side of the central row so as to form a circle. It was apparently meant for sitting, and is quite different in construction from the platforms[3] of Stratum III, which are made of concentric rings of masonry, and are described further below in connection with Trench V.

Lay out of the Workmen's Quarters.

In the southern 130 ft. of this trench are three narrow parallel alleys running from east to west, which have been designated on the plan (Pl. XI) as Lanes I, II and III. They are intersected at right angles by still narrower cross lanes numbered IV, V, VI, VII, VIII and IX. Going from north to south, each of the latter crosses Lane II with a slight eastward deviation[4] at its point of juncture with the former and terminates towards the south in Lane III, and towards the

[1] Its shape is similar to that illustrated in *M. I. C.*, Pl. LXXXVI, 14.

[2] For similar patterns at Mohenjo-daro, *cf. Ibid.*, Pl. CLVII, 4 and 5.

[3] See p. 74 *infra*.

[4] This deviation is apparently due to the unequal width of houses in Blocks I and II.

north in Lane I. Between them, all these lanes enclose fourteen small houses belonging to the IVth stratum. More of them are likely to be recovered on the east and possibly also on the west. Of those that have been uncovered so far, seven are situate in Block I, which is enclosed on the north and south by Lanes II and III, and seven in Block II, which is bounded by Lanes I and II. The cross Lanes IV to IX have the effect of leaving each house open on all four sides, and from this, despite the very fragmentary nature of the remains in Stratum IV, it may be inferred that originally there was a narrow lane to the west of Houses 1 and 2, and that a series of cross lanes on the east, with some more houses of the same kind, is likely to be recovered by excavation to the east of Houses 13 and 14 (Pl. XIV, *a* and *b*). It may be observed that the cross lanes which were originally meant to keep the houses open on all sides and to provide through communication between Lanes I and III were subsequently closed at one or the other end, so as to block the public passage through them to Lanes II and III. But as apparently this blocking did not interfere with the free passage of the inmates of houses in Block I to Lanes II and III and of those in Block II to Lanes I and II, I infer that the cross lanes were the private property of the houses between which they lie. As against this, the Lanes I to III, which were evidently meant for the public, are not blocked anywhere. It seems, therefore, likely that before sanctioning the lay out plan of houses comprising this quarter the municipal authorities insisted on the cross lanes being left for reasons of sanitation without acquiring them for the public use. Further, it may be added that immediately along the north of Lane I and the south of Lane III there are other parallel lanes which show that Lanes I and III were specially meant for the Workmen's Quarters.[1]

Their plan.

Unfortunately, these houses have all but perished. However haphazard their construction may now appear, they were all carefully planned, and, with the partial exception of Houses 5 and 9, closely resemble one another. Pl. XIV shows that in many cases the original walls are now represented by nothing but a few brickbats belonging to their cores, and in some cases by mud brick or only a rammed bed of earth for laying the foundation on. But for the data supplied by Houses 1 to 4, their plans would irrevocably have been lost. Briefly, each house is rectangular and consists of three rooms, or of a courtyard and two rooms, *viz.*, a small and irregularly shaped room alongside the entrance opposite which the corner is filled in solid and a fair sized room equal to the width of the house at the back of the courtyard (Pl. XV, *a*). The entrance itself takes the form of an oblique passage so planned as to prevent anyone looking into the courtyard from the outside.

[1] The houses described below are very small providing only a limited amount of accommodation. The find of several furnaces belonging to Strata III and IV in this part would seem to suggest that some workmen or artisans were living here. At Tell El Amarna the Workmen's Cottages and dwellings in the Workmen's Village, which are identical in every respect, "consist of an entrance hall with a closet at one end, a main living-room sometimes with a column, and two small rooms behind, bed-room and kitchen" (John Pendlebury's, *Tell-El-Amarna*, p 118.) The above village is walled and planned in six blocks which are separated from each other by narrow parallel lanes. The cottages being built in continuous rows have no cross lanes and open only on two sides (*vide* Plan in Sir Leonard Woolley's, *Digging up the Past*, Pl. XVI). In these, as in the Harappā Workmen's Quarters, the accommodation is strictly limited.

Of the above mentioned houses, House 1 is better preserved than the others, and I shall, therefore, take it as a model and make use of House 4 in which the solidly filled in corner is more than usually well-preserved (Pl. XIII, *d*, left ground, centre) to help out my description. Unfortunately, even this house is not complete, though enough of it is left for us to understand and reconstruct the plan more or less accurately (Pl. XIII, *b*, foreground). It measures 55 ft. 4 in. from north to south and 29 ft. 3 in. from east to west. At its south-east corner is a quadrilateral-shaped room which is larger than the corresponding rooms in the remaining houses. Excepting its oblique west wall, the walls of this room are at right angles to each other, the greatest and shortest inner lengths being 13 ft. 3 in. and 11 ft. 3 in. respectively, and the width about 7 ft. It was entered from Lane IV by a small doorway 3 ft. 3 in. wide. On the north side of this room is the courtyard, measuring 22 ft. 9 in. by 20 ft. 6 in., which was entered from Lane III through a slanting passage, 4 ft. wide, left between the room referred to above and the solidly filled in corner. To judge from the remains of a pavement[1] surviving along three sides of the courtyard and also by the dilapidated pavings in the courtyards of some other houses in this quarter, it is likely that in every house the courtyard was paved. In its east wall was a slit, intended no doubt for drainage, which was originally 1 ft. 10 in. wide but later on narrowed down to 1 ft. 1 in. At the north end of the house is a large room measuring 23 ft. 2 in. by 16 ft. 4 in. Unfortunately, its east wall is fragmentary, while the west and partially destroyed south wall are too low—in fact nothing more than mere foundations—to show how it was entered into. The solid mass of masonry at the south-west corner of this house is much ruined, but its shape, which is similar to that of the corresponding corner in House 8, may be reconstructed by referring to the same or to the corresponding corners of Houses 2 and 4 (Pl. XV, *a*), which are better preserved. At the entrance to the oblique passage there are angular chases at opposite points in the corner of the room and the solid filling opposite seemingly for putting in the door frame. These chases are very clearly seen in Houses 4 and 8. **Description of House 1.**

The only outstanding find in this section is a large collection of jewellery (No. 8060) found in the courtyard of House 2 (square I 14/1) at a depth of 7 ft. 8 in. to 8 ft. 4 in. below the surface (Pl. CXXXVII), of which a detailed list is given below. In most cases the arrangement of objects as shown in the plate has been reconstructed from the position in which they were found lying on the ground without any container, and is borne out in several cases by the jewellery from Mohenjo-daro to which reference is made in cases of similar ornament. In some cases, however, the restorations are purely conjectural. **Collection of jewellery No. 8060.**

Pl. CXXXVII, 1-31—

(*a*) No. 14. Hollow armlet of gold sheet tapering both ways from the centre. The sheet is rounded inwards and the line of juncture is not soldered. At each end there is a pin-hole for attachment. Diam. 3¼ in. Cf. *M. I. C.*, Pl. CLI, A, 2, 3, 9 and 10.

[1] The pavement along the east wall is slightly later and contemporary with the narrowing down of the slit in the courtyard.

(*b*) No. 1. Hollow elliptical bangle broken in two parts, similar to the armlet. Diam. 2⅜ in.

(*c*) No. 2. Conical gold ornament for the forehead with doubled rim and with a strong silver hook for attachment inside at the apex. Ht. 1 3/16 in.; diam. at base 1¼ in. How this ornament was actually worn is illustrated by the terracotta figurine No. 53 in Pl. LXXVII, which shows several similar cones worn over the plait of hair from the forehead to the top of the head-dress. Also cf. *M. I. C.*, Pl. CXLVIII, A, 2.

(*d*) No. 8. Heart-shaped pendent in repoussé, with two gold hooks on the underside for suspension. It is made of gold sheet beaten out from behind into three concentric heart-shaped designs in which the sunken surfaces between the undulations are inlaid with ribbed bands of blue faience.

(*e*) No. 15. Brooch, shaped like the figure 8[1]. It consists of a strong flat silver plate to which are soldered three bands of gold symmetrically bent so as to form the figure 8 which is then inlaid with two rows of tiny, cylindrical beads of burnt steatite capped with gold ends. Each of the two loops of the 8-shaped figure has two pin-holes for attachment. L. 2¼ in.; w. 1⅛ in. It could have been worn in front by attachment to the dress or on the hair as shown in the terracotta figurine No. 24 in Pl. LXXVI.

(*f*) No. 7. Necklace consisting of 240 round gold beads arranged in four rows with four spacers and two terminals. Cf. *M. I. C.*, Pl. CXLIX, 3.

(*g*) No. 3. Two wristlets (?) each consisting of 69 round gold beads and two terminals arranged in three rows. One of them has two spacers and the other only one. Its beads are similar to those of necklace *f*, but the size of spacers and terminals is suggestive of the ornament being small rather than a long necklace.

(*h*) Nos. 6 and 20. Two sets each consisting of 27 hollow conical bosses with gold hooks soldered inside at the apex. Besides these, there is one spare boss of a little larger size (No. 16). They may be compared to the bosses tucked up in the loin cloth of the terracotta male figure No. 12 in Pl. LXXVI and were probably meant for a similar use. Although, they could also be worn on the braids of hair[2] as shown in figure 23, Pl. LXXVI, and in figure 60, Pl. LXXVII, they would surely be too numerous for the hair if, as I assume, they belong to a single set.

(*i*) No. 18. A string of 27 gold beads of various shapes.

(*j*) No. 28. 70 miscellaneous beads, caps or ends, etc., of gold, one spacer with two holes, and one terminal.

---

[1] Such figures are also carved on the 'Table of libation with six jugs from Phaestus'. *Cf.* M. P. Nilsson, *The Minoan-Mycenaean Religion*, p. 129, Fig. 30, and are also painted on a bowl from Sphoungaras, *Ibid.*, p. 120, Fig. 24.

[2] They are rather small for being worn on the hair.

Six necklaces mixed—

(*k*) Necklace No. 9 consists of 13 pendents, 4 long facetted gold beads, 2 cylindrical gold end pieces, 26 cylindrical beads of burnt steatite with gold ends, and 8 beads of banded agate. Of the pendents, the central three are of polished jasper, rectangular in section and tapering downwards, while the others of jade are oval in shape and lentoid in section. The tip of each pendent consists of a tubular bead of burnt steatite with gold ends, followed by a tiny gold cylinder and two discs with a disc of burnt steatite between them. The various parts of each pendent were threaded together by means of a copper wire looped at the upper end.

Necklace No. 10 consists of 13 pendents, 7 oval beads of blue faience, lentoid in section, of which 6 have gold caps at the ends, 26 cylindrical steatite beads with gold ends, 2 cylindrical gold end pieces, 3 beads of agate, and 2 of hæmatite.

Necklace No. 11 consists of 13 pendents, 8 oval beads of burnt steatite with gold ends, and 4 without, all lentoid in section, alternating with 26 cylindrical beads of burnt steatite with gold ends. At each end there is a cylindrical gold bead.

Necklace No. 12 consists of 13 pendents, 9 oval beads of blue faience with gold ends lentoid in section, 1 with only one gold end and 2 without. The faience beads come alternately with 26 cylindrical beads of burnt steatite with gold ends. At each end there is a cylindrical gold bead.

Necklace No. 13 consists of 7 pendents, 26 cylindrical beads of burnt steatite with gold ends including 2 of faience, and 18 oval beads of banded agate and hæmatite, lentoid in section.

Necklace No. 17 consists of 8 barrel-shaped beads of green jade, and 26 discoid, hollow beads of gold lentoid in section.

(*l*) *Three necklaces of carnelian.*—Necklace No. 31 consists of 68 round beads, No. 30 of 35 discoid beads lentoid in section, and No. 24 of 19 flat and other beads.

(*m*) *Two necklaces of burnt steatite.*—Necklace No. 27 consists of 7 oval beads, lentoid in section, 4 barrel-shaped, and 47 cylindrical beads, and No. 19 of two tips of pendent beads with gold ends and 8 tubular beads of which 2 have gold ends.

(*n*) *Two strings of faience beads.*—No. 21 has 14 round and discoid beads, and No. 5, 10 beads of various shapes. Three of the latter have gold ends.

(*o*) *One string of shell beads.*—No. 25 comprises 155 beads which are discoid, lentoid, cylindrical, etc.

(*p*) *Silver.*—No. 4. One hollow fragmentary bangle of silver[1] sheet, highly corroded, and a number of silver beads lumped together by corrosion.

[1] According to Khan Bahadur Mohammad Sana Ullah, Archæological Chemist, this bangle is of almost pure silver, free from lead, and contains only a slight impurity of copper.

(*q*) *Mixed lot.*—No. 23. A small lot of broken pendent beads with some gold ends here and there.

Stray finds. Among other interesting antiquities of Stratum IV the following were found scattered over the whole trench :—

1. Fragment of a small unicorn seal with only part of one pictogram surviving. No. 8630; Square I 13/5; Depth 8 ft. 6 in. b.s.
2. Fragment of a unicorn seal with only three pictograms left. Pl. XC, 220. Side $1\frac{1}{16}$ in. No. 10318; Square I 13/13; Depth 7 ft. 2 in. b.s.
3. Small fragment of a unicorn seal. Pl. XC, 216. L. $\frac{3}{16}$ in. No. 11797; Square I 12/15; Depth 10 ft. b.s.
4. Tiny, four-sided, bar-shaped seal inscribed with symbols like V and III on the opposite sides, dotted circles on top, and a double parallel groove on the underside. Pl. XCV, 401. Size $\frac{7}{16}\times\frac{1}{4}\times\frac{7}{16}$ in. No. 8148; Square H 12/23; Depth 7 ft. b.s.
5. Fragment of a tiny rectangular seal; similar to No. 458 in Pl. XCVI, W. $\frac{1}{4}$ in. No. 10223; Square H 11/25; Depth 7 ft. 2 in. b.s.
6. Tiny, rectangular seal with 2 pictograms on one face, and 3 dotted circles on the other. Pl. XCVI, 466. Size $\frac{3}{8}\times\frac{1}{4}$ in. No. 10224; Square H 11/25; Depth 7 ft. 2 in. b. s.
7. Tiny, discoid seal inscribed on both faces. Pl. XCV, 412. Diam. 11/20 in. No. 9014; Square I 12/7; Depth 7 ft. 7 in. b.s.
8. Tiny, discoid seal with inscription on one face and a dotted circle on the other. Pl. XCV, 413. Diam. $\frac{1}{2}$ in. No. 9086; Square I 12/2; Depth 8 ft. 7 in. b.s.
9. Tiny, rectangular seal inscribed on both faces; similar to No. 457 in Pl. XCVI. Size $\frac{3}{8}\times\frac{1}{4}$ in. No. 9057; Square I 12/4; Depth 9 ft. b.s.
10. Tiny, rectangular seal inscribed on both faces. Pl. XCVII, 498. Size $\frac{11}{20}\times\frac{3}{10}$ in. No. 9082; Square I 12/5; Depth 10 ft. b.s.
11. Tiny, fish-shaped seal inscribed on both sides. Pl. XCV, 428. Size $\frac{3}{5}\times\frac{3}{10}$ in. No. 8080; Square I 12/5; Depth 10 ft. 3 in. b.s.
12. *Triratna-shaped,* steatite pendent or terminal with three equidistant vertical holes. Pl. CXXXIX, 32. Size $\frac{3}{5}\times\frac{3}{10}$ in. No. 9084; Square I 12/9; Depth 9 ft. 6 in. b.s.
13. Cubical stone weight. Wt. 13·75 gms.; size ·73×·73×·57 in. No. 10195; Square I 13/3; Depth 9 ft. 6 in. b.s.
14. Frustum of a small faience cone with a circle incised on top and bottom. Ht. $\frac{1}{2}$ in. No. 9083; Square I 12/5; Depth 10 ft. b.s.
15. Faience frustum similar to No. 14. Ht. $\frac{1}{4}$ in. No. 10040; Square I 13/2; Depth 10 ft. b.s.
16. Copper knife blade with straight edge, well preserved. Pl. CXXV, 30. L. $3\frac{1}{4}$ in. No. 10225; Square H 11/25; Depth 7 ft. 2 in. b.s.
17. Copper bangle in 2 pieces. Pl. CXXV, 61. Diam. $1\frac{3}{4}$ in. No. 8930; Square I 15/6; Depth 8 ft. 10 in. b.s.

18. Pottery jar-stand. Ht. 5¼ in.; diam. 10½ in. No. 10181; Square I 13/8; Depth 8 ft. 9 in. b.s.

Deep Digging.

In the middle section of this trench was sunk a deep pit measuring 73 ft. from north to south by 53 ft. from east to west, which has been indicated on the plan by a dotted line (Pl. XI). Beginning from the surface, six strata of occupation were brought to light in the first 17 ft., and as the two pits, one to north and the other to south, into which it is divided at a lower level, grew very narrow at a depth of 23 ft. below the surface, the digging could not be carried down further. Below the IVth stratum there was a very thick, continuous mass of burnt brick and terracotta nodules[1] which seemed to be still frequent at the depth where work had to be stopped. The lower limit of the IVth stratum is 10 ft. 2 in., of the Vth 13 ft. 5 in., and of the VIth 17 ft. 5 in. The Vth stratum, however, in so far as it is represented in this limited section, is quite poor as compared with the IVth or the VIth. In fact, there is nothing more of it but a few small bits of walls set at odd angles with the cardinal points. Nevertheless, this stratum is instructive in one respect; it gives us the first clear indication that, as we go deeper, the size of the bossed square seals, or of the rectangular (plano-convex) seals and sealings, which are usually associated with the upper strata, tends to diminish and to prepare, as it were, the way for a large variety of tiny seals which are common in the lower levels. This is clear from the seals which preponderate among the following antiquities from this stratum:—

Relative depth of Strata V and VI.

Finds.

Stratum V—

1. Unicorn seal with 5 pictograms. Pl. LXXXIX, 164. $\frac{9}{16}$ in. sq. No. 11795; Square I 13/11; Depth 10 ft. 3 in. b.s.
2. Unicorn seal (fragmentary) showing hind part of the animal and front lower legs. Pl. XC, 174. L. 1¼ in. No. 11682; Square I 12/20; Depth 11 ft. b.s.
3. Unicorn seal with 7 pictograms. Pl. LXXXIX, 162. $\frac{11}{16}$ in. sq. No. 12066; Square I 13/12; Depth 11 ft. 8 in. b.s.
4. Unicorn seal (fragmentary) with 5 pictograms. Pl. LXXXIX, 145. Side ⅞ in. No. 11696; Square I 12/15; Depth 12 ft. 6 in. b.s.
5. Rectangular, plano-convex faience sealing inscribed on both sides. Pl. XCIV, 364. Size $\frac{7}{12} \times \frac{1}{2}$ in. No. 10363; Square I 13/2; Depth 11 ft. 6 in. b.s.
6. Tiny, rectangular seal (fragmentary) inscribed on both sides. Pl. XCVII, 537. L. ⅜ in. No. 12067; Square I 13/12; Depth 11 ft. 8 in. b.s.
7. Tiny, four-sided, bar-shaped seal with 2 pictograms on one face, and 2, 3 and 4 circles on the remaining three faces. Did it also serve the purpose of a gaming or divining die[2] (?). Pl. XCVII, 572. Size $\frac{3}{8} \times \frac{3}{16} \times \frac{5}{16}$ in. No. 11695; Square I 13/22; Depth 12 ft. b.s.

[1] For masses of such nodules in Trench I in another part of this mound, see p. 81 *infra*.

[2] This seal is unique in having such arrangement of circles.

8. Tiny, triangular prism seal inscribed on three faces. Pl. XCVIII, 586. L. $\frac{3}{8}$ in. No. 11715; Square I 13/21; Depth 13 ft. 3 in. b.s.

9. Tiny, cylindrical seal inscribed with 2 pictograms round the circumference, and a circle at each end. Pl. XCVII, 561. L. $\frac{3}{8}$ in.; diam. $\frac{3}{16}$ in. No. 11794; Square I 13/16; Depth 13 ft. 3 in. b.s.

10. Rectangular, faience sealing with 3 pictograms on one side and a bison bending over a trough on the other. Pl. C, 659. Rare in being of the tiny size like the faience sealings No. 10226 with a unicorn, or No. 2276 (Pl. XCVIII, 601) with a goat and inscription on each of the two faces. Size $\frac{3}{8}\times\frac{3}{8}$ in. No. 11714; Square I 13/16 Depth 12 ft. b.s.

11. Stopper-shaped, unfinished stone object. Pl. CXVII, 7. A similar object in shell was found at Mohenjo-daro.[1] L. $1\frac{1}{3}$ in. No. 11674; Square I 13/18; Depth 11 ft. b.s.

12. Miniature, pottery goblet with pointed base. Ht. $2\frac{1}{3}$ in. No. 11681; Square I 13/23; Depth 11 ft. 3 in. b.s.

Stratum VI. The VIth stratum is represented by an oblique wall, 18 ft. long, and three small bits of walls. The following objects were recovered from it—

1. Unicorn seal with 6 pictograms. Pl. LXXXIX, 141. $\frac{7}{8}$ in. sq No. 11849; Square I 13/18; Depth 13 to 14 ft. b.s.

2. Unicorn seal with 2 pictograms. Pl. LXXXIX, 165. $\frac{11}{16}$ in. sq. No. 11850; Square I 13/17; Depth 16 ft. b.s.

3. Tiny, discoid seal inscribed on both faces. Pl. XCV, 412. Diam. $\frac{1}{2}$ in. No. 11796; Square I 13/22; Depth 13 ft. 8 in. b.s.

4. Tiny, rectangular seal inscribed on both faces, broken at the right end. Pl. XCVI, 481. Size $\frac{11}{16}\times\frac{7}{16}$ in. No. 11798; Square I 13/17; Depth 13 ft. 9 in. b.s.

5. Tiny, rectangular seal inscribed on both faces, slightly broken. Pl. XCVI, 478. Size $\frac{11}{16}\times\frac{3}{8}$ in. No. 11756; Square I 13/11; Depth 14 ft. b.s.

6. Two fragments of a tiny rectangular seal inscribed on both faces. No. 11856; Square I 13/22; Depth 14 ft. b.s.

7. Tiny, rectangular seal inscribed on both faces (in three fragments). Pl. XCVII, 517. L. $\frac{3}{8}$ in. No. 11757; Square I 13/11; Depth 14 ft. b.s.

8. Tiny, rectangular seal inscribed on both faces and with a pair of circles on each of the two longer sides. Pl. XCVII, 573. Size $\frac{5}{8}\times\frac{1}{4}$ in. No. 11854; Square I 13/17; Depth 14 ft. b.s.

9. Tiny, rectangular seal inscribed on both faces. Pl. XCVII, 514. Size $\frac{9}{16}\times\frac{5}{16}$ in. No. 11853; Squares I 13/17 and 18; Depth 13 to 14 ft. b.s.

10. Tiny, fish-shaped seal inscribed on both faces. Pl. XCVII, 571. L. $\frac{7}{16}$ in. No. 11855; Square I 13/17; Depth 14 ft. b.s.

---

[1] *Cf. M. I. C.*, Pl. CLVI, 6.

11. Tiny, hare-shaped seal inscribed on one side only. Pl. XCV, 424. L. $\frac{3}{8}$ in. No. 11852; Square I 13/17; Depth 14 ft. b.s.
12. Tiny, heart-shaped seal with pictograms on one side, and 3 circles in triangular formation on the other. Pl. XCV, 418. L. $\frac{7}{16}$ in. No. 11793; Square I 13/21; Depth 14 ft. b.s.
13. Tiny, tortoise-shaped seal with pictograms on the underside, and rows of circles on the convex face or top shell. Pl. XCV, 426. L. $\frac{1}{2}$ in. No. 11848; Square I 13/18; Depth 14 ft. b.s.
14. Short, tapering granite celt with a broad and sharp cutting edge chipped off by use. This is the smallest and the only celt of this stone recovered at Harappā. Pl. CXVII, 58. L. $3\frac{3}{8}$ in.; w. at cutting edge $2\frac{1}{4}$ in. No. 12225; Square I 13/23; Depth 16 ft. b.s.
15. Miniature silver boss inlaid at the top with a cylindrical bit of shell. Pl. CXXV, 51. Diam. $\frac{3}{8}$ in. No. 11793; Square I 13/21; Depth 14 ft. b.s.
16. Three pieces of twisted gold foil. No. 11847; Square I 13/17; Depth 14 ft. b.s.
17. Terracotta ram in which the pairs of fore and hind legs are not separated from each other. L. $2\frac{1}{4}$ in. No, 11861; Squares I 13/17 and 18; Depth 13 to 14 ft. b.s.
18. Two copper spear-heads. Pl. CXXV, 71 and 73. L. $6\frac{1}{4}$ and 4 in.; w. $1\frac{3}{8}$ and $1\frac{5}{8}$ in. No. 11858; Square I 13/17; Depth 14 ft. b.s.
19. Flat, narrow and thin copper scraper, tang broken. L. $6\frac{3}{4}$ in. No. 11948; Square I 13/17; Depth 19 ft. b.s.

It will be seen from the above list of the finds of Stratum VI that as against two bossed seals engraved with the figure of the unicorn, which are only $\frac{7}{8}$ and $\frac{11}{16}$ in. square, there are no less than eleven of small size seven being rectangular, one shaped as a fish, one as a hare, one as a tortoise, and another one like a heart. Here, I must also draw the reader's attention to the short granite celt No. 14 of the above list of which the edge was chipped off by use. This is the only finished stone celt, as it is also the smallest one ever recovered at Harappā. The few examples of larger stone celts, none of which is finished, are exclusively of chert, and of an apparently late date. This one is smaller than even the smallest of metal celts.[1] It is also interesting to note that in this stratum were found three twisted pieces of gold foil and a miniature silver boss inlaid at the top with a cylindrical bit of conch shell, which carry the use of gold and silver, as well as the process of inlay, to the Early Intermediate Period at Harappā. A few feet lower than the foundation of the VIth stratum was discovered, at a depth of 19 ft. 8 in., a primitive type of toy dog (No. 11982, l. $2\frac{1}{4}$ in.) with its front and hind legs jugate and not separate from each other. An animal toy with legs similarly made has been mentioned above among the finds of Stratum VI. Another similar toy (No. 4067)[2] was found at a depth of 18 ft. in Trench I in this mound, and two

Large preponderance of early seals.

A rare granite celt.

Gold and silver used very early.

Archaic terracotta animal figurines.

---

[1] *Cf.* Pls. CXXIII, 1-21 and CXXIV, 36-39.

[2] *Cf.* Pl. LXXIX. 82.

more[1] (Nos. J172 and J185) at depths of 14 ft. 8 in. and 14 ft. 9 in. below the surface in Trench III sunk in the valley between the Mounds AB and D.

Trench V.

Trench V is 280 ft. long from east to west: owing to subsequent additions it is 57 ft. wide in the last 90 ft. at the eastern end and 111 ft. over the remaining portion (Pl. XVI, *c*). In it, the Ist stratum is represented by a few bits of walls which stand in the higher eastern section and have already been referred to in the introductory remarks regarding these trenches.[2] A number of minor antiquities, however, were found scattered in this trench at a level higher than that of the IInd stratum and included the following objects. In addition to them was found a small pottery group comprising twelve goblets with pointed bases (No. 9031) from square J 12/10—

1. Fragment of a unicorn seal. Pl. XC, 194. L. $\frac{1}{10}$ in. No. 8646; Square K 12/19; Depth 2 ft. 11 in. b.s.
2. Rectangular and plano-convex steatite seal with 2 pictograms. This is the smallest seal of its kind.[3] Pl. XCIX, 633. Size $\frac{7}{16} \times \frac{3}{16}$ in. No. 10420; from surface.
3. Rectangular, terracotta sealing from the same mould as No. 314[4] in Pl. XCIII. It has 4 pictograms on one side and on the other a two-horned animal which is otherwise exactly similar to the unicorns like whom he has the incense-burner in the usual position under the neck. Size $\frac{11}{16} \times \frac{7}{16}$ in. No. 10965; from spoil earth.
4. Cuboid chert weight, the smallest so far found. Wt. ·95 gm.; size ·3×·3×·25 in. No. 10443; Square J 12/18; Depth 2 ft. b.s.
5. Cuboid chert weight. Wt. 7·9 gms.; size ·6×·6×·5 in. No. 10522; Square K 12/13; Depth 2 ft. 6 in. b.s.
6. Polished chert ball of grey and chocolate colours. Diam. 11/12 in. No. 9097; Square K 12/9; Depth 3 ft. b.s.
7. Limestone *liṅgam* smoothed all over. Pl. CXVII, 18. Ht. 6 in.; diam. at base $4\frac{1}{2}$ in. No. 10496; Square J 12/18; Depth 3 ft. 4 in. b.s.
8. Small hemisphere of burnt steatite, holed in the underside. Diam. $\frac{3}{8}$ in. No. 8720; Square J 12/19; Depth 3 ft. 6 in. b.s.
9. Cubical stone die with one to six marks on its sides, *viz.*, 1 opposite 2, 3 opposite 4, and 5 opposite 6. Pl. CXX, 46. Size $1\frac{11}{16}$ in. cube. No. 8670; Square K 12/24; Depth 4 ft. 6 in. b.s.
10. Small, conical faience boss, hook missing. Retains traces of white glaze. Diam. $\frac{3}{4}$ in. No. 8575; Square K 12/10; Depth 2 ft. b.s.
11. Tiny, couchant faience ram, holed across the neck for suspension. Pl. LXXVIII, 43. L. 1 in. No. 8601; Square K 12/5; Depth 3 ft. 4 in. b.s.

---

[1] *Cf.* Pl. LXXIX, 63 and 61.

[2] See pp. 52-53 *supra*.

[3] This seal and sealing No. 3, which are of small size, must have come up as the result of promiscuous digging for which Harappā has been so notorious.

[4] See p. 29 *supra*.

12. Faience ram similar to No. 11. Pl. LXXVIII, 42. L. 1 in. No. 8602; Square J 12/24; Depth 3 ft. 6 in. b.s.
13. Miniature wavy ring of faience. Pl. CXVII, 13. Diam. 11/16 in. No. 10548; Square J 12/23; Depth 3 ft. 6 in. b.s.
14. Upper part of a red washed pottery standard dish. Diam. 13¾ in.; ht. 4 in. No. 10855; from surface.
15. Squat, open-mouthed pottery vase with concave upper portion. Ht. 4¼ in.; diam. 4 in. No. 8632; Square K 12/24; Depth 3 ft. b.s.
16. Two inscribed potsherds. L. 3¾ and 4¼ in. Nos. 10375 and 10376; Square J 12; Depth 3 to 6 ft. b.s.
17. Two sherds of a dish painted with a deer. The painting is reminiscent of those on the Cemetery flat covers. Diam. 6¾ in. No. 8686; Square K 12; Depth 3 to 6 ft. b.s.
18. Painted potsherd showing a cow suckling her calf, a peacock, tree and lattice pattern. Compared with animal figures on burial pottery the figures on this are rather crude. Pl. LXIX, 12. Size 5¾×4 in. No. 8096; Square K 12/20; Depth 4 ft. 5 in. b.s.
19. Terracotta figure of a ram with nail incision on the body indicating fleece. Pl. LXXVIII, 41. L. 2¾ in. No. 10383; from spoil earth.

Stratum II. Fragmentary nature of remains.

The IInd stratum is also very fragmentary, being represented by one fairly long wall to the west of the well in this trench, two smaller walls further west, several broken bits between the well and the eastern end of the trench, two fragments of drains in squares J 12/23 and K 12/8 lying close to the northern edge, and a few broken pavements, of which one in square J 12/23 is relatively larger. This stratum yielded more finds than the Ist, and included four groups of antiquities which I shall describe first. Group No. 8892 from square I 12/19 is of pottery and comprised four goblets with pointed bases of which two are stamped with the potter's seal (Pl. CII, 23 and 24), a small goblet broken at the neck, a large spoon, another vase, and a lid found betwen 4 and 5 ft. below the surface. Close to this in square I 12/14 was another sub-group No. 8893 which comprised two complete and fragments of about 30 goblets with pointed bases, a broken basin, a crushed *hāndi*-shaped vase and a terracotta whorl. The second group (No. 8611) was found near the well at a depth of 4 ft. below the surface, and consisted of six complete and two fragmentary goblets with pointed bases (Pl. XVIII, *c*). On the above-mentioned pavement in square J 12/23 was recovered the third group (No. 10460) between 3 and 4 ft. below the surface. Besides a number of objects mentioned below, it contained four unfinished, rectangular steatite seals of the plano-convex type showing marks of cutting all over, five broken conch shells, five cores and numerous other fragments of shell weighing about four pounds, as well as a variety of shell details prepared for inlay, *viz.*, three lozenge-shaped, two rectangular, five square, two triangular, one crescent-shaped, one fluted flat piece, six discoid, six bar-shaped, and a tiny ball. This group also comprised a chessman-shaped stone *lingam*, a barrel-shaped unfinished bead of steatite, three pieces of alabaster, a pebble, two terracotta cones, a broken cup,

Three pottery groups and one miscellaneous group.

one wheel, a lid and a ball of the same substance, as well as several animal bones including teeth, long bones, knuckle bones, etc. The variety of these things suggests that the building in which they were found may have been a shop or workshop. The fourth group (No. 10797) consisted only of a jar-stand with horizontal mid-rib, an oval vase, and the lower part of an offerings' dish found in square K 12/19. Among other interesting antiquities of this stratum, which were found widely scattered, are the following:—

1. Unicorn seal with 6 pictograms. Pl. LXXXV, 13. $1\frac{7}{16}$ in. sq. No. 8718; Square I 12/19; Depth 3 ft. 6 in. b.s.
2. Unicorn seal with 5 pictograms, unfinished. Pl. LXXXVII, 44. $1\frac{3}{16}$ in. sq. No. 10625; Square K 12/13; Depth 5 ft. b.s.
3. Unicorn seal with 4 pictograms. Pl. LXXXVIII, 80. $1\frac{1}{16}$ in. sq. No. 10779; Square K 12/18; Depth 8 ft. b.s.
4. Rectangular, plano-convex seal inscribed with 3 pictograms; similar to No. 628 in Pl. XCIX. Size $\frac{9}{16} \times \frac{5}{8}$ in. No. 10485; Square J 12/3; Depth 3 ft. b.s.
5. Rectangular, plano-convex seal inscribed with 7 pictograms. Pl. XCII, 281. Size $1\frac{5}{16} \times \frac{9}{16}$ in. No. 10695; Square K 12/18; Depth 5 ft. 5 in. b.s.
6. Tiny, rectangular seal (fragmentary) inscribed on both faces. Pl. XCV, 403. L. 11/20 in. No. 8102; Square K 12/10; Depth 5 ft. 3 in. b.s.
7. Cylindrical, faience sealing with 4 pictograms on one side, and an acacia tree and a symbol resembling VIII on the other. Pl. XCIX, 646. L. $\frac{13}{16}$ in. No. 8640; Square J 12/4; Depth 3 ft. b.s.
8. Rectangular, faience sealing inscribed on both sides. Pl. XCVIII, 602. Size $\frac{11}{16} \times \frac{5}{16}$ in. No. 10614*a*; Square I 12/11; Depth 2 ft. 9 in. to 3 ft. 3 in. b.s.
9. Oblong, faience sealing, lentoid in section, showing an incense-burner on one side, and 5 blurred pictograms on the other. Pl. XCIII, 320. Size $1\frac{3}{8} \times \frac{7}{16}$ in. No. 10645; Square J 12/19; Depth 4 ft. 6 in. b.s.
10. Rectangular block of chert. Size $13\frac{1}{4} \times 8 \times 4$ to $4\frac{1}{4}$ in. No. 8747; Square J 12/9; Depth 3 ft. 4 in. b.s.
11. Tiny, alabaster lid with knob handle. Pl. LXXXIII, 5. Diam. $\frac{11}{16}$ in. No. 10741; Square L. 12/8; Depth 7 ft. 6 in. b.s.
12. Barrel-shaped, steatite bead with four equidistant bands in relief over the body. The sunk spaces at the ends and between the bands being meant for capping and inlay are rough, but the rest of it is finished and glazed white. It is of unusually large size. Two other zone beads, one of steatite and the other of ivory, are illustrated in Pl. CXXX, 51 and 52. No such bead is known from Mohenjo-daro. Pl. CXXVIII, 19. L. $2\frac{1}{8}$ in.; diam. $1\frac{1}{16}$ in. No. 10700; Square L. 12/9; Depth 7 ft. 6 in. b.s.
13. Hornblende pendent, deeply grooved at the head. Ht. $\frac{7}{16}$ in. No. 10049; Square K 12/9; Depth 8 ft. b.s.

14. Shuttle-shaped chert burnisher, exquisitely polished. Pl. CXVIII, 32. L. $6\frac{5}{16}$ in. No. 10755; Square L. 12/8; Depth 8 ft. b.s.

15. Head of a faience snake in which the tongue was separately inserted. Pl. LXXVIII, 23. L. $\frac{7}{8}$ in. No. 8157; Square I 12/25; Depth 3 ft. 5 in. b.s.

16. Faience ear-button relieved with lezenge-in-circle pattern and cable border. Diam. $\frac{7}{8}$ in. No. 8794; Square L. 12/9; Depth 5 ft. b.s.

17. Plano-convex faience temple disc decorated on obverse with a knob at the centre round which are two dotted circles and a dentate border. It has a segment-shaped hole on the underside which retains an imprint of cotton cloth. Pl. CXXXVIII, 33. Diam. $1\frac{3}{16}$ in. No. 8760; Square L. 12/4; Depth 6 ft. b.s.

18. Knobbed, temple ornament of faience. Pl. LXXXII, 35. Diam. $1\frac{1}{16}$ in. No. 10696; Square K 12/18; Depth 7 ft. 3 in. b.s.

19. Round, copper vase with straight neck and flat bottom. An exactly similar vase was found at Mohenjo-daro.[1] Pl. CXXII, 26. Ht. 6 in.; diam. $5\frac{3}{8}$ in. No. 8250; Square L. 12/5; Depth 5 ft. 6 in. b.s.

20. Thirty eight heart-shaped, shell details for inlay. Size $\frac{7}{16}\times\frac{3}{8}$ to $\frac{3}{16}\times\frac{7}{16}$ in. No. 10692; Square K 12/14; Depth 5 ft. 3 in. b.s.

Pottery vessels—

21. Round jar with ring-base, painted with bands, wavy lines. and dots. Ht. $7\frac{3}{8}$ in.; diam. at mouth $4\frac{3}{4}$ in. No. 8284; Square L. 12/5; Depth 5 ft. b.s.

22. Hand-made, cylindrical cup with three holes at the rim. Pl. LXXI, 69. Diam. $2\frac{1}{2}$ in. No. 8730; Square L. 12/4; Depth 5 ft. b.s.

23. Large cup. Diam. $6\frac{3}{4}$ in. No. 8736; Square L. 12/4; Depth 5 ft. 6 in. b.s.

24. Small, perforated goblet-shaped vase. Ht. $2\frac{1}{4}$ in. No. 8820; Square L. 12/4; Depth 6 ft. 11 in. b.s.

25. Squat, open-mouthed, tapering vase[2]. Diam. $4\frac{3}{8}$ in.; ht. 4 in. No. 10874; Square K 12/13; Depth 8 ft. b.s.

26. Tripod, originally with a seated figure now missing. Ht. $1\frac{3}{8}$ in. No. 10025; Square K 12/10; Depth 5 ft. b.s.

27. Half of a discoid cake mould.[3] Pl. CXX, 27. Diam. $4\frac{1}{8}$ in. No. 9020; Square J 12; Depth 3 to 6 ft. b.s.

28. Discoid whorl with three holes in one line at the centre and grooved rim. Diam. $1\frac{3}{4}$ in. No. 8893*b*; Square I 12/14; Depth 5 ft. b.s.

29. Cubical die marked with 1 opposite 2, 3 opposite 4, and 5 opposite 6. Pl. CXX, 53. Size $1\frac{1}{8}\times1\frac{1}{8}\times1$ in.[4] No. 10697; Square K 12/23; Depth 7 ft. 3 in. b.s.

30. Ball rattle. Diam. $2\frac{3}{4}$ in. No. 10847; Square K 12/13; Depth 8 ft. b.s.

---

[1] *Cf. M. I. C.*, Pl. CXLI, 4 and 11.

[2] *Cf. Ibid.*, Pl. LXXXII, 11.

[3] *Cf. M. I. C.*, Pl. CXXXIII, 7 and 8.

[4] Most of the dice are exact cubes, but this is cuboid.

31. Painted sherd showing a pair of peacocks. Pl. LXIX, 13. No. 8614; Square I 12; Depth 3 to 6 ft. b.s.

32. Sherd painted with chess board and tree patterns. Size 6¼×3¼ in. No. 11065; Square L. 12; Depth 6 to 9 ft. b.s.

Stratum III.

We now come to the IIIrd stratum in connection with which may be mentioned first a scheme of twelve circular platforms occurring in a double row from east to west about the centre of Trench V with additional platforms[1] P1 to P3 in the northern section of Trench IV and P10 and P11 in square J 13. These have been numbered consecutively in the order of their discovery. All of them are nearly equidistant, the intervals between them, centre to centre, being 20 ft. to 20 ft. 6 in. except that between platforms P5 and P6 there is an interval of 40 ft., and that the utterly dilapidated platforms P13 and P15 are built closer to platforms P12 and P14 than the others. The reason for greater distance between platforms P5 and P6 appears to have been that round an existing well of the IVth stratum, which continued to be used at this time, it was felt necessary to allow more space for the public to come and go without let or hinderance (Pl. XI). Similarly, the shorter distance between platforms P12 and P13 and P14 and P15 appears to be due to the existence of contemporary walls close by. Each platform is 11 ft. in diameter, and consists of a single course of four continuous concentric rings of brick-on-edge masonry with a hollow at the centre equal to the length of three bricks. The mortar used in them is mud but the pointing is of gypsum (Pl. XII, *c*). Their purpose is not clear. While digging the hollow of P8 there was found a small quantity of burnt wheat and husked barley and about two pounds of animal bones. Some bits of bones were also found in two or three others. As, however, the bones, etc., lay about a foot below the central hollow, that is to say distinctly below the brickwork of these platforms, and similar fragments of bones were also found sticking at the same level along the edges of the platforms, it appears certain that they were merely a part of the débris and by no means the contents of the hollows.

Twelve Circular platforms. Their alignment, size and construction.

A well of Stratum IV also used with Stratum III.

Slightly to the north, between platforms P4 and P5 is a narrow well, 2 ft. 4 in. in diameter, in which, as in the slightly larger well in Trench IV, the present water level during the winter lies at a depth of 33 ft. below its existing top. This, as will appear from Pl. XVI, *d*, was originally constructed with Stratum IV, when a group of three large cylindrical pottery jars, two of which were lying one above the other, and an oval jar of similar size were placed on two sides of it, apparently for the storage of drinking water for the wayfarers. This well continued to be used along with buildings of the IIIrd stratum. Its ring, however, was not raised, but, as a matter of necessity, head-walls were built on its four sides, of which two are still visible in the photograph forming its south-east corner and presumably rising to a little above the paved floor of the well-chamber, of which also the same corner is preserved. From outside, the latter corner is round.

An excellent statuette of red sandstone.

The most outstanding find from this trench is the small torso[2] (No. 9042, ht. 3¾ in.) of a nude male figure carved in the round in red sandstone. It was

[1] In this square some 40 ft. east of platforms Nos. P10 and P11 two other platforms were found in 1934-35.

[2] It was first described by me in *A. S. R.*, 1928-29, pp. 78-79, Pl. XXXI, *a-d*.

discovered 15 ft. north-west of the well mentioned above and 4 ft. 10 in. below the surface which, owing to a bend at this point, was quite low (Pl. LXXX, *a-d*). It must, therefore, be ascribed to Stratum III. Like the figure of a dancer in dark grey stone[1] (No. Ab959), which was found by Rai Bahadur Daya Ram Sahni near the southern end of the central aisle in the Great Granary, this statuette is incomparably superior to any that has so far been found at Mohenjo-daro.[2] And let me state at the outset that, although a large area—larger than anywhere else at Harappā—has been explored on this mound, not a single object which is not referable to the prehistoric period, has ever been found in it.[3] Indeed, even the things obtained merely by scratching the surface of this mound are all of the Indus Period. The findspot alone of this figure would, therefore, leave little room for doubt as to its prehistoric age, but should there be any doubt on the point it must at once be set at rest when we consider the material, technique and style of the torso. The red sandstone, of which it is carved, like the grey stone of the dancer statuette, was freely imported during the Indus Period at Harappā (where no stone is locally available) and employed for making numerous other objects both small and large. On the other hand, these two stones are not known ever to have been employed in the historic period for making statuary. Pursuant to this point Sir John Marshall has remaked that "among the multitudes of Indo-Hellenistic sculptures in the Panjāb and on the North-West Frontier there is not one that is made from either of these stones."[4] Then as to the technique. We find that in this statuette the head, arms and nipples were made in separate pieces for the attachment of which there are socket-holes in the neck, under the arms and at the breasts. The technique of making this (and the dancer statuette) in parts, though well suited for small figures, is not found, as far as I am aware, in the Indian statuary of the historic period or even in Greek Art. Another point of technique is the use of the tubular drill, which was undoubtedly employed on this statuette in hollowing out the two depressions in front of the shoulders. Part of the central protuberance in them was knocked off as in other stones[5] where this kind of drill was used. It looks as if these depressions were intended to be inlaid with some coloured stone, paste, faience or shell, the protuberance (in so far as it was retained) being required for keying the inlay. We know from the dancer statuette that the nipples of the breasts are inlaid with stone-in-cement, and it may therefore be assumed that corresponding sockets in this statuette, were also intended to be inlaid in like manner.

Circumstances of finding.

Evidence of material and technique.

The pose of the statuette is frontal and therefore quite simple, but its beauty, as pointed out by Sir John Marshall,[6] lies "in the refined and wonderfully truthful modelling of the fleshy parts". Observe in this connection "the subtle flattening of the buttocks and the clever little dimples of the posterior-superior spines

[1] See pp. 22-23 *supra*.

[2] These two are the only human statuettes of stone from Harappā. Compared with them the stone statuary from Mohenjo-daro illustrated in *M. I. C.*, Pls. XCVIII-C is quite poor and crude.

[3] At Harappā there is only one little spot, and that, too, the highest part of the highest Mound AB where Gupta things have been found. Elsewhere every thing belongs to the Indus Period.

[4] *M. I. C.*, p. 45.

[5] *Cf.* stone slabs, Pl. LXXXIII, 28, 30 to 32, and crateriform stands, Nos. 8 and 9 in the same plate.

[6] *M. I. C.*, p. 46.

Style peculiarly Indian.

of the ilium ". As an example of anatomical precision it is indeed perfect, and can bear comparison with the best examples of Greek Art, while among the most ancient statuary it may be compared with the excellent figure of the 'Scribe Accroupi '[1] of the Louvre, IVth-Vth dynasties in Egypt. "And yet the set of the figure, with its rather pronounced abdomen, is characteristically Indian ".[2] However difficult it may be to find a parallel to this and the statuette of the dancer among the human figures at Mohenjo-daro, it cannot be denied that the circumstances of their finding, material, technique and style, afford indisputable evidence of their prehistoric origin. In fact, to those familiar with the glyptic art of the Indus People as represented by the excellent carving of many of the animal figures on the seals it is not a little surprising that the human statuary from Mohenjo-daro should be so poor. Discussing their high artistic merit Sir John Marshall writes[3] "Now, in these two statues it is just this anatomical truth that is so startling; that makes us wonder whether in this all important matter Greek artistry could possibly have been anticipated by sculptors of a far-off age on the banks of the Indus. We know definitely that the Indus engraver could anticipate the Greek in the delineation of the animal forms, and if we compare the statuette of plate X with, for example, seal 337, we must admit that there is a certain kinship between the two, both in the monumental treatment of the figures as a whole and in the perfection of their anatomical details. Experienced sculptors whom I have consulted on the subject take the view that an artist who could engrave the seal in question, would have had little difficulty in carving the statuette."

Other remains of Stratum III.

Except the circular platforms and the well referred to above, the IIIrd stratum is quite poorly represented by the remains of a few pavements, one drain in square J 12/9, the remnants of two rooms enclosing platforms P16 and P17, three or four corners in the eastern section, and some fragmentary walls. Near the drain referred to above was found a lot of broken pottery from which were recovered 18 goblets with pointed bases. It is interesting to record that this little drain is plastered over with a mortar of strange composition[4] (Pl. XVIII, *a*).

Drain with plaster of peculiar composition.

Finds.

The following antiquities of Stratum III were found scattered all over the trench—

1. Unicorn seal (fragmentary) with 4 pictograms. Pl. LXXXVII, 40. $1\frac{3}{8}$ in. sq. No. 10740; Square K 12/23; Depth 8 ft. 9 in. b.s.
2. Rectangular, plano-convex seal with 4 pictograms. Pl. XCII, 282. Size $\frac{13}{16} \times \frac{7}{16}$ in. No. 8350; Square I 12/20; Depth 5 ft. 4 in. b.s.
3. Tiny seal in the form of a couchant hare with a cross-shaped groove on the underside for fixation. Pl. XCVII, 565. Size $\frac{7}{16} \times \frac{3}{8}$ in. No. 10949; Square K 12/14; Depth 9 ft. 7 in. b.s.

---

[1] *C. A. H.*, Vol. of Plates, p. 82 and plate opposite.

[2] *M. I. C.*, p. 46.

[3] *Ibid.*, pp. 46-47.

[4] According to Khan Bahadur Mohammad Sana Ullah this plaster is composed of Calcium Phosphate and Calcium Carbonate, whereas the plasters found so far at Harappā and Mohenjo-daro are composed of Calcium Carbonate and Calcium Sulphate. "Assuming that the original coating was of ordinary lime then Phosphate bearing waters would have transformed it into Calcium Phosphate. As I have written before, it is inconceivable that bone or a Phosphate rock was employed as plaster ....".

4. Cuboid chert weight. Wt. 3·4 gms.; size ·45×·45×·4 in. No. 10738; Square I 12/23; Depth 6 ft. b.s.

5. Tiny bud-shaped pendent of burnt steatite holed across the tang. Pl. CXXXIX, 31. L. 43/100 in. No. 8382*a*; Square J 12/25; Depth 7 ft. 4 in. b.s.

6. Oval bead of burnt steatite (imitation carnelian),[1] lentoid in section with trefoil ornament painted in white. Pl. CXXVIII, 11. Size $\frac{13}{16} \times \frac{5}{8}$ in. No. 8843; Square J 12/18; Depth 7 ft. 8 in. b.s.

7. Large pendent of hornblende deeply grooved at the head. Ht. $1\frac{3}{16}$ in. No. 10970; Square K 12/13; Depth 8 ft. 6 in. b.s.

8. Barrel-shaped bead of yellow carnelian. L. $\frac{11}{16}$ in. No. 10966; Square K 12/13; Depth 8 ft. 6 in. b.s.

9. Cuboid, chert weight. Wt. 13·55 gms.; size ·7×·7×·6 in. No. 10742; Square K 12/19; Depth 8 ft. 6 in. b.s.

10. Small cone of yellow Jaisalmer stone with two deep horinzontal grooves which have the effect of forming a broad band[2] between them. Pl. CXVII, 37. Ht. $\frac{15}{16}$ in. No. 8920; Square L 12/9; Depth 8 ft. 8. in. b.s.

11. Cuboid, chert weight. Wt. 54·6 gms.; size 1·15×1·15×·95 in. No. 10953; Square K 12/13; Depth 9 ft. 8 in. b.s.

12. Cuboid, chert weight. Wt. 3·4 gms.; size ·45×·45×·4 in. No. 10073; Square K 12/9; Depth 10 ft. b.s.

13. Semi-oval terminal[3] of faience with holes for three strands. Pl. CXXXVIII, 49. L. 1 in. No. 8981; Square L 12/9; Depth 9 ft. 6 in. b.s.

14. Ivory disc with an identical scheme of concentric circle decoration on both faces, and a row of circles round the thickness. Pl. CXIX, 55. Diam. 1 in. No. 10800; Square J 12/23; Depth 6 ft. b.s.

15. Long ivory strip with linear decoration, semicircular in section. This is the only example of this shape known from Harappā or Mohenjo-daro. L. $2\frac{3}{4}$ in.; diam. $\frac{3}{8}$ in. No. 8382*b*; Square J 12/25; Depth 7 ft. 4 in. b.s.

16. *Saṅkh* spoon. Size $1\frac{3}{8} \times 1\frac{1}{4}$ in. No. 8814; Square J 12/24; Depth 7 ft. 3 in. b.s.

17. Two pottery bulls' heads with horns twisted round a piece of straw or thin stick which was placed horizontally behind the neck where it has left grooves after the stick was burnt in firing. For fixation each of them has a hole on the underside. Pl. LXXIX, 69 and 70. Ht. $1\frac{5}{8}$ and $1\frac{3}{8}$ in., respectively. No. 10410; Square I 12/23; Depth 6 ft. b.s.

---

[1] For beads and other objects of imitation carnelian from Mohenjo-daro see Mackay in *M. I. C.*, p. 509, Pl. CLVII, 8-12.

[2] This band might represent a ring or *yoni* round the phallic symbol.

[3] Generally the terminals have only one hole through the apex, the strands being controlled by spacers coming in front of the terminals as in the gold necklace illustrated in Pl. CXXXVII, 7. At Mohenjo-daro, however, I found a triangular terminal of faience (Vs 2101) with holes to take four strings. *Cf.* Mackay, *op. cit.*, p. 518.

18. Exquisitely finished pottery bangle with keeled rim. It is made of fine vitreous paste and is of bright red colour[1]. Diam. $4\frac{1}{8}$ in. No. 8989; Square L 12/9; Depth 9 ft. b.s.
19. Bangle similar to No. 18. In both of them the bright red colour is due to their being fired in an oxidizing kiln. Diam. $3\frac{3}{8}$ in. No. 8990; Square L 12/9; Depth 9 ft. b.s.
20. Exquisitely finished pottery bangle of fine vitreous paste with a dark grey, cloudy appearance and metallic ring. This colour is due to ferrous oxide and also indicates that the firing took place in a reducing or smoky atmosphere in the kiln. Pl. CXXXVIII, 1. Diam. $3\frac{1}{4}$ in. No. 8986; Square L 12/9; Depth 9 ft. 6 in. b.s.

Remains of Stratum IV. The IVth stratum is but partially excavated. At several places it seems to have totally disappeared, and at many others no more than the last course or two of its foundations have survived. However, the floor levels of this and of the following stratum were clearly indicated at several points by the find of a number of broken earthenware jars. At the western end of the trench in squares **An utterly ruined house.** I 12/18 and 19 there are distinct indications of three or four rooms, forming the south-west part of a house which has all but disappeared. At present, there are two rooms (Nos. 1 and 2) on the west with the indication of another room (No. 3) in continuation with them to the north. Abutting on to the east of rooms 1 and 2 is a long room No. 4. From near the north-west corner of room No. 1 starts an underground drain, which is met in room No. 4 by another drain from the north. To the south-east of this house there are several fairly good but stray walls of Stratum IV. Beneath another wall in square J 12/25 were found at a **A collection of bovine bones.** depth of 9 to 10 ft. below the surface two bovine leg bones, two foreparts of horned skulls (Pl. XVI, *b*), and a copper spear-head with long tip showing clear marks of a wooden handle over its lower part (Pl. CXXV, 76). Near the east end of this trench in square L 12/4 is a rectangular platform with mud core which is secured on all sides by a surround of brick-on-edge laid lengthwise. This unsubstantial construction was probably due to the necessity of economising bricks.[2]

Finds. The following finds may be recorded from Stratum IV:—

1. Unicorn seal with 5 pictograms, lower left end broken. Pl. LXXXVII, 56. $1\frac{1}{4}$ in. sq. No. 8921; Square I 12/19; Depth 7 ft. 4 in. b.s.
2. Unicorn seal with 3 pictograms. Pl. LXXXVIII, 77. $1\frac{3}{16}$ in. sq. No. 10927; Square I 12/24; Depth 7 ft. 9 in. b.s.
3. Fragment of a unicorn seal. Pl. XC, 187. L. $\frac{15}{16}$ in. No. 11021; Square J 12/14; Depth 9 ft. b.s.
4. Tiny, triangular prism seal with 4 pictograms on one side, 1 on the second, and fish on the third. Pl. XCVIII, 591. Size $\frac{3}{8}\times\frac{1}{4}$ in. No. 8480; Square I 13/21; Depth 7 ft. 9 in. b.s.
5. Prism seal, similar to No. 4. Size $\frac{1}{4}\times\frac{1}{4}$ in. No. 11371; Square I 12/5; Depth 10 ft. 6 in. b.s.

[1] For the composition and analysis of similar earthenware bangles *cf.* Khan Bahadur Mohammad Sana Ullah in *M. I. C.*, p. 686, also Table I on p. 689.

[2] For a similar platform in the Extension of Pits I and II in Mound AB, see p. 154 *infra*.

6. Tiny, rectangular faience sealing inscribed on both sides. Pl. XCVIII, 603. Size $\frac{5}{16} \times \frac{5}{16}$ in. No. 11022; Square K 12/4; Depth 9 ft. 4 in. b.s.
7. Oblong faience sealing, double-convex in section, with a foliated twig on both sides. Pl. CI, 705. L. 1 in. No. 9040; Square J 12/14; Depth 9 ft. 6 in. b.s.
8. Oblong terracotta sealing, double-convex in section, inscribed on both sides. Twisted in firing. Pl. CI, 704. Size $1\frac{3}{16} \times \frac{5}{16}$ in. No. 11064; Square I 12/12; Depth 8 ft. 7 in. b.s.
9. Numerous tiny discoid beads and some cylindrical beads of burnt steatite. No. 10983; Square J 12/19; Depth 8 ft. b.s.
10. Barrel-shaped bead of riband jasper (?). L. $\frac{5}{8}$ in. No. 11074; Square J 12/3; Depth 8 ft. b.s.
11. Cuboid chert weight. Wt. 53·6 gms.; size 1·15×1·15×1 in. No. 11072; Square I 12/23; Depth 8 ft. 9 in. b.s.
12. Barrel-shaped bead of black stone with a bluish white band round the middle. Pl. CXXVIII, 35. L. $\frac{3}{8}$ in. No. 10918; Square K 12/23; Depth 12 ft. b.s.
13. Perforated, cylindrical pottery vase with a large hole through the bottom. Ht. 6 in; diam. $2\frac{3}{4}$ in. No. 8902; Square I 12/19; Depth 7 ft. b.s.
14. Pottery jar-stand with concave body. Ht. 6 in; diam. at top $10\frac{1}{2}$ in. No. 10950; Square J 12/24; Depth 8 ft. b.s.

Stratum V.

Near the eastern end of this trench we dug a little deeper over an area of 29 by 19 ft. Along its northern edge was found in the deeper part, 13 ft. 8 in. below the surface, a group of pottery (Nos. 10247-10249) covered over with fallen bricks and bits of charcoal—apparently the débris of a wall which stood immediately to its north (Pl. XVIII, *b*). The pottery comprised a jar, crushed to bits with its stand, another jar-stand close by, a large but fragmentary handled lid, a bowl, a painted standard dish,[1] a medium-sized oval jar with flat bottom, an entirely crushed, small *hāṇḍi* with a flange round the neck. and fragments of three other jars. The above-mentioned plate has a tall stand (Pl. LXXII, 8), deep cup, and large lip, the cup being painted with a tree, the lip with wicker basket patterns (Pl. LXIX, 10), and the stem with a leafy device. At this place were also found two inscribed potsherds (No. 10284, Pl. CII, 5, and No. 10309).

A pottery group.

Specimens of wheat, barley and sesamum.

In conclusion, I must refer to a few things of general interest found at different levels in this trench. Among them are a quantity of lumped and burnt sesamum found at a depth of 6 ft. in square L 12/4, and some burnt grains of wheat and peas[2] in the hollow of circular platform P8. Regarding wheat Rai Sahib Jai Chand Luthra, Associate Professor of Botany at the Panjāb Agricultural College, Lyallpur, writes as follows:—"(1) No. 5653(*a*). These are grains of wheat.

---

[1] This was broken in two parts but has since been joined.

[2] See also pp. 466-67 *infra*.

Resemble closely the grains of *Triticum Compactum*[1] (Dwarf Wheat). These wheats are grown in dry parts. (2) No. 3429. These are grains of common husked barley. (3) A mass of seeds of sesamum (*Til*) "[2].

A coral. Another object is a hemispherical piece of coral (No. 8990) measuring 3⅞ in. across, which was found at a depth of 8 ft. below the surface in square I 12/24. According to Dr. Baini Prashad, Director, Zoological Survey of India, it is a specimen of *Favia fabus* (Förskal), which species has a very wide distribution in the Indian Ocean. Still another object of interest to be mentioned is a piece of yellow arsenic (*hartāl*), No. 10046, found 10 ft. 6 in. below the surface in square K 12/14. **Arsenic.** Arsenic, as we know, was probably used both as a medicine and poison, and also as an alloy to harden copper tools.[3]

Trench I.

Situation. Simultaneously with the clearance of the Great Granary Area, a large trench marked I on the plan, measuring 224 ft. from north to south by 68 ft. wide, was sunk in the Eastern Section of this mound due east of Trenches V and Ai described above (Pl. I). The ground covered by it has a gentle slope from south to north, but along the eastern edge of the trench it rises slightly in the northern portion after forming a little bend. Being sunk mainly with the object of uncovering all the strata of occupation in this mound, the trench was dug to different levels for preserving the remains uncovered, as will appear from its sectional elevation (Pl. XIX). In the northern part, occupied by the deep digging, it attained a maximum depth of 30 ft., which is also the present spring level of the sub-soil water (Pl. XXI, *b*).

Discovery of eight strata and their relative difference. In this trench, up to a depth of 25 ft. 6 in., eight strata of occupation—fragmentary in each case—have been brought to light. Beginning from the surface, Strata I and II are extremely fragmentary, but the IIIrd though better in point of structural remains than the upper two, is inferior in this respect to Strata IV, V, VI and VII. Of the VIIIth, only a poor and fragmentary drain, and a few bricks laid flat—obviously the core of a wall—are all that have been recovered so far. The first three strata follow each other in quick succession, and at some places are closely packed one over the other. They may be taken together to represent the last or Late Period. The IVth, Vth, VIth and VIIth strata though definitely earlier than the first three, also do not appear to have been separated from each other by a very great length of time, as the débris of about 9 ft. between them is more or less evenly distributed. Taken together they form the Intermediate Period, allowing a difference of about three centuries between the IVth and VIIth strata. There is, however, nearly 5 ft. of débris between the VIIth stratum as represented by the bed of a deep underground drain in the northern part of this trench and a feeble surface drain of the VIIIth stratum referred to

[1] Some of these charred grains were also examined by the Director, Royal Botanic Gardens, Kew, Surrey, England, who wrote to the Director General of Archæology that " This specimen, owing to being so completely carbonised, cannot be identified with certainty, but it appears to be a species of *Triticum* (wheat)."

[2] Specimens of wheat and barley were also found at Mohenjo-daro. *Cf. M. I. C.*, p. 27. These two cereals, as well as sesamum, are still cultivated in the Panjāb.

[3] *Cf. M. I. C.*, p. 690, where Khan Bahadur Mohammad Sana Ullah refers to these properties of arsenic.

below in the account of the Deep Digging. In any case, very little is known at present of the VIIIth stratum. A little below this there is nothing but sand.

Causes of the fragmentary nature of remains.

Apropos of the fragmentary nature of the above remains it may be added that several tunnels made by the present day brick-diggers were also met with in this trench down to a maximum depth of 12 ft. To that may be due, in no small measure, the fragmentary nature of the first four strata, but from the incompleteness of the remaining four, which occur at a great depth, where brick digging would hardly have been paying, it is obvious that in ancient times, too, each successive settlement must have drawn freely upon the ruins of earlier structures for the building materials for their own houses.

Abundance of nodule deposits below 10 ft.

A general phenomenon observed throughout this trench is the frequent appearance of very thick and uneven layers of brick concrete, or, more commonly, of terracotta nodules which are met with at all depths, and, although it would therefore be difficult to assign them to any particular level, it may be stated with a fair degree of accuracy that from a depth of 10 ft. below the surface down to the end of the VIIth stratum their appearance becomes more common. On the other hand, potsherds were more in evidence up to 8 ft. and then grew less by degrees up to 18 ft., and below that were relatively scarce.

Finds from Stratum I.

The first stratum goes down to 4 ft. below the surface and is represented only by a few bits of walls in the southern portion which is a little higher. Among smaller objects found scattered at this level were the following:—

1. Unicorn seal with 4 pictograms. Pl. LXXXVII, 57. $1\frac{1}{16}$ in. sq. No. 1240; Square M 10/20; Depth 2 ft. b.s.
2. Lower half of a badly corroded unicorn seal showing only the incense-burner and body of the animal. Pl. XC, 173. $1\frac{3}{8}$ in sq. No. 12442; Square M 12/20, Depth 3 ft. 5 in. b.s.
3. Unicorn seal fragment showing only the incense-burner and mutilated forepart of the animal. Pl. XC, 184. L. $\frac{13}{16}$ in. No. 1384; Square M 10/20; Depth 4 ft. b.s.
4. Tiny rectangular steatite seal inscribed on both faces. Pl. XCVII, 518. Size $\frac{7}{16}\times\frac{1}{4}$ in. No. 12420; from surface.
5. Rectangular, plano-convex steatite seal with 5 pictograms. Pl. XCII, 283. Size $1\frac{3}{32}\times\frac{7}{16}$ in. No. 21; Square M 11/11; Depth 1 ft. 9 in. b.s.
6. Rectangular, plano-convex steatite seal with 2 pictograms surviving, fragmentary. Pl. XCII. 295. L. $\frac{5}{16}$ in.; w. $\frac{9}{16}$ in. No. 2893; Square M 10/10; Depth 3 ft. b.s.
7. Rectangular, plano-convex steatite seal with 5 pictograms surviving. Left part broken. Pl. XCII, 287. L. $1\frac{1}{16}$ in.; W. $\frac{1}{2}$ in. No. 398; Square M 11/15; Depth 3 ft. b.s.
8. Rectangular, plano-convex steatite seal with 4 pictograms on one face, and 1 on the thickness of the lower side, the latter being at the right instead of the left end. It appears to be an example of the writing being boustrophedon.[1] Pl. XCII, 276. Size $\frac{5}{8}\times\frac{1}{2}$ in. No. 2630; Square M 12/17; Depth 4 ft. b.s.

[1] For examples of such writing at Mohenjo-daro *cf.* Sir John Marshall. *op. cit.*, p. 40 and footnote 1.

9. Steatite block of a rectangular, plano-convex seal with unfinished pictograms. Pl. XCII, 302. Size $1\frac{3}{8}\times\frac{13}{16}$ in. No. 1239; Square M 12/7; Depth 4 ft. b.s.

10. Tiny rectangular faience sealing with 4 pictograms on one side, and 1 on the other. Pl. XCVIII, 605. Size $\frac{9}{16}\times\frac{5}{16}$ in. No. 12416; Square M 12/21; Depth 3 ft. 9 in. b.s.

11. Rectangular terracotta sealing with 5 pictograms on one face, and a crocodile (*Gavialis gangeticus*) preying on fishes (in a river) on the other. Pl. XCIV, 337. Size $1\frac{5}{8}\times\frac{1}{2}$ in. No. 2430; Square M 10/10; Depth 1 ft. b.s.

12. Cylindrical terracotta sealing showing an acacia tree on one side, and 5 pictograms on the other. Pl. XCIII, 327. L. $1\frac{5}{16}$ in. No. 12415*a*; Square M 11/25; Depth 2 ft. b.s.

13. Cylindrical terracotta sealing showing an acacia tree enclosed by a platform on one side, and 3 pictograms on the other. Pl. XCIII, 323. L. 1 in. No. 2982; Square M 10/10; Depth 3 ft. b.s.

14. Cylindrical terracotta sealing similar to No. 13. L. 1 in. No. 7098; Square M 12/13; Depth 3 ft. b.s.

15. Alabaster ring with a socket in thickness. Pl. LXXXIII, 25. Diam. 3 in. No. 540; Square M 12/18; Depth 1 ft. b.s.

16. Flat, oval pebble holed at the narrower end, probably a token. L. $4\frac{1}{2}$ in. No. 12425; Square M 12/28; Depth 1 ft. b.s.

17. Large, smoothed sandstone *liṅgam* partly broken in the upper portion. This is the largest example from Harappā. Pl. CXVII, 4. Ht. 18 in.; basal diam. 10 in. No. 12466; Square M 12/25; Depth 1 ft. 2 in. b.s.

18. Fragment of the funnel-shaped foot of a white limestone offerings' dish. Pl. LXXXIII, 7. L. $8\frac{3}{4}$ in. No. 576; Square M 12/18; Depth 2 ft. 6 in. b.s.

19. Cubical weight of white limestone. Wt. 25·2 gms.; size ·9×·9×·8 in. No. 12440; Square M 12/23; Depth 3 ft. 9 in. b.s.

20. Cubical weight of dark grey stone with white bands. Wt. 6·45 gms.; size ·6×·6×·4 in. No. 12417; Square M 12/22; Depth 3 ft. 10 in. b.s.

21. Two chessman-shaped stone objects, and a hornblende pendent grooved at the neck. Ht. $\frac{13}{16}$, $\frac{13}{16}$ and $\frac{3}{8}$ in. respectively. No. 12433; Square M 12/22; Depth 3 ft. 11 in. b.s.

22. Tapering cylindrical steatite bead with vertically corrugated surface. Pl. CXXVIII, 17. L. $\frac{11}{16}$ in. No. 1977; Square M 10/25; Depth 4 ft. b.s.

23. Large cubical chert weight, much damaged. Pl. CXVIII, 13. Wt. 2,652·8 gms.; size 4·3×4·3×3·2 in. No. 635; Square M 12/17; Depth 4 ft. b.s.

24. Tiny faience bird. Pl. LXXVIII, 4. L. $\frac{3}{4}$ in. No. 12419; from surface.

25. Knob-headed faience ear-button with a circumscribed incurved lozenge at the centre enclosed by a petalled border. Pl. CXXXIX, 10. Diam. 1 in. No. 2935; Square M 10/10; Depth 4 ft. b.s.
26. Mussel shell. Pl. LXXXII, 5. Size 2¾ × 2½ in. No. 2973; Square M 9/25; Depth 2 ft. 6 in. b.s.
27. Cylindrical pottery vessel with flat base and slightly tapering sides. It has a flange at neck and is decorated with five pairs of black bands. Pl. LXXII, 23. Ht. 9½ in.; diam. of mouth 9⅜ in. No. 2484; Square M 10/10; Depth 1 ft. 2 in. b.s.
28. Terracotta ball inscribed with 2 pictograms.[1] Pl. CXX, 30. Diam. 1 1/16 in. No. 12422; Square M 12/25; Depth 3 ft. 5 in. b.s.
29. Six inscribed potsherds. L. 6½ to 4 in. No. 12430; from surface.
30. Two inscribed potsherds. Pl. CI. 708. No. 4682; from spoil earth.
31. Sherd of a dish with deeply incised inscription. Pl. CII, 18. Size 5¼ × ¼ in. No. 2358; Square M 11; Depth 0-3 ft. b.s.

The IInd stratum goes down from 4 ft. to 5 ft. 6 in. below the surface. It is represented in the southern part of the trench by only one small wall in square M 12/12, and along the north-east cutting in square M 10/25 by the remains of two rooms, in one of which is a small pavement (3 ft. 2 in. square) at the corner, and three stouter bits round them. The following finds of this stratum were recovered widely scattered about:— **Stratum II.**

1. Unicorn seal with 3 pictograms. Pl. LXXXVI, 30. 1¼ in. sq. No. 868; Square M 11/19; Depth 4 ft. 6 in. b.s.
2. Unicorn seal with 5 pictograms, lower left corner broken. Pl. LXXXVII, 46. 1¼ in. sq. No. 483; Square M 11/15; Depth 5 ft. b.s.
3. Unicorn seal with 4 pictograms. Pl. LXXXVIII, 92. 13/16 in. sq. No. 1199; Square M 12/17; Depth 5 ft. 6 in. b.s.
4. Terracotta, bossed square seal with 4 blurred pictograms in upper field. The boss is very rough. Pl. XCI, 258. 1 in. sq. No. 3130; Square M 11/6; Depth 5 ft. 6 in. b.s.
5. Tiny rectangular steatite seal with 4 pictograms on one side and 1 on the other. Pl. XCVII, 519. Size ⅜ × ⅜ in. No. 12461; Square M 12/19; Depth 5 ft. 6 in. b.s.
6. Bossed faience sealing showing a *svastika*. Pl. XCV, 399. ⅞ in. sq. No. 59; Square M 12/11; Depth 4 ft. 8 in. b.s.
7. Oval steatite bead lenticular in section. Its surface is painted red to simulate carnelian, and over this are trefoil designs[2] in black with a white border. Size 1⅛ × 1 in. No. 12445; Square M 12/23; Depth 4 ft. 6 in. b.s.
8. Tapering stone pendent deeply grooved at the head. The stone is of dull green colour mottled black. Ht. 7/16 in. No. 7334; Square M 12/8; Depth 4 ft. 10 in. b.s.

---

[1] This is the only inscribed ball so far recovered at Harappā.

[2] See also H. C. Beck, Chap. XV, Pt. 1, p. 396 *infra*. This is serially numbered 57 in his list.

9. Cubical chert weight. Wt. 26·95 gms.; size ·95×·95×·65 in. No. 7416 Square M 12/8; Depth 5 ft. b.s.
10. Cubical chert weight. Wt. 27·3 gms.; size ·95×·95×·7 in. No. 855; Square M 11/19; Depth 5 ft. b.s.
11. Thick alabaster disc with a deep semicircular groove across one face which is pierced through at the centre by a couple of holes. Diam. $1\frac{3}{4}$ in.; ht. $\frac{11}{16}$ in. No. 12437; Square M 12/22; Depth 5 ft. 3 in. b.s.
12. Thick, rectangular steatite amulet with two holes across the length. Size $1\frac{1}{2}\times1\times\frac{7}{16}$ in. No. 7468; Square M 12/9; Depth 5 ft. 6 in. b.s.
13. Faience lozenge with concave, bevelled edges. Size $1\frac{1}{4}$ in Square. No. 12438; Square M 11/25; Depth 5 ft. b.s.
14. Fragmentary copper spear-head with pointed tip. The tang is holed at the lower end. Pl. CXXV, 77. L. $8\frac{3}{8}$ in. No. 10104; Square M 10/25; Depth 5 ft. b.s.
15. Bone rod. L. $5\frac{3}{8}$ in. No. 515; Square M 11/20; Depth 5 ft. 6 in. b.s.
16. Seated terracotta male figure in prayerful attitude with hands folded and legs drawn up in front. Pl. LXXVI, 10. Ht. $2\frac{1}{8}$ in. No. 847; Square M 11/16; Depth 4 ft. 3 in. b.s.
17. Terracotta cubical die, partly broken, marked with 1 opposite 2, 3 opposite 5 and 4 opposite 6. Pl. CXX, 52. Size $1\frac{1}{8}\times1\frac{1}{8}\times1\frac{1}{4}$ in. No. 12423; Square M 12/22; Depth 4 ft. 10 in. b.s.
18. Inscribed potsherd. No. 12569; Square M 12; Depth 3 to 6 ft. b.s.

Stratum III.

Three mud huts.

The IIIrd stratum goes down from 5 ft. 7 in. to 8 ft. 7 in. below the surface. At the southern end of the trench is a row of three mud huts lying from east to west, each measuring 13 ft. 6 in. by 7 ft. 6 in. to 9 ft. 6 in., and separated from one another by narrow passages 2 ft. 6 in. and 3 ft. 6 in. wide (Pl. XX, *b*, foreground). Perched over and slightly projecting from the west wall of the middle room is a wall of the Ist stratum made of burnt bricks (Pl. XX, *d*). Except in one case, the thickness of the east and west walls of the huts is greater than that of the north and south walls. Of these, the stouter walls are built of lumps of wet clay, readily obtained from the river close by, chopped into shape. In the lower portion, the core of these walls was occasionally strengthened by the addition of some burnt brickbats. On the contrary, the thinner walls are made exclusively of mud brick on a foundation of rammed clay. In this connection I may add that, at the present day, the Oḍ and Paṭhān coolies in the neighbourhood while constructing mud huts employ an iron chopper, locally known as *ṭokā*, for dressing walls and some such device seems to have been used in squaring up these ancient mud walls.

Other remains of Stratum III.

To the north of these in square M 12/17 is a broken pavement. Over the rest of the trench this stratum is represented by a number of disconnected walls occurring mostly in the southern but to some extent also in the northern section. In addition to these, may be mentioned, in square M 11/18, a drain connected with a small paved sink (Pl. XX, *a*, centre foreground), and in square M 11/16 a fragmentary pavement with a small drain at the northern edge of the Deep Digging.

A group of pottery.

A number of finds were made in the central portion of the trench, and some of them deserve detailed notice. An interesting group of pottery was found in square M 12/17 at a depth of 5 ft. 9 in. below the surface (Nos. 3821 and 10367). It comprised one well preserved and two mutilated troughs, a crushed round jar, and three oval *ghaṛās* with flat bottom lying on their sides. One of the *ghaṛās* is painted with black bands (partial view, Pl. XXIII, *d*). Near them, and forming part of the same group were found (some two years later) four medium-sized and three small cylindrical vases, one of the latter being perforated and pierced with a large hole at the bottom. With them were also found a number of broken and unbroken curry stones.

A group of seals, etc.

In the centre of the trench in square M 11/15 were discovered at a depth of 5 ft. 9 in. below the surface two important finds, Nos. 113, etc., and No. 277, the latter lying 15 ft. due west of the former. The former group comprised 6 seals, 9 cubical weights[1] of chert (No. 120), 4 conch shells, a dozen terracotta beads, some pottery bangles and vases (Pl. XXII, *a*). Four of the seals (Nos. 115, 116, 117, and 145) exhibit the unicorn (Pls. LXXXV, 9 and 5, LXXXVIII, 78 and LXXXVI, 16), the fifth (No. 114) is rectangular, plane on one side and convex on the other (Pl. XCII, 270), while the sixth (No. 113), with its upper part broken, shows a procession of seven men wearing kilts and wigs (?) marching from right to left (Pl. XCI, 251).[*] In front of the procession is an inscription of seven letters in two lines.

A wonderful copper jar.

No. 277 is a well preserved, round copper jar, concave in the upper portion and covered with a shallow, inverted dish (Pl. XXII, *b*)[2]. It was found buried in the soil quite unconnected with any wall or building; and its underside was thoroughly blackened with soot. Very likely it was a cooking pot. Owing to corrosion, the lid was tightly jammed and a 5 in. square hole had to be sawn open at the top to remove the contents (Pl. CXXIV, 28) before it was chemically cleaned (Pl. CXXIV, 27). Including the 1 in. deep cover it is 9½ in. in height, and 8 in. in diameter at the mouth, the greatest diameter being 10⅜ in. To our delight, it was found to contain in a wonderful state of preservation all the weapons, tools, utensils, ornaments, etc., illustrated in Pls. CXXIII and CXXIV, 1-21 and 23-25. The vessel itself is made in two parts; the upper part, which resembles a pottery jar-stand in shape, being lapped on to the round lower part (Pl. CXXI, 14). On the inside, there are traces of the two parts having been hammered out of sheet metal and then joined, but no hammer marks are visible outside. Among the contents of this remarkable vessel was an assortment of

---

[1] Their sizes range between ·5 in. cube and 1×·65×·6 in.

[2] In shape, this vessel is similar to E. 2044 found at Mohenjo-daro, *cf. M. I. C.*, Pl. CXL, 18, and Pl. CXLI, 12. Later, in 1936 two similar jars (Nos. 13303 *b* and *c*) were also found at Harappā in the eastward extension of Area J, stratum II. Their height is 6·5 and 7 in. respectively. Jar 13303*c* contained the following objects of copper, *viz.*, a round vase (ht. and diam. 2 in. each); two knobbed convex temple ornaments each with a hook for attachment on the inside (ht. ·8 and ·7 in.; diam. 2·5 in. each); four solid bangles ranging in diameters from 1·7 to 2 in. and a thick rectangular piece measuring ·8×·7×·35 in.

weapons, implements, and tools, unequalled by all the other metal finds from Harappā. They are briefly described below:—

Implements and weapons of copper or bronze,[1] *Pl. CXXIII*, 1-67.

Axes without shoulders.

Nos. 1-4 (277*a*/5-277*a*/8). For No. 4 see also Pl. CXXI, 1. Four axes without shoulders, and with straight sides and the lower edge well rounded. L. 5⅛ to 6⅞ in.; w. across the cutting edge 2¾ to 3⅛ in.; w. across the butt end 2 to 2⅛ in. They are similar to the two short and broad axes (Vs. 1450)[2] found by the writer at Mohenjo-daro.

Axes shouldered.

Nos. 5-8 and 10-13 (277*a*/1-277*a*/4, 277*a*/9, 277*a*/14, 277*a*/15 and 277*a*/19) are eight shouldered axes with the cutting edge rounded. L. 3⅞ to 8 in.: w. across the cutting edge 2½ to 4½ in.; w. across the butt end 1⅞ to 2⅞ in. Of these, No. 10 is only the lower part with the cutting edge, but Nos. 5, 6 (see also Pl. CXXI. 2 and 3), 7 and 8 are exceptionally large and strong. The cutting edge of No. 6 is very broad and more prominently shouldered than of any other.[3] One of the Mohenjo-daro axes[4] also has a distinct shoulder and a sharp rounded edge. According to Sir Flinders Petrie the shorter axes with deep and circular edge are not suited for cleaving nor for light wood-cutting, but rather suggest a fighting axe.[5] Nos. 6-8 and 13 are examples which would be suitable for this purpose.

Axes, long and narrow.

Nos. 14-21 (277*a*/10-277*a*/13, 277*a*/16-277*a*/18 and 277*a*/20) are eight long and narrow blade-axes in which the shoulders are incipient, or much less marked, but the lower edge is more or less rounded. L. 4⅛ to 8½ in.; w. across the cutting edge 1¾ to 2⅞ in.; and w. across the butt end 1⅛ to 1⅞ in. Of these, No. 16 is only a fragment of the body deeply inscribed with pictograms, of which only two are now left. No. 20 is similar to a blade-axe (Vs. 1450)[6] found by me at Mohenjo-daro. Some of these, for instance Nos. 15 and 17 have a chisel like edge which shows that they were probably meant for light wood-cutting. A very similar celt[7] was found at Chāndpur in the Bijnor District of the United Provinces. Celt No. 18 (see also Pl. CXXI, 13) shows raised edges in the upper part and as its butt is not burred it could only have been intended for vertical hafting.

Double axes.

Nos. 22 and 23 (277*b*/1 and 227*b*/2) are two unfinished double axes of which the former is broken entirely, and the latter partly across one cutting edge.[8] L. 2⅜ and 2⅝ in.; w. across the cutting edge 3⅞ and 3¼ in. (Pls. CXXIII 22 and 23, and CXXI, 8).

Daggers with tapering sides and curved tip.

Nos. 24 and 25 (277*f*/6 and 277*f*/7) are two daggers with longer tangs than Nos. 26-32 and their tips are curved back. Of these, No. 24 (see also Pl. CXXII,

---

[1] Without analysis it cannot be definitely stated which of them are copper and which bronze.

[2] *Cf. M. I. C.*, Pl. CXXXIX, 2 and 3.

[3] For a similar axe from Italy *cf.* Sir Flinders Petrie, *Tools and Weapons*, Pl. I. 27.

[4] *M. I. C.*, Pl. CXXXVIII, 3 and 3*a*, and Pl. CXXXIX, 4.

[5] Petrie, *op. cit.*, p. 7.

[6] *Cf. M. I. C.*, Pl. CXXXVIII, 1, and Pl. CXXXIX, 1.

[7] *Cf.* Indian Antiquary, Vol. XXXIV, Pl. I, 12.

[8] For double axes from various countries *cf.* Petrie, *op. cit.*, Pl. XII, 21-33, but the Harappā examples have no socket hole through the centre as in Nos. 21-26 of the above plate, nor are they long like Nos. 27-33. In Minoan Civilization the double axe was a very popular cult object. *Cf.* M. P. Nilsson, *The Minoan Mycenaean Religion*, pp. 162-200.

6) is 8¼ in. long and 1⅝ in. broad and its tip has a marked backward curve,[1] and No. 25 (see also Pl. CXXII, 5) is 9¼ in. long and 2⅛ in. broad. The latter has three pictograms on the obverse face, and its tang is formed below the broadest part by deep concave curves along the sides. Both of them are edged only on the convex side.

Daggers with tapering sides.

Nos. 26-32 (277f/1-277f/5 and d15 and d16) are seven daggers tapering along both edges and with longer tangs. L. 6 to 9½ in.; w. 1⅜ to 1¾ in. In Nos. 27-30 (see also Pl. CXXII, 2-4) the upper end of the tang joins the body by means of an inward or concave curve as in No. 25 described above, while in the remaining three, *i.e.*, 26, 31 and 32, the curvature of the upper portion sweeps round right down to the tang as in No. 24. Nos. 29 and 30 are very faintly inscribed, but the writing cannot be made out. In every case, the cutting edge is fairly sharp, but the back edge is blunt and thick—thickest near the tang and gradually thinning out towards the tip as shown in Pl. CXXII, 1-4.

Mace-head.

No. 33 (277h, see also Pl. CXXI, 9) is a round mace-head with a cylindrical hole across the centre. It has a rim at the upper edge. Ht. 1⅞ in.; diam. 2 in.; diam. of hole ⅞ in. Half of a similar marble mace-head (No. 34 in. Pl. CXXIII, No. 573, ht. 2⅝ in., diam. 3 in.) was also found within a few feet from the copper jar No. 277. Several examples of stone mace-heads of different shapes have been found both at Harappā (*cf.* Pl. LXXXIII, 14-16, 19-22 and 24) and Mohenjo-daro,[2] but, as yet, the above is the only example of a metal mace-head.

Spear-heads.

Nos. 35-47 (277d/1 and 277d/13) are thirteen spear-heads (?)[3] with long, thick and flat tangs. L. 4⅝ to 8⅝ in.: w. 1¼ to 4 in. Of these, No. 47 is broken in the upper part and of No. 35, which is the broadest of all, only the lower part has survived. All of them, it may be observed, are remarkably thin and have no mid-rib along the vertical axis where they are slightly thicker than at the edges as shown in Pl. CXXI, 20-28. The edge, however, is sharp all round, and most of them are shaped like an oval leaf with or without the projecting tip. In both Nos. 41 and 42 there are three rivet holes, two in the lower, broad part of the blade, and the third at the lower end of the tang for wooden hafting. In No. 37 also there were apparently three such holes, but of these the lower one has disappeared with the breaking of the tang. Most of them, and especially Nos. 36-39 and 42, show a concavity or irregularity at one or other point along their edges.

Chisels.

Nos. 49-58 (277k/1, 277k/2, 277k/4-277k/6 and 277k/7-277k/11) are ten bare metal chisels none of which was intended to have a handle. They are all made

---

[1] With this *cf.* restored diagram in *M. I. C.*, Pl. CXXV, 6, and also Pl. CXXXVII, 3, which Mr. Mackay calls as leather cutter. That, however, has no vertical rib. The Harappā examples appear to be a bit too long for leather cutters and their back edge is not sufficiently thick to allow of free force being exerted by the forefinger in the actual process of cutting. I, therefore, do not agree with Mr. Mackay's opinion that No. 24 is a leather cutter as stated by him in *M. I. C.*, p. 500. I may also add that in No. 25, which is also meant for a like purpose, the tip is not so much curved back. Probably both of them are daggers.

[2] *M. I. C.*, Pl. CXXXIV, 25-30.

[3] Most of these may have been flaying knives, some resembling those from Egypt. *Cf.* Petrie, *Tools and Weapons*, Pl. XXIII, K1 and Pl. XXXI, 2-4. They have also a marked resemblance with those found at Mohenjo-daro and illustrated in *M. I. C.*, Pl. CXXXVI, especially *cf.* Nos. 2, 4 and 8 with the Harappā examples illustrated in Pl. CXXIII, 38, 40, 45 and 46. It is beyond question that the Indus People consumed plenty of animal food, and at Harappā animal bones are so ubiquitious that they are found wherever one puts spade into ground. Flaying knives must therefore have been a real necessity for every day use.

of cast bars; of Nos. 49 and 55 the section is circular, of No. 56 square, and of the remaining seven rectangular. Except the square headed chisel No. 56, which does not appear to have been much used, all others are considerably burred at the butt with hammer strokes.[1] They may be divided into two classes: (*a*) those which have long and broad shanks, and (*b*) those which are without shanks. To the former class belong Nos. 49-53 in each of which the upper portion is broader and thinner than the lower portion. They are sharply sloped at the edge which in Nos. 49 (Pl. CXXI, 15) and 52 is but incipiently broader than the lower part, a bit more splayed in No. 53, but is markedly well developed in the beautiful examples Nos. 50 and 51 (Pl. CXXI, 16 and 17). They are $4\frac{5}{8}$ to $7\frac{1}{2}$ in. long, $\frac{1}{4}$ to $\frac{1}{2}$ in. broad at the cutting edge, and $\frac{3}{8}$ to $\frac{5}{8}$ in. broad at the butt end, and their greatest thickness is $\frac{1}{4}$ to $\frac{5}{16}$ in. Among them, Nos. 50 and 51 are similar to the Mohenjo-daro chisel illustrated in *M. I. C.*, Pl. CXXXVII, 8. They have also interesting parallels in the two square bronze forms from Peschiera[2] in North Italy. Nos. 54-58 (Pl. CXXI, 10, 11, 18 and 19) are without shanks. Their structure and thickness, except at the sharp edges and burred butt, is more uniform as compared with that of the shanked chisels, and their sides run parallel. They are also smaller in size, being $2\frac{5}{8}$ to $5\frac{1}{4}$ in. long, $\frac{1}{4}$ to $\frac{11}{16}$ in. broad at the cutting edge and $\frac{1}{8}$ to $\frac{3}{8}$ in. thick. Of these, the square headed chisel No. 56, being exceptionally strong, may have been intended for stone cutting, while others of rectangular or round section may have been used for other purposes.[3] Thick square chisels are even now used for cutting stones, along with others of round or hexagonal section.

Cast bars for making chisels.

Nos. 59 and 60 (277k/3 and 277k/13) are two thick bars, one rectangular and the other square in section. The former is $5\frac{7}{8}$ in. long and $\frac{3}{8}\times\frac{1}{4}$ in. in section, and the latter is $4\frac{3}{4}$ in. long and $\frac{1}{4}$ in. square in section. They are only cast bars, but No. 60 also shows a few hammer marks. There is no doubt that they were both intended to be hammered out as chisels of one or the other kind described above.[4] A third piece, No. 48, is only a flat corroded strip $2\frac{5}{8}\times\frac{5}{16}$ in., with a thickness of $\frac{1}{16}$ to $\frac{1}{32}$ in. only. This would hardly make a chisel.

Saws.

Nos. 61 and 62 (277d/14 and 277g/2) are saws, with only one dentate cutting edge. Of these, the former (Pl. CXXI, 32) tapers along both sides and has a long tang formed by deep concave curves in the lower part. Its tip is broken and the present length is $5\frac{3}{8}$ in. and width $1\frac{3}{8}$ in. No. 62 is the lower part of a saw with straight edge and back, but its upper part is broken. The edge gradually narrows down in a dilated curve to form a short tang. It has three good rivet holes, two set obliquely in the lower part of the blade to allow of more space between them for a firmer grip, and the third in the tang for fixation to a wooden handle. Existing length 5 in., w. $2\frac{3}{8}$ in. This is somewhat similar to the Mohenjo-daro example,[5] and suggests that in that only a little

[1] As these were used without handles, Mr. Mackay's opinion that "the long flattened shanks certainly appear to have been made expressly to be fixed in handles...." seems untenable, *cf. M. I. C.*, p. 502.

[2] *Cf.* Petrie, *op. cit.*, p. 20, Pl. XXI, C 7-8.

[3] *Cf.* Petrie, *op. cit.*, p. 20, para. 49.

[4] To judge by its length the longer bar was probably intended for a shanked chisel.

[5] *Cf. M. I. C.*, p. 501, Pl. CXXXVII, 6, and Pl. CXXXVIII, 4.

and not much of the lower end of the tang could have been lost in the break.

Arrow-head.

No. 63 (277c) is a sharp edged arrow-head with an exceptionally long tang. It is also illustrated in Pl. CXXI, 31. L. 5¾ in.; w. 2 in.

Dagger with mid-rib.

No. 64 (277e/2), see also Pl. CXXII, 7, is the tip of what may be a double-edged dagger with mid-rib or reinforcing seam. Though small, this fragment resembles the tip of the Fatehpur daggers, especially No. 3 illustrated by Mr. V. A. Smith in Pl. III of the *Indian Antiquary,* Vol. XXXIV. Like them, too, this was found to be nearly 98 per cent. copper.[1] No. 65 (277d/17), which is only a fragment 1¾ in. across, is probably the body of a double-edged dagger and might even be a part of No. 64, as it is appreciably thicker along the vertical axis. It does not, however, form a mid-rib.

Lance-head.

No. 66 (277c/1) also illustrated in Pl. CXXI, 30, is a lance-head with a short tang and vertical mid-rib from which the edge thins out all round. It was in process of being hammered out into shape and is not finished. To this is due a little denting of the edge. It is 6½ in. long and 2 in. wide.

Chopper.

No. 67 (277g/1) also illustrated in Pl. CXXI, 29, is a semi-oval chopper with short tang. Its tip is pointed and curved back causing a little concavity at this point in the back edge, which is otherwise almost straight and much thicker than the cutting edge. It still retains the sharp edge and is a strong, dependable implement.[2] L. 7⅝ in., w. 2⅜ in.

Miscellaneous objects, Pl. CXXIV, 1-21 and 23-25.

Bangles, solid and hollow, finished, and in process of manufacture.

Nos. 1-13 are several finished and unfinished bangles. They comprise five solid bangles (Nos. 1-4 and 7, inner diam. 1⅝ to 2½ in.) including one fragmentary, an uneven rod (No. 4, 1·6 in.) which was being beaten out into a solid bangle; one complete (diam. 1⅞ in.), and fragments of two hollow bangles made of sheet metal (Nos. 11-13); two flat strips (Nos. 8 and 9), broader at the centre for making hollow bangles (L. 6⅜ and 6¼ in., greatest w. 1½ in.); two other flat strips which were being beaten out and flattened (Nos. 6 and 10), thus showing a still earlier stage in the process of manufacture.

Beam of a weighing scale.

No. 14 is the beam of a weighing scale tapering both ways from the centre which is indicated by an incised line. The ends are flattened to hold the suspended threads from slipping down. Bronze. L. 4⅜ in.

Rectangular pieces.

Nos. 15-18 are four thick rectangular pieces roughly measuring ⅜×⅜×¼ in.

Stilus.

No. 19 is a stilus 5¼ in. long. Its lower end is sharp and pointed, and the upper thinner than the rest. Whether the upper end was intended for insertion into a wooden handle, is doubtful.

Terminal.

No. 20 is a hollow, semicircular terminal of cast copper with a hole at the apex for strings to pass through. Ht. 1¼ in.; diam. 2⅜ in. Similar terminals are also found in gold, faience, and terracotta.

---

[1] Analysed by Khan Bahadur Mohammad Sana Ullah.

[2] It has a certain amount of resemblance with the Egyptian straight backed knives, which, however, have long tangs serving as handles, and in which the tip is not curved back. *Cf.* Petrie, *op. cit.,* Pl. XXIX, 227, 239, and 240.

No. 21 consists of two large, thick pieces of copper probably belonging to one and the same object with prominent hammer marks on both sides. Greatest length 11 in.; w. 3¼ in.

Bowl.

No. 23 is a bowl with tapering sides. Ht. 1⅛ in.; diam. 3⅝ in.

Nos. 24 and 25 are two large, folded sheets of copper. Size 8×6¼ and 5¾×5 in.

Lump of löllingite.

In addition to the objects described above there were found in the same jar several lumps or pieces of copper, and a black lump of löllingite. For the analysis of the latter, as well as of one celt and one dagger belonging to this lot, I am indebted to Khan Bahadur M. Sana Ullah, Archæological Chemist, who writes that "the broken celt a/21 (Pl. CXXIII, 9) is composed of bronze, containing about 8 per cent. tin, and the double edged dagger e/2 (Pl. CXXIII, 64) is nearly pure 98 per cent. copper. The black lump, is the natural mineral 'löllingite',[1] an arsenide of Iron."

Analysis of two objects.

Similarity of the Harappā celts with those from other Indian sites.

Here it may be recalled that some of the celts described above resemble those from the famous Gungeria hoard[2] found in the Bālāghāt District of the Central Provinces, and some others are similar to those from Biṭhūr in the Cawnpore District, Pariār[3] (also written as Parihāra) in the Unao District, and Chāndpur[4] in the Bijnor District of the United Provinces.

More finds from the central area.

Several other interesting finds from this area yet remain to be recorded. Of these, I shall deal with the seals first. Two are square ones of steatite, of which No. 627, broken in the lower half, exhibits the figure of a buffalo (Pl. XCI, 240) similar to the Sumerian prototype which Gilgamesh is seen watering,[5] and No. 2333, also fragmentary, shows the forepart of a bison bending over a deep trough, of which the lower part is ornamented by a railing-like motif (Pl. XCI, 242). The third one, No. 581, is a small rectangular seal of the same substance, plane on one side and convex on the other (Pl. XCII, 284). In addition to these, were found two oblong faience sealings, of which No. 615 is flat and inscribed on one face only (similar to No. 654 in Pl. C), and No. 80 double-convex in section and inscribed on both faces, one face also showing an incense-burner athwart the letters (Pl. XCIII, 321). The other objects comprised one hemispherical alabaster mace-head, pierced with a rectangular hole (No. 644, Pl. LXXXIII, 24), two chert weights[6] (Nos. 7587 and 10274), a well polished chocolate-coloured stone ball of the size of a child's marble (No. 709), an excellent biconical agate bead[7] (No. 202, Pl. CXXVIII, 33), a hornblende pendent (No. 7588), a small bugle-shaped pendent of burnt steatite (No. 656), a fragmentary, trepezoidal, convex faience pendent (No. 7538) relieved on the face with a series of overlapping crescent shaped fluting,[8] and a *śaṅkh* spoon (2972).

---

[1] For the description and analysis of löllingite, *cf.* Khan Bahadur M. Sana Ullah in *M. I. C.*, p. 690.

[2] *Cf. Indian Antiquary*, Vol. XXXIV, p. 233, Pl. V, 4, with Harappā Pl. CXXIII, 6.

[3] *Ibid.*, Vol. XXXVI, pp. 53-54, Pl. VI, 1st row, 2 and 3, and 2nd row, 1, and Pl. VII, 1, 4, and 5.

[4] *Ibid.*, Vol. XXXIV, Pl. I, 8-14.

[5] *Cf.* L. W. King, *History of Sumer and Akkad*, on cover.

[6] Wt. 13·67 and 52·25 gms.; size ·75×·75×·5 and 1·15×1·15×·8 in.

[7] The choice of stone is very good but the bead was not yet polished.

[8] *Cf. M. I. C.*, p. 573, and Pl. CLVII, 43 and 45. These, though fragmentary, being similar to No. 7538 described above, might also be pendents.

In the southern part of the trench was found in square M 12/13 a large trough (No. 470) which contained two goblets with pointed bases, each stamped with the same seal, which may be the potter's name (Pl. CII, 21). Again, in this part, in square M 12/7 was found the fragment of an inscribed goblet (No. 7856, similar to No. 73 in Pl. CIV), and, close by, a medium-sized, squat, tapering vase (No. 626, 9¼ in. in height, Pl. LXXII, 21). **Southern Section.**

From the northern part of the trench there is but little to record. At its north-east end were found a unicorn seal (No. 3459, Pl. LXXXVIII, 89), and an inscribed goblet with pointed base (No. 3262, Pl. CII, 21). In the centre of the northern part in square M 11/11 was found an oblong, double convex faience sealing (No. 94) having three pictograms on one side, and on the other a large acacia tree enclosed in a railing[1] which is but faintly visible now (Pl. XCIII, 326). In the adjoining square M 11/16 is a small broken pavement with a little drain to south. With this were found two large, napiform jars (No. 1033 A and B)[2] of symmetrical and well rounded body decorated with pairs of black bands on deep red ground. They are among the best examples of potter's art from Harappā. Of these, B lay to the south under the drain mentioned above, and A along the west, only half buried, as its upper part stood above the pavement (Pl. XXIII, *a*). Close to it is a hollow rectangular shaft, measuring 3 ft. 4 in. by 2 ft. 5 in. internally, which stands to a height of 5 ft. 7 in. and was probably used as a granary. Its walls are only half a brick in thickness, being constructed entirely of courses laid stretcherwise. **Northern Section.** **Two large jars connected with a pavement.**

The following finds were also made in this section :—

1. Discoid ring of burnt steatite with undulating top. Diam. 5/16 in. No. 12481 ; Square M 12/22 ; Depth 8 ft. b.s.
2. Tiny, plum-shaped soapstone ear-drop. Ht. ½ in. No. 12488 ; Square M 12/22 ; Depth 8 ft. b.s.
3. Small rectangular sandstone block with grooves on four sides formed by sharpening tools. Size 3×2×1¼ in. No. 12506 ; Square M 12/22 ; Depth 8 ft. b.s.
4. Faience squirrel of the usual type, posed sitting with tail upraised and eating fruit held in its forepaws. Ht. 1 in. No. 12443 ; Square M 12/22 ; Depth 6 ft. 4 in. b.s.
5. Tiny, conical faience boss holed at opposite ends of the rim. Ht. ⅜ in. No. 12478 ; Square M 11/25 ; Depth 7 ft. 2 in. b.s.
6. Faience, chessman-shaped object holed in the underside. Ht. 1 1/16 in. No. 12517 ; Square M 12/23 ; Depth 7 ft. 6 in. b.s.
7. Tanged chisel, extremely rusted. Rare. The tang was apparently meant for insertion into a handle. Pl. CXXV, 18. L. 3¼ in. No. 12486 ; Square M 12/21 ; Depth 7 ft. 2 in. b.s.
8. A better class terracotta bust of a female figure larger than the usual size, details missing. Pl. LXXVII, 57. Ht. 3¾ in. No. 12475 ; Square M 12/22 ; Depth 7 ft. 2 in. b.s.

---

[1] A clearer railing is seen on terracotta sealing No. 5617 (Pl. XCIII 325) found in the Southern Extension of the Great Granary Area, *vide* p. 31 *supra*.

[2] For their contents see Chap. VIII, pp. 254-55 *infra*.

Three natural divisions from the IVth stratum downwards.

From the IVth stratum downwards, it would, perhaps, be better to take into account the three natural divisions of this trench into which it has been divided by digging it to different levels (Pl. XIX, section on AB). Starting at the southern end, a higher terrace, 24 ft. long, had to be left for the preservation of the three mud huts described on p. 84 in connection with Stratum III. The Deep Digging in the northern part, which takes the form of a prominent pit between the southern and northern sections, divides the remaining 200 ft. of this trench into three unequal parts, *viz.*, (1) The section south of the Deep Digging, (2) The Deep Digging, and (3) The section north of the Deep Digging. None of them being, in any way, connected one with the other, I shall deal with each one of them separately.

The Deep Digging.

Remains in the Deep Digging.

The Deep Digging measures 68 ft. from east to west by 40 ft. across and is bounded on the north by a west to east drain[1] belonging to Strata VI and VII, and on the south by two long walls of Stratum V in one alignment (Pl. XIX). Leaving out the western 18 ft., where its depth is only 20 ft., the rest of it was dug to 35 ft. below the surface (Pl. XIX, section on AB). The only fragments of walls or large pottery vessels met with in this area were four little remnants of walls of the VIth stratum in Squares M 11/13 and M 11/8 at a depth of 16 ft. 6 in. below the surface; a shallow pottery feeding-trough found at a depth of 20 ft. (Pl. XXIII, *f*); and a crushed earthenware *ghaṛā* of the VIIth stratum which was recovered at a lower level below this trough; a little haphazard drain, and the remains of the core of a wall of the VIIIth stratum at a depth of 24 ft. 6 in. Thus from the surface downwards there was virtually nothing to impede our digging and for this reason the place proved to be an ideal one for deep excavation. Although, however, so free of any structural or bulky remains, this spot has proved one of the richest in Harappā for small seals—so much so that when digging in other parts of the site was proving over monotonous, I sometimes turned back to this spot in the knowledge that I was sure to make some interesting finds there. Here, let me also add that Pl. XXI, *b* furnishes a good illustration of how the various strata rise one above the other from the earliest stratum marked by a few bricks standing out in the Deep Digging to the second stratum over which stands a man in the corner of the trench.

Finds.

The following are the finds recovered from the Deep Digging stratum by stratum :—

Stratum IV—

1. Unicorn seal fragment showing only the incense-burner and head of the animal. Pl. XC, 179. 1$\frac{1}{16}$ in. sq. No. 2695; Square M 11/22; Depth 8 ft. 9 in. b.s.
2. Bossed, square terracotta seal with indistinct pictograms. Pl. XC, 223. 1 in. sq. No. 2125; Square M 11/23; Depth 9 ft. b.s.

[1] This drain was first constructed with the VIIth stratum and repaired with the VIth.

3. Tiny, circular steatite seal with 2 pictograms on one side, and 1 on the other. Pl. XCVII, 551. Diam. $\frac{1}{2}$ in. No. 3961; Square M 11/8; Depth 9 ft. 6 in. b.s.
4. Corner fragment of a tiny rectangular steatite seal. L. $\frac{1}{4}$ in. No. 4104; Square M 11/12; Depth 10 ft. b.s.
5. Tiny, rectangular steatite seal with 3 pictograms on one side, and 1 on the other. Size $\frac{1}{2}\times\frac{1}{4}$ in. No. 3286; Square M 11/21; Depth 10 ft. b.s.
6. Tiny, rectangular steatite seal with 2 pictograms on one side, and 1 surviving on the other. Fragmentary. Pl. XCVII, 546. No. 10067; Square M 11/22; Depth 11 ft. b.s.

Stratum V—

1. Bossed steatite seal (fragmentary) showing a bison bent over a trough and 3 pictograms surviving in the upper field. Pl. XCI, 243. $\frac{11}{16}$ in. sq. No. 1276; Square M 11/12; Depth 13 ft. b.s.
2. Tiny, oval seal of burnt steatite with 3 pictograms on one side, and 1 on the other; similar to No. 543 in Pl. XCVII. Size $\frac{7}{16}\times\frac{5}{16}$ in. No. 1261; Square M 11/17; Depth 11 ft. 4 in. b.s.
3. Bossed steatite seal showing a bull grazing in a trough.[1] Mark the two curved horns and short hump which are characteristics of the Indian bull (*Bos indicus*). Pl. XCI, 239. It is one of the rare examples where a bull is shown bending over a trough. Also *cf.* Pl. XCI, 238. 11/16 in. sq. No. 4042; Square M 11/7; Depth 11 ft. 6 in. b.s.
4. Fragmentary, circular steatite seal inscribed on both sides. Diam. in. No. 4103; Square M 11/8; Depth 11 ft. 6 in. b.s.
5. Tiny shield-shaped steatite seal with pictograms on both sides, fragmentary. Pl. XCVII, 557. L. $\frac{3}{8}$ in.; w. $\frac{7}{16}$ in. No. 4041; Square M 11/8; Depth 11 ft. 6 in. b.s.
6. Tiny, three-sided prism seal of steatite with 3 pictograms on one side, 1 on the second, and 3 dotted circles on the third. Pl. XCVII, 574. L. $\frac{9}{16}$ in.; w. $\frac{1}{4}$ in. No. 2999; Square M 11/17; Depth 11 ft. 8 in. b.s.
7. Tiny, rectangular steatite seal (fragmentary) inscribed on both sides. Pl. XCVI, 483. Size $\frac{5}{8}\times\frac{1}{2}$ in. No. 4043; Square M 11/7; Depth 11 ft. 8 in. b.s.
8. Tiny seal of burnt steatite carved as hare. It has three pictograms on one side, and a cross-shaped groove on the underside for fixation. Pl. XCV, 422. L. $\frac{9}{16}$ in. No. 1203; Square M 11/17; Depth 12 ft. b.s.

---

[1] Regarding the significance of the trough placed before various animals depicted on the seals *cf.* Sir John Marshall, *op. cit.*, pp. 70-71. The two examples above cited appear to be oxen, which should therefore be included in the category of animals shown feeding from a trough.

9. Tiny, three-sided prism seal of steatite with 3 pictograms on one side, 1 on the second, and 3 dotted circles on the third. Pl. XCVII, 575. L. $\frac{1}{2}$ in.; w. $\frac{3}{16}$ in. No. 1262; Square M 11/18; Depth 12 ft. b.s.

10. Two tiny seals similar to No. 9. Each $\frac{3}{16}$ in. long and $\frac{1}{4}$ in. wide. No. 1260; Square M 11/17; Depth 12 ft. b.s.

11. Tiny seal similar to No. 9. L. $\frac{3}{8}$ in.; w. $\frac{1}{4}$ in. No. 1264; Square M 11/17; Depth 12 ft. b.s.

12. Tiny seal similar to No. 9. L. $\frac{7}{16}$ in.; w. $\frac{5}{16}$ in. No. 2917; Square M 11/17; Depth 12 ft. b.s.

13. Tiny, rectangular steatite seal with 3 pictograms on one face, and 1 on the other; similar to No. 509 in. Pl. XCVII. L. $\frac{1}{2}$ in.; w. $\frac{3}{16}$ in. No. 3026; Square M 11/22; Depth 12 ft. b.s.

14. Tiny, rectangular steatite seal (fragmentary) inscribed on both sides. Pl. XCVII, 525. W. $\frac{3}{8}$ in. No. 4044; Square M 11/17; Depth 12 ft. b.s.

15. Tiny, rectangular steatite seal with 3 pictograms on one face, and 1 on the other. Right end broken; similar to No. 508 in Pl. XCVII. L. $\frac{1}{2}$ in.; w. $\frac{5}{16}$ in. No. 1242; Square M 11/17; Depth 12 ft. b.s.

16. Tiny, rectangular steatite seal, fragmentary; similar to No. 502 in Pl. XCVII. L. $\frac{3}{8}$ in.; w. $\frac{1}{4}$ in. No. 1263; Square M 11/17; Depth 12 ft. b.s.

17. Tiny, oval seal of burnt steatite with 3 pictograms on one side, and 1 on the other; similar to No. 542 in Pl. XCVII. Size $\frac{7}{16}\times\frac{1}{4}$ in. No. 3025; Square M 11/22; Depth 12 ft. b.s.

18. Fragment of a tiny, rectangular steatite seal with 2 pictograms on one side, and part of one on the other; similar to No. 509 in Pl. XCVII. W. $\frac{5}{16}$ in. No. 2918; Square M 11/23; Depth 12 ft. b.s.

19. Tiny seal similar to No. 9 above. L. $\frac{7}{16}$ in.; w. $\frac{1}{4}$ in. No. 2894; Square M 11/23; Depth 12 ft. b.s.

20. Tiny, three-sided prism seal of steatite with 3 pictograms on one side, crocodile on the second, and 3 dotted circles on the third. Pl. XCVII, 578. L. 11/16 in.; w. $\frac{3}{8}$ in. No. 2895; Square M 11/23; Depth 12 ft. 3 in. b.s.

21. Tiny, rectangular steatite seal with 2 pictograms on one face, and 1 on the other; slightly broken; similar to No. 502 in Pl. XCVII. Size $\frac{7}{16}\times\frac{1}{4}$ in. No. 2897; Square M 11/23; Depth 12 ft. 3 in. b.s.

22. Tiny steatite seal carved as couchant hare. It is inscribed with 2 pictograms on one side, and a cross-shaped groove on the under-side. Pl. XCV, 425. Size $\frac{1}{2}\times\frac{5}{12}$ in. No. 4179; Square M 11/7; Depth 12 ft. 6 in. b.s.

23. Fragment of a tiny, rectangular steatite seal. W. $\frac{1}{4}$ in. No. 4180; Square M 11/8; Depth 12 ft. 6 in. b.s.

24. Tiny, rectangular steatite seal with 2 pictograms on one side, and 1 on the other. Pl. XCVII, 502. Size $\frac{1}{4}\times\frac{1}{4}$ in. No. 4105; Square M 11/13; Depth 12 ft. 6 in. b.s.

25. Tiny, shield-shaped steatite seal with 3 pictograms on one face, and 1 on the other. Pl. XCVII, 564. L. $\frac{5}{16}$ in.; w. $\frac{3}{8}$ in. No. 1171; Square M 11/13; Depth 12 ft. 9 in. b.s.

26. Tiny seal similar to No. 9 above. L. $\frac{5}{16}$ in.; w. $\frac{1}{4}$ in. No. 1277; Square M 11/18; Depth 13 ft. b.s.

27. Tiny seal similar to No. 9 above. L. $\frac{3}{8}$ in.; w. $\frac{5}{16}$ in. No. 1278; Square M 11/18; Depth 13 ft. b.s.

28. Tiny seal similar to No. 9 above. L. $\frac{5}{16}$ in.; w. $\frac{1}{4}$ in. No. 1279; Square M 11/18; Depth 13 ft. b.s.

29. Tiny, rectangular steatite seal with 3 pictograms on one side, and 1 on the other. Pl. XCVII, 509. Size $\frac{3}{8}\times\frac{1}{4}$ in. No. 1280; Square M 11/18; Depth 13 ft. b.s.

30. Tiny seal similar to No. 24 above. Size $\frac{7}{16}\times\frac{5}{16}$ in. No. 4253; Square M 11/8; Depth 13 ft. b.s.

31. Small corner fragment of a square steatite seal with 2 pictograms. Pl. CI, 696. L. $\frac{7}{16}$ in. No. 4252; Square M 11/7; Depth 13 ft. 4 in. b.s.

32. Tiny seal similar to No. 9 above. L. $\frac{1}{4}$ in.; w. $\frac{5}{16}$ in. No. 1348; Square M 11/18; Depth 13 ft. 6 in. b.s.

33. Tiny seal similar to No. 24 above. Size $\frac{5}{16}\times\frac{5}{16}$ in. No. 1172; Square M 11/18; Depth 13 ft. 7 in. b.s.

34. Tiny seal similar to No. 17 above. Size $\frac{1}{4}\times\frac{1}{4}$ in. No. 3091; Square M 11/17; Depth 13 ft. 7 in. b.s.

35. Tiny, rectangular steatite seal with 4 pictograms on one side, and 3 on the other. It is a good example of scribbled writing. Pl. XCVI, 480. Size $\frac{5}{16}\times\frac{3}{8}$ in. No. 1497; Square M 11/18; Depth 14 ft. 4 in. b.s.

36. Oblong, faience sealing, double convex in section, with 4 pictograms on one side, and 2 pictograms and an incense-burner athwart the writing on the other. Pl. XCIII, 321. L. 1 in.; w. $\frac{1}{2}$ in. No. 2993; Square M 11/17; Depth 11 ft. 8 in. b.s.

37. Tiny, bud-shaped ear-drop of burnt steatite with a holed tang for attachment. Pl. CXXXIX, 31. Ht. $\frac{3}{8}$ in. No. 10068; Square M 11/22; Depth 11 ft. b.s.

38. Small copper chisel. L. $1\frac{3}{8}$ in.; w. $\frac{5}{16}$ in.; th. $\frac{1}{16}$ to $\frac{1}{8}$ in. No. 4257; Square M 11/7; Depth 13 ft. 2 in. b.s.

39. Goblet with pointed base impressed with potter's seal. Pl. CII, 21. Ht. $6\frac{3}{8}$ in. No. 1087 a/1, Square M 11/13; Depth 12 ft. b.s.

40. Hand-made, open-mouthed carinated pottery vase. Ht. $2\frac{3}{16}$ in.; diam. $2\frac{1}{16}$ in. No. 4224; Square M 11/8; Depth 13 ft. 4 in. b.s.

Stratum VI—

1. Tiny steatite seal carved as a running hare with 1 pictogram on one side, and a cross-shaped groove on the underside for fixation. Pl. XCV, 424. L. and ht. 5/16 in. No. 1654; Square M 11/12; Depth 15 ft. b.s.
2. Tiny, three-sided prism seal of steatite with 3 pictograms on one side, crocodile on the second, and 3 dotted circles on the third. Pl. XCVII, 578. L. ½ in.; w. 3/16 in. No. 1665; Square M 11/18; Depth 15 ft. b.s.
3. Tiny, oval seal of steatite with 3 pictograms on one side, and 1 on the other; similar to No. 544 in Pl. XCVII. Size 9/16×½ in. No. 3173; Square M 11/18; Depth 15 ft. b.s.
4. Tiny, three-sided prism seal of steatite with 4 pictograms on one side, 1 on the second, and 3 dotted circles on the third. Pl. XCVIII, 587. Size 9/16×½ in. No. 559; Square M 11/12; Depth 15 ft. 6 in. b.s.
5. Tiny, equilateral triangular steatite seal (fragmentary) with 1 pictogram on one side and 3 dotted circles in a triangular scheme on the other. Pl. XCVII, 513. Each side ½ in. No. 4427; Square M 11/13; Depth 16 ft. 8 in. b.s.
6. Fragment of a tiny, rectangular steatite seal showing part of a pictogram on one side, and staff of the incense-burner on the other. L. ⅜ in.; w. 5/16 in. No. 4428; Square M 11/8; Depth 16 ft. 8 in. b.s.
7. Tiny, rectangular faience sealing with 3 pictograms on one side, and 1 on the other. It is unusually thick for its size. Pl. C, 683. Size ½×3/16×3/16 in. No. 558; Square M 11/12; Depth 15 ft. 6 in. b.s.
8. Cubical chert weight. Pl. CXVIII, 8. Wt. 27·45 gms.; size ·95×·95×·65 in. No. 4066; Square M 11/23; Depth 18 ft. 6 in. b.s.
9. Hand-made, round pottery vase with flat bottom and flared mouth. Ht. 2½ in. No. 4466; Square M 11/8; Depth 16 ft. 2 in. b.s.
10. Terracotta animal figure, mouth and forelegs broken. On either side of its body are embossed two flowers in a shield-shaped[1] pattern indicating trappings. Pl. LXXIX, 47. L. 2·8 in. No. 4067; Square M 11/22; Depth 18 ft. b.s.

Stratum VII.

In the VIIth stratum I also brought to light a crushed earthenware *ghaṛā* at a depth of 21 ft. (square M 11/13), which, being in a very fragmentary condition, was left *in situ*. In the eastern portion of the Deep Digging there were found at the same level and scattered over a space of 20 ft. by 17 ft. 8 in. a number of hardened bovine bones including the forepart of a skull with two horns (Pl. XXII, *d*). Regarding the hardening of these bones as well as of two other groups found in Strata V and VI of the Great Granary Area an interesting phenomenon has been observed, *viz.*, that the bones tend to become harder

Hardened bovine bones at a depth of 21 ft.

Probable cause of hardness.

[1] The shield resembles seals of this shape, *e.g.*, No. 25 of Stratum V above.

and less spongy as the soil itself is harder and more impervious to water. Commencing in Trench I at a depth of 10 ft. the soil is peculiarly hard down up to a depth of 25 ft. below the surface (Pl. XXII, *d*). This compressed layer gradually becomes deeper green in colour as its depth increases. Samples of this soil were sent for analysis to Khan Bahadur M. Sana Ullah, Archæological Chemist in India, who writes that "hardness in clays may be due to (*a*) metamorphic changes, or to (*b*) pressure. As I have found no evidence of metamorphic changes, there is no doubt that the hardness of this stratum is due to pressure exerted by the superincumbent layers of earth. A direct proof of this view is furnished by the fact that these clods have now become quite soft. The preservation of bones is evidently due to the stoppage of the percolation of water through this highly compressed stratum".

Finds.

The following finds were associated with the VIIth stratum:—

1. Square, bossed steatite seal carved with a life-like Brāhmanī bull (*Bos indicus*). All the three pictograms in the upper field are damaged. Pl. XC, 236. It was found under one of the cattle bones mentioned above. 1¼ in. sq. No. 4299; Square M 11/17; Depth 20 ft. 9 in. b.s.
2. Tiny, rectangular steatite seal with 4 pictograms on one side, and a crocodile on the other. Pl. XCVI, 430. Size ⅝ × 5/16 in. No. 1234; Square M 11/13; Depth 19 ft. b.s.
3. Two potsherds painted with black bands. Size 8×6 in. and 4×3¾ in. No. 7864; Square M 11/8 and 13; Depth 20 to 21 ft. b.s.
4. Flat and shallow pottery trough[1] for feeding cattle. Rim turned down. Pl. LXX, 4. Ht. 9 in.; diam. 2 ft. 3 in. No. 3685; Square M 11/13; Depth 20 ft. 6 in. b.s.
5. Pottery vase with a long spout (slightly curved up to prevent spilling) taking off horizontally from the bottom of the vessel. Shows traces of red wash. Pl. LXXI, 90. L. 4¾ in.; ht. 1¾ in.; diam. at rim 2 in. No. 4127; Square M 11/23; Depth 21 ft. b.s.

Cutting in the Deep Digging.

From Pl. XXII, *c* it will be apparent that in this trench the above-mentioned hard and compact stratum of soil is both preceded, as well as followed, by a much softer stratum which is seen extending from the surface of the mound to the bottom of the rain-cut along the western edge of the trench, and also for some distance higher than the head of the man standing at the bottom of the Deep Digging. Below the drain of the VIIIth stratum in square M 11/18 the soil is undisturbed for 3 ft., and then followed by a deposit of sand which has been cut through for another 7 ft. where the level of sub-soil water has been reached. At this level, sand is also found in the dry bed of the river immediately to the north of the mound, and it is possible that below the VIIIth stratum virgin soil has already been reached.[2]

---

[1] This to some extent resembles troughs figured on the seals. *Cf.* Pl. XCI, 238, 241-46, and 253. Also *cf.* seals figured in *M. I. C.*, Pls. CX and CXI. The troughs depicted on the seals, especially their turned down edges would seem somewhat exaggerated for pottery.

[2] During the flood of 23rd September, 1932 at Jubbulpur many feet of sand was deposited by the Narbada during the course of a single night, but such occurrences are exceptional.

The following three terracotta objects were found in connection with the VIIIth stratum at a depth of 23 ft. below the surface—

1. Hollow flesh rubber, square in section, holed on one side. No. 7421; Square M 11/17.
2. Fragment of a long, cylindrical vase. No. 7210; Square M 11/17.
3. Tiger with broken legs. No. 7179; Square M 11/18.

Section south of the Deep Digging.

The section south of the Deep Digging is 120 ft. long from north to south, and was dug to an average depth of 17 ft. 6 in. bringing to light the remains of Strata IV to VI, in addition to the three upper strata already described. For convenience, this area may be further sub-divided into the northern, middle and southern portions. Of these, the northern portion is only 20 ft. long covered by squares M 11/9, 14, 19, and 24, the middle portion 40 ft., embracing squares M 11/10, 15, 20, and 25, and M 12/6, 11, 16, and 21; while the southern portion covers the remaining 60 ft. between squares M 12/7 to 9, and M 12/22 to 24.

Stratum IV.

Northern Portion.

The IVth stratum lies between $8\frac{1}{2}$ and 11 ft. below the surface. In the northern portion of this section there are no structural remains worth recording. From square M 11/19, however, was recovered at a depth of 9 ft. below the surface a crescent-shaped, unbored and unfinished pendent of banded agate, which well deserves notice. It is 2 in. across, lentoid in section, and is broadest at the centre from where the ends are tapered (Pl. CXXXIX, 1). It has an elongated lozenge-shaped red band at the centre with a remarkably symmetrical series of vertical stripes of the same colour on either side, which considerably enhance its beauty.

A Crescent-shaped agate pendent.

Middle Portion.

In the middle portion of this section there are the remains of two rooms in squares M 11/15 and M 11/20. Of these, the eastern one is 7 ft. wide internally; of the western only the southern and eastern walls remain. To the east and west of these rooms are a few other bits of walls, but none of them calls for any remark. The following finds associated with this stratum were recovered from this portion:—

1. Unicorn seal with 8 pictograms. Pl. LXXXVI, 28. $1\frac{1}{2}$ in. sq. No. 12493; Square M 11/25; Depth 8 ft. 8 in. b.s.
2. Unicorn seal with 5 pictograms. In this the open-work of the incense-burner is finer than usual. Pl. LXXXVIII, 100. $1\frac{1}{16}$ in. sq. No. 741; Square M 11/15; Depth 10 ft. 11 in. b.s.
3. Rectangular limestone tablet inscribed with some indistinct marks on obverse, reverse and two sides. Size $\frac{3}{16} \times \frac{7}{16} \times \frac{3}{16}$ in. No. 12494; Square M 11/25; Depth 8 ft. 8 in. b.s.
4. Cylindrical terracotta sealing with 11 pictograms on one side, and crocodile (*Gavialis gangeticus*) on the other; similar to Nos. 334-336 in Pl. XCVII. L. $1\frac{3}{16}$ in.; diam. $\frac{3}{8}$ in. No. 768; Square M 12/16; Depth 10 ft. b.s.

5. Cubical chert weight, slightly chipped off. Wt. 52·3 gms.; size 1·15×1·15×·9 in. No. 12500; Square M 12/21; Depth 8 ft. 8 in. b.s.
6. Barrel-shaped stone bead of bright red colour, damaged. L. ⅜ in. No. 12495; Square M 11/25; Depth 8 ft. 8 in. b.s.
7. Chessman-shaped alabaster object, badly cracked. Ht. 1⅜ in. No. 12507; Square M 12/21; Depth 10 ft. 2 in. b.s.
8. Fragmentary copper spear-head. L. 3½ in. No. 12550; Square M 11/25; Depth 10 ft. b.s.
9. Inscribed potsherd. Pl. CI, 713. No. 4332; Square M 11; Depth 9 to 12 ft. b.s.

Structure in the Southern Portion.

In the remaining 60 ft., constituting the southern portion, there is a substantially built corner of a structure standing to a height of 3 ft. 6 in. in square M 12/12, and in squares M 12/18, 19, and 24, are the remains of a very poorly constructed house (No. 1) consisting of three rooms and a courtyard (Pl. XIX). Rooms Nos. 1 and 2 lie to the north and No. 3 is to the east of the courtyard No. 4, in which there is a pair of rectangular hearths of unequal size constructed side by side (Pl. XXIII, *c*, foreground). The walls of these hearths are only half a brick thick, the east wall of the smaller hearth being composed of two rows of brick-on-edge making up the same thickness. The larger hearth measures 3 ft. 3 in. by 1 ft. 6 in., and the smaller one 2 ft. 6 in. by 1 ft. 6 in. Both of them contained ashes and charcoal, and also some fragments of terracotta cakes, nodules, and one or two bones from the surrounding debris. Here, attention may also be drawn to two pilasters abutting on to each other and projecting from the curtain walls behind the hearths. Evidently they were constructed as supports, since all the walls of this house are only half a brick in thickness. In this section there may also be mentioned a 15 ft. long wall in square M 12/14, which is 2 ft. 8 in. thick. To its west is a small brick edging on both sides of which were recovered some bovine bones including two hoofed lower legs.

Miniature copper chariot.

A very important and interesting object found in the southern portion is an extremely delicate miniature of a two-wheeled copper chariot (No. 355, Pl. CXXV, 35) which has been pieced together from numerous fragments recovered at a depth of 10 ft. 6 in. below the surface in square M 12/13. The chariot is open both front and back, and has a gabled roof which, like the side walls, is relieved with simple linear decoration. The driver is seated in front on a raised seat, but the animal supposed to be yoked to the chariot, the poles, the wheels and the axle are all missing. The chariot is very small—no more than two inches in height, and the details—particularly the face of the driver—very obscure. All that can be said is that the face appears to be somewhat round, with flat and moderately high pitched nose. His hair seems to be plaited and bound into a knot behind the head. As an instance of a covered chariot[1]

[1] Mackay has since found two charming copper toy carts from Chānuh-daro in the Nawabshah District of Sind. Describing them he says "One, with solid wheels complete and the driver seated in front holding a stick or whip, had unfortunately been badly bent, probably by the child that played with it. The other is a village cart, with a pent-roof canopy but unluckily without its wheels". *Cf. A. S. R.* for 1935-36, p. 42. The latter with a pent-roof is similar to the Harappā, example.

this is the first example from the Indus Valley sites, antedating the earliest use of a wheeled vehicle in Egypt by several centuries. The various examples of war chariots on the mosaic standard at Ur[1] (cir. 3500 B.C.) are all four wheeled and without a roof, nor is there any roof on the somewhat carefully modelled terracotta chariot of Ishtar with a high dash-board from Emete Ursag.[2]

Other finds. The following antiquities belonging to Stratum IV were also found in this section—

1. Unicorn seal with 6 pictograms. Pl. LXXXIX, 118. $\frac{3}{4}$ in. sq. No. 12537; Square M 12/18; Depth 10 ft. 3 in. b.s.
2. Tiny, rectangular steatite seal inscribed on both faces. Pl. XCVII, 499. Size $\frac{11}{16}\times\frac{3}{8}$ in. No. 12534; Square M 12/24; Depth 10 ft. b.s.
3. Discoid faience sealing with 7 pictograms on one side and 1 on the other. Pl. XCV, 371. Diam. 11/16 in. No. 12538; Square M 12/18; Depth 10 ft. 3 in. b.s.
4. Two cubical chert weights. Wt. 54·35 and 135·9 gms.; size 1·15×1·15×·95 and 1·65×1·65×1·15 in. respectively. No. 771; Square M 12/18; Depth 9 ft. b.s.
5. Thin, semicircular and tanged object of burnt steatite with one hole at the upper edge and another one in the tang for fixation. Probably meant for inlay. Pl. CXXXIX, 47. Size $\frac{13}{16}\times\frac{5}{8}$ in. No. 10050; Square M 12/8; Depth 9 ft. 6 in. b.s.
6. Cubical chert weight. Wt. 27·3 gms.; size ·95×·85×·75 in. No. 10051; Square M 12/8; Depth 9 ft. 6 in. b.s.
7. Circular, plano-convex temple ornament of burnt steatite with a segment-shaped hole on the underside. Diam. $\frac{11}{16}$ in. No. 274; Square M 12/15; Depth 10 ft. b.s.
8. Two hornblende pendents grooved at the head. Ht. $\frac{1}{2}$ in. and $\frac{7}{16}$ in. No. 10077; Square M 12/7; Depth 10 ft. 6 in. b.s.
9. A fragmentary faience disc with a raised tubular hole across the diameter projecting equally on both faces. Diam. 2¼ in. No. 12508; Square M 12/22; Depth 10 ft. b.s.

Stratum V.

Structures in the Northern Portion. The Vth stratum in this area, of which the level corresponds with that of the Great Granary, lies between 11 ft. and 14 ft. 6 in. below the surface. Belonging to this and immediately south of the Deep Digging in square M 11/19 is a neatly laid rectangular pavement which measures 17 ft. 10 in. by 6 ft. 10 in. (Pl. XXI, *d*). **An excellent pavement.** It is composed of well-rubbed bricks laid flat and has the usual brick edging, which, in turn, is backed by a course of half brick thickness. In its west wall is a large reveal, 8 ft. 5 in. long and 9½ in. deep, and along its north is a thick and long wall running east and west, which is constructed promis-

---

[1] *Cf.* C. L. Woolley, The *Sumerians*, p. 50 ff. Pl. opposite p. 50.

[2] *Cf.* S. Langdon, *Excavations at Kish*, Vol. I, Pl. VII, 2.

cuously of burnt and sun-dried bricks. About 18 ft. west of this pavement and built, with or without bonding, against the south face of the above long wall, which is still partly buried under the western edge of the trench, are two rooms of House 2 (Pl. XIX). In the parti-wall of room No. 2, which has been but partially cleared, is a deep recess measuring 3 ft. 6 in. by 1 ft. 3 in., which was later filled solid with mud to act as foundation for a wall of the IVth stratum. At this time also the eastern room No. 1 was partitioned by another wall. Originally, this latter room was very long and narrow measuring 21 ft. 6 in. from north to south and only 4 ft. across. The western room is much larger and contains a small drain covered by brick-on-edge. On the other side of the same thick wall of mixed construction, and built without bonding behind rooms 1 and 2, is another long and narrow chamber No. 3 (16 ft. 9 in. by 3 ft. 8 in.) with walls only half a brick in thickness. **Remains of House 2.**

The following finds may be mentioned from this portion :— **Finds.**

1. Fragmentary unicorn seal with 3 pictograms surviving. $\frac{11}{16}$ in. sq. No. 2693 ; Square M 11/19 ; Depth 12 ft. b.s.
2. Unicorn seal (damaged) with 2 pictograms surviving. Pl. LXXXIX, 149. $\frac{3}{4}$ in. sq. No. 2726 ; Square M 11/24 ; Depth 12 ft. 8 in. b.s.
3. Tiny, oval seal of burnt steatite with 3 pictograms on one side, and 1 on the other ; similar to No. 544 in Pl. XCVII. Size $\frac{5}{16} \times \frac{3}{16}$ in. No. 3173 ; Square M 11/24 ; Depth 12 ft. b.s.
4. Shield-shaped faience sealing with 4 pictograms on one face, and 1 pictogram enclosed by two dots on the other. Pl. XCV, 369. Size $\frac{3}{4} \times \frac{1}{2}$ in. No. 1235 ; Square M 11/19 ; Depth 12 ft. 9. in. b.s.
5. Cylindrical faience sealing with 2 pictograms on one side, and 1 on the other ; similar to No. 594 in Pl. XCVIII. L. $\frac{3}{4}$ in. ; diam. $\frac{5}{16}$ in. No. 4298 ; Square M 11/9 ; Depth 12 ft. 10 in. b.s.
6. Tiny, rectangular faience sealing with 3 pictograms on one side, and 1 on the other. Pl. C, 691. Size $\frac{7}{16} \times \frac{1}{2}$ in. No. 2787 ; Square M 11/24 ; Depth 13 ft. 4 in. b.s.

In the middle portion there is not a single complete room, but it will appear from Pl. XX, *c* that there are two neatly built pilasters on either side of the man figured in it. To his left is another pilaster, and two pillars in the foreground. Their construction, as well as that of the rectangular pavement described in the Northern Portion, is markedly superior to the remains of Stratum IV. I may, however, point out that in the pilasters behind the man's head some mud bricks were put in at convenient intervals, both in the same and in alternate courses, but they do not mar the neatness of the construction. The following antiquities were found in this portion :— **Remains in the Middle Portion.** **Finds.**

1. Unicorn seal with 4 pictograms, incense-burner partly broken. Pl. LXXXIX, 107. 1 in. sq. No. 3757 ; Square M 12/16 ; Depth 13 ft. 7 in. b.s.
2. Tiny, rectangular steatite seal with 4 pictograms on one face, and crocodile on the other. Pl. XCVI, 435. Size $\frac{5}{8} \times \frac{5}{16}$ in. No. 2570 ; Square M 11/25 ; Depth 11 ft. 6 in. b.s.

3. Tiny, lanceolate steatite seal with 3 pictograms on one side, and 1 on the other; similar to No. 553 in Pl. XCVII. L. $\frac{9}{16}$ in.; w. $\frac{1}{4}$ in. No. 12574; Square M 11/25; Depth 12 ft. b.s.
4. Tiny, rectangular steatite seal with 4 pictograms on one side, and 1 on the other. Pl. XCVI, 451. Size $\frac{11}{16}\times\frac{3}{8}$ in. No. 995; Square M 12/16; Depth 13 ft. b.s.
5. Tiny, rectangular steatite seal with 3 pictograms on one side, and 1 on the other. Pl. XCVI, 456. Size $\frac{9}{16}\times\frac{9}{16}$ in. No. 12516; Square M 12/21; Depth 14 ft. 2 in. b.s.
6. Tiny, rectangular steatite seal with 2 pictograms (which do not resemble those on any other similar seal so far found) on one side, and a fish touching a dotted circle on the other.[1] Rare. Pl. XCVII, 521. Size $\frac{7}{16}\times\frac{1}{4}$ in. No. 12576; Square M 11/20; Depth 14 ft. 6 in. b.s.
7. Tiny, rectangular steatite seal with 4 pictograms on one side, and crocodile on the other. Pl. XCVI, 436. Size $\frac{1}{2}\times\frac{5}{16}$ in. No. 12575; Square M 11/25; Depth 18 ft. 7 in. b.s.
8. Rectangular faience sealing, semicircular in section, with 4 pictograms on one face, and 1 on the other. Pl. C, 684. L. $\frac{11}{16}$ in.; w. $\frac{5}{16}$ in. No. 1032; Square M 11/20; Depth 13 ft. b.s.
9. Tapering flint celt with straight cutting edge. Workmanship rough. Pl. CXVII, 57. Size $9\frac{3}{8}\times4\frac{1}{2}$ in.; greatest th. $1\frac{5}{8}$ in. No. 1034; Square M 12/6; Depth 13 ft. b.s.
10. Couchant, faience ram holed across the neck for suspension. Pl. LXXVIII, 45. L. 1 in. No. 944; Square M 11/20; Depth 12 ft. b.s.
11. Three inscribed potsherds. Pl. CI, 710 and 712. No. 12642; Square M 12; Depth 9 to 12 ft. b.s.; from the washing tub.
12. Inscribed potsherd. Pl. CIV, 78. No. 12659; Square M 12; Depth 9 to 12 ft. b.s.; from the washing tub.

Southern portion. **Two mangers.** In the southern portion, there are the remains of two pillars—one rectangular and the other square—, and two circular mangers standing side by side in square M 12/19 (Pl. XXIII, *c*, centre). As usual, both of them are paved and lined with brick-on-edge. Internally, the western manger is 3 ft. in diameter, and the eastern one 2 ft. 6 in. only. More finds were made in this portion **Finds.** than in the other two. A list of them is given below:—

1. Right upper fragment of a unicorn seal with only two pictograms surviving. Pl. XCIX, 622. L. $\frac{3}{4}$ in. No. 1379; Square M 12/7; Depth 12 ft. b.s.
2. Unicorn seal with 2 pictograms. Pl. LXXXVI, 31. $1\frac{1}{4}$ in. sq. No. 12561; Square M 12/19; Depth 12 ft. 7 in. b.s.

---

[1] Now-a-days it is the practice among pious Hindus to put nose-rings of gold or silver on fishes in sacred rivers or tanks, *e.g.*, in the Ganges at Hardwar. Could the symbol of fish touching a dotted circle have represented a similar practice?

3. Tiny seal of burnt steatite somewhat resembling a boy's writing board (*kāshṭha phalaka*). Pl. XCV, 416. Size ½×⅜ in. No. 10301; Square M 12/17; Depth 11 ft. 9 in. b.s.
4. Fragment of a tiny, fish-shaped (?) steatite seal. Pl. XCVII, 560. L. ⅜ in. No. 12515; Square M 12/22; Depth 12 ft. 3 in. b.s.
5. Tiny, three-sided prism seal of steatite with 3 pictograms on one side, 2 on the second, and 2 circles on the third. Pl. XCVII, 580. L. $\frac{9}{16}$ in.; w. ¼ in. No. 12546; Square M 12/17; Depth 14 ft. 6 in. b.s.
6. Crescent-shaped faience sealing with 3 pictograms on one face, and VIII—like symbol on the other. Unique in this shape. Pl. XCV, 387. Diam. 1 in. No. 12544; Square M 12/24; Depth 11 ft. 8 in. b.s.
7. Tiny, wedge-shaped faience sealing. Pl. XCVIII, 610. Rare. L. $\frac{9}{16}$ in.; greatest w. ¼ in. No. 12562; Square M 12/18; Depth 12 ft. 7 in. b.s.
8. Cylindrical faience sealing with 4 pictograms on one side, and 1 pictogram and an acacia tree athwart the writing on the other; similar to No. 646 in Pl. XCIX. L. $\frac{13}{16}$ in.; diam. $\frac{5}{16}$ in. No. 385; Square M 12/14; Depth 13 ft. b.s.
9. Cylindrical faience sealing similar to No. 8. L. ¾ in. No. 12548; Square M 12/17; Depth 13 ft. 2 in. b.s.
10. Cylindrical faience sealing with 3 pictograms on one side, and an acacia tree on the other. Pl. C, 690. L. ½ in.; diam. $\frac{5}{16}$ in. No. 10162; Square M 12/13; Depth 13 ft. 9 in. b.s.
11. Terracotta discoid sealing with blurred pictograms on one side, and a circumscribed lozenge with incurving sides on the other. Pl. XCV, 377. Diam. ⅜ in. No. 12514; Square M 12/22; Depth 12 ft. 5 in. b.s.
12. Cubical chert weight. Pl. CXVIII, 15. Wt. 27·25 gms.; size ·95×·9×·7 in. No. 1356; Square M 12/7; Depth 12 ft. b.s.
13. Flattish, oval steatite bead lentoid in section. It is painted red to simulate carnelian and then overlaid with trefoil decoration in white. Pl. CXXVIII, 11. Size ⅝×⅜ in. No. 10163; Square M 12/7; Depth 13 ft. 9 in. b.s.
14. Badly rusted copper spear-head with broken tang. L. 9 in. No. 12545; Square M 12/19; Depth 11 ft. 2 in. b.s.
15. Bronze blade-axe with tapering sides, rounded at the cutting edge. L. 6⅜ in.; w. across the cutting 2⅜ in.; w. across the butt end 2 in. No. 384; Square M 12/14; Depth 13 ft. b.s.
16. Ivory stilus with a sharp point at one end. Pl. CXIX, 25. L. 3⅜ in. No. 1169; Square M 12/18; Depth 12 ft. 5 in. b.s.

Stratum VI.

Structural remains of the VIth stratum stand at a depth of 14 ft. 7 in. to 18 ft. 6 in. below the surface, or 1·21 to 1·68 ft. below the foundation of the **Structural remains.**

Great Granary. They are mostly buried under heaps of earth which now support the remains of the five upper strata. In Pl. XX, *c* is also seen at the lowest level an east and west wall of the VIth stratum standing to a maximum height of 7 ft. 7 in., and 30 ft. north of this is another contemporary wall also going in the same direction. There are no other structures worth recording in this stratum. At a depth of 15 ft. below the surface in square M 12/16 and at the spot indicated by the man standing in the above-mentioned photograph, were found numerous fragments of tiny, discoid and extremely thin lanceolate[1] seals of burnt steatite and steatite paste. Those that could be pieced together are described[2] in the list of finds given below. Due west of these, and along the edge of the trench were found two pottery jar-stands, and a large jar (No. 3822) inscribed with three pictograms (Pl. XXIII, *e*). One of the jar-stands has a horizontally fluted mid-rib, and the other[3] is of a type common both at Harappā and Mohenjo-daro.

Inscribed pottery jar and jar-stands.

Group of antiquities No. 10185.

In the southern portion of this section was found a group of antiquities (No. 10185) in square M 12/7 at a depth of 15 ft. 8 in. below the surface. It comprised a unicorn seal $\frac{13}{16}$ in. square with 4 pictograms (Pl. LXXXVIII, 90), another square seal with the effigy of an elephant and six pictograms measuring $\frac{13}{16}$ in. square (Pl. XCI, 229), a tiny oval seal of steatite ($\frac{1}{2}$ by $\frac{5}{16}$ in.) with 3 pictograms on one side and 1 on the other (similar to No. 548 in Pl. XCVII), numerous thin, discoid beads of burnt steatite, 11 round and 5 tubular beads of faience, 7 miscellaneous beads of faience and stone, a thin semicircular tanged object of burnt steatite with two rivet holes for fixation (similar to No. 47 in Pl. CXXXIX), two equally thin but discoid objects of the same substance each with two pairs of holes at opposite points along the edge (Pl. CXXXIX, 48), a shouldered blade-axe of copper (L. $5\frac{1}{4}$ in.) with indistinct marks, a copper terminal, two chert cores, and fragments of pestles.

Finds of Stratum VI.

The following objects were recovered from the section south of the Deep Digging :—

Northern portion—

1. Tiny, discoid steatite seal with 4 pictograms on one side, and fish on the other. Pl. XCV, 411. Diam. $\frac{1}{2}$ in. No. 3171 ; Square M 11/19 ; Depth 17 ft. b.s.
2. Tiny, rectangular steatite seal with incense-burner on one face, and 1 pictogram on the other. Pl. XCVI, 441. Size $\frac{3}{8} \times \frac{5}{16}$ in. No. 1498 ; Square M 11/14 ; Depth 17 ft. b.s.
3. Tiny, rectangular steatite seal with one pictogram on either face. Pl. XCVI, 474. Size $\frac{1}{2} \times \frac{1}{2}$ in. No. 3278 ; Square M 11/19 ; Depth 18 ft. b.s.

---

[1] These are thinner than any other tiny seals found so far, their thickness being no more than $\frac{1}{12}$th in.

[2] See item 4 under Middle Portion below.

[3] Jar-stands of this type found at *Ādichanallūr* in the Madras Presidency belong to a later age. *Cf.* A. Rea, *Catalogue of Prehistoric Antiquities, Ādichanallūr and Perumbair*, Pls. VII and VIII.

Middle portion—

1. Fragment of a unicorn seal with 3 pictograms. L. $\frac{3}{4}$ in. No. 1080; Square M 12/16; Depth 15 ft. b.s.
2. Unicorn seal with 2 pictograms. Pl. LXXXIX, 115. $\frac{15}{16}$ in. sq. No. 1265; Square M 11/10; Depth 15 ft. 6 in. b.s.
3. Unicorn seal with 4 pictograms, slightly chipped off. Pl. LXXXIX, 130. $\frac{7}{8}$ in. sq. No. 517; Square M 12/11; Depth 16 ft. b.s.
4. Three tiny and extremely thin lanceolate steatite seals with 3 pictograms on one side, and 1 on the other. Pl. XCVII, 553-555. L. $\frac{5}{8}$ in.; w. $\frac{1}{4}$ in.; th. $\frac{1}{16}$ in. No. 1154 c, d and e; Square M 12/16; Depth 15 ft. b.s.
5. Tiny, rectangular steatite seal with 4 pictograms on one side, and a crocodile on the other. Pl. XCVI, 432. Size $\frac{7}{16} \times \frac{5}{16}$ in. No. 1425 Square M 12/16; Depth 16 ft. b.s.
6. Tiny, rectangular steatite seal with 4 pictograms on one side, and a crocodile on the other. Size $\frac{7}{16} \times \frac{1}{4}$ in. No. 3791; Square M 11/20; Depth 17 ft. b.s.
7. Tiny, hemispherical steatite seal with 2 pictograms on its plane face.[1] Pl. XCV, 414. Diam. $\frac{3}{8}$ in. No. 1423; Square M 11/20; Depth 17 ft. b.s.
8. Tiny, rectangular steatite seal with 4 pictograms on one face, and 2 on the other. Pl. XCVI, 487. Size $\frac{5}{8} \times \frac{5}{16}$ in. No. 1419; Square M 11/10; Depth 17 ft. 6 in. b.s.
9. Tiny, four-sided, bar-shaped steatite seal with 3 pictograms on one side, fish on the second, 2 dotted circles on the third, and 2 parallel grooves on the fourth. Pl. XCIX, 635. Size $\frac{1}{2} \times \frac{1}{4} \times \frac{3}{16}$ in. No. 3897; Square M 12/6; Depth 17 ft. 9 in. b.s.
10. Tiny, rectangular faience sealing with 3 pictograms on one side, and 1 on the other. Pl. C, 678. Size $\frac{7}{16} \times \frac{5}{16}$ in. No. 657; Square M 11/15; Depth 16 ft. 6 in. b.s.
11. Discoid, grey stone mace-head, double convex in section. The central hole is splayed out on both sides from $\frac{13}{16}$ to $1\frac{1}{4}$ in. Pl. LXXXIII, 14. Diam. $4\frac{3}{4}$ in. No. 1162; Square M 12/20; Depth 15 ft. b.s.

Southern portion—

1. Bossless,[2] rectangular seal of black steatite showing a man attacking a tiger from a *machān* set up on an acacia tree, and the tail of another tiger. The left part is unfortunately broken. Pl. XCI, 248. L. $\frac{15}{16}$ in.; w. $\frac{9}{16}$ in. No. 1380; Square M 12/12; Depth 14 ft. 9 in. b.s.

---

[1] Such seals have only one face, the round portion with bevelled edge being always roughly cut and meant for inlay.

[2] The preserved part of this seal is apparently more than half the length, and as such it is certain that it had no boss on reverse. This is the only example of its kind at Harappā. At Mohenjo-daro, however, there are six examples of rectangular seals with no boss, five in steatite and one in faience, but five of them are pierced with a small hole across the centre which is not the case with this seal. *Cf.* Mackay in *M. I. C.*, p. 373.

2. Tiny, rectangular steatite seal rounded at one end with 3 pictograms on one side, and 1 on the other. Pl. XCVII, 497. Size $\frac{3}{8}\times\frac{5}{16}$ in. No. 10186; Square M 12/9; Depth 15 ft. 8 in. b.s.
3. Tiny, rectangular steatite seal with 4 pictograms on one side, and 1 on the other, fragmentary. Pl. XCVII, 522. Size $\frac{1}{2}\times\frac{1}{4}$ in. No. 12581; Square M 12/23; Depth 16 ft. 9 in. b.s.
4. Tiny, rectangular steatite seal with 3 pictograms on one side, and 1 on the other. Slightly chipped off on one side. Pl. XCVII, 506. Size $\frac{7}{16}\times\frac{5}{16}$ in. No. 737; Square M 12/13; Depth 18 ft. b.s.
5. Tiny, rectangular faience sealing with 4 pictograms on one side, and 1 on the other. Pl. XCVIII, 604. Size $\frac{3}{8}\times\frac{5}{16}$ in. No. 12549; Square M 12/7; Depth 14 ft. 9 in. b.s.
6. Tiny, rectangular faience sealing with 4 pictograms on one side, and 1 on the other. Pl. XCIV, 361. Size $\frac{3}{8}\times\frac{3}{8}$ in. No. 3789; Square M 12/7; Depth 17 ft. 6 in. b.s.
7. Small ring of copper wire, highly rusted. Diam. $\frac{3}{8}$ in. No. 12580; Square M 12/23; Depth 15 ft. 5 in. b.s.

Section north of the Deep Digging.

A well-built drain of Stratum VII.

In the northern section I shall first describe a well-built paved drain of the VIIth stratum which has been discovered at a depth of 22 ft. along the northern edge of the Deep Digging. It has been traced going from west to east right across the trench and found buried under its edges. It is 1 ft. 7 in. wide and at present stands to a height of about 2 ft. at the centre. With the VIth stratum it was utilised again by raising its walls another 2 ft. At this time, it was also fed by a small drain coming from the north. Its walls, as repaired, were reinforced by a packing of rammed mud from behind. This device might also have been employed to strengthen it originally, but that cannot be ascertained now. Like the large drain to be mentioned below in connection with the excavations in Mound AB,[1] it was found chocked with broken earthenware vases, potsherds, some entire vessels and numerous bones discoloured green. In it was also found a bossed steatite seal (1 in. square) bearing an inscription of 5 pictograms in two lines on the right, and, opposite them, an incense-burner, without any animal, in the left ground[2] (No. 10102, Pl. XCI, 256). In the outer mud packing of the drain, to which I have just referred, was found, in square M 11/11, at a depth of 19 ft. 2 in., a tiny, rectangular steatite seal (No. 1219, size $\frac{1}{4}$ by $\frac{1}{2}$ in.) with 2 pictograms on one side and one on the other (similar to No. 431 in Pl. XCVI).

In the remaining 37 ft. of the northern section, the excavation has generally penetrated up to the Vth stratum only, except at the centre, where over a small

---

[1] See pp. 165-66 *infra*.

[2] Here the incense-burner itself seems to be an object of worship, and as it is peculiarly associated with the unicorn it might symbolise him, in the same manner as the *liṅgam* symbolises the god Śiva. *Cf.* Sir John Marshall, *op. cit.*, p. 69.

space it has gone down to the VIth stratum also. In the western half of this portion, there is a complete room of the IVth stratum measuring 17 by 9 to 10 ft. which was repaired in connection with the IIIrd stratum. To its east is a very much dilapidated brick-on-edge pavement, of which the greater part has sagged. **Stratum IV.**

The following objects of Stratum IV were found scattered in the northern section :— **Finds of Stratum IV.**

1. Unicorn seal with 4 pictograms. Pl. LXXXIX, 125. $\frac{7}{8}$ in. sq. No. 1009; Square M 11/16; Depth 9 ft. b.s.
2. Unicorn seal with 4 pictograms surviving, right part broken. Pl. LXXXVIII, 95. $\frac{11}{16}$ in. sq. No. 2930; Square M 11/21; Depth 10 ft. b.s.
3. Tiny, rectangular steatite seal rounded at the left end. It has 4 pictograms on one face, and 1 on the other. Pl. XCVII, 562. Size $\frac{11}{16}\times\frac{7}{16}$ in. No. 3397; Square M 11/21; Depth 10 ft. 5 in. b.s.
4. Oblong terracotta sealing, lentoid in section, with 4 pictograms on one side, and an anchor[1] on the other. Pl. XCIV, 341. L. $1\frac{3}{8}$ in. No. 10103; Square M 10/25; Depth 7 ft. 6 in. b.s.
5. Seven rectangular terracotta sealings with 4 pictograms on either face, distorted in firing. They are all from the same mould. Pl. XCIV, 343. L. $1\frac{1}{4}$ to $1\frac{1}{2}$ in.; w. $\frac{9}{16}$ to $\frac{47}{100}$ in. No. 1646; Square M 10/15; Depth 9 ft. b.s.
6. Rectangular terracotta sealing with 3 pictograms on one face only, distorted in firing. Pl. XCIV, 366. Size $1\times\frac{7}{8}$ in. No. 2057; Square M 10/20; Depth 11 ft. b.s.
7. Rough, tapering flint axe, unfinished. L. $12\frac{7}{8}$ in.; w. across the cutting edge $5\frac{1}{2}$ in.; w. across the butt end 3 in.; th. $1\frac{1}{4}$ to 2 in. No. 3083; Square M 11/6; Depth 10 ft. b.s.
8. Rectangular granite weight. Wt. 6·95 gms.; size ·8×·5×·4 in. No. 4068; Square M 11/6; Depth 11 ft. b.s.
9. Rectangular amulet of burnt steatite with a pair of holes drilled across the length. Size $1\times\frac{3}{4}\times\frac{5}{16}$ in. No. 715; Square M 11/6; Depth 11 ft. b.s.
10. Copper spoon (in imitation of a river shell) with two holes at the upper edge for suspension. Pl. CXXIV, 32. L. $3\frac{7}{8}$ in.; w. 2 in. No. 10129a, Square M 10/15; Depth 7 ft. 6 in. b.s.

Stratum V.

Some 6 ft. north, and running parallel to the large drain of the VIIth stratum described above, is a thick wall of the Vth stratum whose western part appears to have been raised in connection with the above-mentioned room of the IVth stratum. Against its south face were found resting, one over the other in

[1] It is remarkable that the shape of the anchor is similar to that of a modern fluked anchor. This is the only seal with this device.

two columns, five badly crushed earthenware jars (No. 851, Pl. XXI, *c*), and about 20 ft. further north lay another broken jar of the Vth stratum in which was found a human tibia[1] (No. 3686, Pl. XXIII, *b*). This jar also contained, as usual, a small quantity of tiny bones, two triangular pottery cakes, a small vase, two tiny lids, a discoid paste bead, potsherds, pieces of charcoal and brick-bats.[2] In the eastern half of this section there are but a few fragments of walls which do not call for any remark. The following objects of Stratum V were found in this portion :—

A jar with human tibia.

1. Unicorn seal broken across the upper part. Pl. LXXXVII, 64. 1 in. sq. No. 1720; Square M 10/20; Depth 11 ft. 1 in. b.s.
2. Two rectangular terracotta sealings from the same mould, each with 4 pictograms on one side, and 3 incense-burners[3] alternating with four vertical rows of four circles each on the other; similar to No. 322 in Pl. XCIII. Size 1⅛ × 7/16 in. No. 1791; Square M 10/20; Depth 11 ft. 3 in. b.s.
3. Rectangular faience sealing lentoid in section, with 3 pictograms on one side, and 1 on the other. Slightly bent in firing. Pl. XCIV, 357. Size 11/16 × 3/8 in. No. 3890; Square M 11/6; Depth 11 ft. 4 in. b.s.
4. Fragment of a tiny shield-shaped seal of burnt steatite with 2 pictograms surviving on one face, and 1 on the other. Pl. XCVII, 558. L. 5/8 in. No. 3027; Square M 11/21; Depth 12 ft. b.s.
5. Tiny, rectangular steatite seal with 3 pictograms on one side, and 1 on the other; similar to No. 509 in Pl. XCVII. Size 3/8 × 1/4 in. No. 2056; Square M 10/20; Depth 12 ft. b.s.
6. Tiny, rectangular steatite seal with 2 pictograms on one side, and 1 on the other; similar to No. 502 in Pl. XCVII. Size 1/2 × 1/4 in. No. 1963; Square M 11/11; Depth 12 ft. 4 in. b.s.
7. Tiny, rectangular steatite seal with 3 pictograms on one side, and 1 on the other; similar to No. 508 in Pl. XCVII. Size 7/16 × 5/16 in. No. 2569; Square M 10/20; Depth 12 ft. 6 in. b.s.
8. Tiny, rectangular steatite seal with 3 pictograms on one side, and 1 on the other. Pl. XCVI, 461. Size 11/16 × 5/16 in. No. 3668; Square M 10/15; Depth 13 ft. b.s.
9. Tiny, three-sided prism seal of steatite with 3 pictograms on one side, 1 on the second, and 3 dotted circles on the third; similar to No. 575 in Pl. XCVII. L. 7/16 in.; w. 1/4 in. No. 3509; Square M 11/21; Depth 13 ft. 6 in. b.s.

---

[1] With the exception of the pot-burials from the Cemetery H this is the only jar containing a human bone. The bone is not charred.

[2] For a discussion of the contents of such jars *cf.* Sir John Marshall, *op. cit.*, pp. 86-89. See also Chap. VIII *infra*.

[3] Except the three examples mentioned above, on no other seal or sealing from Harappā or Mohenjo-daro is there more than one incense-burner.

10. Tiny, three-sided prism seal of steatite with 5 pictograms on one side, 4 on the second, and 2 dotted circles on the third. This is rare, not only by reason of the larger number of pictograms on two sides but also for the omission of the usual symbol resembling the Roman numerals VII, VIII, VIIII, or the like. Pl. XCVIII, 584. L. $\frac{11}{16}$ in.; w. $\frac{1}{4}$ in. No. 3508; Square M 11/21; Depth 13 ft. 6 in. b.s.

11. Fragment of a tiny, rectangular steatite seal with 1 pictogram surviving on one side, and the tail of a fish on the other. Pl. XCVII, 533. W. $\frac{3}{8}$ in. No. 3576; Square M 11/21; Depth 14 ft. 6 in. b.s.

12. Discoid faience sealing with 5 pictograms on one side, and 1 on the other. Pl. C, 666. Diam. $\frac{1}{2}$ in. No. 4078; Square M 11/11; Depth 13 ft. 3 in. b.s.

Stratum VI.

In this section there is only one thick wall of the VIth stratum in square M 10/20, and only a portion of it could be uncovered, since it lay buried under a wall of Stratum III. The following finds deserve notice:—

1. Tiny, rectangular steatite seal with 4 pictograms on one side, and 3 on the other. Pl. XCVI, 485. Size $\frac{9}{16}\times\frac{9}{16}$ in. No. 2728; Square M 10/15; Depth 15 ft. b.s.

2. Tiny, oval steatite seal with 3 pictograms on one side, and 1 on the other; similar to No. 542 in Pl. XCVII. Size $\frac{9}{16}\times\frac{5}{16}$ in. No. 2483; Square M 11/11; Depth 15 ft. b.s.

3. Tiny seal similar to No. 2. Size $\frac{5}{16}\times\frac{1}{4}$ in. No. 2366; Square M 10/20; Depth 15 ft. 3 in. b.s.

4. Tiny seal similar to No. 2. Size $\frac{3}{8}\times\frac{5}{16}$ in. No. 2357; Square M 10/20; Depth 15 ft. 3 in. b.s.

5. Tiny seal similar to No. 2. Size $\frac{3}{8}\times\frac{5}{16}$ in. No. 2356; Square M 10/20; Depth 15 ft. 3 in. b.s.

6. Tiny seal similar to No. 2. Size $\frac{3}{8}\times\frac{5}{16}$ in. No. 2355; Square M 10/20; Depth 15 ft. 3 in. b.s.

7. Upper half of a tiny seal similar to No. 2. L. $\frac{5}{16}$ in. No. 2480; Square M 10/15; Depth 15 ft. 3 in. b.s.

8. Tiny, oval steatite seal with 2 pictograms on one side, and 1 on the other, fragmentary. Pl. XCVI, 468. L. $\frac{1}{2}$ in. No. 2632: Square M 11/16; Depth 15 ft. 3 in. b.s.

9. Tiny, rectangular steatite seal with 2 pictograms on one side, and part of one on the other, damaged. Pl. XCVI, 473. Size $\frac{7}{16}\times\frac{1}{4}$ in. No. 2481; Square M 11/16; Depth 15 ft. 8 in. b.s.

10. Tiny, rectangular steatite seal with 4 pictograms on one side, and a crocodile on the other. Pl. XCVI, 434. Size $\frac{9}{16}\times\frac{1}{2}$ in. No. 2542; Square M 11/11; Depth 16 ft. b.s.

11. Tiny, rectangular steatite seal with 4 pictograms on one side and a crocodile on the other; similar to Nos. 430-31, 433-35 in Pl. XCVI. Size $\frac{1}{2}\times\frac{5}{16}$ in. No. 2645; Square M 10/15; Depth 16 ft. b.s.
12. Tiny, rectangular steatite seal with 2 pictograms on one side, and 1 on the other. Pl. XCVII, 501. Size $\frac{1}{2}\times\frac{1}{4}$ in. No. 2544; Square M 11/11; Depth 16 ft. b.s.
13. Tiny, rectangular steatite seal with 6 pictograms on one side, and 3 on the other. It also has two dotted circles[1] on the thickness of each of its longer sides. Pl. XCVII, 573. Size $\frac{7}{8}\times\frac{5}{16}\times\frac{1}{8}$ in. No. 3758; Square M 11/20; Depth 16 ft. b.s.
14. Tiny, oval steatite seal with 3 pictograms on one side, and 1 on the other; similar to No. 543 in Pl. XCVII. Size $\frac{3}{16}\times\frac{3}{16}$ in. No. 2648; Square M 11/16; Depth 16 ft. b.s.
15. Tiny, oval steatite seal with 3 pictograms on one side, and 1 on the other. Pl. XCVII, 548. Size[2] $\frac{5}{16}\times\frac{1}{4}$ in. No. 2642; Square M 11/16; Depth 16 ft. b.s.
16. Tiny, leaf-shaped steatite seal with 2 pictograms on one side, and 4 dotted circles on the other. Pl. XCV, 417. Size $\frac{3}{16}\times\frac{5}{16}$ in. No. 2534; Square M 11/11; Depth 16 ft. 2 in. b.s.
17. Tiny, rectangular steatite seal with 4 pictograms on one side, and a crocodile on the other. Pl. XCVI, 431. Size $\frac{5}{16}\times\frac{1}{4}$ in. No. 614; Square M 11/11; Depth 16 ft. 8 in. b.s.
18. Tiny, rectangular steatite seal with 2 pictograms on one side, and 1 on the other. Pl. XCVII, 503. Size $\frac{5}{16}\times\frac{1}{2}$ in. No. 2698; Square M 10/15; Depth 17 ft. b.s.
19. Cylindrical faience sealing with 3 pictograms on one side, and 2 on the other. Pl. XCVIII, 594. L. $\frac{11}{16}$ in.; diam. $\frac{3}{8}$ in. No. 2543; Square M 11/11; Depth 16 ft. 3 in. b.s.
20. Hornblende pendent deeply grooved at the head and with top rounded. Ht. $\frac{1}{2}$ in. No. 4822; Square M 11/6; Depth 17 ft. 9 in. b.s.
21. Flat-bottomed, oval pottery goblet with high neck and slightly flared mouth. Has deep red slip. Pl. LXXI, 33. Ht. $4\frac{1}{4}$ in.; diam. at rim $2\frac{3}{8}$ in. No. 2485; Square M 10/15; Depth 15 ft. 6 in. b.s.

Trench III.

Shape and depth of the trench.

About 80 ft. north of Trench I, and in the highest part of the eastern section of this mound, were sunk two trenches, each originally measuring 100 by 20 ft. and intersecting each other at the centre at right angles. Later, the whole of the southern area of this cross was linked up, and a further extension 20 ft. wide also made along the south. In its present form, therefore, it is a rectangle measuring 100 ft. from east to west by 80 ft. from north to south with a tongue 40 by 20 ft. projecting from the centre of the north side. The

[1] No other seal of this type is so inscribed.
[2] This is the smallest seal from Harappā.

whole of this excavation has been designated Trench III on the plan (Pl. XXIV). The original arms of its cross, shown by dotted lines, were dug between 11 ft. 6 in. and 22 ft. below the surface, while the rest of it was excavated to an average depth of 8 ft. 4 in. only.

Stratification. In this trench were brought to light the fragmentary remains of seven strata corresponding to those in Trench I, and of these the IVth is relatively better preserved. The Ist stratum goes down to 3 ft. 10 in. below the surface, the IInd to 6 ft., the IIIrd to 7 ft., the IVth to 10 ft., the Vth to 14 ft. 6 in., the VIth to 18 ft. 6 in., and the VIIth to 22 ft. Here, too, the first three strata follow each other in quick succession and are definitely late with but little interval between the IInd and the IIIrd, but in the following strata the interval is more clearly marked.

Stratum I. Of the Ist stratum there is but one bit of wall in square N 9/10 and a broken pavement at the north end of the projecting arm. The following objects were found in this stratum :—

1. Fragmentary unicorn seal without any pictograms. Pl. LXXXVII, 41. Size 1⅜ in. sq. No. 3957; Square N 9/15; Depth 3 ft. b.s.
2. Fragmentary seal with the figure of an elephant. Pictograms all lost. Pl. XCI, 226. 2 in. sq. No. 4824; Square N 10/11; Depth 4 ft. b.s.
3. Cylindrical faience sealing with 2 pictograms on one side, and 1 on the other. Corroded. Pl. XCVIII, 613. L. $\frac{5}{16}$ in. No. 4521; from surface.
4. Cylindrical terracotta sealing with 3 pictograms on one side, and a large acacia tree on the other. Pl. XCIII, 328. L. 1¼ in. No. 4076; Square N 9/19; Depth 3 ft. 6 in. b.s.
5. Alabaster chessman-shaped object. Ht. ⅜ in. No. 4883; from surface.
6. Elliptical bead of burnt steatite, lentoid in section. L. ⅜ in. No. 5131; Square M 10/21; Depth 3 ft. 2 in. b.s.
7. Stone tetrahedron. Ht. 2¾ in.; w. at base 2¼ in. No. 5364; Square M 10/25; Depth 4 ft. b.s.
8. Faience pendent set with copper. It has a long cylindrical knob holed across the end for fixation. Pl. CXXXIX, 25. L. ⅜ in. No. 5030; Square N 10/1; Depth 3 ft. b.s.
9. Chessman-shaped faience object coated with white glaze. Ht. ⅞ in. No. 5627; Squares M 10/21; Depth 4 ft. b.s.
10. Napiform miniature vase of faience. Ht. ½ in. No. 5321; Square M 10/21; Depth 4 ft. b.s.
11. Thick, coarse pottery basin with tapering sides. Ht. 6¼ in.; diam. 13⅜ in. No. 2978; Square N 9/20; Depth 1 ft. b.s.
12. Cocoanut-shaped pottery vase. Ht. 3 in. No. 5124; Square M 10/21; Depth 3 ft. 2 in. b.s.
13. Tapering pottery tumbler with traces of green paint. Ht. 2⅞ in. No. 5323; Square M 10/21 Depth 3 ft. 6 in. b.s.

14. Miniature, tapering pottery tumbler. Ht. 1⅝ in. No. 5135; Square N 10/16; Depth 3 ft. 10 in. b.s.
15. Sherd of a squat, bulgy vase painted with deer (?), fishes, and stars. Pl. LXV, 2. L. 8 in. No. 3098; Square N 9/19; Depth 1 ft. 3 in. b.s.
16. Sherd of a flanged bowl-like cover painted with deer and stars. I have not come across any other vessel of this shape. Its painting and deep red wash and of No. 15 are reminiscent of burial pottery. Pl. LXVI, 45. L. 5¼ in. No. 1179; Square N 9/9; Depth 2 ft. 9 in. b.s.
17. Sherd painted with a tree, dotted circles, etc. Pl. LXVII, 3. L. ·8 in. No. 4689; Square N 10/16; Depth 0 to 3 ft. b.s.
18. Sherd painted with a peacock. This fragment is typical of an ellipsoid burial jar. Pl. LXV, 10. L. 7¾ in. No. 1990; Square M 9; Depth 3 to 6 ft. b.s.
19. Potsherd painted with rows of net patterns undulating downwards. Pl. LXVII, 21. L. 6¾ in. No. 3448; Square M 9; Depth 3 to 6 ft. b.s.

Stratum II.

The IInd stratum is hardly better, being represented by no more than a few broken bits of walls, two of which are of mud. Along the eastern edge of the trench may, however, be noticed a circular granary 2 ft. 10 in. in diameter (Pl. XXV, *a*, to left of the man). In the southern portion, in square N 10/11 were found three broken potsherds at a depth of 5 ft. 2 in. below the surface. The patterns painted on them deserve notice (Pl. LXIX, 1, 3 and 4). Although belonging to the same jar they do not unfortunately join, as some of the intermediate pieces are missing, and the complete scheme of their decoration is not apparent. As much of it as survives is divided into three bands, separated from one another by black lines. The uppermost band takes the form of a deep wavy roll within the undulations of which are chequered objects somewhat resembling wicker-work baskets. The middle band was divided by broad uprights of chess-board and diamond chequer patterns into a number of panels containing trees, human figures, deer and birds. The lowest band, which shows indications of circumscribed four-pointed stars,[1] such as were fretted out of shell, has all but disappeared. To revert to the middle band, one fragment (No. 3) shows in the left hand panel the ends of boughs of a tree with a bird seated on one of them, while the rest of the space is occupied by a doe in front of a plant suckling her young, a cock, a star (?), a fish and a butterfly. In the extreme left of the right hand compartment across the chess-board chequer is a man with one hand raised aloft and the other to his head. Beside him is a child whose arms are half raised, as if in alarm. In the rest of the field are two fishes and a cock. Of the other two sherds, No. 1 merely shows a tree and part of a diamond chequer, and No. 4 a tree, one arm and head of a man, a cobra and a star (?).

Three potsherds with interesting paintings.

---

[1] *Cf. M. I. C.*, Pl. CLV, 48 and 49.

The following stray objects were also found associated with this stratum:—

1. Unicorn seal with 10 pictograms. Pl. LXXXVI, 19. $1\frac{1}{4}$ in sq. No. 3170; Square N 9/5; Depth 5 ft. b.s. **Other finds.**
2. Fragment of a unicorn seal with 2 pictograms. Pl. XC, 217. L. $\frac{3}{4}$ in. No. 5367; Square N 10/6; Depth 6 ft. b.s.
3. Steatite seal broken in the process of manufacture with possibly 3 pictograms. Pl. CI, 699. Size $\frac{7}{8}\times\frac{9}{16}$ in. No. 5219; Square N 10/1; Depth 4 ft. 6 in. b.s.
4. Rectangular faience sealing with 6 pictograms. Pl. XCIV, 367a. Size $1\times\frac{7}{16}$ in. No. 1338; Square N $\frac{9}{16}$; Depth 4 ft. 3 in. b.s.
5. Cylindrical terracotta sealing with 3 pictograms on one side, and a faint acacia tree on the other. Pl. XCIII, 323. L. 1 in. No. 5312; Square M 10/21; Depth 5 ft. 2 in. b.s.
6. Chert core. L. $1\frac{3}{8}$ in. No. 1300; Square N 9/6; Depth 4 ft. b.s.
7. Cuboid chert weight, chipped off. Wt. 26·5 gms.; size 1×·95×·65 in. No. 5380; Square M 10/21; Depth 4 ft. 3 in. b.s.
8. Cuboid chert weight, chipped off. Wt. 129·3 gms.; size 1·55×1·55×1·25 in. No. 7099; Square N 9/10; Depth 4 ft. 3 in. b.s.
9. Cuboid chert weight. Wt. 3·4 gms.; size ·45×·45×·4 in. No. 5461; Square M 10/21; Depth 5 ft. 6 in. b.s.
10. Plum-shaped, soapstone ear-drop. L. $\frac{11}{16}$ in. No. 5382; Square N 10/6; Depth 5 ft. 6 in. b.s.
11. Cuboid granite weight. Wt. 53·9 gms.; size 1·6×1·05×·8 in.[1] No. 5448; Square N 10/6; Depth 6 ft. b.s.
12. Faience chessman-shaped object with green glaze. Ht. $\frac{13}{16}$ in. No. 5325; Square N 10/6; Depth 5 ft. 6 in. b.s.
13. Goblet-shaped ivory terminal pierced with a vertical hole. Pl. CXIX, 7. Ht. $1\frac{1}{4}$ in. No. 5449; Square N 10/6; Depth 5 ft. b.s.
14. Cocoanut-shaped pottery vase. Ht. $2\frac{3}{8}$ in. No. 5462; Square M 10/21; Depth 5 ft. 6 in. b.s.
15. Inscribed potsherd. Pl. CII, 18. No. 4171; Square N 9; Depth 3 to 6 ft. b.s.

Stratum III. Of the IIIrd stratum there are several broken walls, coming mostly in the western two-thirds of the main trench. In square N 10/1 is a broken pavement over which was found a pottery group (No. 5630), between 5 ft. 6 in. and 8 ft. below the surface. At its top came a large and badly crushed jar containing a goblet with pointed base, three fragmentary, cylindrical vases, some nodules, and tiny pieces of bones. Below them were three medium-sized *gharās* including two badly crushed ones, four goblets with pointed bases, five cylindrical vases of different sizes, two animal toys, fragments of pottery bangles, cakes, and potsherds. The only preserved *gharā* in this group was full of small, unbaked clay tetrahedrons rounded and holed at each end. Some of these had been crushed under the weight of others. This *gharā* also contained a few

Pottery group No. 5630.

[1] Two of its dimensions are a bit unusual as the top and bottom are usually square or nearly so.

tiny bones. Two discoid paste beads and a faience sealing were found mixed in the débris of this group. Still further down, the third layer consisted of a medium-sized *ghaṛā*, a squat pot, two goblets with pointed bases, three oval and four cylindrical vases, a terracotta cone, etc.

Pottery group No. 5723.

Twenty-two feet west of the above and close to the south-west edge of the trench was found another group of pottery (No. 5723, Pl. XXV, *b*) in square M 10/21 at a depth of 5 to 7 ft. below the surface. It consisted of a number of plain and painted vases, a toy bull, one chert scraper, beads, broken bangles, and fallen bricks. Among the painted vases are one complete and seven fragmentary tapering tumblers, one complete and four fragmentary elegant goblets, and five cocoanut-shaped vases with just a hole at the top as in the natural fruit. With the exception of two tumblers and a goblet which are coated with a green slip, the surface of others is painted white. Some of the latter wares are polychrome and have leafy decoration executed in green and red pigments over white ground (*e.g.*, Pl. LXXI, 23).

Abundance of potsherds and earthenware jars.

With this stratum potsherds were found in great abundance, and a number of broken jars were noticed resting generally against bits of walls in the south-west part of the trench. Among the latter may be mentioned a crushed, earthenware trough (No. 7867)—since joined—from square N 9/10 which lay at a depth of 6 ft. 4 in. below the surface. It is the largest trough yet found at Harappâ, being 2 ft. 9¼ in. high, and 2 ft. 5¼ in. in diameter. Like other troughs, it is painted with black bands and had the more or less usual contents which are typical of the post-cremation urns.[1]

Finds.

The following objects were found scattered in Stratum III :—

1. Unicorn seal with 5 pictograms. Pl. LXXXVIII, 83. 1$\frac{1}{16}$ in. sq. No. 1591 ; Square N 9/3 ; Depth 6 ft. 9 in. b.s.
2. Rectangular faience sealing with 6 pictograms ; similar to No. 367a in Pl. XCIV. Size $\frac{13}{16} \times \frac{5}{16}$ in. No. 1399 ; Square N 9/10 ; Depth 6 ft. b.s.
3. Rectangular and plano-convex terracotta sealing with very faint inscription. Pl. XCIV, 367. L. 1 in. No. 5622 ; Square M 10/21 ; Depth 6 ft. 2 in. b.s.
4. Cylindrical terracotta sealing with 4 pictograms on one side, and an acacia tree on the other. Pl. XCIV, 329. L. 1$\frac{3}{8}$ in. No. 4129 ; Square N 9/20 ; Depth 6 ft. 6 in. b.s.
5. Ill-baked, discoid terracotta sealing with faint inscription on both sides. Pl. C, 662. Diam. $\frac{5}{8}$ in. No. 5621 ; Square N 10/1 ; Depth 6 ft. 9 in. b.s.
6. Ovoid bead of bluish white stone mottled red, lentoid in section. L. $\frac{13}{16}$ in. No. 5456 ; Square N 10/6 ; Depth 6 ft. 4 in. b.s.
7. Hornblende pendent, deeply grooved at the head. Ht. $\frac{5}{8}$ in. No. 5719 ; Square N 10/1 ; Depth 6 ft. 9 in. b.s.
8. Barrel-shaped, unfinished bead of banded agate. L. $\frac{3}{4}$ in. No. 5670 ; Square M 10/21 ; Depth 7 ft. b.s.

---

[1] For its shape and contents see pp. 262-63 *infra*.

9. Tiny, faience squirrel sitting with tail upturned and eating a fruit held in its forepaws.[1] Ht. $\frac{3}{8}$ in. No. 3248; Square N 9/4; Depth 6 ft. b.s.
10. Faience squirrel, neck and forelegs broken. No. 5624; Square N 10/1; Depth 6 ft. 11 in. b.s.
11. Chessman-shaped object of faience with green glaze. Holed on the underside. Ht. $1\frac{1}{8}$ in. No. 5665; Square M 10/21; Depth 7 ft. b.s.
12. Biconical gold bead. L. $\frac{3}{4}$ in. No. 4247; Square N 9/19; Depth 6 ft. 6 in. b.s.
13. Chessman-shaped object of shell, burnt. Ht. $1\frac{1}{3}$ in. No. 5665; Square M 10/21; Depth 7 ft. b.s.
14. Squat, biconvex pottery vase painted horizontally with alternate rows of dots and bands. Pl. LXIX, 7. Ht. $4\frac{5}{8}$ in.; diam. at mouth 3·1 in.; diam. at centre 5·7 in. No. 3281; Square N 9/5; Depth 6 ft. 9 in. b.s.

Stratum IV. We now come to the IVth stratum in which there are definite traces of buildings almost everywhere over rather more than the southern half of this trench (Pl. XXIV). Right down at the centre is the fragmentary House 1, consisting of two rooms (Nos. 1 and 2) on the north, a narrow room (No. 3), **Houses 1 and 2.** of which the greater portion has perished, and part of a fine pavement on the east, and the remains of a courtyard (No. 4) at the south-west. Rooms 1 and 2 are each 6 ft. 10 in. wide internally, the former being 10 ft. and the latter 8 ft. 6 in. long. The width of this house is 23 ft. 6 in.; the length can no longer be determined. In room No. 2 were found a rectangular, plano-convex steatite seal inscribed with three pictograms (No. 4396, Pl. XCII, 285) and a couchant, faience ram (No. 4622) bored across the neck for suspension. The latter got slightly distorted in the firing. In room No. 1 was found a pear-shaped pottery vase with flat bottom painted with a series of black bands (Pl. LXXI, 30), and in the courtyard an interesting terracotta toy of a female figure kneading dough in a shallow, rectangular vessel (No. 1668, Pl. LXXVI, 23.) Immediately to its east and separated by a narrow passage or perhaps a lane, which is but barely indicated, are the remains of another house (No. 2), of which the west wall is seen close to the broken jar in Pl. XXV, *a*. The adjoining corner, which stands highest, is not bonded with the west wall, nor is the wall behind it, but there is no doubt that both of them were built in connection with this house. Contemporary with this is a broken corner further east, and to the west of House 1 three corners, and a broken and covered drain in square M 9/24. In the western part, in square N 9/4 was found a large napiform jar (No. 3925) at a depth of 11 ft. 3 in. below the surface. It is 3 ft. high and 1 ft. **Jar No. 3925.** 4 in. in diameter at the mouth. Like other jars, it is washed red and painted with black bands. On examination, it was found to contain 7 complete and 48 fragmentary goblets with pointed bases, 7 cylindrical vases, and numerous

[1] This invariably is the pose of squirrels found at Harappā or Mohenjo-daro, *cf.* Sir John Marshall, *op. cit.*, p. 43, Pl. XCVI, 7.

fragments of cylindrical, long oval, and other vases, triangular cakes, balls, tiny lids, and toys, 2 river shells, 2 fragments of an ivory rod, much hardened animal bones, and traces of decayed grain.[1]

Finds. The following interesting objects were also picked up from the IVth stratum :—

1. Unicorn seal with 3 pictograms. Pl. LXXXVIII, 74. 1 in. sq. No. 5810, Square N 10/16; Depth 9 ft. 6 in. b.s.
2. *Svastika* faience sealing; similar to No. 399 in Pl. XCV. 5/8 in. sq. No. 4226; Square N 9/15; Depth 8 ft. 2 in. b.s.
3. Triangular inlay object of finely ribbed steatite with chamfered edges and two keyholes on the underside for fixation. Pl. CXXXIX, 71. It is similar to some of the objects recovered from the well in Trench IV.[2] L. across 1¼ in. No. 5808; Square M 10/21; Depth 7 ft. 4 in. b.s.
4. Tooth-shaped bead of burnt steatite. Pl. CXXVIII, 29. L. 3/16 in. No. 2250; Square N 9/13; Depth 7 ft. 6 in. b.s.
5. Large, grey sandstone *liṅgam* rough on the underside. Pl. CXVII, 5. It is larger than the *liṅgam* found previously in Trench Ai in this mound, and smaller than No. 12466 from Trench I. Ht. 15¼ in.; diam. 9 in. No. 3463; Square M 9/25; Depth 7 ft. 10 in. b.s.
6. Alabaster ear-button. L. 3/4 in. No. 4174; Square N 9/20; Depth 8 ft. b.s.
7. Large currystone. L. 1 ft. 5 in. No. 4225; Square N 9/15; Depth 8 ft. 5 in. b.s.
8. Cuboid chert weight. Wt. 6·62 gms.; size ·55×·55×·45 in. No. 5946; Square M 10/21; Depth 8 ft. 7 in. b.s.
9. Granite disc. Pl. CXX, 60. Diam. 1⅜ in. No. 4292; Square N 9/15; Depth 9 ft. 6 in. b.s.
10. Large currystone. L. 2 ft. No. 6018; Square M 10/21; Depth 9 ft. 8 in. b.s.
11. Stone pestle. L. 9 in. No. 6019; Square N 10/6; Depth 10 ft. b.s.
12. Cog-wheel-shaped faience nose-disc. Pl. CXXXIX, 18. Diam. ⅞ in. No. 2123; Square N 9/13; Depth 7 ft. 2 in. b.s.
13. Faience ear-stud. Pl. CXXXIX, 28. L. 7/16 in. No. 5566; Square N 10/6; Depth 7 ft. 4 in. b.s.
14. Heart-shaped faience pendent. Pl. CXXXIX, 5. L. 13/16 in. No. 1682; Square M 9/23; Depth 8 ft. b.s.
15. Cog-wheel-shaped paste nose-disc. Diam. 7/16 in. No. 5718; Square N 10/6; Depth 8 ft. 4 in. b.s.
16. Two extremely fragmentary but identical ivory cones with flat horizontal rim at the base. On the underside each of them has at the centre a rectangular, vertical hole 1½×⅜ in. reaching up to the apex, and this is bisected at right angles by a round hole bored through

[1] These contents are typical of the post-cremation burial urns, see Chap. VIII *infra*.

[2] For the description of the above objects see p. 61 *supra*.

the body just above the rim. May have been used as *chauks*, or conical ornaments for the head. Pl. CXXXVIII, 24 and 25. Ht. 1¾ in. and 1 3/16 in.; diam. 2 7/16 in. No. 5722; Square M 10/21; Depth 7 ft. 1 in. b.s.

17. Small shell spoon. Pl. LXXXII, 3. L. 2 in. No. 5805; Square N 10/1; Depth 8 ft. 8 in. b.s.

Pottery objects—

18. Three (fragmentary) tapering tumblers with traces of white slip. They are similar to those found in the pottery group No. 5723 described above. Ht. 3¼, 3¼ and 2 in. No. 5806; Square M 10/21; Depth 7 ft. 8 in. b.s.
19. Small goblet with pointed base. Body scored. Ht. 2¼ in. No. 5870; Square M 10/21; Depth 8 ft. 2 in. b.s.
20. Biconvex vase with flat bottom. Pl. LXXI, 47. Ht. 5¼ in. No. 5945; Square M 10/21; Depth 8 ft. 8 in. b.s.
21. Cup with 2 handles; cf. Pl. LXXI, 64. Diam. 2¼ in. No. 4338; Square N 9/20; Depth 10 ft. b.s.
22. Whistling hen. Ht. 2¾ in. No. 5567; Square N 10/6; Depth 7 ft. 4 in. b.s.
23. Hand-made cage. Pl. CXX, 25. Ht. 2¼ in. No. 4173; Square N 9/20; Depth 8 ft. b.s.
24. Ball rattle from a very fragmentary round jar. Diam. 1⅜ in. No. 7823; Square N 10/1; Depth 9 ft. b.s.

Strata V and VI. As already stated, only the original cross trench was dug deeper, and therefore Strata V to VII are confined to that portion alone. In the northern arm, and at the centre of the original cross are seen one fairly well preserved corner, and four or five fragments of walls of the Vth stratum between the foundation of which and that of the IVth there is a distinct interval. At a lower level were found two walls of the VIth stratum, one in the southern arm of the abovementioned cross, and the other in the northern arm, but the latter is buried below the corner of the Vth stratum. The following finds were made in connection with these strata :—

Vth stratum—

1. Unicorn seal with 2 pictograms. Pl. LXXXIX, 124. 15/16 in. sq. No. 2531; Square N 9/13; Depth 10 ft. 4 in. b.s.
2. Unicorn seal very much chipped off, only 2 pictograms surviving. Pl. XC, 177. 1 1/16 in. sq. No. 1962; Square N 9/7; Depth 11 ft. b.s.
3. Unicorn seal with 2 pictograms. Pl. LXXXVI, 29. 1¼ in. sq. No. 1842; Square N 9/10; Depth 12 ft. b.s.
4. Fragment of a unicorn seal with 4 pictograms. Pl. LXXXIX. 153. L. ⅞ in. No. 2786; Square N 9/18; Depth 13 ft. 2 in. b.s.

5. Thick, unfinished seal of black soapstone engraved with the figure of a unicorn. The upper field is plain, and the legend is inscribed on the thickness of the upper and left sides. In the impression in both cases there is a blank space at the right end of the inscription suggesting that the script was written from right to left.[1] Pl. LXXXIX, 123. $\frac{7}{8}$ in. sq. No. 2785; Square N 9/13; Depth 14 ft. b.s.
6. Unicorn seal, pictograms broken away. Pl. XC, 182. $\frac{11}{16}$ in. sq. No. 2811; Square N 9/13; Depth 14 ft. 4 in. b.s.
7. Tiny, rectangular steatite seal inscribed on both faces, fragmentary. Pl. XCVI, 475. Size $\frac{11}{16} \times \frac{3}{8}$ in. No. 2730; Square N 9/13; Depth 13 ft. 4 in. b.s.
8. Slatestone ring with undulating top. Diam. $2\frac{3}{4}$ in. No. 2517; Square N 9/18; Depth 10 ft. 2 in. b.s.
9. Oval steatite bead, lentoid in section. Size $1\frac{1}{8} \times \frac{7}{8}$ in. No. 1910; Square N 9/7; Depth 11 ft. b.s.
10. Shuttle-shaped stone burnisher, broken. Pl. CXVIII, 36. L. $2\frac{3}{4}$ in. No. 1849; Square N 9/9; Depth 11 ft. 3 in. b.s.
11. Yellow Jaisalmer stone frustum of a cone with a tube-drill hole at the top. Ht. $1\frac{13}{16}$ in.; diam. $1\frac{1}{16}$ in. No. 2681; Square N 9/18; Depth 11 ft. 6 in. b.s.
12. Stone chessman-shaped object, holed on the underside. Ht. $\frac{7}{8}$ in. No. 4477; Square N 9/20; Depth 11 ft. 6 in. b.s.
13. Forepart of a stone mongoose, broken. Pl. LXXVIII, 25. L. $6\frac{1}{4}$ in. No. 2086; Square N 9/8; Depth 13 ft. 6 in. b.s.
14. Plano-convex, discoid temple ornament of shell of which it is the only example at Harappā. It is holed on the underside precisely like those of faience and steatite.[2] Diam. $1\frac{3}{8}$ in. No. 4690; Square N 9/20; Depth 11 ft. 6 in. b.s.
15. Pottery cup on a short stand with three equidistant holes below the rim. Pl. LXXI, 84. Ht. 2 in. No. 4626; Square N 9/15; Depth 10 ft. 6 in. b.s.
16. Discoid, convex terracotta temple ornament decorated with two concentric rows of dots along the rim. Knobbed at the centre. Diam. $2\frac{1}{4}$ in. No. 4183; Square M 9/23; Depth 10 ft. 11 in. b.s.

VIth stratum—

1. Broken unicorn seal with only 5 pictograms surviving. Pl. LXXXVII, 67. $1\frac{1}{8}$ in. sq. No. 2118; Square N 9/9; Depth 15 ft. b.s.
2. Unicorn seal with only 3 pictograms surviving. Pl. LXXXIX, 159. $\frac{3}{4}$ in. sq. No. 2121; Square N 9/9; Depth 15 ft. b.s.

---

[1] This was the usual direction of Indus writing. *Cf.* Sir John Marshall, *op. cit.*, p. 40.

[2] For its hole *cf. M. I. C.*, Pl. CLV, 6.

3. Unicorn seal (broken) with only one pictogram surviving. The size of this seal is unusual for such depth. Pl. LXXXV, 11. 1 13/16 in. sq. No. 2253; Square N 9/9; Depth 15 ft. 3 in. b.s.
4. Unicorn seal (broken) with only 2 pictograms left. Pl. LXXXVII, 59. 1 3/16 in. sq. No. 2254; Square N 9/9; Depth 15 ft. 3 in. b.s.
5. Unicorn seal fragment. Pl. XC, 192. L. 3/4 in. No. 2259; Square N 9/9; Depth 15 ft. 3 in. b.s.
6. Bit of a unicorn seal. Pl. XC, 208. No. 2694; Square N 9/9; Depth 15 ft. 3 in. b.s.
7. Unicorn seal (broken) with only 3 pictograms surviving. Pl. LXXXIX, 140. 1 in. sq. No. 2390; Square N 9/10; Depth 15 ft. 5 in. b.s.
8. Unicorn seal fragment. Pl. LXXXVI, 32. 1 1/4 in. sq. No. 2392; Square N 9/9; Depth 15 ft. 5 in. b.s.
9. Unicorn seal, upper part broken. Pl. LXXXIX, 127. 13/16 in. sq. No. 2476; Square N 9/9; Depth 15 ft. 10 in. b.s.
10. Unicorn seal (fragment) with trace of only one pictogram. Pl. XC, 197. 11/16 in. sq. No. 2530; Square N 9/9; Depth 10 ft. 4 in. b.s.
11. Unicorn seal with the upper part and left lower corner broken. Pl. LXXXVII, 62. 1 1/16 in. sq. No. 2255; Square N 9/9; Depth 16 ft. 3 in. b.s.
12. Unicorn seal with only 2 pictograms surviving. Pl. LXXXIX, 146. 13/16 in. sq. No. 2532; Square N 9/9; Depth 17 ft. 6 in. b.s.
13. Unfinished, bossless seal with 4 pictograms. Pl. XCI, 260. 1 in. sq. No. 2731; Square N 9/8; Depth 18 ft. 6 in. b.s.
14. Tiny, rectangular steatite seal rounded at one end. It is inscribed with 5 pictograms on one side, and 1 on the other. Pl. XCV, 404. Size 13/20×3/10 in. No. 2257; Square N 9/9; Depth 15 ft. 3 in. b.s.
15. Tiny, rectangular steatite seal (fragmentary) inscribed on both sides. Pl. XCVII, 528. W. 5/16 in. No. 2477; Square N 9/9; Depth 15 ft. 8 in. b.s.
16. Tiny, rectangular steatite seal with 3 pictograms on one side, and 1 on the other. Pl. XCVI, 463. Size 3/8×5/16 in. No. 2431; Square N 9/10; Depth 16 ft. 4 in. b.s.
17. Tiny, rectangular steatite seal with 3 pictograms on one side, and 1 on the other; similar to No. 508 in Pl. XCVII. Size 3/8×1/4 in. No. 2696; Square N 9/9; Depth 16 ft. 6 in. b.s.
18. Tiny, triangular prism seal of steatite with 4 pictograms on one side, 1 on the second, and 3 dotted circles on the third. Pl. XCVIII, 582. L. 1/2 in. No. 2528; Square N 9/10; Depth 17 ft. 10 in. b.s.
19. Tiny, triangular prism seal of steatite with 5 pictograms on one side, 1 on the second, and a diagonal cross on the third. Pl. XCVIII, 581. L. 5/8 in. No. 2429; Square N 9/3; Depth 18 ft. 5 in. b.s.

20. Rectangular faience sealing with 3 pictograms on one side, and 1 on the other. Pl. XCIV, 353. Size $\frac{3}{4} \times \frac{3}{8}$ in. No. 2177; Square N 9/9; Depth 15 ft. 2 in. b.s.
21. Rectangular faience sealing with 4 pictograms on either side. Pl. XCIV, 356. Size $\frac{5}{16} \times \frac{1}{4}$ in. No. 2270; Square N 9/3; Depth 16 ft. 2 in. b.s.
22. Rectangular faience sealing with 4 pictograms on one side, and 1 on the other; broken at one end. Pl. XCIV, 354. W. $\frac{7}{16}$ in. No. 2478; Square N 9/10; Depth 16 ft. 5 in. b.s.
23. Cylindrical faience sealing with 3 pictograms on one side, and an acacia tree on the other. Pl. XCIX, 650. L. $\frac{1}{2}$ in. No. 2697; Square N 9/9; Depth 11 ft. 6 in. b.s.
24. Wedge-shaped faience sealing with 3 pictograms on one side, and 1 on the other. Pl. C, 682. L. $\frac{9}{16}$ in. No. 2325; Square N 9/3; Depth 16 ft. 9 in. b.s.
25. Oblong terracotta sealing, plano-convex in section, showing on one side a man carrying a large incense-burner along which are 3 pictograms, and on the other an incense-burner on either side of which are 2 pictograms. The incense-burner,[1] be it noted, is precisely similar to what is found under the neck of unicorns. Pl. XCIII, 309. L. $1\frac{1}{8}$ in. No. 2262; Square N 9/3; Depth 14 ft. 8 in. b.s.
26. Tiny faience fish. Pl. LXXVIII, 20. L. 1 in. No. 2391; Square N 9/10; Depth 15 ft. 9 in. b.s.
27. Oval pottery vase with flared mouth and flat bottom. Lower part rough. Ht. $8\frac{1}{4}$ in. No. 2330; Square N 9/6; Depth 15 ft. 9 in. b.s.

Explanation of the preponderance of unicorn seals.

It will be observed that among the seals from the Vth and VIth strata there is quite a large number of the unicorn ones which are not usually found at such a depth. With the exception of seal No. 1842,[2] however, they are all either broken or unfinished, some of them being mere fragments; and the seal No. 1842, moreover, is also much worn. The uselessness of the above unicorn seals coupled with the manner in which they were found intermixed with large dumps of nodules, potsherds, etc., thrown in as filling for the foundations of the IVth stratum easily explains how they found their way to such a great depth. This explanation is further confirmed by the fact that most of them were found in the western and southern arms of the original trench where the filling is more abundant. Another thing which also points to the same conclusion is that whereas the unicorn seals are broken, the tiny ones, which are usually associated with the Vth and VIth strata, are generally entire despite their delicate fabric. It may therefore be assumed that, unlike the unicorn seals, the tiny seals could not have been thrown in at a later time.

---

[1] This, among others, is one of the sealings which clearly suggests that the incense-burner itself was an object of worship or veneration. *Cf.* Sir John Marshall, *op. cit.*, p. 69.

[2] Serial No. 3 of Stratum V.

Stratum VII.

Only one wall of the VIIth stratum was recovered in the southern arm of the original trench at a depth of about 21 ft., but, owing to the edges being treacherous, it had to be covered up again. The following four antiquities are assignable to this stratum :—

1. Unfinished, bossless steatite seal with indistinct pictograms. Pl. XC, 225. $\frac{11}{16}$ in. sq. No. 2394 ; Square N 9/3 ; Depth 20 ft. b.s.
2. Tiny, rectangular steatite seal with 3 pictograms on one side, and 1 on the other ; similar to No. 508 in Pl. XCVII. Size $\frac{7}{16} \times \frac{1}{4}$ in. No. 2569 ; Square N 9/10 ; Depth 19 ft. b.s.
3. Tiny, rectangular steatite seal, broken and chipped, with only 1 pictogram surviving. W. $\frac{3}{8}$ in. No. 2631 ; Square N 9/9 ; Depth 19 ft. 3 in. b.s.
4. Tiny, rectangular steatite seal with 3 pictograms on one side, and 1 on the other. Pl. XCVII, 508. Size $\frac{7}{16} \times \frac{1}{4}$ in. No. 2568 ; Square N 9/10 ; Depth 19 ft. 6 in. b.s.

Trench VI.

Locale and extent of the trench.

Due east of Trenches I and III, and at a considerably lower level in the eastern slope of this mound, was sunk a large trench measuring 318 ft. long from north to south by 65 ft. wide on the average, but in the southern 53 ft. its average width diminishes to 49 ft. only. Along its eastern edge, which is appreciably lower than the opposite one, were sunk two subsidiary trenches called Extension I and Extension II, each going towards the east and terminating at the foot of the mound. Of these, Extension I is 73 ft. long by 42 ft. wide and Extension II is 56 ft. long and 25 ft. wide. The whole of the main trench together with the subsidiary extensions has been named Trench VI (Pl. XXVI). The configuration of the ground covered by it varies a great deal. Although at this point the slope of the mound is greatest towards the east, it is also quite marked towards the north, while towards the south, which is only a continuation of the eastern foot of the mound, the surface is generally low (between 532 and 534 ft. above the mean sea-level).

Configuration.

Higher and lower portions of the trench and their stratification.

Leaving out the southern 120 ft. of the trench, a 30 ft. wide strip along its western edge was found to be generally higher than the rest of it, but even here there is a gradual slope both ways from the centre (Pl. XXVI, section on AB). For the purpose of stratification, therefore, the high western strip mentioned above has to be taken separately from the rest of the main trench in which five strata of occupation have been uncovered so far. Although here the excavation has gone lower than the present silted-up bed of the *Sukhrāvā*, the virgin soil has not been reached yet. In the raised portion, Stratum I goes down to 4 ft., II to 6 ft., III to about 9 ft., IV to 11 ft., and V lower than 11 ft., whereas over the remainder of the trench Stratum I goes down to 2 ft., II to $4\frac{1}{2}$ ft., III to $7\frac{1}{2}$ ft., IV to 10 ft., and V below 10 ft. Let me, however, add that at this spot the above limits of Strata I and II are a little misleading, since actually there is not much difference between the levels from which they rise, especially in the higher portion at the centre. Indeed, it is often difficult to distinguish

Confusion between Strata I and II.

them from one another, the apparent difference in their level being merely due to their depth below the surface which has no relation to the level of their foundation. Their remnants in the northern and central sections of the trench can hardly be correlated, and a certain amount of arbitrary distinction has therefore been unavoidable (Pl. XXVII, *b*, background). On the other hand, there

Clear interval between the remaining strata.

is a distinct interval between the IInd and IIIrd strata as clearly indicated by the walls, and the position of earthenware jars in the northern portion of this trench (Pl. XXVIII, *c*). Nor is there any confusion between the two lower strata. The three upper strata are comparatively fragmentary, but were nevertheless prolific in portable finds. Of these, the first two are of poor construction and definitely late. They may be taken to correspond with the three upper strata in the remaining trenches all of which were sunk from much higher levels.

Reason for excavating here.

Before proceeding to give a detailed description of this trench, let me state that this lower part was excavated in the hope that here it might be possible to avoid some of the superficial strata which are necessarily met with everywhere in the higher parts of this mound, and at the same time to penetrate more quickly to the better class buildings such as the Great Granary. This hope was only partly realised. In the IVth stratum we brought to light the eastern part of the large house No. 1 (Pl. XV, *b*) described below, which is encumbered only by a few unconnected walls of Strata II and III (Pl. XXVIII, *a*). On the other hand, its western part, coming, as it does, under the raised part of this trench, is broken or much interfered with by many mutilated structures of Strata I to III.

Stratum I.

Stratum I is represented in the middle and northern sections only. It consists of a few fragmentary walls and two circular granaries both situated in square O 10/24, of which the complete one is 3 ft. 1 in. in diameter and survives to a height of 3 ft. 3 in. (Pl. XXVIII, *a*). The following finds were associated with this stratum :—

1. Unicorn seal with 5 pictograms, fragmentary. Pl. LXXXVII, 52. $1\frac{3}{8}$ in. sq. No. 11369; from the surface of the mound.
2. Lower part of a unicorn seal showing the animal and part of the incense-burner. Pl. LXXXVII, 65. $1\frac{1}{16}$ in. sq. No. 11163; Square P 10/5; Depth 2 ft. b.s.
3. Fragment of a unicorn seal with 4 pictograms only. Pl. XC, 211. $\frac{3}{4}$ in. sq. No. 11233; Square O 10/19; Depth 3 ft. b.s.
4. Rectangular, plano-convex steatite seal with only 5 pictograms surviving, right half broken. Pl. XCIX, 634. L. $\frac{11}{16}$ in. No. 10831; Square O 10/21; Depth 2 ft. 3 in. b.s.
5. Tiny, rectangular steatite seal rounded at one end, and inscribed with 4 pictograms on one face only. Unfinished. Pl. XCVII, 563. Size $\frac{5}{8}\times\frac{3}{8}$ in. No. 12104; Square O 11/23; Depth 1 ft. b.s.
6. Tiny, rectangular steatite piece cut into the shape of a seal. Size $\frac{11}{16}\times\frac{5}{16}$ in. No. 11012; Square O 9/22; Depth 2 ft. b.s.
7. Exquisitely finished, oval bead of banded agate, lentoid in section. Pl. CXXVIII, 34. L. 1 in. No. 10820; Square O 10/21; Depth 1 ft. b.s.

8. Red sandstone cubical die marked with 1 opposite 2, 3 opposite 5, and 4 opposite 6.[1] Pl. CXX, 52. Side 1¼ in. No. 11201: Square O 9/18; Depth 2 ft. 3 in. b.s.
9. Double-convex, discoid limestone mace-head, damaged at the edge. Diam. 3⅝ in. No. 11000; Square O 9/23; Depth 3 ft. 6 in. b.s.
10. Cuboid chert weight. Wt. 13·8 gms.; size ·75×·75×·55 in. No. 10942; Square O 10/23; Depth 3 ft. 10 in. b.s.
11. Low copper ring-stand with concave moulding at the base. Pls. CXXII, 29, and CXXIV, 33. Diam. 3⅞ in. No. 10824; Square P 9/3; Depth 8 in. b.s.
12. Leaf-shaped, double edged copper dagger with raised mid-rib,[2] and three holes for fixation including one at the far end of the tang. Pl. CXXIV, 49. L. 11½ in.; w. 2 7/16 in. No. 10916; Square O 10/21; Depth 2 ft. 6 in. b.s.
13. Curved, copper knife blade, broken. Pl. CXXV, 31. L. 3 7/16 in. No. 10881; Square O 10/24; Depth 3 ft. 10 in b.s.
14. Tiny, barrel-shaped gold bead, distorted. L. 3/16 in. No. 11250; Square O 9/26; from surface.
15. Trough-shaped pottery cup with pointed base, painted with a series of black bands. Ht. 2⅜ in. No. 10600; Square P 9/3; Depth 1 ft. 6 in. b.s.
16. Pottery wheel inscribed with a symbol resembling IV. Diam. 1⅝ in. No. 11211; Square O 10/16; Depth 3 ft. b.s.

Stratum II. Fragmentary nature of remains.

The IInd stratum has many more fragmentary remains than the 1st, confined mostly to the raised belt along the western edge of the trench. They comprise a number of broken pavements and drains, two rooms, one in square O 10/18 and 19, and the other in squares O 9/20 and 25—and a circular paved manger in square O 10/18, which is 3 ft. 2 in. in diameter, and lined, as usual, with standing bricks. In addition to these, there are a few more fragmentary pavings and bits of walls which are widely scattered over the remaining portion of the trench.

Pottery group, etc., in a small room.

In the northern room (square O 9/20 and 25), of which the construction is very poor, were found together a medium-sized biconvex vase—painted with a tree, birds, cross-hatched net patterns, etc.—, a broken standard dish, a vase of rough make, one goblet, a dish, one biconvex and two *hāṇḍi*-shaped vases, a goblet with pointed base, an oval jar, fragments of two long oval vases, and broken bits of animal bones among which was a piece of a jaw. Some of the bones were charred and at one point the earth was ashy. A little above these objects were recovered a saucer-like copper lid (Pls. CXXII, 31, and CXXIV, 34), some fragments of a copper rod, and a unicorn seal[3] (Pl. XCIX, 615). About

[1] For the arrangement of marks on Mohenjo-daro dice which are all of terracotta, *cf.* Mackay in *M. I. C.*, pp. 551-52.

[2] This is one of the rare weapons with a clear mid-rib from Harappā. No such example is known from Mohenjo-daro.

[3] The last three things are numbered 11296 *a* to *c*.

30 ft. north of this room were found, in squares O 9/18 and 23, 59 tiny, socketted cone frustums, mostly of hornblende, 11 plano-convex bead-like tops of the above, a hornblende pendent grooved at the head, 3 tiny stone balls, 20 miscellaneous beads, a terracotta conical *liṅgam*, a copper chisel, one rod, and a terminal of the same substance—all within 1 ft. and 4 ft. 4 in. below the surface (No. 11116 *a* to *g*). Nearby again, were found at a depth of 4 to 6 ft. 5 more conical grey stone frustums of which No. 11178 has a holed disc of burnt steatite fixed with cement on the top. This latter shows how the holed, plano-convex bead-like members mentioned above were fixed at the head of frustums. With these were also recovered two barrel-shaped beads—one of steatite and the other of carnelian—a round faience bead, a charred ivory stilus (11061*a*), a tiny, leaf-shaped faience sealing (No. 11330, Pl. XCIX, 644) with 4 pictograms on one side and a fish in relief on the other, a faience finger-ring with linear decoration (No. 10993), and a tiny faience parrot with two depressions at the wings for inlay, in which traces of red colour were detected when found (No. 11259, Pl. LXXVIII, 2). The eyes of the parrot are indicated by a transverse hole, and there is a deep socket on the underside for separate insertion of the feet.

Group No. 11116 and other things.

Finds.

The following interesting objects of Stratum II were found scattered in this stratum :—

1. Unicorn seal with 2 pictograms, damaged. Pl. LXXXIX, 160. Size $\frac{7}{8} \times \frac{13}{16}$ in. No. 11716; Square Q 10/4; Depth 2 ft. 4 in. b.s. Mark its irregular shape which may be due to aberration in the stone.
2. Square seal with 5 pictograms only. The animal is broken off. Pl. XCIX, 623. $\frac{7}{8}$ in. sq. No. 11500; Square P 10/10; Depth 3 ft. 3 in. b.s.
3. Unicorn seal with 4 pictograms. With this were found 2 faience and 12 steatite beads mixed up in some broken pottery. Pl. LXXXIX, 112. $\frac{7}{8}$ in. sq. No. 10835*a*; Square P 9/5; Depth 3 ft. b.s.
4. Left part of a unicorn seal showing only 2 pictograms, head of the animal, and incense-burner. Pl. LXXXV, 7. $1\frac{13}{16}$ in. sq. No. 11476; Square P 10/16; Depth 3 ft. 9 in. b.s.
5. Fragmentary unicorn seal with only 4 pictograms and part of the animal surviving. Pl. LXXXVII, 61. L. $1\frac{1}{16}$ in. No. 12185; Square O 11/18; Depth 4 ft. 2 in. b.s.
6. Rough piece of limestone incised with a pictogram and other marks. Size $\frac{5}{8} \times \frac{7}{16}$ in. No. 10802; Square P 9/5; Depth 4 ft. 4 in. b.s.
7. Fragment of a unicorn seal showing forepart of the animal, incense-burner, and one pictogram. Pl. XC, 206. $\frac{7}{8}$ in. sq. No. 11039; Square O 9/25; Depth 4 ft. 6 in. b.s.
8. Fragment of a unicorn seal showing part of the animal, incense-burner, and one pictogram. Pl. XC, 180. $1\frac{1}{16}$ in. sq. No. 11038; Square O 10/24; Depth 5 ft. b.s.
9. Fragmentary unicorn seal with 6 pictograms. Pl. LXXXIX, 109. $1\frac{1}{16}$ in. sq. No. 12139: Square O 8/20; Depth 5 ft. 4 in. b.s.

10. Unicorn seal with 4 pictograms. Knob and edge broken. Pl. LXXXIX, 148. $\frac{11}{16}$ in. sq. No. 11304; Square O 10/19; Depth 5 ft. 8 in. b.s.

11. Unicorn seal with 6 pictograms. Pl. LXXXVIII, 87. $1\frac{1}{4}$ in. sq. No. 11331; Square O 9/17; Depth 5 ft. 10 in. b.s.

12. Square seal engraved with a Brāhmanī bull. It is chipped off in the upper part on obverse and lower part on reverse. Pl. XCI, 234. $\frac{15}{16}$ in. sq. No. 10995; Square O 10/22; Depth 5 ft. 6 in. b.s.

13. Unfinished steatite seal with 3 pictograms on one face, and 1 on the upper thickness. Pl. XCI, 259. $1\frac{1}{16}$ in. sq. No. 11040; Square O 10/23; Depth 6 ft. b.s.

14. Tiny, perforated cylinder seal of steatite inscribed with 4 pictograms round the circumference. Pl. XCV, 409. Diam. $\frac{3}{8}$ in. No. 12150; Square P 11/5; Depth 2 ft. 6 in. b.s.

15. Tiny, rectangular steatite seal with one pictogram on one face only, unfinished. Pl. XCVII, 515. Size $\frac{7}{16}\times\frac{5}{16}$ in. No. 10998; Square O 10/25; Depth 3 ft. 6 in. b.s.

16. Tiny, triangular steatite seal with 3 or 4 faint pictograms on one side, and 1 on the other. Broken at one corner. Pl. XCV, 420. Side $\frac{3}{8}$ in. No. 10999; Square O 9/24; Depth 4 ft. b.s.

17. Tiny, rectangular steatite seal with 4 pictograms on one side, and 1 on the other. Pl. XCVI, 444. Size $\frac{7}{12}\times\frac{3}{8}$ in. No. 11291; Square O 9/21; Depth 4 ft. 3 in. b.s.

18. Three-sided, prism sealing of faience with 5 pictograms on one side, 2 on the second, and a crocodile on the third. Pl. XCVIII, 597. L. $\frac{11}{16}$ in. No. 10960; Square O 10/22; Depth 5 ft. b.s.

19. Tiny, rectangular steatite seal with 2 pictograms on one side, and 1 on the other. Pl. XCVI, 470. Size $\frac{5}{16}\times\frac{3}{16}$ in. No. 10994; Square O 10/22; Depth 5 ft. 6 in. b.s.

20. Seal of the couchant hare type inscribed with 2 pictograms on one side only. Pl. XCV, 421. Size $\frac{1}{2}\times\frac{3}{8}$ in. No. 11268; Square O 10/17; Depth 6 ft. b.s.

21. Rectangular faience sealing rounded at one end. It has 4 pictograms on one side, and 1 on the other. Pl. XCVIII, 606; Size $\frac{3}{8}\times\frac{5}{16}$ in. No. 11417; Square P 11/1; Depth 3 ft. b.s.

22. Rectangular faience sealing with 6 pictograms on one side, and 1 on the other. Pl. XCIV, 358. Size $\frac{11}{16}\times\frac{3}{8}$ in. No. 10997; Square O 10/24; Depth 4 ft. b.s.

23. Three-sided, prism sealing of faience with 6 pictograms on one side, 1 on the second, and an indistinct figure on the third. Pl. XCVIII, 596. L. $\frac{11}{16}$ in. No. 11511; Square P 11/6; Depth 4 ft. 2 in. b. s.

24. Oblong faience sealing, lentoid in section, showing an acacia tree on one side, and 4 pictograms on the other. Pl. XCIV, 331. Size $1\times\frac{5}{8}$ in. No. 11244; Square O 10/16: Depth 5 ft. 6 in. b.s.

25. Hexagonal faience sealing with 4 pictograms on one side, and an acacia tree and VII on the other; similar to No. 324 in Pl. XCIII. Size 13/16 × 7/16 in. No. 11358; Square O 10/19; Depth 5 ft. 6 in. b.s.

26. Chessman-shaped object of yellow Jaisalmer stone. Ht. 13/16 in. No. 11409; Square P 11/6; Depth 2 ft. 4 in. b.s.

27. Barrel-shaped steatite bead. L. 3/4 in. No. 10567; Square P 10/4; Depth 3 ft. b.s.

28. Cuboid chert weight. Wt. 13·8 gms.; size ·7×·7×·62 in. No. 10631; Square P 10/4; Depth 3 ft. b.s.

29. Cuboid weight of banded agate. Wt. 27·1 gms.; size ·9×·9×·8 in. No. 10632; Square P 10/4; Depth 3 ft. b.s.

30. Cuboid weight of dark grey chert. Wt. 26·5 gms.; size ·9×·9×·75 in. No. 11421; Square P 11/1; Depth 3 ft. 4 in. b.s.

31. Cuboid chert weight, broken. Wt. 132·0 gms.; size 1·6×1·6×1·25 in. No. 11241; Square O 10/16; Depth 4 ft. 7 in. b.s.

32. Rectangular strip of copper with straw marks on the rusted surface. Pl. CXXV, 17. L. 2 3/8 in. No. 11328; Square O 10/21; Depth 3 ft. b.s.

33. Copper strip gradually thinning towards one end, and possibly intended for a chisel. L. 3 1/8 in. No. 11086; Square O 10/24; Depth 4 ft. 6 in. b.s.

34. Flat copper scraper with rounded edge. Pl. CXXV, 38. L. 3 1/16 in. No. 11292; Square O 9/20; Depth 5 ft. 4 in. b.s.

35. Tiny, conical gold boss with a hook inside. Diam. 3/8 in. No. 11515; Square P 10/20; Depth 3 ft. 2 in. b.s.

Pottery—

36. Bath-tub-shaped cup with spout at one end, and 4 holes through the bottom. Pl. LXXI, 75. L. 5 3/8 in.; ht. 2 1/4 in. No. 12141; Square O 8/21; Depth 5 ft. 4 in. b.s.

37. Large, crude bull's head painted with bands, dotted circles, and comb pattern. Pl. LXXIX, 73. It was found at the eastern foot of the mound below the level of adjoining fields in Extension I of this trench. Its painting, texture, and red glaze are reminiscent of burial pottery. Close to it was found a jar of burial type with a flange round the body. This bull's head, it must be pointed out, is quite different from all other terracottas of which multitudes have been found on this site. L. 4 3/4 in. No. 11698; Square Q 10/5; Depth 3 ft. b.s.

38. Ball rattle. Diam. 1 3/8 in. No. 11422; Square O 11/21; Depth 4 ft. 2 in. b.s.

39. Five sherds of painted saucers similar in respect of shape, size and paintings to those of Stratum II from the Cemetery H. L. 3 1/4 to 4 3/8 in. No. 10910; Square O 9; Depth 0 to 3 ft. b.s.

Remains of Stratum III.

The IIIrd stratum, which here probably corresponds with the IVth in other trenches of this mound, is represented in the southern section of this trench by a large, dilapidated, brick-on-edge pavement along the western edge, three fragmentary pavements to its east, three exceptionally thick walls, the remains of a room in square P 11/8, and some isolated, broken walls. In the northern part of the middle section there are four or five walls of considerable length where the floor level of this stratum was indicated by the presence of several broken jars and a line of five *gharās* and one jar-stand in square O 9/23 (Pl. XXVIII, *c*), but in the northern section there is only one thick wall and two or three fragments.

Pavement with gypsum pointing and jar-stands.

The above-mentioned brick-on-edge pavement, which lies in squares O 10/20 and 25 and O 11/16 is built in two sections each made of finely rubbed bricks with neat gypsum pointing. Its edging has disappeared. In its raised section are embedded seven jar-stands which are 7 to 8 in. in diameter, and while clearing one of them yielded a lanceolate faience sealing (No. 11381) inscribed on both sides (Pl. C, 673). In the adjoining part of the floor, which is only a few inches lower, there is an opening for a similar jar-stand (Pl. XXVII, *b*, fore-ground).

Second occupation of House 1.

The above remains of Stratum III are clearly distinguishable from those of the two upper strata by their distinctly lower level and superior construction. It also appears that at a still lower level the eastern rooms of the large house No. 1 of Stratum IV described below[1] were again utilised in connection with the IIIrd stratum by filling them with rammed clay up to their present height, at which level the old doors were closed with brick-work masonry (Pl. XXVII, *a*). At this time, two new walls, one along the east and the other along the north, were constructed inside the earlier room No. 3 (Pl. XXVIII, *a*, middle room). But in room No. 5, to the south, the original walls were rasied, and a new pavement was constructed at a higher level.

Finds.

Scattered throughout the trench were found the following interesting objects—all belonging to Stratum III:—

1. Unicorn seal with all but one pictogram lost in the break. Pl. XC, 183. $\frac{5}{8}$ in. sq. No. 11329; Square P 8/5; Depth 5 ft. b.s.
2. Unicorn seal with 2 pictograms. Pl. LXXXIX, 129. $\frac{13}{16}$ in. sq. No. 10815; Square P 10/2; Depth 5 ft. 6 in. b.s.
3. Unicorn seal with 2 pictograms. Pl. LXXXIX, 166. $\frac{11}{16}$ in. sq. No. 12215; Square P 11/5; Depth 5 ft. 9 in. b.s.
4. Fragment of a unicorn (?) seal. Pl. XC, 212. No. 12332; Square P 11/9; Depth 6 ft. b.s.
5. Unicorn seal, fragmentary, with only part of a pictogram surviving. Pl. LXXXIX, 151. $\frac{13}{16}$ in. sq. No. 11318; Square O 9/23; Depth 6 ft. 6 in. b.s.
6. Fragment of a bossed seal. L. 1 in. No. 12322; Square O 11/17; Depth 6 ft. 6 in. b.s.

---

[1] See pp. 131-32 *infra*.

7. Upper half of a unicorn seal with 2 pictograms. Pl. LXXXIX, 155. $\frac{11}{16}$ in. sq. No. 10818; Square P 10/4; Depth 6 ft. 6 in. b.s.
8. Unicorn seal with 7 pictograms, fragmentary. Pl. LXXXIX, 111. $\frac{15}{16}$ in. sq. No. 11368; Square O 10/19; Depth 6 ft. 6 in. b.s.
9. Lower half of an unfinished unicorn seal. Pl. LXXXVII, 66. $\frac{7}{8}$ in. sq. No. 12140; Square O 8/20; Depth 6 ft. 10 in. b.s.
10. Unicorn seal with 5 pictograms. Pl. LXXXVIII, 101. $\frac{15}{16}$ in. sq. No. 11359; Square O 10/19; Depth 6 ft. 10 in. b.s.
11. Lower part of a unicorn seal showing only the legs of the animal and the staff of the incense-burner. Pl. XC, 215. $\frac{7}{8}$ in. sq. No. 12268; Square P 11/1; Depth 7 ft. b.s.
12. Unicorn seal with 4 pictograms. Pl. LXXXIX, 134. $\frac{7}{8}$ in. sq. No. 12251; Square P 11/11; Depth 7 ft. 4 in. b.s.
13. Left hand triangular fragment of a unicorn seal showing only part of a pictogram and body of the animal. Pl. XC, 191. L. $\frac{5}{8}$ in. No. 11342; Square O 9/18; Depth 8 ft. b.s.
14. Unicorn seal with 5 pictograms surviving, fragmentary. Pl. LXXXVII, 49. $1\frac{1}{4}$ in. sq. No. 11332; Square O 10/18; Depth 8 ft. 1 in. b.s.
15. Triangular fragment of a small, unfinished, steatite seal showing only 2 pictograms. Pl. XCVII, 567. L. $\frac{7}{16}$ in. No. 11432; Square O 11/21; Depth 5 ft. 2 in. b.s.
16. Fragment of a steatite seal showing 3 damaged pictograms. Size $\frac{5}{8}\times\frac{1}{2}$ in. No. 11394; Square O 10/17; Depth 8 ft. b.s.
17. Fragment of a rectangular, plano-convex steatite seal showing 2 damaged pictograms. It is unusual in being bored horizontally across the length instead of vertically through the thickness. Pl. XCII, 290. Size $\frac{7}{16}\times\frac{5}{16}$ in. No. 11370; Square O 10/24; Depth 8 ft. 8 in. b.s.
18. Tiny, rectangular steatite seal with 4 pictograms on one side, and 3 on the other. Pl. XCVI, 447. Size $\frac{5}{8}\times\frac{5}{16}$ in. No. 10830; Square P 10/5; Depth 5 ft. 6 in. b.s.
19. Tiny, rectangular steatite seal with 4 pictograms on one side, and 2 on the other. Pl. XCVI, 472. Size $\frac{5}{8}\times\frac{5}{16}$ in. No. 12216; Square P 11/5; Depth 5 ft. 9 in. b.s.
20. Tiny, three-sided prism seal of steatite with 3 pictograms on one side, 1 on the second, and 3 dotted circles on the third, fragmentary; similar to No. 647 in Pl. XCIX. L. $\frac{5}{8}$ in. No. 12327; Square O 11/22; Depth 6 ft. 6 in. b.s.
21. Tiny, rectangular steatite seal with 5 pictograms on one side, and 3 on the other. Pl. XCVI, 449. Size $\frac{3}{4}\times\frac{1}{2}$ in. No. 11077; Square O 10/22; Depth 6 ft. 8 in. b.s.
22. Tiny, rectangular steatite seal with 3 pictograms on one side, and 1 on the other. Pl. XCVI, 459. Size $\frac{1}{2}\times\frac{5}{16}$ in. No. 11085; Square O 10/22; Depth 7 ft. 4 in. b.s.

23. Fragment of a tiny rectangular steatite seal with only 2 pictograms surviving on one side, and dotted circles on the other, L. $\frac{7}{16}$ in. No. 11317; Square O 10/23; Depth 7 ft. 5 in. b.s.

24. Tiny, leaf-shaped steatite seal with 1 pictogram on one side, and dotted circles on the other. Pl. XCVII, 559. Size $\frac{11}{16} \times \frac{3}{8}$ in. No. 11305; Square O 10/17; Depth 8 ft. b.s.

25. Tiny, steatite seal shaped like the Indian boy's writing board (*Kāshṭha-phalaka*) with 3 pictograms on one side, and 3 dotted circles on the other. Pl. XCV, 408. Size $\frac{11}{16} \times \frac{5}{8}$ in. No. 11334; Square O 10/18; Depth 8 ft. 1 in. b.s.

26. Fragment of a fish-shaped faience sealing with 3 pictograms on one side, and part of one on the other. Pl. XCV, 384. L. $\frac{5}{8}$ in. No. 12329; Square O 11/25; Depth 5 ft. 9 in. b.s.

27. Tiny, discoid faience sealing with 2 pictograms on one side, and 1 on the other. Pl. XCV, 374. Diam. $\frac{3}{8}$ in. No. 11027; Square P 10/2; Depth 6 ft. b.s.

28. Cylindrical faience sealing with 3 pictograms on one side, and 1 on the other; similar to No. 687 in Pl. C. L. $\frac{1}{4}$ in. No. 12160; Square O 9/16; Depth 6 ft. 5 in. b.s.

29. Tiny, rectangular faience sealing with 3 pictograms on one side, and 1 on the other. Pl. C, 681. Size $\frac{5}{16} \times \frac{1}{4}$ in. No. 11348; Square O 9/18; Depth 8 ft. b.s.

30. Tiny, discoid faience sealing showing a tortoise in high relief on one side, and 1 pictogram on the other. Pl. C, 663. Diam. $\frac{1}{2}$ in. No. 11341; Square O 9/18; Depth 7 ft. 6 in. b.s.

31. Fish-shaped faience sealing with 4 pictograms on one side, and 3 on the other. Pl. XCV, 427. L. $\frac{3}{8}$ in. No. 12380; Square O 11/25; Depth 8 ft. b.s.

32. Triangular, prism sealing of terracotta with a blurred, legendary scene on each side. One face shows a god standing. His right arm is profusely ornamented, but the left is altogether blurred. The second face depicts a tall, stalwart man engaged in fighting a bison which has been firmly caught by the horns. The scene may be a representation of Ea-bani fighting a bison in a jungle. The third face shows, to left, a figure—probably a god—seated in a typical attitude of *yoga*[1] (cf. the following sealing, Pl. XCIII, 303) with another figure to right seated on haunches. Pl. XCIII, 310. Size $\frac{5}{8} \times \frac{1}{2}$ in. No. 11306; Square O 10/19; Depth 6 ft. 6 in. b.s.

33. Oblong, terracotta sealing with legendary scenes on both faces depicted probably from left to right as may be judged by the position of three pictograms at the right end of the reverse. Pl. XCIII, 303. First, on the obverse, is the familiar scene of a man attacking a

[1] *Cf.* Sir John Marshall, *op. cit.*, p. 52 ff. and Pl. XII, 17, also Pl. CXVIII, 11.

tiger from a *machān* erected on an acacia[1] tree, then a god (?) "seated on a low Indian throne in a typical attitude of *yoga*, with legs bent double beneath him, heel to heel, and toes turned downwards. His arms are outstretched, his hands, (presumably) with thumbs to front resting on knees. From wrist to shoulder the arms are covered with bangles".[2] From behind his head-dress there is a long, tassel-like appendage to right, which perhaps is faintly seen on the standing figure on reverse also. Of the animals to his right, the one in the enclosure has a short, bushy tail and bovine legs, and its head is turned backwards. It may be a goat. Below the projection may be a hare or kid, and above it an animal with long body and short legs of which the figure is altogether blurred. From left to right, on the reverse, is a humpless bull standing by a trident-headed post with his head bent down a little, then a standing figure, possibly a god, in front of a two-storeyed structure, followed by three pictograms at the right end. The structure, which appears to have been of wood, is of unusual interest. It looks like a combined side elevation and perspective of a double storeyed room preceded by a porch—both of open work in front, but seemingly the two storeyed room is closed by lattice work on the rear side and crowned at the corners by somewhat conical finials. It is not clear what the bifurcated object hanging down from a projection in front of the terrace is intended to represent. Below this is seen a domical object over the porch. The structure is probably of a sacred character, and in view of the trident post and bull[3]—which are peculiarly associated with Śiva whose prototype has been found at Mohenjo-daro,[4] the possibility of the standing figure being ultimately identified as another form of the same god may not be altogether ruled out. Size 1$\frac{15}{16}$ × $\frac{3}{8}$ in. No. 11466; Square O 10/25; Depth 7 ft. 5 in. b.s.

34. Cubical chert weight. Wt. 6·9 gms.; size ·55×·55×·5 in. No. 11517; Square P 10/15; Depth 4 ft. 8 in. b.s.

35. Stone chessman-shaped object with a dotted circle on top, and hole on the underside. Ht. $\frac{5}{8}$ in. No. 11424; Square P 11/6; Depth 5 ft. 2 in. b.s.

36. Three barrel-shaped faience beads decorated with black bands at the ends and rows of dots of the same colour over the body. Rare. Pl. CXXVIII, 9. Each $\frac{3}{8}$ in. long. No. 10685*a*; Square P 9/5; Depth 3 to 5 ft. b.s.

---

[1] For similar representations at Mohenjo-daro *cf. M. I. C.*, Pl. CXI, 353 and 355. At p. 71 thereof Sir John Marshall suggests that such seals may have been used as protective amulets against tigers or other jungle animals. Also *cf.* Harappā Pl. XCI, 248, and Pl. XCIII, 308.

[2] This exactly is Sir John Marshall's description of the pose of the prototype of the historic Śiva referred to in footnote 1 above.

[3] The Nandi bull is always installed in front of a Śiva temple, but usually it is posed seated.

[4] *Cf.* Sir John Marshall, *op. cit.*, p. 52 ff. and Pl. XII, 17.

37. Faience ball with incised, linear decoration hatched in opposite direction in each quarter. Pl. CXX, 41. Diam. 1 in. No. 11479; Square P 9/15; Depth 7 ft. 2 in. b.s.

38. Long copper dagger with concave edges and short tang. Pl. CXXIV, 48. L. 10¾ in.; w. 2¾ in. No. 11289; Square O 10/17; Depth 7 ft. b.s.

39. Copper tanged chisel. Rare.[1] Pl. CXXV, 18. L. 5 in. No. 12253; Square P 11/11; Depth 7 ft. 4 in. b.s.

40. Terracotta tetrahedron. Ht. ⅝ in. No. 11030; Square O 10/25; Depth 4 ft. 6 in. b.s.

41. Short, thick terracotta cone with a shallow socket on top. Ht. 4 in.; diam. 3¼ in. No. 11475; Square P 9/15; Depth 6 ft. 4 in. b.s.

Stratum IV.

The eastern part of a well-to-do house.

Lower down, at the centre of this trench, is a large house—No. 1 of the IVth stratum—the plan of whose eastern part is quite clear, but its western part is broken, and partly buried under the edge of the trench (Pl. XXVI). Apparently, it was a well-to-do house with a frontage of over 100 ft. on the east, on which side there is a narrow well 2 ft. 6 in. in diameter sunk in the open plinth (Pl. XV, *b*). Though primarily meant for the inmates of this house, its situation on the open plinth suggests that it was equally accessible to the neighbours. To north, opposite the well is a small room No. 7 measuring 7 ft. 5 in. by 7 ft. 2 in., which from its size and situation at the entrance to the inner apartments seems probably to have been a porter's lodge.[2] At this point starts a Z-shaped gallery (No. 6), 3 ft. wide, giving access first to room No. 5, which measures 10 ft. 6 in. by 7 ft. 2 in., and then to closet No. 4, which is 11 ft. 5 in. long by 3 ft. 6 in. wide. Across this closet are the women's apartments Nos. 3 and 2 on the plan (Pl. XXVII, *a*). Of these, the former is 16 ft. 8 in. by 12 ft. and the latter 12 ft. by 8 ft. 8 in. To west of room No. 2 is a large dilapidated room No. 1, of which the extent is partially indicated by the remains of a brick pavement. The north wall of these two rooms is very substantially built and placed directly over an existing wall of Stratum V as shown by the offset in the right fore-ground of Pl. XXVIII, *a*. Besides the door opening into room No. 2, room No. 3 also opens on the west into what is obviously the remains of a large courtyard (No. 8) 43 ft. 9 in. long from north to south, and on the south into closet No. 4 mentioned above. From the gallery opposite room No. 7 there is another opening into the courtyard, and at this place there are clear indications of a set of at least three more rooms, of which Nos. 9 and 11 opening on the terrace round the well could be conveniently used as guest rooms and No. 10, which lies behind room No. 9, by the male inmates. At this point there were probably more rooms towards the west, but they cannot be traced any longer. In like manner, it is possible that the gallery-room No. 5 on account of its situation adjoining the inner apartments may have been intended for female guests.

---

[1] This is the only other example of a tanged chisel from Harappā, none being found at Mohenjo-daro. The tang was presumably inserted in a wooden handle.

[2] For a similar situation of the porter's lodge in House XIII, Vs Area, at Mohenjo-daro *cf.* Sir John Marshall, *op. cit.* p.20.

Later secretions. As already pointed out, parts of this house appear to have been utilised again when the IIIrd stratum was in occupation, and the well was also raised higher and reused. At this time all the old doors—3 ft. 5 in. to 3 ft. 9 in. wide—were bricked up at a higher level above the new filling of rammed mud which was now put in the rooms. The walls of this house are quite substantial, except the one on the extreme east, which is much thinner. On the inner side, this is faced with burnt bricks but the outside shows alternate courses of burnt and sun-dried bricks. **Constructional peculiarity.** In reality this wall, as it stands now, represents merely the finished interior face, its present outer surface being really the core. There is little doubt that its outer face, as shown on the plan and isometric projection (Pls. XXVI and XV, *b*), was supplied by raising a very long wall of the Vth stratum which stood immediately in front and a part of which was actually utilised for raising the east wall of room No. 2 (square P 10/1).

Remains of Stratum IV in the northern section. In the northern section of this trench have been recovered traces of 4 or 5 rooms constituting house No. 2. These, too, are reared on walls of the Vth stratum. Some of them are of the same mixed construction as the outer face of the east wall of house No. 1 just described (Pl. XXVII, *d*).

The following finds were associated with this stratum :—

1. Fragment of a unicorn seal with part of only one pictogram surviving. Pl. XC, 175. $1\frac{1}{4}$ in. sq. No. 12323 ; Square P 11/1 ; Depth 7 ft. 6 in. b.s.
2. Unicorn seal with 5 pictograms. Lower part broken. Pl. LXXXVII, 55. $1\frac{1}{16}$ in. sq. No. 11379 ; Square O 9/23 ; Depth 9 ft. b.s.
3. Fragment of a unicorn seal with only 2 pictograms and part of the animal's head surviving. Pl. LXXXIX, 154. $\frac{11}{16}$ in. sq. No. 11361 ; Square O 10/17 ; Depth 9 ft. 7 in. b.s.
4. Steatite seal showing a tiger with a trough in front and a pictogram above. Pl. XCI, 246. $\frac{11}{16}$ in. sq. No. 11110 ; Square P 10/3 ; Depth 7 ft. 8 in. b.s.
5. Two fragments of a steatite seal with only one pictogram surviving. Pl. XCII, 290. Size $\frac{3}{4}\times\frac{3}{4}$ in. No. 11377 ; Square O 9/18 ; Depth 9 ft. 8 in. b.s.
6. Upper left corner of a steatite seal with only 2 pictograms. Pl. CI, 695. L. $\frac{11}{16}$ in. No. 11392 ; Square O 9/18 ; Depth 10 ft. 6 in. b.s.
7. Tiny, rectangular steatite seal with 3 pictograms on one side, and 1 on the other ; similar to No. 509 in Pl. XCVII. Size $\frac{1}{2}\times\frac{3}{8}$ in. No. 11380 ; Square O 9/23 ; Depth 9 ft. b.s.
8. Tiny, rectangular steatite seal with 3 pictograms on one side, and a *pīpal* (*ficus religiosa*) leaf on the other. Pl. XCVI, 439. Size $\frac{3}{8}\times\frac{5}{16}$ in. No. 11372 ; Square O 10/18 ; Depth 10 ft. b.s.
9. Tiny, three-sided prism seal of steatite with 4 pictograms on one side, and 1 on the second, the third side being plain. Pl. XCVII, 579. Size $\frac{3}{8}\times\frac{5}{16}$ in. No. 11390 ; Square O 9/19 ; Depth 10 ft. b.s.

10. Tiny, rectangular steatite seal with 3 pictograms on one side, and 1 on the other. Slightly damaged; similar to No. 531 in Pl. XCVII. L. $\frac{1}{2}$ in. No. 11391; Square O 9/18; Depth 10 ft. 6 in. b.s.
11. Thick, fragmentary rectangular faience sealing with 3 pictograms on one side, and rectilinear patterns on the other. Pl. C, 656. L. $\frac{3}{4}$ in.; w. $\frac{1}{2}$ in. No. 11516; Square P 10/15; Depth 4 ft. 8 in. b.s.
12. Tiny, discoid faience sealing with 4 pictograms on one side, and 1 on the other. Pl. XCV, 375. Diam. $\frac{7}{16}$ in. No. 11333; Square O 9/20; Depth 10 ft. b.s.
13. Brick inscribed with 3 pictograms on one face, right side broken. Pl. CII, 11. L. 8 in.; w. 5 in.; th. 2 in. No. 11343; Square O 9/17; Depth 9 ft. 6 in. b.s.
14. Shapeless, terracotta sealing with 3 blurred pictograms on one side, and two parallel grooves made by pressing wet clay on a reed mat on the other. Pl. CI, 707. Size $1\times\frac{3}{4}$ in. No. 11393; Square O 9/18; Depth 10 ft. 1 in. b.s.
15. Two tiny cone frustums of hornblende holed at the top. Pl. CXXXIX, 36. Ht. $\frac{7}{16}$ in. No. 11346; Square O 9/23; Depth 9 ft. 6 in. b.s.
16. Copper celt with tapering sides, sharp cutting edge and burred butt. Pl. CXXIV, 39. L. $4\frac{1}{16}$ in.; w. $2\frac{1}{4}$ in. No. 11154; Square P 10/1; Depth 8 ft. 4 in. b.s.
17. Copper imitation of a river shell which bore impressions of straw or wood on its rusted surface. In fragments. No. 11356; Square O 9/19; Depth 9 ft. 1 in. b.s.

Stratum V.

Except in the narrow strip along the eastern edge of the trench, the Vth stratum has nowhere been dug completely, since it lies buried beneath later structures. Nevertheless, in this limited section, it is worth noticing that there are two long walls standing about 8 ft. apart which run more or less parallel to each other for over 200 ft. from north to south (Pl. XXVIII, *d*, left ground). Of these, the outer or eastern one was rebuilt in sections in connection with the IVth stratum, and is tilted outwards in the southern part where it survives to an average height of 4 to 5 ft. At the north end of the inner wall is a small stretch of exceptionally thick wall which, though not bonded, forms a continuation of it (Pl. XXVI). The space enclosed by the above long walls is obviously a lane with two paved sinks in it, 43 ft. apart. The southern sink (No. 1) measures 4 ft. by 2 ft. 10 in., and is now 3 ft. deep. At its bottom was a 10 in. thick layer of earth containing decayed cereals on which lay about 200 earthenware vases—mostly the sherds of goblets with pointed bases, a female figurine, a toy bull, a pottery bead, brickbats and animal bones. Among the latter were a large cattle bone, one jaw, ribs, leg and knuckle bones (Pl. XXV, *c*). These contents were obviously thrown in as rubbish, most of the pottery being the drinking vessels thrown away after use, as is done to this day by the Hindu population in India.[1]

Two long walls probably forming the sides of a lane.

Two sinks.

[1] The idea in throwing away earthenware vessels which have once been held to the mouth, is that they become impure, since unlike metal vessels, they cannot be cleaned with mud or ashes.

Sink No. 2, which measures 3 ft. 10 in. by 2 ft. 9 in., contained nothing. Its west wall is battered.

The following antiquities were found in connection with the Vth stratum:—

1. Unicorn seal (fragmentary) with one complete and two mutilated pictograms surviving. Pl. LXXXIX, 136. $\frac{3}{4}$ in sq. No. 12180; Square O 9/18; Depth 11 ft. 4 in. b.s.
2. Unicorn seal showing only the mutilated animal and incense-burner; inscription lost. Pl. LXXXIX, 157. $\frac{11}{16}$ in. sq. No. 12179; Square O 9/18; Depth 11 ft. 4 in. b.s.
3. Fragment of a unicorn seal showing only one pictogram and head of the animal. Pl. LXXXIX, 158. L. $\frac{3}{8}$ in. No. 12181; Square O 9/18; Depth 11 ft. 4 in. b.s.
4. Tiny, rectangular and plano-convex steatite seal showing only one pictogram. Unfinished. This shape is rare among tiny seals. Pl. XCVII, 540. Size $\frac{3}{4}\times\frac{3}{8}$ in. No. 11440; Square P 11/1; Depth 7 ft. b.s.
5. Tiny, rectangular bar-shaped steatite seal with 5, 4, and 1 pictograms respectively on three faces, and two dotted circles on the fourth. Pl. XCVIII, 583. Size $\frac{5}{8}\times\frac{1}{4}\times\frac{1}{8}$ in. No. 11349; Square O 10/16; Depth 11 ft. 4 in. b.s.
6. Fragment of a three-sided, prism seal of steatite with only 1 pictogram surviving on one side, the other two sides being plain. L. $\frac{5}{8}$ in. No. 11420; Square O 10/16; Depth 12 ft. 8 in. b.s.

Extension II. We come now to the two eastward extensions to which I referred at the beginning of the account of this trench. Of these, Extension II is totally devoid of structural remains except a circular manger edged off with standing bricks, and three or four bits of walls which were hidden in the débris, consisting of potsherds and bones lying helter skelter. The potsherds, however, are not without interest, as they belong to two distinct classes, *viz.*, (*a*) to the types of vessels which are usually found in the mounds, and (*b*) to a variety of other vessels which are peculiar to the two strata of burial pottery found in the Cemetery H.[1]

Sherds of burial and non-burial types of pottery. Among those of the latter class, which are typical of the upper stratum in the Cemetery, were collared necks of ellipsoid and other jars (Pl. LXXIII, 44 and 49), fragments of jars with a flange round the neck or cordon round the body, and sherds which bear on them the finger-tip and finger-slip[2] patterns (Pl. LXXIII, 46 and 55). Those which represent the IInd stratum were the stands or bottom fragments of squat and ribbed offering dishes (Pl. LXXIII, 58 and 59) or of plates (Pl. LXXIII, 56, 57 and 61), necks of *kalaśas*[3] (Pl. LXXIII, 63), flasks (Pl. LXXIII, 50 and 52), ring-bases of the latter, as well as fragments of saucers, flat covers (Pl. LXXIII, 45) and bowls (Pl. LXXIII, 60).

In this connection let me add that almost everywhere to the east of Trench VI fragments typical of burial pottery were picked up at or near the surface of this mound, and they were still more common on Mound AB.

---

[1] For the description of Cemetery H see Chap. VI.

[2] For an explanation of the finger-tip and finger-slip patterns see p. 204 *infra*.

[3] These were cocoanut-shaped water vessels with long, splayed-out necks.

Extension I has revealed the back part of a house which runs right under unacquired and cultivated fields (Pl. XXVIII, *b*) and points to the desirability of excavating these low grounds when funds permit. As these walls stand at the foot of the mound, their low level does not necessarily indicate that they belong to an earlier stratum. Their construction and the find of a flanged round jar (No. 12266) typical of Stratum I in the Cemetery H are indicative of a late date for these walls, which cannot as yet be correlated. To the same conclusion we are also led by the crude, but red and highly glazed terracotta bull's head[1] (No. 11698, Pl. LXXIX, 73) which is painted with devices similar to those on the burial pots, and which is unlike any terracotta figurine so far found from the Indus Valley Sites. **Extension I.**

The following seven finds were made from the spoil earth, and as five of them are seals of the tiny size they may be presumed to have been recovered from early strata :— **Finds from spoil earth.**

1. Fragment of a unicorn seal showing only the standard and part of the animal. Pl. XC, 202. L. $\frac{9}{16}$ in. No. 12381.
2. Tiny, rectangular steatite seal inscribed on both faces, fragmentary. Its preserved end is pierced with a hole[2] which cuts through a pictogram on either side. Pl. XCVI, 491. L. $\frac{1}{2}$ in.; w. $\frac{3}{8}$ in. No. 12101.
3. Tiny, hare-shaped steatite seal, uninscribed. It has a cross-shaped groove for fixation on the underside; similar to No. 422 in Pl. XCV. L. $\frac{7}{16}$ in. No. 12384.
4. Fragment of a tiny rectangular steatite seal with only 2 pictograms surviving on either side. Pl. XCVII, 517. No. 12099.
5. Tiny, three-sided prism seal of steatite with 2 pictograms on one side, and 1 on each of the other two sides. Pl. XCVIII, 588. L. $\frac{3}{8}$ in. No. 12102.
6. Cubical chert weight. Pl. CXVIII, 25. Wt. 6·95 gms.; size ·57 × 57 × ·5 in. No. 12383.
7. Brick bearing on one side impression of a cloth, and of the feet of a dog. Size $10\frac{3}{4} \times 5\frac{1}{4} \times 2\frac{1}{4}$ in. No. 11355; from the heap of bricks near Trench III.

[1] For its description see item 37 under Stratum II, p. 136 *supra*.

[2] It is just possible that the other end broke when drilling a hole, for with two holes the seal could be tied on the arm as an amulet.

CHAPTER III.

Mound AB.

Mound AB. Configuration.

Due south of Mound F, and across the village road going west to the hamlet of Hāfiz Bullah, stands Mound AB—the highest of all the mounds at Harappā (Pl. I). Roughly, it is a parallelogram in shape, measuring some 1,450 ft. from north to south by 800 ft. from east to west. It rises quite abruptly above the surrounding plain, the contour lines, as will appear from the site plan (Pl. I), following one another in quick succession along the slopes on all sides. Elsewhere at Harappā, such steep slopes are found only on Mound E. Crowning its north-east edge, and orientated from north to south, is the tomb of a Muhammadan saint named Nūr Shāh, constructed of bricks extracted from the ancient ruins. This tomb, enclosed by a brick wall, is 46 ft. long and 3 ft. 6 in. broad. From its size, it is known as the tomb of *Naugazā*,[1] literally a man nine yards in stature. Not far from this, but at a higher level and apparently to the west,

Structures seen on it by General Cunningham.

General Cunningham reported that he traced the remains of flights of steps on both the eastern and western faces of this mound, as well as the basement of a large square building.[2] As none of these remains now exist it may be that they were dug away, after Cunningham's time, for the sake of their bricks.

Exploitation for bricks.

During the last century, a light railway appears to have been constructed up to the mounds for carrying brick ballast, and I myself picked up a fish-plate belonging to this railway on the east bank of the modern irrigation distributary shown between Mounds AB and E (Pl. I). This and the neighbouring Mound E have suffered most from brick-diggers. According to Cunningham,[3] bricks from Harappā were converted into more than 100 miles of railroad ballast, and the extent to which this mound was exploited can be gauged from the two large ravines which were cut almost across its entire width from east to west, as well as from other large ravines on the north and south, not to mention innumerable smaller entrenchments and tunnels sunk in every direction. And in this connection it may also be observed that the prosperous little town of Harappā, with a population of about 3,000, and houses[4] chiefly of burnt brick, came to possess its first brick kiln only after the mounds had been brought under the protection of the Ancient Monuments Preservation Act in 1920.

Divisions of Mound AB.

The two east to west ravines, referred to above, divide this mound into three parts, of which the middle one, lying between the two ravines is the smallest. In the middle and southern sections, which are connected by a narrow neck, there is an irregular eminence indicated by the 580 ft. contour line, and in the northern section there is one eminence a few feet higher near the north-western edge of the mound, and another one still higher between this and the *Naugazā* tomb (590 ft. above the mean sea-level).

---

[1] The word *Naugazā* is also interpreted by some people as Naughāzi or new victor in the cause of Islam.

[2] *C. S. R.*, Vol. V, p. 106.

[3] *Ibid.*, p. 107.

[4] These houses are one, two, and sometimes even three storeys high.

Excavation B.

Mr. Sahni's trench.

In the northern portion of this mound, Rai Bahadur Daya Ram Sahni excavated a considerable area (B) in the years 1920-21, 1923-24 and 1924-25. He began by sinking a trial trench 55 ft. long by 20 ft. wide, a little to the west of and parallel to the tomb of *Naugazā*. This trench was extended to a length of over 160 ft., and later on, at right angles to it, he sank two subsidiary trenches towards the west which cut across the highest portion of the mound, the northern one distinguished as D trench, and the southern one as Bg. On these being linked up the whole excavation was called B (Pl. XXIX). This area is now an irregular polygon measuring some 160 ft. from east to west by 100 ft. from north to south increasing to 160 ft. along the eastern side.

Original ground level and stratification.

From the highest point—590 ft. above the sea-level—the ground covered by this excavation falls some 20 ft. in level towards the south and east (Pl. XXIX, Section of Trench B), so that for a space of about 40 ft. along its eastern edge we come almost at once to the IVth stratum of remains, without encountering any of the three upper strata. On the other hand, in the middle part of this area, the IVth stratum is reached at a depth of 12 to 21 ft. below the surface. To avoid confusion on the part of the reader, a word must be said here in regard to the method of recording followed during the time of the Rai Bahadur. It appears that the depth of antiquities was then recorded sometimes from the highest point of the mound, that is to say from 590 ft. above the sea-level, and at others from the surface of the ground at the point where the find was made, which, as already mentioned, might be as much as 21 ft. lower.

Stratum I.

In the high western part (Pl. XXX, *d*, left back-ground) in square P 18/4, Rai Bahadur Daya Ram Sahni found, 6 ft. below the highest point of the mound, a few walls composed of brickbats of the Indus period taken from the site together with bricks of larger size, measuring 14 to 15 by 9½ to 10½ by 2½ in. These larger bricks are assignable to the early Gupta period. Three feet lower down, he also found another structure of similar bricks, to which probably belonged three fragmentary terracotta panels in high relief figured in Pl. LXXII, 52, 53 and 55. Of these, No. 52 (B404) shows the headless figure of a votary kneeling down in prayer, perhaps, before a deity whose right lower leg is all that now survives. Whether what hangs down from the votary's right arm is the end of the scarf or some other part of the drapery is not clear. On the pedestal is shown a railing which, as I have pointed out elsewhere,[1] had been a familiar motif in connection with sacred trees, as far back as the Indus period. No. 52 (B1686) is a headless female figure, who, to judge by the cylindrical drum (?) (*mṛidaṅga*) held between her hands, is a musician. She is standing behind a railing in an easy posture with the hips thrown out towards the right. The folds of her scarf, *dhotī*, and upper garment are clearly indicated. The third panel (No. 55) is very much mutilated and shows nothing but the legs of a standing figure.

Brick remains and panels of the Gupta period confined to the highest terrace.

Gupta bricks, spouts and cast terracotta beads.

Along with the above terracotta panels there were also recovered a number of bricks carved with full or half blown lotus rosettes, foliage, bead-and-reel motifs, etc. (Pl. LXXII, 45, 46, 54 and 60-62), three pottery spouts with narrow

[1] *Cf.* p. 24 *supra.*

apertures; and two small cast heads of terracotta (Pl. LXXII, 56 and 57). On the steep slope (Pl. XXX, *a*) opposite the door to the tomb of *Naugazā* Mr. Sahni recovered two more similar cast heads and a few carved bricks (Pl. LXXII, 58 and 59). All the four terracotta heads, including No. 59 of which the head-dress is lost and the left side repaired, appear to have been cast in the same mould. From the above finds it is evident that in early Gupta times the summit of this, the highest mound at Harappā, was crowned by some edifice or group of edifices which, like those on the highest eminence at Mohenjo-daro,[1] were presumably Buddhist.

Stratum II—the latest remains of the Indus period.

The IInd stratum was found at a depth of 4 to 6 ft. below the Gupta remains, and is confined to the raised central part of the mound. To the north, in square P 18/1 along the edge of the excavation, was a circular granary (ht. 6 ft., diam. 4 ft. 2 in.) made of bricks laid stretcherwise (Pl. XXX, *d*, along the right edge and Pl. XXIX, plan and section), and at the centre, about 40 ft. south of this, a rough, square brick platform, on which was found, lying upside down, a large, crushed earthenware bowl filled with ashes and charcoal. Some 8 ft. again, to the east of the latter were the T-shaped remains of two rooms. Two noticeable features of these, which they share with other late remains of Stratum II of the Indus period, are (1) that their construction is extremely poor, and (2) that they are composed mainly of brickbats. The following small objects were recovered from this stratum:—

Finds.

1. Tiny conical limestone *liṅgam*, surface corroded. Ht. 11/16 in. No. Bg3; Depth 2 ft. b.s.
2. Fragmentary unicorn seal with 3 pictograms. Pl. LXXXVII, 42. 1 7/16 in. sq. No. Bg7; Depth 3 ft. b.s.
3. Rough stone ball. Diam. 1 1/8 in. No. B75; Depth 3 ft. 5 in. b.s.
4. Open-mouthed, pedestalled earthenware vase adorned with a row of four deer in two pairs, each pair alternating with a cog-wheel-shaped, circumscribed orb. Above them and enclosed by bands are rows of leaves alternating with fishes. Pl. LXXIII, 51. The shape, ware and paintings are typical of several vases of Stratum II from the northern extension of the Western Section of the Cemetery H. It was found at the foot of the granary mentioned above. Ht. 5 3/4 in.; diam. at mouth 5 1/4 in. No. D27; Depth 4 ft. b.s.
5. Cubical chert weight. Wt. 28·6 gms.; size ·9×·9×·8 in. No. Bg14; Depth 4 ft. b.s.
6. Fragmentary unicorn seal with 3 pictograms surviving. Pl. LXXXVI, 24. 1 3/8 in. sq. No. B101; Depth 5 ft. b.s.
7. Tiny cubical chert weight, the smallest found at Harappā. Wt. 1·3 gms.; size ·32×·32×·3 in. No. Bg23; Depth 5 ft. b.s.
8. Tiny cubical chert weight. Wt. 6·9 gms.; size ·57×·57×·5 in. No. Bg22; Depth 5 ft. b.s.
9. Small quartzite cone, unfinished. Ht. 3/4 in. No. B1826; Depth 5 ft. b.s.

[1] *Cf. M. I. C.*, pp. 113-23.

To the west, in squares Q 18/17 and 18, was a broken rectangular pavement of the IIIrd stratum with brick edging. It is in two parts and measures 10 ft. from north to south by 4 ft. across (Pl. XXX, *b*). In its southern half is a narrow, unpaved chamber (1 ft. 5 in. by 1 ft. 4 in.) lined with brick-on-edge. A similar chamber was found in the large rectangular floor of Stratum V, and two more in other parts of Trench 1 in Mound F. At the bottom of this chamber, Rai Bahadur Daya Ram Sahni found some fragments of charred bones which led him to think that this was a *samādhi*,[1] but as similar bones are still found in the débris immediately under the foundation of the same flooring, those recovered by the Rai Bahadur probably also formed part of the débris. Twenty feet east of this floor is a wall of Stratum III, and 40 ft. further on in the same direction are the remains of a brick-on-edge pavement in squares P 18/8 and 13, and the fragment of a wall in square P 18/9. The following six antiquities were found in connection with this stratum :—

1. Small conical *liṅgam* of hornblende with a white vertical band across the centre. Ht. $\frac{11}{16}$ in. No. B625 ; Depth 7 ft. 8 in. b.s.
2. Right half of a rectangular and plano-convex steatite seal with 5 pictograms surviving. Pl. XCII, 288. Size $1\frac{1}{3} \times \frac{3}{8}$ in. No. D38 : Depth 8 ft. b.s.
3. Hornblende pendent, deeply grooved at the head. Cf. Pl. CXXXIX, 37 and 39. Ht. $\frac{1}{4}$ in. No. D22 ; Depth 8 ft. b.s.
4. Block of grey sandstone roughly resembling a (?) tortoise-shell. Pl. CXVII, 8. Size 2 ft. 5 in. × 2 ft. 7 in. No. B1514 ; Depth 9 ft. b.s.
5. Faience chessman-shaped object. Ht. $\frac{3}{8}$ in. No. B1470 ; Depth 9 ft. b.s.
6. Block of red sandstone carved somewhat in the shape of a tortoise-shell with a shallow oval cavity scooped out on the underside. Size $20 \times 17\frac{1}{3}$ in. No. B1515 ; Depth 11 ft. b.s.

Strata IV and V.

Very little is left of the IVth stratum. The next stratum below revealed, in squares P 18/2 and 7, a solidly built niche at a depth of 24 ft. below the summit of the mound. It measures 8 ft. 4 in. by 5 ft. 2 in. externally, and is composed of bricks of the usual size, *viz.*, $11 \times 5\frac{1}{4} \times 2\frac{1}{2}$ in. Later, it was repaired with larger bricks measuring $14 \times 7 \times 3\frac{1}{2}$ in. On its paved floor Mr. Sahni found a broken, medium-sized earthenware jar, a number of goblets with pointed bases, numerous potsherds and charcoal. Some bones were also found in these vessels. Special interest, however, attaches to a number of fragments[2] mostly of undulating grey stone rings of different sizes, arc-shaped pieces of red standstone with raised flat bands in parallel curves (Pl. LXXXIII, 33 and 35), and some objects of yellow limestone, which were found to the north and north-east of the above-mentioned niche. To the east of these finds were recovered some more red sandstone objects of smaller size with shapes suggestive of round *liṅgams* (Pl. LXXXIII, 26 and

Paved niche.

Fragments of stone rings and other objects.

---

[1] *A. S. R.* for 1924-25, p. 78.

[2] Some of them are inscribed with a number of lines which may be pictographic, *cf.* Pl. CIII, 54-57.

27). oblong shafts rectangular in section (Pl. LXXXIII, 29) blocks finished on three faces (Pl. LXXXIII, 31), and other non-descript pieces of stone. Some interesting pieces from among them are given in the list of finds below.

Two stone rings and a large disc known to Cunningham.

From this same spot probably came two large undulating rings of yellow Jaisalmer stone, and a disc of grey stone which are now lying near the tomb of *Naugazā* (Pl. CXVII, 1, 2 and 16). Each of the rings is 2 ft. in diameter, 1 ft. 1½ in. in height and pierced through the centre with a hole 10¼ in. in diameter. The disc, with a diameter of 2 ft. 9 in., is finished on the face and contiguous edge which tapers out for 3 inches. These three stone objects were also known to Sir Alexander Cunningham who mentions the local legend that two of them were the thumb rings, and the large disc, the '*nag*', or gem of the ring[1] of the *Naugazā*, notwithstanding that the so-called gem is larger than the ring.

A stone ring without undulations.

The Rai Bahadur recovered one undulating ring of yellow stone from the village (Pl. CXVII, 6) and a round one of dull grey stone with a yellowish band (diam. 1 ft. 8 in., and diam. of hole 10 in.) at the centre from the Harappā Police Station (Pl. CXVII, 3). Unlike the former, the latter has no undulations at the top or bottom. It is similar to a large collection of stone rings found by Rai Bahadur Daya Ram Sahni in Room 49, House V, Block 2 of Section B of the Hr. Area at Mohenjo-daro.[2] These large stone rings and many of the miniature ones, fashioned out of stone, shell, faience, and imitation carnelian, are undoubtedly cult-objects, as shown by Sir John Marshall, probably symbolizing the *Yoni* or female principle.[3]

Stone objects.

Some of the more interesting stone objects, other than rings, are described below. Those whose depth ranges from 4 ft. 6 in. to 6 ft. 6 in. were found towards the eastern edge of the trench, and the others with progressively increasing depth, more towards the west reaching a point opposite the paved niche referred to above.

1. Fragment of a red sandstone block with two raised bands (15/16 in. wide) in parallel curves. Pl. LXXXIII, 33. Size 5×3¼ in. No. B1; Depth 4 ft. 6 in. b.s.
2. Fragment of a small polished red sandstone pillar or *liṅgam* split vertically. Ht. 4¼ in.; diam. 4¼ in. No. B2; Depth 4 ft. 6 in. b.s.
3. Fragment of a red sandstone slab polished on the only existing face. L. 6 in. No. B19; Depth 6 ft. b.s.
4. Fragment of a light grey sandstone slab rectangular in section and polished on three sides, one side being broken. On one side it shows a tubular drill hole 1⅜ in. in depth and diameter. L. 7 in.; th. 3½ in. No. B17; Depth 6 ft. b.s.
5. Fragment of a stone pillar similar to No. 2 above. Ht. 4¼ in.; diam. 4⅜ in. No. B102; Depth 6 ft. b.s.

---

[1] *C. S. R.*, Vol. V, p. 106, Pl. XXXIII, 8 and 9.

[2] *Cf. M. I. C.*, p. 191, and also Pl. XXXVIII, f, which shows a row of limestone rings found in chamber 74, Block 3, L. Area.

[3] *Ibid.*, pp. 64-66.

6. Fragment of a block of greyish sandstone with red veins, polished on three sides. It has a tubular drill hole $\frac{13}{16}$ in. in diameter on one face, and a tapering flat rib in relief on the other. Size 5×4½ in. No. B20; Depth 8 ft. b.s.

7. Fragment of a grey stone channel (?) with straight sides. Pl. LXXXIII, 34. Size 4¾×3¾ in. No. B22; Depth 6 ft. b.s.

8. Fragment of a stone pillar or *liṅgam* similar to No. 2 above, of which three-fourths of the circumference is preserved. The broken vertical section shows small aggregates of fossilised mussel shell. Pl. LXXXIII, 27. Ht. 3¾ in.; diam. 4 in. No. B14; Depth 6 ft. b.s.

9. Red sandstone fragment with three finished and polished faces, the fourth being broken. Originally it appears to have been rectangular in section. L. 6 in.; th. 4⅜ in. No. B16; Depth 6 ft. b.s.

10. Fragment of a reddish grey stone, probably of a four-sided prism, split vertically. It is polished on the three preserved faces. Size 4¾×3¾×3½ in. No. B103; Depth 6 ft. 6 in. b.s.

11. Conical grey stone *liṅgam* with two irregular bands over the body. Ht. ¾ in. No. B743; Depth 12 ft. b.s.

12. Fragment of a stone pillar similar to No. 2 above. Ht. 4 in.; diam. 4½ in. No. B134; Depth 12 ft. b.s.

13. Arc-shaped, red sandstone fragment with a raised rib 1½ in. wide parallel to the perimeter, a tubular drill socket on the underside, etc. Ht. 3½ in. No. B755; Depth 15 ft. b.s.

14. Fragment of a pentagonal red sandstone slab inscribed with 5 pictograms. Pl. XCVIII, 599. Size 5¼×4¾×1 in. No. B951; Depth 16 ft. b.s.

15. Rectangular block of yellow sandstone with a number of tubular drill holes. It is dressed but not polished. Pl. LXXXIII, 28. Size 8½×5¼×3¼ in. No. B815; Depth 19 ft. b.s.

16. Fragment of a flat grey stone with indications of three tubular drill holes side by side. Size 6×5¼ in. No. B815; Depth 19 ft. b.s.

17. A grey stone fragment, roughly tetrahedron-shaped, with slightly convex and rounded sides. The base is flat, and has two small tubular drill holes. There is also one large and one small tubular hole in one of the sides. Pl. LXXXIII, 36. This object has the semblance of a rather pointed hoof. L. 6¾ in. No. B1659; Depth 21 ft. b.s.

18. Chessman-shaped faience object. Ht. ¾ in. No. B1106; Depth 14 ft. b.s.

19. Thick, discoid faience bead with sets of oblique lines hatched in an opposite direction in each quarter of the circumference. Diam. ⅞ in. No. B1257; Depth 14 ft. b.s.

20. Faience sealing with chequered pattern of 12 squares enclosed by two successive squares. Pl. XCV, 395. 11/16 in. sq. No. B1114; Depth 17 ft. b.s.
21. Bronze bowl[1] (*katōrā*) with plain thick rim, slightly damaged at bottom. Diam. 6½ in.; ht. 2¼ in. No. B958; Depth 18 ft. b.s.
22. Tapering ivory baluster with cross-hatched decoration at the ends and curved flutes in the intervening space. Pl. CXIX, 31. L. 2 in. No. B976; Depth 16 ft. b.s.

Colour and technique of the above stone objects.

The first seventeen objects mentioned above are interesting as most of them are made either of grey stone like the statuette of the dancer No. Ab959[2] (Pl. LXXXI), or of red sandstone like the nude male torso No. 9042[3] (Pl. LXXX), both of which were found in the lower Mound F. Not only that, but these stone objects also exhibit, like the statuettes, the use of both pointed and tubular drill, and an equally good polish. Another point of technique that should be noticed is that the raised, flat bands in parallel curves[4] on the arc-shaped stones (*e.g.* Pl. LXXXIII, 33 and 35) were first sawn in short lengths with a small, straight edged saw and then gradually converted into a curve, the portion between the raised bands being cut away with the help of a chisel leaving a more or less rough surface between the finished bands.

A large heap of animal bones.

In association with this stratum, and in the central part of the excavation, Rai Bahadur Daya Ram Sahni found a remarkably large heap of loose animal bones (B954), which deserves special mention (Pl. XXX, c). Writing about them in the *A. S. R.* for 1924-25 (p. 79) he says " I had them examined by a professor of the Veterinary College at Lahore and they are stated to include besides many others, which on account of their fragmentary condition are not identifiable, a skull with a few molars of a dog, the upper jaw of a sheep, the lower jaw with two or three molars and hocks (Tibia Tarsal) of an ox, and a large number of bones of a horse or horses, *viz.*, the radius and ulna combined, scapula, humerus, occipital, etc. **************** They may be the remains of a big animal sacrifice ". Several smaller collections of animal bones, almost entirely of cattle, which I found at very low levels in Mound F,[5] Area J, and in the Deep Digging in the Cemetery H[6] were not piled up as these, but lay scattered about, so that only a few bones were ever heaped up together.

Stratum V re-utilised with Stratum IV.

The Vth stratum is distinguished by the massiveness of its brick structures. Along the eastern edge of the original Trench B (which was 160 ft. long from north to south and 20 to 45 ft. wide) it is clear that the buildings of the Vth stratum had been repaired and re-utilised in later times, so that there is absolutely no

---

[1] *Cf. A. S. R.*, for 1924-25, p. 79. Its shape is notoriously modern.

[2] For description of the dancer see pp. 22-23 *supra*.

[3] For its description, see pp. 74-76 *supra*.

[4] This motif of raised bands in parallel curves became very popular in Buddhist architecture, *e.g.*, over the façades of Chaitya caves. We know, too, that several other motifs, such as the railing, tree worship, *svastika* symbol, etc., were also anticipated by the Indus people. For tree worship, etc., *cf.* Sir John Marshall, *op. cit.*, pp. 63-66.

[5] See pp. 34 and 96-97 *supra*.

[6] See p. 232 *infra*.

interval between the Vth and IVth strata (Pl. XXX, *a*, right hand background). A number of tunnels sunk by brick-diggers were met with at this level, particularly towards the north, with the result that what now survives is a more or less confused mass of remains in which the lay-out of the walls is far from clear. Nevertheless, the Rai Bahadur notices two brick structures in the Vth stratum. "One of these", he says, "is a square room with thick walls and paved interior which was divided into two smaller chambers at a later date".[1] The other structure, in squares P 18/20, 25, etc., is a jumble of brick remains in which there is a thick wall some 30 ft. long from east to west to the north face of which was found sticking a small unicorn seal ($\frac{5}{8}$ in. sq., No. B230) with three pictograms (Pl. LXXXIX, 135).

A complete room. In squares P 18/11 and 12 are the remains of an oblong room measuring 14 by 12 ft. internally (Pl. XXX, *d*, right hand, centre), but its walls are not bonded with one another. Its west wall, which is the thickest and rises from a greater depth, was originally constructed with the VIth stratum and subsequently raised. In contact with and parallel to its north wall is a slightly earlier wall which is seen projecting from below the east wall of this room. Alongside of it is a small rectangular drain built across the wall.

The following antiquities were found in association with the Vth stratum :—

Finds.

1. Thick, discoid faience bead incised with cross-hatched pattern. Diam. $\frac{3}{8}$ in. No. B959; Depth 18 ft. b.s.
2. Discoid faience stand with deeply scored tubular projection in the centre. Ht. $\frac{11}{16}$ in.; diam. $1\frac{3}{8}$ in. No. B192; Depth 19 ft. b.s.
3. Knobbed faience lid. Diam. $1\frac{1}{8}$ in. No. B207; Depth 19 ft. b.s.
4. Rough shell ring. $1\frac{7}{8}$ in. wide; diam. $3\frac{1}{4}$ in. No. B1578; Depth 19 ft. b.s.
5. Plano-convex, rectangular steatite seal with 5 pictograms. It is without the usual white glaze. Pl. XCII, 296. Size $1\frac{3}{16} \times \frac{7}{16}$ in. No. B191; Depth 20 ft. b.s.
6. Miniature, open-mouthed earthenware vase with well-defined base. Pl. CXXXIX, 49. Ht. $\frac{3}{8}$ in. No. B1388; Depth 20 ft. b.s.

Remains of Stratum VI. Between the Vth and the VIth strata, except at the room mentioned above, there is generally a layer of débris 2 ft. 6 in. to 3 ft. 3 in. in thickness (Pl. XXIX section). Remains of Stratum VI are scarce, consisting of only a few fragmentary walls in squares P 17/20 and 25 and P 18/8, 12 and 19, two pavements in squares P 18/12 and 13, one of which is composed of well-rubbed bricks of a slightly smaller size, *viz.*, $10\frac{1}{4}$ to 10 by 5 to $4\frac{3}{4}$ by 2 in.,[2] and two rough pavements existing side by side at a higher level in square P 18/17. These latter, on account of their roughness and higher level, appear to be the bottom remains of refuse pits of the Vth stratum. Here, in association with the VIth stratum were found at a depth of 24 ft. below the surface a number of copper pieces in the form of small contiguous circles somewhat resembling the pods of an acacia tree (Pl. CXXIV, 35).

---

[1] This room is not clear now.

[2] Before being chiselled these bricks were presumably of the usual size.

Remains and finds of Stratum VII.

Along the centre of the eastern edge of this excavation, over an area measuring about 40 ft. sq. were exposed at a lower level a few walls and pavements of the VIIth stratum, together with the following antiquities :—

1. Fragment of a unicorn (?) seal with 3 pictograms surviving. Pl. XCIX, 625. L. $1\frac{3}{16}$ in. No. B1522; Depth 24 ft. b.s.
2. Barrel-shaped bead of banded agate. L. $\frac{7}{16}$ in. No. B1180; Depth 24 ft. b.s.
3. Plano-convex, discoid steatite temple ornament. Diam. $\frac{5}{16}$ in. No. B1373; Depth 26 ft. b.s.
4. Miniature faience goblet. Pl. LXXXII, 26. Ht. $\frac{5}{8}$ in. No. B1372; Depth 26 ft. b.s.
5. Unicorn seal with 2 pictograms. Pl. LXXXVIII, 93. 1 in. sq. No. B1341; Depth 28 ft. b.s.

Finds from the surface and unrecorded depth.

The following two objects were found at the surface of the trench :—

1. Plano-convex, rectangular steatite seal[1] with 5 pictograms. Size $1\times\frac{5}{8}$ in. From the summit of the mound to the west of *Naugazā*.
2. Fragmentary, rectangular steatite pendent with cross-hatched pattern on both sides. Size $\frac{5}{16}\times\frac{1}{2}$ in. No. B1465; from surface.

In respect of the following three finds the depth does not appear to have been recorded :—

1. Mason's plummet of steatite, pear-shaped. Pl. CXVII, 9. Ht. $1\frac{1}{4}$ in.; diam. 1 in. No. B241.
2. Limestone ball, probably a child's play marble. Diam. $\frac{11}{16}$ in. No. B562; Depth 3 to 5 ft. b.s.
3. Quarter of a hollow hemisphere of shell with a deep line incised along its perimeter. Length of chord $2\frac{3}{16}$ in.

TRENCH E.

To the south of Excavation B and in the bed of the adjoining deep ravine, the Rai Bahadur cut another shallow trench designated E in which he found the following objects :—

1. Terracotta *liṅgam.* Ht. $\frac{5}{8}$ in. No. E1269.
2. A bunch[2] of three copper instruments connected together by their looped ends. One of the instruments is a double-edged knife, the second a pricker, and the third a pair of pincers. They probably constituted a surgical (?) set. Pl. CXXV, 1. L. $4\frac{3}{8}$, 5, and $5\frac{1}{4}$ in. respectively. No. E3; Depth 3 ft. b.s.
3. Fossilised, bivalve mussel shell. L. $1\frac{1}{8}$ in. No. E25; Depth 3 ft. b.s.

---

[1] This must obviously have been cast out by brick-diggers, since otherwise it could not have lain above the Gupta remains.

[2] For similar bunches of toilet articles *cf.* Petrie, *Tools and weapons* p. 52, Pl. LXIV, figs. 46, 48, and 50-52.

Extension of Pits I and II.

Along with other excavations during the working season of 1924-25 Rai Bahadur Daya Ram Sahni sank four pits in the southern part of this mound, each measuring 50 ft. sq. Of these, I linked up Pits I and II in the year 1926-27 by sinking between them a long, narrow trench, measuring 260 ft. from east to west and varying in width from 13 to 30 ft. The reason for extending this particular part of the excavation was that in Pit I a gable-roofed drain of Stratum IV, going from west to east, had already been brought to light by the Rai Bahadur, and this I was anxious to follow up and ascertain what buildings it was connected with. Accordingly, in the year 1927-28 the whole length of this trench except 66 ft. at its eastern end, was expanded into a large rectangle measuring 194 ft. from east to west by 137 ft. from north to south (Pl. XXXI).

Position of the excavation. **And Division into the Eastern, Middle and Western Sections.**

As will be seen from the site plan (Pl. I) this area lies immediately south of the second large ravine referred to on p. 136 above. Owing to differences in the levels and irregularities in the stratification of the remains, it will be convenient to divide this area into three sections—Western, Middle and Eastern, and I would ask the reader to bear in mind that the division between the Western and Middle sections coincides with a line drawn north to south at a distance of about 80 ft. from the western side of the excavation. The dividing line between the Middle and Eastern sections is less precise but approximately at the same distance from the eastern side of the area.

The main excavation was carried to an average depth of between 10 and 12 ft.; the projecting tongue towards the east to a depth of 16 to 20 ft. In the Middle and Eastern sections, Stratum I goes down to 4 ft. 4 in. below the surface, Stratum II from 4 ft. 5 in. to 6 ft. 9 in., Stratum III from 6 ft. 10 in. to 9 ft. 6 in., Stratum IV from 9 ft. 7 in. to 10 ft. 10 in., and Stratum V from 10 ft. 11 in. to 12 ft. 2 in. But in the eastern tongue all antiquities found lower than 12 ft. below the surface must be relegated to the VIth and earlier strata the limits of which it is not possible to define at present. As against this, in the Western Section Stratum I goes down to 2 ft. 8 in., Stratum II from 2 ft. 9 in. to 5 ft. 1 in., Stratum III from 5 ft. 2 in. to 7 ft. 2 in. and Stratum IV, below which the excavation was not carried down in this section, from 7 ft. 3 in. to 10 ft. 3 in. It should be clearly understood, however, that in places the brick remains are so disconnected and fragmentary that the stratification is far from certain.

Original Pits I and II.

Pits I and II, excavated by Mr. Sahni, lay in one line from north to south and have since merged in the Eastern Section of this excavation. The antiquities found by him will be described with others found in the same strata; and are distinguished by the prefixes PI and PII to their numbers, according as they emanated from Pit I or Pit II.

Stratum I.

In this excavation the structural remains appertaining to Stratum I are few and far between, consisting, in the Eastern Section of a small chamber, 4 ft. 8 in. by 3 ft. 8 in., in square Q 24/12, of a bit of wall to its north, and of some traces of a mud hut to its extreme south, on the edge of the area; while in the Western Section there is only one wall in square P 24/8. Among the minor antiquities from Stratum I, special mention should be made of a carinated copper

Copper jar No. PII-13. pot (PII-13) found by Rai Bahadur Daya Ram Sahni in Pit II at a depth of 3 ft. 6 in. below the surface (Pls. CXXIV, 26 and CXXII, 24). It has straight rim and is of about the same size as the remarkable copper vessel No. 277[1] which I found in Trench I, Mound F. Like that one, it was covered by a shallow, inverted dish but its contents proved to be nothing more than "broken copper dishes, common earth, and two or three teeth of a wild beast".[2] Besides this copper pot the objects from Stratum I included the following:—

Other minor antiquities.

1. Unicorn seal with 3 pictograms. Pl. LXXXIX, 117. $\frac{7}{8}$ in. sq. No. PI-4; Depth 2 ft. 6 in. b.s.
2. Unicorn seal with 6 pictograms. Pl. LXXXVII, 45. $1\frac{7}{16}$ in. sq. No. 2879; Square R 24/2; Depth 3 ft. b.s.
3. Tiny, rectangular steatite seal with 3 pictograms on one side, and 1 on the other. Pl. XCVII, 499. Size $\frac{3}{16}\times\frac{3}{16}$ in. No. PII-1; Depth 1 ft. b.s.
4. Rectangular, plano-convex steatite seal with 6 pictograms. Pl. XCII, 272. Size $1\frac{3}{8}\times\frac{5}{16}$ in. No. PI-2; Depth 1 ft. 8 in. b.s.
5. Bar-shaped, terracotta sealing, square in section. On obverse it shows 3 pictograms and a man standing in front of a tiger with something like a drum held in his hands, and on reverse a row of 5 *svastikas* enclosed in square panels and the same 3 pictograms repeated at the right end. Pl. XCIII, 306. Size $1\frac{3}{16}\times\frac{5}{16}\times\frac{5}{16}$ in. No. 201; Square Q 24/22; Depth 1 ft. 3 in. b.s.
6. Fragmentary chert flake tapering towards the lower end, well polished. Size $2\frac{1}{8}\times\frac{5}{8}$ in. No. 4820; from surface.
7. Cubical chert weight. Wt. 6·72 gms.; size ·6×·6×·4 in. No. 4250; Square Q 24/21; Depth 1 ft. b.s.
8. Cubical chert weight. Wt. 28·25 gms.; size ·95×·95×·65 in. No. 3663; Square Q 23/10; Depth 1 ft. b.s.
9. Cog-wheel-shaped steatite disc decorated with incised circles at the centre and along the perimeter. Pl. CXXXIX, 45. Diam. $\frac{11}{16}$ in. No. 4817; Square P 24/11; Depth 1 ft. 6 in. b.s.
10. Small *liṅgam* of grey stone mottled white. Pl. CXVII, 24. Ht. $\frac{3}{4}$ in. No. 5329; Square P 24/6; Depth 2 ft. b.s.
11. Cubical chert weight. Wt. 3·4 gms.; size ·47×·47×·35 in. No. 4373; Square Q 25/6; Depth 2 ft. b.s.
12. Chessman-shaped object of lapis lazuli, the only one in this stone. Ht. 1 in. No. 4367; Square Q 24/21; Depth 3 ft. b.s.
13. Cubical weight of granite. Wt. 27·65 gms.; size ·9×·9×·65 in. No. 4368; Square Q 24/21; Depth 3 ft. b.s.
14. Cubical chert weight, the largest so far found. Pl. CXVIII, 3. Wt. 2,703·9 gms.; size 4·2×4·2×3·7 in. No. 7168; Square Q 23/15; Depth 4 ft. b.s.

---

[1] See Chap. II, p. 85 *supra*.

[2] *A. S. R.* for 1924-25, p. 80.

15. Cubical chert weight. Wt. 1·75 gms.; size ·4×·4×·3 in. No. 3831; Square Q 24/23; Depth 4 ft. b.s.
16. Glazed faience bangle. It still retains its fine original blue colour. Pl. CXXXVIII, 9. Diam. 2$\frac{3}{4}$ in. No. 2851; Square R 24/7; Depth 5 in. b.s.
17. Faience tetrahedron with a hole through two adjacent sides, and a blind hole in the third. Pl. CXX, 56. Two sides $\frac{11}{16}$ in. each, and one $\frac{5}{8}$ in. No. 5291; Square P 24/24; Depth 2 ft. 6 in. b.s.
18. Faience toy sieve, fragmentary. Diam. 1$\frac{1}{16}$ in. No. 4221; Square Q 25/16; Depth 3 ft. b.s.
19. Tiny faience bowl. Pl. CXXXIX, 51. Ht. $\frac{1}{8}$ in.; diam. $\frac{5}{16}$ in. No. 4219; Square Q 25/16; Depth 3 ft. b.s.
20. Copper spear-head. L. 7$\frac{5}{8}$ in. No. 4370; Square Q 24/1; Depth 1 ft. b.s.
21. Bronze celt, slightly shouldered, cutting edge broken. L. 6$\frac{3}{8}$ in.; width across the cutting edge 3$\frac{1}{4}$ in., and at the butt end 2$\frac{1}{4}$ in. No. PII-2; Depth 1 ft. 3 in. b.s.
22. Copper bar, rectangular in section. L. 3 in.; section $\frac{5}{16}$×$\frac{3}{16}$ in. No. 5187; Square Q 24/4; Depth 2 ft. b.s.
23. Spiral ring of copper wire. Pl. CXXV, 56. Diam. $\frac{5}{8}$ in. No. 4870; Square P 24/6; Depth 2 ft. 3 in. b.s.
24. Carinated copper pot, concave above shoulder; its lid was in several fragments. Pl. CXXIV, 26. Ht. 7$\frac{7}{8}$ in.; diam. 7$\frac{3}{4}$ in. No. PII-13; Depth 3 ft. 6 in. b.s.
25. Broken ivory strip with a rivet hole and serrated lower end. It is decorated with a row of incised circles on both faces. Pl. CXIX, 42. L. 2$\frac{1}{8}$ in.; w. $\frac{7}{16}$ in. No. 7045; Square Q 23/15; Depth 2 ft. 6 in. b.s.
26. Fragmentary ivory comb with a handle at one end. It is decorated with two rows of concentric circles on either face. Only one of its teeth is now left. Pl. CXIX, 6. Ht. 3$\frac{13}{16}$ in. No. 7038; Square Q 23/15; Depth 2 ft. 6 in. b.s.
27. Perforated cylindrical earthenware vase with a hole 1$\frac{3}{4}$ in. in diameter at the bottom. The vase is broken horizontally. Diam. 5 in.; ht. 3$\frac{3}{4}$ in. No. 2549; Square R 24/21; from surface.
28. Oval neck of an ellipsoid earthenware jar with four pairs of holes in the flange. This shape is typical of many jars from Stratum I in the Cemetery H. Pl. LXXIII, 42. Greater diam. 6$\frac{3}{4}$ in. No. 3882; Square Q 24/24; Depth 1 ft. b.s.
29. Medium-sized, oval earthenware vase. Ht. 8 in. No. 2711; Square Q 24/19; Depth 4 ft. b.s.
30. Pear-shaped earthenware vase with flat bottom. It is painted between bands with trees, birds, and wavy lines in the manner of burial pottery. Its fabric also is equally fine. Pl. LXXIII, 73. Ht. 2$\frac{5}{16}$ in. No. 616; Square P 24/22; Depth 4 ft. 2 in. b.s.

31. Large, fragmentary brick with lozenge pattern incised on one side. L. 13 in.; th. 3$\frac{1}{4}$ to 3$\frac{3}{4}$ in.; w. 9 in. No. 5602; Square P 23/10; Depth 1 ft. b.s.

32. Terracotta toy-cart shaped rather like a modern tipping truck. Pl. CXX, 4. Ht. 3$\frac{3}{8}$ in.; L. 3$\frac{3}{4}$ in.; w. 3 in. No. 4867; Square P 24/16; Depth 2 ft. b.s.

33. Sherd of a dish showing part of a pictogram. Pl. CII, 17. Size 7×5 in. No. 1210; Square R 24/7; Depth 3 ft. b.s.

Stratum II.

In the East and Middle Sections Stratum II lies between 4 ft. 5 in. and 6 ft. 9 in., and in the Western Section between 2 ft. 9 in. and 5 ft. 1 in. below the surface. From this stratum downwards, the southern part of the Middle Section becomes more and more productive in finds, though here, too, the structural remains continue very poor (Pl. XXXI). This portion is bounded on the north by a long, gable-roofed drain of the IVth stratum, on the west by a reservoir of the IIIrd and a dilapidated pavement of the IInd stratum, on the south by the edge of the excavation, and on the east by the line of squares Q 24/8, 9, 10 and Q 25/6. In this portion, close to the southern edge of the trench, there are several remains of Stratum II consisting of three corners, a few walls, and a small pavement. The following antiquities were found in it:—

Remains and finds from southern part of Middle Section.

1. Unicorn seal with 4 pictograms, damaged. Pl. LXXXVII, 54. 1$\frac{1}{16}$ in. sq. No. 1314; Square P. 24/23; Depth 4 ft. b.s.

2. Two fragments of a unicorn seal showing 2 pictograms, head of the animal, and incense-burner. L. $\frac{7}{10}$ in. No. 5759; Square Q 25/1; Depth 5 ft. b.s.

3. Unicorn seal with 8 pictograms. Pl. LXXXV, 1. 2$\frac{5}{8}$ in. sq. No. 3716; Square Q 24/9; Depth 5 ft. 6 in. b.s.

4. Unicorn seal with 8 pictograms. Pl. LXXXVI, 22. 1$\frac{5}{16}$ in. sq. No. 3725; Square Q 24/10; Depth 5 ft. 9 in. b.s.

5. Bossed faience sealing with a *svastika* in relief. Similar to No. 396 in Pl. XCV. $\frac{5}{8}$ in. sq. No. 5639; Square Q 24/4; Depth 4 ft. 6 in. b.s.

6. Small conical stone *liṅgam*. Pl. CXVII, 20. Ht. 1$\frac{3}{16}$ in. No. 5427; Square P 24/24; Depth 3 ft. 6 in. b.s.

7. Cross-shaped bead of burnt steatite bored across one arm which is square in section, while the other arm is tapering and pointed at both ends. Pl. CXXVIII, 27. Size $\frac{1}{2}$×$\frac{1}{2}$ in. No. 4556; Square Q 24/9; Depth 3 ft. 8 in. b.s.

8. Cubical limestone weight, Wt. 3·3 gms.; size ·45×·45×·4 in. No. 5505; Square Q 24/5; Depth 3 ft. 10 in. b.s.

9. Plum-shaped, sonpstone ear-drop. Ht. $\frac{5}{8}$ in. No. 5292; Square P 24/9; Depth 4 ft. b.s.

10. Cubical chert weight. Wt. 3·5 gms.; size ·45×·45×·4 in. No. 5580; Square P 24/24; Depth 4 ft. 3 in. b.s.

11. Conical finial of hornblende with a vertical tubular drill hole in the underside and a lateral hole at the base. Ht. 2⅜ in.; diam. at base 2¼ in. No. 4605; Square Q 24/9; Depth 4 ft. 6 in. b.s.
12. Miniature conical *liṅgam* of chalcedony, well polished. Pl. CXVII, 15. Ht. 13/16 in. No. 4602; Square Q 24/3; Depth 4 ft. 7 in. b.s.
13. Tiny ball of hornblende. Diam. ⅜ in. No. 5824; Square P 24/24; Depth 5 ft. 6 in. b.s.
14. Small conical *liṅgam* of yellow Jaisalmer stone with three equidistant vertical grooves meeting at the apex. Pl. CXVII, 34., Ht. 1¼ in. No. 3717; Square Q 24/9; Depth 5 ft. 6 in. b.s. For a similar object *Cf. M. I. C.*, Pl. CLVII, 61.
15. Chert core. Size 4⅛×1⅞×1⅛ in. No. 5901; Square Q 25/1; Depth 6 ft. b.s.
16. Four-legged sandstone for grinding curries. Pl. CXVII, 51. Size 16½×13×4 in. No. 4713; Square Q 24/9; Depth 6 ft. 4 in. b.s.
17. Fragment of a faience object with raised pattern in black glaze. Pl. LXXXII, 13. Size 15/16×⅝ in. No. 5472; Square P 24/24; Depth 3 ft. 6 in. b.s.
18. Fragment of a thick, deeply serrated bangle of green faience. Pl. CXXXVIII, 12. L. 2¾ in. No. 4655; Square Q 25/6; Depth 4 ft. b.s.
19. Pendent of burnt steatite, shaped like a lemon leaf. It is chamfered and holed at the base for attachment. Pl. CXXXIX, 4. L. 1⅝ in.; w. 13/16 in. No. 5679; Square P 25/21; Depth 4 ft. 8 in. b.s.
20. Perforated, miniature cylindrical faience bottle with mouldings around neck and holed at the bottom. Pl. LXXXII, 10. Ht. 2 1/16 in.; diam. at bottom ⅝ in. No. 7024; Square P 24/10; Depth 5 ft., b.s.
21. Faience button with indented border. Pl. CXXXIX, 21. Diam. ¾ in. No. 5822; Square P 25/21; Depth 5 ft. 5 in. b.s.
22. Fragment of a hollow cylinder of imitation carnelian painted in white with bands and curved lines. Pl. LXXXIII, 44. Diam. 1 in.; ht. 1¼ in. No. 5467; Square P 24/24; Depth 3 ft. 6 in. b.s.
23. Heart-shaped shell object with bevelled edge for inlay. Pl. CXXXIX, 84. Greatest diam. ¾ in. No. 3718; Square Q 25/6; Depth 5 ft. 3 in. b.s.
24. Fragmentary shell spoon. L. 4¼ in. No. 5829; Square Q 25/1; Depth 5 ft. 5 in. b.s.
25. Terracotta ball with nail incisions. Diam. 1¼ in. No. 4612; Square Q 24/8; Depth 4 ft. 9 in. b.s.
26. Terracotta hen on stand with outstretched wings. Pl. LXXVIII, 14. Ht. 2⅜ in. No. 5827; Square Q 25/1; Depth 5 ft. 5 in. b.s.

Uncommon pottery forms.

In the northern part of the Middle Section and across the gable-roofed drain, where there are no structural remains of Stratum II, were found the following antiquities which include two cylindrical pottery bottles with flared mouths (Pls. LXX, 27, and LXXI, 4 and 5) and several flesh rubbers of uncommon forms

(Pls. LXX, 26 and LXXI, 11-13) the former being the only examples of their kind so far found at Harappā or Mohenjo-daro.

1. Cubical chert weight. Wt. 3·3 gms.; size ·47×·45×·37 in. No. 4912; Square P 23/25; Depth 3 ft. 6 in. b.s.
2. Fragmentary faience terminal, semi-oval in shape. L. $\frac{3}{4}$ in.; w. $\frac{1}{2}$ in. No. 7146; Square Q 23/5; Depth 4 ft. 6 in. b.s.
3. Copper spear-head with short tang, broken along the cutting edge, the back edge being concave. L. 4 in.; w. $1\frac{5}{8}$ in. No. 7303; Square Q 23/5; Depth 4 ft. b.s.
4. Four-sided, hollow pottery flesh rubber (fragmentary) with convex surface rubbed on all sides. L. 4 in. No. 5097; Square P. 24/21; Depth 5 ft. b.s.
5. Two cylindrical earthenware bottles with flared mouths. Rare. Pl. LXXI, 4 and 5. Ht. $7\frac{1}{2}$ and $7\frac{1}{4}$ in. No. 4383; Square P 24/21; Depth 5 ft. 9 in. b.s.
6. Small, round earthenware vase with long, concave neck. It is red-washed and painted with a row of leaves enclosed by bands. The ware is similar to some found in the Cemetery H. Ht. $2\frac{1}{4}$ in No. 7408; Square P 23/25; Depth 6 ft. b.s.

Western Section. Southern part.

In the southern part of the Western Section are the remains of a large pavement in square P 25/21, and close to it on the north, a small square pavement. No finds, however, were made in association with them, and the five antiquities mentioned below came from the area to the north-west of the latter pavement.

1. Upper half of a unicorn seal with 4 pictograms. Pl. LXXXVIII, 69. $1\frac{5}{8}$ in. sq. No. 5383; Square P 24/9; Depth 4 ft. 6 in. b.s.
2. Discoid button of steatite paste. Pl. CXXXIX, 44. Diam. $\frac{5}{16}$ in. No. 5585; Square P24/14; Depth 5 ft. 6 in. b.s.
3. Biconical bead of *sang-i-abri.* No. 5915; Square P. 24/9; Depth 6 ft. 6 in. b.s.
4. Alabaster pedestal (similar to the one illustrated in Pl. LXXXIII, 8), broken on one side. Having been rendered unserviceable it was being sawn vertically from top and bottom for making smaller objects. Diam. $6\frac{1}{2}$ in.; ht. $2\frac{3}{8}$ in. No. 7397; Square P 24/9; Depth 6 ft. 6 in. b.s.
5. Shallow earthenware crucible, oval at base and with straight sides. Pl. LXXI, 80. Size $1\frac{5}{8}\times\frac{13}{16}$ in. No. 1322; Square P 24/8; Depth 3 ft. b.s.

Structures and finds in its northern part.

In the northern part of the Western Section there are a few isolated bits of walls of Stratum II, and in square P 24/11 is a small pavement built against an existing wall of Stratum III. Close to this pavement were found the following seven objects:—

1. Unicorn seal with 5 pictograms. Pl. LXXXVIII, 97. $\frac{3}{4}$ in. sq. No. 5082; Square P 24/11; Depth 5 ft. 10 in. b.s.
2. Unicorn seal with 2 pictograms. Pl. LXXXVI, 18. $1\frac{1}{4}$ in. sq. No. 5083; Square P 24/11; Depth 6 ft. b.s.

3. Small bronze chisel $\frac{1}{4}\times\frac{3}{16}$ in. in section, unfinished. L. $1\frac{3}{8}$ in. No. 5087; Square P 24/11; Depth 6 ft. b.s.
4. Short, thick ivory stilus with a sharp point. Pl. CXIX, 12. L. $1\frac{7}{8}$ in. No. 4956; Square P 24/11; Depth 4 ft. b.s.

Pottery.

5. Painted upper part of a standard cup. Diam. at rim $3\frac{3}{8}$ in. No. 4955; Square P 24/11; Depth 4 ft. b.s.
6. Whistling hen (*ghuggu*). L. $2\frac{3}{8}$ in.; ht. $2\frac{1}{4}$ in. No. 4958; Square P 24/11; Depth 4 ft. b.s.
7. Hen on standard base. Pl. LXXVIII, 13. Ht. $3\frac{1}{8}$ in. No. 5092; Square P 24/11; Depth 6 ft. b.s.

The following objects of Stratum II were found widely distributed over the whole trench:— Stray finds.

1. Unicorn seal with 10 pictograms. Pl. LXXXV, 14. $1\frac{11}{16}$ in. sq. No. 7411; Square Q 23/15; Depth 6 ft. 4 in. b.s.
2. Fragmentary, rectangular, plano-convex steatite seal with 3 pictograms surviving. Pl. XCII, 292. Size $1\frac{1}{4}\times\frac{1}{2}$ in. No. 7409; Square Q 23/10; Depth 6 ft. b.s.
3. Rectangular steatite seal with 2 pictograms, unfinished. Rough boss at the back. Pl. XCII, 298. Size $1\times\frac{7}{12}$ in. No. 4432; Square P 24/16; Depth 6 ft. 1 in. b.s.
4. Fragment of a chert polisher, semi-oval in section. L. $1\frac{7}{16}$ in. No. 5648; Square P 23/10; Depth 3 ft. b.s.
5. Cubical limestone weight. Wt. 6·85 gms.; size ·7×·65×·35 in. No. 7512; Square P 25/11; Depth 3 ft. b.s.
6. Cubical chert weight. Wt. 6·85 gms.; size ·6×·6×·45 in. No. 5426; Square P 24/7; Depth 4 ft. b.s.
7. Broad chert knife with a rough mid-rib on one side. Pl. CXVIII, 45. Size $5\frac{3}{8}\times1\frac{3}{8}$ in. No. 3727; Square Q 24/14; Depth 5 ft. b.s.
8. Cubical chert Weight chipped off along the edges. Wt. 27·3 gms.; size ·9×·9×·8 in. No. 7664; Square P 25/11; Depth 5 ft. b.s.
9. Cubical limestone weight. Wt. 2·75 gms.; size ·4×·4×·35 in. No. 5012; Square P 24/16; Depth 5 ft. b.s.
10. Long-barrel object of hornblende, probably a weight. L. $3\frac{3}{8}$ in. No. 4374; Square Q 25/16; Depth 5 ft. b.s.
11. Cubical chert weight. Wt. 27·0 gms.; size ·95×·95×·7 in. No. 7640; Square Q 23/10; Depth 6 ft. b.s.
12. Discoid button of steatite paste. Pl. CXXXIX, 30. Diam. $\frac{3}{8}$ in. No. 5477; Square P 23/10; Depth 5 ft. b.s.
13. Tiny copper ball (?). Pl. CXXV, 11. Diam. $\frac{3}{16}$ in. No. 4377; Square Q 25/16; Depth 5 ft. b.s.
14. Earthenware lamp-stand with marks of burning. Pl. LXXI, 82. Ht. $4\frac{3}{4}$ in. No. 7304; Square P 23/15; Depth 4 ft. b.s.
15. Convex potsherd pierced through with a row of oblong apertures and bands of incised cross hatching above and below. Pl. LXXII, 33. Size $5\times4\frac{1}{4}$ in. No. 7089; Square P 24/20; Depth 5 ft. b.s.

Finds from Pits I and II.

There were no brick remains of Stratum II in Pits I or II, but the following antiquities were found in them by the Rai Bahadur :—

1. Unicorn seal with 9 pictograms; broken at the lower right corner. Pl. LXXXVI, 25. $1\frac{1}{4}$ in. sq. No. PII-21; Depth 5 ft. b.s.
2. Unicorn seal with 5 pictograms. Pl. LXXXV, 6. $2\frac{1}{16}$ in. sq. No. PI-39; Depth 5 ft. b.s.
3. Unicorn seal with 8 pictograms. Pl. LXXXV, 3. $2\frac{1}{4}$ in. sq. No. PI-40; Depth 5 ft. b.s.
4. Unicorn seal with 5 pictograms, lower right corner broken. Pl. LXXXV, 8. $1\frac{1}{2}$ in. sq. No. PI-41; Depth 5 ft. b.s.
5. Unicorn seal with 8 pictograms. Pl. LXXXV, 4. $1\frac{3}{8}$ in. sq. No. PI-42; Depth 5 ft. b.s.
6. Unicorn seal with 4 pictograms. Pl. LXXXVIII, 99. $\frac{3}{4}$ in. sq. No. PII-23; Depth 5 ft. 6 in. b.s.
7. Unicorn seal with 2 pictograms. Pl. LXXXVIII, 91. 1 in. sq. No. PII-53; Depth 5 ft. 10 in. b.s.
8. Rectangular, plano-convex steatite seal with 3 pictograms. Pl. XCII, 289. Size $\frac{11}{16} \times \frac{3}{8}$ in. No. PI-44; Depth 6 ft. b.s.
9. Four-petalled flower cone of red sandstone[1] with a cylindrical hole through the centre and a tubular drill socket in the side. Pl. LXXXIII, 21. Ht. $2\frac{3}{4}$ in.; diam. $3\frac{1}{4}$ in. No. PII-20; Depth 5 ft. b.s.
10. Two hornblende pendents, deeply grooved at the neck. Ht. $\frac{5}{8}$ and $\frac{9}{16}$ in. No. PI-70 and 71; Depth 6 ft. 6 in. b.s.
11. A small faience flower with six petals. Damaged. Diam. 1 in. No. PI-58; Depth 5 ft. 3 in. b.s.

Finds from the north-east corner of the excavation.

At the north-east corner of the excavation were found the following objects in the adjoining squares Q 23/20, 25, and Q 24/21 :—

1. Rectangular, plano-convex steatite seal with 12 pictograms, chipped off at both ends. Pl. XCII, 271. Size $2\frac{1}{2} \times \frac{3}{4}$ in. No. 7354; Square Q 23/20; Depth 6 ft. 2 in. b.s.
2. Chessman-shaped stone object. Ht. $\frac{13}{16}$ in. No. 4387; Square Q 24/21; Depth 4 ft. b.s.
3. Small, rectangular object of yellow sandstone with two adjoining holes, each measuring $\frac{11}{16} \times \frac{3}{16}$ in. One of the holes was closed by a piece of shell inlay. Projecting on either side of the base is a short flange $\frac{1}{8}$th in. long by which it could be slided into a case. Size $1\frac{7}{8} \times \frac{7}{16} \times \frac{3}{8}$ in. No. 4435; Square Q 24/21; Depth 5 ft. 8 in. b.s.
4. Fragmentary flint tablet (?), chipped on both faces. Size $3\frac{3}{4} \times 1\frac{3}{8}$ in. No. 444; Square Q 24/21; Depth 6 ft. b.s.
5. Two-holed rectangular steatite amulet. Size $\frac{13}{16} \times \frac{13}{16} \times \frac{1}{4}$ in. No. 4510; Square Q 24/21; Depth 8 ft. b.s.

[1] This stone is the same as that of the red sandstone torso of a nude male figure No. 9042, see pp. 74-76 *supra*.

6. Chessman-shaped faience object with a hole at bottom. Ht. 1⅛ in. No. 7573*b*; Square Q 23/20; Depth 6 ft. b.s.
7. Copper bare metal chisel $\frac{3}{16}$th in. square in section; the edge is slightly splayed. *Cf.* chisel No. 277k/2, Pl. CXXIII, 52. L. 5⅜ in.; w. at edge $\frac{3}{16}$ in.; w. at butt end ¼ in. No. 4384; Square Q 24/21; Depth 4 ft. b.s.
8. Small, flat bottomed earthenware vase painted with bands. Such vases are now-a-days used as inkpots by small boys in India. Ht. 1⅞ in. No. 4448; Square Q 24/21; Depth 5 ft. b.s.
9. Broad, squat earthenware vase with narrow mouth. Pl. LXXI, 26. Ht. 4 in. No. 3291; Square Q 23/25; Depth 5 ft. 3 in. b.s.
10. Small blackware vase. Ht. 2 in. No. 4438; Square Q 24/21; Depth 5 ft. 6 in. b.s.
11. 42 double convex, discoid beads of terracotta, and a faience chessman-shaped object found together. Pl. CXXVIII, 4. No. 7573*a*; Square Q 23/20; Depth 6 ft. b.s.

Still further east, on the slope of the mound where the trench projects beyond the rectangle, were discovered the undermentioned four objects. but no brick remains came to light. **Finds from the east end.**

1. Unfinished, rectangular steatite seal with 10 pictograms along three edges of the face. Pl. XCI, 254. Size $1\frac{1}{2}\times1\frac{7}{16}$ in. No. 2789; Square R 24/12; Depth 6 ft. b.s. This is much nearer a square than the ordinary rectangular seals of which the length considerably exceeds the width.
2. Half of a shuttle-shaped chert burnisher. Pl. CXVIII, 33. L. 3¼ in. No. 2469; Square R 24/7; Depth 4 ft. 6 in. b.s.
3. Quadrilateral-shaped, polished red sandstone slab 2⅞ in. thick with one tubular drill hole in each of the four sides. The holes are 1⅛ to 1¼ in. deep and $\frac{15}{16}$ to 1 in. in diameter. The faces and sides are all finished. There are two arc-shaped cuts along one of the oblique sides, but as the slab is broken at one point its shape is not certain. It may have been pentagonal instead of quadrilateral. Pl. LXXXIII, 30. Size $16\frac{3}{4}\times13$ in. No. 2847; Square R 24/7; Depth 7 ft. b.s.
4. Hornblende pendent, deeply grooved at the head. Ht. ½ in. No. 2790; Square R 24/12; Depth 7 ft. b.s.

In the Middle and Eastern Sections Stratum III lies between 6 ft. 10 in. and 9 ft. 6 in. below the surface, and in the Western Section between 5 ft. 2 in. and 7 ft. 2 in. With the exception of the northern part of the Middle Section, where it does not seem to exist at all, it is represented everywhere by mere fragments of buildings, without one single complete room. The number of antiquities, however, found in this stratum was considerable. **Stratum III.**

To begin first with the Western Section, which is divided across the middle by an open space which was already in existence during the fourth period of **Western Section.**

occupation (Pl. XXXI). At the west end of this space, and running north to south at right angles to it, there was a broad passage near the western limit of the excavation between Houses 1 and 2. Of the westernmost House 1 there are only two adjacent walls surviving—one with a little projection. Here, as shown on the plan, were found two small earthenware jars lying close to each other. Eastward, on the other side of the passage, are the remains of House 2 in which there is a large but dilapidated brick-on-edge pavement, measuring 18 ft. 3 in. by 11 ft. 3 in. This pavement is laid on a bed of rammed concrete over which again there is a 2 to 3 in. thick layer of fine gravel or *bajri* (Pl. XXXII, *d*, foreground). Near its northern edge are two rectangular depressions with an interval of 2 ft. between them and at the centre of each is an approximately circular brick, 5¼ in. in diameter. In this house was found at a depth of 7 ft. below the surface half of a tiny rectangular faience sealing (No. 4765, Pl. XCVIII, 595) showing an animal—probably a goat—and VIII on one side, and three pictograms on the other. Its existing length is only ⅜ in. A few feet to the south-east of this pavement was a fragmentary rectangular platform with brick edging round a mud core. Its west side is 6 ft. long.

A brick-on-edge pavement with two depressions.

Platform with mud core.

A saucer-shaped depression.

To the north-east of the above pavement was discovered, in squares P 24/18 and 19 an irregular and shallow saucer-shaped depression sunk in hard earth (Pl. XXXIII, *c*). It is 11 ft. 6 in. in diameter and 1 ft. 10 in. deep, and had a filmy coating of bluish green earth with a soft, soapy feel. According to Khan Bahadur Mohammad Sana Ullah, Archæological Chemist in India, it is Fuller's earth (*Multāni matti*) which until very recently was used by women in the Panjāb for washing and cleaning purposes. He infers that this earth was imported and used during the Indus Period at Harappā. Later on, a rectangular pillar was built inside this depression and two walls along its outer edge.

Finds from the northern part of the Western Section.

North of the open space referred to above were found the following three objects :—

1. Rectangular, plano-convex seal[1] of blue faience with 3 pictograms. Rare. Faience sealings are common but not seals. Pl. XCIX, 629. Size 13/16 × ½ in. No. 4703; Square P 24/8; Depth 7 ft. b.s.
2. Fragment of the rim of an open-mouthed copper vessel. L. 3⅝ in. No. 7642; Square P 24/9; Depth 7 ft. b.s.
3. Terracotta ball honeycombed with holes. Pl. CXX, 36. Diam. 1⅞ in. No. 6050; Square P 24/9; Depth 7 ft. b.s.

Buildings of Stratum III constructed against a wall of Stratum V.

One of the most noticeable features in this section is an east-west wall on the northern side of the open space referred to above (Pl. XXXIII, *b*). It is 53 ft. long, 2 ft. thick, and is broken at both ends. Originally constructed during the Vth period of occupation it was subsequently used both in the IVth and the IIIrd periods. In the foreground of the above photograph may be seen, one above the other, the openings of two small wall drains, and by their side a

[1] It is possible, however that being made of faience it was a sealing rather than a seal in which case the mould would have been in relief.

water chute 10½ in. wide with sloping back. The chute and the upper drain are contemporary with the IVth stratum, but the lower opening probably belonged to the Vth. Against the north face of this wall were built structures of both the IVth and IIIrd strata, the former being mostly buried below the latter, while in their turn structures of the IIIrd were overlaid by an oblique drain, a fragmentary brick-on-edge pavement, and one or two bits of walls of Stratum II some of which may be seen at a higher level in the above photograph. Of the IIIrd stratum, there is an incomplete room in front of the man figured in the photograph, a broken drain to the south of this room, and another drain to the man's left, which emptied itself down into the drain of the IVth stratum alongside the water chute. Behind this complex, a little towards the north-west, are the remains of a larger room of Stratum III, of which the west and south walls are missing.

Gable-roofed drain of Stratum IV.

The open space in front of the long wall, and the water chute and drain openings referred to above all drained away towards the east through a gable-roofed drain which has been traced for a length of 130 ft. (Pl. XXXI). This drain, originally constructed in the IVth Period, was subsequently utilised by builders of the IIIrd Period. At its western end, abutting on to south were found four large earthenware jars (Pl. XXXIII, *a*). Of these, the higher one belonged to the IInd stratum, and the remaining three to the IIIrd. Of the latter, the right hand jar had no connection with the drain, but the other two, which are connected with each other and enclosed round the mouth by square brick reservoirs,[1] were embedded in the ground (Pl. XXXIII, *a*). Spill water from the eastern jar flowed through a narrow and shallow drain into the western jar (Pl. XXXIV, *c*), which is embedded at a lower level, since it was also fed from the south by another contemporary drain with a 6-inch sq. opening (Pl. XXXII, *b*, right ground centre). To lodge silt in the two jars and ensure proper functioning of the gable-roofed drain only the surplus water from the western jar was allowed to pass into it by means of an overflow channel seen in Pl. XXXIII, *a*. West of these jars this drain now extends for 3 ft. 4 in. only. At this point its roof is flat, not gabled.

Spill water jars in connection with the above drain.

Two rubbish-pits along the drain.

At a distance of 50 ft. from the existing west end of this drain there is a jar lined rubbish-pit 1 ft. 11 in. deep, and 53 ft., still further east, another brick-lined pit 2 ft. 7 in. sq. and 1 ft. 7 in. deep. Both of these pits belong to the IVth stratum and were constructed along with the original drain.

A drain of Stratum V buried below the above drain.

The gable-roofed drain, described above, having ended abruptly on the east, I dug deeper at this point and discovered, 4 ft. 4 in. below its foundation, another well-built drain of the Vth stratum laid in a packing of mud bricks (Pl. XXXII, *c*). This drain is 2 ft. wide, 2 ft. 3 in. high, and its walls, supported from behind as they are by a solid mass of mud bricks, are only one brick thick. This is the best and largest drain at Harappā—larger even than the drain[2] of Stratum VI found alongside the Deep Digging in Trench I, Mound F. Like the latter, it is neatly paved with well rubbed brick-on-edge which, in this case, is laid on a properly sloped bed of flat bricks. The drain has a sharp gradient towards the east:

---

[1] Reservoir on the western jar has a larger capacity.

[2] For a description of this drain see p. 106 *supra*.

for 100 ft. it runs in the same alignment under the gable-roofed drain above it, then turns round to north, widens out, and is ultimately lost in a great mass of débris. For about 20 ft. at its eastern end, which projects beyond the upper drain. it is much dilapidated showing only the south wall and a part of the pavement. At this place it was tunnelled to a length of 15 ft. and found completely choked with earth and potsherds discoloured green. A large majority of the sherds were fragments of goblets with pointed bases evidently used as drinking vessels and thrown away after use as is still the custom in India.

Remains and finds of Stratum III in the Middle Section, southern part.

In the southern part of the Middle Section of this excavation are the remains of two pavements, several fragments of walls, and a few corners, none of which is more than a few feet in length. Nevertheless, this area, more than any other, was prolific in small finds among which the undermentioned deserve notice:—

1. Unicorn seal with 5 pictograms, upper left corner broken. Pl. LXXXVIII, 73. $1\frac{1}{16}$ in. sq. No. 7006; Square Q 24/5; Depth 7 ft. 6 in. b.s.
2. Seal in the making, showing 2 pictograms and unfinished body of unicorn. Pl. XC, 169. $1\frac{3}{16}$ in. sq. No. 7113; Square Q 24/5; Depth 8 ft. 6 in. b.s.
3. Rectangular, plano-convex steatite seal, fragmentary, with only 2 pictograms surviving. Pl. XCII, 293. L. $\frac{5}{8}$ in.; w. $\frac{1}{2}$ in. No. 4795; Square Q 24/3; Depth 7 ft. 6 in. b.s.
4. Tiny, cylindrical steatite seal with 6 pictograms round the circumference, VIII-like symbol on top, and a dotted circle at the bottom. Pl. XCV, 409*a*. Diam. $\frac{1}{3}$ in.; ht. $\frac{1}{4}$ in. No. 7121; Square Q 24/3; Depth 8 ft. b.s.
5. Tiny, rectangular steatite seal with 3 pictograms on one side, and 2 on the other. Pl. XCVI, 482. Size $\frac{7}{12}\times\frac{1}{4}$ in. No. 7155; Square P 24/25; Depth 8 ft. 6 in. b.s.
6. Bossed faience seal with 2 pictograms. Rare. Pl. XCV, 382. $\frac{5}{8}$ in. sq. No. 5975; Square Q 24/5; Depth 6 ft. 8 in. b.s.
7. Tiny, oval faience sealing with 5 pictograms on one side, and 1 on the other. Pl. C, 674. Size $\frac{5}{8}\times\frac{3}{8}$ in. No. 5974; Square Q 24/5; Depth 7 ft. 6 in. b.s.
8. Faience sealing embossed with a *svastika*. Similar to No. 399 in Pl. XCV. $\frac{5}{8}$ in. sq. No. 4762: Square Q 24/9; Depth 7 ft. 9 in. b.s.
9. Tiny, rectangular faience sealing, fragmentary, with 2 pictograms on one side, and a double-line diagonal cross enclosed in a square on the other. Pl. XCIX, 648. L. $\frac{7}{16}$ in.; w. $\frac{3}{8}$ in. No. 7156; Square P 24/25; Depth 8 ft. 6 in. b.s.
10. Cubical chert weight, broken diagonally. Wt. 98·24 gms.; size 1·52 ×1·52×1·3 in. No. 6059; Square Q 24/4; Depth 7 ft. b.s.
11. Oval steatite bead, lentoid in section. Drilled with circles in trefoil form for inlay.[1] L. $\frac{7}{8}$ in. No. 4774; Square Q 24/3; Depth 7 ft. b.s.

[1] For similar patterning *cf. M. I. C.*, Pl. CXLVI, 53.

12. Fragmentary arc-shaped tube of yellow Jaisalmer stone. Pl. LXXXIII, 45. L. 4 in.; diam. 2 in. No. 4799; Square Q 24/10; Depth 7 ft. 6 in. b.s.
13. Globular bead of burnt steatite with a broad raised band round the centre. Diam. $\frac{5}{8}$ in. No. 7097; Square Q 24/3; Depth 8 ft. b.s.
14. Cubical chert weight. Wt. 54·0 gms.; size 1·25×1·25×·8 in. No. 4993; Square Q 25/6; Depth 8 ft. 4 in. b.s.
15. Alabaster ball. Diam. $1\frac{3}{8}$ in. No. 4939; Square Q 24/8; Depth 8 ft. 6 in. b.s.
16. Hornblende pendent, deeply grooved at the head. Ht. $\frac{15}{16}$ in. No. 7157; Square P 24/25; Depth 8 ft. 6 in. b.s.
17. Cubical weight of cherty limestone, damaged. Wt. 52·2 gms.; size 1·15×1·15×·9 in. No. 5086; Square Q 25/6; Depth 8 ft. 6 in. b.s.
18. Barrel-shaped stone bead. L. $\frac{13}{16}$ in. No. 7438; Square Q 24/3; Depth 9 ft. b.s.
19. Cog-wheel faience disc, fragmentary. Diam. $\frac{13}{16}$ in. No. 7007; Square Q 24/4; Depth 7 ft. b.s.
20. Tiny, lozenge-shaped piece of faience with concave edges for inlay. Bears traces of red paint. L. $\frac{11}{32}$ in. No. 6058; Square Q 24/4; Depth 7 ft. b.s.
21. Fragment of a faience vase with black glaze at the neck where the surface has become rough as the glaze has run down owing to intense vitrification. Pl. LXXXII, 21. Size $1\frac{13}{16}\times1\frac{1}{4}$ in. No. 6054; Square Q 24/4; Depth 7 ft. b.s.
22. Faience button with indented border, knob broken. Diam. $\frac{5}{8}$ in. No. 7008; Square Q 24/5; Depth 7 ft. 6 in. b.s.
23. Fragment of a small, faience vase with 6 black bands. Pl. LXXXII, 20. Ht. 2 in. No. 4801; Square Q 24/9; Depth 7 ft. 6 in. b.s.
24. Faience finger-ring with fluted surface. Pl. CXXXIX, 43. Diam. $\frac{15}{16}$ in. No. 4766; Square Q 24/3; Depth 7 ft. 6 in. b.s.
25. Faience tetrahedron incised with a circle on each face. Pl. CXX, 55. Size $\frac{7}{16}\times\frac{7}{16}\times\frac{3}{8}$ in. No. 4763; Square Q 24/3; Depth 7 ft. 6 in. b.s.
26. Closed faience tube, fragmentary. L. $1\frac{1}{4}$ in.; diam. $\frac{3}{8}$ in. No. 7017; Square Q 25/1; Depth 7 ft. 6 in. b.s.
27. Tiny, couchant faience ram holed across the neck for suspension. L. 1 in. No. 4865; Square Q 24/3; Depth 7 ft. 9 in. b.s.
28. Conical faience ornament with a loop on the inside below the apex for attachment. It was worn on the forehead as shown on terracotta figurines Nos. 23 and 30 in Pl. LXXVI. A similar ornament of gold was also found in the jewellery lot No. 8060 from Trench IV, Mound F. Pl. CXXXVII, 2. Ht. $\frac{13}{16}$ in.; diam. 1 in. No. 7082; Square P 24/24; Depth 8 ft. b.s.

29. Bossed, faience amulet divided into four quadrants, each quadrant having a set of four lines alternately vertical and horizontal. Pl. XCV, 389. ¾ in. sq. No. 4846; Square Q 24/3; Depth 8 ft. 3 in. b.s.
30. Bronze chisel with broad cutting edge, 3/16 × 3/16 in. in section. Slightly bent in the lower portion. L. 2¼ in. No. 7016; Square P 24/24; Depth 7 ft. b.s.
31. Copper stilus, broken. L. 4 in. No. 5980; Square Q 24/5; Depth 7 ft. b.s.
32. Tiny silver boss. Diam. ¼ in. No. 4857; Square Q 24/8; Depth 8 ft. b.s.
33. Bronze knife blade with an almost straight edge and broad tang (⅝ × 7/16 in.) in which there is a rivet hole. Pl. CXXV, 28. L. 2 9/16 in.; w. ½ in. No. 4863; Square Q 24/8; Depth 8 ft. b.s.
34. Numerous copper pieces weighing about two lbs. No. 7018; Squares Q 24/3 and 4; Depth 6 to 8 ft. b.s.
35. Tiny, semicircular gold terminal. Diam. ⅜ in. No. 4907; Square Q 24/8; Depth 8 ft. 8 in. b.s
36. Lead vase, much corroded and fragmentary. Ht. 2 in. No. 6051; Square Q 24/5; Depth 8 ft. b.s.
37. Ivory rod with bird-like head. Pl. LXXVIII, 19. L. 1½ in. No. 4997; Square Q 24/9; Depth 7 ft. b.s.
38. Club-shaped ivory rod, fragmentary. Pl. CXIX, 45. L. 2⅜ in. No. 7015; Square Q 24/4; Depth 7 ft. b.s.
39. Tanged, oval ivory object with a sharp edge, split vertically Pl. CXIX, 56. L. 2⅝ in. No. 7083; Square Q 24/4; Depth 7 ft. 6 in. b.s.
40. Small shell spoon. L. 2⅜ in. No. 6057; Square Q 24/4; Depth 7 ft. b.s.

Remains in the Eastern Section. In the southern part of the Eastern Section the only structural remains worth noticing are, three pavements of flat bricks. One of these is at the south-east corner of House V, the second one (with brick edging and with a depression for a *gharā*) is in square Q 24/20 against the north face of a wall of Stratum III, and the third one is in square Q 25/21. In square Q 24/15, was found an exceptionally interesting and well-made pottery trough No. 3868 with fine red wash and black bands. **Post-cremation trough No. 3868.** It is cylindrical in the upper portion and tapers in the lower part to a narrow bottom, being 2 ft. high and 1 ft. 11 in. in diameter at the mouth (Pl. XXXIV, *b*). It contained a much decayed tortoise-shell, a few bones of birds or other animals, several vases, a small painted dish, a river shell, numerous beads of carnelian, paste and faience, some ashes, bits of charcoal, etc. This is one of the favourite shapes of post-cremation urns of which I have exhumed over 230 examples at Harappā. The evidence furnished by them and by those from Mohenjo-daro, as well as by a large number of post-cremation urns found by Sir Aurel Stein both in Northern and Southern Balūchistān at sites where there is reason to suspect the presence of especially strong influence from the Indus side, has been discussed at length by Sir John Marshall in *M. I. C.*, pp. 86-89, and as I myself entirely concur in the conclusions drawn by him, it is unnecessary for me to go over the same ground again.

Finds from the northern part. In the northern part of this section is a curved drain covered with flat bricks, and several isolated bits of walls to the west of it. In the north-east corner, close to the drain, were discovered the following objects belonging to Stratum III :—

1. Chessman-shaped object of shell. Ht. $1\frac{1}{8}$ in. No. 7522 ; Square Q 23/25 ; Depth 9 ft. b.s.
2. Spiral finger-ring of copper. Diam. $\frac{5}{8}$ in. ; ht. $\frac{3}{16}$ in. No. 4554 ; Square Q 24/16 ; Depth 9 ft. b.s.
3. Semicircular faience terminal. Diam. $1\frac{3}{16}$ in. No. 4737 ; Square Q 24/21 ; Depth 8 ft. 9 in. b.s.
4. Bossed faience amulet with cross-hatched pattern. Pl. XCV, 393. $\frac{7}{12}$ in. sq. No. 7582 ; Square Q 23/15 ; Depth 8 ft. 6 in. b.s.
5. Faience flower petal with indented edge. L. $\frac{7}{8}$ in. No. 4664 ; Square Q 24/21 ; Depth 7 ft. 6 in. b.s.
6. Tiny, couchant faience ram. L. 1 in. No. 7551 ; Square Q 23/20 ; Depth 7 ft. b.s.
7. Cubical chert weight. Wt. 25·95 gms. ; size 1×1×·7 in. No. 4509 ; Square Q 24/21 ; Depth 8 ft. b.s.
8. Double-convex, discoid steatite bead bored axially, and carved on either side with a different kind of cross whose arms are decorated with rows of incised lines. The spaces between the arms are similarly decorated. Pl. CXXVIII, 30. Diam. $\frac{1}{4}$ in. No. 4684 ; Square Q 24/21 ; Depth 8 ft. b.s.
9. Cubical chert weight, unfinished. Size 1·6×1·5×1·37 in. No. 7521 ; Square Q 23/25 ; Depth 7 ft. 6 in. b.s.
10. Cubical chert weight. Wt. 3·55 gms. ; size ·45×·4×·4 in. No. 7569 ; Square Q 23/25 ; Depth 7 ft. b.s.
11. Plum-shaped, soapstone ear-drop. Pl. CXXXIX, 33. Ht. $\frac{5}{8}$ in. No. 4503 ; Square Q 24/16 ; Depth 7 ft. b.s.
12. Flint core. Size $4\frac{3}{8}\times1\frac{1}{2}\times\frac{7}{8}$ in. No. 7553 ; Square Q 23/25 ; Depth 7 ft. b.s.

Finds from Pits I and II. From the original Pits I and II were recovered the following six objects belonging to Stratum III :—

1. Unicorn seal with 3 pictograms. Pl. LXXXIX, 120. $\frac{11}{16}$ in. sq. No. PII-71 ; Depth 8 ft. 6 in. b.s.
2. Fragmentary unicorn seal, upper part with pictograms broken. Pl. LXXXVII, 58. $1\frac{3}{16}$ in. sq. No. PII-82 ; Depth 9 ft. 6 in. b.s.
3. Square block of hornblende finished on the face and sides but with a rough protuberance on reverse. Pl. LXXXIII, 12. $2\frac{3}{8}$ in. sq. ; th. $1\frac{1}{2}$ in. No. PII-61 ; Depth 7 ft. 6 in. b.s.
4. Cubical limestone weight. Wt. 133·3 gms. ; size 1·6×1·6×1·1 in. No. PI-87 ; Depth 9 ft. b.s.

5. Cog-wheel faience disc. Diam. $\frac{3}{4}$ in. No. PI-124; Depth 8 ft. b.s.
6. Faience squirrel with tail upturned and munching something held in its fore-paws. Ht. $\frac{15}{16}$ in. No. PI-85; Depth 8 ft. 6 in. b.s.

Charred wheat. Near the centre, and along the eastern cutting of the above pits was found scattered in the débris of Stratum III, a quantity of charred wheat.

Fragmentary nature of all strata. Pl. XXXII, *a*, gives a fairly clear idea of the extremely fragmentary nature of the brick remains in this area. Such as they are, the best preserved of the walls and chambers belong to the IVth stratum; those of the IIIrd, are much more dilapidated, while in the IInd and Ist strata there are hardly any remains at all.

Scattered finds of Stratum III. Widely scattered among the fragments of masonry were found the following antiquities belonging to Stratum III:—

1. Fragment of a unicorn seal showing forelegs of the animal and incense-burner. Pl. XC, 195. L. $1\frac{1}{4}$ in. No. 7691; Square P 25/11; Depth 6 ft. 9 in. b.s.
2. Fragment of a unicorn seal showing the mouth and horn of the animal, and part of the incense-burner. L. $1\frac{5}{16}$ in. No. 7364; Square P 23/15; Depth 7 ft. b.s.
3. Unicorn seal with traces of 3 damaged pictograms. Broken across the right hand portion. Pl. LXXXVII, 38. $1\frac{3}{8}$ in. sq. No. 3772; Square Q 24/6; Depth 7 ft. 6 in. b.s.
4. Fragmentary unicorn seal showing only the body of the animal. Pl. XC, 209. $\frac{11}{16}$ in. sq. No. 2793; Square R 24/12; Depth 8 ft. b.s.
5. Unicorn seal with 3 pictograms. Pl. LXXXIX, 142. $\frac{11}{16}$ in. sq. No. 3803; Square Q 24/14; Depth 8 ft. b.s.
6. Elephant seal with 5 pictograms. Pl. XCI, 230. $\frac{7}{8}$ in. sq. No. 3771; Square Q 24/2; Depth 8 ft. b.s.
7. Rectangular, plano-convex steatite seal with 3 pictograms. Pl. XCII, 267. Size $1\frac{3}{16} \times \frac{5}{8}$ in. No. 5542; Square P 24/6; Depth 6 ft. b.s.
8. Fragment of a tiny, rectangular steatite seal with 2 pictograms surviving on one side, and VII-like symbol on the other. L. $\frac{7}{16}$ in. No. 4552; Square Q 24/1; Depth 7 ft. 10 in. b.s.
9. Tiny, rectangular faience sealing with 5 pictograms. Pl. C, 669. Size $\frac{3}{4} \times \frac{5}{16}$ in. No. 1876; Square P 24/17; Depth 6 ft. 10 in. b.s.
10. Steatite ear-drop, plum-shaped. Pl. CXXXIX, 24. Ht. $\frac{9}{16}$ in. No. 6001; Square P 24/19; Depth 6 ft. 6 in. b.s.
11. Hornblende pendent, deeply grooved at the head. Ht. $\frac{11}{16}$ in. No. 7725; Square P 25/11; Depth 6 ft. 6 in. b.s.
12. Plano-convex, discoid alabaster base with a socketed projection on top. Pl. LXXXIII, 10. Diam. $2\frac{3}{4}$ in.; ht. $1\frac{1}{8}$ in. No. 5228; Square Q 24/1; Depth 7 ft. b.s.
13. Half of a shuttle-shaped chert burnisher. Pl. CXVIII, 34. L. $3\frac{1}{8}$ in. No. 3143; Square R 24/3; Depth 8 ft. b.s.

14. Alabaster ring flattened on both sides. Diam. $1\frac{3}{8}$ in. No. 7509; Square Q 24/15; Depth 9 ft. b.s.
15. Tiny, round steatite vase with a cylindrical hole to indicate its capacity. Pl. CXXXIX, 58. Ht. $\frac{1}{2}$ in. No. 3825; Square Q 24/15; Depth 9 ft. b.s.
16. Tiny, couchant faience ram, holed across the neck for suspension. L. 1 in. No. 7305; Square P 23/15; Depth 5 ft. 6 in. b.s.
17. Miniature faience goblet. Pl. LXXXII, 26. Ht. $1\frac{1}{2}$ in. No. 4764; Square Q 24/23; Depth 7 ft. b.s.
18. Rectangular, plano-convex faience amulet. Size $1\frac{11}{16}\times\frac{5}{8}$ in. No. 7465; Square Q 23/10; Depth 7 ft. b.s.
19. Faience ear-stud relieved with a lozenge in cable border. Edge broken. Diam. $\frac{13}{16}$ in. No. 5785; Square P 23/10; Depth 7 ft. b.s.
20. Short bronze chisel $\frac{1}{4}\times\frac{3}{16}$ in. in section. Cutting edge damaged and the lower part bent. L. $1\frac{5}{8}$ in.; edge $\frac{3}{8}$ in. No. 5600; Square P 24/6; Depth 7 ft. b.s.
21. Ivory stilus or pin with long pointed end. Pl. CXIX, 22. L. $3\frac{5}{16}$ in. No. 5103; Square P 24/11; Depth 6 ft. 8 in b.s.
22. Oval shell bowl. Pl. LXXXII, 6. Size $5\frac{5}{8}\times3\frac{3}{4}$ in. No. 2714; Square R 24/11; Depth 8 ft. 7 in. b.s.
23. Squat, earthenware vase with broad mouth and flat bottom, painted with a series of bands, and with a broad band over the neck. Ht. $2\frac{1}{2}$ in.; diam. $3\frac{1}{4}$ in. No. 7556; Square P 23/25; Depth 8 ft. 4 in. b.s.
24. Small, round pottery vase. Ht. $1\frac{5}{8}$ in. No. 7523; Square P 23/25; Depth 8 ft. 8 in. b.s.

A fractional burial.

Between the IIIrd and IVth strata there came to light in this digging, an interesting fractional burial—the only one so far found in the higher mounds. It was found in squares Q 24/10 and Q 25/6, at a depth of 10 ft. 10 in. to 11 ft. 4 in. below the surface (Pl. XXXII, *b*, below the shed), and consisted of two fragmentary human skulls (Nos. 5440 B and C), one lower jaw (No. 5440A), and some other bones, a tubular bead of terracotta and one fragment of the base of an offerings' dish. The burial had been made in the deserted corner of a house of the IVth stratum and some brick edging had been added on the east and south sides to form a more defined enclosure, measuring 10 ft. 10 in. from north to south and 9 ft. 11 in. from east to west up to the broken end of the south edging (Pl. XXXIII, *f*). The brick edging, however, which alone is contemporary with the burial, is not, it should be observed, at right angles to the older walls of the house. Evidently, this burial took place at a time when the IVth stratum of buildings had fallen to ruins and the IIIrd had not yet come into existence.[1] As pointed out by Sir John Marshall this burial is contemporary with the Indus remains of Mohenjo-daro of about the Late III Period.[2]

[1] In *M. I. C.*, p. 84 this burial has been assigned through an error to a time between the IVth and Vth strata. In *A. S. R.* for 1927-28, pp. 85-86, however, the correct facts are given.

[2] *M. I. C.*, p. 84.

Its details. As regards the details of this burial,[1] the lower jaw No. 5440A lay near the centre of the brick edging on the south side, skull 5440B was lying on its right side in the centre of the enclosure with its lower jaw immediately in front, while the second skull, 5440C was partially inclined on the left side. Only a very small fraction of other bones was recovered, mostly scattered round skull 5440B, but none of them was found in the natural physical order. On the contrary, several ribs were lying behind skull 5440B. From the position in which the bones were found it looks as if the corpses were exposed to birds and beasts of prey before being buried. This inference is borne out by the numerous fractional burials enclosed in jars which I found in Stratum I of the Cemetery H. For, if the whole of this fractional burial had been removed and consigned to an urn, the result would hardly have been distinguishable from the contents, for example, of pot-burial No. 3934*c*,[2] which, in its turn, is in no way different from the other pot-burials.[3] The skulls in this burial, be it added, are brachycephalic with high-pitched nose, belonging to the Alpine type.[4]

Bones apparently exposed.

Stratum IV. We come now to the IVth stratum when this area was bisected from east to west by the long gable-roofed drain and a wall of Stratum V already described. In the southern part of the Eastern[5] Section, in squares Q 24/14, 19, and 24, were discovered in the original Pit II the fragmentary remains of House 5 of the IVth stratum. The house has all but perished; at present it measures 27 ft. 7 in. from west to east by 19 ft. 6 in. from north to south, and appears to have consisted of four rooms, *i.e.*, two in front towards the south, and two, at the back entered from the front. The south-eastern room has a doorway opening 4 ft. 2 in. wide; the other doorways have disappeared. The width of the front rooms is 5 ft. 10 in., and of the back ones 7 ft. 6 in., the length of the largest room being 15 ft. 2 in. In this house was found a small, bossed faience sealing (No. PII-86, $\frac{7}{16}$ in. sq.) relieved with two rows of rectilinear patterns.

Pit II, House 5.

Charcoal of bamboo and pine varieties. In the Middle Section (south) to the west of this structure, are several other walls including a broken wall (Pl. XXXIV, *e*) about 4 ft. 6 in. high in square Q 24/9, on either side of which, as well as in the surrounding area, was a quantity of charcoal of *Bambusa*, *Saccharum arundinaceum*, and pine wood.[6] A large,

---

[1] In a personal communication to me Dr. Guha doubts the authenticity of this burial and regards it as one of the modern graves. In support of this view he quotes Dr. D. N Wadia of the Geological Survey of India who found skull No. 5540C to possess higher specific gravity as compared with bones from Cemetery H and Area G. The archæological evidence, however, detailed above leaves no possible doubt as to the genuineness of this burial. The better preservation of the bones is likely to be due to the following reasons. First, the quantity of saltpetre in Mound AB is appreciably less than in the Cemetery H or Area G. Secondly Mound AB being high and this burial being found deep down in it there would be less infiltration than in the burials in Area G and Cemetery H which are nearer the surface and have been flooded by rain water from the mounds for thousands of years. In these two parts of the site saltpetre was bound to have been more destructive.

[2] *Cf.* p. 211 *infra*.

[3] *Cf. A. S. R.* for 1927-28, pp. 86-87.

[4] *M. I. C.*, p. 108.

[5] For division of this excavation into the Eastern, Middle and Western Sections see p. 145 *supra*.

[6] Three samples of this charcoal were examined by Mr. V. Narayanaswami of the Botanical Survey of India who writes "(1) is the charcoal of a *Bambusa* from the nature of the closed and scattered vascular bundles seen in the cross-section and the hollow internodes, (2) is the charcoal of *Saccharum arundinaceum* compared with a cross-section of the same from a herbarium specimen and found to agree, and (3) is the charcoal of a pine wood, confirmed by the presence of resin ducts in the numerous annular rings'.

shallow earthenware trough[1] of an uncommon type, which is somewhat akin to the troughs depicted on seals, was found crushed on a bit of wall in square Q 24/4. The following antiquities also were found near by :—

1. Tiny, polished ball of chalcedony. Diam. 7/16 in. No. 7293; Square Q 24/4; Depth 10 ft. b.s.
2. Rectangular, double-holed steatite amulet. Size 11/16×1/4 in. No. 7295; Square Q 24/8; Depth 10 ft. b.s.
3. Miniature faience goblet with pointed base, scored round the centre. Fragmentary. Pl. LXXXII, 17. Ht. 1½ in. No. 5142; Square Q 24/3; Depth 10 ft. b.s.
4. Long, pointed bone rod or stilus, broken at one end. Pl. CXIX, 21. L. 5 in. No. 4896; Square Q 24/9; Depth 10 ft. b.s.

Reed and bamboo huts. Large quantities of charcoal of the pine variety as well as of bamboos and reeds and heaps of ashes were commonly met with throughout the south-west quarter of this area, and this, coupled with the fact that some of the walls were of mud, suggests that most of the habitations here were probably reed and bamboo huts of the poor.

Western Section, southern part. In the southern part of the Western Section very little belonging to the IVth stratum had been brought to light, but the following finds may be noticed :—

Group from square P 24/19—

1. Barrel-shaped object of hornblende, polished. L. 4 3/16 in. No. 7013; Depth 7 ft. 6 in. b.s.
2. Small chalcedony *liṅgam*. Ht. 13/16 in. No. 7493; Depth 7 ft. 6 in. b.s.
3. Plum-shaped soapstone ear-drop. Ht. 5/16 in. No. 7205; Depth 9 ft. 6 in. b.s.
4. Cog-wheel faience disc. Pl. CXXXIX, 16. Diam. ¾ in. No. 7547; Depth 9 ft. 6 in. b.s.
5. Half of an earthenware bangle with heart-shaped designs in red on white ground. Its outer edge tapers to a point. Pl. CXXXVIII, 7. Diam. 3¾ in. No. 7129; Depth 8 ft. 6 in. b.s.

Miscellaneous—

1. Unicorn seal with 4 pictograms. Pl. LXXXIX, 128. 13/16 in. sq. No. 1500; Square P 24/8; Depth 9 ft. 2 in. b.s.
2. Rectangular, plano-convex steatite seal with 3 pictograms. Pl. XCII, 280. Size 1 1/16×⅝ in. No. 2187; Square P 24/8; Depth 9 ft. b.s.
3. Round alabaster bead. Diam. 1¼ in. No. 7495; Square P 24/10; Depth 8 ft. b.s.
4. Small stone cylinder. Diam. ⅜ in.; ht. 7/16 in. No. 4881; Square Q 24/9; Depth 8 ft. b.s.
5. Double-convex, discoid bead of carnelian, flattened at top and bottom. Diam. ¾ in. No. 7039; Square P 24/9; Depth 8 ft. 5 in. b.s.

---

[1] The only other shallow trough from Harappā was found in Stratum VI, Trench I, Mound F. *Cf.* p. 144 *supra*.

6. Fragment of a round stone mace-head showing vertical grooves at opposite points of the central hole. They were probably meant for inserting a flanged handle. Pl. LXXXIII, 22. Diam. 3$\frac{5}{8}$ in. No. 7127; Square P 24/14; Depth 8 ft. 6 in. b.s.
7. Chert core. Size 4$\frac{3}{4}$×1$\frac{1}{2}$×$\frac{3}{4}$ in. No. 7172; Square P 24/14; Depth 9 ft. b.s.
8. Shell ball, plain. Diam. 1$\frac{1}{4}$ in. No. 7436; Square P 24/9; Depth 7 ft. 6 in. b.s.
9. Small, globular earthenware vase with long, painted neck and flared mouth. Ht. 1$\frac{3}{4}$ in. No. 4729; Square P 24/13; Depth 7 ft. 3 in. b.s.
10. Terracotta male figure holding a duck in arms, legs broken. Pl. LXXVI, 14. Ht. 3 in. No. 4925; Square P 24/9; Depth 9 ft. 2 in. b.s.

Western Section, northern part.

Remains and antiquities of Stratum IV.

In the northern part of the Western Section are several fragmentary brick remains. These comprise the south-east corner of a room in squares P 23/5 and 10, the T-shaped remains of two rooms in square P 24/11, of which one wall is over 19 ft. long, various fragments of walls, and three broken pavements of which the one in square P 24/2, measures 6 ft. 3 in. by 5 ft. 10 in. In this section, were found the undermentioned antiquities in the adjoining squares P 24/6, 11, and 16, between 7 ft. 5 in. and 10 ft. below the surface :—

1. Unicorn seal with 4 pictograms. Pl. LXXXVI, 33. 1$\frac{3}{16}$ in. sq. No. 4553; Square P 24/16; Depth 7 ft. 5 in. b.s.
2. Unicorn seal with 4 pictograms. Pl. LXXXIX, 143. $\frac{11}{16}$ in. sq. No. 5634; Square P 24/6; Depth 7 ft. 6 in. b.s.
3. Fragmentary seal with the figure of a composite monster with 4 pictograms surviving. Pl. XCIX, 623. L. $\frac{11}{16}$ in. No. 5633; Square P 24/11; Depth 8 ft. b.s.
4. Tiny, rectangular steatite seal with 3 pictograms on one side, and 1 on the other. Pl. XCVI, 490. Size $\frac{1}{2}$×$\frac{1}{4}$ in. No. 5152; Square P 24/16; Depth 8 ft. b.s.
5. Tiny, rectangular steatite seal with 3 pictograms on one side, and 2 pictograms with a dotted circle at each end on the other. Pl. XCVI, 465. Size $\frac{1}{2}$×$\frac{1}{4}$ in. No. 5180; Square P 24/11; Depth 10 ft. b.s.
6. Tiny, rectangular steatite seal (fragmentary) with 2 pictograms surviving on one side, and 1 on the other. W. $\frac{1}{4}$ in.; L. $\frac{3}{8}$ in. No. 5181; Square P 24/11; Depth 10 ft. b.s.
7. Plum-shaped, steatite ear-drop with a rusted copper wire projecting at the head. Ht. $\frac{3}{8}$ in. No. 5652; Square P 24/11; Depth 8 ft. b.s.
8. Heart-shaped steatite pendent holed at the upper and lower ends. Apex broken. Size $\frac{11}{16}$×$\frac{9}{16}$ in. No. 5784; Square P 24/11; Depth 8 ft. b.s.
9. Chessman-shaped object of yellow Jaisalmer stone. Ht. $\frac{13}{16}$ in. No. 5776; Square P 24/6; Depth 8 ft. b.s.

10. Cog-wheel shaped faience disc. Diam. $\frac{11}{16}$ in. No. 5179; Square P 24/11; Depth 7 ft. 6 in. b.s.
11. Hexagonal faience bead with mid-rib for hole along the longer axis.[1] Pl. CXXVIII, 13. Two shorter sides $\frac{7}{16}$ in. each. No. 5706; Square P 24/11; Depth 8 ft. 4 in. b.s.
12. Copper bead. Diam. $\frac{5}{16}$ in. No. 5853; Square P 24/6; Depth 8 ft. 6 in. b.s.
13. Half of a shell wavy ring. Pl. CXVII, 10. Diam. 1 in. No. 5854; Square P 24/6; Depth 9 ft. b.s.
14. Long, oval earthenware vase. Ht. 12 in. No. 5153; Square P 24/11; Depth 8 ft. 2 in. b.s.

Two earthenware jars.

Besides the above finds may also be mentioned two earthenware jars which were found near the north-west corner of this excavation in square P 23/5. Of these, No. 5919 was a large, inscribed jar which lay crushed at a depth of 10 ft. below the surface. It contained small pieces of animal bones, bits of charcoal, and among the pottery objects a bull's head, pieces of a standard dish, of perforated and other vases, and of dishes, etc., a fragmentary wheel, broken bangles, and some triangular cakes. Up to four-fifths of its height this jar was filled with porous earth mixed with some decayed cereal on which were impressions of leaves. The other jar, No. 7765, was found at a depth of 9 ft. 5 in. Its contents were similar, but in the porous earth it retained a few vestiges of seeds of the melon species.

Eastern Section, northern part.

Of Stratum IV, there is nothing to record from the northern part of the Middle Section and I therefore pass on to the northern part of the Eastern Section. Here, there is a small, brick enclosed pavement 2 ft. 6 in. by 2 ft. 3 in., in square Q 24/16, the corner of two walls to its east, and four bits of walls to the north and north-east. Here, too, in square Q 24/21, were found the following 3 objects :—

1. Conical stone *lingam*. Pl. CXVII, 19. Ht. $1\frac{1}{8}$ in. No. 4519; Depth 10 ft. b.s.
2. Cubical chert weight. Wt. 3·6 gms.; size ·55×·5×·3 in. No. 4620; Depth 10 ft. b.s.
3. Long barrel-shaped, hollow pottery flesh rubber holed at top. Ht. $7\frac{3}{4}$ in.; diam. $2\frac{3}{4}$ in. No. 4651; Depth 10 ft. b.s.

Scattered finds belonging to Stratum IV.

Besides the foregoing minor antiquities from the various sections, the following objects from Stratum IV also deserve mention :—

1. Lower half of a unicorn seal. Pl. LXXXVIII, 70. $1\frac{1}{4}$ in. sq. No. 5777; Square P 24/2; Depth 9 ft. b.s.
2. Unicorn seal with 5 pictograms, upper left corner slightly broken. Pl. LXXXVI, 34. No. 4991; Square Q 25/21; Depth 10 ft. 9 in. b.s.
3. Fragmentary sealing of green faience with a double outlined cross at the centre and a tiny square at each corner. *Cf.* No. 391 in Pl XCV. $\frac{3}{4}$ in. sq. No. 5635; Square P 24/1; Depth 8 ft. b.s.

---

[1] For other beads with mid-rib from Harappā see Pl. CXXX, 53-56 and Pl. CXXXIII, 3.

4. Tiny, rectangular faience sealing with 5 pictograms on one side, and 1 on the other. Similar to No. 346 in Pl. XCIV. Size $\frac{7}{8}\times\frac{7}{16}$ in. No. 7537; Square P 23/15; Depth 9 ft. b.s.
5. *Svastika* faience sealing. Similar to No. 396 in Pl. XCV. $\frac{9}{16}$ in. sq. No. 4603; Square Q 24/21; Depth 10 ft. b.s.
6. Barrel-shaped bead of agate. L. $\frac{5}{8}$ in. No. 6070; Square P 24/4; Depth 7 ft. 6 in. b.s.
7. Hornblende pendent, deeply grooved at the head. Ht. $\frac{7}{16}$ in. No. 7166; Square P 24/4; Depth 8 ft. 6 in. b.s.
8. Short, polished cylindrical weight of dark green stone. Pl. CXVIII, 29. Ht. $\frac{13}{16}$ in.; diam. $\frac{11}{16}$ in. No. 4881; Square Q 24/9; Depth 8 ft. b.s.
9. Hornblende pendent, deeply grooved at the head. Ht. $\frac{1}{2}$ in. No. 4668; Square P 24/22; Depth 10 ft. b.s.
10. Hornblende pendent, similar to above. Ht. $\frac{7}{16}$ in. No. 4992; Square P 25/21; Depth 10 ft. 9 in. b.s.
11. Plano-convex disc of steatite paste holed through the centre. Diam. $\frac{5}{8}$ in. No. 5783; Square P 24/2; Depth 8 ft. b.s.
12. Knobbed, ear-stud of steatite paste. Diam. $\frac{5}{8}$ in. No. 5632; Square P 24/7; Depth 8 ft. b.s.
13. Small, round faience vase with flat, projecting base. Pl. LXXXII, 12. Ht. and diam. 1 in. No. 7762; Square P 23/15; Depth 9 ft. 6 in. b.s.
14. Tiny, couchant faience ram holed across the neck for suspension. L. 1 in. No. 7545; Square P 24/20; Depth 10 ft. b.s.
15. Faience ear-button with rough knob. Diam. $\frac{3}{4}$ in. No. 4704; Square P 24/21; Depth 10 ft. b.s.
16. Fragment of a deeply serrated bangle of white faience. Originally it may have had a green or blue glaze. L. across $2\frac{3}{4}$ in. No. 4652; Square Q 25/16; Depth 10 ft. 6 in. b.s.
17. Copper rod, rectangular in the upper part but rounded and pointed at the lower end; tip broken. L. $3\frac{5}{8}$ in. No. 2551; Square Q 24/18; Depth 10 ft. 6 in. b.s.
18. Oval earthenware goblet with straight neck. Ht. $4\frac{1}{2}$ in. No. 7365; Square P 23/15; Depth 7 ft. 6 in. b.s.
19. Oval pottery vase with broad mouth and flat bottom. Ht. $8\frac{1}{8}$ in.; diam. at mouth 4 in. No. 7716; Square P 24/12; Depth 10 ft. b.s.
20. Pottery spoon in imitation of shell prototype. L. 5 in.; w. $4\frac{1}{8}$ in. No. 4879; Square P 24/18; Depth 10 ft. 3 in. b.s.
21. Terracotta quadruped with holed and flattened neck for fixing a revolving head on. Pl. CXX, 17, lower part. L. $2\frac{3}{4}$ in. No. 7492; Square P 24/20; Depth 8 ft. b.s.
22. Sherd of a goblet with pointed base showing 6 pictograms. Pl. CII, 27. Size $4\frac{5}{8}\times3\frac{3}{8}$ in. No. 1160; Square P 14/12; Depth 7 ft. 4 in. b.s.

Stratum V.

Middle Section, northern part.

In the northern part of the Middle Section an area measuring 51 by 48 ft. was selected for deep digging, but as a number of pavements lying close to one another, and some fragmentary walls of Stratum V quickly appeared within 2 ft. 3 in. of the nearby surface further progress at this place became impossible (Pl. XXXII, *b*). At the south-west corner of this deeper digging, alongside the western end of the covered drain, is a paved pit (No. 2) of Stratum IV measuring 5 ft. 2 in. by 3 ft. 3 in. internally and 4 ft. 9 in. deep (Pl. XXXII, *b*, right, centre ground). Immediately behind it, but on a higher level, is part of a similar pit (No. 1) belonging to Stratum III.

Two paved pits of Strata IV and III.

Antiquities of Stratum V.

No antiquities were recovered from the above deep digging, but at a higher level in the tongue which projects beyond the main excavation, and at one place in the Eastern Section, which was dug slightly deeper and then refilled, were found the following antiquities of Stratum V:—

1. Tiny, hemispherical steatite seal with 2 pictograms on the plane face. From the roughness of its lower side, bevelled edge, and flattish bottom it would appear to have been used as the bezel of a ring. The few seals of this type so far recovered are always inscribed with the same two pictograms. Similar to No. 414 in Pl. XCV. Diam. $\frac{3}{8}$ in. No. 3851 ; Square Q 25/11.
2. Rectangular faience sealing with 6 pictograms. Similar to No. 367*a* in Pl. XCIV. Size $1 \times \frac{5}{8}$ in. No. 1877 ; Square R 24/6.
3. Faience squirrel with upturned tail munching something held in its forepaws. Pl. LXXVIII, 28. Ht. $\frac{15}{16}$ in. No. 2713 ; Square R 24/16.
4. Four sided ivory baluster with rows of horizontal lines and incised circles on opposite faces. Pl. CXIX, 47. Ht. 2 in. No. 3694 ; Square Q 24/22.

Stratum VI.

Towards the east the projecting tongue of the trench was dug deeper in order to follow up the large drain[1] of Stratum V. Only two walls of Stratum VI were discovered in it, but the following antiquities were recovered between 12 ft. 5 in. and 19 ft. 10 in. below the surface and may be relegated to the VIth and earlier strata, the precise depths of which have not yet been ascertained :—

1. Unicorn seal with 4 pictograms. Unglazed. Pl. LXXXIX, 116. $\frac{7}{8}$ in. sq. No. 2463 ; Square R 24/17 ; Depth 19 ft. 6 in. b.s.
2. Rectangular, plano-convex steatite seal with 4 pictograms, damaged. Pl. XCII, 265. Size $1\frac{1}{4} \times \frac{5}{8}$ in. No. 7546 ; Square P 24/22 ; Depth 13 ft. 6 in. b.s.
3. Shield-shaped, tiny steatite seal with 2 pictograms on one side, and 1 on the other. Pl. XCV, 407. L. $\frac{3}{4}$ in. ; w. $\frac{9}{16}$ in. No. 1722 ; Square R 24/7 ; Depth 15 ft. 6 in. b.s.

[1] For the description of this drain see pp. 155-56 *supra*.

4. *Svastika* faience sealing. Similar to No. 396 in Pl. XCV. $\frac{11}{16}$ in. sq. No. 2545; Square R 24/16; Depth 19 ft. 10 in. b.s. or 8 ft. 10 in. below drain of Stratum IV.
5. Long, barrel-shaped object of hornblende. L. $2\frac{1}{4}$ in. No. 7597; Square P 24/21; Depth 13 ft. b.s.
6. Half of a highly polished lentoid agate bead. L. $\frac{3}{4}$ in.; w. $\frac{3}{8}$ in. No. 7574; Square P 24/21; Depth 13 ft. 6 in. b.s.
7. Plain, faience tetrahedron. Pl. CXX, 56. Three sides $\frac{13}{16}$ in., and one $\frac{3}{4}$ in. No. 1059; Square R 24/2; Depth 18 ft. b.s.
8. Copper arrow-head, bifurcated at the lower end. Pl. CXXV, 14. L. $1\frac{3}{16}$ in. No. 2454; Square R 24/16; Depth 18 ft. 2 in. b.s.
9. Shell ball decorated with six double circles incised round the circumference. Pl. CXX, 40. Diam. $1\frac{3}{16}$ in. No. 1323; Square P 24/17; Depth 12 ft. 5 in. b.s.
10. Pottery corn-measure (*ṭopā*) with flat bottom and concave sides. Pl. LXXII, 17. Ht. $2\frac{1}{2}$ in.; diam. $4\frac{3}{4}$ in. No. 2676*b*; Square P 24/8; Depth 12 ft. 8 in. b.s.
11. Terracotta hen whistle. Pl. CXX, 19. L. $2\frac{3}{8}$ in. No. 7515; Square P 24/22; Depth 13 ft. b.s.

The following two objects were found in the spoil earth of this excavation :—

1. Faience bull head with flowing dewlap and deep sockets in the eyes for inlay. On either side of the head are two holes, which were probably meant for fixing ears and horns. Pl. LXXIX, 67. L. $2\frac{1}{4}$ in. No. 2649.
2. Miniature, open-mouthed pottery vase. Ht. $\frac{7}{16}$ in. No. 2650.

Pits III and IV.

Situation and surface level. Close to the Extension of Pits I and II are two more pits numbered III and IV, each measuring 50 ft. sq. These along with the first two were excavated by the Rai Bahadur. Pit III, situated about 16 ft. to the south of the excavation described above, was sunk from a slightly higher level than the remaining three. The first three pits stood in one line from north to south, but the IVth lies about 70 ft. due south-west of Pit III.

Pit III. Pit III was excavated to a depth of 6 to 10 ft. below the surface and revealed one corner of a room belonging to Stratum III, which is overlaid by a fragmentary paving of Stratum II (Pl. XXXIV, *d*). In this the following antiquities were found at the depths noted against each :—

1. Triangular prism sealing of faience with 5 pictograms on one face, acacia tree and VIII-like symbol on the second, and dotted circles on the third. Pl. XCVIII, 598. Size $\frac{11}{16} \times \frac{5}{16}$ in. No. 11373; from surface.
2. Fragmentary unicorn seal showing forepart of the animal and incense-burner. Pl. XC, 221. $1\frac{1}{2}$ in. sq. No. PIII-54; Depth 7 ft. 6 in. b.s.

3. Rectangular, plano-convex steatite seal with 4 pictograms. Pl. XCII, 265. Size 1$\frac{1}{2}$×$\frac{7}{8}$ in. No. PIII-7; Depth 5 ft. b.s.
4. Left half of a rectangular, plano-convex seal with 3 pictograms surviving. Pl. XCII, 291. L. 1$\frac{1}{8}$ in.; w. $\frac{3}{16}$ in. No. PIII-38; Depth 6 ft. 10 in. b.s.
5. Alabaster pedestal with a shallow socket on top and 3 holes on the underside. Pl. LXXXIII, 9. Ht. 1$\frac{1}{8}$ in.; diam. 3$\frac{3}{8}$ in. No. PIII-56; Depth 8 ft. 3 in. b.s.
6. Two alabaster pedestals similar to above. Pl. LXXXIII, 8. Ht. 1$\frac{3}{16}$ in.; diam. 3$\frac{1}{2}$ in. each. No. PIII-74; Depth 9 ft. b.s.
7. Fragment of faience lotus fruit.[1] Diam. 2$\frac{5}{16}$ in. No. PIII-18; Depth 5 ft. 6 in. b.s.
8. Miniature ivory pillar (fragmentary) with a blind hole at top and bottom. It is decorated with two undulating bands alternating with horizontal rings. Pl. CXIX, 9. Ht. 1$\frac{1}{4}$ in. No. PIII-9; Depth 5 ft. 6 in. b.s.

Remains and antiquities of Pit IV.

Pit IV was excavated to a depth of 10 ft. to 11 ft. 6 in. On its eastern side was found a small room of Stratum IV which measures 7 ft. 7 in. by 6 ft. 8 in. internally, and is bisected by a covered drain coming from the north side. Behind this room, a little higher than the drain, was a fragmentary brick-on-edge pavement of Stratum III, with a contemporary wall to its left (Pl. XXXIV, *a*). In the west part of this pit there are four or five broken walls of the IIIrd stratum. The following antiquities belonging to Strata I and IV were found here. Of these, the unique rhomboidal seal with undulating edges, engraved with the figure of a flying eagle, deserves special notice.

Stratum I—

1. Fragment of a rectangular steatite seal with two pictograms surviving. L. $\frac{3}{8}$ in. No. PIV-19; Depth 1 ft. 8 in. b.s.
2. Rhomboidal steatite seal with undulating edges. On one side is a flying eagle with snakes (?) above the wings. On the other, is a cross with triangles between the arms. Pl. XCI, 255. Diagonals 1$\frac{3}{8}$ and 1$\frac{1}{4}$ in. No. PIV-85; Depth 2 ft. b.s.

Stratum IV—

1. Unicorn seal with 3 pictograms. Pl. LXXXVIII, 96. 1 in. sq. No. PIV-99; Depth 9 ft. b.s.
2. Unicorn seal with 9 pictograms, broken in the lower part. Pl. LXXXVI, 20. 1$\frac{13}{16}$ in. sq. No. PIV-114; Depth 11 ft. b.s.
3. Fragment of a hemispherical faience *chauk* or head ornament with rolled cable rim, and a circular hole at base. The exterior is ornamented with three concentric and hatched wavy bands in relief. Pl. CXXXVIII, 28. Diam. 2$\frac{1}{4}$ in.; ht. 1$\frac{1}{8}$ in. No. PIV-100; Depth 10 ft. b.s.

---

[1] For similar lotus fruit from Mohenjo-daro *cf. M. I. C.*, Pl. CLVIII, 4 and 6.

Trench at the southern edge of Mound AB.

About 40 ft. south of Pit IV, described above, a large trench was sunk at the southern edge of Mound AB measuring 187 ft. from north to south by 90 ft. from east to west (Pl. XXXV). Part of this trench, which I shall refer to as Section I, was cut in the flat top of the mound; but part of it, which I shall refer to as Section II, extended down the slope of the mound towards the south.

In this trench, remains of six strata have been brought to light. Of these, the Ist and the IInd come fairly close to each other, but between the remaining four strata there is a varying amount of débris. In Section I, the Ist stratum goes down to 3 ft. below the surface, the IInd to 6 ft., the IIIrd to 9 ft. 3 in., the IVth to 12 ft., the Vth to 16 ft., and the VIth to 17 ft. 6 in. In Section II there were no remains of the three upper strata. The IVth stratum lies between 11 ft. 9 in. and 13 ft. 3 in., the Vth between 13 ft. 3 in. and 15 ft., and the VIth between 16 and 17 ft. below the flat top of the mound (Pl. XXXV).

Primary object of the trench.

The primary object of sinking this particular trench was to connect up this part of the site with the Cemetery H which lies further to the south, and establish, if possible, the relationship between their several strata. To facilitate the digging, advantage was taken of an existing deep ravine (Pl. XXXVI, *a*), probably the result of old-time brick-digging, and this was extended on all sides during the working season of 1930-31. But owing, unfortunately, to drastic retrenchment in departmental expenditure during the following year this project had to be given up.

Remains of Strata I and II.

The Ist stratum in this trench is confined to the eastern and northern portions of Section I where it is represented by a thick, segment shaped wall, and several other broken, isolated pieces of walls which are best seen in Pl. XXXVI, *c*. No antiquities, however, were recovered from this stratum. The IInd stratum is hardly better preserved, being represented by only two walls buried underneath the segment shaped wall mentioned above, a small pavement, and a few other scattered fragments of brickwork (Pl. XXXV). The following objects, however, were found associated with this stratum :—

Finds of Stratum II.

1. Unicorn seal with 5 pictograms. Pl. LXXXIX, 132. 7/8 in. sq. No. 12164; Square R 28/2; Depth 4 ft. 4 in. b.s.
2. Fragment of a unicorn seal showing only the forelegs of the animal. Pl. XC, 203. L. 5/8 in. No. 11588; Square Q 27/15; Depth 5 ft. b.s.
3. Unicorn seal with 2 pictograms. After being damaged at the upper left corner of the reverse it was in process of being cut into pieces by a cross-shaped groove visible on the face. Pl. LXXXIX, 156. 11/16 in. sq. No. 11554; Square R 27/2; Depth 5 ft. 2 in. b.s.
4. Fragment of a rectangular, plano-convex, steatite seal with only 1 pictogram surviving. Pl. XCII, 299. L. 1 1/8 in. No. 12178; Square Q 28/12; Depth 4 ft. 4 in. b.s.
5. Faience bar, triangular in section, with a row of circles incised on each of the three sides. One end broken. This is the only example of its kind in faience, all other similar objects being made of bone or

ivory. L. ⅜ in. No. 11513; Square Q 27/13; Depth 3 ft. 7 in. b.s.

6. Well modelled, miniature bull-head of shell drilled with holes for inlaying eyes and horns. The folds of skin are indicated by raised bands in parallel curves, and there is a chain round the neck possibly for suspending a bell. Pl. LXXIX, 68. L. 1⅜ in. No. 11566; Square Q 28/22; Depth 6 ft. b.s.

Remains of Stratum III. **Well with double ring.**

The remains in the IIIrd stratum comprise three or four broken pavements in Section I, four or five corner walls widely scattered about, several other fragments of walls, and a large well in square Q 27/19, which was found at a depth of 8 ft. 2 in. below the surface (Pl. XXXVI, *f*). A curious feature of this well is that it is composed of two concentric rings of masonry of which the outer one is 7 ft. 3 in. in diameter and the inner one 3 ft. 9 in., the interval of 1 ft. between them being filled with pure indurated clay. The former is built of whole bricks of the usual size, *viz.*, 11 by 5½ by 2¾ in., and the latter entirely of wedge-shaped bricks 9¾ to 10 in. long by 5 in. broad, tapering to 3¼ in. at the smaller end, by 2 in. thick. All these bricks were made apparently by chiselling bricks of the ordinary size. In this connection it is noteworthy that with one exception[1] wedge-shaped bricks have not been found in any other ancient well at Harappā, and at Mohenjo-daro, where they are common, the angle of the wedge is not, as a rule, so sharp. Let me add that whereas the inner face of the outer ring, which was never exposed, is entire, it is much dilapidated in the inner ring of which the shaft has been traced to a depth of 62 ft. where its masonry was found somewhat disturbed and it was risky to dig deeper. It is twice as deep as any of the other wells so far unearthed at Harappā,[2] and probably that is the reason why the outer ring, which must have been very costly, was considered indispensable for additional strength. The following objects (No. 12106 *a-j*) were found inside the well at the depths noted against them:—

a. One cylindrical faience bead. L. ·35 in. Depth 6 ft.

b. One chert weight. Wt. 27·3 gms.; size ·90×·85×·80 in. Depth 30 ft.

c. Fragment of a chert weight. Depth 32 ft.

d. One terracotta cone. Ht. 2·3 in. Depth 39 ft.

e. One chert weight. Wt. 54·1 gms.; size 1·15×1·15×·95 in. Depth 39 ft.

f. Two bricks measuring 14×7½×3¼ and 11½×5¾×3¼ in. Depth 40 ft.

g. Two terracotta balls and one ring. Diam. 1·1, 1·0, and 1 in. respectively. Depth 47 ft.

h. Three terracotta balls. Diam. 1·2, 1·2 and 1·7 in. Depth 50 ft.

i. One stone ball and one terracotta wheel. Diam. 1·3 and 2·7 in. respectively. Depth 53 ft.

j. One terracotta ball. Diam. 1·1 in. Depth 59 ft.

---

[1] Somewhat wedge-shaped bricks are also found on the well in Trench VI, Mound F, but they are not well chiselled.

[2] Three of these wells were found in Trenches IV, V and VI in Mound F, and the fourth in Trench II in Area G.

Finds.

Besides the finds of this stratum mentioned below, a few crushed earthenware jars were brought to light in the south-eastern portion of Section I:—

1. T-shaped tablet of black steatite inscribed with a row of three *svastikas* above and one below. There is a groove at each end of the horizontal limb, intended for metal attachments, and its right position appears to have been as shown in the illustration. Pl. XCII, 278. Size 1¾ × 15/16 in. No. 11649; Square Q 27/20; Depth 9 ft. 3 in. b.s.
2. Tiny, rectangular steatite seal with 2 pictograms. Size 11/16 × 3/8 in. No. 11626; Square R 27/4; Depth 9 ft. 4 in. b.s.
3. Tapering hornblende pendent. Ht. ¾ in. No. 11594; Square Q 28/6; Depth 7 ft. 2 in. b.s.
4. Two well-polished balls, one of carnelian and the other of limestone. The latter retains traces of white paint. Diam. 13/16 and 11/16 in. No. 12048; Square R 28/2; Depth 10 ft. b.s.
5. Miniature faience ram holed across the neck for suspension. Pl. LXXVIII, 44. L. 1 1/16 in. No. 11611; Square R 27/4; Depth 7 ft. b.s.
6. Miniature, squat earthenware vase. Ht. ⅜ in. No. 11535; Square R 27/4; Depth 6 ft. 6 in. b.s.
7. Terracotta rattling ball with a short handle. Pl. CXX, 32. L. 2¾ in. No. 11605; Square Q 27/9; Depth 6 ft. 9 in. b.s.
8. Well modelled terracotta monkey climbing the branch of a tree. Pl. LXXVIII, 35. Ht. 2¼ in. No. 11625; Square Q 27/22; Depth 8 ft. 8 in. b.s.

Stratum IV. Pavement with several partitions.

There are several walls of the IVth stratum scattered about in Section I, and about 12 ft. below the surface immediately west of the well mentioned above are the remains of a large, contemporary brick-on-edge pavement. Broken on all sides it is now 35 ft. from east to west with a maximum width of 11 ft. (Pl. XXXVI, *d*). Crossing it at right angles at a higher level is a wall of the IIIrd stratum. This pavement is divided into eleven rectangular spaces by ten small parapets, each built of two courses of half brick thickness at intervals of 2 to 3 ft. 4 in. As the parapets are not precisely parallel to each other, the width of the partitions varies somewhat. This pavement was found covered with quantities of wood and bamboo charcoal—probably the remains of a thatched roof. An abundance of charcoal in the northern part of Section II also indicates that the buildings in the IVth stratum were generally destroyed by fire. About 20 ft. west of the well, at the place where an abundance of charcoal is seen to the left of the high wall of Stratum III (Pl. XXXVI, *d*), were found two very much decayed and distorted copper bangles together with the following three objects:—

Probably covered with thatched roof. Destruction of Stratum IV by fire.

1. Copper gouge (in two pieces) with semicircular cutting edge. Pl. CXXV, 40. L. 4¼ in. No. 12392*a*; Square Q 27/14; Depth 11 ft. 6 in. b.s.
2. Similar copper gouge fitted with an alabaster handle. Pl. CXXV, 41. L. 5⅓ in. No. 12392*b*; Square Q 27/14; Depth 11 ft. 6 in. b.s.

3. Copper bowl with flared sides and flat rim, repaired. Pl. CXXIV, 22. Diam. 5¾ in.; ht. 2⅝ in. No. 12392c; Square Q 27/14; Depth 11 ft. 6 in. b.s.

Another pavement. The above-mentioned brick-on-edge pavement has a counterpart to the east of the well. But this is more dilapidated and does not show any partitioning parapets. At present, its greatest length is 14 ft. from east to west and maximum width only 8 ft. On it was found a copper razor (size 2¼ × 2⅝ in.) of the "Irish" pattern (Pl. CXXV, 46) already known from several examples at Harappā and Mohenjo-daro.[1]

Finds. The following eight objects were found in association with Stratum IV:—

1. Unicorn seal with 5 pictograms. Pl. LXXXIX, 114. 1⅛ in. sq. No. 11705; Square R 28/3; Depth 10 ft. 8 in. b.s.
2. Unicorn seal with 3 pictograms, unfinished. Pl. LXXXVIII, 98. 1 in. sq. No. 11768; Square Q 28/16; Depth 11 ft. 6 in. b.s.
3. Small fragment of a unicorn seal showing the hind part of the animal. L. 7/16 in. No. 12363; Square Q 27/14; Depth 11 ft. 8 in. b.s.
4. Chessman-shaped object of pale carnelian. Ht. ⅞ in. No. 12352; Square R 29/1; Depth 3 ft. b.s.
5. Conical faience *liṅgam*[2] with horizontal grooves. Pl. CXVII, 27. Ht. 1⅛ in. No. 12292; Square Q 28/6; Depth 12 ft. b.s.
6. Well modelled, faience duck with two deep holes for separate insertion of feet. Neck and tail broken. Pl. LXXVIII, 18. L. 1¼ in. No. 11893; Square Q 28/21; Depth 13 ft. b.s.
7. Corner fragment of a terracotta screen perforated with intersecting circles. Pl. LXXII, 29. L. 7½ in. No. 12390; Square Q 29/17; Depth 3 ft. b.s.
8. Fragment of a round vase painted with four bird-headed, human figures advancing to left hand-in-hand between two deer (?).[3] The lower legs of the therianthropic figures are not shown being apparently hidden in the double band which probably represents a river—possibly the prototype of the Vaitarṇi river. The painting is typical of the Cemetery H ware. Pl. LXIX, 18. Similar therianthropic figures[4] are found on burial pot No. H206*b* (Pl. LXII, 1, *a* and *b*). No. 11995; Square Q 28 (from washing tub); Depth 6 to 9 ft. b.s.

---

[1] *Cf.* Pl. CXXV, 47. Also *cf. M. I. C.*, Pl. CXXXVII, 6, and Pl. CXXXVIII, 12.

[2] Similar *liṅgams* have also been found at Mohenjo-daro, *cf. op. cit.*, Pl. CLIII, 27 and 28.

[3] On a shell tablet from Phæstus are shown four dæmons with animals' heads advancing towards the left, each with its left arm hanging down, and the right holding a staff, as tall as the figure itself. Three have quadrupeds' heads, the third being horned, although its species is uncertain [perhaps dog (?), boar and bull]; the fourth has a bird's head. *Cf.* M. P. Nilsson, *The Minoan Mycenæan Religion*, p. 320, fig. 96, and footnote 2 which refers to the opinion of Hogarth who calls the figures on the Phæstus tablet as "first cousins of Nilotic divinities", but according to Nilsson the resemblance to Babylonian figures is much more striking and evident. In support of this he says that "The figures and their attitudes recall so strongly the rows of animal-headed dæmons on some Babylonian and Assyrian amulets, *e.g.*, the second zone of the 'Hades tablet' or a similar tablet from Assur (fig. 97), that they are without the slightest doubt to be derived from Babylonian prototypes, even if the examples quoted may be later in date. Babylonian seal cylinders, imported into Crete in Middle Minoan I and imitated here *testify* the connexion, though Babylonian influence on Minoan art is questionable".

[4] Regarding the semi-divine nature and popularity of therianthropic figures with the Indus people *cf.* Sir John Marshall, *op. cit.*, pp. 66-68.

Bath with drain in Section II.

In the northern part of Section II is a small paved bath of the IVth stratum made of extremely well-rubbed bricks in squares Q 28/18 and 23, from which a covered drain goes eastward for a length of 26 ft. and is met by another covered drain coming from the north-east. No sink or common drain was recovered at their terminus, but there can be little doubt that they drained away towards the east into the depression between Mounds AB and E. There are no finds worth recording from this area.

Stratum V. Row of earthenware jars.

At a distance of 80 ft. from the northern edge of this trench was discovered a remarkably long row of 54 earthenware jars belonging to Stratum V, at a depth of 15 ft. 9 in. to 16 ft. 6 in. below the surface (Pl. XXXVI, *b*). This row extends for 109 ft. from east to west and cuts across the entire width of the trench. All the jars comprising it, except two, are broken, and in some cases were piled two or even three deep, above one another (Fig. *b*). They appear to have been

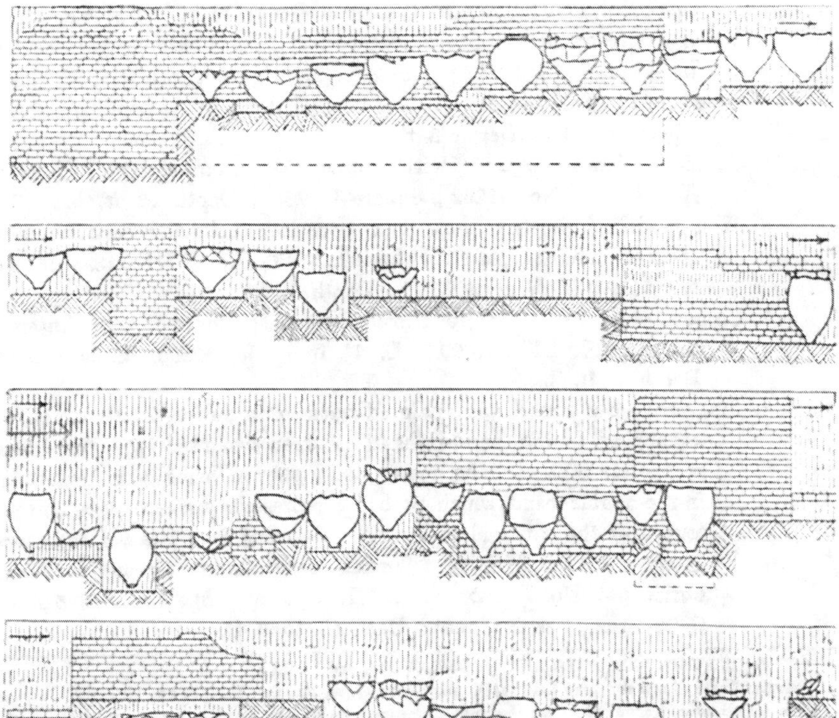

SCALE 1 in. = 5 ft.

FIG. *b*.—MOUND AB, TRENCH AT THE SOUTHERN EDGE, ROW OF POST-CREMATION URNS, LOOKING SOUTH.

placed against the back wall of several houses which stood in a line immediately to their south. Originally constructed during the VIth period of occupation, this wall was repaired and utilised again in the following period. Its present height varies between 1 ft. 3 in. and 6 ft. 6 in. I have not met with a similar row of jars elsewhere at Harappā. Their contents are typical of the post-crema-

Probably post-cremation urns.

tion urns with which we are so familiar at Harappā, and are tabulated separately.[1] Almost invariably they contained bones of small quadrupeds, birds or fish accompanied, in many cases, by some pottery goblets with pointed bases, bowls, saucers and other small vessels, human and animal toys, balls, beads, bangles, toy-carts, wheels, triangular cakes, river shells, decayed grain, ashes and charcoal. These contents are strikingly similar to those of the post-cremation urns from Balūchistān. "Of such urns a large number were found by Sir Aurel Stein in both northern and southern Balūchistān, but only at sites where the red-and-black or *Mehī* wares predominated and where there is reason to suspect the presence of specially strong influence from the Indus side, *e.g.*, at Dabar-kot, Periāno-Ghuṇḍai, Mughal-Ghuṇḍai, Mehī, and Suktagen-dor. On all these sites the burial customs seem to have been identical; the cinerary urns, that is to say, were buried either within or in close proximity to dwelling-houses and contained precisely the same sort of small vessels, animal remains and other objects as are found in the urns at Harappā and Mohenjo-daro, generally with human bones and ashes intermixed, but not infrequently without them. Side by side with the urn-burials at Mehī Sir Aurel found also several examples of the cremated bones having been left on the spot where the pyre was made, and vessels and other objects subsequently placed near them. Such burials he took to represent a transitional stage leading on to the deposit of the entire body in the earth, as at Nāl and Shāhī-tump; but the processes of cremation and inhumation are so fundamentally distinct that this view must obviously remain open to question."[2]

Absence of human bones not altogether surprising.

As regards the disposal of cremated bones, several years ago I pointed out to Sir John Marshall that among Hindus in many parts of the Panjāb the practice which obtains now is for the bones to be gathered together on the fourth day, washed and pounded, and then committed to the Ganges at Hardwar, or, in the case of poor people, to the nearest river. Some such custom may well have been in vogue among the Indus people also: only the ashes from the cremated pyre may have been taken up and deposited in these urns with offerings to the dead. Even if pounded bones were consigned to these jars, they could hardly be recognized now. In most countries the solemn rites connected with the disposal of the dead are apt to change but little, and in a conservative country like India a continuity of the old customs would be more than probable.

Group of finds.

Only the western half of Section I was dug deep enough to reach the Vth stratum. A few feet to the north of the above-mentioned row of jars in square O 27/15 is a substantial masonry pillar 4 ft. 3 in. high, which originally measured 4 by 3 ft., but with the IVth stratum was enlarged to 4 ft. sq. Besides this, there is one wall, the fragment of a pavement, and one or two other walls buried under structures of the IVth stratum. Close to the pillar and in the adjoining square Q 27/20 were found at a depth of 13 ft. to 15 ft. 6 in. below the surface, 9 *svastika* faience sealings $\frac{5}{8}$ to $\frac{11}{16}$ in. sq. (*cf.* Pl. XCV, 392 and 396-99), 20 chert scrapers, 41 fragments of shell bangles, 2 diamond shaped tablets of the same

---

[1] See pp. 272-74 *infra*. Similar urns have also been found at Mohenjo-daro. For a discussion of their contents and probable purpose *cf.* Sir John Marshall, *op. cit.*, pp. 86-89.

[2] Sir John Marshall, *op. cit.*, p. 89.

substance, a miniature, round pottery vase, and 112 miscellaneous beads. To the south of the row of jars, are several walls of Stratum V including a fairly good section of walling in squares Q 28/16 and 17. Among them, in the squares Q 28/11, 12 and 16, were found the following objects:—

1. Unicorn seal with 2 pictograms. Unique inasmuch as there is no incense-burner in front of the animal and that in the impression the animal faces left instead of the usual right.[1] Pl. XCIX, 617. $\frac{7}{8}$ in. sq. No. 12002; Square Q 28/16; Depth 14 ft. b.s.
2. Unicorn seal with 4 pictograms. Pl. LXXXIX, 138. $\frac{7}{8}$ in. sq. No. 12035; Square Q 28/11; Depth 14 ft. b.s.
3. *Svastika* faience sealing, the largest so far found at Harappā. Pl. XCV, 397. $1\frac{3}{16}$ in. sq. No. 11931; Square Q 28/11; Depth 14 ft. b.s.
4. *Svastika* faience sealing, similar to No. 396 in Pl. XCV. $\frac{11}{16}$ in. sq. No. 12064; Square Q 28/16; Depth 15 ft. 10 in. b.s.
5. Upper part of the blade of a curved copper knife. Pl. CXXV, 29. L. $3\frac{1}{4}$ in. No. 12113; Square Q 28/11; Depth 15 ft. 6 in. b.s.
6. Leaf-shaped copper spear-head with long tip and short tang. It is broken along one edge, but the irregular curvature of the preserved opposite edge clearly indicates that it was re-sharpened. Size $6\frac{3}{4}\times2\frac{1}{4}$ in. No. 12114; Square Q 28/12; Depth 15 ft. 6 in. b.s.
7. Copper spear-head with prolonged point. Pl. CXXIV, 45. L. 10 in.; w. $2\frac{1}{4}$ in. No. 12115; Square Q 28/12; Depth 15 ft. 6 in. b.s.
8. Copper spear-head with prolonged point, fragmentary. Pl. CXXV, 74. L. $7\frac{3}{8}$ in. No. 12177; Square Q 28/12; Depth 15 ft. 6 in. b.s.

Scattered finds. In addition to the above antiquities were found widely scattered over the deeper portions of the trench the following objects associated with Stratum V:—

1. Fragmentary unicorn seal with only one pictogram surviving. Pl. XC, 178. 1 in. sq. No. 11837; Square Q 27/14; Depth 13 ft. 1 in. b.s.
2. Fragment of a unicorn seal with only 4 pictograms surviving. Pl. XC, 172. $1\frac{3}{8}$ in. sq. No. 12149; Square Q 28/9; Depth 15 ft. 6 in. b.s.
3. *Svastika* faience sealing, damaged; similar to No. 396 in Pl. XCV. $\frac{5}{8}$ in. sq. No. 12031; Square Q 28/22; Depth 13 ft. b.s.
4. Well polished ball of hornblende. Diam. $\frac{13}{16}$ in. No. 11867; Square Q 28/11; Depth 13 ft. 4 in. b.s.
5. Chessman-shaped object of palish carnelian. Ht. 1 in. No. 12062; Square Q 27/20; Depth 13 ft. 6 in. b.s.
6. Cross-shaped steatite bead, one arm partly broken. L. $\frac{5}{8}$ in. No. 12086; Square Q 28/6; Depth 14 ft. b.s.

---

[1] In *M. I. C.*, seal No. 167 in Pl. CVIII also the animal is shown facing left, and from the above Harappā seal it is probable that there the object below the head of the unicorn is no other than the third letter of the inscription. *Cf.* Sir John Marshall, *op. cit.*, p. 69, footnote 2.

7. Well polished, square block of *sang-i-abri*, with concave edges, slightly damaged. Pl. CXVII, 61. This stone is of rare occurrence at Harappā, only one fluted piece No. 11994, and a bead being found. No example of this stone has been published from Mohenjo-daro. Size $7\frac{3}{8} \times 7\frac{1}{4} \times 2\frac{3}{8}$ in. No. 11952; Square Q 28/21; Depth 14 ft. b.s.
8. Fragment of *sang-i-abri* slab with parallel fluting. Pl. LXXXIII, 51. In this piece the red colour predominates as compared with the yellow colour of the square block No. 11952. Size $4\frac{3}{8} \times 3\frac{1}{2}$ in. No. 11994; Square Q 27/23; Depth 14 ft. 4 in. b.s.
9. Small undulating ring-stone, fragmentary. Pl. CXVII, 16. Diam. $3\frac{3}{8}$ in. No. 12050; Square R 28/1; Depth 14 ft. 6 in. b.s.
10. Two equal cubical chert weights. Wt. 26·75 gms.; size ·97×·95×·65 in. No. 12356; Square R 27/5; Depth 16 ft. 5 in. b.s.
11. Hollow, faience nose-disc with ribbed surface. Diam. $\frac{1}{4}$ in. No. 12027; Square Q 28/17; Depth 13 ft. 5 in. b.s.
12. Fragment of faience snake with two holes at the top for the insertion of fangs. Pl. LXXVIII, 24. L. $1\frac{3}{8}$ in. No. 12358; Square R 27/5; Depth 16 ft. 5 in. b.s.
13. Two copper spear-heads, one with long and the other with short tang. Pl. CXXV, 68 and 70. L. $6\frac{11}{16}$ and 6 in. No. 12001 *a* and *b*; Square Q 28/8; Depth 13 ft. 10 in. b.s.
14. Copper hasp (?). Pl. CXXV, 57. L. $2\frac{1}{4}$ in. No. 12024; Square Q 28/17; Depth 14 ft. 9 in. b.s.
15. Fragmentary wheel-shaped object of imitation carnelian with fish scale pattern round the hub on the outer side, and two circles of dots one on either side of a circular band on the inner. Pl. LXXXIII, 43. Diam. $1\frac{7}{8}$ in. No. 12375; Square R 27/5; Depth 13 ft. 6 in. b.s.
16. Knobbed ivory handle, round in section, upper part broken. Pl. CXIX, 8. L. $1\frac{3}{4}$ in. No. 12061; Square Q 28/16; Depth 15 ft. 10 in. b.s.
17. Terracotta female figure seated on a three-legged stool and holding an object in her left hand. Besides the usual crescent-shaped head-dress, she wears on the left side of her forehead a string of four conical bosses like those found in the jewellery group No. 8060 from Trench IV in Mound F. Pl. LXXVI, 26. Ht. $5\frac{1}{4}$ in. No. 11932; Square Q 27/20; Depth 14 ft. b.s.
18. Seated terracotta male figure with hands folded in worship. He is kneeling on his left leg, while the right is stretched out in front. Pl. LXXVI, 7. Ht. $2\frac{1}{4}$ in. No. 12023; Square Q 28/17; Depth 14 ft. 9 in. b.s.
19. Terracotta lion or tiger reclining at full length. Pl. LXXIX, 87. L. $3\frac{3}{8}$ in. No. 12173; Square Q 28/12; Depth 15 ft. 8 in. b.s.

The greater part of Section II is occupied by a mass of mud brick filling which measures about 70 ft. from east to west by over 50 ft. from north to south and **Infilling of mud bricks.**

has a maximum depth of 5 ft. 9 in. (Pl. XXXVI, *e*). The size of bricks varies from 1 ft. 1 in. to 1 ft. 7 in. in length by $6\frac{1}{2}$ to $9\frac{1}{4}$ in. in width by 3 to 5 in. in thickness. Coming, as it does, under the slope of the mound and being isolated from structural remains, it is difficult to say precisely to which particular stratum this filling should be assigned. In the western 25 ft., however, it descends to the level of the VIth stratum where it is 3 to 4 ft. lower than the rest, and as it also goes underneath the bath of Stratum IV in squares Q 28/18 and 23, it seems originally to have been started with the Vth stratum and enlarged again with the IVth. The following objects were found on this filling, the variation in their depth below the surface being due to the sharp fall of the mound; the faience sealing No. 12066 was found close to its foot:—

Its probable date.

1. Bossed seal with the device of a *Brāhmanī* bull and 3 pictograms. Lower part broken. Pl. XCI, 237. $1\frac{3}{16}$ in sq. No. 12132; Square Q 28/18; Depth 15 ft. 2 in. b.s.
2. Bossed seal engraved with the figure of a composite monster and with 5 pictograms surviving. Only the erect tail of the animal and part of the haunches are now left. Pl. XCI, 250. L. $\frac{15}{16}$ in. No. 12131; Square Q 28/18; Depth 15 ft. 2 in. b.s.
3. Discoid, faience sealing double convex in section with 3 blurred pictograms on one side only. Pl. XCV, 380. Diam. $\frac{3}{4}$ in. No. 12060; Square Q 28/25; Depth 13 ft. b.s.
4. *Svastika* faience sealing, broken at one corner. It is similar to No. 396 in Pl. XCV. $\frac{5}{8}$ in. sq. No. 12133; Square Q 28/23; Depth 14 ft. 10 in. b.s.

South of this floor are fragments of two thick walls of the Vth stratum, and close to one of them lay a broken earthenware jar.

A fragmentary house of Stratum VI.

Stratum VI was reached only in the western part of this trench between the *kachchā* infilling and the long row of jars described above (Pl. XXXV). At this place it is represented by the remains of a house of which there are a few long walls running east and west. The following two objects were found in it:—

1. Fragmentary bronze axe with broad, well tapered cutting edge; the back probably had a ring socket. Pl. CXXII, 18, and Pl. CXXIV, 40. W. at cutting edge $3\frac{3}{4}$ in.; greatest th. $\frac{5}{16}$ in. No. 12393; Square Q 28/11; Depth 17 ft. 2 in. b.s.
2. Sherd painted with human figures, fishes, etc. The centre figure is carrying a cross-pole with a net or basket suspended from either end. Pl. LXIX, 16. L. $11\frac{3}{4}$ in. No. 12395; Square Q 28; Depth 15 to 18 ft. b.s. From the washing tub.

Group of finds No. 12387.

At the foot of the mound and round the junction of squares Q 29/11, 12, 16, and 17 were recovered from a small pit measuring 12 ft. each way the following group of objects No. 12387, between 2 ft. 6 in. and 4 ft. 6 in. below the surface:—

1. 682 terracotta cones, circular in section, and painted with horizontal bands of blue on white ground, or of white or blue on red ground. All of them are holed at bottom. Probably gamesmen. Pl. CXVII, 39-42. Ht. $\frac{11}{16}$ to 1 in.

2. 37 four-sided pyramidal terracotta cones[1] with concave sides, painted white. Probably gamesmen. Pl. CXVII, 45 and 46. Ht. 1 in.
3. Alabaster cone. Pl. CXVII, 21. Ht. ⅞ in.
4. 27 terracotta bangles, including one of superior finish. Diam. 2·5 to 3·5 in.
5. Pottery feeding-vase (?) with narrow spout resembling a smoking pipe in shape. Pl. LXXI, 89. L. 4⅝ in.; ht. 3 in.
6. Closed, cylindrical pottery lamp with spout for wick. Pl. LXXI, 87. Ht. 3½ in.; diam. at top 2¼ in.
7. Conical alabaster lid with projecting lip. Holed through the centre. Pl. LXXXIII, 1. Diam. 1⅝ in.; ht. ⅞ in.
8. Unfinished, rectangular[2] unicorn seal of black steatite with 3 pictograms. The knob at the back having broken, the seal was pierced by two holes through the body of the animal. Pl. LXXXIX, 167. Size 13/16 × 9/16 in.
9. Two semicircular terracotta terminals each with three holes for holding different strings. L. of each 1·3 in.
10. Four terracotta spacers. L. 1·2, 1·1, 1 and 1 in. respectively.
11. Six horn discs. Diam. ⅞ to 3/16 in.
12. Plano-convex, discoid hornblende pendent grooved at the rim, fragmentary. Diam. 7/16 in.
13. Some charred wheat, charcoal, and potsherds were also found with these objects.

The undermentioned two objects were found from the spoil earth of this trench :— **Finds from spoil earth.**

1. Hornblende pendent, deeply grooved at the head. Ht. 7/16 in. No. 11482; Square Q 28/11.
2. Nude, terracotta male figure as if in the act of exercising, with the arms thrown out and legs doubled up. Right lower leg broken. Wears necklace (?) of two strands. Pl. LXXVI, 13. Ht. 3¼ in. No. 11484; Square Q 28/11.

---

[1] The objects mentioned under 1 and 2 above are not well burnt, their colours are not properly fixed, and do not stand washing.

[2] Rectangular unicorn seals of this type are rare.

CHAPTER IV.

Area J.

Area J comprises a small, low Mound (D) situated to the south of Mound AB, and the depression lying between them (Pl. I). Three trenches were sunk in this area, one from east to west in the depression (No. III), and the other two (Nos. I and II) at right angles to it in Mound D. Trench III is about 220 ft. long by 20 ft. wide and, with the exception of the deep digging, to which I shall return presently, was dug to a varying depth ranging between 3 ft. 10 in. and 7 ft. below the surface (Pl. XXXVIII, *d*). Three fragmentary strata of occupation have been uncovered in it (Pl. XXXVII), the first one going down to a little over 2 ft., the second to about 4 ft., and the third to 7 ft.

Stratification.

Stratum I.

Despite the fact that there are no more than two pieces of walling in Stratum I, the eastern portion was found to be particularly rich in small antiquities among which the following deserve notice:—

1. Unicorn seal with 3 pictograms. Pl. LXXXIX, 163. $\frac{11}{16}$ in. sq. No. J20; Square S 30/1; Depth 1 ft. 6 in. b.s.
2. Lower part of a unicorn seal showing only legs and part of the body of the animal. Pl. LXXXVII, 63. $1\frac{1}{8}$ in. sq. No. J21; Square S 30/1; Depth 1 ft. 6 in. b.s.
3. Upper part of a unicorn seal with 5 pictograms. Pl. LXXXIX, 152. $1\frac{1}{16}$ in. sq. No. J28; Square S 29/10; Depth 2 ft. 2 in. b.s.
4. Fragment of a unicorn seal with only two pictograms surviving. Pl. XC, 198. 1 in. sq. No. J41; Square S 29/5; Depth 2 ft. 10 in. b.s.
5. Unicorn seal with 7 pictograms. Pl. LXXXVIII, 103. $1\frac{1}{4}$ in. sq. No. J46; Square S 30/6; Depth 3 ft. 2 in. b.s.
6. Oblong, faience sealing, lentoid in section, showing 4 pictograms on one side, and an acacia tree surrounded by a platform on the other. Pl. XCIV, 332. L. $\frac{5}{8}$ in. No. J10; Square S 30/1; Depth 1 ft. b.s.
7. Oblong, faience sealing from the same mould as No. 6, broken at the right end. L. $\frac{3}{4}$ in. No. J29; Square S 30/6; Depth 2 ft. b.s.
8. Cubical chert weight. Wt. 13·65 gms.; size ·75×·75×·6 in. No. J13; Square S 29/20; Depth 1 ft. b.s.
9. Cubical chert weight. Wt. 13·08 gms.; size ·7×·7×·57 in. No. J12; Square S 29/5; Depth 1 ft. b.s.
10. Cubical chert weight. Wt. 54·6 gms.; size 1·1×1·1×1 in. No. J49; Square S 30/16; Depth 2 ft. b.s.
11. Miniature faience goblet with remnant of green glaze inside. Pl. LXXXII, 25. Ht. $1\frac{7}{16}$ in. No. J11; Square S 29/20; Depth 1 ft. b.s.

12. Copper antimony rod stopper showing on top a dog biting the ear of a goat. Pl. CXXV, 34 and 36. L. 4¼ in. No. J19; Square S 30/16; Depth 1 ft. b.s.
13. Copper spear-head of the usual shape but with a broad and long tang. Pl. CXXV, 67. L. 6⅞ in.; w. 2 in.; w. of tang ¾ in. No. J38; Square S 30/11; Depth 2 ft. b.s.
14. Finger ring of copper wire with a silver bezel soldered on the joint. Pl. CXXV, 49. Size ⅞×¾ in. No. J47; Square S 29/20; Depth 2 ft. b.s.

Stratum II. Of the IInd stratum there is a wall at the west end of the trench, and close by a small corner of a room enclosing a broken *ghaṛā*. Further east is the northern part of another small room, two other walls which are seen higher in the foreground of Pl. XXXVIII, *d*, an L-shaped corner with a pilaster at the point where it meets Trench II, and the remains of a pavement at the east end on which rested a broken *ghaṛā*. No finds were recovered from this stratum.

Stratum III. Such as they are, the buildings of the IIIrd stratum are mainly of mud, though occasionally of mud brick also, burnt brick being exceptional. To the east of the deep digging are two small *kachchā* rooms. Immediately to their west was found (in square S 29/15 at a depth of 6 ft. 4 in. below the surface) a long, perforated, cylindrical pottery-heater (No. J148; ht. 1 ft. 7 in.; diam. 6½ in.) pierced with a large hole through the bottom[1] (Pl. LXXII, 6). This is the largest vessel of its kind yet found at Harappā. **Perforated heater.**

Finds from the western part of the trench. In the western part, between the break and squares R 29/10 and R 30/6 are four mud walls, which are partly buried under the edges of the trench. The space immediately to the west of the break was dug to a depth of 7 ft. and yielded the following:—

1. Oblong, faience sealing,[2] lentoid in section, with 4 pictograms on one side, and an acacia tree enclosed in a platform on the other. L. 15/16 in. No. J121; Square R 30/11; Depth 5 ft. 6 in. b.s.
2. Pottery disc simulating *shīsham* (*Dalbergia latifolia*) leaf on either side. Pl. LXXI, 72. Diam. 1⅜ in. No. J106; Square R 30/11; Depth 4 ft. b.s.
3. Ring-based, carinated pottery vase with flanged neck. It is painted alternately with rows of flying kites and birds (?), and its shape, superior red slip, and texture, as well as paintings are typical of the Cemetery H wares. Pl. LXXIII, 39. Ht. 5⅛ in.; diam. 2¼ in. No. J176; Square R 30/11; Depth 7 ft. b.s.

13 ft. west of the western mud wall lay a group of four broken *ghaṛās* in square R 30/6, and a little further on, part of a paved room in squares R 30/1 and R 29/5 (w. 9 ft. 10 in.).

---

[1] Numerous similar heaters have also been found at Mohenjo-daro, *cf.* Mackay in *M. I. C.*, p. 313, Pl. LXXVIII, 3, and Pl. LXXXIV, 3-18. The bottom hole in a few of the larger vessels at Harappā is, however, much larger and without smaller holes around it such as are found in the Mohenjo-daro vessels.

[2] This is from the same mould as No. 6 on p. 180 *supra*.

Deep digging.

East of the break a pit was sunk about 40 ft. long from east to west by 20 ft. wide and 20 ft. deep. In its western part were found three crushed earthenware jars between 8 ft. and 12 ft. below the surface. One of these (No. J166) was *deg*-shaped with long, narrow, tapering bottom; the second one was cylindrical, painted with linear and geometrical patterns; and the third one was of the common napiform shape. Still further down, between 14 and 16 ft. below the surface, were found a few terracotta animal toys with their fore and hind legs fashioned in a single piece, *i.e.*, without a division between the two legs. They are described in the list below, but it may be observed here that animal toys of such archaic type have only been found from the Vth stratum downwards in the deep diggings in Trenches I and IV of the low Mound F, and in the deep digging in the north-east part of the Eastern Section of the Cemetery H, where only one specimen was unearthed. So far as I am aware, such toys are not found at Mohenjo-daro, where the early Harappā seals also have not yet been found.

Primitive animal toys.

Rubbish heaps.

From a depth of 12 to 20 ft. in this pit were found regular lines of ashes or ashy earth mixed with potsherds, brickbats, and nodules, but no structures were met with below the IIIrd stratum. The size of this deep pit is too small to enable me to state whether originally it was an open space or not, but evidently the sweepings and refuse of neighbouring houses were thrown in here. The following finds were recovered from it, but in the absence of structural remains they cannot be assigned to any particular strata:—

Finds.

1. Large copper spear-head. Pl. CXXV, 65. L. 10⅛ in.; w. 2⅝ in. No. J125; Square S 29/15; Depth 8 ft. 10 in. b.s.
2. Flat, unfinished strip of copper, thinned at one end, and possibly intended for a cobbler's awl. L. 4⅜ in. No. J124; Square S 29/15; Depth 10 ft. 8 in. b.s.
3. Small, round earthenware vase with deeply scored body. Ht. 2¼ in. No. J80; Square S 29/5; Depth 8 ft. b.s.
4. Square, bossed seal showing only the hind quarters of a rhinoceros (?), fragmentary. No pictograms were inscribed in the upper field. Pl. XCI, 252. ⅝ in. sq. No. J139; Square S 29/15; Depth 12 ft. b.s.
5. Humped earthenware bull with fore and hind legs fashioned in single pieces. Pl. LXXIX, 63. L. 2⅜ in. No. J172; Square S 30/6; Depth 14 ft. 8 in. b.s.
6. Humped bull similar to No. J172. Pl. LXXIX, 61. L. 3 in. No. J185; Square S 29/5; Depth 14 ft. 9 in. b.s.
7. Humped bull similar to No. J172. Pl. LXXIX, 62. L. 3 in. No. J188; Square S 29/5; Depth 16 ft. b.s.

Mound D.

Two trenches running parallel to each other with a distance of over 110 ft. between them were sunk in Mound D. Of these, Trench I cuts across the mound from north to south; Trench II extends southward only as far as the ridge.

Trench I.

Stratification.

Trench I, which lies to the west, was first begun late in the year 1927-28 but only partially excavated then. In 1930-31 the work was resumed, and a number of mud brick houses of the IIIrd and IVth strata were brought to light. The ridge of this mound appears to have been occupied by structures of Strata I and II only. Trench I measures 147 ft. from north to south by 61 ft. from east to west (Pl. XXXVII). In order to reach the IVth stratum it was sunk below the ridge to a depth of 10 to 11 ft., at the northern end between 3½ ft. and 5½ ft., and at the southern end between 1 and 2 ft. only. In the Northern Section which extends for 50 ft. from that extremity the Ist stratum was non-existent; the IInd was represented only by a few broken household pots and other finds which lay between 1 ft. 6 in. and 2 ft. below the surface (Pl. XXXVIII, *b*); the IIIrd stratum lies between 2 ft. and 4½ ft. below the surface, and the IVth descends to 6½ ft. In the Middle Section of this trench, which covers about 70 ft., the Ist stratum goes down to 2 ft., the IInd to a little over 5 ft., the IIIrd to 6¼ ft., and the IVth to 9½ ft. In the Southern Section, which occupies the remaining 27 ft. the two upper strata are non-existent, the IIIrd is found to a depth of 1½ ft. followed by a few remains of the IVth stratum which come close to the surface along the southern edge.

Finds from Stratum I.

The following finds were recovered from Stratum I:—

1. Unicorn seal with 6 pictograms. Pl. LXXXIX, 113. 1 3/16 in. sq. No. J500; Square Q 30/20; Depth 1 ft. 3 in. b.s.
2. Unicorn seal with 6 pictograms, lower right part broken. Pl. LXXXVI 36. 1¼ in. sq. No. 4079; Square Q 30/13; Depth 2 ft. 1 in. b.s.
3. Tiny, triangular steatite seal with 4 pictograms on one side, and 1 on the other. Pl. XCV, 419. Side ¾ in. No. 4080; Square Q 30/13; Depth 1 ft. b.s.
4. Fragment of a tiny, rectangular steatite seal inscribed on both sides. Pl. XCVII, 524. W. 5/16 in. No. J532; Square Q 30/23; Depth 1 ft. 3 in. b.s.
5. Fragment of a rectangular faience sealing with pictograms on both sides. Pl. XCIX, 636. W. 5/16 in. No. 3943; Square Q 31/11; Depth 5 in. b.s.
6. Cylindrical terracotta sealing with 2 pictograms and 2 dots on one side, and 1 pictogram on the other. Pl. C, 675. L. ⅝ in. No. J466; Square Q 30/18; Depth 7 in. b.s.
7. Cylindrical terracotta sealing with 4 pictograms on one side, and crocodile on the other. Slightly curved in firing. Pl. XCIV, 338. L. 1⅛ in. No. J478; Square Q 30/23; Depth 9 in. b.s.
8. A lot of 74 thin, disc beads of steatite paste of three sizes, mostly larger than the usual size. Diam. 13/32, ⅜ and ¼ in. No. 4155; Square Q 30/20; Depth 1 ft. b.s.
9. Cubical limestone weight. Wt. 6·55 gms.; size ·57×·57×·47 in. No. J513· Square Q 31/17; Depth 1 ft. 9 in. b.s.

10. Rectangular steatite amulet with 2 parallel holes, slightly damaged. Size 1×$\frac{11}{16}$ in. No. J512; Square Q 31/18; Depth 1 ft. 9 in. b.s.
11. Cubical chert weight. Wt. 54·25 gms.; size 1·15×1·15×·95 in. No. 3979; Square Q 31/16; Depth 2 ft. 9 in. b.s.
12. Chessman-shaped object of green jasper. Ht. $\frac{7}{8}$ in. No. 3951; Square Q 31/18; Depth 3 ft. b.s.
13. Square, steatite amulet incised with three rows of three double concentric circles. It has a cylindrical, holed projection for a knob at the back. Pl. XCV, 388. $\frac{3}{4}$ in. sq. No. 4156; Square Q 30/19; Depth 1 ft. b.s.
14. Ivory spatula. Pl. CXIX, 57. L. 6$\frac{1}{4}$ in. No. 4164; Square Q 30/20; Depth 1 ft. 6 in. b.s.
15. Inscribed potsherd. No. 4320; Square Q 31; Depth 3 ft. b.s.

Stratum II. Finds of Stratum II were recovered in two groups in the Central Section, the first group lying to the north in square Q 30/15, and the second to the south in squares Q 31/13, 18, and 23. The former group comprises the undermentioned seven objects:—

1. Steatite seal showing a bison bending over a trough and 7 pictograms. Pl. XCI, 245. $\frac{13}{16}$ in. sq. No. J361; Square Q 30/15; Depth 3 ft. 4 in. b.s.
2. Unicorn seal with 6 pictograms, fragmentary. Pl. LXXXIX, 131. 1$\frac{1}{16}$ in. sq. No. J548; Square Q 30/20; Depth 4 ft. 7 in. b.s.
3. Cubical chert weight. Wt. 27·32 gms.; size ·95×·9×·75 in. No. 4009; Square Q 30/15; Depth 3 ft. 2 in. b.s.
4. Cubical chert weight. Wt. 13·9 gms.; size ·7×·7×·6 in. No. 4054; Square Q 30/15; Depth 4 ft. b.s.
5. Chert tablet, broken. L. 2$\frac{3}{8}$ in. No. 4087; Square Q 30/15; Depth 4 ft. b.s.
6. Faience baluster triangular in section incised with a row of circles on each face in imitation of ivory prototypes; broken at one end. L. 1 in. No. 4017; Square Q 30/15; Depth 4 ft. b.s.
7. Flat-bottomed, squat flask with narrow neck, painted in bands with *pīpal* (*ficus religiosa*) leaves. Pl. LXXI, 26. Ht. 4$\frac{1}{4}$ in.; diam. 6 in. No. 4053; Square Q 30/15; Depth 4 ft. b.s.

The southern group comprised the following six objects:—

1. Unicorn seal with 4 pictograms. Pl. LXXXVI, 35. 1$\frac{1}{12}$ in. sq. No. 3975; Square Q 31/18; Depth 4 ft. b.s.
2. Tiny, rectangular steatite seal rounded at one end, and inscribed with 4 pictograms on one side, and 1 on the other; unglazed. Pl. XCVII, 562. Size $\frac{11}{16}$×$\frac{7}{16}$ in. No. J575; Square Q 31/18; Depth 4 ft. b.s.
3. Rectangular terracotta sealing with 7 pictograms on one side, and 5 on the other: twisted in firing. Pl. XCIV, 349. Size 1×$\frac{7}{16}$ in. No. J455; Square Q 31/13; Depth 4 ft. b.s.

4. Carnelian spheroid flattened at top and base. Probably a weight.[1] Pl. CXVIII, 30 and Pl. CXX, 58. Diam. 1⅛ in.; ht. ⅞ in. No. J576; Square Q 31/18; Depth 4 ft. b.s.
5. Cubical chert weight, fragmentary. Wt. 101·83 gms.; No. 3976; Square Q 31/18; Depth 4 ft. b.s.
6. Barrel-shaped weight[2] of soapstone broken at one end. Wt. 36·9 gms. L. 2⅜ in. No. J577; Square Q 31/23; Depth 4 ft. 7 in. b.s.

Stratum III.

In the IIIrd stratum were exposed the remains of four[3] *kachchā* houses occupying the greater part of the trench, a paved bath (5 ft.×4 ft. 5 in.) in the middle of the Central Section with two earthenware *gharās* embedded against its south side, evidently for the bath water, and some more fragments of walls of burnt brick masonry (Pl. XXXVIII, *a*). Besides these remains, along the northern edge of the trench was a drain which comes down from the higher ground on the north and turns westward in square Q 30/17 (Pl. XXXVIII, *b*, background). This has been traced for a length of 45 ft. only.

***Kachchā* houses.**

The four *kachchā* houses, referred to above, are constructed mainly of mud bricks with an occasional patch, corner, or pilaster of burnt brick masonry. Three of these houses, numbered 1 to 3, are partially buried under the eastern edge of the trench (Pl. XXXVII). The west part of House 1 comprises a large, rectangular courtyard (No. 1) and a side room (No. 2), with three more partially excavated rooms (Nos. 3 to 5) at the back. Of House 2 only three rooms are visible and none of them is complete, while of House 3 only some fragments have survived. House 4 consists of four parts (Pl. XXXVIII, *b*). Of these, No. 1 appears to have been the courtyard, of which the west and south walls were originally constructed during the fourth period. When it was reconstructed in the following period the doorway in its west wall, which is of burnt brick masonry, was filled up with mud bricks. Room No. 2 is in the north-east corner of this court, and adjoining it on the east side of the court are two other rooms, Nos. 3 and 4. The following objects were found in Room No. 3:—

Finds from House 4.

1. Unicorn seal with 3 pictograms. Pl. LXXXIX, 126. 1⅛ in. sq. No. J481; Square Q 30/14; Depth 5 ft. 7 in. b.s.
2. Triangular, prismatic faience sealing with 5 pictograms on one side, 1 on the second, and a fish on the third. Pl. XCIX, 645. L. 11/16 in. No. J359; Square Q 30/14; Depth 2 ft. 10 in. b.s.
3. Circular faience sealing with 3 pictograms on one side, and 1 on the other. Pl. XCV, 370. Diam. ½ in. No. J394; Square Q 30/14; Depth 3 ft. 9 in. b.s.
4. Triangular, prismatic faience sealing with some blurred pictograms on one side, 1 on the second, and a fish on the third. Pl. XCIX, 642. L. ⅝ in. No. J619; Square Q 30/13; Depth 4 ft. 7 in. b.s.

---

[1] Six weights of this type have been found at Mohenjo-daro. *Cf. M. I. C.*, p. 462, Pl. CXXXI, 60 and 61.

[2] For weights of this type from Mohenjo-daro, *cf. M. I. C.*, p. 463, Pl. CLIV, 5 and 8.

[3] The greater part of House 1 as it has survived really belongs to Stratum IV, but its higher walls which are buried under the eastern edge of the trench were renovated with Stratum III with which it has been described now.

Other finds. The following antiquities belonging to Stratum III were found widely scattered over the whole trench :—

1. Steatite seal showing a bison (*Bos gaurus*) bending over a trough; fragmentary. $\frac{3}{4}$ in. sq. No. J482; Square Q 30/15; Depth 6 ft. b.s.
2. Unicorn seal with 6 pictograms, very well engraved. Pl. LXXXIX, 106. $1\frac{3}{8}$ in. sq. No. J579; Square Q 31/16; Depth 6 ft. b.s.
3. Unicorn seal with 3 pictograms. Pl. LXXXIX, 122. $\frac{3}{4}$ in. sq. No. 4015; Square Q 30/18; Depth 7 ft. b.s.
4. Tiny, oval steatite seal inscribed on both sides; fragmentary. Pl. XCVII, 545. W. $\frac{5}{16}$ in. No. J523; Square Q 30/13; Depth 4 ft. 8 in. b.s.
5. Tiny, rectangular steatite seal with 4 pictograms on one side, and 1 on the other. Pl. XCVI, 445. Size $\frac{11}{16}\times\frac{3}{8}$ in. No. J582; Square Q 30/18; Depth 5 ft. b.s.
6. Tiny, rectangular steatite seal with 3 pictograms on one side, and 1 on the other; similar to No. 458 in Pl. XCVI. Size $\frac{5}{16}\times\frac{5}{16}$ in. No. J402; Square Q 31/18; Depth 5 ft. 4 in. b.s.
7. Tiny, square steatite seal with 2 pictograms on one side, and 1 on the other. This shape is unique among seals of this class. Pl. XCV, 406. $\frac{7}{16}$ in. sq. No. J581; Square O 31/17; Depth 6 ft. 4 in. b.s.
8. Two fragments of a tiny, rectangular seal inscribed on both sides. Pl. XCVII, 531. Size $\frac{3}{8}\times\frac{1}{4}$ in. No. 4051; Square Q 31/12; Depth 8 ft. b.s.
9. Cylindrical faience sealing showing 4 pictograms on one side, and VIII-like symbol and acacia tree on the other. Similar to No. 646 in Pl. XCIX. L. $\frac{13}{16}$ in. No. J533; Square Q 30/19; Depth 2 ft. 7 in. b.s.
10. Rectangular faience sealing with 4 pictograms on one side, and 1 on the other. Pl. XCIV, 355. Size $\frac{3}{4}\times\frac{5}{8}$ in. No. J494; Square Q 30/8; Depth 3 ft. 8 in. b.s.
11. Rectangular faience sealing with 2 pictograms on one side, and 1 on the other. Much distorted in firing. Pl. C, 686. Size $\frac{5}{8}\times\frac{3}{16}\times\frac{5}{8}$ in. No. J403; Square Q 30/19; Depth 4 ft. b.s.
12. Rectangular faience sealing with 5 pictograms on one side, and 1 on the other. Pl. XCIV, 350. Size $\frac{3}{4}\times\frac{5}{8}$ in. No. J463; Square Q 30/14; Depth 4 ft. 5 in. b.s.
13. Rectangular faience sealing with 6 pictograms on one side, and 1 on the other. Pl. XCIV, 345. Size $\frac{7}{8}\times\frac{7}{16}$ in. No. J462; Square Q 30/15; Depth 6 ft. 2 in. b.s.
14. Shield-shaped faience sealing with 3 pictograms on one side, and 1 on the other. Pl. XCV, 376. Size $\frac{11}{16}\times\frac{5}{8}$ in. No. J449; Square Q 31/7; Depth 6 ft. 10 in. b.s.
15. Oblong terracotta sealing, lentoid in section, with blurred pictograms on both sides. L. $\frac{7}{8}$ in. No. J503; Square Q 30/8; Depth 4 ft. 2 in. b.s.

16. Cubical limestone weight. Wt. 2·9 gms.; size ·43×·43×·35 in. No. J598; Square Q 31/22; Depth 5 ft. 9 in. b.s.
17. Sharp-edged, bronze smoothing plane (?) similar to the one illustrated in Pl. CXXIV, 36. Upper part missing. L. $3\frac{1}{4}$ in.; w. at cutting edge $1\frac{1}{2}$ in.; th. $\frac{1}{16}$ in. No. J562; Square Q 30/20; Depth 6 ft. b.s.
18. Conical steatite ear-drop with a holed projection at top for suspension. Pl. CXXXIX, 31. Ht. $\frac{5}{16}$ in. No. J594; Square Q 30/20; Depth 5 ft. 7 in. b.s.
19. Terracotta hare in which the pairs of fore and hind legs are not separated from each other. Pl. LXXIX, 46. L. $2\frac{1}{4}$ in. No. J587; Square Q 31/16; Depth 5 ft. 3 in. b.s.

Remains of Stratum IV.

The IVth stratum is at present represented only by the earlier parts of the courtyard of House 4 referred to above, by the western part of House 1 and a few other walls. In the courtyard of House 4 were found the undermentioned copper weapons belonging to the IVth stratum:—

1. Dagger, tang broken. The original shape of one edge has been modified, probably by sharpening. Pl. CXXIV, 46. L. $8\frac{3}{8}$ in.; w. $1\frac{5}{8}$ in. No. J483; Square Q 30/14; Depth 5 ft. 7 in. b.s.
2. Leaf-shaped spear-head with long tang. It has two rivet holes near the centre and one at the far end of the tang. Its form is early, mark particularly the position of the holes. Pl. CXXV, 72. L. $6\frac{1}{2}$ in.; w. 2 in. No. J485; Square Q 30/14; Depth 5 ft. 7 in. b.s.
3. Spear-head with broad tang, tip broken. Early type. Pl. CXXV, 69. L. $6\frac{1}{4}$ in.; w. 2 in. No. J484; Square Q 30/14; Depth 5 ft. 2 in. b.s.

Scattered finds.

The following objects of Stratum IV were found widely scattered:—

1. Tiny, rectangular steatite seal inscribed on both sides; fragmentary. L. $\frac{3}{8}$ in.; w. $\frac{5}{16}$ in. No. J586; Square Q 30/19; Depth 6 ft. b.s.
2. Tiny, rectangular steatite seal with 2 pictograms on one side, and 1 on the other. Pl. XCVI, 479. Size $\frac{11}{16}\times\frac{5}{16}$ in. No. J580; Square Q 30/20; Depth 6 ft. 7 in. b.s.
3. Fragment of a tiny, rectangular steatite seal inscribed on both sides. Pl. XCVI, 496. W. $\frac{1}{4}$ in. No. J450; Square Q 31/16; Depth 7 ft. b.s.
4. Thick, rectangular steatite seal, roughly inscribed on both sides. Its script seems to be peculiar. Size $\frac{3}{8}\times\frac{7}{16}\times\frac{1}{4}$ in. No. J531; Square Q 30/13; Depth 5 ft. 5 in. b.s.
5. Fish-shaped faience sealing with 4 pictograms on one side, and 3 on the other; similar to No. 658 in Pl. C. L. $\frac{7}{8}$ in. No. J493; Square Q 30/10; Depth 7 ft. 4 in. b.s.
6. Circular faience sealing with 2 pictograms on one side, and 1 on the other. Pl. XCV, 378. Diam. $\frac{7}{16}$ in. No. J593; Square Q 31/16; Depth 7 ft. 9 in. b.s.

7. Square, bossed faience sealing with two concentric squares enclosed by a border of short vertical strokes; broken. Pl. XCV, 383. $\frac{7}{16}$ in. sq. No. J583; Square Q 31/22; Depth 8 ft. b.s.
8. Rectangular faience sealing with 2 pictograms surviving on one side and an animal with broken head—probably a unicorn—on the other. Pl. C, 677. L. $\frac{7}{16}$ in.; w. $\frac{5}{16}$ in. No. J409; Square Q 31/17; Depth 9 ft. b.s.
9. Cubical chert weight. Wt. 1·7 gms.; size ·35×·35×·30 in. No. J451; Square Q 31/7; Depth 7 ft. 6 in. b.s.
10. Flat-based, squat earthenware flask with a hole for the mouth; decorated with bands. Pl. LXXI, 29. Ht. 3½ in.; diam. 4 in. No. J179; Square S 30/11; Depth 11 ft. 7 in. b.s.

Trench II.

Trench II is 70 ft. long with an average width of 32 ft. (Pl. XXXVII). In this trench also, remains of four strata were uncovered, which with the exception of a couple of walls belonging to the IInd and IIIrd strata, are all confined to its southern half (Pl. XXXVIII, *c*). The Ist stratum goes down to about 3 ft. below the surface, the IInd to 5½ ft., the IIIrd to 8½ ft., and the IVth to 12 ft.

Stratum I. In the Ist stratum, which is represented by three fragments of walling near the eastern edge of the trench, the following two objects were found:—

1. Tiny, rectangular steatite seal with 5 pictograms on one side, and 4 on the other. Pl. XCVI, 477. Size $\frac{5}{8}\times\frac{5}{16}$ in. No. J213; Square S 30/7; Depth 2 ft. b.s.
2. Tiny, rectangular steatite seal with 4 pictograms on one side, and 1 on the other. Pl. XCVII, 510. Size $\frac{5}{16}\times\frac{5}{16}$ in. No. J30; Square S 30/6; Depth 2 ft. 6 in. b.s.

Stratum II. Of the IInd stratum there are two walls alongside the eastern edge of the trench, and the northern one of these has two recesses, each 2 ft. wide and 9 in. deep. The following six objects associated with this stratum were found in square S 30/4:—

1. Unicorn seal with 6 pictograms. Pl. LXXXVIII, 104. 1¼ in. sq. No. J273; Depth 4 ft. b.s.
2. Tiny, rectangular steatite seal with 4 pictograms on one side, and 3 on the other. Pl. XCVI, 471. Size $\frac{11}{16}\times\frac{1}{2}$ in. No. J274; Depth 4 ft. 5 in. b.s.
3. Tiny, triangular prism seal of steatite with 5 pictograms on one side, 2 on the second, and 1 on the third. Rare, in that it is inscribed on all the three faces. Pl. XCVIII, 589. L. ½ in. No. J212; Depth 4 ft. 6 in. b.s.
4. Fragment of a tiny, rectangular steatite seal inscribed on both sides. W. ⅜ in. No. J279; Depth 5 ft. 2 in. b.s.

5. Discoid faience sealing with 4 pictograms on one side, and 1 on the other. Pl. XCV, 381. Diam. ½ in. No. J275; Depth 4 ft. 8 in. b.s.
6. Alabaster cylinder, ovoid in section. May have been prepared for cutting oval tablets similar to Nos. 52-55 in Pl. CXVII. L. 4 in.; diam. 3¼ in. No. J277; Depth 4 ft. 4 in. b.s.

The following finds of Stratum II were found scattered in the trench:— **Scattered finds.**

1. Tiny, rectangular steatite seal with 6 pictograms on one side, and 4 on the other. Pl. XCVI, 446. Size ⅜×⅜ in. No. J630; Square S 30/1; Depth 3 ft. 6 in. b.s.
2. Tiny, rectangular steatite seal with 4 pictograms on one side, and 1 on the other. Pl. XCVI, 492. Size 7/16×5/16 in. No. J229; Square S 30/3; Depth 5 ft. 2 in. b.s.
3. Oblong faience sealing, semicircular in section, with 4 pictograms on one side, and 1 on the other. Pl. C, 689. L. 11/16 in. No. J228; Square S 30/8; Depth 4 ft. 8 in. b.s.
4. Fragment of a tiny, rectangular faience sealing inscribed on both sides. Pl. XCVIII, 609. W. ⅝ in. No. J284; Square S 30/3; Depth 5 ft. 5 in. b.s.
5. Body of a well-modelled steatite bird with traces of wings and left leg surviving. Pl. LXXVIII, 1. L. 1 11/16 in. No. J320; Square S 30/1; Depth 5 ft. b.s.
6. Miniature faience ram. L. 1 in. No. J269; Square S 30/4; Depth 3 ft. 6 in. b.s.
7. Fragmentary copper spear-head with 2½ in. long tang holed at the lower end. Pl. CXXV, 66. L. 4¾ in; w. 2 in. No. J220; Square S 30/8; Depth 5 ft. 6 in. b.s.

The IIIrd stratum in this trench is slightly better preserved and represented by a nearly complete room situated in squares S 30/8 and 9 with L-shaped remains of an apartment in front of it to the west. The following antiquities were recovered from Stratum III:— **Stratum III.**

1. Tiny, rectangular steatite seal with 4 pictograms on one side, and 3 on the other. Pl. XCVI, 472. Size 5/16×5/16 in. No. J235; Square S 30/8; Depth 7 ft. 4 in. b.s.
2. Tiny, triangular prism sealing of faience with pictograms on two sides, and circles on the third; fragmentary. Pl. XCIX, 649. L. ½ in. No. J219; Square S 30/9; Depth 7 ft. 10 in. b.s.
3. Rectangular faience sealing with 2 pictograms on one side, and 1 on the other. Pl. C, 680. Size 5/16×5/16 in. No. J283; Square S 30/4; Depth 6 ft. 9 in. b.s.
4. Tiny faience bird. Pl. LXXVIII, 4. L. 5/16 in. No. J223; Square S 30/3; Depth 6 ft. 2 in. b.s.

The remains in the IVth stratum comprise a spacious room measuring 26 ft. 6 in. by 9 ft. 10 in. situated along the south end of the trench, and a mud wall **A large room of Stratum IV.**

nearly parallel to it at a distance of 19 to 20 ft. The following objects were found in the room :—

1. Tiny, rectangular steatite seal inscribed on both sides; fragmentary. Pl. XCVII, 523. L. $\frac{3}{8}$ in.; w. $\frac{5}{16}$ in. No. J250; Depth 9 ft. 11 in. b.s.
2. Tiny, rectangular steatite seal with 3 pictograms on one side, and fish on the other. Pl. XCVI, 437. Size $\frac{3}{16}\times\frac{5}{16}$ in. No. J256; Depth 10 ft. 8 in. b.s.
3. Tiny, fish-shaped steatite seal with 4 pictograms on one side, and 3 on the other. Pl. XCV, 427. Size $\frac{3}{16}\times\frac{1}{4}$ in. No. J329; Depth 10 ft. 9 in. b.s.
4. Heart-shaped faience seal with 4 pictograms on one side, and 2 on the other. Pl. XCV, 415. Size $\frac{5}{8}\times\frac{5}{16}$ in. No. J321; Depth 10 ft. 6 in. b.s.
5. Terracotta ball rattle perforated on one side. Pl. CXX, 31. Diam. 2 in. No. J338; Depth 12 ft. b.s.

Other finds.

The following four objects were recovered to the south of the above-mentioned room :—

1. Square bossed seal inscribed with a running hare and perhaps a pictogram above its head; fragmentary. This is the only bossed seal with figure of a hare. Pl. XCVII, 568. $\frac{9}{16}$ in. sq. No. J337; Square S 30/2; Depth 9 ft. 6 in. b.s.
2. Small silver vase of thin sheet, broken at bottom. Shows numerous hammer marks both inside and out. Pl. CXXV, 53. Ht. $1\frac{3}{16}$ in.; diam. $1\frac{1}{16}$ in. No. J339; Square S 30/8; Depth 9 ft. 7 in. b.s.
3. Finger ring of thick gold wire, square in section, distorted. Pl. CXXV, 55. Diam. $\frac{11}{16}$ in. No. J260; Square S 30/8; Depth 9 ft. b.s.
4. Terracotta dog with pairs of fore and hind legs not separated from each other. L. $2\frac{1}{4}$ in. No. J353; Square S 30/8; Depth 8 ft. 9 in. b.s.

Data regarding the comparatively early age of Area J.

Before concluding this account of Area J, it remains to emphasize two features. One is that the level of the ground here is much below that of Mound AB; the other is that the minor antiquities found here are of a distinctly early type. Thus, among the seals and sealings, a large proportion consist of the tiny varieties which, as I have stated elsewhere,[1] were almost invariably associated with the early strata in Mound F, and found in lesser numbers in the early strata in Mound AB.[2] Then there are the copper weapons which, with the exception of spear-head No. J125 (Pl. CXXV, 65), show markedly primitive shapes (*cf.* Pl. CXXIV, 46 and Pl. CXXV, 66-69 and 72), their tangs being comparatively long, and in many cases unusually broad; and in spite of this, unprovided with

[1] See p. 324 ff. *infra*.

[2] Several tiny seals were also found near the surface of this mound, but that would not be surprising when it is remembered that this mound is also the most exploited and that some of these seals would naturally have been dug up and thrown out with earth on the surface.

one exception,[1] with rivet holes for attachment. Again, there are the animal toys mentioned above with their front and hind legs fashioned in single pieces[2] instead of being separated, and I have already pointed out in connection with the deep digging in Trenches I and IV in Mound F that animal toys of this type are confined to the earliest strata at Harappā. Taken together, this evidence points to the conclusion that Area J is almost contemporary with Mound F, and earlier than the late occupations on Mound AB.[3]

---

[1] The sole exception is the spear-head No. J485 (Pl. CXXV, 72) in which the two upper holes are placed so high up the blade that much of it would be needlessly covered by the wooden haft, and moreover they are also carelessly and clumsily punched at uneven distances from the edges. The fine spear-head No. J125 (Pl. CXXV, 65) referred to above, is among the largest specimens from Harappā, but does not betray the existence of a vertical mid-rib.

[2] In Balūchistān, however, animal toys with the legs treated in this manner are quite common. Among the sites in Gedrosia they have been found at Shāhī-tump, Mehī, Mēn, etc. *Cf.* Sir Aurel Stein, *Mem. A.S.I.*, No. 43, Pls. XIV, XXVII, and XXXI.

[3] For the comparative chronology of mounds and correlation of different strata in them, see p. 15 ff. *supra*.

CHAPTER V.

Area G.

Locale and level. Immediately south of the Lahore-Multan road and opposite the mound occupied by the local Police Station, a hexagonal piece of land, measuring about 10 acres, was acquired for exploration late in the year 1928-29. This area has been designated G. Like Area H, it is low-lying, being some 4 to 8 ft. below the latter. Its north-eastern part is level with the fields to the east; the rest, which is a bit higher, first rises gradually towards the south and then falls again. Not long ago it formed part of the military encamping ground. Of all the land round about Harappā this area is most highly charged with salpetre, and this explains why the antiquities found in it are specially liable to crumble unless prompt measures are taken to preserve them (Pl. I).

Trenches I, II and III. At present, this area is divided by an oblique irrigation channel into two parts; one to the north, the other to the south. Here two trial trenches, each 10 ft. wide, were sunk. No. I is 280 ft. long from east to west, and runs across the centre of the northern half; No. II, which is 400 ft. long, crosses the southern portion from north to south. Later on, traces of two brick walls were noticed in a disused, modern irrigation channel which ran along the western end of Trench I, and here, too, a rectangular area was dug measuring 127 ft. from north-east to south-west by 60 ft. wide. This is distinguished as Trench III. As both Trenches I and III were sunk in the Northern Section, I shall describe them first.

Trench I.

Finds. Trench I was dug to an average depth of 5 ft. 6 in. and yielded the following objects which have been arranged according to the strata in which they were found:—

Stratum I—

1. Chert flake. Pl. CXVIII, 38. L. 3¼ in. No. G31; Square AN 36/ 25; Depth 2 ft. b.s.
2. Unbored, barrel-shaped bead of carnelian. L. ⅜ in. No. G46; Square AM 36/25; Depth 2 ft. b.s.

Stratum II—

1. Long-barrel bead of light grey limestone with black stripes. Pl. CXXVIII, 49. L. 2⅜ in. No. G50; Square AO 36/5; Depth 3 ft. 4 in. b.s.
2. Fragmentary earthenware basin with tapering sides and perforated bottom. Diam. 10¼ in.; ht. 3⅜ in. No. G43; Square AN 36/10; Depth 3 ft. b.s.

3. Terracotta cubical die glazed red and marked with 1 opposite 6, 2 opposite 5, and 3 opposite 4.[1] Pl. CXX, 54. 1¼ in. cube. No. G72; Square AO 36/5; Depth 3 ft. 2 in. b.s.

Stratum III—

1. Bottom of an earthenware inscribed with one pictogram. Pl. CIII, 40. Size 7×3¾ in. No. G276; Square AO 36; Depth 3 to 6 ft. b.s.
2. Potsherd with 4 pictograms, broken horizontally. Pl. CIII, 43. Size 4¾×4¼ in. No. G277; Square AN 36; Depth 3 to 6 ft. b.s.
3. Sherd showing one pictogram. L. 7⅜ in. No. G278; Square AO 36; Depth 3 to 6 ft. b.s.
4. Neck fragment of a pot showing one pictogram. Pl. CIV. 75. L. 5¼ in. No. G279; Square AN 36; Depth 3 to 6 ft. b.s.
5. Inscribed sherd of a thick ware showing part of a pictogram. Pl. CIV, 67. L. 3¼ in. No. G280; Square AO 36; Depth 3 to 6 ft. b.s.
6. Neck fragment of a vase showing one pictogram. L. 4¼ in. No. G282; Square AO 36; Depth 3 to 6 ft. b.s.
7. Neck fragment of a vase with one pictogram. L. 4¼ in. No. G283; Square AN 36; Depth 3 to 6 ft. b.s.
8. Inscribed sherd showing part of a pictogram. L. 4 in. No. G284; Square AO 36; Depth 3 to 6 ft. b.s.
9. Fragment of the neck of a flanged pot with white slip. Its lower part is painted with crude peacock and leafy devices. Pl. LXIX, 13. Size 6×2½ in. No. G155; Square AO 36; Depth 3 to 6 ft. b.s.
10. Cubical chert weight of yellow tint. This colour is rare in chert. Wt. 26·6 gms.; size ·9×·9×·7 in. No. G248; Square AM 36/10; Depth 6 ft. b.s.

Superabundance of saltpetre. Only three bits of walls, standing widely apart from one another, were brought to light in this trench; for the rest it was full of crumbling potsherds and loose earth highly charged with saltpetre.

Trench III.

Nature of remains. The structural remains in Area G, so far as it has been examined, are extremely poor. Altogether, four strata of occupation are indicated in Trench III, mostly by broken bits of walls (Pl. XXXIX). Beside several fragmentary walls of Stratum II, there are the remains of two fairly large rooms in the Southern

[1] This resembles the modern dice inasmuch as the sum of the numbers on any of the two opposite sides is equal to seven. This is the only known example with such numbering from Harappā or Mohenjo-daro. *Cf.* Mackay in *M. I. C.*, Vol. II, pp. 551-52, and footnote 1 on p. 552. Also *cf.* pp. 456-57 *infra*.

Section (Pl. LVIII, *a*). In the south-west corner of the larger room is a closet, partitioned into two, in which was found a rectangular faience sealing (G113) described below.

Finds. The following objects were recovered from the strata under which they are mentioned :—

Stratum I—

1. Fragmentary unicorn seal showing only the body of the animal and incense-burner. Pl. XC, 201. L. $\frac{3}{4}$ in. No. G201; Square AM 35/14; Depth 3 ft. b.s.

2. Tiny, rectangular faience sealing with 6 pictograms; similar to No. 367*a* in Pl. XCIV. Size $\frac{11}{16}\times\frac{7}{16}$ in. No. G113; Square AM 35/23; Depth 2 ft. b.s.

3. Oblong faience sealing, lentoid in section, with 3 pictograms on one face, 2 pictograms and upper part of an incense-burner on the other; similar to No. 321 in Pl. XCIII. L. $\frac{5}{8}$ in.; w. $\frac{3}{8}$ in. No. G175; Square AM 35/20; Depth 3 ft. b.s.

4. Barrel-shaped stone bead. L. $\frac{1}{2}$ in. No. G111; Square AM 35/23; Depth 1 ft. b.s.

5. Yellow limestone ball. Diam. $1\frac{1}{8}$ in. No. G197; Square AM 35/20; Depth 3 ft. b.s.

6. Small oval pottery vase with narrow neck. Ht. $2\frac{3}{8}$ in. No. G126; Square AM 35/23; Depth 3 ft. b.s.

7. Handled pottery cup. Diam. $3\frac{5}{8}$ in.; ht. $2\frac{1}{2}$ in. No. G176; Square AM 35/20; Depth 3 ft. b.s.

Stratum II—

1. Steatite amulet with cross hatched incisions on both faces. It is holed across the tang for suspension round the neck. Pl. CXXXVIII, 44. Size $\frac{7}{8}\times\frac{11}{16}$ in. No. G193; Square AM 35/20; Depth 3 ft. 6 in. b.s.

2. Two barrel-shaped beads of banded stone. Pl. CXXVIII, 36. L. $\frac{5}{8}$ and $\frac{7}{16}$ in. No. G203; Square AM 35/22; Depth 4 ft. b.s.

3. Holed alabaster disc. Diam. $1\frac{1}{8}$ in. No. G230; Square AM 35/17; Depth 4 ft. 3 in. b.s.

4. Bar-shaped, ivory baluster with linear decoration, rectangular in section. L. $2\frac{3}{8}$ in. No. G239*e*; Square AM 35/14; Depth 4 ft. b.s.

5. Quarter of a shell hemisphere with lines incised along its perimeter. Size $1\frac{3}{8}\times1\frac{3}{16}$ in. No. G205; Square AM 35/19; Depth 4 ft. b.s.

A cinerary urn.

In addition to the above antiquities were recovered from this trench an open-mouthed, flanged pottery vase, fragment of a large pottery dish (G223), and a terracotta chessman-shaped object (G204). Here, too, was found a fragmentary earthenware jar lying at a depth of 4 ft. below the surface. Among its contents were a goblet with pointed base, two small cylindrical vases, an ivory baluster with incised decoration, a river shell, numerous sherds—mostly of goblets with pointed bases, pieces of triangular cakes and bangles, a clay ball, and some animal bones. These contents are similar to those of numerous post-cremation[1] urns which have been recovered in large numbers from the various mounds.

Trench II.

An interesting sealing.

Trench II was dug to an average depth of 7 ft. In its northern portion were found, among other objects, 31 cylindrical terracotta sealings described below, each with a unicorn on one side and four pictograms on the other (G256, etc.; Pl. XCIII, 315), and an interesting, oblong faience sealing, plano-convex in section (No. G107; Pl. XCIII, 316). The latter shows on the plane face a deity standing to right under an arch voluted at the lower ends and made of what appears to be the bent bough of a *pīpal* (*ficus religiosa*) tree. Facing the deity is the half-kneeling figure of a suppliant with hands raised in prayer, and, behind him, a goat of inordinately large size. But whether the goat, as suggested by Sir John Marshall,[2] is one of the intermediary deities (represented in Mesopotamia in anthropomorphic form, and at Mohenjo-daro as a composite creature) come to introduce the worshipper to the divinity, or is merely a well fed animal brought as an offering by the votary, it would be difficult to affirm. It should be noted, however, that the animal is not bound, or captive in any way, and this circumstance militates against its being an offering. Unfortunately, it is not possible to determine the sex of the deity, as the sealing shows no details —a defect which is invariably shared by other sealings also.

The following antiquities from the northern part of this trench deserve notice :—

1. Cylindrical terracotta sealing with a unicorn on one side, and 4 blurred pictograms on the other. A number of sealings from the same mould were also found in this trench. Pl. XCIII, 315. L. $1\frac{13}{16}$ in.; diam. $\frac{5}{16}$ in. No. G8; Square AM 40/24; Depth 8 in. b.s.
2. Cylindrical terracotta sealing from the same mould as No. G8. No. G58; Square AM 40/21; Depth 2 ft. 6 in. b.s.
3. Cylindrical terracotta sealing from the same mould as No. G8. No. G80; Square AM 40/21; Depth 3 ft. b.s.
4. Chert knife with midrib. Pl. CXVIII, 42. L. $3\frac{1}{4}$ in. No. G67; Square AM 40/23; Depth 2 ft. 10 in. b.s.
5. Fine pottery goblet. Ht. $3\frac{3}{8}$ in. No. G16; Square AM 42/22; Depth 1 ft. 10 in. b.s.

[1] See Chap. VIII, *infra*. Also *cf.* Sir John Marshall, *op. cit.*, pp. 87-89.

[2] *M. I. C.*, pp. 64-65, Pl. XII, 18.

6. Pottery vase with flat base. Ht. 2¼ in. No. G56; Square AM 40/25; Depth 2 ft. b.s.

Stratum II—

1. Unicorn seal with 6 pictograms. Pl. LXXXV, 15. 1 3/16 in. sq. No. G217; Square AN 40/25; Depth 3 ft. b.s.
2. Fragment of a unicorn seal showing only 2 pictograms and upper part of the animal and incense-burner. Pl. XC, 181. L. ¾ in. No. G104; Square AM 40/24; Depth 4 ft. b.s.
3. Tiny pottery disc incised with two circles of dots along the rim and with two holes for suspension. Diam. 1⅝ in. No. G245; Square AN 39/6; Depth 4 ft. 9 in. b.s.
4. Two inscribed potsherds showing 1 and 3 pictograms respectively. Pl. CIII, 35 and 51. L. 5 and 5¾ in. No. G267; Square AN 40; Depth 3 to 6 ft. b.s.

Stratum III—

1. 28 cylindrical terracotta sealings from the same mould as Nos. G8, G58 and G80.[1] No. G256; Squares AM 40/21 and AN 40/1; Depth up to 7 ft. b.s.
2. Fragment of an earthenware cage with a bird perched on top. Pl. CXX, 24. Ht. 2⅜ in. No. G144; Square AM 40/24; Depth 7 ft. b.s.

Three interesting terracotta figures.

In addition to the above finds there are three small terracottas which deserve notice. One of these (G38) shows a basket containing eatables carried on the head of a figure (Pl. LXXVII, 59). The second one (G185) exhibits a spirally conical[2] treatment of the hair which is bound with a fillet[3] round the forehead (Pl. LXXVI, 19). The third one is a low stool with a foot-board in front (G183) on which is a pair of human feet (Pl. LXXVI, 25).

Southern portion.

Group G15.

I now pass on to the southern portion of this trench in which were found in square AM 43/21, lying one below the other, in soft and pure silt, two groups of pottery; Nos. G15 and G130. Of these, the former lay only 2 ft. below the surface and consisted of three small jars of medium size, two dishes decorated with black bands, and an offerings' dish (Pl. XLII, *a*). The latter is rather squat as compared with similar standard dishes from the mounds. To their left, lying a little higher and almost in contact with the surface, were two entirely crushed *gharās*. Further down, between 5 ft. 9 in. and 6 ft. 6 in. below the

---

[1] Identical sealings described under Stratum I above are likely to have come up as the result of later brick digging.

[2] So far as I am aware there is no other figure at Harappā or Mohenjo-daro showing a similar treatment of the hair. A head found by me at the latter site (*cf. M. I. C.*, Pl. XCV, 23) seems to show a conical head-dress which, unlike this, is not turned into a spiral cone.

[3] For a plain gold fillet, *cf.* Pl. CXXX VII, 22.

surface, lay the much larger second group, G130 (Pl. XLI, *b*) which comprised the following vessels:— **Group G130.**

1. Medium-sized, globular jar resting on ring-stand, and covered with handled lid.[1] Pl. LXX, 16. It has incipient neck and is painted with three sets of black bands on red glazed surface. Ht. 8¾ in. The lid and stand were both broken. Diam. of lid, 6½ in.
2. Squat vase with flat base covered with a deep cup. Pl. LXX, 20. Ht. 6¼ in.
3. Three complete and three broken oval jars of ordinary make. Pl. LXX, 23. Ht. 5¾ to 7 in.
4. Two open-mouthed, oval goblets with flat base. Pl. LXX, 28. Ht. 6 in.
5. One goblet with standard foot. Pl. LXX, 5. Ht. 8¼ in.
6. Eight long, slender vases with flat base and flared mouth. Pl. LXX, 35. Ht. 5½ to 6 in.
7. Offerings' cup or censer. Pl. LXX, 6. Ht. 11 in.
8. Offerings' dish. Pl. LXX, 12. Diam. 12 in.
9. Twenty flat shallow dishes. Pl. LXX, 8. Diam. 11 to 11½ in.
10. Five saucers[2] with tapering sides of which three are broken. Diam. 7¾ to 8¼ in.

All the above vessels are flat at bottom, and, except the oval vases, are painted with a red slip, though none of them is well burnt. The covered jars 1 and 2 contained nothing but layers of percolated earth.

Close to the southern extremity of this trench was discovered, in the same soft soil, a well 3 ft. 3 in. in diameter, in which the present water level was 25 ft. below the top, or about 31 ft. below the surface. Sherds of a very large and thick type of jar were found in it. **A well.**

About 140 ft. north of the well mentioned above, in squares AN 42/21 and 22 a large group of human and animal remains was discovered in February, 1929, which, owing at that time to insurmountable difficulties in preserving them before removal, had to be covered up again temporarily with soil. In consultation with the Archæological Chemist it was also decided to keep the covering earth moderately moist, more particularly during the hottest part of summer, so that the saltpetre with which this soil is highly charged, might be allowed to evaporate as far as possible, and so do less damage. The course adopted proved more efficacious than we had hoped, and when the remains were uncovered again, after nine months, we found that they had suffered no further visible harm, though they were too fragile and delicate to remain *in situ* for long so as to admit of really comprehensive photographs being taken of them. For this reason, I thought it advisable to prepare two plans to the same scale showing precisely the **Group of skeletal remains No. G289. Its discovery and temporary covering up.**

[1] *Cf.* this lid with similar lids on burial-pots of Stratum I from the Cemetery H, *e.g.*, on Nos. H250. 7435d, and 3934b, Pl. LXI, 1, 3 and 7.

[2] They are plain and exactly similar to saucers of Stratum II from the Cemetery H, Pl. LX, 21-23.

Necessity of two plans and the method of their plotting.

position of all the bones and pottery. These two plans have since been combined into one, the remains shown in black representing those belonging to the upper layer; the remains in red those belonging to the lower. By this combined plan a fair idea can be formed of how the remains were actually lying over one another in the ground. It is to be remarked, however, that no attempt has been made in this plan to show, by foreshortening or otherwise, the inclination at which many of the bones and other objects were lying; and as a result, some of the bones appear nearer to adjacent objects than they actually were. But this is a defect that could not be avoided. For convenience of plotting, the area was arbitrarily divided into four divisions marked I, II, III and IV on the plan (Pl. XL). The whole find, being indivisible, has been numbered G289, but in each division, the pottery has been numbered alphabetically, *e.g.*, P*a*, P*b*, etc., while the bones have been numbered numerically, the skulls being distinguished from other bones by prefixing the letter 'S' to their respective serial numbers. On the other hand, bones lumped together are distinguished by the prefix 'L' in front of their respective numerals. Thus, S11 in a particular division indicates that in that division the 11th bone was a skull, etc.

Method of recording.

Composition and extent of the group.

The remains in this group, which were found tightly packed together between 4 ft. and 5 ft. 10 in. below the surface (Fig. *c*), comprised 20 complete human

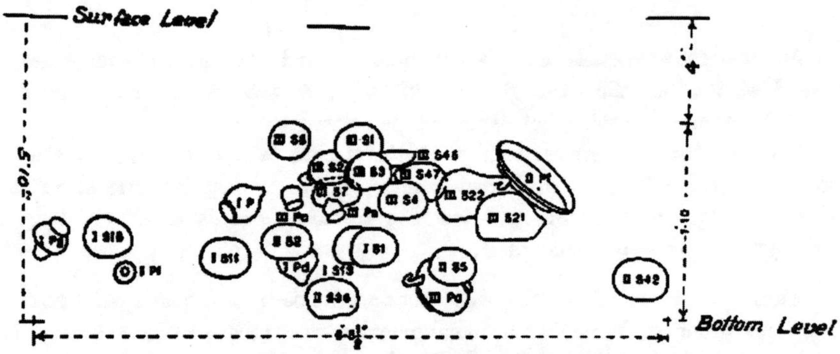

FIG. c.—SECTIONAL VIEW OF FIND G 289 (SKULLS AND POTTERY) LOOKING NORTH.

skulls and fragments of a few others, 10 lower jaws, parts of vertebral columns, bones of hips, legs and arms, as well as some animal bones, and a considerable amount of pottery. For clarity, I have divided the group into four parts and shall describe, division by division, the principal bones and pottery.

Division I.

In Division I were found four skulls Nos. S1, S11, S13 and S15. S1 lay near the point of intersection of the axial lines, and S11 about 2 ft. to its south-west. Between these two skulls was a human jaw No. 4, and long bones Nos. 3 and 8. Below the latter was a large, flat animal bone, No. 24—probably a haunch. Three feet west of jaw No. 4 was another jaw, No. 5, with the fragmentary bones Nos. 6 and 10 alongside it. Near skull S11 lay fragments of bones, a goblet with pointed base P*b*, and a little further south a long bone, No. 17. Below the goblet P*b*, were recovered a jaw No. 12 and long bones Nos.

20, 22, and 23, and close by lay another goblet with pointed base Pd, and the upper part of the stem of an offerings' dish Pe. About a foot to the east and south-west respectively of S11 were lying skulls Nos. S13 and S15. Near the latter lay a fragmentary bone No. 16, a vase Pf, a goblet with pointed base Pg, and, further south, another similar goblet Ph. Immediately to the north and west of S13 were two more goblets with pointed bases Pj and Pi, both of which were lying in contact with a leg bone No. 14.

Division II. In the southern part of Division II were lying, roughly in a line from east to west, two skulls S2 and S5, a lower jaw No. 3, and five vases Pa to Pe, the latter consisting of three oval vases, one goblet with pointed base, and a smaller goblet of oval shape. Immediately to the north of Pa and Pc, respectively, were skull S36 at a lower level and some metacarpal bones No. 32. Further up in the same direction lay an animal hip bone No. 33, and the remains of a human spine No. 28, which partially covered a bovine jaw No. 27. Within a foot from the northern end of the above spine lay inclined five long bones Nos. 11 to 15, and close by a rib No. 17. Intermingled with them were two offerings' dishes, of which Pg, which was lying upside down, is complete, and Pf merely the top dish. Bones Nos. 15 and 17 lay in them. About 6 in. below the top dish Pf was recovered a lower human jaw No. 19 probably belonging to the neighbouring skull S18, and over a foot to its south-east, but at a lower level, lay the severed head of skeleton No. 42, which was orientated approximately from north-west to south-east (Pl. XLI, *a*). From the upper end of the spine to the lower end of the femurs the skeleton was intact, but the left femur lay sloping as it had sunk a little. To the right of the thorax was a long bone No. 43, and below the femurs two other leg bones, probably a tibia and fibula No. 41. Close to the latter was a broken saucer Pj, and, further down, a cylindrical vase Pl and a goblet Pk. There were numerous other bones in this division which need not be noticed.

Division III. Group of five skulls. From here I pass on to Division III. In its lower angle were lying, disjointed and damaged, five human skulls Nos. S1 to S4, and S7 (Pl. XLI, *a* in front of the graduated staff, and Pl. XLII, *c*, left ground). Their tops came within 4 ft. to 4 ft. 6 in. of the surface. To the left of S4 was a goblet Pa, and to its right a squat and round, medium-sized vase with ring-base Pd which was hidden under two long bones Nos. 9 and 11, and the part of a spine No. 12 lying close by. Touching the skull S7 was a pottery saucer Pb, in contact with which was another vase Pc. Near by lay the fragment of a skull No. S13. About 12 and 15 in. respectively to its north and north-east lay skulls No. S8, and Nos. S46 and S47. Below skull S46 were a long bone No. 67, and a broken human spine No. 69, the western end of which was resting partly on an inverted lower jaw No. 68. Between these skulls and Pb were found on a lower plane the leg bone No. 18, and part of the spine No. 19 of an animal—probably the *canis familiaris*. A little to the east and north-east of skull S47 were recovered several leg and arm bones Nos. 26 to 39, 50, 51 and 70 (Pl. XLI, *a*, right background). Of these, Nos. 26 to 33 were crumbled.

Another group of three skulls.

Between the above-mentioned long bones and skulls S1 to S4 were found three more skulls numbered S21 to S23, which lay closely packed in numerous long bones. Skull S22 had toppled over S23, but S21 and S23 apparently lay side by side on the same level (Pl. XLII, *b*). Besides these, were fragments of two more skulls numbered S24 and S25, the former lying immediately to the west of S22, and the latter in front of S21 and S23. Mixed up with these bones, but at a lower level, were recovered two fragments of the leg of an animal (Nos. 64 and 65), and vases P*e* and P*f*, the former being painted (Pl. XLII, *d*).

Division IV.

In Division IV were found, between 4 ft. 3 in. and 4 ft. 9 in. below the surface, only two small vases P*a* and P*c*, and a broken goblet with pointed base P*b*.[1]

Probable date of the group, and Area G.

From the foregoing account it is quite clear that the human remains described above were freely mixed with typical Harappā pottery of the Indus Period, and also with some animal bones, which included those of cattle. The number of goblets with pointed bases was larger than that of any other vessels, and the presence of the two offerings' dishes (P*f* and P*g*) in Division II is of more than ordinary interest as here their funerary nature is hardly open to doubt. As we shall presently see in Chapter VI on the Cemetery H, such dishes figured frequently among the sepulchral furniture, but here it is important to point out that these specimens, as well as those found in the two pottery groups G15 and G130 already described from this part of the trench, are more closely allied in shape to offerings' dishes found in the mounds than to those from the Cemetery H. The strong, squat dishes with horizontally ribbed stands, and the still shorter and finer ones with a deeper cup from the Cemetery H (Pl. LXI, 21 and 22 and Pl. LI, *d*) are noticeably different from these, and, to my mind, show a higher degree of development than those from the mounds. At the same time it is evident that the fundamental structure and purpose of the vessel remained the same, *i.e.*, in every case they were raised on hollow, funnel-shaped stands, and were designed as eating plates for the living as well as for the dead. Hence whatever may be the interval in time between the mounds and the Cemetery H, the Area G very likely stands between the two.

---

[1] In square R 37 about 250 ft. south of the Eastern Section of Cemetery H were recovered in the beginning of 1938 the remains of nine human bodies (Nos. H 779 *a-f* and H 780-782) and a large number of flat bottomed funeral pottery which is remarkably similar to that previously found from Area G in Groups G15, G130 and the multiple burial G289. In this case, the corpses were laid from north to south and the head was turned a little to the left. Although the human burials came within 1 ft. 6 in. and 2 ft. 6 in. of the surface, the accompanying pottery disposed in two layers went down to 4 ft. 6 in. Of the six bodies lying to west and forming one group (No. H 779 *a-f*), only one was somewhat complete, the others being fractional and mutilated. The pottery found with the above nine burials comprised globular jars with flat bottom which are with or without an incipient flange at the neck and were sometimes covered with handled lids; standard dishes and cups, the latter being cylindrical or more or less carinated; shallow plain dishes; long slender vases with flat base and flared mouth; goblets with or without standard feet; oval or squat vases with flat bottom; flanged *hāndi*; jar-stands; two tall crateriform jars and a few other shapes which might well be found by further exploration of Area G. For the similarity of the above pottery with that of Area G *cf.* p. 196 ff. *supra* and Pl. LXX, 5, 6, 8, 11, 12, 16, 17, 20, 22, 23, 34, 35 and 36. In this connection it should also be added that the disposition of this pottery is not much different from that of the multiple burial G289.

Eighteen further burials brought to light here in 1938-39 were accompanied by similar pottery. Among them, however, two skeletons (Nos. H 793 and H 794) wore necklaces of thick steatite disc beads; another (No. H 804) a conch shell armlet on the right arm and anklets—each comprised of three strings—of very thin and tiny disc beads of steatite on both legs; and a fourth one (No. H 808) yielded from below the left pelvic bone two short-barrel beads of gold and carnelian.

Identification of human skulls.

Dr. B. S. Guha,[1] Anthropologist of the Zoological Survey of India, has given me the following identification of the human skulls in this group, and I have added notes against them to show how they were lying in the ground before removal. A reference to the plan and photographs already mentioned in the text will explain my notes clearly.—

Skulls in Division I.	S1—child.	Were lying apart from each other.
	S11—male—adult.	
	S13—female—adult.	
	S15—child.	
Skulls in Division II.	S2—adult—sex (?).	Were lying fairly close to each other, but not together.
	S5—adult—female.	
	S36—adult—female (?).	
	S18—adult—male.	
	S42—adult—male.	This is part of skeleton No. 43.
Skulls in Division III	S1—child.	Lay piled up together with I S1 and II S18.
	S2—adult—male.	
	S3—adult—sex (?).	
	S4—child.	
	S7—adult—male.	
	S8—child.	Lay close to S46 and S47.
	S21—adult—female (?).	Lay piled up together.
	S22—adult—male.	
	S23—adult—male.	
	S24—adult—sex (?). (Are fragments of skulls.)	
	S25—adult—sex (?). (Are fragments of skulls.)	
	S46—adult—male.	Lay together.
	S47—adult—male.	Lay together.
	S13—Fragment of the skull of a child (?).	

Position of heads and pottery.

From the plan it is apparent that all the heads lay severed and most of those in Division III were either actually piled up, or somehow came to lie over one another. In most cases the pottery, where it occurs, was found close to the skulls, but in some instances it had apparently rolled away. It is also noteworthy that in proportion to the twenty skulls, most of which were found crowded

[1] Personal communication.

in Division III, the quantity of human bones was small. What there were consisted mainly of the long bones of legs and arms; the ribs and phalanges of hands and feet were very few. With the sole exception of skeleton No. 42 in Division II, in which the skull lay alongside the trunk (which was still connected with the femurs), there was not a single instance in which the principal members of the body did not lie separated. Nothing whatever was found in the way of personal ornaments, nor was there any other indication to suggest that the dead included some principal person for whom the rest, as well as the animals, might have been sacrificed. In other words, there is nothing in this group which points to human sacrifice such as was found by Sir Leonard Woolley in the graves of the Kings of Ur.[1] The skeleton No. II 42 was lying at a short distance apart from the others, but that by itself is no sufficient reason for regarding it as the skeleton of a chief or other important personage. Whether, therefore, this heap of mangled and mutilated remains resulted from a massacre of the men, women, and children represented in it, who were subsequently disposed of in accordance with the then existing custom of fractional burial, or whether this is an example of a multiple burial after exposure of the victims of some raid, accident or epidemic, is a question that must remain open. In either case, the presence of the sacrificed animals, and of the pottery intended for the use of the dead leaves little doubt that the burial was conducted, as far as possible, on orthodox lines, though it is very different from the burial of the fourteen complete skeletons found by Mr. Hargreaves at Mohenjo-daro in Room 74 of House V, HR Area, Section B.[2]

No ornaments.

No trace of human sacrifice.

Multiple tragedy possibly due to a raid, accident or epidemic.

Their disposal in orthodox manner.

Site used for dumping rubbish.

Such remains of buildings—and they were few and far between—as were found in these trial trenches were enveloped in masses of burnt clay nodules, ashes and potsherds, the whole descending to a depth of 5 to 7 ft.[3] from the surface. The nodules, which constituted the bulk of this débris, had no doubt been used, as they are commonly used at Mohenjo-daro, for the foundations of these or later buildings; the potsherds were mainly broken goblets with pointed bases.

Two deep pits.

Find of a bovine skull in one and of two tiny seals in the other.

Two pits were also sunk in this area; one at the northern end of Trench II; the other at the southern edge of Trench III. In the former was found the forepart of a bovine skull at a depth of 13 ft. below the surface; in the latter were recovered a few remains belonging to Strata III and IV at depths of 8 ft., and 11 ft. 6 in. respectively. Two tiny, rectangular seals (No. G257, and No. G262; Pl. XCVII, 516), which are typical of early strata in the mounds, were found at depths of 9 ft. 6 in. and 10 ft. respectively below the surface. Both of them may be assigned to the IVth stratum.

---

[1] *Cf. Ur of the Chaldees*, pp. 33 *et seq.*, and Pl. II.

[2] *Cf. M. I. C.*, p. 79.

[3] Very similar is the condition of the two or three upper strata in Mounds F and AB.

CHAPTER VI.

Area H : The prehistoric cemetery.

Cemetery H is situated at the foot of Mounds D and E on either side of a modern irrigation channel about 150 yards to the north-north-west of the small Archæological Museum where the ground slopes down gradually from north to south and from west to east (Pl. I). Standing as it does at the southern foot of the mounds, water rushes over it with much force after a heavy shower, and it was due to this circumstance that the neck of one of a group of four burial-pots (No. 3934 a-d),[1] which lay concealed almost immediately below the surface in square S 34/7, became uncovered (Pl. XLIII). In digging it out the remaining three jars were also brought to light and removed for examination to the museum (Pl. LVII, *a*). Then, in February 1928, only three feet to the south, was recovered another group of seven jars No. 7435 a-g[2] (Pl. XLVI, *a*), which on examination all proved to be pot-burials. **Accidental discovery.**

With the existence of this Cemetery thus established, I at once took steps to acquire a sufficient area at this place to allow of digging being done on a reasonably extensive scale. Yet in spite of the pressure I was able to exert, the land could not be acquired till late in the working season of 1928-29, when little could be done. During the following two field seasons of 1929-30 and 1930-31, however, a special push was made with this work, and by 1933-34 an area of some 3,800 square yards, or a little over three quarters of an acre, was explored. As will be seen from the plan (Pl. I), part of the excavated area lies to the east, part to the west of the modern irrigation channel, the eastern part averaging 145 ft. from north to south by 140 ft. from east to west, and the western 185 ft. from north to south by 55 ft. from east to west. In the Eastern Section the excavation was carried down to an average depth of 5 ft. 6 in.; in the Western a foot and half lower. Some 20 ft. north of the Western Section another excavation was made measuring 61 ft. from north to south by 65 ft. from east to west, which was dug to an average depth of 5 ft. From its centre towards the north, projects a tongue measuring 30 by 20 ft., in which the depth of the digging varied from 6 to 11 ft., since the ground here rises somewhat towards the slope of Mound D. This second excavation on the west of the irrigation channel has been designated "the Extension" of the Western Section. **Acquisition of land, etc.** **Extent of excavation.**

Throughout this area structural remains are very scanty; in the Eastern Section, in squares S 33/10 and S 34/6, there is a broken culvert-like structure, which is standing to a height of 2 ft. and has a span of 2 ft. 2 in. Over a part of its west wall are the remains of the corner of a building belonging to the latest stratum. Around this structure, for about 60 ft. from east to west and 40 ft. from north to south was a thick bed of burnt clay nodules which started from a depth of 2 ft. 6 in. and ended at 5 ft. below the surface. Doubtless they formed part of the foundations of this or other buildings. Further north and north-east, again, was **Traces of structural remains.**

[1] For their description see pp. 211-12 *infra*.

[2] See p. 212 *infra*.

Two distinct strata-the upper one of Pot-burials and the lower one of Earth-burials.

soft sandy soil—very much like river silt. From this culvert-like structure or thereabouts as far as the western, southern and eastern edges of the Eastern Section, as well as from the southern portion of the Western Section and its Extension came one after the other a rich collection of grave pottery: more than 120 burial-pots from the upper stratum, and beneath them a series of entirely different earth-burials. In these earth-burials, as we shall see presently, the corpses entire or fractional were laid in graves in the ground accompanied as a rule, but not invariably, by funeral pottery consisting of water-pots (Pl. LX, type E), bowls (Pl. LX, type B), offerings' dishes or plates (Pl. LX, type F), saucers (Pl. LXI, type K), flat covers (Pl. LXI, type M), flasks (Pl. LXI, type G), round vases (Pl. LXI, type I), etc.

Pots of Stratum I crushed by traffic.

In the stratum above these earth-burials only pot-burials were found (Pls. XLV, *a*; XLVI; XLVII, *a* and *d*; and L, *a* and *d*). Being generally in contact with or near the present surface, the pots were usually found crushed to pieces and often had their upper parts destroyed by the traffic passing above them.

Their shape and size.

The shapes of these pots are various (Pl. LIX, *a*); the commoner forms among them being round (Pl. LX, type C), ellipsoid (Pl. LX, type A) or carinated (Pl. LX, type D). Their height ranges from 9¾ to 23¾ in. The round ones are either plain or painted, but if painted they are flanged at the neck (*cf.* Pl. LX, 12) and, like the ellipsoid jars, have sometimes a ring-base. The plain jars have their lower portion roughened by "finger-tip" or "finger-groove" patterns. The former pattern was obtained by beating the body of a wet jar with a special dabber, which was prepared by impressing the finger-tips on its surface before it was put in the kiln (*cf.* Pls. LIX, *a*, 10; and LX, 14). The other pattern was made simply by passing the fingers over the wet clay while the jar was still being turned on the wheel (Pls. LIX, *a*, 8; and LX, 13). The finger grooves so made generally run parallel, but there is some irregularity at the points where the fingers start fresh grooving.

Technique.

The structure of these pots exhibits some interesting points of technique. Thus, in preparation for both, the "finger-tip" and "finger-groove" patterns wet clay was applied to the lower portion of sun-dried jars before they were fired. Similarly, the neck flange was also added afterwards. Smaller jars were at once finished on the wheel, but the larger ones were made in two parts, the upper being then joined to the lower. In several instances the mid-joint is readily observable, and in one or two cases it is quite clumsily made. The ellipsoid jars invariably have a short, straight, collared rim with or without a flange (Pl. LX, type A; and Pl. LIX, *a*, 1-5 and 9), and this type of neck is common to all burial-pots except those with the finger-tip pattern (*cf.* Pl. LIX, *a*, 10). Some of the ellipsoid jars (without flange) are severely plain, some are decorated merely with bands, but there are a few others with elaborate paintings. Pots of the carinated type are all painted and flanged at the neck, but, with one exception (Pl. LX, 17), are much smaller in size. They are concave above, and convex below, and have a distinct, projecting base (Pl. LX, 15-17). All burial-pots were originally covered or stoppered with inverted bowls, vases, handled lids, potsherds or bricks, and occasionally the lid was further secured by covering it with a sherd (*cf.* Pl. XLIV).

Method of description.

The burials in both strata have been numbered in the order in which they were found and are therefore somewhat irregular, but in the following pages I shall describe the various burials square by square starting with the north-west corner in each section and proceeding by successive series of squares regularly from north to south, so that the reader may find no difficulty in following my description.

Pot-burials of Stratum I.

Contents different from those of post cremation urns.

By way of introduction let me make a few general remarks, in the first place, regarding the contents, usually similar, of burial-pots, since that will obviate the necessity of my describing the contents[1] of each individual pot though I shall have to deal later on with certain peculiarities in the contents of some of the pot-burials. With two or three exceptions the burial-pots contained, as I have said, nothing but human remains which were placed direct at their bottom, and usually filled no more than the lower half of jars, the upper part, despite the covers or stoppers on them, being filled with soft, percolated earth. Small earthernware vessels, such as drinking goblets with pointed bases, cylindrical vases, etc., or toys and cakes, which are commonly found in the much larger post-cremation burial urns from the mounds were in all cases conspicuous by their absence. Another thing which struck me at once about these pot-burials was the way in which the bones were found indiscriminately packed at the bottom of jars whose size and shape precluded the possiblility of their ever having been used for complete burials[2]. In this connection, the group of two skulls, one mandible and a few other bones discovered by me in 1927-28 in a small enclosure dating between the IVth and IIIrd strata in Mound AB and described in Chapter III, pp. 161-62, had already pointed to the conclusion that one method of disposing of the dead practised at Harappā was to expose[3] the corpse or corpses to birds and beasts of prey, and subsequently to deposit in an urn whatever might be left of the excarnated remains. And there can be no doubt that this was the method adopted in these pot-burials in Cemetery H. For, if the remains in the aforesaid enclosure in Mound AB had been taken up and deposited in an urn the result would have been little different from the contents of the multiple burial found in pot No. 3934c. A further feature to be borne in mind is that these burial-pots from Cemetery H are very different in their shape and in the realistic motifs of their paintings from the jars with geometric[4] and other patterns found in the mounds.

Suggestion of exposure of the dead.

Shape and decoration of burial-pots.

---

[1] The contents of all burial-pots containing human remains have been tabulated in Appendix I, pp. 242-45 *infra*.

[2] I do not include pots containing whole babies in embryonic position.

[3] A. B. Keith in his *Religion and Philosophy of the Veda*, writing about the disposal of the dead (pp. 417-18) says "Other modes of disposal of the dead are referred to in the Ṛigveda and the Atharva Veda. The dead might be cast away (*paroptāḥ*); or they might be exposed (*uddhitāḥ*). The latter expression seems to mean exposed on trees, a practice which was known in later India, and which is referred to in the Śatapatha Brāhmaṇa, being prescribed as the expiation in the case in which a cow is slaughtered and found to be in calf, as regards the disposal of the embryo. But these ideas are of no importance for Vedic India in general; the rite of burning is the rite which has won approval in the sūtras, and that of burying the body is there severely restricted." It is important to note that burial and even exposure were known to Vedic Āryans and if they were restricted by them, it does not follow that they were not the usual methods of disposing of the dead among the non-Āryan people with whom we are concerned in the Cemetery at Harappā.

[4] Realistic paintings occur but very seldom on jars from the mounds, and where they do their execution is quite different. *Cf.* p. 246 *infra*.

EASTERN SECTION (see Pls. XLIII, XLIV and XLIX).

Two isolated jars.

Beginning with the north-west part of the Eastern Section of the Cemetery, square R 34/17 contained two burial pots, Nos. H250 and H252. Of these, the former is ellipsoid in shape, has a ring-base and flange round the neck, and was covered with a handled lid (Pl. LXI, 3). It is painted with rows of fishes, birds, leaves, etc. (Pl. LXII, 7). No. H252 also has a ring-base, but its shape is round and the upper part broken.

Mixed group No. H231 comprising pottery of Strata I and II, etc.

Squares R 33/25 and R 34/21. These squares have been taken together as they contained the burial group No. H231, and two isolated pots Nos. H186 and H235. No. H231 comprised five jars, of which *a*, *b* and *c* are ellipsoid in shape and *d* and *i* broken *gharās* both decorated with the finger-tip pattern (Pl. XLVII, *d*). Of the ellipsoid jars, *a* was effectively covered with a large, inverted, hemispherical bowl and is remarkably intact. It is painted at the shoulder with two rows of flying kites (?) alternating with pairs of horns[1] containing leaves. Pot *b*, with the finger-groove pattern on its lower part, was covered with an inverted, round vase, and lay slightly inclined to the north-east. A curious feature was that between jars *a* and *d* was a sub-group of smaller vessels *e* consisting of a bowl, three saucers and one flask, to the south of which again was another sub-group *f* comprising a small vase placed in another bowl broken in two pieces, two saucers and one flask. Two feet to the south-east of *f* was a third sub-group *g* comprising a bowl, one saucer with a small vase, as in *f*, and a flask on either side. Between the burial-pots *a* and *b*, but at a higher level was found a fragmentary flat cover *h* painted on the underside with fishes and the foreparts of *markhor*[2] goat (Pl. LXIV, 14). Here it is important to notice that the smaller vessels *e-h*, which lay interspersed between the larger burial-pots, are typical of the funeral pottery of Stratum II, which, as a rule, is found at a distinctly lower level than the pot-burials. This commingling of pottery from the two strata is probably due to the fact that at this particular point the ground was somewhat higher when the older earth-burials were made, but had been levelled down to an appreciable extent before the pot-burials which succeeded them. Or it may be that these particular graves of the lower stratum were nearer the surface than was usually the case. (Pl. XLIV, 3rd row.)

Possible reason for the mixing of pottery.

Pots H186 and H235 are round and ellipsoid *gharās*, the former was covered by the broken bottom of a ring-based jar, while the latter was closed by an extremely fragmentary round vase. It is flanged at the neck and has cordon round the body: its upper part is painted in six compartments with two rows of six leaves each.

Group H206, etc.

Squares R 34/22 and R 34/23. In these two squares were found one isolated jar, No. H251, and an important group of eleven jars No. H206 a-k (Pl. XLVI, *c*). No. H251 is a round jar of small size covered with a handled lid. It has ring-base and a flange round the neck, but is not painted and lay underneath a wall of Stratum I.

---

[1] See footnote 1 on p. 211 *infra*.

[2] See footnote 2 on p. 214 *infra*.

Instructive mythological paintings on jars H206 a-b. Peacock in relation to the dead.

Of the group No. H206, jars *b*, *h*, *g*, *c*, *d*, and *e* lay roughly on an arc, and *a* and *f* to the west of *e*. Jars *a-d* are ellipsoid in shape; *f-h*, which have lost their upper part, are round; *e*, the lower part of another round jar, had a cordon round the body; *i* was a crushed oval vase; while *j* and *k* are the familiar drinking goblets with pointed bases which, probably, were only a part of the débris. The pot *a*, which was covered with an inverted bowl (Pl. LVII, *b*, left hand jar), is decorated at the shoulder with three flying peacocks alternating with stars (Pl. LXII, 2). Placed horizontally in the body of each peacock is a therianthropic[1] figure probably representing the *sūkshma śarīra* or ethereal body of the dead being carried to heaven. From this, and also from the frequent recurrence of the peacock motif—often with horns[2]—on other burial-pots, it is evident that the peacock was regarded with peculiar sanctity in connection with the cult of the dead. Jar *b* was covered with an inverted bowl, completely smashed (Pl. LVII, *b*, middle jar). It is painted in two bands; the lower one with rows of leaves alternating with pairs of stars, the upper with more elaborate scenes, seemingly of a mythological character (Pl. LXII, 1, *a* and *b*). In the upper band, on opposite sides of the jar, are two similar groups of figures showing a bovine animal—probably a bull—with long, incurving horns on either side of a beaked human figure[3] who has secured them by the neck with ropes held in hands and under the feet, and who also has a bow and arrow in his left hand.[4] This creature is human but for the beak and wavy lines rising from his head. In the left hand representation (Pl. LXII, 1*a*), the animal on the left is being attacked by a hound which has caught its tail in his mouth. It will also be noticed that the hind quarters of this animal are shown in outline only, while in the right-hand one they are blocked in. Behind the hound are two horned peacocks in flight (Pl. LXII, 1*a*). The scene evidently proceeds from left to right where the principal representation is again repeated with some difference (Pl. LXII, 1*b*). To the right of the left hand scene, that is to say between the two principal representations, is a goat of inordinately large size whose enormous horns are ornamented with eight trident-like devices, and whose hind-quarters, like those of the left hand bull, are also shown in outline only. The trident associated with Śiva, whose prototype[5] has been found at Mohenjo-daro, and with other deities, as well as the horns (with which the trident was to become intimately connected), were regarded as emblems of divinity by the Indus People, and it is not unlikely that the supernatural size of this goat and the trident-shaped crests have a similar significance[6].

Description of paintings.

On the other side of the jar is a repetition of the scene already described, but with this difference that each of the bulls is now bedecked with a trident-shaped crest between the horns, similar to the crests on the horns of the divine goat, and that the tail of the left hand animal is missing—having seemingly been bitten

---

[1] For therianthropic figures in the Indus Culture *cf. M. I. C.*, pp. 66-68.

[2] For the divine nature of horns *cf.* Sir John Marshall *Ibid.*, pp. 54-55.

[3] The human figures on the burial-pot No. 7435e (Pl. LXII, 13), and on sherd No. 11995 (Pl. LXIX, 18) are also beaked. For beaked figures also *cf.* M. P. Nilsson, *The Minoan Mycenaean Religion*, pp. 320-21, fig. 96.

[4] Ṛigveda, X, 18, 9 refers to bow (and arrow) being placed with a dead man.

[5] *Cf.* Sir John Marshall, *op. cit.*, Pl. XII, figs. 17, 18, and 22.

[6] *Ibid.*, pp. 54-55 where the significance of the horns of divinity and the *triśūla* is explained.

off by the hound. Between the bulls and the composite being are two small peacocks, presumably the same that are seen behind the hound in the left hand scene and are now reduced in size for want of space. The peacocks, like the goat and the two composite beings in these scenes, are facing right and this may be taken to be the direction in which the figures were depicted as moving, though exigencies of composition demanded that the two bulls should face one another with the composite being between. As a matter of fact the latter, who, I think, was the embodiment of the dead person, was, as I shall presently explain, meant to be following the cattle, which in virtue of their having been sacrificed or given in gift to a priest, were privileged to take with them the spirit of the dead person to the 'Abode of Bliss'. The rest of the available space is filled with stars, birds, leaves, etc.

Possible interpretation of the paintings.

That this elaborate painting, occurring as it does, on a burial-pot is meant to portray what was believed to happen to the dead person there can hardly be any doubt. It appears to me that the hound in the left hand scene, may, like the two hounds of Yama[1], be the hound of Hades and that the right hand scene, where the cattle are now decked with trident crests, depicts them in the 'Abode of Bliss,' after they have passed through the intermediate Hades. The goat between the two scenes, as we shall presently see, was also a sort of 'pathfinder' and a deified intermediary, an inference which, as I have already observed, may be drawn both from its large size and the crests on its horns.

Bulls probably prototypes of the Anustaraṇi and Vaitaraṇi cows.

In discussing early Indo-Āryan customs regarding the Dead and Disposal of the Dead, Professor Hillebrandt says "The living are bound to prepare the way for the dead in the other world, to provide them with food for their great journey into Yama's realm and to supply them with means for crossing the rivers. These ends are served by the Utkrānti or Vaitaraṇi cow, which in some cases has been presented to the Brāhmaṇs before his death by the deceased himself or his son. The same was originally, no doubt, the purpose also of the Anustaraṇi cow, which is led along in the funeral train, and whose members are finally laid upon those of the dead, its kidneys being deposited in his hands as food for Yama's dogs. The streams which have to be crossed are probably indicated by the piece of reed which is introduced into the wall of the tomb which is meant to serve as a boat."[2] In the light of this passage, I suggest that the bulls anticipated the sacred Āryan cows, and that the left hand one, which is without the entrails is perhaps to be identified with the prototype of the Anustaraṇi, and the right hand one with that of the Vaitaraṇi cow. Some of the oldest references to the former are in *Ṛigveda*, X, 16, 7; *Aśvalāyana Ghṛihya Sūtra*, IV, 3; *Aitareya Brāhmaṇa*, III, 3, 8; and *Kātyāyana Srauta Sūtra*, XXV, 7, 30; and to the latter in *Rāmāyaṇa*, IV, 44, 65; *Mahābhārata*, II, 373, and III, 6054 and 8148; and *Harivaṁśa*, 7736 and 9511. The hound, as already remarked, is reminiscent of Yama's dogs. In connection with the outlined hind-quarters of the goat it is interesting to point out that in *Ṛigveda*, X, 16, a funeral hymn

Hound reminiscent of Yama's dogs.

---

[1] *Ṛigveda*, X, 14. 10-12.
[2] *E. R. E.*, Vol. 4, p. 475.

addressed to Agni (Fire), the deity at the time of cremating a dead body, is thus exhorted in verse 1 :—

> " Burn him not up, nor quite consume him, Agni ; let not his body or his skin be scattered.
>
> O *Jātavedas*, when thou hast matured him, then send him, on his way unto the Fathers."

Sacrifice of goat in the Ṛigveda.

Again in verse 4 of the same hymn Agni is asked in the following words to consume only the goat that was slaughtered and laid limb by limb on the corpse :—

> " Thy portion is the goat : with heat consume him, let thy fierce flame, thy glowing splendour, burn him.
>
> With thine auspicious forms, O Jātavedas, bear this man to the region of the pious."[1]

Significance of the sacrifice of the goat and the bull.

In the scenes portrayed on this jar the only indication of the slaughter of the goat, as well as of the prototype of the Anustaraṇi cow, is afforded by the absence of the entrails, but in view of the verses quoted above there is no doubt that the sacrifice of these animals was intended to protect the dead person from the fire, whose fury was to be exhausted on the limbs of the goat and presumably also of the bull. Moreover, according to the *Ṛigveda*, the duty of Agni (*Jātavedas*) was to mature the dead man and to send him to the region of the pious, or the Fathers, as stated in verses 1 and 4 of the hymn quoted above. Let me support this by a quotation from Keith.[2] " The practice of enveloping the body of the dead in the limbs of the cow is a curious one, and offers possibilities of different explanations. But it is clearly the view of the Ṛigveda that the heat of the fire is to exhaust its fury on the members of the goat and presumably also of the cow, and it may be that the offering was a sort of substitution for the dead himself, so that evil powers might assail it in place of him. The goat stands in another category : it may be compared to the goat which is slain with the sacrificial horse to show it the way : in the passage to the next world the journey may be trackless and the sure-footed goat will find the way."[3] Thus the goat was also a kind of path-finder and in a way the fore-runner of the spirit of the dead man. Having shown the way, presumably to the " Land of Bliss," the function of the goat was over, and it was no longer required in the right hand scene.

Parallelism of beliefs with those of the Ṛigveda.

As pointed out above, the paintings can hardly fail to recall to mind the parallelism, with some of the rites, ritual, and beliefs contained in hymns 14, 16, and 18 of the Xth Maṇḍala of the *Ṛigveda*, but as here the paintings are connected with post exposure fractional burials and not with cremation the comparison cannot be carried further. Nevertheless, the similarity of beliefs, as far as it goes, is very striking. It is however, not intended to suggest more than a comparison, for the connexions or affinities between the Vedic Āryans and the cultures connected with the Harappā burials are not yet quite clear.

---

[1] R. T. H. Griffith, *Translation of the Hymns of the Ṛigveda*, third edition, Vol. II, p. 402.

[2] A. B. Keith, *Religion and Philosophy of the Veda*, p. 423.

[3] According to *Atharva Veda*, XVIII, 2, 22, the *Maruts* are to cool the dead through the goat, perhaps by using up the power of the fire on it.

The idea of the Vaitaraṇi stream on the way to the Land of Bliss.

As pointed out by Professor Hillebrandt, one of the essential services for the dead is to provide them with the means for crossing the rivers. A glance at Pl. LXII, 1*a* and 1*b* will show that along the upper and lower ends of the painted frieze there are wavy lines probably representing the rippled surface of waters may be of the Vaitaraṇi stream or its prototype—and that the bulls, the goat, as well as the spirit of the dead person are shown with feet invisible or immersed in water.[1] That the Abode of Bliss or Elysium as understood by the Egyptians, or the Minoans who, according to M. P. Nilsson,[2] borrowed the idea from the former, was situated beyond the seas where the Blest were carried bodily by means of boats is in a way similar to the Hindu idea that every dead person on his way to the "Land of Bliss" has to cross the Vaitaraṇi (literally "difficult to cross") stream. Regarding the Egyptian idea M. P. Nilsson says "It is difficult to pass over the waters encircling the islands of the Blest. Hence they sometimes pray to the divine birds, the falcon of Horus or the ibis of Thoth, to carry them over, but usually they trust in a ferryman called 'Face-behind,' who brings both the gods and the deceased to these islands."[3] In Egypt the occasional reference of prayers to the divine birds, the falcon of Horus or the ibis of Thoth, may be paralleled in the present instance by a beaked head being given to the spirit of the dead man.

Isolated pots.

Square S 33/5. In this square there were only two burial-pots, numbered H165 *a* and *b*. Both the pots are round; pot *a*—decorated with the finger-grove pattern—was closed with an inverted round vase of medium size and again covered with a sherd, whereas pot *b* was covered only with a sherd (Pl. XLIV, 3rd row, end).

Square S 34/1. In this square were found four isolated pots, Nos. H156, H147, H149 and H150, and a group of six jars, No. H148 *a-f*, which partly extended over the adjoining squares S 34/2 and S 34/7. Pot H156 is a round *ghaṛā* of fine texture painted with leaves at the shoulder. It was covered with a handled lid. H147 is a round jar covered with a potsherd and H149 merely the body of a large jar whose bottom and upper part are missing. Pot H150 is ellipsoid in shape and distorted in the lower part (Pl. LIX, *a*, 2). It is flattish at the bottom and was closed with an inverted round vase with ring-base. At the shoulder it is painted with a frieze of five conventionalised peacocks (Pl. LXII, 6).

Group H148.

Of the group H148 (Pl. XLVII, *a*, right ground) pots *d* and *e* are round, fragmentary *ghaṛās* of medium size whose lower part is separated by a rough chevron, and the body honey-combed with the finger-tip pattern. Jars *b*, *c* and *f* survive only in the lower half, but *a* is complete and was covered with a tarboosh-shaped lid (Pls. LXI, 2; and LIX, *a*, 9). It has ring-base, cordon round the body and flange at the neck. In the lower part below the shoulder cordon it takes the form of an almost hemispherical bowl, but above the shoulder it tapers gradually towards the neck where the flange is grooved horizontally and pierced through

[1] That the feet of the hound are visible is presumably due to its attack being depicted in the Hades and not in the stream.

[2] *The Minoan Mycenaean Religion*, p. 545.

[3] *Ibid.*, pp. 545-46.

with three vertical, equidistant holes. Above the shoulder it is decorated with five flying peacocks alternating with rows of birds (?) (Pl. LXII, 8). Its lid, pierced by two holes at opposite points of the rim, is also decorated with what looks like four pairs of horns each separated from the other by a star and containing two or three fishes[1] in it (Pl. LXII, 10).

Square S 34/2. In this there were only two jars, H151 *a* and *b*, the former being a medium-sized *ghaṛā* covered with an inverted flask and tilted towards the north, and the latter an open-mouthed, carinated pot covered with a handled lid. The neck flange of this pot is horizontally grooved and holed like that of H148 *a*. Its concave upper portion is decorated with two rows of flying kites(?) alternating with leafy patterns (Pl. LIX, *a*, 7).

Three groups and one other jar.

Square S 34/4. This square contained three groups of burial-pots, Nos. H152 *a-c*, H153 *a-e*, H154 *a-d* and another pot H230 (Pl. XLV, *a*, left gound, and Pl. XLVI, *a*, background). Of group No. H152, all the three jars were broken at the top, *c* being extremely fragmentary. A few feet to their west lay the second group, No. H153, comprising five jars. Of these, *a*, which is globular, has ring-base and a flange round the neck which is pierced with three equidistant pairs of holes. It is painted at the shoulder with wavy lines, dotted circles, and stars. Jars *b*, *c*, and *d* are all broken in the upper part, while of *e*, which is round and the smallest in the group, the surface was badly corroded by saltpetre. Between jars H153*a* and H152*c* lay a round broken *ghaṛā* (No. H230) decorated with the finger-tip pattern. A few feet to the south-east of this was the third group, No. H154, consisting of four jars. Of these, *a* is ellipsoid in shape, but the other three are small, round *ghaṛās*. The former was covered with fragments of another jar, *b* with an inverted shallow basin, and *c* and *d* only with potsherds. Round the shoulder, *a* is painted with three long-horned and humped quadrupeds, apparently bulls, birds and stars (Pl. LXII, 5).

Square S 34/5. In this there were only two jars, No. H155 being a small round *ghaṛā* broken in the upper part and another extremely fragmentary jar which was not considered worth recording.

Group No. 3934.

Square S 34/7. Groups[2] Nos. H62 *d* and *e* and 3934 *a-d* were recovered from this square. The former consisted of two broken jars of which only the lower portion had survived. The latter group, being the first to be accidentally exposed after a heavy rain, is important in having actually led to the discovery of the Cemetery. Three jars of this group are illustrated in Pl. LVII, *a*. As the examination of this and of the following group No. 7435 *a-g* actually revealed the existence of the Cemetery here I shall deal with their contents also.

Contents of the first four pot-burials.

Of group No. 3934, pot *a* (Pl. LVII, 3) which is the best preserved, contained nothing; in *b* (Pl. LVII, 2) was a clay ball and a flat, feather-like ornament of ivory with linear decoration (Pl. CXIX, 44); *d* was very fragmentary; and *c* (Pl. LVII, 1) surviving only in the lower half, contained near the bottom three

[1] Sir John Marshall thinks that these are some kind of weapon, *viz*., a trident-head, or arrow-head, or spear-head like the double axe set between the horns in Crete.

[2] Being discovered before the regular excavation of the Cemetery these groups have not been shown in the section.

fragmentary human skulls, and one fragment of a leg bone. Only a little of the upper half of one of these skulls was preserved, while of the remaining two, nothing but filmy impressions were left on the endo-cranial cast of earth which had filled their hollows.

Group No. 7435. Square S 34/8. In this and in part of square S 34/13 were discovered seven more jars numbered 7435 *a-g* which lay about 3 ft. to the south of the above group No. 3934 (Pl. XLVI, *e*). Their tops came to within 3 to 6 in. below the surface, and they varied in height from 9 to 22 in. Of these, five were covered with shallow, bowl-like lids, which in two cases have narrow projections at the top for convenient handling. Except the round broken pot *g*, the other jars of this group are better preserved and painted in the upper portion. Of *c*, the cover also is painted and holed through the centre. In each of the pots *a*, *d* and *f* the flange below their mouth has four equidistant holes. Pots *b* and *c* of this group are flat at bottom, but *d* and *g* are globular. The largest pot *e* is ellipsoid in shape but flat at bottom, while *b*, *d*, and *f* are provided with ring-bases. Pot *a* is painted with horizontal rows of wavy lines alternating with highly conventionalised trees, separated from one another by stars (Pl. LXIII, 19); *b* with similar rows of wavy lines and trees between which are rows of flying birds (Pl. LXIII, 18); *c* and *d* only with wavy lines and stars; *e* with flying peacocks alternating with fantastic animals (Pl. LXII, 13); and *f* with peacocks with trident tails, wavy lines ending in stars or rayed orbs, and rows of leaves linked together (Pl. LXII, 15). The scene on pot *e* is very elaborate. The animals are male—seemingly bulls with bird-like heads and a curious device around the neck. In the case of the second bull from the left, what I have taken to be the bird-headed[1] spirit of the dead is apparently carried on the animal's back, whereas on the third figure it becomes a part and parcel of the animal's head which is therefore longer than that of other cattle on this jar. On the other hand, on pot No. H206*a* (Pl. LXII, 2) the spirit of the dead (in a therianthropic form) is carried in the body of a flying peacock.

Shape of pots.

Paintings.

Contents. Inside pots *a*, *c* and *g* were found fragmentary skulls and long bones, etc., which, according to Dr. B. S. Guha,[2] Anthropologist of the Zoological Survey of India, are those of babies, but as pot *g* was uncovered and broken it also contained several extraneous brickbats which had damaged the fragile bones. Pot *b* contained an adult's skull with more or less complete cranium which was packed round with other bones. Its occipital region was in contact with the bottom and the facial portion towards the mouth of the jar. Pots *d* and *f* had tiny pieces of babies' bones, and the latter also had a few bits of decayed charcoal and potsherds, but *e*, which was the largest of the group, contained nothing.

Square S 34/10. No. H146 *a* and *b* were merely the lower parts of two jars.

There were two jars in square S 34/13. Of these, H61 was broken up to the shoulders, but painted and hedged round the mouth by standing bricks; and No. H83 was a round *ghaṛā* decorated with the finger-tip pattern and closed at the mouth by an inverted vase.

---

[1] A similar form is given to the spirit of the dead person on the burial-pot No. H206b. Also *cf.* Pl. LXII, 1*a* and 1*b*.

[2] Personal communication.

Several isolated jars.

Squares S 34/17, S 34/18 and S 34/19 contained seven burial-pots, Nos. H166, H167, H168, H614, H187, H169, and H170. Of these, H168 with flanged neck and ring-base was covered with a broken lid ; and H614, a round *gharā* relieved with the finger-tip pattern, was closed by an inverted, round vase. The other jars were all fragmentary.

The Eastern Section was extended at the south-east part as shown in the plan (Pl. XLIII). In this were recovered several burial-pots, a square pavement and two bits of walls of Stratum I in the corresponding squares S 34/17 and S 34/23, and a corner of a building belonging to Stratum II in squares S 34/20 and S 34/25 (Pl. XLVI, *b*).

In Square S 34/22 were found three pots, Nos. H615, H617 and H618, all round in shape. Of these, the first two have the finger-tip pattern, but only the first one was complete and closed with a round, inverted vase.

In the adjoining square S 34/23 were recovered only two jars. One of these, H616, which was almost entire, was closed by an inverted round vase and secured by bricks round its base; it was decorated with the finger-tip pattern. The second one (H626) was merely the broken bottom of a jar decorated with the finger-groove pattern. In square T 34/2 was another jar bearing the finger-tip pattern, which was also closed by a round vase like Jar H618.

Group H620.

In the next two squares, T 34/3 and T 34/4, were one group, H620 *a-d*, and four other jars, Nos. H622, H623, H624 and H625. Group H620 comprised two jars and two vases. Of these, *a* is a large carinated pot, much larger than the three examples found before (Pl. LXI, 17). It was originally covered with a large, inverted and painted bowl, of which two or three fragments survived a few inches higher than its mouth (Pl. LXIII, 13). Its flange is broken at three places and the body crushed on one side. The painting on its concave upper part is divided by broad horizontal bands into two tiers, each subdivided into a number of triangular panels decorated with rows of flying birds or fishes (?) (Pl. LXIII, 1*a* and 1*b*). Placed on either side of this jar were a minature, carinated vase *c* (Pl. LX, 24) with a closely fitted flask inside which had crushed its walls, and a neckless, round vase *d* ; while just a little apart, was an ellipsoid jar *b* with the usual collared rim. This latter was broken into several pieces and painted with bands only. Its mouth was tightly closed with the lower part of a cover of some sort. Four feet to the south-west of this jar was the bottom fragment of a jar No. H621, and 6¼ ft. to the south-east the lower half of jar No. H622 with the finger-tip pattern. Four feet to the east of H622 lay jar No. H623, which, too, was broken in the upper part. This is painted in two tiers: the upper one showing rows of birds (which look like arrow-heads) alternating with rows of double lozenges flanked by leaves, and the lower one with alternate groups of different birds (Pl. LXIII, 7). Seven feet to the north-east of jar H620*a* was the lower portion of jar H624, and 10 ft. roughly east was jar H625 decorated with the finger-tip pattern and inclined to the north-east. It was closed with an inverted, round vase, and secured with brickbats round the base. Part of this jar had disappeared, and the rest was crushed. Jars H621 and H644 found in squares S 34/24 and T 34/5 were too fragmentary to call for any remarks.

Some more isolated pots.

WESTERN SECTION (see Pls. XLVIII and XLIX).

Profusion of pot-burials in the southern portion.

In the Western Section of the Cemetery pot-burials were found grouped in the southern portion and scattered in the north-east, whereas in the greater part of this excavation they were entirely absent. First of all may be described four groups, Nos. H245-H248 (Pl. L, *d*) which came in squares Q 34/23 and Q 34/24. The groups H245 and H246 were larger than the other two. The former group lay a few feet north of the latter and comprised seven jars, of which *d-g* were utterly crushed, while *a-c* were but slightly damaged. Pot *a* is ellipsoid in shape; it has ring-base, cordon round the body and flanged neck and was covered with a handled lid on which, again, was placed a potsherd. It is painted at the shoulder with two highly stereotyped peacocks in flight which alternate with panels formed of wavy lines with rayed orbs inside and a row of fishes(?) along the upper fringe. The rest of the space is filled with smaller orbs (Pl. LXII, 3). Its lid, too, is painted with bands, rough triangles, and wavy lines. Jars *b* and *c* are also ellipsoid in shape, but without the flange, cordon or ring-base. Of these, *b* was covered with an inverted bowl which was crushed to pieces (Pl. LVII, *b*, 3). On this pot, the decoration consists of pairs of peacock heads joined U-wise, alternating with rayed orbs or stars. Crowning the peacock-heads are pairs of sacred horns, with twin leaves[1] set between. (Pl. LXII, 4.) The painting on *c* is in two registers and consists of rows of leaves (?), oblique wavy lines, pairs of horns, stars and (?) fishes (Pl. LXII, 12).

Group H245.

Paintings on jars; *a-c*.

Group H246; its orientation and preservation.

The southern group, H246, consisted of nine jars *a-i*. Of these, *a* and *f-i* lay roughly in a line from north to south, and, with the exception of *f* are smaller in size, while *b-e* were lying in a quadrilateral formation to their west. Jars *a*, *b*, *e* and *h* were covered with inverted bowls which had been crushed to pieces, *c* and *d* with large potsherds; while of *f*, *g* and *i* the upper portion itself had perished (Pl. L, *d*, right hand group). With the exception of *h* and *i*, all the other jars of this group are painted, but on *f* the decoration was destroyed by the action of saltpetre. Among these, *a* is carinated and painted in the upper portion with three sets of tassel-like motifs, each alternating with a star-in-crescent pattern. Pots *b* and *f-i* are round, but of these *b*, *f* and *g* have ring-bases. Pot *g* is decorated with leaves, pairs of horns, sets of wavy lines, etc. Pots *c-e* are ellipsoid in shape, and of these, *c* is painted only with black bands, *d* with sets of crescents, and *e* with *markhor* goat,[2] trees, and birds in the upper tier, and stars-in-crescent, and birds, in the lower (Pl. LXII, 11). The right hand goat in the illustration has a trident between its horns—doubtless as a mark of its sanctity.

Paintings on jars of this group.

Both the jars of group H247 are ellipsoid in shape and were covered with inverted bowls; of *b* the lid again was covered with a potsherd. Pot *a* is

[1] For similar twins, triplets, quadruplets, etc. of leaves see Pl. LXIV, 18-20 and 24, also Pl. LXII, 15 and Pl. LXIII, 16.

[2] It might as well be deer but for the horns which resemble those of a *markhor* (*capra falconeri*), *cf.* R. Lydekker, *The Game Animals of India, Burma, Malaya and Tibet* (1924 edn.), p. 123, fig. 17, and p. 125, fig. 18. The *markhor* is likely to have been invested with sanctity owing to its reputed character as a snake eater. I believe this very animal is depicted in the heads on the vases illustrated in Pl. LXIII, 9; Pl. LVIII, *c*, 6 and Pl. LXVI, 59. And perhaps, too, the pairs of horns above the peacock-heads in Pl. LXII, 4; and the independent motif evolved from them as seen in Pl. LXII, 10, 12, etc. also represents the same animal.

decorated with bands and wavy lines, and *b*, with stars in the lower register and stars and wavy lines in the upper. The latter, it may be added, shows several thread marks in the lower part. Group H248 lay a few feet to the north-east of H247 and consisted of three jars. Of these, *a* and *b* were placed side by side with a standing brick in between, while of *c* practically nothing remained. The carinated jar *a* was covered with a handled lid, and painted with trees, fishes, stars, etc.: *b* is ellipsoid and has a cordon round the body and flanged neck. It was covered with a potsherd, and is decorated in two rows of compartments with star and wavy line motifs (pl. LXIII, 20). **Group H247 and H248.**

In square Q 34/25 were found three jars. Of these, H349 lay in a tilted position, split vertically. It appears to have been painted with straight and wavy lines. A few feet to its south-east and on either side of a broken wall lay the other two jars, Nos. H346 *a-b*. The former is ellipsoid in shape, and was covered with a broken bowl. It is painted in two tiers with sets of leaves alternating with wavy lines (Pl. LXII, 9). Pot *b* is round, but a part of its upper portion, which is painted alternately with sets of vertical and wavy lines, is missing. **Five jars scattered about in the southern portion.**

Square R 34/3 contained a cracked, roundish jar, No. H344, covered with an inverted bowl. It is painted with bands only. Nothing was left of the other jar indicated in this square.

In square R 33/14 were five jars, Nos. H253 *a* and *b*, H254, and H255 *a* and *b*. Both jars comprising group H253 were ellipsoid in shape and found crushed. Of these, *a* was covered with the upper part of a stout and squat offerings' dish of Stratum II. It is painted merely with bands; whereas *b* shows stars, wavy lines, and leaves in the upper tier, and two circumscribed, rayed orbs in the lower. H254 is a round *ghaṛā* which was covered with a potsherd and brick, and has the finger-tip pattern on its lower portion. Pot H255*a* is ellipsoid in shape and was covered with a broken jar, while *b* is merely the lower part of a round *ghaṛā* decorated with the finger-tip pattern. **Pot-burials in the north-eastern portion.**

In square R 34/11 lay inclined a smashed pot, H342*a*, decorated with the finger-groove pattern and covered with the fragments of a small, globular jar. Close by, on either side of it, were found two other jars Nos. H342*b* and H343.

Pots Nos. H256, H263 and an unnumbered one found along the eastern edge of this section were very fragmentary and do not deserve notice.

Extension of the Western Section (see Pls. XLVIII, and XLIX, section on GH).

Over a greater part of this extension both the strata of burials were found to continue. The pot-burials came, as usual, just below the surface (Pl. L, *a*), and the earth-burials, which in this trench are all fractional, were separated from them by a lesser interval (Pl. L, *b*) than in the Eastern Section (Pl. XLIX, section on GH). **Difference in the level of pot and earth burials.**

In the whole of this extension there is but one wall. It stands close to the eastern edge, rises from a depth of 5¼ ft. below the surface and is about 11 ft. long. Among the burial-pots in this area the first to claim our attention lay in square R 32/14 and is the lower part of a medium-sized round jar,

No. H681, which is painted with black bands only. In the next square, R 32/15, there were five jars. Of these, H683 and H710 were very fragmentary and H684 the fragment of a large jar decorated with the finger-tip pattern. Unlike other jars with similar decoration it has black bands in the upper part, where the surface is polished red and adorned with a horned animal's head similar to the heads depicted on H702c[1] (*cf.* Pl. LXIII, 9). Both the remaining jars, Nos. H682 and H685, were round. The former was tilted towards the south-east and very much crushed. It is decorated only with bands, and appears to have been closed with a round vase of which pieces were found close to its mouth. The latter is broken through at one point, and had been bent in course of firing. It is painted at the shoulder with peacock headed V-shaped designs, each containing two dotted circles which alternate with stars.

Several isolated jars.

East of the above jars were discovered six burial-pots in square R 32/20. Of these, No. H672 was a badly crushed, ellipsoid jar painted in two rows one below the other. The lower row consists only of two circumscribed, rayed-orbs, and the upper one, so far as it survives, shows a peacock enclosed by couples of V-shaped slanting strokes, etc. From inside it was recovered a painted, round vase (Pl. LXIII, 11). About eight and twelve feet respectively due north-east of this were jars H673 and H674. The former is oval in shape and was tilted towards the west. It has wide mouth and short, plano-convex neck, an incipient cordon (1/5th in. wide) at the shoulder, and projecting base. It was covered with an inverted, round vase and enclosed by bricks at the base (Pl. XLIX, section on GH and Pl. LIX, *a*, 6). Like most of the jars with the finger-tip or finger-groove patterns, it contained a baby in embryonic position (Pl. LVII, *c*, 1). Like them, too, it is without any painting. The *gharā* H674, which bears the finger-tip pattern, was also secured by brickbats round the neck. Five feet south-east of H673 was an uncovered, round vase No. H675, which is decorated with two rayed-orbs opposite each other, but only one of them survives now. About four feet to the east of H675 was another round jar H677, which again was enclosed by bricks round the shoulder. Nearly four feet to the south of this was the fragmentary lower portion of jar H676.

Jar H673 containing a baby in embryonic position.

In square R 32/24 was found the lower half of a round jar marked with the finger-tip pattern (H679), and in each of the squares R 33/16 and R 32/25 there was a broken and unmarked jar.

Miscellaneous paintings.

Having described the pot-burials, a few words may be added here about the nature of the miscellaneous designs on the pots other than the therianthropic and animal figures to which I have already referred. For instance, the stars and what I have described as "rayed-orbs" may well have been meant to symbolise the heaven and sun; the wavy lines, continuous triangles or fishes may have represented the waters; the leaves, plants and trees vegetation in general;[2] and the flying birds doubtless served to symbolise the air through which the

[1] For the proposed identification of this animal with *markhor* see footnote 2 on p. 214 *supra*.

[2] Some such belief appears to have been expressed in *Ṛigveda*, X, 16, 3. I quote its translation by Griffiths. Addressing the corpse, the *Ṛishi* says:—

"The Sun receive thine eye, the wind thy spirit; go, as thy merit is, to earth or heaven.
Go, if it be thy lot, unto the waters; go, make thine home in plants with all thy members."

soul of a dead person made its way to the realms beyond.[1] In connection with the latter belief we may recall the therianthropic figures with birds' heads on pot-burials Nos. H206*b* and *a* (Pl. LXII, 1*a*, 1*b* and 2) and 7435*e* (Pl. LXII, 13).[2] This belief is supported by the painting on jar No. H206*a* where the actual vehicle for carrying the soul (?) of the departed is the peacock. Be this as it may, it was obviously not considered obligatory that all or, indeed, any of the above-mentioned motifs should be painted on every burial-pot, for we have seen that some of the pots are without any paintings, while others are decorated merely with bands.

Size of pots unsuited for complete burials.

The size and shape of the jars in Stratum I preclude the possibility of their having contained whole bodies of adults or even of grown-up children whether at full length or in a crouching position. The height of the jars ranges from 9⅞ to 23⅞ in., and diameter at the mouth from 6¼ to 9¼ in. Round *ghaṛās* with the finger-tip pattern have their rims slightly everted (Pls. LIX, 10 and LXI, 14). In all other cases, the jars have straight, plano-convex, collared rim (Pl. LXI, types A; C, 12 and 13; and D). It may be observed, too, that, in many cases, the mouth opening was slightly oval and not exactly circular—possibly to make it more convenient for taking in the skull. The purpose of the holes, which in many cases pierced the neck, was no doubt to enable strings to be passed through them and over the covers, though even if there had been no holes at all, the strings could still have been tied securely beneath the flange.

Their contents presuppose exposure of the dead bodies.

Besides the eleven pot-burials discovered up to 1928-29 the contents of which have already been described,[3] one hundred and twenty-four other pot-burials were subsequently found in the Cemetery and their contents examined. Of these, 35 contained bones of adults—young or old, 21 of children, 6 whose age is doubtful, and 11 of babies or infants, while 51 were without bones and filled only with percolated earth. The quantity of bones in the pots differs very widely. From the data so far unearthed, it may be stated with reasonable certainty that bodies of adults and grown-up children were almost invariably exposed to birds and beasts of prey, and after a short period, the exact duration of which we have no means of determining at present, such bones as remained were collected and deposited in pots or burial urns.[4] Usually, the skull or its fragments, leg and arm bones, part of the vertebral column, pelvis, shoulder blade, some other long bones with a few comparatively of the smaller bones formed the entire collection

---

[1] In the *Baudhāyana Dharmasūtra*, II, 14, 9 and 10 it is recorded "that the birds at the offering of the dead should receive lumps of food just like the Fathers, on the ground that in the form of birds the Fathers go about". *Vide* A. B. Keith, *op. cit.* p. 415. The paintings we are discussing are much older. It may, however, be observed that the *Pitaras* (Fathers) are only one degree removed from the 'Pretas' which term is applied to the dead before their funeral rites are performed, on the completion of which they are supposed to be immediately transformed into *Pitaras* (Fathers).

[2] *Cf.* pp. 207 ff. and 212 *supra*.

[3] See pp. 211-12 *supra*.

[4] In the oldest culture of Elam, *i.e.*, in Susa Ia "The dead were buried individually, sometimes flexed, sometimes extended, as in the al'Ubaid phase of Sumer. More often, however, the burial was secondary; the bones were only interred after the flesh had decayed, probably that is, after exposure, and the skeleton is often incomplete. This rite was characteristic of Elam in subsequent periods also; the previous exposure of the corpse may be the origin of Zoroastrian and Parsi usage which has only dispensed with the subsequent interment." Gordon Childe, *New Light on the Most Ancient East*, pp. 232-33.

of a dead body. As the lighter and more fleshy bones could be easily carried away by birds and beasts, the quantity left necessarily varied under different circumstances.

Usual contents.

Examples of the average contents of the jars with adults' bones are furnished by jars Nos. H245*a*, H249, H61 and H206 (Pl. LIV, *a-d*): the smallest number of bones, consisting of only two fragments of a leg bone, was found in jar No. H245*c* (Pl. LV, *c*). Other jars containing very few bones were H146, H624, H672, H682, H231*a*, H154*a*, H245*f*, and H153*c* two of which are illustrated in Pl. LV, *a* and *b*. The jars with numerous bones clearly show us how their contents were packed in. Not infrequently the skull was placed on one side touching the wall of the urn, while the leg and arm bones were laid obliquely or horizontally intersecting one another in all positions, and other bones were inserted wherever possible. In several cases, the skull was found in the centre, or a little away from it, and the long bones stood erect. It should, however, be added that the skulls were usually placed upright, though in several cases they were found upside down or on one or the other cheek, having presumably turned over. In some instances they were found inverted at the bottom of the jar with the cranium in contact with its surface.

Occasional presence of bones from other bodies.

As a rule, one jar was meant only for the bones of a single individual,[1] but an exception is furnished by jar No. 3934*c* which contained three skulls. The duplication of small bones occurs also in several other pots. Thus, in pot No. H247*a* were found mixed up with the bones of an adult, a humerus, piece of a skull and of an os innominatum, one femur and two tibias of a child; and in H167, containing the remains of a grown-up young person, one mandible, four phalanges, one tarsal, five metatarsals, and one shaft of a long bone of a child; whereas in pots H246*e* and H255*a* were found only one piece each of a second sacrum; in H245*a* only a fragment of the skull of a child; in H154*a* one extra tibia, one fibula and one patella of a child and three metatarsals each of two other adults; and in H62*d* and H249 three and one epiphyses respectively, of the long bones of children. From these examples it may be surmised that, at the time of collecting the bones, small pieces of bone lying about on the exposed ground got mixed up with the remains of the corpse or corpses and were inadvertently buried with them.

Three jars with some exceptional contents.

Where, as in most cases, the quantity of bones was considerable, they were found to rise 5 to 10 in. above the bottom of urns. In jar No. H245*a* (*cf.* Pl. LIV, *d*), however, the bones rose to 17¼ in. above the bottom. This is very exceptional, as, except in the carinated pots whose size is much smaller than that of others, the bones were usually confined to the lower half. Jar No. H154*a*, which contained the bones of an adult, also had inside, rising a little above the skull, a small bi-convex, narrow-necked and painted vase with splayed neck and projecting base (Pls. LV, *b* and LVIII, *b*, 9); while No. H231*b*, with the bones of a young person, had two cog-wheel shaped nose discs of steatite holed through the centre and incised with a circle on either face (*cf.* Pl. CXXXIX, 18-20). Jar No. H149 deserves special notice. It is of the round type, surviving

[1] For the detailed contents of each pot see Appendix I, pp. 242-45 *infra*.

only to two-thirds of its original height. When found, it was full of ashy earth freely mixed with pieces of charcoal, some blackened potsherds, and numerous fragments of charred[1] and uncharred bones, including one charred bone of a bird. Unlike other jars, which merely contained human bones, this had fragments of two triangular cakes, one drinking goblet with pointed base typical of the Indus Period, and one dish, a terracotta ball, and pieces of a bangle, and a stone pestle. The majority of the bones contained in it were completely charred, others only slightly calcined, while others bore no traces of fire at all. It may be, therefore, that in this case the body was first exposed, and then partially burnt, and that subsequently the remains were taken up and buried.[2] The other contents of this pot are equally exceptional. They call to mind some of the contents of the large, post-cremation urns so well known from the mounds at Harappā and Mohenjo-daro.

Babies buried entire in embryonic position.

One ellipsoid, one oval and nine round jars, Nos. H673, H148*a*, H156, H83, H165*b*, H169, H619, H625, H679, H165*a*, and H622, were used for the burial of infants or babies. Of these, six had the finger-tip and two the finger-groove patterns on their lower part. Bodies of infants were not exposed. Pls. LV, *e*, and LVI, *a-d* furnish conclusive proof that babies were first tied up in the embryonic position, then probably wrapped in a piece of cloth[3] and so placed in the urn. Thus jars H83 and H165*a* (Pls. LV, *e*, and LVI, *a*) make it clear that the head was still connected with the spinal column, and that the thorax, though bent, was in its natural position, while the legs were doubled up and the metatarsals were in front of the lower legs. In the former case, the right arm was bent and placed over the abdomen, as the radius and ulna cover some of the lower ribs. In this connection it may be recalled that in the southern Panjāb even to this day Hindu babies up to about eighteen months[4] of age are buried and not cremated, though at some places by the river side they are wrapped in cloth and submerged in the river with a *gharā* filled with water and attached to it. The reason for not exposing babies may have originated in the fact that by exposure there was a fair chance of the whole body being carried away by birds or beasts of prey, and in that case no part or bone would have been left for burial in an urn. The idea of burying babies in a crouching position appears to have been

---

[1] Dr. Guha, who examined these bones, writes that "a large number of broken pieces of bones show undoubted evidence of calcination".

[2] Some such practice appears to have been alluded to in *Ṛigveda*, X. 16, 6 whose translation I quote from Griffith :—

"What wound soe'er the dark bird hath inflicted, the emmet, or the serpent or the jackal.
May Agni who devoureth all things heal it, and Soma who hath passed into the Brāhmaṇa."

Also see Gordon Childe, *op. cit.*, p. 244, who referring to a burial from Musyān writes "One tomb at the latter site contained the remains of two skeletons; the excavators also speak of partial cremation, perhaps comparable to the rite reported by Woolley from Ur. The vaulted tombs, the multiple interments, and the partial cremations might result from Babylonian influence".

[3] This inference appears justified from the position of babies in the jars. To secure the body in this posture cloth or string must necessarily have been required but neither of them could possibly be expected to have survived. Since cloth was manufactured by the Indus People it is likely that babies, to be secured in the embryonic position, were probably first tied with string and then wrapped up, as now, in a piece of cloth.

[4] A. B. Keith in his *Religion and Philosophy of the Veda*, p. 417, writes "Burning is normally preferred, the chief exceptions being very holy ascetics and infants under two years of age but the existence of burial cannot be denied for any period".

suggested by their embryonic pre-natal existence, and perhaps also by the belief that so placed the children might soon be reborn.

Bones are generally found in a crumbled condition,[1] but the degree of their preservation varies greatly. It was observed that in some cases bones of adult persons had utterly decayed, while those of infants were much better preserved.

Earth-burials of Stratum II.

Nature of earth-burials.

I now come to the lower (IInd) stratum. In this a number of human remains, apparently consigned to graves in the ground, were found both in the Eastern Section (Pl. XLV, *b*), and in the Northern Extension of the Western Section (Pl. L, *b*). The burials, however, differ considerably from one another; most of those in the Eastern Section were whole burials, whereas those in the latter were invariably fractional. In both areas, there was a complete absence of pot-burials in the lower level, and, on the other hand, the graves in this earlier level were distinguished by the presence of funeral furniture quite different from any thing found with the later pot-burials above them. Such furniture, with the food and drink which accompanied it, was intended, of course, for the use of the departed (Pl. LIX, *b*).[2]

Eastern Section (see Pls. XLIII and XLIV).

Burial No. H710.

Square R 34/17. The first earth-burial to be described is No. H710. It is the skeleton of an adult female orientated approximately from east to west (Pl. LI, *b*). It was fully stretched, and, except the cranium, was fairly well preserved. The head was turned on the left cheek, the left arm was bent up and placed over the shoulder, and the right forearm was bent so as to place the hand between the left arm and pelvis. The feet were also turned to left. No pottery was found with this.

Burial No. H695.

Square R 34/21. In this square, was lying supine, almost from east to west skeleton No. H695 of an adult male with large and well developed bones (Pl. LI, *c*). The left leg was almost straight, but the right was slightly inflexed, the humeri ran parallel to the thorax and the left hand was placed on the right, which lay over the abdomen, while the metacarpals and ungual phalanges had slipped into the pelvic cavity. There was no trace of the metatarsals or the foot phalanges. The skull with the mandible was slightly inclined to right. In course of clearing, an animal phalange was picked up near it. Four[3] sub-groups of vessels, all typical of the pottery of Stratum II, *viz.*, H231 *e*, *f*, *g*, and *h* were found to some extent mixed up with the later pot-burial group H231 *a*-*d* and *i*, but there can be virtually no doubt that they belonged to the earlier earth-burial.

Burial No. H698.

Square R 34/22. This square contained four earth-burials, Nos. H698, H696, H697 and H485, and two isolated ribbed food plates, H505 and H506 (*cf.* Pl. LX, 21). Burial No. H698 is the skeleton of an adult male stretched at full length from west to east. This direction is rare. Most of it had sunk below the

---

[1] For the decay of bones, see Dr. M. A. Hamid and Khan Bahadur Mohammad Sana Ullah's note, pp. 238-40 *infra*.

[2] For the early Āryan belief in life hereafter see *Rigveda*, X, hymns 15-18.

[3] These have already been described with the pot-burial group H231, see p. 206 *supra*.

original bed. The head was turned on the left cheek, the hands crossed each other over the right side of the pelvis with the left placed over the right (Pl. LII, *a*). Another unusual feature was that all the pottery lay crowded together at the feet; it consisted of a medium-sized painted jar *a* (Pl. LX, 19), with wide open mouth, and projecting ring-base in place of the usual *kalaśa*,[1] two saucers *b*, one of which lay under the feet, one flask *c* of the usual type, two other flasks of a larger size, *d*, and four small round vases, *e* (Pl. LXI, 13) with long splayed necks. The water jar touched the right foot, the large flasks lay parallel to the lower legs, and the rest of the pottery was arranged on either side of the water-pot. To left, alongside the skeleton, extending from the thorax down to the knees, was laid, in a line, the dismembered body of a ruminant, which, according to Dr. B. S. Guha, Anthropologist of the Zoological Survey of India, was a small sheep or goat[2] (H698*f*). That the animal had been sacrificed[3] and intentionally cut to pieces does not admit of any doubt, as the ribs lay uppermost, with the lower jaw in two fragments below, then some long bones and vertebræ, while some of the animal's ribs[4] were found placed in the deadman's hands. The human skull was damaged on the right parietal side, but the bones were in good condition; the height of the man was apparently above normal.

Unusual position of pottery.

Goat offered as a sacrifice for the dead.

Burial No. H696.

Burial No. H696, again of an adult male, lay from north-east to south-west (Pl. LI, *a*). Near its head were found two ring-based, medium-sized, open-mouthed water-pots (Pl. LXI, 12), each closed with a flask such as were generally used to stopper the water-pots, or placed inside the bowls.[5] One of the flasks was turned upside down. The water-pots are painted at the shoulder with rows of conventionalised leaves (?) alternating with a winged figure-of-8 (Pl. LXIII, 6). This skeleton was lying on the left side with legs inflexed, the right being placed over the left. His left arm was laid parallel to the body, but the right was bent at the elbow with the hand placed over the left forearm. The middle portion of the skeleton was missing.

Burial No. H697: pottery resembling that from the mounds.

About 13 ft. east-north-east of the above skeleton was found the burial No. H697: of an adult male lying from east to west (Pl. LIII, *d*). Though the legs of this skeleton were bent, the body was lying supine, and it must therefore be inferred that the thorax got pressed down at a later date. The head, however, was still turned on the left cheek, the left arm was folded up with the hand on the shoulder, and the right bent at the elbow with the hand resting a little below the heart. The legs were almost doubled at the knees with the right placed over the left. All but the lower part of the skull had disappeared, and excepting the bones of the left arm, the rest of the skeleton was also fragmentary. In this burial, again, the pottery and its arrangement were in some respects different from what is usually found with the earth-burials in this section. Thus, in place

[1] Shorn of the neck the *kalaśa* (water-pot) resembles the shape of a cocoanut; see Pl. LIX, *b*, 4, and Pl. LX, 18 and 20.

[2] Personal communication.

[3] For the sacrifice of goat *cf.* *Ṛigveda*, X, 16, 4.

[4] Were they to be offered to the watch dog of Yama or the hound of Hades(?). For the dogs of Yama see *Ṛigveda*, X, 14, 10-12.

[5] *Cf.* Pl. LIII, *b* and c and Pl. LIX, *b*, 1.

of the flat covers and saucers we have here wide cups and handled lids—the latter being in no way different from their prototypes found in the mounds. Among the grave furniture there were two broken cups, one within the other lying close to the mouth, two more touching them behind, one lying between the knees and the left arm, while nearer the feet were an offerings' plate (*c*) of the usual type, two handled lids and two cups (*e*), one crushed bowl (*b*) of a thinner fabric than usual, containing a round vase, and a small *ghaṛā* (*a*) in place of the usual *kalaśa*. The *ghaṛā* was tilted and originally covered with two cups, one of which was still sticking to it, while another lay at the feet over a sherd of the bowl. As to the character of the pottery, it appears to be mixed, the food plate being typical of Stratum II in the Cemetery (*cf.* Pl. LX, 22), while on the other hand, the common *ghaṛā*, cups and lids are more akin in shape and fabric to the pottery from the mounds than from the Cemetery.

Burial No. H485.

The fourth burial, No. H485, in this square was of a young adult male lying approximately from east to west (Pl. LI, *e*). The ground under this burial, appears to have sunk both above and below the pelvis which therefore lay higher than the rest of the body.[1] The feet, knees, and left hand were missing; and the skull and other bones had crumbled. No pottery was found with this. Two squat and ribbed offerings' dishes, Nos. H505 and H506, were also found in this square.

Burial No. H488.

Square R 34/23. In this square was found the complete burial, No. H488, of an adult female lying from north-east to south-west. It was fully stretched and better preserved than most of the others, but the feet were missing (Pl. LI, *f*). The head with gaping mouth lay on the left cheek, and arms alongside the body. Like skeleton No. H485, it was laid on the back. About a foot from its head lay a mass of animal bones, No. H507, in which some teeth were also noticeable, and a little further on was a *kalaśa* (No. H508) closed with a flask. The animal bones were lying approximately on the same plane as the skeleton, but the *kalaśa* stood considerably lower, possibly because its lower part had been buried in the ground.

Dismembered burial No. H636.

In square S 33/5 and partly in square R 33/25 was found a dismembered human skeleton No. H636 of an adult lying from north-east to south-west. The legs and feet were disconnected from the upper portion which did not lie in the natural position. Thus the skull, of which only the left half remained, lay between the two humeri and pointed towards the feet, while the inverted mandible rested partly under the left cheek and partly under the head of the right humerus. The arms were apparently doubled up since the left forearm was found to cover the upper part of the left humerus and the right forearm lay in a corresponding position. Immediately behind the left humerus, which was in contact with the hind part of the broken skull, were vertebrae and several ribs. Three carpals were found from within the mandible. The legs, which were even more fragmentary and in an advanced stage of decay, were flexed, the left being placed over the right. Only a little of the lower portion of the femurs remained, but the lower legs, though broken, did for the most part survive. Several metatarsals, tarsals,

---

[1] The unevenness of the body is not apparent in the photograph, as it was taken from above.

and phalanges lay jumbled together at the lower end of the legs. No pottery was found with this skeleton.

Square S 34/1 contained two burials and some pottery. Of these, No. H502*g*, which was lying from north-east to south-west, was the skeleton of an adult male with large and well developed bones (Pl. LIII, *c*). In this case, the head was turned on the left cheek and the legs were inflexed. The right forearm was originally placed across the abdomen as indicated by the hand which lay between the lower ribs and the left os innominatum, as well as by the radius and ulna crossing over the right part of the thorax. The left arm was doubled up alongside the body. The pottery, which lay on the head side, consisted of two *kalaśas* (*a*) each closed with a flask, a plain bowl (*b*) with a flask inside, one large flask (*e*) which lay close to the smashed *kalaśas* on the right, two saucers (*c*), and five flat covers (*d*), four of which were broken. Between the saucers and flat covers were a few fragmentary animal bones, No. H503. **Burial No. H502.**

About 8 ft. south-east of the above burial was brought to light the second skeleton, No. H501*a*, of a young person (Pl. LIII, *b*). It lay completely on the right side with legs inflexed. The lower jaw was slightly displaced and the head completely crushed. The arms were bent upwards and the hands placed in front of the face. Close to the head were found a *kalaśa* (*b*) and a bowl with a flask inside (*d*) with eight saucers and flat covers (*c*) lying between them, while opposite the lower legs lay inclined a stout offerings' dish (*e*). Interspersed between the saucers and flat covers were some stray animal bones, including ribs, long bones, and a few phalanges. **Burial No. H501.**

In this square were also found two *kalaśas* (Nos. H504 and H234*a*), an offerings' dish (No. H234*b*), and a bowl (No. H512). **Unconnected funerary vessels.**

Square S 34/2 contained one burial and a separate group of pottery. Of these, skeleton No. H484*a* of a man of tall stature was lying from north-east to south-west (Pl. LIII, *a*). Its position, as compared with that of burial No. H501*a*, was reversed in so far as the body was partially turned on the left side. The skull, which was broken, lay on the left cheek, and the lower jaw was broken in two pieces. The left hand was placed over the heart and the right over the abdomen. Below the lower jaw was a small, narrow-necked, bulgy vase (*b*), close to the right shoulder two flasks and a bowl (*c*), and near the head a *kalaśa* closed with a flask (*d*). Between the above *kalaśa* and the bowl were animal bones including a jaw (*e*). Compared with other skeletons, the bones of this and of skeleton No. H502*g* are appreciably larger. **Burial No. H484.**

In this square also lay a group of pottery No. H487 *a-d*, comprising a shattered bowl of a larger size than usual (containing a small vase painted with bands), two globular vases of comparatively rough make lying one over the other, one complete and one broken offerings' plate of the usual type, and a smashed saucer (Pl. XLVII, *c*, right foreground). No human remains were found with this group, and it is possible that this pottery was placed with burial No. H485[1], already described, in square R 34/22. **Pottery group No. H487.**

[1] See p. 222 *supra*.

Fractional burial No. H486. In square S 34/3 the only burial (No. H486) was fractional and consisted only of a broken skull (*a*), close to which were placed one *kalaśa* closed with a flask, a deep bowl, another small *kalaśa*, an offerings' standard dish, one flask, a round vase covered with a saucer, and eleven other saucers (*b*).

Burial No. H88. Square S 34/6 contained two burials and a lot of pottery. Of these, burial No. H88, of an adult female (?), lay from south-east to north-west. The body was fully stretched, the right hand was placed over the left forearm, and the legs were doubled up. Bowl No. H64 with a flask inside apparently belonged to this burial. Immediately to its north were some highly decayed animal bones. **Dismembered burial No. H184.** About 3 ft. south-west of this was the dismembered skeleton No. H184*k* of an adult male, which lay roughly from east to west (Pl. LII, *c*). Of this, the legs, arms, skull, and trunk were lying completely severed. Thus, one femur lay between two tibias, part of the other femur was lying near the pelvis, which again lay alongside the crushed ribs and spinal column, while between the thorax and one tibia was the utterly crushed skull, of which naught but a part of the upper jaw was left. Immediately to its east and south was a group of pottery, comprising two long-necked *kalaśas*, four flasks (of which one is painted), one bowl, a vase, an offerings' standard dish, eight flat covers, each with a pair of holes, and five saucers (No. H184 *a-i*). Close to the latter were found the vertebral column and other bones of an animal (No. H184*j*). Within a few feet to the south-east and resting on a slightly higher plane was the leg bone of an animal (No. H483). Six feet due south of this skeleton was a row of eighteen flasks, one bowl, and two *kalaśas* (No. H157 *a-d*), apparently belonging to some other fractional burial, of which no trace is now left. Nos. H132, H164 and H190 also found in this square were all flasks, the first mentioned being painted with stars, etc.

In the next square, S 34/7, were found two long-necked, graceful flasks (H62*a*) and two saucers (H62*b* and *c*). Further on, in square S 34/9, were recovered some fragments of human bones.

Fractional burial No. H307. Close to the present southern boundary of this section and lying in squares S 34/5 and S 34/10, was discovered a fractional burial of an adult male No. H307*a* orientated approximately from south-west to north-east (Pl. LII, *d*). It consisted of the spinal column, hip bone and femurs which were connected with each other, and of the severed head which was lying close to the left femur. To its north and west were stray animal bones (No. H307*b*), such as ribs, joint bones, etc. No pottery was found with this burial.

In square S 34/11 and partly in S 34/12, were found one deep bowl and seven saucers (H63 *a* and *b*), as well as a round painted vase with long, splayed neck (H86*a*) and two fragmentary saucers (H86*b*).

Burial No. H306. The last burial in this section (No. H306) was found lying from north-east to south-west in square S 34/19 (Pl. LII, *b*). This burial is complete and consists of the skeleton of an adult stretched at full length. It was lying on the back, but the head was turned over on the right cheek, the forearms were crossed over the abdomen, and the left hand was placed on the right forearm. One bowl and a flask lay close to the head.

EARTH-BURIALS IN THE EXTENSION OF THE WESTERN SECTION.

(See Pls. XLVIII and XLIX—section on GH.)

No earth-burials of Stratum II were found in the main Western Section, but in its Extension several fractional burials were recovered below the level of the pot-burials (Pl. L, *b*). Squares R 32/15 and R 33/11 contained four burials. The first one of these (No. H701) consisted only of a squat, open-mouthed vase with projecting ring-base (*cf.* Pl. LXI, type H) containing a round flask (*cf.* Pl. LXI, type G). The squat vase was adorned with V-shaped linear decoration below the neck (Pl. LXIII, 3), and the flask with linear decoration at the shoulder and three circumscribed and rayed-orbs over the body (Pl. LXI, 10). No bones were found near this burial. To the west of this was recovered the dismembered skeleton of a young person (No. H700) at a depth of 2·3 ft. below datum line. In this case the skull, which was broken into several parts, lay towards the east, and the mandible, which was in its original position, showed that only 12 teeth had been cut, and one was sprouting. The arms and other bones were badly broken, and some of them lay along the left of the head. With this were found placed a plain, red washed, footless dish of thick ware (*cf.* Pl. LXI, type L), and a squat, medium-sized vase with broad mouth and ring-base (diam. 6¾ in.) containing a round vase with long, splayed neck as in the flasks (Pl. L, *d*, foreground). From this, and some other examples to be mentioned below, it may be inferred that the squat, open-mouthed vase with the round vase inside was used as a substitute for the customary large bowl which, as we have seen in the Eastern Section, usually contained a flask, and possibly also for the *kalaśa* or water-pot as well, which frequently occurred with earth-burials in the Eastern Section, since no water-pot is found in company with them. Similarly, the flat dish took the place of the standard dish.

Burial No. H701.

Fractional burials H699 and H700.

Change of pottery.

9 ft. 8 in. to the north-east of H700 was the third fractional burial, No. H702 *a-c* (Pl. L, *c*, right background). It consisted of two fragments of femurs in conjunction with a plain dish (*a* ; diam. 10¼ in.), a round flask (*c*) painted alternately with three stars and three *markhor*[1] heads (Pls. LXI, 14, LXIII, 9 and LVIII, *c*, 6), and a round, *loṭā*-shaped vase (*b* ; Pl. LXI, 17) painted at the shoulder with birds (Pls. LVIII, *c*, 7, and LXIII, 2).

8 ft. 6 in. to the south-east of H700 was the much mutilated fourth burial, No. H707, which lay very unevenly from east to west. All that could be recovered of this was the crushed head, arms doubled up under the breast, and a part of the badly mutilated spinal column (Pl. L, *b*, left foreground). No pottery accompanied it. In the adjoining square R 33/16, 3 ft. 9 in. to the north-east of H707, was a round pot-burial (H709) with thick rim, of which the mouth was closed by an inverted round pot. The cover and the jar, which had completely turned over, were smashed. It is worth remarking that this jar stood at a lower level than the head of skeleton No. H707, with human bones on either side—those to its left being a clavicle and bit of another long bone, and to its

Fractional burial.

An anciently disturbed burial.

[1] See footnote 2 on p. 214

right vertebræ and ribs (H708). It seems therefore that there was a fractional burial on this spot, which was disturbed when the jar No. H709 was deposited here. That the jar, in this case, was buried deeper than usual, calls for no special explanation. It was probably a matter of chance, or there may have once been a depression at this point. It should be noticed, however, that the jar, which was empty, differed somewhat in shape from others found in this Cemetery.

Fractional burials H703 and H704.

Two burials were found in square R 32/20. Of these, No. H703 (Pl. LXI, 11) was a squat water-pot containing a round flask. The water-pot is painted with three winged figure-of-8 devices alternating with groups of oblique lines (Pl. LXIII, 8). The flask is painted with three circumscribed and rayed orbs (Pl. LVIII, *c*, 2). Twelve feet south-east of H703 was found a crushed, open-mouthed, squat vase with ring-base (H704) containing, as usual, a round flask which is painted with sets of dotted circles and triangles. At a slightly lower level than this lay the parietal fragments of a human skull without any other bone.

Burial No. H706.

In square R 33/16 was found the upper part of the skeleton of an adult female, No. H699, consisting only of the body up to the thorax and the upper part of the arms. The head lay to the north, and seemingly no pottery accompanied this burial (Pl. LI, *d*).

In square R 32/25 were found a fragmentary flask, crushed, squat vase with a flask inside (H705), and the burial group H706, comprising a plain, footless, thickware dish (*a*), like those found with burials H701 and H702, and a medium-sized, round vase (*b*) with prominent neck and ring-base (Pl. LXI, 16), closed with a pear-shaped flask (Pl. LVIII, *c*, 4). Of these remains, the medium-sized vase is painted in two tiers—the lower with three circumscribed and rayed orbs; the upper with a frieze of three peacocks all facing right, between which the blank spaces are filled with a vertical row of three dotted circles each (Pl. LXIII, 12). The covering flask is also painted in two tiers: the lower one with two circumscribed and rayed orbs, and the upper one with winged figure-of-8 devices alternating with triangular motifs (Pl. LXIII, 4).

In the IInd stratum in squares R 32/14 and R 32/15 was traced an L-shaped edging of painted potsherds similar to the pottery from the mounds. Within this edging were some bits of animal bones.

Directions of burials.

From the foregoing account of Stratum II it will appear that in the Eastern Section the prevailing direction in which the dead bodies were laid in the graves was from the north-east to south-west (Pl. XLIII). Skeletons Nos. H695, H697, and H710[1] were, however, orientated from east to west, while No. H698 is the only instance where the body was laid from west to east. In one complete (H88) and two incomplete burials (H184k and H307a) the bodies were lying in other directions also. Only five skeletons, *viz.*, Nos. H484*a*, H501*a*, H502, H696, and H697, were laid to rest with the legs inflexed;[2] in other cases, where the skeletons were entire, the legs were fully stretched.

Burials with or without pottery.

In most burials, some grave furniture in the shape of funeral pottery was placed with the dead persons, but no pottery

[1] This is not exact east and west but only approximately so.

[2] The common attitude of repose.

was found with skeletons Nos. H88, H485, H488, H695,[1] and H710, nor with the incomplete burials Nos. H307*a*, H636, H699 and H707.

Grouping and frequency of funeral pottery.

Fairly large groups of pottery characteristic of Stratum II were found with burials Nos. H501, H502, H697, and H698. Where the pots were few, they were generally placed fairly close to the head. Of most frequent occurrence was the water-pot (Pls. LX, type E; and LXI, type H), which usually took the form of a cocoanut-shaped *kalaśa* with long splayed out neck (Pls. LIX, *b*. 4; and LX, 18 and 20), a small round *ghaṛā* (Pl. LIII, *d*), an open-mouthed, round pot with a small standard base (Pls. LIX, *b*, 3; and LX, 19), or an open-mouthed, squat vase with ring-base (Pl. LXI, type H). Wherever the last of these occurs, it also does duty for the bowl. But whatever its shape might be, the water-pot was usually closed with or contained a flask, or else it had some other kind of lid or stopper on it. Next in the order of frequency to the water-pot, were the bowl with or without a flask inside (Pls. LIX, *b*, 1 and 2; and LX, type B), and the food plates or dishes with or without a stand (Pls. LIX, *b*, 5 and 9; LX, type F; and LXI, type L). Of far less frequent occurrence were the flasks (Pls. LIX, *b*, 7, 8, 10 and 11; and LXI, type G), saucers and flat covers (Pls. LIX, *b*, 6 and 12; and LXI, types K and M), but whenever they came as separate vessels and not merely as stoppers or covers they were usually found in fairly large numbers.

Kalaśas.

The *kalaśas* are generally larger than the other types of water-pots. They vary in height from 11¾ to 20 in., and most of them contained gypsum crystals formed at the bottom—a fact which points to their use for keeping water. The flask over the water-pot was not only a convenient stopper, but handy for drinking water which the dead person required during his long journey to the other world.

Offerings' dishes or plates.

The offerings' dishes (*e.g.*, Pls. LIX, *b*, 5; and LX, 21) are squat, strong and well made, with raised horizontal mouldings on the base. They are different alike in shape, size, and texture from the stemmed dishes found in the mounds and Area G. No less different are the offerings' dishes like those illustrated in Pls. LIX, *b*, 9; and LX, 22. These have a deeper bowl, are of smaller size and of a thinner fabric than the last mentioned. They closely resemble the offering stand No. S. D. 229, illustrated in Pls. LXXVIII, 8, and LXXIX, 4 of *M. I. C.* A vessel generally similar to these offerings' dishes has been found in many of the pre-Sargonic burials discovered in the Sumerian Palace at Kish. Along with them in every case was found a water-jar and a plate with a hollow stem "similar to the 'Champagne vases' found in the lower strata of Carchemish". "They are made of coarse clay, generally red in colour, and made in two pieces, the base and stem being one and the dish the second part." According to Professor Langdon they were intended to be used as eating plates.[2] The Harappā offerings' dishes are of similar structure but their stems with pronounced horizontal mouldings are shorter; otherwise their shape and technique are

[1] It is, however, probable, as already pointed out, that bowl No. H64 was associated with burial No. H88; the group of pottery No. H487 with burial No. H488; and the pottery sub-groups No. H231 *e-g* with burial No. H695.

[2] S. Langdon, *Excavations at Kish*, Vol. I, pp. 75-76, Pls. XIV, 4, and XV, 1.

much the same. In a word, the Harappā dishes are a little more squat, of finer texture and stronger built. In most cases, the dishes with horizontal mouldings on the base have a hole through the centre which connects the bowl of the dish with the hollow stem (Pl. LX, 21). At Kish, "Nearly every one (of the dishes) has four holes at the base which are evidently ventilation holes to cool the stem, which would otherwise become very hot". Professor Langdon believes that "The hollow stems were intended to contain charcoal, and in this manner the food was kept warm". The same purpose could also have been served, to some extent, by the central hole in some of the Harappā offerings' dishes, though the explanation suggested by Prof. Langdon is questionable. The similarity of the plates of Kish and Harappā is instructive for the evidence it furnishes of cultural contact, particularly as in both cases they were associated with earth-burials and intended as food plates.

Bowls, saucers, and flat covers.

The bowls are severely plain (Pls. LIX, *b*, 1 and 2; and LX, type B); in most cases they contained nothing except flasks. The saucers are deep with the lip well splayed out (Pls. LIX, *b*, 6; and LXI, type K). In some cases they are painted with chevrons and holed at the rim, while the flat shallow covers invariably have a couple of holes at the rim (Pls. LIX, *b*, 12; and LXI, type M). Doubtless the purpose of these holes was for tying them to a larger vessel, though it should be noted that there was no direct evidence of this in the positions in which they were found. In every case they are painted on the underside. Their ornaments consist of deer, peacocks, trees, leaves, stars, birds, fishes, hands, tassels, etc. (Pl. LXIV), most of which, it should be remarked, were reproduced later on the burial jars of the upper stratum.

Paintings on flat covers.

Flasks.

Most of the flasks have a pear-shaped body, long and gracefully splayed out neck, and well defined base (Pl. LXI, type G), but others, especially those from the Extension of the Western Section, are round and have no projecting base (Pl. LXI, type I). Some of the flasks and vases are of extremely fine and delicate texture with bright red polish over the surface (Pl. LVIII, *b*, 3-8, *c*, 2 and 6). Of these, a few are painted with simple designs consisting of lines and chevrons, stars in circles or crescents, and with a dark slip over the neck (Pl. LVIII, *b*, 3, 5, 6 and 8); in others only the neck is painted.

Composition of rubbish in the Cemetery.

A common feature of the débris in the Cemetery Area was that the whole of the Western Section, and the western and eastern parts of the Eastern Section were littered with a thick layer of countless potsherds far outnumbering any that have yet been found at any one place at Harappā.[1] The sherds represented almost all types of earthenware vessels in common use on the mounds. Among these heaps, the typical Indus goblets with pointed bases far exceeded all other vessels in numbers. Fragments of oval and round *gharās*; dishes with incurving or splayed out rim; medium-sized, cylindrical vases; round jars with thick walls and painted with black bands; long oval, *hāṇḍi*-shaped, and crude carinated vases, as well as sherds of troughs—all these were found in large numbers.[2]

[1] Area G was also full of potsherds, but there the numbers were appreciably smaller as compared with those from the Cemetery H. Both areas appear to have been used for dumping broken ware and rubbish.

[2] The above enumeration of shapes indicates their order of frequency.

Apart from this pottery and the earth and pot-burials described above the Cemetery area yielded a number of small antiquities unconnected with the graves. Some of these objects may have been swept down in course of centuries from the mounds, others were presumably dumped in with broken pottery long before this area came to be used as a cemetery. Below is a list of these objects :—

Eastern Section.

Stratum I—

1. Fragment of a unicorn seal with only one pictogram surviving. Pl. XCII, 277. L. $\frac{5}{8}$ in. No. H604; Square S 34/23; Depth 6 in. b.s.
2. Fragment of a seal showing three pictograms, the head of a unicorn, and an incense-burner. Pl. XC, 185. L. $\frac{7}{8}$ in. No. H30; Square S 35/10; Depth 1 ft. 3 in. b.s.
3. Rectangular, plano-convex steatite seal with 7 pictograms surviving. Pl. CI, 698. L. $1\frac{1}{16}$ in.; W. $\frac{5}{8}$ in. No. H160; Square S 33/10; Depth 2 ft. 6 in. b.s.
4. Fragment of a hexagonal faience sealing with one pictogram on either face; similar to No. 324 in Pl. XCIII. L. $\frac{3}{8}$ in.; w. $\frac{3}{8}$ in. No. H91; Square S 34/20; Depth 3 in. b.s.
5. Tiny stone *lingam*. Ht. $\frac{13}{16}$ in. No. H95; Square S 34/10; Depth 1 ft. b.s.
6. Shuttle-shaped chert polisher, fragmentary. Pl. CXVIII, 55. L. $\frac{13}{16}$ in. No. H33; Square S 34/9; Depth 1 ft. 6 in. b.s.
7. Cog-wheel shaped faience nose-ring, slightly damaged. Diam. $\frac{7}{8}$ in. No. H123; Square S 34/16; Depth 1 ft. 9 in. b.s.
8. Tiny, couchant faience ram, holed across the neck for suspension. L. 1 in. No. H183; Square S 34/6; Depth 3 ft. b.s.
9. Carinated pottery vase. Ht. $3\frac{1}{8}$ in. No. H20; Square S 34/7; Depth 6 in. b.s.
10. Terracotta toy representing two squirrels (?) one going up and the other coming down the stump of a tree. Pl. LXXVIII, 33. Ht. $2\frac{3}{4}$ in. No. H21; Square S 35/10; Depth 1 ft. 3 in. b.s.
11. Terracotta male figure with hands folded in worship; fragmentary. Ht. 2 in. No. H233; Square R 34/20; Depth 1 ft. 10 in. b.s.

Stratum II—

1. Unicorn seal with 5 pictograms. Pl. LXXXVIII, 79. $1\frac{1}{8}$ in. sq. No. H220; Square S 34/16; Depth 3 ft. 5 in. b.s.
2. Shield-shaped faience sealing with 5 pictograms on one side, and 1 on the other. Pl. XCV, 368. Size $\frac{15}{16} \times \frac{1}{16}$ in. No. H550; Square S 34/9; Depth 5 ft. 3 in. b.s.
3. Cubical chert weight. Wt. 6·6 gms.; size ·55×·53×·45 in. No. H70; Square S 34/11; Depth 3 ft. 6 in. b.s.

4. Plano-convex. discoid bead of banded stone. Diam. 11/16 in. No. H232; Square S 34/1; Depth 3 ft. 10 in. b.s.
5. Cog-wheel shaped steatite disc with a large hole at the centre and a small one on either side touching the former. Pl. CXXXIX, 15. Diam. 1 1/16 in. No. H450; Square S 34/17; Depth 4 ft. 5 in. b.s.
6. Fragmentary steatite object relieved with a series of crescentic ribs. It is holed across the width. Pl. CXXXIX, 42. Size 1⅜×1 in. No. H469; Square S 34/1; Depth 4 ft. 10 in. b.s.
7. Flower-shaped steatite pendent with eight petals. inlaid alternately with lapis lazuli and dark red stone. On reverse, it is decorated with a scheme of incised, concentric circles. Three inlaid pieces of lapis lazuli and one of red stone survive. Pl. CXXXIX, 7. Diam. ¾ in. No. H500; Square R 34/22; Depth 5 ft. b.s.
8. Tiny. couchant faience ram. L. 1 in. No. H221; Square S 34/16; Depth 3 ft. 5 in. b.s.
9. Cubical faience die marked with 1 opposite 2, 3 opposite 4, and 5 opposite 6. Pl. CXX. 51. ⅜ in. cube. No. H413; Square S 34/17; Depth 3 ft. 8 in. b.s.
10. Flower-shaped faience pendent with only a part of one petal surviving. Pl. CXXVIII. 28. Diam. 2¼ in. No. H412; Square S 34/18; Depth 3 ft. 8 in. b.s.
11. Small, narrow-necked vase of black pottery. Ht. 2¼ in. No. H218; Square S 34/1; Depth 3 ft. 7 in. b.s.
12. Tiny pottery vase. Ht. 7/16 in. No. H468; Square S 34/1; Depth 4 ft. 10 in. b.s.
13. Terracotta toy showing in relief a crocodile and its young basking in the sun; fragmentary. Pl. LXXVIII, 22. Size 3¼×½ in. No. H417; Square R 34/22; Depth 3 ft. 6 in. b.s.

Stratum III—

1. Tiny bead of thin gold leaf, distorted. L. 3/16 in. No. H586; Square S 33/15; Depth 6 ft. 11 in. b.s.
2. Fine earthenware vase painted with two peacocks facing right. Pl. LVIII, *b*, 1. Ht. 2⅜ in. No. H607; Square S 33/15; Depth 8 ft. 2 in. b.s. Its fabric and paintings are reminiscent of burial pottery.

Stratum IV—

1. Biconical agate bead, fragmentary. L. 1½ in. No. H692; Square S 34/12; Depth 10 ft. b.s.
2. Cubical chert weight. Wt. 27·45 gms.; size ·9×·9×·77 in. No. H666; Square S 33/15; Depth 11 ft. 8 in. b.s.

From spoil earth—

1. Fragmentary, rectangular faience sealing with 2 pictograms surviving on one side and 1 on the other. Pl. XCIV, 359. L. 11/16 in.; w. ⅜ in. No. H715.

Western Section.

Stratum II—

1. Discoid faience sealing with 4 pictograms on one face, and 1 on the other. Pl. CI, 702. Diam. 5/16 in. No. H297; Square R 34/2; Depth 4 ft. b.s.
2. Cuboid faience sealing showing an acacia tree enclosed in a platform on one face and 2 pictograms on the opposite face, each of the remaining four sides being inscribed with a dotted circle. Pl. CI, 703. Side ½ in.; th. ⅜ in. No. H441e; Square Q 34/19; Depth 6 ft. 8 in. b.s.
3. Cuboid chert weight. Wt. 6·85 gms.; size ·55×·55×·5 in. No. H539; Square R 34/5; Depth 4 ft. 6 in. b.s.
4. Cuboid chert weight, unfinished. Size 1·85×1·7×1·2 in. No. H386; Square R 34/8; Depth 5 ft. 6 in. b.s.
5. Barrel-shaped bead of sard. Pl. CXXVIII, 34. L. ⅜ in. No. H475; Square R 33/18; Depth 7 ft. 5 in. b.s.
6. Forty-four thick, discoid steatite beads. Diam. ⅜ in. No. H515; Square R 33/18; Depth 7 ft. 6 in. b.s.
7. Tiny, bud-shaped faience pendent with a holed projection at the base. Broken. L. 3/16 in. No. H317; Square R 34/4; Depth 3 ft. 10 in. b.s.

Stratum III—

1. Fragment of a unicorn seal showing hind part of the animal and 2 pictograms. Pl. CI, 697. 1 in. sq. No. H540; Square R 33/13; Depth 8 ft. 1 in. b.s.

Extension of the Western Section.

Stratum I—

1. Faience ear stud. L. 7/16 in. No. H663; Square R 32/24; Depth 3 ft. b.s.

Stratum II—

1. Rectangular, plano-convex steatite seal with 5 pictograms. Pl. XCIX, 630. Size 11/16 × 7/16 in. No. H605; Square R 32/18; Depth 4 ft. 6 in. b.s.
2. Faience ball incised with a row of four double concentric circles round the circumference, and two on the remaining spaces. Pl. CXX, 41. Diam. 1⅓ in. No. H665; Square R 32/14; Depth 4 ft. 2 in. b.s.

Structural remains in the Western Section.

In the Western Section, below the level of Stratum II (which, however, was not represented here by any earth-burials) were brought to light the remains of three rooms. These were found in the southern part and consisted of a wall 40 ft. long from east to west, two parti-walls going northwards, the T-shaped remains of another structure, and a broken bit of wall (Pl. XLVIII). Immediately south of the above long wall and close to the western edge of this section was found, at a depth of 5 ft. below the surface, a small group of non-burial

A group on non-burial pottery and two other finds.

pottery, No. H441 *a-d*. It comprised a large goblet with pointed base (*a*), a similar goblet of the usual size, and a fine oval vase (*b*), a small napiform jar lying over two crushed *hāṇḍis*, and a cylindrical cup (*c*), and lastly a crushed, globular vase (*d*) (Pl. XLIX, section on EF). Later, in course of clearing, there came to light at the same level and near the south-west corner of this section, a shallow, red washed, pottery trough with everted rim and flat bottom (H568; diam. 17¼ in.; ht. 6 in.). This is different both from the large troughs found in the mounds, and from the funeral bowls of Stratum II (Pl. XLIX, section on EF).

Deep Digging in the Eastern Section.

A large pit, measuring 78 ft. from north to south by 37 ft. wide, was sunk along the north-east corner of the Eastern Section and excavated to a depth of 15 ft. In its northern portion was found, lying on its side in a bed of silt, an ellipsoid jar with collared rim (No. H627) at a depth of 7 ft. 9 in. below the surface, that is to say at a level considerably lower than that of the IInd stratum.

Finds of burial and non-burial types of pottery.

At a depth of 9 ft. and close to the eastern edge of this pit, were found together, but completely broken, the tapering bottom of a medium-sized, earthenware jar, a small *ghaṛā*, and a deep basin with tapering sides—all similar to such vessels found in the mounds. They lay in a four feet thick layer of rubbish consisting of foundation nodules, potsherds, brickbats and ashes. In the southern portion, which was characterised by the absence of soft soil, there were brickbats and potsherds galore and among them part of an upper jaw, hip and other pieces of bovine bones. In the middle portion, however, the soil was hard and absolutely free from such débris.

Group of bones.

Further down and scattered over an area of 30 by 11 ft. in the western half of the southern portion of the deep digging were discovered, at a depth of 11 ft., a large number of fragmentary cattle and other bones. Among them were one complete humerus and the upper part of another, one hip bone and the fragment of another, one scapula, large fragments of three lower jaws, fragments of four horns, pieces of two antlers, a heel consisting of calcaneum, astragalus, and cuboid, a metatarsal and six other fragmentary bones. There were also some phalanges, one vertebra, one fragment of a rib, three heads of femurs, four astragali, and several other bones. In this connection it may be recalled that cattle bones were also recovered at a few places in the earlier strata in Mound F, *viz.*, in the deep digging in Trench I, and in the south-east and south-west corners of the Great Granary.[1] In all these cases, the bones were found lying in a compressed layer of stiff soil which had hardened and preserved them.[2]

Continuity of the Indus sherds in the Cemetery.

Pl. XLVII, *b*, shows a thick layer of soft, riverine deposit casually interrupted by a pocket of rubbish of which the component sherds belong to vessels which were in common use on the mounds. One of these pockets, which is seen in the background, went down to a depth of 15 ft. below the surface. Moreover, from the surface downwards enormous heaps of potsherds were found over a greater part of the area explored in the Cemetery, and the sherds from these deposits, like those from the lower pockets, belong to vessels which were in every day use on the mounds.

---

[1] See pp. 34, 45 and 96 *supra*.

[2] This is the view of the Archæological Chemist in India, *vide* pp. 96-97 *supra*.

Links and parallelism of burial pottery with that from Area G and the mounds.

The offerings' dishes or plates[1] with broad, stemmed bases from the Cemetery presuppose a long period of development. Though their shapes differ considerably from the tall dishes found in the mounds, the connection between them can be seen in the intermediate stage represented by two offerings' dishes (Pl. LXX, 10 and 14) from Area G. An important point worth remembering in respect of their form and structure is that in all cases the dishes, whether they come from the Cemetery, Area G, or the mounds, have a broad base and hollow stem to which the dish was added as a second member, so that, all along, the fundamental conception of this vessel remained the same. Again, the thick dishes of red ware without a standard base (Pl. LXI, 25), of which several examples were found in the Extension of the Western Section of the Cemetery, are also not without parallels from the mounds ;[2] and the carinated pots of Stratum I (Pl. LX, type D) from the Cemetery H were anticipated by a number of small vases of the same shape which were recovered at varying depth from the several mounds, *e.g.*, Nos. 852 and 19 (Pl. LXXIII, 64 and 65) from Mound F ; Nos. 655 and B1566 (Pl. LXXIII, 70 and 72) from Mound AB ; and J176 (Pl. LXXIII, 39) from Area J. Furthermore, the squat, medium-sized, round water pots with broad mouth and well-defined ring-base (Pl. LXI, type H), which were recovered from Stratum II of the Extension of the Western Section of the Cemetery, resemble vase No. D27 (Pl. LXXIII, 51) which was found 4 ft. below the surface in Trench B near the Tomb of *Naugazā*, and No. 5191 (Pl. LXXIII, 40) found in the Extension of Pits I and II in the same mound at a depth of over 3 ft. The round *loṭā*-shaped, medium-sized vase No. H702b (Pl. LXI, 17), also from the Extension of the Western Section, is paralleled by No. 4165 (Pl. LXXIII, 53) found at a depth of 2 ft. 9 in. below the surface in Mound D, and also by sherd No. PIV-64 (Pl. LXXIII, 54) from Pit IV at a depth of 6 ft. below the surface of Mound AB. Let it also be added that on the last four examples cited above even the paintings are similar to those on the examples from Cemetery H. Again, in the round Cemetery vases, with or without a ring-base, this resemblance in shape, as well as decoration, is put beyond question when we compare vases Nos. 1022[3] and D28[4] (Pl. LXXIII, 50 and 52) with Nos. H702c and H703b from the Cemetery (*cf.* Pl. LXI, 14), or the painting on vase No. 1284 (Pl. LXXIII, 68) which was found 3 ft. below the surface in Trench I, Mound F, with  motif which is employed to fill the space around the deer and peacock on the flat covers illustrated in Pl. LXIV, 4, 5 and 8.

Links with Mound F.

This evident relationship between the burial pottery and the pottery from the mounds was brought out still more clearly by the discovery of a heap of potsherds and animal bones (Pl. XXVII, *c*) in Extension II of Trench VI on the eastern slope of Mound F. These sherds comprised numerous fragments which were typical of the burial pottery from the Cemetery, and ohters equally typical of secular wares found in the mounds. Among the former were many

[1] *Cf. M. I. C.*, Pls. LXXVIII, 8, and LXXIX, 4.

[2] Dish No. 4509, which was found on a small paving in the Eastern Extension of the Great Granary Area, is of a very similar shape.

[3] This was found in the Great Granary Area at a depth of 2 ft. below surface.

[4] This was found in Trench B near the tomb of *Naugazā* at a depth of 4 ft. below surface.

characteristic collared rims with or without a flange (*e.g.*, Pl. LXXIII, 42, 44, and 49), fragments of jars with the finger-groove or finger-tip patterning on them (Pl. LXXIII, 46 and 55), several ring-bases and necks of flasks like those used to stopper the burial jars in Stratum I. In addition to them, there were several fragments typical of the funeral pottery of Stratum II including the upper and lower parts of squat offerings' dishes (Pl. LXXIII, 47, 58 and 59), three fragments of offerings' plates (Pl. LXXIII, 57, 61, and 62), two necks of *kalaśas* (Pl. LXXIII, 63), a fragment of the upper part of a bowl (Pl. LXXIII, 60), two halves and smaller fragments of flat, painted covers (Pl. LXXIII. 45). Already before the discovery of this heap, we had picked up to the south of it and not far away, a few fragments of flat painted covers typical of Stratum II in the Cemetery. Besides the above examples, fragments of squat and ribbed offerings' dishes, necks of *kalaśas*, and fragments of the body of jars with the finger-groove and finger-tip patterning on them were also found near the surface of the Trench at the Southern Edge of Mound AB, as well as elsewhere on the same mound. The cumulative evidence of these potsherds found in large numbers on and near the surface of the eastern slope of Mound F, and from all over the highest Mound AB, which is one of the latest mounds at Harappā, throws a valuable side light on the date of the Cemetery H, which may confidently be assigned to the latest period of the prehistoric Indus Culture, as it manifested itself at Harappā after Mohenjo-daro had ceased to be. In this view I am confirmed by the comparatively bold and highly developed forms of the burial pottery as a whole, and also by the distinctly more advanced character of their paintings as compared with those on the bulk of the pottery from the mounds. Parenthetically, however, let me add that there are several examples of burial-pots in which the lower parts, which were separately made, are not symmetrically joined with the upper part. Similarly also, there are a number of flasks of which the forms are imperfectly developed. These defects, however, are likely to have been due merely to inferior workmanship or cheaper production.

With Mound AB.

More developed forms.

Little Stratigraphical difference between Strata I and II.

Now, as sherds typical of burial pottery of Strata I and II were, in many cases, found mixed up together on the mounds, it is unlikely that the two strata were separated from each other by any very great length of time, and the fact that in the Cemetery itself there is not much débris between them lends further support to this view. Further, in so far as earth-burials must be inhumed at a safely low level, the mere fact that pot-burials lay above them or at a higher level would not necessarily indicate an earlier date for the former; indeed it is quite conceivable that the two strata, which are not separated by any structural remains, may be more or less contemporary. On the other hand, so far as the methods of disposing of the dead are concerned, there is a radical difference between earth-burials, complete or fractional, of the IInd stratum, and the later post-exposure pot-burials of the top stratum, so much so that it is difficult to escape the conclusion that this sudden and startling change from one kind of burial to the other within a comparatively short space of time was due to some racial or cultural upheaval brought about by the immigration of a foreign people into this district of the Panjāb. And

Sudden change in burial customs explained.

the craniological evidence summarised below by Dr.[1] Guha goes to support this inference; for it indicates that the large-headed dolichocephalic type with well-developed supraorbital ridges and high cranial roof, long face and prominent nose which has been recovered from the earth-burials of Stratum II had undergone a definite admixture with a small low-headed type of people, by the time we come to the pot-burials of the upper stratum. In other words, that, while the skulls from Area G and from the IInd stratum of the Cemetery show a continuity of the Indus People of Harappā and Mohenjo-daro, a fresh element in the population is evidenced by the skulls recovered from the top stratum of the Cemetery.

Conclusion.

In describing the IInd stratum I observed that while some of the earth-burials were unaccompanied by any pottery at all, in others the pottery varied in quantity, and in others new types of vessels came into common use. Thus, in the Extension of the Western Section, flat dishes took the place of the standard offerings' dishes and a single vessel was substituted for the bowl and water-pot which were commonly met with in the Eastern Section. In this way, not only a marked change had taken place in the character of funeral pottery, but more important still was the unexpected change from complete to fractional burials, which were rare in the Eastern Section. But whether this change from complete to fractional burials, with the simplification of the pottery forms, marked an intermediate stage between the fractional burials of the Eastern Section and the post-exposure pot-burials of Stratum I is open to question. That the fractional burials of Stratum II had undergone previous exposure seems to me highly probable, since otherwise many of them could hardly have been so fragmentary; in any case they were invariably inhumed directly in the earth, in contrast with the later burials of Stratum I which were inhumed in pots.

Inference from parallels to burial pottery.

The burials described above in the Ist and IInd strata of this Cemetery are quite distinct from the post-cremation burials which were the fashion during the Indus Period, as evidenced by many examples both at Harappā and Mohenjo-daro.[2] Nevertheless, in view of the marked similarity of much of the later pottery found on the city sites with that found in these burials, it is impossible, as I have already pointed out, to divorce the latter from the Indus Culture, or to assume a complete break in the continuity of that culture. In my view, the burials belong to the latest phase of the Indus Culture represented at Harappā—a phase which was not reached at Mohenjo-daro—but I think that substantial changes must have been introduced into this culture as a result of foreign conquest or immigration and that these changes are sufficient to explain the new fashions in burial practices. In order to show more clearly the relationship between the pottery from the city and that from the Cemetery I have tabulated separately in Chapter VII, 95 examples of painted pottery from the mounds. Their shapes, texture and paintings are so typical of the Cemetery wares that they are virtually indistinguishable (Pls. LXV and LXVI).

[1] See pp. 238-39 *infra*.
[2] See chap. VIII *infra*, and Sir John Marshall, *op. cit.*, pp. 86-89.

Evidence of fractional burial from Mound AB.

Apropos of the pot-burials, I must once again refer to my discovery of a group of two human skulls, one lower jaw, and some other bones in Mound[1] AB. They came to light at a depth of 10 to 11 ft. below the surface between the IIIrd and IVth strata. As already pointed out, if these remains had been deposited in an urn, instead of in the earth the result would not be far different from such a pot-burial as No. 3934c.[2] This find, which has been assigned by Sir John Marshall to about the Late III Period of Mohenjo-daro,[3] provides another link between the Cemetery and the town settlements.

Earth-Burials of Nāl, Musyān, and Shāhi-tump.

In Balūchistān, both at Nāl in the Jhalāwān District to the east, and at Shāhī-tump near Turbat to the south-west earth-burials were found by Mr. Hargreaves and Sir Aurel Stein. Summarizing the results of these discoveries Sir John Marshall writes[4] "At the former site some of the skeletons were provided with definite graves, others were laid in the bare earth, but in no case were they accompanied by pottery or other sepulchral furniture, though some of them had beads and other simple personal ornaments.

"These complete burials at Nāl are ascribed by Mr. Hargreaves to the same age as the fractional burials on the same site, in which, as we shall presently see, the human remains were accompanied by numerous vessels containing food and drink, and by other objects for the use of the dead. If Mr. Hargreaves is correct in this view—and there is no reason to question it—then the complete as well as the fractional burials at Nāl must be contemporary with the typical Nāl pottery which, according to Sir Aurel Stein, does not make its appearance until relatively late in the Chalcolithic Age. Complete and fractional burials are found also side by side at Musyān in Western Persia, and are seemingly contemporary, but in that area fractional burials appear to be the exception rather than the rule, whereas at Nāl it is just the reverse.

"The burials of Shāhī-tump, which occur in the latest strata on the top of the mounds, are believed by Sir Aurel Stein to be slightly earlier than those of Nāl. The bodies are laid in the earth, generally on their backs or left sides, and facing the north. About them, especially at the head and back were many bowls and other vessels of earthenware, containing the charred bones of lambs, goats, and other burnt offerings for the dead. With them, too, was a variety of other articles such as stone beads, copper celts, spear-heads and the like".

Their comparison and contrast with the Harappā earth-burials.

In general the earth-burials of Stratum II of the Cemetery H at Harappā are comparable, so far as the method of inhumation is concerned, to those of Nāl and Musyān, and the complete burials also to those of Shāhī-tump. Nevertheless, it may be added that at Harappā the fractional earth-burials are neither exceptional as at Musyān, nor of such frequent occurrence as they are at Nāl, though the evidence so far recovered points to a preponderance of complete burials. The shapes, as well as the paintings on the burial pottery from Nāl and Shāhī-tump are entirely different from those of the funerary vessels from the

[1] *Cf.* pp. 161-62 *supra.*

[2] For contents of this pot see pp. 211-12 *supra.*

[3] *Cf. M. I. C.*, p. 84.

[4] *Ibid.*, pp. 81-82.

IInd stratum in the Harappā Cemetery. In no case were the latter accompanied by any weapons, personal ornaments[1], or even beads. On the other hand, the charred bones of lambs, goats, etc., which Sir Aurel Stein found in the Balūchī graves were paralleled in several earth-burials at Harappā by the sacrifice of sheep or goat which in one case (burial No. H698) was laid alongside the dead body, and in several others its remains were found lying between the grave furniture and the dead person. In this connection it may be recalled, again, that in *Ṛigveda*, X, 16, 4, Agni is asked to consume the sacrificed goat which is his share and to carry, without injuring, the dead man to the region of the pious. And here, too, I must remind the reader of the identification which I proposed of the pre-Āryan bulls painted on the burial-pot No. H206b with the prototypes of the Anustaraṇi and Vaitaraṇi cows[2] of the Ṛigvedic Āryans. Let it be added that the Āryan custom of sacrificing a cow or goat alluded to in the Ṛigveda relates to cremation,[3] not to burial, though the reference to the removal of the bow (and arrow) from the dead man's hands by the younger brother of the deceased points clearly to burial.[4] Cremation and burial were both practised by the Ṛigvedic Āryans.[5] Nor is there any reason why the pre-existing non-Āryan sacrifice, which may well have been borrowed by the Āryans, should not have been modified by them to suit their own customs and beliefs. Clearly there is an *a priori* probability of such borrowing on the part of the Vedic Āryans from a people whom they found in possession of a relatively advanced state of civilization.[6]

Evidence of paintings.

Before leaving the subject of collateral evidence from Balūchistān, it may be added that there are many significant parallels between the burial pottery from Harappā and many of the wares collected by Sir Aurel Stein from Chalcolithic sites not only in Balūchistān but in Gedrosia as well. The superior Cemetery wares from Harappā with bright red or pink colouring are analogous to some of the pottery from Moghal-Ghuṇḍai and Periano-Ghuṇḍai in Zhob valley and Mehi in Gedrosia; and the similarity between them is observable not only in the fabric, but in the shapes of some of the vessels and in some of their paintings. Thus the row of 'flying birds'[7] motif (separated by sets of vertical lines) on sherd M.M.E.6 from Moghal Ghuṇḍai,[8] and the same motif placed in various positions on sherds P23, P.S.W. 34, P.N.E. 1 from Periano Ghuṇḍai,[9] etc., is almost identical with the accessory ornaments on the pots illustrated in Pl. LXII, 1*b* and 11, etc. Again, the double line chevron on Mehi II.8.1, Mehi II.9.13,[10] etc.,

Evidence of Balūchistān pottery.

[1] A female earth-burial No. H 788 recently found in the Eastern Section of the Cemetery (Square S 34/6) which was accompanied by the usual grave furniture wore a gold bangle on her left wrist.

[2] See p. 208 *supra*.

[3] X, 16. 4.

[4] X, 18, 9.

[5] A. B. Keith, *Religion and Philosophy of the Veda*, p. 417.

[6] Sir John Marshall, *op. cit.*, Preface, pp. V-VIII.

[7] Sir Aurel Stein calls it 'sigma' motif. *Cf. Mem. A. S. I.*, No. 43, p. 34 (Pl. I, Z. W. 1) and p. 36 (Pl. II, B. R. 3), etc.

[8] *Mem. A. S. I.*, No. 37, Pl. XI.

[9] *Ibid.*, Pls. V and VII.

[10] *Mem. A. S. I.*, No. 43, Pl. XXX.

may be matched by paintings on the Harappā pots figured in Pl. LXIII, 1*a* and 1*b*, 19, etc. In addition to the above, there are a few more sites in Gedrosia, notably Gate-dap and Kambar ḍamb where, despite its different colour and fabric, some of the pottery shows a distinct resemblance in painted designs to some of the Harappā Cemetery wares. For instance, the wavy line motifs turned to one side or the other on sherds G.D.6[1] and Kamb. 42 (unillustrated) resemble those on the burial-pots illustrated in the Harappā Pl. LXII, 1*b* over and behind the right hand animal and on No. 14 of the same plate. Again, the continuous double line chevron on the open bowl Kamb. 2[2] may be compared with the Harappā paintings in Pl. LXIII, 1*a* and 1*b* and 21. The highly conventionalised tree motif on Kamb. 1[3] and Kamb. 17 (unillustrated) has close parallels in the paintings on the Harappā pots figured in Pl. LXIII, 15, 19 and, particularly, 18. Although such examples may easily be multiplied, the above will suffice for my present purpose as I wish merely to draw attention to the cultural connection evidenced by these ceramic wares between Harappā and some of the Chalcolithic sites in North Balūchistān and Gedrosia. This evidence taken with what has already been said in comparing the earth-burials of Stratum II with those of Nāl, Musyān and Shāhī-tump would seem to indicate for the Cemetery a date intermediate between certain sites in Northern Balūchistān and Gedrosia to which pointed reference has been called above and the earth-burials of Nāl.

Racial types represented by the Cemetery.

As to the craniological evidence recovered from the Cemetery H, Dr. B. S. Guha, Anthropologist to the *Zoological Survey of India*, observes as follows: " From the foregoing account of the comparative characters of the skulls it is clear that the racial types represented in the collection comprise a large-headed, dolichocephalic people with well-developed supra-orbital ridges and high cranial roof, long face and prominent nose. This type is represented specially in the open burial remains but is also found in the G site; and in the Jar-burials there is at least one skeleton, *viz.*, No. H 255, which definitely belongs to this type. This type is closely allied to the Mohenjo-daro I, and SK1 M 28 excavated by Dr. Mackay from Mohenjo-daro subsequently. It resembles also in shape and proportions, the Al-'Ubaid skulls and the 'massive' type of Kish crania described by Keith and Buxton and the predynastic Kawamil skulls from Upper Egypt.

" To conclude this brief review of the racial types found at Harappā, there is no reason to doubt the continued presence of the races of the Late Indus Valley Period of Mohenjo-daro in the earlier epochs as seen from the G site and open burial remains. But with the introduction of the Jar-burials indicating probably a considerable gap of time,[4] a definite admixture with a small, low-headed race, such as is seen among the present aboriginal population of India, is strongly indicated. The Harappā remains also demonstrate the presence of a non-Armenoid, and probably also of an Armenoid-Alpine-race in the Indus Valley during

---

[1] *Mem. A. S. I.*, No. 43, Pl. XX.

[2] & [3] *Ibid.*, Pl. XXV.

[4] See, however, pp. 10, 11 & 234. M. S. Vats.

the Chalcolithic times, whose presence was surmised at Mohenjo-daro from the presence of a single skull of a child."[1]

Note on the decay of human skulls from the Cemetery H by Dr. M. A. Hamid, Assistant Archæological Chemist.

The following is the analysis of the specimen of soil:—

	Per cent.
Moisture	1·09
Gypsum	0·29
Sodium chloride and other salts	0·29
Lime	4·22
Magnesia	0·57
Carbon dioxide	2·98
Phosphoric and hydride	0·99
Ferric oxide alumina	9·53
Insolubles	77·14
Carbonaceous matter, etc.	2·70
TOTAL	99·80

Bone consists of (1) combustible organic matter and (2) non-combustible inorganic matter. The non-combustible inorganic or mineral matter is composed chiefly of phosphate and in lesser amount of carbonate of lime besides very small amounts of magnesium, chlorine, fluorine, etc. Lime even if added intentionally in the caustic form would soon change to carbonate in the presence of so much decaying organic matter. It seems to me that the disintegration of skulls is due not to the presence of lime but to the scarcity of it.

The proportion of fatty and mineral matter in the bones varies with age. Thus in the children it has been found that the ash increases with the advance in years. It would appear, therefore, that the skulls of the infants are more liable to disintegration and decay (due to the scarcity of lime salts and predominance of organic matter) than those of adults. It may be that the jars in which the bones have disintegrated contained skulls of infants.[2]

Khan Bahadur Mohammad Sana Ullah, Archæological Chemist in India, agrees with the above conclusions of Dr. M. A. Hamid, subject to the following remarks:—

Bones are composed of organic and inorganic matter. When bones are buried in the soil, the former constituent undergoes decomposition rapidly, giving rise to the formation of carbonic acid and ammonium compounds besides other products. The inorganic or mineral residue consists chiefly of calcium phosphate and lesser amounts of calcium carbonate. This substance undergoes hydrolysis in waters charged with carbonic acid, resulting in its gradual dissolution, but

[1] Personal communication.

[2] This is interesting, but the conclusion is not justified by facts since in many cases bones of infants are much better preserved whereas those of adults have utterly crumbled. A more probable reason for the preservation or decay of bones might have been found in the immediate environments of each burial and other contributory causes. —M. S. VATS.

this reaction is retarded or stopped altogether if sufficient lime or other calcium salts are present. It is, therefore, obvious that if lime had been added intentionally, it would have acted rather as a preservative, and not as a destructive agent of the bones, as has been suggested. The presence of about 4 per cent. lime in the earth cannot be intentional, as small amounts of lime are invariably present in the soils.

Moreover, the presence of ammonium salts, chlorides and sulphates in the percolating waters would also tend to increase the dissolution of the mineral or inorganic portion. The ammonium salts are formed, as stated above, by the decomposition of the organic matter of the bones themselves, as well as that which is generally present in the soil. The soil at Harappā is also heavily charged with alkaline chlorides and sulphates. It is, however, obvious that the conditions prevailing in the soil where these skulls were found, are all favourable to the gradual dissolution of the bony material. I might add that the broken condition of the jars would facilitate the elimination of the solution resulting from these reactions and thus prevent the concentration of calcium salts. It is on this account that something of the bones still remains in the closed jars, which have been found intact, while mere traces of the skulls have remained in the broken ones.

APPENDIX I.

Table of the Contents of Burial-pots of Stratum I from the Cemetery H.

APPEN

TABLE OF THE CONTENTS OF BURIAL-POTS OF

Abbreviations used

Plus	+
Fragments	†
Child	(O)
Left	(L)
Duplicate	*

Serial Number.	Field register number.	Shape of pot.	Height in inches.	Reference to types in Pl. LXI.	Skull.	Mandible.	Vertebræ.	Sacrum.	Sternum.	Ribs.	Clavicle.	Scapula.	Humerus.	Ulna.	Radius.	Carpals.
1	2	3	4	5	6		7		8	9	10	11	12	13	14	15
1	H61	Ellipsoid . . .	19½	A, 5 & 8	1	1†	5+1	1	..	2	1	1(L)	2	2	1†	..
2	H146b	Do. . . .	14½	A, 5 & 8	1	1	5	..	..	1	1(R)	..	..	..	..	..
3	H153a	Ellipsoid, with neck flange and ring-base.	14½	A, 3, 4 and 7.	1	1	8	..	1	3	1(R)	1(R)	2	2	2	..
4	H153c	Ellipsoid . . .	13	A, 5 & 8	1†	..	..	..	..	..	..	..	..	..	..	..
5	H156d	Do. (fragments) .	17½	A, 5 & 8	1†	..	..	..	..	4†	..	2	2+1†	2	1†(R)	..
6	H154a	Ellipsoid, with neck flange.	21½	A, 6	1	..	14	1	..	10	2	1†(L)	3	2	2	1
7	H168	Ellipsoid . . .	..	A, 5 & 8	1	1	9	1	..	2	1(R)	..	2	2	2	..
8	H206a	Do. . . .	23½	A, 5 & 8	1	1	22	1	..	16†+1	2	2	2	2	2	..
9	H206c	Do. . . .	22	A, 5 & 8	..	1	10	1	1	..	1(R)	2	2	2	2	11
10	H206d	Do. . . .	22	A, 5 & 8	1	1	23	1	..	11	2	2	2	2	2	13
11	H206f	Do. . . .	21½	A, 5 & 8	1	1	13	1	..	2	2	2	2	2	1(R)	4
12	H206g	Round (fragmentary) .	13½	C, 12	..	..	..	..	..	..	..	1(R)	..	..	..	..
13	H231a	Ellipsoid . . .	22	A, 5 & 8	1†	1†	1	..	..	4	1(R)	..	..	..	2	..
14	H231b	Do. . . .	..	A, 5 & 8	1†	..	..	..	..	10	1(R)	1†	1†(R)	1†(R)	4†	..
15	H245a	Ellipsoid with flange at neck and cordon round body.	23	A, 1, and 2	1	1	24	1	..	13	1(L)	2	..	..	..	..
16	H245c	Ellipsoid, with neck flange.	22	A, 6	..	..	..	..	..	..	..	..	1†	..	1†	..
17	H245d	Ellipsoid . . .	18	A, 5 & 8	1†	..	..	..	..	11	2	..	2	2	1(R)	..
18	H245e	Do. . . .	19	A, 5 & 8	1	1	18	1	1	4	1(R)	2	2	2	2	4
19	H246c	Do. . . .	..	A, 5 & 8	1	1	5	1	..	..	2	1(L)	2†	2†	1†(R)	1
20	H246d	Do. . . .	..	A, 5 & 8	0	1	17	1	..	20†	..	1(L)	..	..	..	..
21	H246e	Do. . . .	21	A, 5 & 8	1	1†	31	1+1*	1	8	1†(R)	2	2	2	2	10
22	H247a	Ellipsoid, with neck flange.	21½	A, 6	1† (O)	..	16	1	..	21	2	2	2+1 (O)	2	2	5
23	H247b	Do. . .	..	A, 6	1	1	19	1	1	7	2	2	2	2	2	6
24	H249	Ellipsoid . . .	20	A, 5 & 8	1	..	2	..	..	..	1†	..	2	2	2+1 (O)	..
25	H250	Do. . . .	18	A, 5 & 8	1†	..	19	1(O)	..	10	2	2	1†	..	1†	..
26	H253b	Do. . . .	..	A, 5 & 8	1†	1	..	..	..	..	..	2	2	1†	..	..
27	H255a	Do. . . .	19½	A, 5 & 8	1	1	21	1+1*	1	6	2	2	2	2	2	12
28	H344	Do. . . .	19½	A, 5 & 8	1	1	..	..	..	2	1†(R)	..	2†	..	2†	..
29	H346a	Ellipsoid, with neck flange.	22	A, 6	1†	..	1†	1†	..	1	..	..	..	..	..	..
30	H346b	Round (fragmentary) .	13½	C, 12	1	1	14	..	..	8	2	2	2	2	2	..

DIX I.

Stratum I from the Cemetery H.

in the table :—

Right . . . . . (R)
Shafts of long bones . . . SLB
Heads of long bones . . . HLB
Epiphyses . . . . Epi

Metacarpals. 16	Ungual phalanges. 17	Os innominatum. 18	Femur. 19	Patella. 20	Tibia. 21	Fibula. 22	Tarsals. 23	Metatarsals. 24	Phalanges. 25	Unidentified fragments. 26	Representing one or more skeletons. 27	Animal bones accompanying. 28	Remarks. 29	Serial Number. 1
..	..	1†(L)	2	..	2	1†	2	..	..	2	1	..		1
..	5	..	..	..	..	..	6	4	..	6SLB+4	1	..	Bones worn out.	2
6	3	2	1†	..	1†	2	2	8	2	6SLB+1	1	..	Most of the long bones were fragmentary.	3
..	..	..	..	..	..	..	..	..	..	..	1	..	Contained only a fragment of skull.	4
..	..	1†(R)	2	..	1	2	11	6	5	..	1	..	Skull represented by left maxilla and zygoma.	5
5	11	2	2	1(O)	2+1† (O)	1+1 (O)	4	6−3* −2*	6	..	4	..	Also contained one patella, one tibia, and one fibula of a child and metatarsals of two other adults.	6
2	3	2	2	..	2	2	5	4	1	3	1	..	Bones worn out.	7
0	7	2	2	1 (L)	2	2	6	7	7	106LB+5	1	..	Bones worn out.	8
7	11	2	2	2	2	2	14	9	7	..	1	..		9
10	15	2	2	2	2	2	16	10	19	45LB+2	1	..		10
1	3	1(L)	2	1(L)	2	2	5	6	6	..	1	2 fragments of animal ribs (?).		11
..	..	..	..	..	..	..	..	..	..	..	1	..	Contained one scapula only.	12
..	..	2†	1(R)	..	2	..	..	1	..	15LB	1	..	Bones fragmentary.	13
1	2	1†	2	..	2	..	..	1	..	1	1	2 long bones of a bird (?).		14
1	2	2	2	..	..	1	..	..	..	..	2	..	Also contained small fragments of the skull of an infant.	15
..	1	..	Fragments of the shaft of long bones.							4	1	..	Represented only by 7 bits of bones.	16
..	5	2	1(L)	..	..	..	..	7	..	7SLB	1	Bones of 2 rodents (?).	Bones much worn out.	17
8	7	2	2	2	2	2	9	4	6	..	1	..		18
8	14	2†	2†	2	2†	0	1	0	7	..	1	..		19
..	..	1(L)	2	..	..	1†	1	..	..	25LB+2	1	..		20
6	9	2	2	1(L)	2	2	10	4	7	..	2	..	Also contained fragment of a second sacrum.	21
7	11	2+1 †(O)	2+1 (O)	2	2+2 (O)	2	10	7	3	6SLB	2	..	Mixed with the fragments of a child's skeleton.	22
10	14	2	2	1(R)	2	2	9	5	5	..	1	..		23
3	2	1†(R)	2	..	1†	..	3	4	5	..	2	..	Also contained one epiphysis of radius of a child.	24
..	4	7	2	..	2	2	1	4	1	2	1	..	Bones much worn out.	25
2	8	..	2	..	2	2	1	2	..	..	1	..		26
10	16	2	2	1(L)	2	2	14	10	14	..	2	..	Also contained fragment of a second sacrum.	27
..	..	1†(R)	2†	..	2†	..	2	5	2	..	1	..	Most of the bones were very fragmentary.	28
..	..	..	..	..	..	..	..	..	..	..	1	..	Represented only by 4 bits of bones.	29
4	14	2	2	..	2	1†	4	6	5	7	1	..	Bones much worn out.	30

APPEN

Serial number. 1	Field register number. 2	Shape of pot. 3	Height in inches. 4	Reference to types in Pl. LXI. 5	Skull. 6	Mandible. 6	Vertebræ. 7	Sacrum. 7	Sternum. 8	Ribs. 9	Clavicle. 10	Scapula. 11	Humerus. 12	Ulna. 13	Radius. 14	Carpals. 15
31	H620b	Ellipsoid, with neck flange.	23	A, 5 & 8	1	1	5	..	..	1	..	1(L)	2	1(L)	1(L)	..
32	H151b	Carinated . . .	8½	D, 15-17									Fourteen fragments of the			
33	H167	Do. . . .	22	D, 15-17	1?	1?	..	..	..	5?	..	..	..	1?	..	..
					..	1? (O)	..	..	..	..	..	..	..	..	..	..
34	H62d	Round, with finger-tip patterning (fragmentary).	15½	C, 14	2?	..	..	..	..	..	..	..	..	..	..	..
35	H62e	Do. (fragmentary) .	14½	C, 14	..	..	..	..	..	2	..	1?	..	..	..	..
36	H88	Do. .	18½	C, 14	1	1	19	..	..	4	1(L)	2	2	2	1(L)	..
37	H246a	Do. (fragmentary) .	..	C, 14	1?	..	..	..	..	..	..	..	..	..	..	..
38	H148b	Do. .	11	C, 14	1	1	..	..	..	..	..	..	..	2	..	..
39	H152c	Do. .	17½	C, 14								Unidentified fragments of charred				
40	H187	Do. (fragmentary) .	13½	C, 14	1?	..	..	..	..	..	..	..	..	..	..	..
41	H206b	Round, with finger-groove patterning.	13½	C, 13	1?	1?								Two fragments		
42	H231c	Do. .	..	C, 13	1?	..	22	..	..	14	1?	2?	1(R)	1(R)	1(L)	..
43	H231d	Round, with finger-tip patterning.	12	C, 14	..	..	..	..	..	..	..	..	..	..	..	..
44	H154b	Round, with neck flange.	14½	C, 12									Twenty fragments of charred			
45	H235	Ellipsoid, with neck flange and cordon round body.	14½	A, 1 & 2	..	..	..	..	..	..	..	..	..	..	..	..
46	H251	Round, with neck flange.	..	C, 12	1?	1? (O)	..	..	..	3	..	..	..	..	..	..
47	H342a	Round, with finger-groove patterning (fragmentary).	20	C, 13	1?	..	..	..	..	..	..	..	..	..	..	..
48	H148a	Ellipsoid, with flange at neck and cordon round body.	..	A, 2	Babies buried in embryonic position.											
49	H156	Round . . .	17	..												
50	H165a	Round, with finger-groove patterning.	13	C, 13												
51	H185b	Round, with finger-tip patterning.	14½	C, 14												
52	H169	Round (fragmentary) .	..	..												
53	H619	Round, with finger-tip patterning.	15	C, 14												
54	H622	Round, with finger-groove patterning.	9½	C, 13												
55	H625	Round, with finger-tip patterning.	14	C, 14												
56	H673	Oval, with projecting base.	12½	..												
57	H679	Round, with finger-tip patterning.	8	C, 14												

In jars Nos. H150, H346a, H246b, H673 and H697

DIX I—*concld.*

Metacarpals. 16	Ungual phalanges. 17	Os innominatum. 18	Femur. 19	Patella. 20	Tibia. 21	Fibula. 22	Tarsals. 23	Metatarsals. 24	Phalanges. 25	Unidentified fragments. 26	Representing one or more skeletons. 27	Animal bones accompanying. 28	REMARKS. 29	Serial Number. 1
10	3	1(L)	2	..	2	2	2	..	..	..	1	..	Bones much worn out.	31
shafts of long bones.								2	2	3	1	..	All very much fragmentary.	32
..	..	..	..	..	..	..	..	3†	..	33LB	2	..	Bones very much fragmentary. Also contained fragmentary mandible, etc., of a child.	33
..	4(O)	..	..	..	..	..	1	4(O)	..	1(O)5LB	..	..		
..	1	3†	..	..	..	..	2	..	..	9+43LB	2	..	Bones very few and fragmentary, also contained 3 fragments of epiphyses of long bones of a child.	34
..	..	..	..	..	..	..	..	..	..	3	1	..	Bones very few and fragmentary.	35
..	5	2	1†	..	1†	2	..	10 (2)	..	..	1	..	Contained a baby laid in embryonic position.	36
..	..	..	..	..	..	..	..	..	..	..	1	..	Contained only a skull fragment.	37
..	..	..	..	..	..	..	..	..	..	188LB+1	1	..	Bones fragmentary.	38
and uncharred bones.								12	..	..	1	..	Bones fragmentary.	39
..	..	..	..	..	..	..	..	..	..	75LB	1	..	Bones fragmentary.	40
of long bones.											1	..	Contained only four fragments of bones.	41
..	7	2	4	..	..	2	1	3	3	9Epi	1	Bones of a rodent.	Bones worn out.	42
..	..	..	..	..	..	..	..	..	..	..	..	Antler (?)	.	43
and uncharred bones (unidentified).													Bones fragmentary.	44
..	..	..	2	..	2	1†	5	5	9	..	1	..	Contained bones only of the lower extremity.	45
..	..	..	..	..	..	..	..	..	..	125LB	3	..		46
..	..	..	..	..	..	..	..	..	..	..	1	..	Contained only a skull fragment.	47
														48
														49
														50
														51
														52
														53
														54
														55
														56
														57

the bones were preserved in position for exhibition.

CHAPTER VII.

Painted Potsherds from various mounds and their Classification.

See Pls. LXV—LXVIII.

Fundamental difference between burial and household pottery.

The painted potsherds figured in the above-mentioned plates, which were found in various mounds and trenches, belong to two distinct classes. Those illustrated in Pls. LXV and LXVI are entirely similar in texture, wash, shape, and paintings to the burial pottery from Strata I and II in the Cemetery H, and so dissimilar from the ordinary household ware, found at Harappā and Mohenjo-daro (Pls. LXVII and LXVIII) that even a small fragment among the latter can be picked out at a glance.

Difference in the composition and mixing of clay.

Whereas the household pottery is usually made of a comparatively coarse clay, the clay of the burial ware is of fine grain, better levigated and puddled, a little softer, and therefore a trifle more plastic—characteristics which are commonly shared by the better class post-cremation urns from the mounds, *e.g.*, the large and well made deeper troughs and the napiform jars. And whereas the prevailing colour of the household ware that is the red-and-black[1] Indus ware is light red or salmon on which the painting is executed in black, sherds of the other class are of a decidedly deeper red colour with brighter slip on which the black painting becomes automatically more pronounced.

Difference in colour.

Shapes.

Again, with the exception of two examples, *viz.*, medium-sized, squat jars (Nos. 2 and 46), and a flanged, bowl-like cover (No. 45) the shapes of the vessels represented by the sherds figured in Pls. LXV and LXVI, are similar to those found in Strata I and II of Cemetery H (Pls. LX and LXI), but in sharp contrast with the shapes of the household vessels.

Paintings.

Paintings on this burial pottery betray a distinct preference for animal motifs, such as the goat, deer, bull and peacock, kites and fishes, as well as, for plants, trees, stars, leaves, etc. On the other hand, household wares show an equally strong bias in favour of geometrical patterns and other linear forms. True, animal forms are sometimes also depicted on household potsherds; for instance, the peacock on Nos. 51-53, and 56 and fish on Nos. 57 and 58 in Pl. LXVIII, but the delineation differs from that of corresponding figures on Nos. 7-11, and 15-19 and 21 in Pl. LXV.

Different treatment of accidental common motifs.

Below is a tabulated list of the potsherds figured in Pls. LXV and LXVI with remarks on their shapes and paintings with special reference to analogues among the Cemetery H wares. The remarks on the sherds in Pls. LXVII and LXVIII are concerned only with their paintings, since their shapes, which are typical of the Indus wares, are already well-known from *M. I. C.*

[1] For the explanation of this nomenclature *cf.* Sir John Marshall, *op. cit.*, p. 97.

Descriptive Table of sherds illustrated in Pls. LXV and LXVI, with shapes and paintings typical of burial pottery from the Cemetery H.

For reference to types see Pls. LX and LXI.

Serial No.	Register No.	Depth in feet.	Stratum.	Mound and Trench.	Description.	Type.	Description of paintings and references to similar paintings on burial pottery.
1	6140	0·5	I	F. Trench IV .	Fragment of the upper part of a large, ellipsoid jar.	A	Nos. 1-6 exhibit the figures of deer. *Cf.* Pl. LXIV, 1-6.
2	3098	1·25	I	F. Trench III .	Fragment of the upper part of a medium-sized squat jar; shape not represented in burial pottery.	..	
3	11738	0·3	I	AB. Trench at the southern Edge.	Fragment of the upper part of a large, ellipsoid jar.	A	
4	11481	0·3	I	F. Trench VI .	Ditto . .	A	
5	12305	15-18	VII	AB. Trench at the Southern Edge.	Ditto . .	A	
6	3352	0·3	I	Area J. Trench III.	Half of a flat cover . .	M	
7	5194	3-6	II	AB. Extension of Pits I and II.	Fragment of a large thick walled jar. Shape not clear.	..	Nos. 7-11 are decorated with peacocks of which 7-9, and 11 resemble the peacock illustrated in Pl. LXIV, 8, while No. 10 is similar to the peacock in Pl. LXIII, 12.
8	7447	0·3	I	Ditto .	Fragment of a large ellipsoid jar.	A	
9	7417	0·3	I	Ditto .	Ditto . .	A	
10	1900	3-6	II	F. Trench III .	Ditto . .	A	
11	B354	0·4	II	AB. Trench B.	Ditto . .	A	
12	..	..	..	..	Fragment of a large footless dish.	L	Decorated with figures standing round the centre of the dish. The design is not paralleled by any known painting on burial pottery.
13	3098	1·25	I	F. Trench III .	Fragment of a large ellipsoid jar.	A	Nos. 13 and 14 are decorated with the figures of quadrupeds whose body is drawn only in outline. Standing on the body of No. 13 is the lower part of a human figure.
14	..	..	..	..	Ditto . .	A	
15	11744	0·3	I	AB. Trench at the Southern Edge.	Fragment of a very large and thick ellipsoid (?) jar.	A (?)	Nos. 15-19, 21 and 73 are decorated with fishes. *Cf.* Pl. LXIII 1 (*a* and *b*), and Pl. LXII. 3, 7 and 10.
16	A610	2	I	F. Great Granary Area.	Fragment of a water-pot .	E, 19	
17	B1290	7·5	II	AB. Trench B.	Half of a tarboosh-shaped lid such as covered pot-burial No. H148a of type A.	*Cf.* lid of No. 2, Pl. LX.	
18	10836	0·3	I	F. Trench IV .	Fragment of a round jar .	C	
19	B1391	20	IV	AB. Trench B .	Ditto . . .	C	
20	11438	9-12	IV	F. Trench VI .	Fragment of a round jar .	C	This is painted with peacocks of which only the tails are left. *Cf.* Pl. LXII, 6.
21	..	..	..	..	Fragment of a food plate .	F, 21	
22	11737	0·3	I	AB. Trench at the Southern Edge.	Fragment of a round jar .	C	Decorated with halves of birds(?). *Cf.* Pl. LXII, 16.
23	3177	3-6	II	Area J. Trench III.	Fragment of the upper part of a round jar.	C	Nos. 23 and 24 are decorated with the same comb-like motif as No. 80.
24	4037	2	..	F. Great Granary Area.	Ditto . .	C	
25	11775	0·3	I	AB. Trench at the Southern Edge.	Ditto . .	C	Nos. 25, and 33-35 exhibit the common star motif. *Cf.* Pl. LXIII, 10.
26	PIV-38	3	I	AB. Pit IV .	Ditto . .	C	Nos. 26-30 exhibit circumscribed and rayed orbs, and No. 31 a spoked wheel. *Cf.* Pl. LXIII, 4, 10, 12 and 14.
27	11063	3-6	II	F. Trench VI .	Ditto . .	C	
28	11851	0·3	I	AB. Trench at the Southern Edge.	Ditto . .	C	
29	1606	2	I	F. Trench I .	Fragment of a round vase .	H, 16	
30	..	..	..	..	Ditto . . .	H, 16	

Descriptive Table of sherds—contd.

Serial No.	Register No.	Depth in feet.	Stratum.	Mound and Trench.	Description.	Type.	Description of paintings and references to similar paintings on burial pottery.
31	11415	0-3	I	F. Trench VI .	Centre fragment of an offerings' dish.	F, 21	
32	B747	15	III	AB. Trench B .	Fragment of the upper part of an ellipsoid jar.	A	
33	11758	0-3	I	AB. Trench at the Southern Edge.	Fragment of an ellipsoid jar .	A	
34	11096	3-6	II	F. Trench VI .	Fragment of the upper part of an ellipsoid jar.	A	
35	11740	0-3	I	AB. Trench at the Southern Edge.	Fragment of a bowl-like lid .	*Cf.* lid of No. 1 in Pl. LXI.	
36	8776	0-3	I	F. Trench IV .	Fragment of a small round jar	C	Motif uncertain.
37	..	..	..	..	Ditto . .	C	Common wavy line motif. *Cf.* Pl. LXII, 3 and 12.
38	11851	0-3	I	AB. Trench at the Southern Edge.	Ditto . .	C	For the chevrons (*cf.* Nos. 76, 88 89). See Pl. LXIII, 3 and 14.
39	11777	3-6	II	Ditto .	Fragment of an ellipsoid jar .	A	Rectangular chessboard pattern with leafy border, *cf.* Pl. LXIII, 15.
40	11161	3-6	II	F. Trench VI .	Fragment of a flat cover .	M	Nos. 40-42 are decorated with flying birds. With Nos. 40 and 41 *cf.* Pl. LXIII, 7, lower tier and with No. 42 Pl. LXIV, 13.
41	11890	0-3	I	AB. Trench at the Southern Edge.	Fragment of a carinated pot	D	
42	1324	3	I	AB. Extension of Pits I and II.	Fragment of a round jar .	C	
43	849	From spoil earth.		F. Trench I .	Fragment of a flat cover .	M	For the plants on Nos. 43 and 44 *cf.* Pl. LXIV, 19, 20, 23 and 24.
44	B876	9	..	AB. Trench B .	Fragment of a tarboosh-shaped lid.	*Cf.* lid of No. 2 in Pl. LXI.	
45	1179	2-75	I	F. Trench III .	Fragment of the lower part of a flanged bowl-like cover. None of the other bowl-like covers from the Cemetery H is so flanged.	..	Nos. 45, 47, 48, 51, 52 and 60 are decorated with deer, stars, etc., *cf.* Pl. LXIV, 1-5.
46	4689	0-3	I	Ditto .	Fragment of the upper part of a medium-sized, squat jar similar to No. 2.	..	Nos. 46, 49, 50, 53 and 55-60 exhibit the figures of humped cattle. To the right of the beast in No. 46 is a human figure with a stick in right (?) hand but the head is missing. On Nos. 55 and 56, are fish in front of cattle, possibly to represent the journey of the animals across the prototype of the Vattaran stream.
47	11995	6-9	III	AB. Trench at the Southern Edge.	Fragment of the upper part of a round jar.	C	This (see also Pl. LXIX, 18) is decorated with four therianthropic figures with beaked heads, as in Pl. LXII, 1 (*a* and *b*), facing left, standing between two deer (?).
48	4037	2	I	F. Great Granary Area.	Ditto . .	C	
49	..	..	..	..	Ditto . .	C	
50	11743	0-3	I	AB. Trench at the Southern Edge.	Ditto . .	A	
51	B220	0-5	I	AB. Trench B .	Fragment of a flat cover .	M	
52	11461	0-5	I	F. Trench VI .	Fragment of the upper part of a round jar.	C	
53	..	..	..	..	Ditto . .	C	
54	1062	4-7	II	AB. Extension of Pits I and II.	Fragment of a flat cover .	M	For painting of this see below Nos. 61-66.
55	4481	6-9	III	F. Trench III .	Fragment of the upper part of a medium-sized, squat jar similar to No. 2.	..	
56	11790	0-3	I	AB. Trench at the Southern Edge.	Fragment of the upper part of a round jar.	C	
57	D14	7-5	III (?)	AB. Trench B .	Fragment of a flat cover .	M	
58	11018	0-3	I	F. Trench VI .	Fragment of a round vase .	I	
59	B776	15-17	IV (?)	AB. Trench B .	Ditto . .	I	
60	11888	0-3	I	AB. Trench at the Southern Edge.	Ditto . .	I	

Descriptive Table of sherds—concld.

Serial No.	Register No.	Depth in feet.	Stratum.	Mound and Trench.	Description.	Type.	Description of paintings and references to similar paintings on burial pottery.
61	11974	0-3	I	AB. Trench at the Southern Edge.	Fragment of the upper part of an ellipsoid jar.	A	Nos. 61-68 are decorated with peacocks, as also is No. 84. On No. 63, however, there are two peacock heads set U-wise as in Pl. LXII, 4, but the painting is very faint. For the favourite peacock motif see Pl. LXII, 2-4, 6 and 8, and Pl. LXIV, 6-8, etc.
62	8775	0-3	I	F. Trench IV .	Ditto . .	A	
63	B1731	2	I	AB. Trench B .	Fragment of the upper part of a round jar.	C	
64	..	..	..	..	Ditto . .	C	
65	8776	0-3	I	F. Trench IV .	Fragment of the upper part of an ellipsoid jar.	A	
66	8363	3-6	II	Ditto .	Ditto . .	A	
67	B1290	7·5	II	AB. Trench B .	Fragment of a bowl or tarboosh-like lid.	*Cf.* covers of Nos. 2 and 3 in Pl. LXI.	
68	B870	15	IV	Ditto .	Fragment of a round vase .	I	
69	..	..	..	..	Fragment of the upper part of a round jar.	C	
70	B887	0-3	I	AB. Trench B .	Fragment of a vessel, shape not clear.	..	Conventional tree with large leaves, *cf.* Pl. LXIII, 19.
71	5466	4-5	II	F. Trench III .	Fragment of a round vase .	I	Hand-like motif, *cf.* Pl. LXIV, 12.
72	11884	0-3	I	AB. Trench at the Southern Edge.	Fragment of a carinated pot	D	(?) Flying bird motif, *cf.* Pls. LXII and LXIII, 7.
73	..	..	..	..	Fragment of a round jar .	C	
74	1022	2	I	F. Great Granary Area.	Upper part of a round vase .	I	Nos. 74-76 are decorated with stars, winged figures-of-8, and chevrons. *Cf.* Pl. LXII, 6, and Pl. LXIII, 1 (*a* and *b*), and 5.
75	PIV-110	10	IV	AB. Pit IV .	Fragment of the upper part of a round jar.	C	
76	19	2-5	I	F. Trench I .	Fragment of a small carinated vase.	D	
77	11220	5-75	II	F. Trench VI .	Fragment of a round jar .	C	The motif of Nos. 77 and 78 consists of leaves radiating from a circle. This motif is so far unrepresented among the paintings on the Cemetery H pottery. The paintings on No. 77 is almost exactly similar to that on sherd No. Ch 210 of Chanhunjo-daro, the ware, painting and wash of which are typical of the Cemetery H pottery.
78	8776	0-3	I	F. Trench IV .	Ditto . .	C	
79	11142	3-6	II	F. Trench VI .	Fragment of the upper part of a round jar.	C	Nos. 79 and 82 are painted with oblique lines, *cf.* Pl. LXII, 12.
80	10061	3-6	II	Ditto .	Fragment of the upper part of an ellipsoid jar.	A	
81	11481	0-3	I	Ditto .	Fragment of the upper part of a round jar.	C	For the leaves of No. 81 *cf.* Pl. LXII, 14 and for Nos. 84-86 *cf.* Pl. LXIV, 18-21.
82	11976	6-0	III	AB. Trench at the Southern Edge.	Fragment of a round jar .	C	
83	7862	0-3	I	F. Trench IV .	Ditto . .	C	
84	PI-110	2	I	AB. Extension of Pits I and II.	Ditto . .	C	
85	11481	0-3	I	F. Trench VI .	Fragment of a small carinated vase.	D	
86	B1674	18	V	AB. Trench B .	Fragment of a round jar .	C	
87	11481	0-3	I	F. Trench VI .	Fragment of a small carinated pot.	D	
88	5191	3-6	II	Ditto .	Fragment of the upper part of a combined water-pot and bowl.	H	For the chevrons of Nos. 88, 89 and 93 see above No. 38. Within the chevrons of No. 89 are representations of hands as in Pl. LXIV, 12 and 16.
89	6085	0-3	I	AB. Extension of Pits I and II.	Ditto . .	H	
90	..	..	..	..	Body of a round vase . .	I	For painting on this *cf.* Pl. LXIV, 24.
91	7258	6-0	III	F. Great Granary Area.	Fragment of a round jar .	C	For the tassel-like motif of Nos. 91 and 92 *cf.* Pl. LXIV, 15.
92	5468	3-5	II	AB. Extension of Pits I and II.	Fragment of an ellipsoid jar .	A	
93	..	..	..	..	Fragment of a carinated pot. Its shape is not quite clear in the photograph.	D	For the chevrons of Nos. 93 and 94, *cf.* Pl. LXIII, 1 (*a* and *b*), etc.
94	1236	4	II	F. Great Granary Area.	Fragment of a carinated vase	D	
95	11366	3-6	II	F. Trench VI .	Ditto . .	D	

See Pls. LXVII and LXVIII.

Household potsherds found at all levels.

Painted Indus potsherds have been found from all mounds, in all trenches, and at all levels. The examples illustrated in Pls. LXVII and LXVIII have been found up to a depth of 17 ft. in Mound F, 18 ft. in Mound AB, 12 ft. in Mound D, 3 ft. in the Cemetery H, and 6 ft. in Area J. This, however, does not mean that they may not be found at still lower levels. Since most of the shapes of secular pottery found in the various mounds at Harappā are similar to those of the Mohenjo-daro wares, it was but natural that in the main their paintings should also be similar. Having described in detail the painted sherds, which are typical of the Cemetery H pottery, it will do for my present purpose to refer only to the principal motifs painted on the sherds illustrated in Pls. LXVII and LXVIII, and to point out their similarity with the paintings on Mohenjo-daro pottery.

Their similarity in shape and paintings to Indus wares of Mohenjo-daro.

Trees.

Nos. 1-10, 12-13, 36-42, and 49-50, are painted with trees whose leaves are hachured in many cases. Trees are also found depicted on Mohenjo-daro pottery. *Cf. M. I. C.*, Pl. LXXXVII, 5.

***Pīpal* leaves.**

Nos. 11, and 43-48 are painted with the device of *pīpal* (*ficus religiosa*) leaves issuing from branches or twigs. This motif, too, is represented at Mohenjo-daro, *op. cit.*, Pl. XC, 18.

Geometrical patterns.

Nos. 15-18, and 22-27 are painted with geometrical patterns which are also familiar from Mohenjo-daro, *op. cit.*, Pl. LXXXVII, 4.

Heart-shaped motif.

Nos. 19 and 32 are painted with heart-shaped patterns which are common in shell both at Harappā and Mohenjo-daro, *op. cit.*, Pl. LXXXVII, 4.

Net patterns (?).

Nos. 20, 21, and 31 are painted with net (?) patterns undulated on one side only. This motif is quite common on Harappā pottery.

Leaves.

Nos. 28-30 are painted with leaves such as are figured in *M. I. C.*, Pl. XCI, 9-11.

Double triangles and chessboard patterns.

Nos. 33-35, 76 and 78 are painted with double triangles and chessboard patterns which are also common at Mohenjo-daro, *op. cit.*, Pl. XCII, 9, 10, 11, etc.

Peacocks.

Nos. 51-53, and 55-56 are painted with peacocks which are not found on the pottery so far published from Mohenjo-daro.

Hen and peacock (?).

No. 54 is painted with a hen and peacock[1] (?) facing each other, and in the upper field there is the lower part of another quadruped, a star and two wavy lines.

Fish.

Nos. 57 and 58 are painted with fish which are fairly common on the painted pottery at Harappā, but have not as yet been found on Mohenjo-daro pottery.

Interlacing circles.

The remaining thirty potsherds are painted with various patterns which are fairly common at Harappā, and most of them are also known from Mohenjo-daro. Among them, however, I may specially refer to the lozenge-in-circle and interlacing circle motifs found on Nos. 65, 67, 75, 77, 79, 84 and 87.

---

[1] This animal is quite differently depicted from those in Pl. LXVIII, 51-53.

CHAPTER VIII.

Household Pottery Jars and Post-cremation Urns from the Mounds together with Tabulation of the latter's contents (see Pl. LXXV, *a*).

Apart from the post-exposure burial jars and the funerary furniture peculiar to Cemetery H which have already been described in Chapter VI, the jars[1] recovered from various mounds at Harappā may be divided into two classes: (*a*) those that were used for household purposes such as storage of water, grain, oil and the like, and (*b*) post-cremation urns whose funerary nature has already been explained by Sir John Marshall in *M. I. C.*[2] largely on the evidence recovered at Harappā and in Balūchistān. With regard to jars of the first category it will suffice to draw attention to some of the popular shapes illustrated in Pl. LXXIV, *a*. Most of them are *gharās*, varying in shape from round to oval, and are coarser in texture and of handier size than the jars of *b* class (Pl. LXXV, *a*). Besides these, they comprise also long, narrow-necked, carrot-shaped jars (Pl. LXXIV, *a*, 5), which are invariably painted black and were presumably half-buried in the ground, and several shallow, open troughs (Pl. LXXIV, *a*, 6 and Pl. LXX, 4) which were used for feeding cattle or as dyeing vats. Three large cylindrical jars, two of which were lying one above the other, and an oval jar of similar size found placed on either side of the well in Trench V, Mound F (Pl. XVI, *d*), were apparently meant for the storage of drinking water for wayfarers. Another medium-sized jar found in the Eastern Extension of the Great Granary Area was half full of triangular terracotta cakes[3] (Pl. VIII, *a*); a *gharā* in Trench III, Mound F, was found filled with unbaked clay tetrahedrons;[4] while a jar[5] (12414) from Trench IV, Mound F, contained a unicorn seal (Pl. LXXXVII, 47), several stone *liṅgams*, an alabaster flower cone, hone, grindstones, etc., and a number of tiny objects of shell. Some 120 examples of household jars have so far been recovered, mostly in a fragmentary condition. **Jars for household economy.**

Of post-cremation urns 230 specimens were found associated with the Late and Middle Periods of Harappā. Most of their shapes are illustrated in Pl. LXXV, *a*. Except No. 5 (see also Pl. LXX, 3), which is perfectly cylindrical, the bases of all the jars illustrated in this plate though flat, are so narrow as to suggest that their lower parts were usually buried in the ground. From the household types of jars they are distinguished by their large size, thick and superior ware, and wide mouth. Most of them are made of fine, well levigated clay in the composition of which a quantity of lime may be presumed from the bright red colour of their wares. Many of the commoner types, *i.e.*, Nos. 1-4 **Post-cremation urns.**

---

[1] This term has been used here in reference to jars of medium or large size only and does not include small vases such as drinking goblets or other handy vessels.

[2] *Cf.* pp. 86-90.

[3] See p. 44 *supra*.

[4] See p. 113 *supra*.

[5] See pp. 56-57 *supra*.

2 x 2

Frequency of types. in Pl. LXXV, *a*, are coated with deep red wash often polished to a smooth and glossy appearance and then decorated with single or double bands in black all over the body.[1] Most frequent among these are the round or oval and large napiform jars (Nos. 1 and 4 respectively) of which about 90 examples of each type have been found. Next to them, with 38 examples, come the deep, wide mouthed crateriform vessels (*e. g.*, No. 2; see also Pl. LXX, 1) sharply tapering downwards to a narrow base. Of the long beaker-like jars with wide, slightly flared mouth (No. 3; see also Pl. LXX, 2) only 15 examples were recovered. The shapes illustrated under Nos. 5-8 in Pl. LXXV, *a* are rare; with them should be included the large pointed *loṭā*-shaped jar illustrated in Pl. XVIII, *g*.

Technique. On account of their large size none of the foregoing types are finished in one piece: Nos. 1-5 are made in two parts, and Nos. 6-8 in three parts, *i.e.*, the neck, the body and the base. In No. 5 the bottom was added to the hollow cylinder; in Nos. 1-4 there is only one joint near the middle. In view of the difficulty of turning vessels of such large dimensions on the wheel, it is not unlikely that jars like No. 4, were first fashioned in moulding pits as country *maṭs* are still fashioned today and then joined up and trued on the wheel. That this was the process followed, is borne out by the striations on the inside of all these jars but the joints are often so skilfully manipulated as to be hardly perceptible in the better finished examples.

Findspots. The post-cremation urns are found both intra and extra mural, that is to say within the houses (generally buried beneath the floors) as well as in streets and under the drains. An astonishingly long row of 54 broken napiform and round jars, apparently buried beneath the surface of a lane, was unearthed in Stratum V. They lay in a line going from east to west across the width of the Trench at the Southern Edge of Mound AB (Pls. LXXV, *b* and XXXVI, *b*).[2] Usually, the contents were found in the lower half of the urns, the upper part being filled with earth, but sometimes there were cereals of some sort below the other contents.

Usual contents. The contents of 178 urns which were found singly and of the row of 54 jars referred to above, have been tabulated separately at the end of this chapter. Usually, the urns contained bones (in some cases charred) of animals, birds, fishes, etc., in varying quantities, but with the exception of No. 11[3 and 4] (3686) found in Trench 1, Mound F, which contained, besides animal bones, an unburnt human tibia (Pl. XXIII, *b*), no other post-cremation urn has ever yielded human bones. The animal bones comprised teeth, joint and long bones, ribs, etc., while those of birds and other small creatures included jaws, vertebræ, legs and the like. The urns also contained goblets with pointed bases, cylindrical vases, human and animal toys, balls, beads, bangles, miniature lids, toy carts, wheels,

---

[1] No. 5 also in the same plate is equally well polished and painted, but is the only example of this shape.

[2] For their description, see pp. 174-75 *supra*, and for table of contents, see pp. 272-74 *infra*.

[3] This was associated with the Vth stratum and may therefore be dated to the Middle II Period of Harappā. For fuller description, see p. 108 *supra*.

[4] This and other numbers mentioned below refer to the serial numbers in the table of contents, pp. 254-71 *infra*.

triangular cakes, river shells, decayed grain, ashes and charcoal.[1] Among smaller vessels, the goblets with pointed bases, which were used as drinking cups, far exceeded all other pottery in number. In ten jars there were over a dozen in each, while in No. 28 (3925) there were as many as 55, including the broken ones. Among the more unusual objects found in these urns the following claim special notice. No. 70 (3868) contained besides other things a tortoise-shell (Pl. XXXIV, *b*); No. 89 (XLIV) about 4 lbs. of animal bones some of which were charred; Nos. 45 (7857), 164 (7198) and two others, antlers, besides which there were numerous pencil-like pieces of slag in No. 45. In No. 35 (5919), which is an inscribed jar,[2] the earth bore impressions of leaves and traces of decayed grain, and in No. 147 (7783) also were impressions of leaves and roots on the earth. Nos. 106[3] (7765) and 116 (10252) (the latter being inscribed) contained vestiges of seeds of the melon species and decayed cereals, the latter also containing traces of chaff, straw and leaves in the earth and a discoid faience sealing (Pl. C, 671). Finally No. 101 (unmarked), of which the contents were covered with greenish earth, contained some decayed cereal to which a number of dead worms were found adhering.

Exceptional contents.

In Chapter III I have already discussed the nature of these urns in connection with the long row of broken jars referred to above,[4] and shall now conclude by quoting Sir John Marshall who has well summed up all available evidence in regard to the post-cremation nature of these urns in his work on Mohenjo-daro.[5] "As a rule, the bones are those of lambs, goats, chickens, etc., and in some cases there are no bones at all. What, then, is the meaning of these numerous urns, with their contents of smaller vases and other articles, not infrequently mingled with ashes, but without any human bones? I think there can be only one answer. It is that they served the same purpose as their counterparts containing human bones and other articles, only that in their case there were no bones left after cremation to be buried. The absence of such bones does not, in effect, present any real difficulty; for it is still a practice in the Panjāb to take the remains of the bones from the funeral pyre, pound them to dust, and then commit them to the river. Some such practice may well have obtained among the Indus people, who may either have buried the pounded dust in these urns, in which case it would scarcely be detectable, or else may have thrown the ashes into the river and buried only an urnful of offerings in the house of the dead."

Evidence suggestive of the post-cremation nature of the urns.

[1] But for the evidence from Balūchistān where along with similar contents such urns were found to contain human bones also, it might have been thought that these were merely in the nature of offerings to the manes or Gods.

[2] & [3] See p. 105 *supra*.

[4] See pp. 174-75 *supra*.

[5] *M. I. C.*, p. 88.

TABLE I.—CONTENTS OF POST-

List of abbre

1. Trench . . . . Tr.
2. Trench at the Southern Edge . . . . . . Tr. S. E.
3. Extension of Pits I and II . . . . . . Ex. P. I & II.

Serial No.	Register number.	Findspot.			Depth below surface.	Stratum.	Measurements.	Description of jar.	Bones of animals and birds with approximate quantity or number.	Pottery.	
		Mound.	Trench.	Square.						Goblets with pointed bases.	Other pottery.
1	2	3	4	5	6	7	8	9	10	11	12
1	182	F	I	M 12/12	6 ft. 6 in.	III	..	Large, in fragments	Very few . .	2 and 2 fragmentary.	....
2	1033A	F	I	M 11/16	5 ft. 6 in.	III	Ht. 3 ft. . .	Large, napiform .	6½ oz. . .	Do. .	2 medium cylindrical and 2 small round vases and 1 fragmentary long oval vase.
3	1033B	F	I	M 11/16	5 ft. 6 in.	III	Ht. 2 ft. 10 in. .	Do. . .	6½ oz. . .	..	....
4	1161	F	I	M 12/17	13 ft.	V	..	Large, fragmentary	A few . .	1 and 1 fragmentary.	....
5	1637	F	III	N 9/0	8 ft. 9 in.	IV	..	Do. . .	One piece . .	..	....
6	2526	F	III	N 9/13	9 ft.	IV	..	Large, round, crushed.	A few . .	..	....
7	2676	AB	Ex. P. I & II.	P 24/8	12 ft. 8 in.	V	..	Large, round .	..	2	1 open squat vase, 1 tiny lid.
8	2875	AB	Ex. P. I & II.	R 24/7	9 ft. 4 in.	III	..	Large round, fragmentary.	A few . .	..	....
9	..	AB	Ex. P. I & II.	Q 24/8	7 ft.	II	..	Do. . .	About 3 oz. .	..	....
10	..	F	I	M 11/16	4 ft. 10 in.	II	..	Do. . .	½ lb. . .	1 and 4 broken (No. 3530).	....
11	3656	F	I	M 10/15	14 ft.	V	..	Do. . .	Human tibia and small animal bones.	..	1 carinated vase and 2 lids.
12	3689	AB	Ex. P. I & II.	P 24/23	8 ft. 8 in.	IV	Diam. at centre 2 ft. 11 in., ht. 3 ft. 1 in.	Large, round, most of upper part missing.	¾ lb. . .	..	....
13	3690	AB	Ex. P. I & II.	P 24/23	11 ft. 6 in.	V	Diam. at mouth 11½ in., ht. 2 ft. 5 in.	Large, round, in fragments.	About 5 oz. including a few charred ones.	1	1 long oval vase and 1 broken oval jar.
14	3692	AB	Ex. P. I & II.	P 24/23	11 ft. 4 in.	V	Diam. at mouth 1 ft. 2 in., ht. 1 ft. 7 in.	Napiform . .	A few . .	1	....
15	3710	F	I	M 12/16	8 ft.	III	Ht. 2 ft. 3 in., diam. at mouth 11 in.	Large, round fragmentary.	½ lb. . .	..	....
16	..	F	G. G. Area.	J 7/10	1 ft. 6 in.	I	..	Do. . .	..	..	....
17	3759	F	G. G. Area.	I 9/8	5 ft. 3 in.	III	Ht. 2 ft. 3 in., diam. at mouth 12½ in.	Large, napiform .	A few . .	..	....
18	3822	F	I	M 12/6	15 ft. 9 in.	VI	Ht. 2 ft. 3 in., diam. at mouth 11 in.	Large, napiform, in sherds.	..	..	....
19	3824	F	G. G. Area.	I 9/3	4 ft. 1 in.	III	..	Large, round, in fragments.	½ lb. . .	1	....
20	..	F	G. G. Area.	I 7/10	9 ft. 10 in.	IV	..	Large, napiform .	½ lb. . .	..	....
21	..	F	G. G. Area.	I 7/9	8 ft. 4 in.	IV	..	Large, napiform, very fragmentary.	½ lb. . .	1 (No. 3828) .	....
22	..	F	G. G. Area.	I 7/10	9 ft. 6 in.	IV	..	Do. . .	½ lb. . .	..	....
23	3847	F	G. G. Area.	I 8/10	4 ft. 9 in.	III	..	Large, round, very fragmentary.	½ lb. . .	2	3 tiny lids .

CREMATION URNS.

viations used :—

4. Great Granary Area . . . . G. G. Area.
5. Terracotta . . . . T. C.

OBJECTS.			Ornaments of pottery, faience, shell, etc. (in case of pottery substance is not specified).	Charcoal, ashes, etc.	Shell, ivory, copper.	Miscellaneous.	REMARKS.	Serial No.
Toys.	Cakes.	Potsherds.						
13	14	15	16	17	18	19	20	1
....	..	Large number . .	....	Small quantity of charcoal.	A small ivory object.	....	....	1
Seated male .	..	Several, miscellaneous	Round faience bead No. 3531f.	Some charcoal	..	....	Nos. 2 and 3 were fragmentary and lay against a small broken pavement. Pl. XXIII, a.	2
....	Fragments .	Of goblets with pointed bases, vases, etc.	Fragments of bangles	..	..	Charred wheat and slag.	....	3
1 ball . .	..	Fragment of a long oval vase.	....	..	..	....	....	4
....	..	Of goblets with pointed bases.	Fragment of a bangle	..	..	....	....	5
Fragmentary female figurine.	..	....	....	..	..	....	....	6
....	..	Of goblets with pointed bases, and of a toy standard dish.	....	..	..	Decayed grain .	It stands under a water rimte near the western end of the trench. All the contents were discoloured green.	7
....	..	Of goblets with pointed bases, long oval vases and other vessels.	....	Charcoal .	..	Do.	....	8
....	..	Do. . .	....	Do. . .	..	Do.	....	9
....	..	Do. . .	Fragments of bangles	..	..	....	....	10
....	2 complete and several fragments.	Miscellaneous . .	Tiny discoid paste bead.	Tiny pieces of charcoal and ashes.	..	....	In its upper half which contained only bricks and brickbats the earth was hard, whereas in the lower containing bones, cakes, and vases, it was greenish, porous and soft mixed with charcoal and ashes. Human tibia lay in the middle. Pl. XXIII, b.	11
....	A fragment .	Miscellaneous, of jars and vases.	....	Pieces of charcoal.	A river shell .	Decayed grain mixed in greenish earth	....	12
....	Fragments .	Miscellaneous . .	Fragment of a bangle	Tiny pieces of charcoal.	..	Decayed grain in lower half.	Its upper half was filled with percolated earth.	13
Fragment of a cart.	Do. .	Do. . .	....	Do. . .	..	Decayed wheat.	....	14
....	..	Of goblets with pointed bases.	....	..	..	....	....	15
....	..	....	....	..	..	....	Only the bottom portion survived.	16
....	Fragments .	A few, of goblets with pointed bases and other vessels.	....	..	..	....	....	17
....	..	2 small, one being of the neck of jar.	....	..	..	....	It is inscribed with 3 pictograms at the shoulder and close to it were two jar stands (No. 3823 A and B). Pl. XXIII, c.	18
One ball, fragmentary horn and a wheel.	Fragments .	Of about 20 goblets with pointed bases and miscellaneous.	Fragments of T. C. and faience bangles, and 1 faience bead.	..	..	A bit of slag.	....	19
Oval cage .	Do. .	Miscellaneous shreds .	1 bangle and some fragments.	..	..	....	For cage see Pl. CXX, 26	20
Rhinoceros .	..	....	....	..	..	....	....	21
....	..	Of goblets with pointed bases and other vases.	Fragments of bangles	..	..	....	....	22
1 big ball .	Fragments .	Of goblets with pointed bases, small jars, vases, etc.	Fragment of a faience bangle.	..	..	Ribbed steatite amulet and some slag.	....	23

TABLE I.—CONTENTS OF POST-

Serial No.	Register number.	Findspot.			Depth below surface.	Stratum.	Measurements.	Description of jar.	Bones of animals and birds with approximate quantity or number.	Pottery.	
		Mound.	Trench.	Square.						Goblets with pointed bases.	Other pottery.
1	2	3	4	5	6	7	8	9	10	11	12
24	3848	F	G. G. Area.	I 9/6	6 ft. 9 in.	IV	..	Large, round, very fragmentary.	½ lb. . .	..	3 tiny lids and fragments of others.
25	3867	F	G. G. Area.	I 9/6	5 ft. 9 in.	III	..	Do. . .	1 lb. . .	..	1 tiny lid . .
26	..	F	III	N 9/4	8 ft. 6 in.	IV	..	Do. . .	A few very thin bones of birds.	2 (3917a)	1 oval vase with marked of bottom (3917a), 1 cylindrical vase and a miniature *handi* painted with black bands (3917b).
27	..	F	I	M 11/18	14 ft. 3 in.	V	..	Large, napiform, fragmentary.	Hardened bones .	..	Medium-sized oval vase and a miniature vase (3922).
28	3925	F	III	N 9/4	11 ft. 3 in.	V	Ht. 3 ft., diam. at neck 1 ft. 4 in.	Large, napiform, neck slightly broken.	Hardened bones of which a few were found sticking to a fragment of goblet with pointed base.	7	7 small cylindrical vases, 3 tiny lids and fragments of lids. A small basin in fragments (diam. 8 in.), and a fragmentary standard cup.
29	3929	F	G. G. Area.	I 9/7	10 ft. 2 in.	V	..	Shaped like a goblet with pointed base. Rare.	Hardened bones .	..	Goblets with pointed bases, a ribbed jar, and other vessels.
30	4317	D	I	Q 31/11	6 ft. 5 in.	II	..	Large, round .	A few, highly decayed.	4	1 small oval vase .
31	..	D	I	Q 30/19	2 ft.	I	..	Large, round, very fragmentary.	Small pieces including a charred one.	..	....
32	4935	F	G. G. Area.	J 8/23	9 ft. 6 in.	IV	..	Do. . .	Three pieces and one tooth.	..	1 small spoon .
33	4989	F	G. G. Area.	K 8/3	10 ft. 6 in.	IV	Ht. 2 ft. 3 in., diam. at mouth 11 in.	Do. . .	Some . . .	..	....
34	5873	F	III	N 10/6	8 ft.	IV	..	Do. . .	..	1	1 cracked long oval vase.
35	5919	AB	Ex. P. I & II.	P 23/10	10 ft.	IV	..	Large, inscribed napiform.	Several, including a few charred pieces of large bones.	..	....
36	..	F	III	N 10/6	9 ft.	IV	..	Large, very fragmentary.	Several pieces .	1	....
37	..	AB	Ex. P. I & II.	P 23/5	7 ft. 6 in.	IV	..	Do. . .	..	..	....
38	7174	AB	Ex. P. I & II.	Q 25/1	9 ft.	III	Ht. 2 ft. 6 in. .	Large, napiform, very fragmentary.	Several . .	..	3 tiny lids and a fragment.
39	7823	F	III	N 10/1	9 ft.	IV	..	Large, round, very fragmentary.	Several, including some pieces of charred bones.	..	....

CREMATION URNS—*contd.*

OBJECTS			Ornaments of pottery, faience, shell, etc. (in case of pottery substance is not specified).	Charcoal, ashes, etc.	Shell, ivory, copper.	Miscellaneous.	REMARKS.	Serial No.
Toys.	Cakes.	Potsherds.						
13	14	15	16	17	18	19	20	1
Fragments of wheels.	Fragments .	Of goblets with pointed bases and other vessels.	4 bangles and fragments, 1 bead, 1 cylindrical faience bead and 1 tiny paste bead.	Bits of charcoal	..	Traces of decayed wheat at bottom.	....	24
1 ball, 1 fragmentary bull and 1 wheel.	Do. .	Do. . .	Fragments of bangles	..	..	....	It has a brick enclosure round the mouth.	25
Leg of a human figure, fragmentary long horn and 1 bull's head with hole for attachment.	Do. .	Large number, including those of small jars, goblets with pointed bases, long oval and cylindrical vases, offerings' dishes, etc.	Fragments of bangles. One round bead of faience and a tiny discoid one of paste (3917h).	Bits of charcoal	Ivory baluster with incised decoration (3917 c). Fragments of a rusted copper ring (3917g).	One fragmentary antler (3917). Decayed grain mixed with greenish earth. Fragmentary square brick. Fragment of a stone hone and some slag.	....	26
....	Do. .	Of several oval vases, *handi*, small jar, basin, dish and other vases.	Fragments of bangles and 1 round faience bead (3922c).	Bits of charcoal, ashes mixed with earth at places.	River shell and one fragmentary ivory rod (3923a).	Decayed grain.	....	27
1 pregnant woman, 1 fragmentary female and a nude male figure. Fragments of human figures and legs. 1 bull. 1 fragmentary animal, horns broken and entire, 2 carts, 2 wheels, 3 balls, and fragments of carts and wheels.	Do. .	Of about 4 dozen goblets with pointed bases, of cylindrical, oval, long oval and other vases, small jars, *handis*, etc.	....	Bits of charcoal	2 river shells and 2 fragments of an ivory rod pointed at both ends.	Decayed grain mixed in greenish earth. One t. c. cone.	In its upper half, the earth was harder than in the lower where it was profusely mixed with decayed grain. In some vases percolated earth was found in layers.	28
....	Do. .	....	Fragments of bangles	..	..	Decayed grain in porous, green earth.	The earth in which the jar was embedded was hard and littered with potsherds, brickbats, nodules and fragments of triangular t. c. cakes and ashes.	29
5 broken animals, 1 female figurine and 1 ball.	Do. .	Of a small oval vase, 2 cylindrical vases, 2 dozen goblets with pointed bases, etc.	2 bangles . .	Pieces of charcoal.	..	1 t. c. tube and a rough discoid tablet convex on both sides where it has a groove in the centre.	It lay near a small *ghara* and both appeared to have been full of grain. The small jar contained nothing else.	30
....	..	Its own sherds and a few more.	....	Bits of charcoal	..	....	It contained porous and flaky earth.	31
1 horn . .	..	Its own and 1 of a goblet with pointed base.	Fragments of bangles. 1 round and 1 tubular bead, 2 round faience beads.	..	..	....	It was partially buried under a later wall.	32
1 ball, 1 bird, and 1 bust of a male figure.	Fragments .	Of 27 goblets with pointed bases and of numerous miscellaneous vessels.	Fragments of bangles and 1 of a faience bangle.	..	..	....	The earth inside was ashy. Some bones were also found sticking outside the jar.	33
....	Do. .	Bottom of a cylindrical vase.	....	..	..	....	....	34
1 bull's head and fragment of a wheel.	Fragments of 7 or 8.	Of an offerings' dish, perforated vase, cylindrical, round and oval vases.	Fragments of bangles	Tiny pieces of charcoal.	1 river shell was found inside a fragmentary oval vase.	One chert scraper and some slag.	The lower 4/5th of this jar contained porous, greenish earth mixed with some decayed cereal and bore leafy impressions.	35
....	Fragments .	Of vases, etc., and of a painted *handi* lying at the bottom of the jar.	Do. .	..	..	1 stone grinder .	The earth inside was hard and greenish and contained some decayed cereal.	36
Cart fragment .	..	Of dishes, a small jar, a goblet with pointed base and a cylindrical trough (?)	Fragment of a bangle	..	..	....	Contained loose earth.	37
....	Fragments of 4 or 5.	Of long, oval and cylindrical vases, of dishes, a small jar and other vessels.	1 bead and fragments of 4 or 5 bangles, 1 paste bead and 2 pieces of a faience bangle.	Tiny pieces of charcoal.	Pieces of river shells.	Pieces of mica, 1 shell and 1 stone disc. Some slag.	The earth in the upper [illegible]th of the jar was hard and probably extraneous, but in the rest it was greenish and porous due to some decayed cereal.	29
Rattle ball .	Fragments of 3 or 4.	Of goblets with pointed bases; of cylindrical, oval, perforated and *handi*-shaped vases.	Fragments of bangles	At places the earth was ashy in the lower half.	..	....	In the upper part, which contained bones, the earth was loose and powdery and in the lower, with which the other contents were associated, it was greenish on account of some decayed cereal and at places it was ashy too.	39

TABLE 1.—CONTENTS OF POST-

Serial No.	Register number.	Findspot.			Depth below surface.	Stratum.	Measurements.	Description of jar.	Bones of animals and birds with approximate quantity or number.	Pottery.	
		Mound.	Trench.	Square.						Goblets with pointed bases.	Other pottery.
1	2	3	4	5	6	7	8	9	10	11	12
40	7841	F	G. G. Area.	I 9/10	3 ft. 10 in.	II	..	Large, round, very fragmentary.	Several . .	..	....
41	..	F	G. G. Area.	I 9/10	4 ft. 3 in.	III	..	Large, round, lower half.	Do. . .	..	....
42	7840	F	G. G. Area.	I 9/14	8 ft.	IV	Ht. about 3 ft. .	Large, round, fragmentary.	Several, including a few charred bones.	..	1 small cylindrical vase.
43	7854	F	G. G. Area.	M 12/8	7 ft. 6 in.	III	..	Do. . .	Several . .	5	2 miniature lids
44	7856	F	I	M 12/7 and 8.	6 ft.	III	..	Large, round, cracked.	Do. . .	..	1 small tumbler and 2 miniature lids.
45	7857	F	G. G. Area.	H 9/23	4 ft. 6 in.	III	..	Very large, round, in pieces.	Several, including an antler in pieces	5	1 medium-sized tumbler.
46	..	F	IV	..	2 ft. 6 in.	II	..	Large, round, very fragmentary.	Several tiny bones	..	....
47	10232C	F	G. G. Area.	J 9/1	15 to 16 ft.	VI	..	..	3 or 4 tiny bits of bones.	..	....
48	..	F	IV	I 14/9	3 ft.	II	..	..	A piece of bone .	..	....
49	..	F	IV	I 11/10	6 ft. 8 in.	III	..	Large, round, very fragmentary.	A few tiny bones .	..	....
50	..	D	I	Q 31/23	1 ft. 3 in.	I	Ht. 1 ft. 6 in. .	Small, napiform, lower half.	½ lb. . . .	..	...
51	..	D	I	Q 31/16	6 in.	I	..	Large, napiform, badly crushed.	A few bits . .	..	....
52	IV	D	I	Q 30/19 and 24.	2 ft. 6 in.	III	..	Large, napiform, bottom portion.	A few pieces, one being calcined.	..	....
53	X	D	I	Q 30/10	3 ft. 3 in.	II	Ht. 2 ft. 6 in. .	Large, napiform, lower half.	½ lb. of which ¼ lb. were of a rodent.	..	2 vases . . .
54	XII	D	III	S 30/1	3 ft. 6 in.	II	..	Large, napiform, bottom portion.	½ lb. including one partially charred.	..	....
55	XXIV	AB	Tr.S.E.	Q 29/21	4 ft.	IV	..	Napiform, lower half.	..	..	....
56	XLII	AB	Tr.S.E.	Q 27/7	8 ft.	III	..	Do. .	4 pieces of large bones, and a broken tooth.	..	....

CREMATION URNS—*contd.*

Objects.			Ornaments of pottery, faience, shell, etc. (in case of pottery substance is not specified).	Charcoal, ashes, etc.	Shell, ivory, copper.	Miscellaneous.	Remarks.	Serial No.
Toys. 13	Cakes. 14	Potsherds. 15	16	17	18	19	20	1
1 ball, a few legs and horns.	Fragments of 3 or 4.	Some, of goblets with pointed bases, of a *handi*, jars and other vessels.	Fragments of 3 or 4 bangles and 2 of faience bangles.	Pieces of charcoal in ashy earth.	A river shell .	....	This was placed in the bottom of a larger jar. In its upper part and along the sides, the earth was hard, but in the lower, porous and powdery. Its colour was pale green just above the bottom.	40
Ram, fragmentary.	Fragments of 4 or 5.	Of about a dozen goblets with pointed bases, of 2 cylindrical vases, 1 trough, 1 jar holed through bottom, 1 dish, 1 *handi*, etc.	....	Tiny pieces of charcoal.	..	....	The earth in this jar was greenish and porous.	41
1 bull, 1 female and 1 leg.	Fragments of about a dozen.	Of about a dozen goblets with pointed bases, of 1 oval and 2 cylindrical vases, jars and other vessels.	Fragments of 4 or 5 bangles, 2 beads of paste, and 1 of faience.	Do. .	..	....	On the missing side of the jar several brickbats got in. The earth in the upper half was hard and contained but a few pieces of bones, brickbats, and fragment of an animal toy. In the lower half it was porous and greenish.	42
Fragment of a female figure.	Fragments of 3 or 4.	Half a basketful of sherds and of goblets with pointed bases and small jars. Of a cylindrical vase, a standard dish, a *handi* and a long oval vase.	....	Do. .	..	Some slag . .	Some of the tiny bones were found inside the goblets with pointed bases.	43
1 ball, 1 animal, head dress of a female and 2 wheels.	Fragments of 2 or 3.	Of about a dozen goblets with pointed bases, 3 miniature and 1 large tumbler, 1 oval vase, 1 handle, of jars, etc.	Fragments of 2 ribbed and 3 or 4 other bangles and 1 small paste bead.	Do. .	A rusted piece of copper and a river shell.	....	Among sherds of goblets one was inscribed and the other bore a seal impression. In its lower half, owing to some decayed cereal, the earth was greenish and porous.	44
1 wheel and 1 ram.	..	Of over a dozen goblets with pointed bases, one tumbler and ½ basketful of other vessels.	Fragments of bangles, a tubular bead and a small faience bead.	..	..	An antler in pieces and long pieces of slag in pencil-like formation weighing about 2 lbs.	....	45
....	Some fragments.	Of a few goblets with pointed bases, dishes, and other jars.	A faience bead (8642b).	..	..	A t. c. lump with impression of closed fist (8642a).	The earth near its bottom was loose and discoloured green.	46
....	..	....	....	..	..	A chert piece.	....	47
....	Fragments .	Of a goblet with pointed base and a few other sherds.	....	Ashes and pieces of charcoal	..	....	This was placed over the bottom of another large jar which was hedged round by standing bricks.	48
....	Do. .	Two each of jars, dishes and bottoms of oval vases. Of 1 vase, and 1 trough.	....	Profusion of ashes and charcoal.	..	....	....	49
....	A few . .	Several, including those of goblets with pointed bases, an oval vase, a dish and a miniature cylindrical vase.	Pieces of t. c., faience and shell bangles.	Bits of charcoal mixed in ashy earth.	..	Decayed cereal	It stood against a *kachcha* wall.	50
....	A few pieces .	3	A bit of bangle .	Do. .	3 pieces of a thin rusted copper rod.	.	....	51
....	Several fragments.	A few, one of them being of a round *ghara*.	....	Do. .	..	Lumps of decayed cereal.	....	52
1 cart, 1 ball .	Do. .	About half a basketful including those of goblets with pointed bases, long oval, cylindrical and other vases.	Fragments of bangles.	Bits of charcoal and ashes.	..	Traces of decayed cereal	The jar stood against a bit of wall.	53
....	2 fragments .	Of 2 vases . .	3 fragments of bangles.	..	..	One tiny rectangular steatite seal inscribed on both sides.	....	54
1 ball, 1 bull and fragment of a cart frame.	..	2 each of goblets with pointed bases and of cylindrical vases.	2 pieces of bangles .	A few bits of charcoal.	..	....	....	55
1 ball, 1 bead .	..	....	....	Bits of charcoal mixed with brownish earth.	..	Fragmentary grindstone.	The jar stood by a wall.	56

TABLE I.—CONTENTS OF POST-

Serial No.	Register number.	Findspot.			Depth below surface.	Stratum.	Measurements.	Description of jar.	Bones of animals and birds with approximate quantity or number	Pottery.	
		Mound.	Trench.	Square.						Goblets with pointed bases.	Other pottery.
1	2	3	4	5	6	7	8	9	10	11	12
57	LI	F	VI	O 11/24	3 ft. 4 in.	II	Diam. at centre 2 ft. 7 in., diam. at mouth 1 ft. 2 in.	Large, napiform, very fragmentary.	½ lb. .	2	1 long oval vase and 1 tumbler.
58	LII	F	VI	O 9/17	5 ft. 6 in.	II	Ht. 2 ft. 2 in., diam. at mouth 9 in., diam. at centre 2 ft. 1 in.	Large, napiform, fragmentary.	About 4 lbs. including a few partially charred.	..	1 miniature lid, 2 pieces of a cart.
59	XIX	D	III	R 30/21	13 ft.	V	..	Mediocre, napiform, bottom portion.	½ lb. including a few partially charred.	..	....
60	XXVIIa	AB	Tr.S.E.	Q 25/22	7 ft. 6 in.	III	..	Napiform, lower part.	1 oz. including two charred ones.	..	....
61	XXXII	AB	Tr.S.E.	Q 25/16	11 ft. 3 in.	IV	Diam. at centre about 2 ft.	Mediocre, napiform, badly crushed.	Piece of a large bone.	..	....
62	XXXVIII	AB	Tr. S.E.	Q 28/1	6 ft. 4 in.	III	..	Large, round, upper half.	1 oz. . . .	..	....
63	XLIX	F	VI	P 11/5	7 ft. 2 in.	III	.	Mediocre, napiform, lower half.	2 small bits of bones	..	....
64	470	F	I	M 12/18	7 ft. 6 in.	III	Diam. 2 ft. 2 in. .	Large trough, fragmentary.	A few large bones .	7 including 2 with seal impressions.	....
65	2666	AB	Pits I & II.	Q 24/14	9 ft. 9 in.	IV	..	Large trough .	10 oz. . . .	..	1 tumbler . .
66	3425	F	I	M 11/21	13 ft. 10 in.	V	..	Large trough, in fragments.	..	..	....
67	3687	F	G. G. Area.	J 7/20	8 ft. 4 in.	IV	Ht. 1 ft. 11 in. .	Do. .	½ lb. . . .	..	....
68	3868	AB	Ex. P. I & II.	Q 24/15	8 ft. 11 in.	III	Ht. 2 ft. 2 in., diam. 1 ft. 11 in.	Large trough .	½ lb. and a decayed tortoise-shell.	..	1 medium-sized and 1 small tumbler (No. 3868b) and a saucer.
69	3880	AB	Ex. P. I & II.	Q 24/14	9 ft. 9 in.	IV	Diam. 1 ft. 1 in. .	Do. . .	½ lb. . . .	..	1 small round vase and 2 medium-sized tumblers.
70	3904	F	G. G. Area.	J 9/25	5 ft. 2 in.	II	Ht. 1 ft. 9 in., diam. 1 ft. 8 in.	Do. . .	Large bones ½ lb. and tiny bones of fish, etc.	..	1 double convex vase of black pottery, 1 small tumbler and 1 lid.
71	3905	F	G. G. Area.	J 9/9	8 ft. 8 in.	III	Diam. 1 ft. 1½ in., ht. 1 ft. 3 in.	Trough . .	A few . . .	..	....
72	3916	F	III	N 9/5	7 ft. 8 in.	IV	..	Large trough, in fragments.	..	..	....
73	4900	AB	Ex. P. I & II.	Q 24/10	7 ft. 8 in.	III	..	Do. .	Several . .	..	....
74	7093	AB	Ex. P. I & II.	Q 24/6	6 ft. 9 in.	II	..	Do. .	Numerous . .	2	....
75	7287	F	G. G. Area.	J 9/9	10 ft. 3 in.	V	.	Trough, fragmentary.	Several, including charred ones near the bottom.	..	....
76	7284	F	G. G. Area.	J 9/10	9 ft. 0 in.	IV	..	Small trough, fragmentary.	2 or 3 pieces .	..	....
77	7764	AB	Ex. P. I & II.	Q 24/2	16 ft. 6 in.	VI	Ht. 2 ft., diam. 2 ft.	Mediocre trough .	Some pieces .	..	3 tiny lids . .
78	..	F	IV	I 15/3 and 4	2 ft.	I	Diam. 2 ft. .	Trough, fragmentary.	A few pieces .	..	....

-Cremation Urns—*contd.*

Objects			Ornaments of pottery, faience, shell, etc. (in case of pottery substance is not specified)	Charcoal, ashes, etc.	Shell, ivory, copper.	Miscellaneous.	Remarks.	Serial No.
Toys.	Cakes.	Potsherds.						
13	14	15	16	17	18	19	20	1
1 wheel and 2 horns of toy animals.	Large number of fragments.	One and half basketfuls including those of 22 goblets with pointed bases, of 4 long oval vases, dishes, etc.	Pieces of t. c. and faience bangles, 2 fragments of a burnt shell pendant, 1 faience ear-stud.		.	Piece of a chert scraper.	The earth in it was slightly grey and mixed with sand.	57
1 wheel and horn of a toy animal.	A few fragments.	About a basketful of miscellaneous vases and vessels.	3 pieces of bangles	..	.	1 stone pestle and piece of a stone object.	The jar was buried under a rectangular brick platform.	58
....	Some fragments.	Numerous, including 2 of dishes, and 1 neck piece of a vase.	2 fragments of bangles.	Bits of charcoal and ashes mixed with earth.	..	....	The jar was resting directly over a thick deposit of burnt and ashy earth.	59
1 fragmentary bull.	2 fragments .	About one and half basketfuls including 2 of oval vases, 4 bottoms of pointed goblets, 2 of cylindrical vases, etc.	4 fragments of bangles.	Bits of charcoal	..	Lumps of decayed cereal.	....	60
....	..	...	A bit of faience bangle.	Bits of charcoal and lumps of ashes.	..	Fragment of a burnt chert scraper.	....	61
....	.	A few, including 1 of vases.	Bits of bangle and 1 tiny faience bead.	Bits of charcoal in greenish grey earth.	..	....	It lay upside down.	62
....	5 pieces .	A few, including 1 of an offerings' dish and stem of the same.	....	Bits of charcoal mixed with earth of pale tinge.	..	....	....	63
2 balls . .	..	A few . . .	Fragment of a bangle and 1 ring, 1 faience bead.	..	1 river shell, 2 fragments of an ivory binster.	....	....	64
1 seated male, 1 animal figure, 1 wheel and balls.	Fragments .	Of goblets with pointed bases, vases, tumblers, etc.	....	Charcoal .	1 river shell	Decayed grain mixed in greenish earth.	....	65
....	Do. .	A few, of vases and dishes.	....	..	A small piece of ivory.	....	....	66
....	Do. .	Of goblets with pointed bases, long oval vases, dishes, basins, etc.	....	..	..	Fragments of tuber .	It was buried under a wall.	67
A ball and fragments of toys.	Do. .	Of goblets with pointed bases, vases, tumblers, dishes, etc.	Fragments of bangles, 3 faience, 1 paste, 1 t.c. and 1 carnelian beads.	Bits of charcoal	1 river shell .	....	For the tortoise-shell and other contents see Pl. XXXIV. b.	68
1 wheel . .	Do. .	Of cylindrical vases and other vessels.	1 bangle and fragments.	..	Rusted copper lumps.	....	....	69
1 female and 1 animal figurine and 1 horn-shaped object	Do. .	Of goblets with pointed bases, tumblers, cups, etc.	Fragments of bangles	..	..	A cubical stone weight	The earth in the trough was soft, porous and greenish and contained decayed grain.	70
....	..	2 or 3 . . .	Do. .	..	..	Some slag . .	....	71
....	..	Of a *handi* and vases .	A few paste beads .	..	..	....	....	72
....	Fragments .	Of 3 or 4 goblets with pointed bases, oval vases, a small jar and other vessels.	....	Abundant charcoal near the bottom.	..	Fragment of a stone quern.	....	73
....	Do. .	Do. .	....	Some pieces of charcoal and ashes in the upper portion.	River shells .	Chert flakes . .	Several tiny bones were found inside goblets with pointed bases.	74
Fragment of a leg.	Several fragments.	A few, *e.g.*, rim of a trough, neck of a jar, bottom of a miniature vase.	....	Bits of decayed charcoal.	..	Piece of a pestle and 1 chert scraper.	The earth, especially in the upper part, was hard and contained some ashes and charcoal.	75
....	Numerous fragments.	....	....	..	..	....	It contained very hard earth.	76
Fragmentary wheel and a stool, fragments of a female figure and a chariot.	..	Quarter basketful of offerings' dishes, of 7 or 8 goblets with pointed bases, vases of sorts and dishes.	....	Tiny pieces of charcoal.	..	....	In its lower portion the earth was greenish and porous as it contained some decayed cereal.	77
....	1 large, in fragments.	A handful of potsherds of a goblet with pointed base and other bases.	....	Some ashes .	..	....	This trough was lying upside down and its bottom was missing.	78

TABLE I.—CONTENTS OF POST-

Serial No.	Register number.	Findspot.			Depth below surface.	Stratum.	Measurements.	Description of jar.	Bones of animals and birds with approximate quantity or number.	Pottery.	
		Mound.	Trench.	Square.						Goblets with pointed bases.	Other pottery.
1	2	3	4	5	6	7	8	9	10	11	12
79	7839	F	G. G. Area.	I 9/3	7 ft.	IV	Ht. 1 ft. 2 in., diam. 2 ft.	Trough . .	A large number .	1 fragmentary	1 tiny lid and 1 tumbler.
80	7867	F	III	N 9/10	3 ft. 6 in. to 6 ft. 4 in.	III	Ht. 2 ft. 9½ in., diam. 2 ft. 5½ in.	Large trough .	½ lb. . . .	1	1 tiny lid . .
81	..	F	III	I 12/3	5 ft. 10 in.	III	..	Trough, bottom portion.	Several . .	..	....
82	..	F	IV	I 12/3	6 ft. 10 in.	IV	..	Medium-sized trough, very fragmentary.	..	2 fragmentary	1 oval vase . .
83	8533	F	IV	I 24/3	8 ft. 6 in.	III	Ht. 2 ft., diam. 1 ft. 11 in.	Large trough, cracked.	A few, including one charred from bottom.	..	....
84	..	F	IV	I 12/4	9 ft. 6 in.	IV	..	Trough, fragmentary.	A few . . .	..	2 oval vases (10313)
85	10385	F	IV	I 12/4	9 ft. 6 in.	IV	..	Large trough, in fragments.	Several . .	..	Small goblet . .
86	XXVII	AB	Tr. S.E.	Q 27/23	13 ft. 3 in.	V	..	Trough, fragmentary.	Do. . .	..	....
87	XXIX	AB	Tr. S.E.	R 28/2	6 ft. 6 in.	III	..	Trough, very fragmentary.	1 oz. including 1 charred.	..	....
88	XXXV	AB	Tr. S.E.	Q 27/20	13 ft. 3 in.	V	Ht. 2 ft., diam. 1 ft. 9 in.	Large trough, fragmentary.	½ lb. . . .	..	....
89	XLIV	F	IV	I 12/15	11 ft. 8 in.	V	Ht. 1 ft. 11 in., diam. 1 ft. 8 in.	Do. .	Large bones weighing about 4 lbs. including some charred ones. These included leg and other long bones, some vertebrae, two canine jaws, ribs, and a number of teeth.	..	....
90	..	F	G. G. Area.	I 9/7	4 ft. 3 in.	III	..	..	Small pieces of bones.	..	....
91	..	F	G. G. Area.	I 9/7	4 ft. 11 in.	III	..	Round, very fragmentary.	7 oz. . . .	..	Some small lids .
92	..	F	G. G. Area.	I 8/9	4 ft. 9 in.	IV	..	Do. .	4 oz. . . .	..	....
93	..	F	G. G. Area.	I 9/6	5 ft. 3 in.	III	..	Do. .	3 oz. . . .	..	....
94	3470	F	G. G. Area.	J 8/22	8 ft. 9 in.	III	Ht. 1 ft. 5 in. .	Do. .	Piece of a bone .	1	A fragmentary tapering vase.
95	..	F	G. G. Area.	J 7/25	10 ft. 8 in.	IV	..	Do. .	A few . . .	..	....
96	..	F	III	N 9/5	7 ft. 3 in.	IV	..	Do. .	..	..	....
97	..	F	III	N 9/5	7 ft. 8 in.	IV	..	Do. .	Several . .	1	1 lid . . .
98	..	F	III	N 9/4	7 ft. 2 in.	IV	..	Do. .	A few . . .	..	Tumbler and a small *handi*.
99	..	F	III	N 9/4 and 9.	9 ft. 3 in.	IV	..	Do. .	½ lb. . . .	..	1 miniature vase and a small lid (3921).

CREMATION URNS—*contd.*

Objects. Toys. 13	Cakes. 14	Potsherds. 15	Ornaments of pottery, faience, shell, etc. (in case of pottery substance is not specified). 16	Charcoal, ashes, etc. 17	Shell, ivory, copper. 18	Miscellaneous. 19	Remarks. 20	Serial No. 1
....	Fragments of about a dozen.	Half a basketful. Of 2 goblets with pointed bases, 1 long oval, 2 cylindrical, 2 *Mandi*-shaped and 2 other vases. Of 1 jar, 1 dish and other vessels.	....	..	..	..	The earth in its lower portion was hard and greenish. Just at the bottom a small quantity of earth was loose, sandy and powdery.	79
1 flower, 1 human figure, 2 human legs, fragment of an animal and 2 tiny balls	1 fragment .	A number, with a majority of goblets with pointed bases.	Fragments of bangles and 1 bead, 1 faience and 1 paste bead, fragment of a faience bangle.	..	..	1 grindstone, 1 chert core, 1 t.c. tube, and several pieces of slag.	This trough lay a little below the foundation of a feeble wall of the 1st stratum and is the largest of all.	80
....	A few fragments.	Of a pointed goblet, thick tumbler, offerings' dish, and miscellaneous vases.	Fragment of a bangle	Pieces of decayed charcoal.	Copper scum .	Some slag . .	Earth in the trough was porous.	81
...	Pieces .	A large number . .	....	Pieces of charcoal and lumps of ashes.	..	Traces of decayed cereal. Fragments of a stone dish.	....	82
...	A piece .	One-sixth basketful, miscellaneous.	1 discoid steatite bead.	..	..	....	....	83
....	Some pieces .	Numerous, of goblets with pointed bases and other small vases.	....	..	..	Traces of decayed cereal.	At the mouth the trough was hedged round with standing bricks.	84
....	Fragments .	Of miscellaneous vessels	....	Tiny pieces of charcoal.	..	Decayed cereal mixed in earth.	On removal of this trough another similar trough was found underneath.	85
...	..	A few . . .	2 bits of faience and t.c. bangles.	Bits of charcoal	Bit of river shell	Traces of decayed cereal. Fragment of an alabaster wavy ring and 1 of a disc.	....	86
....	..	A few, including bottom of a long oval vase, 4 of dishes, and 1 of a tumbler.	....	Charcoal and ashes mixed with earth.	2 river shells .	A stone disc with a diametrical depression on either side.	This trough was lying upside down close to a fragmentary pavement.	87
Bust of a female figure and 2 balls.	Two bits .	About half a basketful, of pointed goblets, 1 small tumbler, dishes, and 1 long oval vase.	3 pieces of bangles, 2 beads, of faience and steatite.	Bits of charcoal	1 small oval shell tablet.	Lumps of decayed cereal, a pebble of chalcedony and pieces of slag.	It lay slightly tilted against a bit of wall.	88
....	Some pieces .	Numerous, including 2 bottoms of goblets with pointed bases, sherds of dishes, 1 long oval vase, etc.	4 discoid steatite beads.	Bits of charcoal mixed with earth.	..	2 lumps of t.c. pressed under a closed fist. Decayed cereals.	The trough lay embedded in a thick layer of rubbish consisting of brickbats, nodules and charcoal.	89
2 balls and fragments of others.	Fragments .	Of goblets, with pointed bases, tumblers, etc.	Fragment of a bangle	..	Fragment of a river shell.	Fragment of a t.c. horn-shaped object.	....	90
Several balls .	Do. .	Of goblets with pointed bases, etc.	Fragments of bangles	..	..	Fragment of a t.c. tube.	This jar lay under No. 92.	91
....	..	Of a goblet with pointed base, 1 long oval vase and 1 tumbler.	Fragment of a bangle	..	..	....	....	92
....	..	Sherds of a dish .	....	.	..	....	....	93
1 rhinoceros, 1 fragmentary wheel.	Fragments .	Sherds of goblets with pointed bases, tumblers, etc.	....	.	Piece of a river shell.	....	....	94
....	Do. .	Of goblets with pointed bases, and small jars.	Fragments of faience and t.c. bangles.	..	..	Traces of decayed grain.	....	95
....	Do. .	Of jars, vases, tumblers and other vessels.	....	..	..	....	....	96
....	..	Of goblets with pointed bases, and of a basin, perforated cylindrical vessel, tumbler, round vases, etc.	Fragments of a bangle and 1 tiny faience bead.	..	Fragments of a pointed ivory rod.	....	....	97
1 ball and fragments of a chariot.	Fragments .	Of goblets with pointed bases, tumblers, basins and dishes.	....	..	..	....	....	98
....	Do. .	A few, of small jars and other vessels.	Fragments of bangles	..	1 river shell .	Decayed grain in greenish earth.	....	99

TABLE I.—CONTENTS OF POST-

Serial No.	Register number.	Findspot.			Depth below surface.	Stratum.	Measurements.	Description of jar.	Bones of animals and birds with approximate quantity or number.	Pottery.	
		Mound.	Trench.	Square.						Goblets with pointed bases.	Other pottery.
1	2	3	4	5	6	7	8	9	10	11	12
100	..	AB	Ex. P. I & II.	O 24/21 and 22.	5 ft. 8 in.	II	..	Round, very fragmentary.	Some . . .	..	....
101	..	F	III	N 10/6	8 ft. 10 in.	IV	..	Do. .	½ lb. . . .	..	....
102	..	F	III	N 10/1	6 ft. 6 in.	III	..	Do. .	..	..	....
103	..	AB	Ex. P. I & II.	Q 25/1	6 ft.	II	..	Do. .	Some . . .	..	....
104	7539	F	G. G. Area.	I 9/20	7 ft. 10 in.	III	..	Do. .	Some including piece of a charred bone.	..	1 small tumbler and 2 tiny lids.
105	7751	AB	Ex. P. I & II.	P 23/15	8 ft.	IV	..	Do. .	Some . . .	..	Squat vase . .
106	7765	AB	Ex. P. I & II.	P 24/5	9 ft. 5 in.	IV	..	Do. .	Several . .	..	4 tiny lids . .
107	..	AB	Ex. P. I & II.	P 25/6	9 ft. 10 in.	IV	..	Do. .	Some . . .	..	....
108	7778	F	G. G. Area.	I 9/3	6 ft. 6 in.	IV	..	Round, lower half	Do. . .	..	1 tiny lid . .
109	..	F	G. G. Area.	I 0/3	7 ft.	IV	..	Small round, very fragmentary.	Do. . .	..	....
110	..	F	IV	I 13/34	1 ft. 9 in.	I	..	Small, round, bottom portion.	A few . . .	..	....
111	7849	F	III	N 9/15	10 ft. 3 in.	V	..	Do. .	Several . .	..	....
112	7851	F	G. G. Area.	I 9/3	3 ft. 10 in.	II	..	Round, crushed .	Do. .	..	2 tiny and 1 large lid, 1 tumbler.
113	7863	F	G. G. Area.	K 9/3	9 ft. 4 in.	III	..	Round, very fragmentary.	Do. . .	..	Long oval vase, fragmentary.
114	.	F	V	K 13/6	2 ft.	I	..	Do. .	A small quantity of decayed bones.	..	....
115	..	F	V	K 11/16	1 ft. 6 in.	I	..	Do. .	A few decayed bones.	..	....

CREMATION URNS—*contd.*

Objects.			Ornaments of pottery, faience, shell, etc. (in case of pottery substance is not specified).	Charcoal, ashes, etc.	Shell, ivory, copper.	Miscellaneous.	Remarks.	Serial No.
Toys.	Cakes.	Potsherds.						
13	14	15	16	17	18	19	20	1
....	..	....	Tiny cylindrical bead. No. 4555.	Tiny pieces of charcoal.	..	....	Earth inside the jar was loose. At bottom it was powdery and discoloured green.	100
....	Some fragments.	Of one goblet with pointed base.	....	Tiny pieces of charcoal and ashes.	..	....	The contents were covered with greenish earth containing some decayed cereal. A number of dead worms were sticking inside the jar.	101
....	Do.	Of goblets with pointed bases and other vases.	....	..	..	Decayed cereal.	....	102
....	..	Of goblets with pointed bases, 1 tumbler, 1 dish and other vessels.	....	..	..	Do.	....	103
....	Fragments of 4 or 5.	7 or 8 small sherds	Fragment of a bangle	..	..	....	....	104
....	Do.	Half a basketful of goblets with pointed bases, of 4 oval vases, 2 tumblers, 3 goblets, 3 lids and other vessels.	1 paste bead	..	..	Decayed grain.	....	105
2 balls	1 fragment	Of goblets with pointed bases and other vessels.	2 pieces of a ribbed faience bangle.	Pieces of charcoal.	..	Some seeds of melon variety and decayed cereals.	....	106
....	..	Of goblets with pointed bases, 1 dish, 1 basin, 3 tumblers, 1 *handi*-shaped and of some other vases.	....	Tiny pieces of charcoal.	1 tiny piece of copper.	....	Earth in the jar was porous and ashy.	107
1 mother suckling a baby.	Fragments of 4 or 5.	Two handfuls, of a small jar, goblets with pointed bases, vases, etc.	1 bead; 1 complete and fragments of 2 or 3 bangles.	..	1 plano-convex piece of shell.	....	....	108
....	..	....	....	Tiny pieces of charcoal.	..	Decayed cereal.	....	109
....	Some fragments.	Of jars, etc.	....	..	..	....	The earth inside it was ashy.	110
1 wheel and 1 chariot with trace of an occupant.	..	Half a basketful, of a dozen goblets with pointed bases, 2 small tumblers, 1 oval vase, 1 dish and other vessels.	Fragment of a bangle and 1 faience bead.	Tiny pieces of charcoal.	1 fragmentary ivory stilus.	1 fragmentary antler	Sherds of goblets with pointed bases retained traces of decayed grain and some also contained tiny bones.	111
1 female figurine and a chariot.	Fragments of 4 or 5.	Of more than a dozen goblets with pointed bases, 2 or 3 long oval, 1 oval, 1 double convex, 1 *handi*-shaped and 2 pointed vases, of 3 or 4 tumblers, 3 or 4 smaller jars, 4 or 5 dishes and a basin.	Fragments of one keeled and of 3 or 4 other bangles, 1 tiny discoid paste bead.	Do.	..	....	It contained hard earth.	112
1 leg	Fragments of 2 or 3.	Of goblets with pointed bases, of 1 dish, 1 basin, 1 small jar, 1 *handi*-shaped vase and of other vessels.	Tubular bead, fragments of 4 or 5 bangles and 1 paste bead.	Ashes and tiny pieces of charcoal mixed with greenish earth.	..	Decayed cereal and lot of slag.	More than half the jar was full of extraneous, ashy earth profusely mixed with slag and nodules. In the upper half it contained a basketful of thin ballast, ashes, tiny pieces of charcoal, 3 or 4 brickbats, a few sherds and pieces of a very decayed bone. In the lower half, with which the majority of contents were associated, the earth was greenish, porous and ashy.	113
....	..	Several, of long oval and perforated vases, of tumblers, and goblets with pointed bases, etc.	1 faience bead	Tiny pieces of charcoal.	..	....	....	114
1 ball	..	A few, of a tumbler and of 1 goblet with pointed base, etc.	1 tiny discoid steatite bead.	Do.	..	....	....	115

TABLE I.—CONTENTS OF POST-

Serial No.	Register number.	Findspot.			Depth below surface.	Stratum.	Measurements.	Description of jar.	Bones of animals and birds with approximate quantity or number.	Pottery.	
		Mound.	Trench.	Square.						Goblets with pointed bases.	Other pottery.
1	2	3	4	5	6	7	8	9	10	11	12
116	10252	F	IV	I 12/4	9 ft.	IV	..	Round, in pieces .	Several . .	..	1 oval vase with long neck and 1 small squat vase.
117	..	F	IV	I 13/14	3 ft.	II	..	Do. . .	Several, and a broken tooth.	..	....
118	10384	F	V	K 12/10 and 15.	7 ft. 3 in.	II	..	Do. .	A few . .	..	....
119	XXV	AB	Tr. S. E.	Q 28/21	13 ft.	V	..	Round, bottom portion.	Several and 1 molar tooth.	..	....
120	XXVI	AB	Tr. S. E.	Q 27/25	12 ft. 5 in.	IV	..	Do. . .	2 oz. . . .	..	....
121	XXX	AB	Tr. S. E.	R 28/2	6 ft.	II	..	Round, fragmentary.	4 fish bones and a few other tiny bones.	..	....
122	XXXI	AB	Tr. S. E.	Q 28/1	13 ft.	V	..	Round, bottom portion.	2 bits . . .	..	2 lids, 1 small vase 1 shallow saucer and 1 tiny vase.
123	3760	F	G. G. Area.	I 9/9	9 ft. 8 in.	V	Ht. 1 ft. 6 in., diam. of mouth 1 ft. 2 in.	Large, oval . .	Very few . .	..	....
124	4360	F	G. G. Area.	K 8/5	4 ft.	II	Ht. 1 ft. 3 in. .	Oval, in fragments	A piece of bone .	..	....
125	5345	F	G. G. Area.	I 9/15	5 ft. 10 in.	III	Ht. 1 ft. 8 in., diam. of mouth 7½ in.	Oval . . .	Do. . .	..	A fragmentary tumbler.
126	5920	AB	Rv. P. I & II.	P 23/10	9 ft.	IV	..	Do. . . .	4 small pieces of charred bones and 3 others.	1	....
127	7289	F	G. G. Area.	I 9/20	9 ft. 6 in.	IV	..	Oval, cracked .	Some . . .	..	....
128	7772	F	G. G. Area.	I 9/2	3 ft. 6 in.	II	..	Do. . .	Do. . . .	2	....
129	7840	F	G. G. Area.	I 9/1	2 ft. 6 in.	II	..	Do. . .	A few . . .	..	....
130	..	F	G. G. Area.	J 9/21	13 ft.	V	Ht. about 1 ft. 1 in.	Oval, very fragmentary.	Do. . . .	..	....
131	7853	F	G. G. Area.	I 9/8	7 ft. 2 in.	IV	Ht. 1 ft. 6 in., diam. at mouth 6 in.	Do. . .	Several . .	..	....
132	7866	F	G. G. Area.	J 9/25	12 ft.	IV	..	Oval . . .	A few . . .	..	....
133	6332	F	V	J 12/25	7 ft. 4 in.	III	..	Oval, very fragmentary.	A fragmentary bone.	2	....
134	..	F	IV	I 14/9	8 ft. 10 in.	III	..	Oval, bottom portion.	Some . . .	..	....
135	V	D	I	Q 30/14	1 ft. 9 in.	II	Ht. about 1 ft. 8 in.	Oval, upper half .	2 small pieces .	..	....

Cremation Urns—*contd.*

Objects. Toys. 13	Cakes. 14	Potsherds. 15	Ornaments of pottery, faience, shell, etc. (in case of pottery substance is not specified). 16	Charcoal, ashes, etc. 17	Shell, ivory, copper. 18	Miscellaneous. 19	Remarks. 20	Serial No. 1
1 wheel . .	Several fragments.	Of a basin, of goblets with pointed bases, tumblers, perforated vases, jars, dishes, etc.	2 pieces of bangles .	Bits of charcoal	2 small pieces of river shell.	Traces of decayed cereal and some slag. A discoid faience sealing lentoid in section (Pl. C, 671).	The earth in the jar was porous and contained traces of decayed cereal. Chaff, straw, melon seeds and leaf impressions. The jar is inscribed in 2 lines with 7 pictograms.	116
....	..	....	....	Tiny pieces of charcoal.	..	Traces of decayed cereal at the bottom.	The jar was covered with a fragmentary dish.	117
....	Some fragments.	Some . . .	Bit of a bangle .	A few pieces of charcoal.	River shell .	Fragments of a chert scraper. Decayed cereal.	....	118
....	..	Numerous, including those of dishes, and of 1 tumbler and 1 goblet with pointed base.	....	..	..	....	At the bottom was a thick layer of ashes in which the sherds were much rooted.	119
2 balls . .	..	A few, including bottom of a goblet with pointed base.	....	..	..	Porous lumps of decayed cereal with occasional marks of chaff.	....	120
....	..	Numerous, including those of a flanged *handi*-shaped vase, of a dish and oval vases.	....	Bits of charcoal and ashes.	..	....	This jar lay embedded in a fragmentary pavement.	121
....	..	2 fragments of a dish and 1 of a tumbler.	44 double convex discoid and 121 biconical beads, 6 steatite beads and a discoid plano-convex faience temple ornament.	..	..	....	....	122
....	Numerous fragments.	2 or 3 bits . .	....	Tiny pieces of charcoal and ashes.	..	....	....	123
....	A few fragments.	Of goblets with pointed bases and other vases.	....	Tiny pieces of charcoal.	..	....	Contained percolated earth.	124
....	..	A few . . .	....	Some .	..	....	....	125
....	..	Of a long oval vase and another vessel.	....	..	..	Decayed cereal.	....	126
....	A fragment .	1 of dish and 1 other .	2 fragments of bangles.	A few tiny pieces of charcoal.	A piece of shell	....	....	127
....	..	Of a small oval vase and 2 of neck of a jar.	....	2 or 3 bits of charcoal.	..	A small faience vase.	....	128
....	..	2 or 3 bits . . .	....	..	..	Piece of slag.	....	129
....	Fragments of 7 or 8.	Some score sherds of a jar, a dish, and other vessels.	Fragments of 2 bangles.	Ashes mixed with tiny pieces of charcoal.	Piece of a river-shell.	....	Earth in the jar was hard but at bottom it was ashy and powdery.	130
Legs of human figurines.	Fragments of 1 or 2.	Of a long oval vase, a goblet with pointed base, and another jar.	Pieces of a few bangles.	Ashes mixed with greenish and porous earth in the lower portion.	Do. . shell.	....	The neck of the jar was encased in a brick reservoir	131
....	..	1 of a goblet with pointed base.	....	..	..	Decayed cereal.	....	132
....	..	A few miscellaneous, including one of an oval vase.	Tiny bud-shaped faience pendant (No. 8382a).	..	Ivory baluster in pieces.	....	....	133
....	1 fragment .	A few, of a goblet with pointed base and of other vases.	....	Some ashes and small pieces of charcoal were found at bottom.	..	....	....	134
....	Do. .	A few . . .	....	..	..	Fragments of a stone pestle.	The earth inside bore faint impressions of some cereal-like seanrum.	135

TABLE I.—CONTENTS OF POST-

Serial No.	Register number.	Findspot.			Depth below surface.	Stratum.	Measurements.	Description of jar.	Bones of animals and birds with approximate quantity or number.	Pottery.	
		Mound.	Trench.	Square.						Goblets with pointed bases.	Other pottery.
1	2	3	4	5	6	7	8	9	10	11	12
136	VII	D	I	Q 31/6	7 ft. 6 in.	IV	Ht. 1 ft. 3 in. .	Oval, fragmentary	A few . . .	..	....
137	XXXIX	AB	Tr. S. E.	R 27/3	14 ft.	IV	..	Large, oval, bottom portion.	Do. .	..	....
138	XL	AB	Tr. S. E.	Q 28/17	9 ft. 7 in.	III	..	Oval, very fragmentary.	2 pieces, charred.	..	....
139	XLI	AB	Tr. S. E.	Q 28/7	1 ft. 6 in.	I	..	Large, oval, bottom portion.	1 oz. . . .	.	....
140	XLIII	F	IV	I 12/15	11 ft. 0 in.	V	Ht. 1 ft. 5½ in. .	Oval, fragmentary	2 oz. . . .	1	....
141	XLVII	F	IV	I 13/23	7 ft. 2 in.	III	..	Do. . .	2 or 3 small bits of bones.	..	....
142	299	F	G. G. Area.	J 9/25	11 ft. 6 in.	IV	..	Large, cylindrical	½ lb. . . .	..	11 small lids . .
143	3577	F	I	M 11/12	11 ft. 5 in.	V	Ht. 2 ft. 4½ in., diam. at mouth 1 ft. 6 in.	Do. . .	½ lb. . .	..	....
144	3683	F	I	M 11/20	9 ft. 11 in.	IV	Ht. 2 ft. 4 in., diam. 1 ft. 3 in.	Large, cylindrical, fragmentary.	..	1 complete, 1 broken.	1 long oval vase .
145	3885	F	G. G. Area.	J 7/20	8 ft. 3 in.	IV	..	Do. . .	½ lb. . .	..	1 tumbler, 2 lids and 1 basin.
146	5872	F .	III	N 10/11	8 ft. 6 in.	IV	..	Large, cylindrical, lower half.	Several . .	1 large and 2 small.	1 oval vase and 1 tumbler.
147	7783	F	G. G. Area.	H 9/23 and I 9/3	7 ft. 3 in.	IV	..	Do. . .	Tiny bones, skull of a small creature and pieces of large bones.	..	1 tiny lid and a fragmentary tumbler.
148	..	F	IV	I 13/16	6 ft. 10 in.	III	..	Cylindrical .	½ lb. . . .	..	....
149	..	F	V	J 12/25	11 ft.	IV	..	Large, cylindrical, flat at base and flanged below rim.	A few pieces .	..	....
150	..	D	I	Q 30/9	2 ft. 2 in.	III	Diam. 1 ft. 4½ in.	Large, cylindrical, upper one-third broken.	1 tooth . .	1	....
151	XI	D	I	Q 31/7 and 8	7 ft. 9 in.	IV	..	Large, cylindrical	About 1½ lbs. .	6	1 long oval vase and 1 large tumbler.
152	XXII	D	III	S 29/15	9 ft.	IV	..	Large, cylindrical, lower half.	A bit . . .	..	....
153	2844a	F	G. G. Area.	I 8/7.	5 ft. 8 in.	III	..	Fragmentary .	Some . . .	..	....
154	2844b	F	G. G. Area.	I 8/7	5 ft. 10 in.	III	..	Do. . .	Do. . .	..	....
155	..	F	I	M 11/7	10 ft.	IV	..	Large, fragmentary.	A few . . .	..	....

Cremation Urns—*contd.*

Objects. Toys.	Cakes.	Potsherds.	Ornaments of pottery, faiance, shell, etc. (in case of pottery substance is not specified).	Charcoal, ashes, etc.	Shell, ivory, copper.	Miscellaneous.	Remarks.	Serial No.
13	14	15	16	17	18	19	20	1
....	Several fragments.	A few . . .	Fragment of a shell bangle.	Pieces of charcoal.	..	Lumps of decayed cereal.	....	136
....	..	Numerous, including 1 of a handi-shaped flanged vase, and 1 of a small painted vase.	2 bits of bangles .	Profusion of ashes and charcoal.	1 small lump of copper, 1 oval shell tablet.	1 piece of chert, and 1 t. c. tetrahedron.	Was partially buried under a later wall.	137
....	..	....	1 discoid bead .	Bits of charcoal	..	....	Immediately below its fragments lay 2 sherds of a large dish in which were found two charred animal, bones.	138
....	..	....	....	Do. . .	..	....	....	139
....	4 pieces .	Several, including those of a goblet with pointed base, and of a long oval vase.	....	Do. . .	..	Decayed cereal.	....	140
....	..	A few . . .	....	Bits of charcoal	..	Lumps of decayed cereal.	In the lumps of decayed cereal there were indications of barley (?) husk.	141
....	Numerous fragments.	Some . .	1 bangle and 1 paste bead.	Some charcoal .	2 fragmentary river shells.	....	....	142
....	..	Bottom of a goblet with pointed base and of another vessel.	1 bangle . .	..	..	Stone pestle and fragments of a grindstone.	....	143
....	..	....	....	..	..	....	....	144
2 balls, 1 seated male, 1 standing female wearing copper armlet, 1 animal, 1 horn, and pieces of cart frames.	Several fragments.	Of more than a dozen goblets with pointed bases, and of an oval vase, round jar, dishes, etc.	Fragments of bangles.	..	..	Decayed grain.	....	145
....	Fragments .	Of a dozen goblets with pointed bases, and of round and oval vases, tumblers and small jars.	1 bangle and some fragments.	A few pieces of charcoal.	..	....	....	146
1 ram . .	Do. .	Half a basketful of goblets with pointed bases, tumblers, etc.	1 bangle and fragments.	..	..	1 thick t. c. ring .	On the greenish earth which filled it were impressions of leaves and roots.	147
....	..	Several . . .	....	Some pieces of charcoal.	..	Stone pestle . .	It lay against a thick wall.	148
....	Several fragments.	Its own, pieces of basins, goblets with pointed bases, etc.	2 fragments of bangles.	Tiny pieces of charcoal in the upper portion.	..	Rough stone ball .	It stood at the end of a small covered drain.	149
....	..	4 fragmentary vases .	Fragment of a bangle	Ashes . .	1 broken river shell.	Decayed cereal.	....	150
2 wheels .	A few . .	Miscellaneous, about half a basketful.	A number of broken bangires.	Bits of charcoal	..	Lumps of decayed cereal.	This was placed on the bottom of a napiform jar and had a brick reservoir above it.	151
....	..	Several, one of them being the socted bottom of a vase.	1 round carnelian bead.	..	..	1 tumbler of steatite.	....	152
....	..	Several . . .	....	..	..	....	....	153
1 female figure and pieces of cart frames.	..	Of goblets with pointed bases.	....	..	..	....	....	154
...	..	A few . . .	....	..	..	....	Round the mouth of this jar was a square brick reservoir.	155

TABLE I.—CONTENTS OF POST-

Serial No.	Register number.	Findspot.			Depth below surface.	Stratum.	Measurements.	Description of jar.	Bones of animals and birds with approximate quantity or number.	Pottery.	
		Mound.	Trench.	Square.						Goblets with pointed bases.	Other pottery.
1	2	3	4	5	6	7	8	9	10	11	12
156	..	AB	Ex. P. I & II.	Q 24/15	5 ft. 3 in.	II	..	Very fragmentary.	¼ lb. . . .	..	....
157	..	AB	Ex. P. I & II.	Q 24/18	5 ft. 3 in.	II	..	Do. . .	1 fragment . .	..	....
158	..	D	I	Q 31/13	4 ft. 6 in.	II	..	Do. . .	A few . . .	..	1 small tumbler.
159	..	D	I	Q 31/10	3 ft.	I	..	Bottom portion .	Some . . .	..	....
160	.	F	G. G. Area.	K 9/2	5 ft. 9 in.	II	..	Do. . .	Do. . .	..	1 globular vase (4630) of black colour.
161	5570	F	III	N 10/1	5 ft.	II	..	Do. . .	5 tiny pieces .	1	3 tumblers . .
162	7090	AB	Ex. P. I & II.	P 24/25	6 ft. 10 in.	III	..	Very fragmentary.	Several . .	1	1 long oval vase, fragmentary.
163	..	AB	Ex. P. I & II.	P 24/21	8 ft.	IV	..	Do. . .	A few . . .	..	....
164	7198	AB	Ex. P. I & II.	P 24/11	6 ft.	III	..	Do. . .	Do. . .	..	1 tumbler . .
165	7737	F	G. G. Area.	I 9/5	3 ft. 4 in.	II	..	Do. . .	3 . . .	3	....
166	7774	F	G. G. Area.	I 9/10	9 ft.	V	..	Do. . .	3 pieces . .	..	....
167	..	F	IV	I 13/23	1 ft.	I	..	Do. . .	1 piece . .	..	....
168	7836a	F	IV	I 14/3	9 in.	I	..	Do. . .	A few . . .	..	....
169	..	F	IV	I 12/10	8 ft. 6 in.	IV	..	Do. . .	Some, including two teeth and a few charred pieces.	..	....
170	10312	F	IV	I 12/7	9 ft. 5 in.	IV	..	Large, shaped like a goblet with pointed base.	A few . . .	..	....
171	XLV	F	IV	I 12/5	11 ft. 4 in.	V	Ht. about 2 ft. .	Squat, tapering .	6 oz. including one charred.	..	A large oval vase with long neck.
172	10360	F	IV	I 11/10	7 ft. 6 in.	IV	..	*Dog*-shaped, with pointed bottom, crushed.	½ lb. . . .	..	2 oval vases, 1 small dish.
173	10377	F	V	J 12/9	9 ft. 8 in.	IV	..	Long, oval, fragmentary.	Numerous, including joint bones, ribs and jaws.	1	..
174	..	F	V	J 12/4	9 ft. 9 in.	IV	..	Do. . .	A few . . .	..	....
175	..	F	IV	J 14/21	6 ft. 6 in.	III	Ht. 2 ft., dia. at centre 2 ft.	Napiform, lower two-third.	2 oz. . . .	..	1 round fragmentary vase.
176	.	F	IV	J 13/12	6 ft.	III	Diam. 2 ft. . .	Large trough, fragmentary.	1 lb . . .	..	....

CREMATION URNS—*concld.*

Objects.			Ornaments of pottery, faience, shell, etc. (in case of pottery substance is not specified).	Charcoal, ashes, etc.	Shell, ivory, copper.	Miscellaneous.	Remarks	Serial No.
Toys.	Cakes.	Potsherds.						
13	14	15	16	17	18	19	20	1
1 ram . .	..	Of a tumbler and of a dish.	....	Some pieces of charcoal.	..	Fragment of a unicorn seal.	....	156
....	..	2 or 3 . . .	....	2 tiny pieces of charcoal.	..	....	....	157
1 female figure .	Fragments of 2 or 3.	....	Fragment of bangles and 1 horn.	Tiny pieces of charcoal.	1 river shell .	Decayed cereals. A piece of slag.	....	158
....	3 fragments .	....	Fragment of a faience bangle.	Do. . .	Do. . .	....	....	159
....	..	....	....	..	..	....	....	160
....	..	....	....	..	..	....	....	161
....	..	....	....	Pieces of charcoal.	..	Decayed cereal	A few long bones were found in the oval vase.	162
....	Fragments of 3 or 4.	Several of a tumbler, an offerings' dish and other vessels.	....	Tiny pieces of charcoal.	..	....	The jar was full of brick bats.	163
....	Fragments .	Some . . .	..	Do. . .		2 fragmentary antlers. Decayed cereal.	....	164
....	..	....	1 small discoid paste bead.	..	..	....	One of the goblets had a series of four vertical strokes incised on it.	165
....	Fragments of 1 or 2.	A handful, including some of a perforated cylindrical vase.	1 complete and 1 broken paste bead.	..	..	....	....	166
....	..	A handful, of 1 goblet with pointed base and of other vessels.	....	..	..	....	....	167
....	..	3 or 4 . . .	....	..	..	....	....	168
....	..	A few . . .	....	..	..	....	....	169
....	..	Several, including 1 of a shallow dish.	Fragment of a cylindrical steatite bead.	Profusion of charcoal and ashes.	A fragmentary lozenge-shaped copper object.	Many t.c. lumps with impressions of a closed fist.	Shape rare.	170
....	Numerous fragments.	Numerous, miscellaneous.	....	Bits of charcoal	..	Lumps of decayed cereal, 5 t. c. lumps with marks of a closed fist.	....	171
....	Several pieces	Several, including bottoms of 2 oval vases and of a pointed goblet.	....	Tiny bits of charcoal.	2 river shells .	Traces of decayed cereal.	Shape rare.	172
....	Fragments .	Of goblets with pointed bases, tumblers and long oval vases, etc.	1 plain (entire) and pieces of ribbed bangles, 6 pieces of faience finger rings, 6 faience beads and 8 tiny discoid steatite beads.	Bits of charcoal	..	....	....	173
....	1 fragment .	Of 3 tumblers, goblets with pointed bases, of 1 long oval vase, 1 red washed dish and 1 perforated vase.	Fragments of thick bangles.	2 or 3 pieces of charcoal.	1 river shell .	....	....	174
....	Do.	A number . . .	....	Charcoal . .	Do. . .	1 rough stone ball.	....	175
....	2 fragments .	Do. . . .	2 fragments of bangles.	Do. . .	..	Decayed cereal.	....	176

TABLE II.—CONTENTS OF THE LONG ROW[1] OF 54 BROKEN JARS DISCOVERED IN A LANE IN THE TRENCH AT THE SOUTHERN EDGE OF MOUND AB IN ASSOCIATION WITH STRATUM V AT A DEPTH OF 15 FT. 9 IN. TO 16 FT. 6 IN. BELOW THE SURFACE.

(Pls. LXXV, *b* and XXXVI, *b*.)

Serial No.	Square.	Measurements.	Bones of animals and birds with approximate quantity or number.	Pottery Objects.				Ornaments (in case of terracotta substance is not specified).	Charcoal, ashes, etc.	Uncommon contents.	Remarks.
				Pottery.	Toys.	Cakes.	Potsherds.				
1	2	3	4	5	6	7	8	9	10	11	12
1	Q 28/1	..	1 oz.	..	..	..	A few . . .	..	Bits of charcoal.	..	
2	Q 28/6	..	1 oz.	..	..	..	Half a basketful, including 1 of a small tumbler.	Thin, discoid paste bead.	Do.	Fragment of a faïence sealing.	
3	Q 28/6	..	3 oz.	..	Female head.	..	Half a basketful, including sherds of a pointed goblet, a perforated vase, a dish and one painted vase.	4 faïence beads	Do.	One piece each of chalcedony and mica.	
4	Q 28/6	Diam. at centre 1 ft. 9 in.	10 oz.	..	..	..	Numerous, including those of tumblers, long oval vases, pointed goblets, dishes and of a flanged vase.	Several pieces of bangles.	Do.	..	
5	Q 28/6	..	8 oz.	..	..	..	Half a basketful, including those of a long oval vase, of a pointed goblet, etc.	..	Do.	..	This jar stood over two other fragmentary Jars Nos. 6 and 7.
6	Q 28/6	..	1 oz.	..	..	..	Of a *ghara*, a long oval vase, a tiny lid, etc.	..	Do.	..	
7	Q 28/6	..	½ oz.	..	..	1 bit	About one-third basketful, including 5 bottoms of pointed goblets.	..	Do.	Decayed cereal	
8	Q 28/6	..	A few	..	..	..	Several .	..	Do.	Lumps of decayed cereal.	
9	Q 28/6	..	1 oz.	..	..	2 bits	A few, including one of a pointed goblet.	2 fragments of bangles.	Do.	1 terracotta lump with impression of closed fist.	Lay immediately north of No. 8 about 2 ft. outside the row.
10	Q 28/6	..	4 oz. including a few charred bits.	..	..	..	Several, including one each of a pointed goblet, a tumbler and a dish.	2 pieces of terracotta and 1 of shell bangles.	Do.	..	Lay about a foot to the north-west of No. 9.
11	Q 28/6	..	A few	..	..	..	A few . .	..	Do.	..	
12	Q 28/6	..	4 oz.	..	..	..	Quarter basketful, including one each of a pointed goblet, a dish and a *ghara*	..	Do.	Lumps of decayed cereal.	
13	Q 28/6	..	1 oz.	..	..	..	One each of a dish and a pointed goblet.	A cylindrical shell bead, fragmentary.	Do.	Decayed cereal	
14	Q 28/6	..	Some tiny bones.	..	..	..	A few, of the jar itself	..	Do.	A fragmentary chert scraper.	
15	Q 28/6	..	1 oz.	..	..	..	A few, of the jar itself and one of a dish.	..	Do.	Piece of a miniature wavy ring of alabaster. Decayed cereal.	
16	Q 28/6	..	½ oz.	..	..	6 fragments.	Several, including those of the jar itself and of a small *ghara*.	3 beads of steatite and 1 of faïence.	Do.	..	
17	Q 28/6	Contents typical but not recorded.									
18	Q 28/6	Diam. at centre 1 ft. 10 in.	1 oz.	A fragmentary long oval vase.	1 wheel	..	Several, including 1 of a pointed goblet and bottom of a *ghara*.	..	Bits of charcoal	Lumps of decayed cereal.	
19	Q 28/11	Diam. at centre 1 ft. 3 in.	4 oz.	1 small tumbler and 1 tiny lid.	1 ball	..	A few, including 1 of a long oval vase.	Thin discoid bead of steatite paste.	Do.	Do.	
20	Q 28/11	..	1 oz. including a few charred ones.	..	1 dog	..	Several, including bottom of an oval jar, and 2 of an oval vase.	..	Do.	Do.	
21	Q 28/11	..	1 oz.	..	Pedestalled bird.	Some fragments.	Numerous, including those of oval and long oval vases and pointed goblets.	Leaf-shaped copper pendant, fragmentary.	Do.	Do.	

[1] Beginning from its western end the jars in this row were numbered 1, 2, 3, 4, etc. Most of them were napiform in shape but some were round, and stood singly touching one another, though in some cases they were piled up two or three one above the other.

TABLE II.—CONTENTS OF THE LONG ROW OF 54 BROKEN JARS—*contd.*

Serial No.	Square.	Measurements.	Bones of animals and birds with approximate quantity or number.	POTTERY OBJECTS.				Ornaments (in case of terracotta substance is not specified).	Charcoal, ashes, etc.	Uncommon contents.	REMARKS.
				Pottery.	Toys.	Cakes.	Potsherds.				
1	2	3	4	5	6	7	8	9	10	11	12
22	Q 28/11	Contents typical but not recorded.									
23	Q 28/11	..	2 oz.	..	..	..	A few including one of a pointed goblet.	..	Bits of charcoal.	Fragment of a greystone pestle. A few lumps of decayed cereal.	
24	Q 28/11	..	..	..	..	2 bits.	Bottom of a goblet with pointed base.	..	Do.	..	Only bottom of the jar survived.
25	Q 28/11	..	6 oz.	2 tiny lids	1 ball	1 fragment.	Several, including one each of a long oval vase and of a small oval jar.	1 fragment of a thick terracotta bangle and one of a shell bangle with midrib.	Do.	1 shell losenge. Some husk and decayed cereal.	Lay above No. 26.
26	Q 28/11	..	4 oz.	..	..	..	Several . . .	..	Do.	Lumps of decayed cereal.	
27	Q 28/11	..	4 oz.	..	..	..	Half a basketful, including 2 of pointed goblets, 2 of dishes, several of a *sherd*, 1 of a tumbler, and of other vases.	Bit of a tubular bead.	Do.	..	
28	Q 28/11	..	6 oz. 1 or 2 pieces bear marks of fire.	1 small vase.	1 wheel	..	About a basketful, including those of goblets with pointed bases tumblers, dishes, long oval vases, etc.	..	Do.	..	
29	Q 28/11	Contents typical but not recorded.									
30	Q 28/11 and 16	..	A few. One piece bears marks of fire.	..	..	A few fragments.	2 of a *sherd* . .	..	..	A small lump of copper and a river shell.	
31	Q 28/11	..	2 oz. Some of the larger bones are charred.	1 tiny lid	Fragmentary wheel and a female torso.	A few fragments	Numerous, including those of a dish, a pointed goblet and an oval vase.	..	Bits of charcoal.	Lumps of decayed cereal.	
32	Q 28/16	..	A small piece	..	..	..	..	..	..	..	Only bottom of the jar survived.
33	Q 28/16	Diam. at centre 1 ft. 8 in.	2 oz.	1 small tumbler	..	..	Numerous . . .	2 fragments of shell bangles and 2 of a terracotta bangle.	..	..	
34	Q 28/16	..	A few tiny bones.	..	..	..	A few . . .	1 lozenge-shaped and 1 tubular bead of faience.	Bits of charcoal.	..	
35	Q 28/16	..	3 oz.	..	..	..	Some, including those of a small jar.	..	Do.	Decayed cereal	
36	Q 27/25 and Q 28/21	..	A few tiny bones.	..	..	..	Several, including one of a pointed goblet and 1 of a vase.	..	Do.	..	Stood over No. 37.
37	Q 27/25 and Q 28/21	..	½ oz. including some tiny charred bones.	..	..	..	Several, including those of a tumbler, a long oval vase, a pointed goblet and of other vases.	2 tubular faience beads.	Do.	..	
38	Q 27/25 and Q 28/21	..	8 oz. including 4 burnt tiny bones.	..	..	Several fragments	A number, including those of dishes, of a goblet with pointed base, a flanged vase and a *sherd*.	..	Do.	..	Among bits of charcoal was found a charred grain of the size and shape of a gram.
39	Q 27/25 and Q 28/21	..	1 oz.	..	..	..	Several, including those of a tumbler, a small oval jar and of another vase.	A thin discoid bead of steatite paste.	Do.	Decayed cereal	
40	Q 27/25 and Q 28/21	..	4 oz.	1 tiny lid.	1 wheel	..	A number, including those of pointed goblets, long oval and cylindrical vases and 3 neck fragments of an oval jar.	2 pieces of bangles.	Do.	..	
41	Q 27/25	..	10 oz. including some charred ones.	1 tiny lid.	..	..	Numerous, including those of a perforated vase and a goblet with pointed base.	Piece of a faience bangle. 4 beads of steatite and faience.	Do.	3 chert flakes.	

TABLE II.—CONTENTS OF THE LONG ROW OF 54 BROKEN JARS—*concld.*

Serial No.	Square.	Measurements.	Bones of animals and birds with approximate quantity or number.	POTTERY OBJECTS.				Ornaments (in case of terracotta substance is not specified).	Charcoal, ashes, etc.	Uncommon contents.	REMARKS.
				Pottery.	Toys.	Cakes.	Potsherds.				
1	2	3	4	5	6	7	8	9	10	11	12
42	Q 27/25	Diam. at centre 2 ft.	2 oz. including several tiny and delicate bones. One large bone was partly charred.	..	..	..	One and a half basketfuls, including those of goblets with pointed bases, 5 of dishes, 1 each of a long oval, cylindrical and round vases, 1 of a small oval jar and 3 of a ghayā.	4 steatite and faience beads and 1 bit of shell bangle.	Bits of charcoal.	Lumps of decayed cereal.	
43	Q 27/25	Diam. at centre 2 ft 1 in.	2 oz. including numerous tiny bones. One large bone bears marks of fire.	1 small lid	..	3 bits.	Half a basketful, including those of a goblet with pointed base, a dish, an oval and a long oval vase.	2 tiny spacers, one of terracotta and the other of faience	Do.	Lumps of decayed cereal.	
44	Q 27/25	Diam. at centre 2 ft.	3 oz.	Do.	Bust of a male figurine, and a tiny ball.	..	Half a basketful, including 1 of a large offering's dish, 1 of an oval jar, and of pointed goblets, dishes and vases.	1 faience bead	Do.	..	
45	Q 27/25 and R 27/5	Diam. at centre, 1 ft. 9 in.	2 oz.	1 goblet with pointed base.	..	..	Numerous, including those of pointed goblets, tumblers, vases and dishes.	6 steatite beads Small pieces of bangles.	Do.	..	
46	R 27/5	..	4 oz	..	1 collared dog and 1 ball.	..	Half a basketful, including those of goblets with pointed bases, 1 of a dish and 1 of a ghayā.	3 faience beads.	Do.	Biconical stone object, fragmentary, 2 pieces of soapstone and 1 of slate stone.	
47	R 27/5	..	6 oz. One bone is charred.	..	1 fragmentary female.	6 fragments.	About a basketful, including those of 3 dishes, 1 tumbler, 1 large oval vase and 4 of pointed goblets.	4 pieces of bangles and 4 faience beads.	Do.	1 piece of soapstone.	
48	R 27/5	Diam. at centre 2 ft.	6 oz.	..	..	..	Several, including those of a dish, 2 of pointed goblets, 2 of a jar painted with bands.	1 tubular steatite bead.	Do.	1 piece of chert scraper.	The earth was greyish at bottom and bore imprints of chaff.
49	R 27/5	..	8 oz. including a few partially charred.	..	..	A few fragments	Quarter basketful, of miscellaneous vases.	2 faience beads and pieces of faience and shell bangles.	Do.	1 lozenge-shaped piece of shell.	
50	R 27/5	Diam. at centre 1 ft. 10 in.	A few pieces.	1 miniature tumbler, 1 goblet with pointed base.	..	..	Its own, and of goblets with pointed bases and of some other vessels.	..	Do.	..	
51	R 27/5	Diam. at centre 1 ft 11 in.	½ lb.	1 goblet with pointed base.	..	..	Its own, and a few of other vessels.	..	Do.	1 piece of soapstone.	
52	R 27/5	Diam. at centre 1 ft. 10 in.	1 large piece of bone.	..	..	..	Several.	..	Charcoal and ashes	..	
53	R 27/5	Diam. at centre 1 ft. 11 in.	4 oz.	..	..	..	Several, miscellaneous	..	Bits of charcoal.	..	
54	R 27/5	Diam. at centre 1 ft. 9 in.	Several pieces.	1 miniature tumbler	..	..	Do.	..	Do.	1 tiny discoid bead of burnt steatite.	

CHAPTER IX.

Plain and Painted Pottery.

In *Mohenjo-daro and the Indus Civilization*[1] Dr. Mackay has fully described the pottery of that site; and has discussed the use of the wheel, the probable method of open firing as suggested by the present day practice in Sind and the Panjāb, the ingredients of the clay, the use of slips and the technique of manufacture. His remarks on these subjects apply with equal force to the pottery of Harappā which is in all main essentials identical with that of Mohenjo-daro. Indeed, almost every type of pottery from Mohenjo-daro illustrated in *M. I. C.*, Pls. LXXIX to LXXXVI, has been found at Harappā, and the correspondence is so close that it would be superfluous to repeat Dr. Mackay's descriptions again. On the other hand, the converse is not equally true, since, as we shall presently see, there are many varieties of vessels found at Harappā, which are not represented at Mohenjo-daro. In colour, the pottery of Harappā, like that of Mohenjo-daro is prevailingly light red and the clay of which it is made, more often that not, has a natural admixture of sand and lime or both, but only in such small quantities that they cannot be easily detected with the naked eye. **Identity with Mohenjo-daro pottery.** **Colour of pottery.**

From the earliest stratum onwards that is, from the eighth in succession from the surface in Mound F, the pottery is usually wheel-made, hand-made examples being confined to small vessels such as those illustrated in Pl. LXXI, 57, 58, 68, 69, etc., which are often the handiwork of children. And in each successive settlement on the town sites, the shapes and decoration of the vessels remain, with few exceptions, unchanged. On the other hand, the Cemetery H pottery is strikingly different from the characteristic pottery of the town sites both at Harappâ and Mohenjo-daro. This Cemetery pottery has already been described in detail in Chapter VI; and here we need only remark that compared with the household pottery, its clay is generally of a finer texture, better levigated and puddled, and at the same time softer and more plastic. It burns a deeper red and has a brighter red slip on it. The distinction between the two classes of pottery is equally observable in their paintings which have little or nothing in common with each others,[2] as the reader may readily perceive if he compares the typical painted potsherds from Cemetery H illustrated in Pls. LXV and LXVI with those of the household vessels illustrated in Pls. LXVII and LXVIII. **Its conservative character.** **Cemetery H pottery.**

In the description, which follows, of these wares I have included only such vessels (all medium-sized or small) as are rare, peculiar or otherwise specially important. For the commoner types the reader should refer to Chapter XVII of *M. I. C.*; and for the larger jars and post-cremation urns to Chapter VIII of this work.

Examples of plain, round dishes have been found in all parts of the site between the Ist and IVth strata, and may, therefore, be ascribed to the Late **Dishes.**

---

[1] Chap. XVII.

[2] For details of difference in their shapes and painting, see Chap. VII. Also Chap. VI on Cemetery H.

2 P 2

and Middle I Periods of Harappā. They are mostly alike in shape, with diameters ranging between 10·3 and 21·5 in. The upper limit is, however, rarely reached, the more popular size being from about 11½ to a little over 13 in. Usually they are very shallow (*e.g.*, Pl. LXXII, 1-3), but one of them (No. 12234), which is also the thickest, is as deep as 3 in. A little of its depth is, however, due to distortion in firing.

Some of them are coarse both inside and out, but more often the interior surface is much better finished than the exterior and in a few cases both surfaces are equally well finished. Dishes of the two latter varieties were always coated with a pink or bright red slip on the finished surface(s). Most of the dishes are plain on the underside[1] but some have a ring-base which was invariably added afterwards and is generally well trimmed. The height of the ring-base varies from 0·15 to 0·5 in., the diameter varying with the size of the dish.

Dishes and Pans (Pl. LXXII, 1-3).

No. 1 (G15e) is shallow and flat at base but is deeper than some of the dishes in the pottery group G130 (Pl. XLI, *b*). Its underside is rough and shows trimming with an edged tool; the interior is coated with a pinkish slip and then decorated with concentric circles in black. It is 13·2 in. in diam. and 1·3 in. deep. Area G, Trench II, Square AM 43/21; Depth 0-2 ft. b. s.; Stratum I. It formed part of the pottery group illustrated in Pl. XLII, *a*.

No. 2 (G15f) was also found with No. 1. This shows a light red slip inside, over which there are traces of concentric circles in black. It measures 11·5 in. in diam. and 1·1 in. deep.

No. 3 (G223) is the largest dish, or perhaps it should rather be called 'pan,' found at Harappā. Its ring-base, which is 11·8 in. in diam., is almost equal to the diameter of an average plate. It is coated both inside and out with a bright red slip which is carefully polished, but the portion enclosed by the ring-base is rough and without a slip. A little less than half of it has survived, its restored diam. being 21·5 in., depth 2 in., maximum th. 0·5 in., and ht. including the ring-base 3 in. Area G, Trench III, Square AM 35/23; Depth 4 ft. b. s.; Stratum II.

Basins. Basins must have been made in fairly large numbers but on account of their steep sides they are never found intact. The two examples illustrated in Pl. LXXII, 4 and 5 have been pieced together from several fragments. They are similar in shape to the basins illustrated in *M. I. C.*, Pl. LXXXII, 27-29, and are quite roughly made.

No. 4 (3885b) measures 9·6 in. in diam., 3·6 in. high and is 0·3 in. thick. Mound F, Great Granary Area, Square J 7/20; Depth 8 ft. 3 in. b. s.; Stratum III.

No. 5 (3886) measures 12·8 in. in diam., 4·1 in. high and is 0·4 in. thick. Mound F, Great Granary Area, Square J 7/25; Depth 7 ft. 9 in. b. s.; Stratum III.

---

[1] For similar dishes *cf. M. I. C.*, Pl. LXXXII, 31, 34 and 35.

Offering-dishes and Censers.

The following varieties of offering-dishes and censers have been found at Harappā :—

Offering-stands.

(*a*) Shallow or moderately deep dishes on tall, broad stands (*e.g.*, Pl. LXXII, 7 and 9).

(*b*) Shallow dishes on squat stands (*e.g.*, Pl. LXXII, 12).

(*c*) Dishes on medium-sized stands with deeper bowl and large lip (*e.g.*, Pl. LXXII, 8).

(*d*) Bowls on squat or tall stands (*e.g.*, Pl. LXXII, 10 and 11).

(*e*) Squat dishes with deep bowls (*e.g.*, Pl. LX, 22).

(*f*) Stronger and larger dishes with ribbed stands (*e.g.*, Pl. LX, 21).

None of the above varieties of standard dishes or bowls have been found lower than the Vth stratum and they may therefore be assigned to the Middle II, Middle I and Late Periods at Harappā. Those of type *a* are similar to the Mohenjo-daro offering-stands illustrated in *M. I. C.*, Pl. LXXIX, 11-13, 15, 21 and 23 ; those of type *b* resemble No. 2 in the same plate ; those of type *e* somewhat resemble No. 4 but have a deeper bowl (Pl. LX, 22). Bowls or offering-stands of the other types have not been found at Mohenjo-daro.

Method of manufacture.

One feature common to most[1] of these offering-stands is that they are made in two parts, namely the upper bowl or dish as one part and the stem or base as the other. With the exception of types *b* and *e* mentioned in the preceding paragraph their shapes are such as to render them easily liable to break. The offering-stands are a superior class of pottery, usually made with great care, and coated with a red slip, in addition to which the stem and inner surface of the dish are painted with a series of black bands. The dishes of type *c* are painted profusely over the stem and lip, the bowl itself being usually left plain on the outside but painted within. Thus, we find that the interior of No. 10249b (Pl. LXXII, 8) is painted with a tree pattern (Pl. LXIX, 10) and in two or three other bowls of the same type (which being fragmentary are not illustrated) there are a number of concentric circles round the centre. Several hand-made, miniature, offering-stands, which have been found, are evidently the handiwork of children.

Slip. **Decoration.** **Miniature examples.**

For the history of the offering-stand in Mesopotamia and elsewhere, the reader should consult *M. I. C.*, pp. 295-6.

No. 11 in Pl. LXX (G289 II Pf) is a shallow bowl from the top of an offering-stand. Its lip is very gracefully splayed out, the ware is particularly fine and finished with a deep red wash, rubbed smooth. The stem was not recovered. This is one of the funerary vessels found with the large group of dismembered human remains (G289) illustrated in Pls. XLII, *c* and XLI, *a*. It measures 13·5 in. in diam. and is 1·5 in. deep. Area G, Trench II, Square AN 42/21, 22 ; Stratum III.

No. 10 (G289 II Pg) in Pl. LXX is another dish found along with No. 11 in association with the same burial group. It is seen upside down in Pl. XLII, *c* by the side of four skulls. Its bowl is uncommonly deep and marks a transition

[1] No. 11 in Pl. LXXII is made in three parts, see p. 279 *infra*.

between the shallow offering-dishes like Nos. 11 and 12 on this plate and the stout, squat and ribbed funeral dishes illustrated in Pl. LX, 21. This particular specimen is quite well preserved but was distorted in firing. It is 9·1 in. high, and 12 in. across the top; the diam. of the base is 11 in.

It may be noticed that the standard dishes described above probably took the place of the present day low metal tripods in use in certain parts of India for supporting food dishes so as to obviate the inconvenience of having to bend too low, when squatting cross-legged at dinner on the floor.

Type a (Pl. LXXII, 7 and 9).

No. 7 (G15d) is also illustrated in Pl. LXX, 14. It is a comparatively squat dish painted with deep red slip all over, which in course of firing was distorted at the base. It measures 9 in. high, 11·8 in. across the top and 12 in. across the base. From the pottery group illustrated in Pl. XLII, *a*. Area G, Trench II, Square AM 43/21 ; near the surface.

No. 9 (G130h) is also illustrated in Pl. LXX, 12. It is rather tall for its size. Retains slight traces of red wash. Measures 11·9 in. high, 11·8 in. across the top and 11·7 in. across the base. From the large pottery group No. G130, where it is seen standing between the censer and flat dishes (Pl. XLI, *b*). Area G, Trench II, Square AM 43/21 ; Stratum III.

Type b (Pl. LXXII, 12).

Rare shapes.

No. 12 (7476) is less than half of a dish resting on a squat stand. The joint is quite rough at one point but over the remaining portion it has been effaced in the final trimming. The colour of the clay is brick red, the dish having a pale red wash, over which is painted in black a series of equidistant concentric circles. This is the only example of its kind from Harappā. It measures 5·3 in. high, 12 in. across the top and 6·2 in. across the base. Mound F, Great Granary Area, Square J 7/19 ; Depth 4 ft. b. s. ; Stratum II.

No. 7736 (unillustrated) is a basin on a short funnel-shaped stand. Less than half of it survives, its restored dimensions being 9·11 in. across the basin and 6 in. across the base. Including the stand it is 4 in. high, the depth of the basin being 2·3 in. Mound F, Great Granary Area, Square K 9 ; Depth 9 to 12 ft. b. s. ; Stratum IV.

Type c (Pl. LXXII, 8).

No. 8 (10249b) is also illustrated in Pl. LXX, 13. It is an example of fine type of offering-dish with deep bowl and well-flared lip coated all over with red slip and profusely painted in black. The stem is painted with leaves and other conventionalised linear patterns, the lip with the curious repeat shown in Pl. LXIX, 10, and the bowl with a tree conventionally treated. The walls of the bowl are decorated inside and out with a series of circles in close succession. It measures 11·4 in. high, 10·8 in. across the top, and 11·7 in. across the base. Mound F, Trench V, Square L 12/4 ; Depth 13 ft. 8 in. b. s. ; Stratum V. *Cf.* also, Pl. XVIII, *b*.

A number of similar offering-dishes of which the bases seldom survive and the lips are invariably broken, have been recovered from various mounds in association with Strata I to IV. Usually, the lip and outer side of the bowl and presumably also the stem were profusely painted with black bands, thick dots and hachured triangles or other linear decorations. The interior of the bowl was sometimes painted with a series of concentric circles. This particular type appears to have been a popular one and it is a pity that no well-preserved examples have been found.

Type d (Pl. LXXII, 10 and 11).

No. 10 (G130g) is also illustrated in Pl. LXX, 6. It is seen in the pottery group G130 standing by the side of the offering-dish in Pl. XLI, *b*. It is a plain, red washed piece with deep cup on a tall stand measuring 11 in. high, 4·6 in. across the cup, and 8·4 in. across the base. It may have been intended as a censer. Area G, Trench II, Square AM 43/21 ; Depth 6 ft. 6 in. b. s. ; Stratum III.

No. 11 (4337) with a segmented stand is more squat than No. 10. It is made in three parts (the cup, the base and the segmented stem) which are rather roughly joined together. The vessel is not quite regular having been distorted in firing. Being underburnt it has a black, smoky appearance. The cup and base are damaged. It measures 7 in. high, 5·2 in. across the cup and 5·5 in. across the base. Mound F, Trench III, Square N 9/20 ; Depth 10 ft. b. s. ; Stratum IV.

A similar stem (No. 842) is now without the cup and base ; when entire it would appear to have been slightly taller than No. 11. This, too, is of black pottery but all well burnt.

Types e and f (Pl. LX, 22 and 21).

These types are confined to Stratum II of Cemetery H where they formed part of the grave furniture. They have already been described at pp. 327-28 *supra*.

Fluted and scored pottery (Pl. LXXI, 14-17 and Pl. LXX, 19, 41 and 42).

This type of pottery is not common at Harappā though more examples of it have been found here than at Mohenjo-daro.[1] It comprises two kinds, *viz.*, (1) small, broad-based, narrow-mouthed flasks and (2) medium-sized vessels which are either round and flattened at base or quite squat. Examples of the flasks are illustrated in Pl. LXXI, 14-17 and Pl. LXX, 41 and 42, and an example of the medium-sized vessels, which are much rougher than the flasks, is illustrated in Pl. LXX, 19. All of them are characterised by deep grooving on the outer face. In all cases the grooving is concentric not spiral. **Fluting.**

Narrow necked vases and flasks (Pl. LXXI, 26-29, Pl. LXXII, 32 and Pl. LXX, 21). **Oil-vases.**

Narrow mouthed vessels were presumably used for oils or other costly liquids : the larger vessels being used for keeping the essential oils, the smaller flasks for daily use. The former are broad, squat vessels to prevent tilting and the

[1] *M. I. C.*, p. 309.

spilling of the contents, while their necks are extremely narrow, ranging in diameter from 0·2 to 0·85 in. only. The openings of Nos. 26 and 29 in Pl. LXXI and of No. 32 in Pl. LXXII are little more than mere holes and the filling and emptying of them would therefore have been a slow process.

Most of these larger vessels are coated with a red or black wash, but whether coated or uncoated great care seems to have been taken to mix and levigate the clay of which they are made. The red washed examples are often decorated with black bands which come either in quick succession or in sets of bands over the upper part (*e.g.*, Pl. LXX, 21). No. 26 illustrated in Pl. LXXI, however, is painted with leafy patterns, now somewhat blurred. In all cases their surface is rubbed smooth.

These larger vases fall into two classes: (*a*) those with a more or less projecting flat or ring-base; and (*b*) those with a flat bottom. The former type preponderates over the latter.

Type a (Pl. LXXI, 26-29 and Pl. LXX, 21).

No. 26 (J109) has an incipient base; it is coated with red slip and painted with leaf patterns in two registers which are separated from each other by sets of black bands. In this case the neck aperture is 0·25 in. in diam. The vase measures 4·2 in. high and has a maximum diam. of 6·5 in. Area J, Trench III, Square S 29/20; Depth 8 ft. 5 in. b. s.; Stratum IV.

No. 27 (2446) is a sharply carinated vessel with a ring-base which was added afterwards. It is made in two parts, the upper part being joined to the lower at the carination, but from outside the joint was effaced in the final trimming up. This particular shape is rare. Above the carination it is painted with a series of black bands of which traces may be seen in another photograph (Pl. LXXIII, 66). Ht. 3·5 in., diam. 5·4 in. Mound F, Great Granary Area, Square J 7/10; Depth 3 ft. b. s.; Stratum I.

No. 28 (3426), with rounded bulbous body, has a flat base added on to it. It was painted with a series of a black bands on a ground of red but the slip had mostly disappeared. Ht. 3·3 in., diam. 4·8 in. at middle. Mound AB, Extension of Pits I and II, Square Q 24/25; Depth 8 ft. b. s.; Stratum III.

No. 29 (J179) is similar to the foregoing in shape but the base is moulded as part of the vessel, not added on as in Nos. 27 and 28. It is coated all over with a cream coloured slip but the upper part was also painted red, with black bands above. Its mouth, of which the lip is broken, is pierced merely with a hole. Ht. 3·2 in., diam. at middle 4·1 in. Area J, Trench III, Square S 30/11; Depth 11 ft. 7 in. b. s.; Stratum V.

No. 21 (840) in Pl. LXX is a squat round vase with small neck and incipient moulded base. It is coated with red slip and decorated above the middle with four sets of black bands. Mound F. Trench IV, Square I 14/8; Depth 5 ft. 2 in. b.s.; Stratum II.

Type b (Pl. LXXII, 32).

Black pottery. No. 32 (4630) in Pl. LXXII is a round vase of black pottery with flat bottom, narrow neck and small lip. It is coated with a black slip, and is 3·8 in. high, the maximum diam. being 4·2 in. Mound F, Great Granary Area, Square K 9/2; Depth 5 ft. 9 in. b. s.; Stratum II.

No. 12623 (not illustrated) is similar in shape and painting to No. 21 in Pl. LXX, with this difference only that though flat at the bottom it has no moulded base. It is 4·5 in. high and is 6·4 in. across the middle. Mound F, Trench IV, Square J 13/3; Depth 7 ft. b. s.; Stratum IV.

Rare shape. No. 4391, also unillustrated, is exceptionally squat, being only slightly round at the base and convex above. Its mouth is broken. Owing to the peculiar shape its height is much smaller than that of other vessels of its size. It measures 4 in. high and has a maximum diam. of 8·7 in. Mound AB, Extension of Pits I and II, Square Q 23/25; Depth 5 ft. 3 in. b. s.; Stratum II.

Date. The above types of narrow-mouthed vases have been found from levels of of different periods. Vases Nos. 26 and 29 in Pl. LXXI may be assigned to the Early Period. Some of the later vases of this type, *e.g.*, No. 21 in Pl. LXX, have well-developed shapes and are carefully painted.

The narrow-mouthed vases illustrated in *M. I. C.*, Pl. LXXXI, under types J and J (*a*), Nos. 13-17, are different in shape, though not in conception, from the Harappā examples.

Flasks (Pl. LXXI, 14-17).

The flasks are all made of a fine, well levigated clay. Two (Nos. 14 and 16) of the four examples are coated with red slip, well polished, which is not found on the other two. Of the latter, No. 17 is painted with four black bands. All these vessels were recovered in the Great Granary Area in association with the IInd stratum and may therefore be dated to the Late Period.

No. 14 (3478) is the lower part of a tapering vase with ring-base. It is very well-made and the bright red slip on it is carefully polished on the outside. It is 2·7 in. across the base. Square J 7/10; Depth 4 ft. b. s.

No. 15 (A3) is also illustrated in Pl. LXX, 41. It is a broad-based, narrow-necked bottle scored above the base and below the shoulder. On the inside it retains marks of finger grooving, but is without any slip. It measures 5·3 in. high by 3·3 in. in diam. Depth 4 ft. 6 in. b. s.

No. 16 (4263) is smaller than No. 15, but the decoration is much the same. It retains traces of a red slip. Ht. 3·5 in., diam. 2·6 in. Square J 9/25; Depth 5 ft. 3 in. b. s.

No. 17 (Ab268) is also illustrated in Pl. LXX, 42. It is a pear-shaped vase with tapering neck and projecting base, and is the only fluted bottle which is quite entire. Ht. 4·3 in., diam. 3·4 in. Depth 5 ft. 3 in. b. s.

No. 12198 (unillustrated) is a deeply fluted fragment of an exceptionally well-made, medium-sized squat jar of the same shape as No. 14. It has a bright red slip which is carefully polished. Mound AB, Trench at the Southern Edge, Square Q 28/21; Depth 16 ft. 6 in. b. s.; Stratum IV. Late Period.

No. 19 (1009) in Pl. LXX is a roundish, medium-sized vessel with flat bottom and fairly broad mouth. This and two other fragmentary examples including the squat vase No. 12046, which is exactly similar to the fluted vase illustrated in

M. I. C., Pl. LXXXIII, 1, are all of rough texture, and would not have served the same purpose as the flasks.

Jar-stand.

No. 18 (2679) in Pl. LXXII is a solitary example of a fluted jar-stand. None like it has been published from Mohenjo-daro. Diam. across the top and base 9 and 9·7 in. respectively, ht. 5 in. Mound F, Trench III, Square N 9/18; Depth 11 ft. 4 in. b. s., Stratum V.

Vases with pedestal bases (Pl. LXXI, 18-20).

Vases of this type are quite common at Harappā and are found in association with the Late and Middle Periods. As a class they are a superior kind of ware, often coated with bright red slip which is sometimes pinkish and in two cases blackish. A few examples are without any slip at all. Their structure is exactly similar to the examples illustrated in *M. I. C.*, Pl. LXXX, 28-34. Three examples with different types of bases are illustrated in Pl. LXXI, 18-20. Their height ranges between 2·1 and 4·25 in.

Ribbed or cordoned pottery (Pl. LXX, 34).

Ribbed pottery is as rare at Harappā as at Mohenjo-daro; less than a dozen examples of this type having been found. It is characterised by a raised rib or cordon at the shoulder and round bottom, the upper part being coated with a red, pink, or black slip, and then painted with red or black bands. The height of complete specimens, which are small, ranges between 2·4 in. and 3·8 in. Most of the medium-sized examples are found blackened with soot on the underside and it may therefore be inferred that like the modern *hānḍi* they were used for cooking purposes. All the five shapes of this type illustrated in *M. I. C.*, Pl. LXXX, 38-42 are paralleled at Harappā. The levels from which they come are Late and Intermediate.

Suspensory vases (*cf. M. I. C.*, p. 293).

Mostly hand-made.

Suspensory vases at Harappā are few, and small in size. Altogether nine examples have been found, and of these all except one are hand-made and quite rough. Four of the hand-made examples are oval, ovoid or goblet-shaped and the other four perfectly cylindrical in which the bottom is roughly joined to the wall. They are likely to have been made by children as playthings and are pierced at the rim with two, three or four holes for suspension by a cord.

One hand-made example is illustrated in Pl. LXXI, 69 (1644). It is 2·1 in. high and 3·1 in. across the mouth.

Wheel-turned example.

No. 33 (unmarked) in Pl. LXX is the only wheel-turned example from Harappā. It has incipient neck pierced with four holes, cylindrical scored body, and round bottom. It appears to belong to the Late Period and its purpose cannot be different from the hand-made examples referred to above.

Spouted vases (Pl. LXXI, 67, 75, 87, 89 and 90).

Spouted vases again are very scarce at Harappā, while at Mohenjo-daro only one doubtful example (D383) has been recovered. This latter is illustrated in *M. I. C.*, Pl. LXXXIII, 20. Dr. Mackay has referred to the great popularity of the spouted jars in Babylonia and Elam throughout a very long period[1] and to the fact that about 2750 B.C. this shape had begun to lose its popularity in Mesopotamia. Altogether seven examples of spouted vases have been recovered here, and of these two are hand-made. With the exception of Ae275 (unillustrated) which is a very late and decadent example from Stratum II, Mound F, all were found in the IVth to VIIIth strata in Mound F and Area J. Apart, too, from the hand-made example illustrated in Pl. LXXI, 75, they are all wheel-made and of good fabric. No. 90 in Pl. LXXI was found in the Deep Digging in Trench I, Mound F, at a depth of 20 ft. below the surface in association with the VIIIth stratum and may be assigned to the early part of the 4th Millenium B.C.

No. 67 (2837) is the spout of a feeding vase (?) similar to No. 89. Like the latter and No. 90, which are described in Chap. XIII,[2] it has only a narrow hole for the jet. Mound F, Trench I, Square M 11/23; Depth 13 ft. b. s.; Stratum V. **Description.**

No. 75 (12141) is hand-made. Its base, pierced with four holes, and the spout were added separately. Apparently it was a toy. Length, including spout, 6 in., w. and ht. 2·3 in. each. Mound F, Trench VI, Square O 8/21; Depth 5 ft. 4 in. b. s.; Stratum IV.

No. 87 (12387f) is a closed, spouted lamp. It is described in the chapter on Household Objects, Tools and Implements.[3]

Corn measures (Pl. LXXII, 15-17).

Of the three vessels which I take to be corn-measures, two (Nos. 15 and 17) resemble jar-stands but are closed like regular vessels at the bottom; the other (No. 16) is globular in the lower part and funnel-shaped above. The latter shape in wood is still used in the Deccan and the Central Provinces for measuring corn. **Corn-measures.**

No. 15 (3154) resembles a jar-stand but has a flat closed-in base. It is 3·2 in. high and its diam. at the mouth is 4·5 in. Mound F, Great Granary Area, Square J 9/7; Depth 2 ft. 6 in. b. s.; Stratum I.

No. 16 (273) is also illustrated in Pl. LXX, 39. It is flat at base, globular in the lower part and funnel-shaped above. Both parts were separately made and joined at the equator. The joints are perceptible both inside and out. It is 4 in. high and 4·2 in. across the mouth. Mound F, Great Granary Area, Square J 8/24; Depth 5 ft. b. s.; Stratum II.

No. 17 (2676b) is similar to No. 15 but its body is more concave and tapering. It is 2·7 in. high and 4·5 in. across the mouth. Mound AB, Extension of Pits I and II, Square P 24/8; Depth 12 ft. 8 in. b. s.; Stratum V.

It is probable that similar vessels illustrated in *M. I. C.*, Pl. LXXXIII under jar-stands Nos. 55 and 56 which have thin bases were also corn measures. Dr. Mackay has rightly pointed out that their use as jar-stands is uncertain.[4]

---

[1] *M. I. C.*, pp. 292-3.
[2] & [3] See p. 375 *infra*.
[4] *M. I. C.*, p. 312.

Unusual vessels.

Cylindrical bottles.

Nos. 4 and 5 (4383) in Pl. LXXI (*cf.* Pl. LXX, 27) are two long, cylindrical bottles with short neck and horizontal rim. They were found together and retain traces of white slip. The ware is fairly coarse and thick with sand added as a dégraissant. These are the only examples of this shape known from Harappā or Mohenjo-daro and belong to the Late Period. Their height is 7·5 and 7·8 in., respectively, and diam. 3 and 2·9 in. across the mouth. Mound AB, Extension of Pits I and II, Square P 24/21; Depth 5 ft. 9 in. b. s.; Stratum III.

Tumblers.

Nos. 9 and 10 (3973 and 1268) in Pl. LXXI are the only specimens of tumblers found at Harappā. They differ from the ordinary beakers illustrated in *M. I. C.*, Pl. LXXX, 9-27 in that the sides are straight and without any rim. In this respect they anticipate their modern counterparts in glass or metal.

No. 9 is also illustrated in Pl. LXX, 37. It is slightly wider at the top than at the base. Ht. 4·6 in., diam. at mouth 2·9 in. Mound D, Trench I, Square Q 31/11; Depth 3 ft. b. s.; Stratum II.

No. 10 is perfectly cylindrical; ht. 2·9 in., diam. 2 in. Mound F, Trench I, Square N 12/16; Depth 16 ft. b. s.; Stratum VI.

Flanged bowl.

No. 23 (2484) in Pl. LXXII is the only example of a flanged bowl of this type so far recovered from Harappā or Mohenjo-daro. It is of pale grey colour and covered with a white slip on which are painted pairs of black bands. It is made in three parts, namely the base, the body up to the flange and the upper portion including the flange. The lines of juncture are visible on the inside but not on the outside. The vessel is 9·6 in. high, and 9·3 in. across the mouth. The flange, which is common among the Cemetery H wares of Stratum I, was intended to support an overlapping cover. Mound F, Trench I, Square M 10/10; Depth 1 ft. 2 in. b. s.; Stratum I.

Nos. 21 (Pl. LXX, 18) and 24 in Pl. LXXII are much smaller in size than the bowl described above but like it are provided with a wide flat base. In all three examples the base was separately made and added on to the upper part.

Heaters (Pl. LXXII, 6).

Base pierced with one hole only.

The curious perforated vessels, of which various types are shown in *M. I. C.*, Pl. LXXXIV, 3-18, were equally common at Harappā and associated mostly with the Late and Middle Periods. I have nothing to add to the remarks made about them by Dr. Mackay[1] except that at Harappā heaters of large size are invariably pierced with a single large hole through the bottom without any of the smaller perforations around such as are seen in *M. I. C.*, Pl. LXXXIV, 13 and 18. The single hole in the base of Nos. 15 and 16 in that plate is much smaller than in the large examples from Harappā.

The tallest heater.

No. 6 (J148) in Pl. LXXII is the tallest heater found at Harappā or Mohenjo-daro. It is well burnt but part of it was blackened in the firing. The perforations are very numerous. Considering its height of 19 in., its walls (0·25 in.) are unusually thin. Diam. 6·2 in. Mound D, Trench III, Square S 29/15; Depth 6 ft. 4 in. b. s.; Stratum III.

---

[1] *M. I. C.*, p. 313.

One wide-shouldered, squat-necked, pointed vase (No. 5804) which is somewhat similar to the specimen figured in *M. I. C.*, Pl. LXXVIII, 16 (left hand one) and two fragments of a round vase have been recovered at Harappā. This 'barbotine' or 'pimpled ware' is extremely rare here as well as at Mohenjo-daro, and the few examples so far found are all of small sized vessels of unusual composition[1] with the "pellets" applied to the surface in a regular scheme and with considerable skill and care. This ware has been found in the Early and Middle Periods at Harappā, and something a little like it has been found at Nāl in Balūchistān (*cf. M. I. C.*, Pl. XCIII, Nos. 24n and 25n). The excrescences on the few vases referred to above are conical in shape, like the bosses seen on the jewellery in Pl. CXXXVII, 6 and 20, and the pellets on the loin-cloth of the male figure illustrated in Pl. LXXVI, 12. **Barbotine or pimpled ware.** **Explanation of pimpled wares.**

No. 5804 (Pl. LXXI, 14*a*) is of light yellow colour and painted round the neck with a slip of dull cream colour. It is broken at one point in the shoulder where the section reveals a dark colour due no doubt to intense vitrification. Its shape is similar to the left hand example illustrated under No. 16 of *M. I. C.*, Pl. LXXVIII, but in this case the neck is everted and the shoulder squatter. It measures 1 in. high and 1·65 in. across the shoulder. Mound F, Trench III, Square N 10/16; Depth 7 ft. b. s.; Stratum III.

No. 1745 (Pl. LXXI, 14*b*) are two sherds of a round vase made of a cream-coloured paste of which the colour is the same throughout; it looks almost like faience. Mound AB, Extension of Pits I and II, Square R 24/7; Depth 15 ft. 6 in. b. s.; Stratum VI.

Incised ware.

Incised pottery is also rare at Harappā, not a single complete vessel having been found. However, there are several fragments which are incised on the inside with the same patterns as those illustrated in *M. I. C.*, Pl. CLVII, 2, 4, 5 and 7, and besides these, there are three fragments of dishes incised on the outside (Pl. LXXII, 35, 36 and 44). Moreover, there are two fragments of troughs which suggest that the flat pieces of incised ware figured in *M. I. C.*, Pl. CLVII, 1, 2, 4, 5 and 7 are from the bottoms of washing or dyeing troughs. The walls of these troughs are vertical and plain, the incised patterning being confined to the bottom which thus treated may have served better for the rubbing and cleansing of garments. **Incised pattern.**

No. 8240 (unillustrated) is part of a vat incised at the bottom with four concentric series of interlacing circles set round a centre circle. Its diameter was 26·5 in., existing height 13 in. and average thickness in the lower part and base 0·8 in. As already remarked in regard to the wide, flat-based vessels illustrated in Pl. LXXII, 21, 23 and 24, the base was separately moulded and joined to the upper ring which is wheel-turned. Flush with the bottom of the trough and surviving on one side only is a hole 0·9 in. in diameter apparently for letting out the water or dye. Mound F, Trench IV, Square I 13/4; Depth 10 to 11 ft. b. s.; Stratum V. **Troughs.**

[1] An analysis of one of these has been given by Dr. M. A. Hamid in *M. I. C.*, p. 316 and attention is invited to the remarks made by him regarding the colour of this ware.

No. 8613 (unillustrated) is a small fragment of the base and side wall of another trough. Its bottom is incised with interlacing circles decorated with zig-zag lines. Its diameter was 15·5 in. and the existing height 4 in.

There are four other fragments of the bottom portions of troughs incised with interlacing circles precisely in the same way as Nos. 2, 4 and 5 in *M. I. C.*, Pl. CLVII. Their thickness varies between 0·45 and 1·05 in.

No. 3063 is the bottom of a much smaller vessel 9 in. in diameter. Its decoration consists of a rosette at the centre made up of five series of crescentic incisions proceeding from left to right.

Incised dishes. There are two classes of dishes with incised decoration at Harappā: (*a*) those which are decorated inside and (*b*) those which are decorated outside. Two of the former class are decorated with a spiral ornament expanding out from the centre and consisting of a succession of semicircular depressions probably made with the half of a hollow reed. This decoration is similar to that on dish No. 7 illustrated in *M. I. C.*, Pl. CLVII.

No. 2647 (unillustrated) is the fragment of a dish with splayed out lip. Of No. 5044 (also unillustrated) only the central part with the ring-base remains. Its central spiral ornament is enclosed by an incised circle round which are two black bands. The exterior of these two dishes is quite rough. On the other hand, the decoration of the following dish is confined to the outside, the interior being left rough.

Nos. 35, 36 and 44 (5384) are three fragments of a dish with well splayed out lip and incised decoration on the underside only. Similar decoration is also found on some of the Harappā painted pottery, *e.g.*, on the sherds illustrated in Pls. LXIX, 9, and LXVII, 28 which were found in the Extension of Pits I and II in Mound AB and belong to the Late Period. The dishes with incised decoration on the inside and the troughs described above belong to the Middle and Early Periods.

Inscribed pottery (Pls. CII, CIII and CIV, Nos. 1-53 and 58-85).

Stamped goblets. Stamped and inscribed pottery, which is hardly found at Mohenjo-daro, is fairly common at Harappā. The inscriptions may be either potters' marks or names of the owners of the vessels. It is noteworthy that scored goblets with pointed bases are the only wares which are stamped, the stamps in their case being presumably potters' seals. Nos. 21, 23, 24 and 46 are each stamped with a different rectangular seal each measuring 0·9 by 0·4 in. Nos. 53, 72, 73[1] and two others (Nos. 7860 and 10589), which are blurred and not illustrated, are impressed with one and the same seal (0·6 by 0·35 in.), and Nos. 74, 76 and several others which are not illustrated are all impressed with another seal consisting of one character only (0·5 in. square).

Inscriptions incised before or after finishing wares. More usually, however, the inscriptions are not stamped but incised, the writing being done either before or after the wares were finished. Where it was done before firing the engravers may be supposed to have been the potters

[1] It will be observed that on this the seal impression is upside down.

themselves. In other cases, it appears to have been the owner of the vessels who inscribed the vessel with his own name or marks. Instances of the latter practice are Nos. 1, 3, 10, 12, 26, 28, 48, 62, 84, 85, etc., in which the inscriptions were engraved by cutting through the red or black slip of the finished wares.

Shapes of inscribed vessels.

Among drinking vessels several goblets with pointed bases bear inscriptions, *e.g.*, Nos. 25, 27 and 75; and so too, do round, water vessels, large household or post-cremation jars, dishes, basins, *hāṇḍis*, discs for rounding *chapatis* (*e.g.*, No. 4). On the large-sized vessels, inscriptions were incised generally round the centre but there are examples in which they are incised close to the bottom, *e.g.*, No. J97 (not illustrated) on which, strangely enough, the inscription is written upside down, while in others (*e.g.*, No. 61) the inscription is on the rim. On smaller vessels the inscriptions were engraved any where (Nos. 4 and 14-18). Here we may notice also some other miscellaneous objects which bear short inscriptions. These include the inscribed red stone pentagonal slab figured in Pl. XCVIII, 599; a long and narrow bronze blade-axe[1] and the curved bronze dagger figured in Pl. CXXIII, Nos. 16 and 25; the stone fragments belonging to undulating ring-stones figured in Pl. CIII, 54-57[2] and certain other stone pieces from Mound AB, Trench B (Stratum IV), though whether the marks on the last mentioned are characters of the Indus Script, is questionable.

Painted pottery.

Painted pottery was as popular at Harappā as it was at Mohenjo-daro, but as a rule only fragments of painted wares have survived. In shape, composition, firing, slip, colouring and decoration, Harappā pottery is so similar to that of Mohenjo-daro that Dr. Mackay's description of the latter[3] is equally good for the former, and little need be added to it.

Classification of painted pottery.

Leaving out the Cemetery H pottery which has already been described in Chapter VI, the pottery from the mounds may be divided broadly into two classes, *viz.*, (*a*) the large, well-made post-cremation urns which are usually coated with a carefully polished, deep red slip but sometimes with a cream-coloured slip; and (*b*) the ordinary household types of jars among which are included the store-jars, water-jars and smaller vessels including goblets, cups, tumblers, etc. The favourite types of jars of the former class are illustrated in Pl. LXXV, *a*. They are usually painted with double black bands on a polished ground of red, but are sometimes left plain (*e.g.*, Nos. 6-8).[4] Household jars of large size, especially those which were used as water-vessels, are often plain though coated sometimes with a cream-coloured slip or wash. On the other hand, a large variety of medium-sized vessels, were richly decorated (*cf.* Pls. LXVII and LXVIII and Pl. LXIX, Nos. 5-7). Such vessels, though relatively numerous, were of course few by comparison with the ordinary unpainted vessels in use for every day purposes and would, it need hardly be said, be regarded as objects of some value.

---

[1] See pp. 86-87 *supra*.

[2] Of these, No. 56 is of yellow Jaisalmer stone: the others of grey stone.

[3] *M. I. C.*, pp. 318-22.

[4] For the description of post-cremation urns see Chap. VIII *supra*.

Polychrome pottery (Pl. LXXI, 21-25).

Polychrome pottery is very rare at Harappā and Mohenjo-daro and at both places it is confined to the Late Period. The few examples so far recovered bear only simple conventional designs. In all the five examples mentioned below, as also in the two illustrated in *M. I. C.*, Pl. LXXXVII, 2 and 3, the clay is covered by a cream-coloured slip on which the other colours are afterwards laid.

Double slip.

No. 21 (7788) is a pomegranate-shaped vase with white slip. Round its shoulders are faint traces of long oval petals which were alternately red and green resembling in shape the petals on No. 3, *M. I. C.*, Pl. LXXXVII. This vase is 2·8 in. high, and the same across the middle. Mound F, Great Granary Area, Square H 9/24; Depth 7 ft. b. s.; Stratum IV.

Nos. 22-25 (No. 5723) were found together in one group of pottery associated with Stratum III, and have already been described in the account of Trench III, Mound F.[1] The colour schemes on Nos. 22, 24 and 25 have entirely faded away but that on No. 23 is much better preserved. It consists of a series of four highly conventionalised, foliate plants each with leaves bifurcating obliquely on either side of the vertical stem. Interspaced between the leaves are triangular motifs pointing downwards. The leaves are all dark red and the triangles green. This decoration, though simple, must have looked quite effective on the white ground. There are also indications of green and red colours on the bichrome goblet No. 24 but whether the cream slip on the coconut-shaped vase No. 22 had any colour scheme on it or not, is difficult to determine.

Paintings.

In this section we are concerned exclusively with paintings on the household jars recovered from the town site, not with the late Cemetery H wares or analogous wares antedating them from the latest settlements on the mounds.

Paintings in black on red or cream ground.

As at Mohenjo-daro, the paintings on our Harappā vessels are invariably arranged in horizontal registers. Sometimes the whole pot is painted, *e.g.*, Nos. 6 and 7 in Pl. LXIX, but sometimes only the upper part. In the latter case the lower part was decorated, if at all, with black bands only. The motifs are either simple black bands and dots as in Pl. LXIX, 7, or linear and geometrical, but sometimes realistic figures, human as well as animal, also occur. The paintings are nearly always executed in black on a carefully prepared ground of red, but in the two following exceptions the ground slip is partly or wholly cream-coloured. No. 13 in Pl. LXIX is a fragment of the body and neck of a squat, *hāṇḍi*-shaped vessel, the neck of which has a bright red slip while the body is cream-coloured. No. 28 in Pl. LXVII which comes from the body of a vessel also has a cream slip with the decoration in black.

Pl. LXIX.

Realistic motifs.

Nos. 1, 3 and 4 are sherds of an elaborately painted jar. The painting consists of three horizontal registers. The topmost register shows curvilinear backet patterns within the bends of a deeply undulating band. The second

[1] See p. 114 *supra*.

register is divided by broad uprights of diamond or chess-board chequers into a number of compartments in which are depicted human figures, birds, fishes, animals and trees. Little survives of the third register which seems to have been adorned with interlacing circles.[1]

Animal forms.

Nos. 11 and 12 also belong to one and the same pot in which the decoration is divided into compartments by broad, cross-hatched uprights with branches and leaves of trees at their sides. No. 11 shows two goats, a highly conventionalised representation of a peacock, and between the feet of the lower goat a grass-hopper. No. 12 has a she-goat suckling her young and a peacock similar to that in No. 11.

No. 13 shows another representation of a peacock holding a plant in its beak and crude caricatures of small birds opposite.

Fisherman with nets.

No. 16 is highly interesting. It shows a fisherman carrying two nets suspended from a pole across his shoulders. He was preceded by another man whose arm can be seen at the extreme right and followed by a quadruped of which very little is left. The cross-hatched lines below apparently represent the rippled surface of a river. A fish and a tortoise (?) with cross-hatched bodies, crabs or star-like objects fill the rest of the field.

Pl. LXVIII.

Peacocks, hen and fishes.

Sherds Nos. 51-53 exhibit peacocks. The conventional treatment of their outspread tails is well illustrated in No. 52. In No. 56 the head of the bird shown against the tree is depicted with much effect. In No. 54, perhaps, a peacock and a pehen are shown facing each other. In Nos. 57 and 58 fishes are drawn quite conventionally.

Blocking and hatching done side by side.

It will be observed that the bodies of men and quadrupeds on sherds Nos. 3, 4, 11, 12 and 16 in Pl. LXIX are with one exception[2] completely blocked in, while the fishes and tortoise on the same sherds, and the peacocks and fishes in Pl. LXVIII, 51-53, 57 and 58 are hatched and not blocked. It seems, therefore, that both methods of drawing were employed side by side and it is not possible to draw a line between them. At Mohenjo-daro animal figures are all hatched without exception,[3] but as pointed out by Dr. Mackay none of them antedates the Late Period. It should also be observed that the animal figures illustrated in *M. I. C.*, Pl. XCII, 20-22 and 25-27 are quite crude compared with the more realistic examples on sherds Nos. 3, 11, 12 and 16 in Pl. LXIX, or even compared with the hatched animal figures on sherds Nos. 51-54 and 56-58 in Pl. LXVIII.

Date of painted pottery.

In connection with the date of these sherds it is to be noted that those figured in Pls. LXVII, LXVIII and LXIX have been found up to a depth of 17 ft. in Mound F, 18 ft. in Mound AB, 12 ft. in Mound D, 6 ft. in Area J, and 3 ft. in the Cemetery H, and it is therefore clear that they are referable to the Early and Middle as well as to the Late Period at Harappā. Dr. Mackay has pointed out that during Susa I Period in Persia the bodies of animals were usually blocked

[1] For their detailed description, see p. 112 *supra*.

[2] The body of the doe in sherd No. 3 is not completely blocked, perhaps, to avoid heaviness.

[3] *M. I. C.*, p. 324.

in entirely and that hatching was done as a rule in Susa II Period and at Musyān and Jamdet Nasr.

Certain animals common to seals and painted pottery.

A point worth noticing is that the animals depicted on stamp seals and larger sealings, with the exception of the goat on faience sealing No. 316, are conspicuous by their absence from painted pottery. Among tiny seals and sealings, however, we find not only the goat on Nos. 595 and 601, but the tortoise on Nos. 426 and 663 and fish on Nos. 427, 428, 658, etc. The bull, buffalo, bison, elephant and tiger which have been depicted with great fidelity on stamp seals and were undoubtedly familiar to the Indus people do not find any place at all on painted pottery.

Tree and plant designs (Pls. LXVII and LXVIII).

Date-palm, acacia and *pīpal* tree.

Some examples of trees have already been referred to in the description of sherds Nos. 1, 3, 4, 11 and 12 in Pl. LXIX. There are four or five other kinds of trees also among which the date-palm may be recognised on sherds Nos. 2, 38, 41 and 55; the acacia on Nos. 9, 40 and 42; and the *pīpal* which is represented only by leafy twigs on Nos. 11 and 43-48. Trees such as those depicted on Nos. 3 and 6 which have single or double long leaves pointed at both ends and the more conventional trees depicted on Nos. 4, 5, 13, 36 and 37 are not susceptible of identification. The latter trees also occur at Mohenjo-daro, for instance, on the painted oval jar illustrated in *M. I. C.*, Pl. LXXXVII, 5, etc. The acacia tree, it may be observed, is very frequently depicted on the seals, especially on the terracotta and faience sealings, and the *pīpal* occurs on seal No. 387 illustrated in *M. I. C.*, Pl. CXII and in the form of a bough bent into an arch which enshrines a deity on the Harappā sealings Nos. 307, 316 and 317.

Comb motif.

The comb motif is clear on sherd No. 82. This motif is very clearly depicted on some of the Nāl pottery, *e.g.*, No. 78 figured in *M. I. C.*, Pl. XCIII, and on the Mohenjo-daro sherd No. 9 in Pl. LXXXIX.

T-shaped motif.

The T-shaped motif on sherd No. 72 also occurs on the soapstone seal No. 278 of which the upper limb is inscribed with three empanelled *svastikas* and a fourth in the lower panel.

Cross-shaped motif.

The cross-shaped motif on sherds Nos. 16 and 17 is represented on a steatite discoid button and a cruciform bead illustrated in Pl. CXXVIII, 27 and 30.

The so-called hide motif.

The so-called hide motif[1] was quite popular and is seen on sherds Nos. 18, 21, 23, 24, 62, 64, 67, 68, 73, 79 and 87. There can be no question that this motif is a mere resultant from the scheme of interlacing circles as illustrated in *M. I. C.*, Pl. XC, 22 and in the Nāl vase illustrated in Pl. XCIII, 27N of the same volume. No special significance need therefore be attached to this as precisely the same shape occurs in stone, faience and shell objects of inlay where no idea of hide could possibly have been present.[2]

Basket motif.

The basket motif was also quite popular and is found both at Harappā and Mohenjo-daro. Here it may be seen on Nos. 85 and 86, as well as on Nos. 1, 3, 4, 8, 10, 14 and 15 in Pl. LXIX.

[1] *M. I. C.*, p. 327.

[2] For similar objects of shell inlay *cf.* *M. I. C.*, Pl. CLV, 58 and the interior of Nos. 48 and 49 on the same plate, also Harappā Pl. CXXXIX, 88.

Heart motif.

The Heart motif, too, is common to both sites. In No. 19 it combines the forms of shell inlay as illustrated in *M. I. C.*, Pl. CLV, 38-47, but in No. 32 only the simple form is repeated, as in *M. I. C.*, Pl. CLV, 39-44.

Fish-scale motif.

The fish-scale motif was also very popular. In No. 74, it occurs in its simple form; in Nos. 15, 70, 71 and 81 it is elaborated by the addition of strokes, dots or repetitions of the motif itself. The same motif is found at Mohenjo-daro also and is well illustrated on the Nāl cup reproduced in *M. I. C.*, Pl. XCIII, 22n.

Rayed circles or orbs.

Rayed circles or orbs, which may represent stars or the solar disc with rays shooting forth, are represented on sherds Nos. 15, 63, etc. This motif retained its vogue even on the later Cemetery H wares,[1] and is also found at Mohenjo-daro.

Simple geometrical motifs.

Elementary geometrical motifs also find a place in these paintings: for instance simple dots are seen on Nos. 7, 18, etc., triangles or double triangles meeting at their apexes on Nos. 33, 35, 76, 82 and 83 and chess-board chequers on Nos. 34, 67 and 78.

[1] *Cf.* Pls. LXXII-LXIV.

CHAPTER X.

Human and Animal Figurines.

Terracotta Human Figurines.

(Pls. LXXVI and LXXVII, 1-69.)

Proportion of male and female figurines. A very large number of human figurines has been found at Harappā at all levels and in all trenches. Nearly two-thirds of them are female and over one-third male, the latter not being so rare as at Mohenjo-daro.[1] The female figures wear only a loin cloth with or without a girdle. The male figures, with the exception of two seated (Nos. 12 and 15) and one standing (No. 19), are all nude. **Their postures.** Usually, the female figures are standing but they are seen in several other postures also, while the male are commonly found seated, either with their arms round the knees (*e.g.*, Nos. 1-5), or in a devotional attitude with hands folded and the legs in front (*e.g.*, Nos. 8-10). In one case one leg is doubled underneath (No. 7); in another the figure is evidently in a squatting posture though the legs are not defined (No. 6).

Classification. The human figures may be divided into three classes: *viz.*, (*a*) those that are funerary in character, (*b*) *ex-voto* offerings, almost exclusively of the great Mother Goddess,[2] and (*c*) toys for children, though it must be admitted that no hard and fast line can be drawn between the three classes. Many of the post-cremation urns,[3] of which I have examined more than two hundred and thirty at Harappā, and of which a large number has been found at Mohenjo-daro also, contained both human and animal figurines, and in such cases the funerary nature of the figurines is hardly open to doubt.[4]

Red paint. Most of the human and animal figures, retain no trace of paint, and it is probable that three-fourths of them were never painted at all, though weathering and the action of saltpetre in the soil may account for the disappearance of the paint from a number of them. As at Mohenjo-daro, the colours used were haematite[5] and yellow ochre for red, and green earth[6] for green. Now-a-days, too, red lead (*sindhūra*), or red ochre (*geru*), mixed with water or oil (not with *ghī*)[7] is applied to sacred images of gods and goddesses as well as their vehicles.

Peculiarities of head-dress. As already pointed out by Dr. Mackay in *M. I. C.*, many of the female figures wear a distinctive head-dress which rises fan-like from the back of the head, in some cases directly from the head as in Nos. 29, 32 and 44, while in others it

---

[1] *Cf. M. I. C.*, pp. 338 and 340.

[2] For worship of the Mother Goddess, *cf.* Sir John Marshall, *M. I. C.*, pp. 49-52.

[3] See Chap. VIII with Tables I and II.

[4] *Cf. M. I. C.*, p. 339. Dr. Mackay's view that "there is no evidence of their being of a funerary nature" cannot be reconciled with facts.

[5] *Cf.* Mackay in *M. I. C.*, p. 341.

[6] Specimens of green earth which was probably imported from Balūchistān have been found both at Harappā and Mohenjo-daro.

[7] *Cf. M. I. C.*, p. 341. I can find no evidence for Dr. Mackay's statement that now-a-days the colour is mixed with *ghī*. The cost of *ghī* would be prohibitive.

forms part of the coiffure, *e.g.*, in Nos. 41-43. Another peculiarity of these figurines is a shell-like object worn on either side of the head sometimes supported by a band or braid of hair, *e.g.*, on Nos. 23, 24, 35-40, and 44-48. Sir John Marshall suggests that these may in reality have been distended ears, the ears having been artificially enlarged and shaped to the form of a hollow shell or cup. Above the forehead and in front of the fan-like head-dress several figures wear flowers (usually three) in the head-dress (Nos. 34-40).

Cones below panniers. The cone on either side of the head-dress seen below the pannier ornament on figures 36-40, 46 and 47 appears to be a separate ornament, and not a corner of the coif as suggested by Dr. Mackay[1] by way of an alternative explanation. That it was a separate ornament is, I think, indicated by the position of somewhat similar cones worn on the heads of figures 23, 26, 30, 31, 51 and 53. Precisely similar cones made of gold were found among the personal ornaments in the jewellery hoard No. 8060 from Trench IV, Mound F (Pl. CXXXVII, 2, 6, 16 and 20).

Jewellery. As at Mohenjo-daro, most of the female figures wear an abundance of jewellery. Among the most common ornaments are a close-fitting collar with a number of pendents, a long necklace, often with a brooch or clasp at the centre, reaching down between the breasts, and a loin girdle, with one to three bosses or clasps. Among the male figurines, jewellery is rare.

Of most of the figures the arms and lower legs are broken, and any armlets, bracelets, or anklets that they may have worn, have disappeared. **Bangle worn by a funerary figure.** Actually the only example of a bangle is that worn on the right arm of the funerary figure No. 48.[2]

Technique. All pottery figures are well burnt and are usually of a dull red or flesh colour. The technique regarding their eyes, nose, mouth and ears, which is identical at Harappā and Mohenjo-daro, has alrady been fully explained by Dr. Mackay[3] and does not call for further discussion.

See Pls. LXXVI and LXXVII.

Seated male figures with hands on knees. No. 1 (1196) is 1·75 in. high. It is of rough workmanship and shows a nude male figure squatting with arms round the knees. Mound F, Great Granary Area, Square J 8/2; Depth 4 ft. b.s.; Stratum II.

No. 2 (23) is 2 in. high. The posture is similar to that of No. 1, but the figure wears a collar pinched and pointed in front. He also wears a perforated cap with turned-up brim. Mound F, Trench I, Square M 11/11, Depth 3 ft. b.s.; Stratum I.

No. 3 (Ab443) is 1·5 in: high and similar to No. I. Mound F, Great Granary Area; Depth 5 ft. b.s.; Stratum II.

No. 4 (4752) is 1·25 in. high. In this the hands merely touch the knees and do not clasp them. Workmanship rough. Mound F, Great Granary Area, Square K 9/3; Depth 8 ft. 2 in. b.s.; Stratum III.

---

[1] *M. I. C.*, p. 339.

[2] This was recovered from the post-cremation burial urn No. 3885. For other contents see Table I, No. 145, p. 268 *supra* and for description p. 298 *infra*.

[3] *M. I. C.*, pp. 340-41.

No. 5 (5060) is 1·4 in. high. This is similar to figures 1-3, but the legs are parted. Workmanship rough. Mound F, Great Granary Area, Square J 9/15; Depth 4 ft. 6 in. b.s.; Stratum II.

Male figures in devotional attitude.

No. 6 (H233) is 2 in. high. It is a squatting male figure with folded hands. The legs are not defined. Cemetery H, Eastern Section, Square R 34/20; Depth 1 ft. 10 in. b.s.; Stratum I.

No. 7 (12023) is 2·4 in. high. This figure is seated with hands folded in devotional attitude and is of better workmanship than Nos. 4-6. Its left leg is doubled, as in a kneeling posture, while the right is stretched out in front. The figure wears a collar made of two dabs of clay. The eyes and mouth are fashioned out of the usual pellets of clay. Mound AB, Trench at the Southern Edge, Square Q 28/17; Depth 14 ft. 9 in. b.s.; Stratum V.

No. 8 (5655) is 1·6 in. high. It is a rough figure seated on its haunches with arms clasped about the knees and hands folded in worship. Mound F, Trench III, Square N 10/21; Depth 6 ft. 8 in. b.s.; Stratum III.

No. 9 (3072) is 1·7 in. high and of very rough workmanship. The legs, which are in one piece, are stretched out in front and the hands folded above the breast. Mound F, Trench I; from spoil earth.

No. 10 (847) is 2·1 in. high and similar to No. 9. Its eyes are made of round pellets holed in the centre to represent pupils, which, as pointed out by Dr. Mackay,[1] were rarely shown. The mouth is open. Mound F, Trench I, Square M 11/16; Depth 4 ft. 3 in. b.s.; Stratum II.

Standing male.

No. 11 (Ab326) is 4·5 in. high. It is a standing nude male figure wearing a broad collar broken in front. The arms and lower legs are missing and the facial features rough. Mound F, Great Granary Area; Depth 5 ft. 6 in. b.s.; Stratum II.

Male figure wearing elaborate necklace and ornamented loin cloth.

No. 12 (1452) is 5·7 in. high. This is an unusually elaborate male figure which, as shown by the break below, was originally seated on a chair which may have been similar to one of the chairs under figures 25-26. Being split vertically nearly half of the right side is missing, together with the legs and arms. The features of the face are fashioned with unwonted care; the eyes are elongated with holes for the pupils; the nostrils are also indicated by holes, and the lips and beard are well modelled.[2] The forehead is receding, the nose prominent. In general appearance this terracotta calls to mind the steatite male statue illustrated in Pl. XCVIII and discussed on pp. 44, 356 and 357 of *M. I. C.* The treatment of the hair may be compared to that of No. 22 figured in *M. I. C.*, Pl. XCV. It was looped round in four long braids, two at the back of the head and one on either cheek, but two of the coils are missing. In the Mohenjo-daro figure referred to above, the side plaits are coiled from right to left, and at the back there is only a single cap-like coil. Dr. Mackay has drawn attention to the custom of wearing coiled plaits at the sides of the head in some Babylonian statues.[3]

Facial features.

Treatment of hair.

---

[1] *Cf. M. I. C.*, p. 342.

[2] *Cf.* Mackay in *M. I. C.*, p. 342 Pl. XCV, 9 and 14, and p. 345, Pl. XCIV, 3 and 4.

[3] *M. I. C.*, p. 343.

Unlike other male figures which, with a few exceptions, are nude, No. 12 wears a kilt studded with bosses, and a necklace of four bands. The ends of these bands were interlaced at the back of the neck. Numerous conical bosses of gold reminding of those studded on the kilt were found in the jewellery group No. 8060[1] from Mound F, Trench IV. Similar bosses are also worn on the heads of figures 23, 26, 30, 31, 51, 53 and 60. It may be inferred, therefore, that the bosses on this figure, represented originals of gold, silver or copper. I do not agree with Dr. Mackay that on figure 10 of *M. I. C.*, Pl. XCV the conical projections on the kilt represent wool.[2] They are more likely to have been ornamental bosses like those portrayed in this terracotta. Mound F, Great Granary Area, Square J 9/24; Depth 8 ft. 9 in. b.s.; Stratum V. **Necklace and bejewelled kilt.**

No. 13 (11484), which is 3·4 in. high, is particularly interesting by reason of its unusual posture. It represents a nude male figure (wearing the usual collar), with the two arms thrown back horizontally, the legs doubled up from the knees, as if the man were going through some physical exercise. From spoil earth. Mound AB, Trench at the Southern Edge. **Physical exercise.**

No. 14 (4925) is 2·9 in. high. This is another nude male figure—legs broken —carrying a duck closely pressed to his breast with both arms. Mound AB, Extension of Pits I and II, Square P 24/9; Depth 9 ft. 2 in. b.s.; Stratum IV. **Figure carrying a duck.**

No. 15 (H596) is 1·7 in. high. It represents a man with long beard, seated on a chair (which has now disappeared) and resting his hands on the knees, as in Fig. 4. Cemetery H, Western Section, Square R 33/4; Depth 2 ft. b.s.; Stratum I. **Bearded male.**

No. 16 (8568) is 3·3 in. high. It represents a seated, bearded, nude male figure with legs stretched out in front. The hair is combed into a single broad plait doubled up and tied with a fillet over the head. Closely similar is the treatment of the hair in the figure illustrated in *M. I. C.*, Pl. XCIV, 3 and 4, though in that case there is no fillet. The fillet is also absent from figures 61 and 62 of Pl. LXXVII. According to Dr. Mackay, the Mohenjo-daro figure referred to above "either wears a cap with a pointed end that is rolled up, or hair twisted into a coil," but judging by the plaited hair on the present figure as well as on figures 61 and 62 below, the second explanation seems the more likely. Mound F, Great Granary Area, Square I 12/10; Depth 3 ft. 6 in. b.s.; Stratum I. **Male figure with plaited hair.**

No. 17 (2194) is 3·1 in. high. This is a nude male figure resting on the right foot and holding a baby(?) in his arms. The figure retains slight traces of paint. Mound AB, Extension of Pits I and II, Square Q 24/14; Depth 6 ft. b.s.; Stratum II. **Male with a baby in lap.**

No. 18 (PIV-69) is 1·5 in. high. This is the bust of a male figure wearing a scarf round his neck. Mound AB, Pit IV; Depth 6 ft. b.s.; Stratum II. **Male wearing scarf.**

No. 19 (G185) is 4·25 in. high. It is a standing male figure wearing a loin cloth of which only a part is now left. The eyes are elongated, the ears mere dabs of clay, and the hair is wound into a spiral cone of which the lower end is secured by a fillet round the forehead. There is another fillet round the neck which may have been the upper part of a necklace. Area G, Trench II, Square AM 40/22; Depth 2 ft. 3 in. b.s.; Stratum I. **Male with a spiral cone of hair.**

---

[1] Pl. CXXXVII, 6, 16 and 20.

[2] *M. I. C.*, p. 342.

Standing male figure.

No. 20 (7102) is 4·7 in. high. It is a standing nude male figure wearing a close fitting necklace. Workmanship rough. Mound F, Great Granary Area, Square K 7/5; Depth 8 ft. 7 in. b.s.; Stratum III.

Horned male figures.

Nos. 21 and 22 (B1704 and A191) are 2·6 and 1·7 in. high respectively. The former is a male figure broken at the waist and showing on the underside marks of breaking off from a seat. It is better made than most of the others and wears a high collar pinched to a point in front. Its eyes are made of round pellets and the mouth of an elongated pellet slit horizontally for the lips. On its head is a rolled bandeau from which protrude a pair of horns. One of the horns is broken, but both are distinctly visible from behind.

The second figure is a male(?) head with prominent horns the upper ends of which are broken. The base of this head is concave and pierced with a hole for attachment.

The above are the only two examples of horned figures in terracotta. At Mohenjo-daro various figures with horned heads have been found. They include the three clay masks illustrate din *M. I. C.*, Pl. XCV, 1 -3, a small horned statuette of copper, the seal No. 357 illustrated in *M. I. C.*, Pl. CXI showing Ea-bani fighting with a lion, and the rectangular copper piece illustrated in Pl. CXVII, 16, of the same monograph. The horns[1] on these figures leave little room for doubt that they are representations of some deity. No. 21 was found at a depth of 2 ft. 6 in. b.s., in Mound F, Great Granary Area, Stratum I; and No. 22 at a depth of 17 ft. b.s., in Mound AB, Trench B, Stratum IV.

Female kneading dough.

No. 23 (1668) is 3·4 in. high. It is a seated female figure kneading dough in a shallow, rectangular trough with straight sides. She wears a fan-like head-dress with pannier[2] ornaments on either side below which is a conical boss. She also wears another conical boss on the top of the head. Mound F, Trench III, Square K 9/10; Depth 9 ft. 6 in. b.s.; Stratum III.

Female wearing brooch.

No. 24 (10216) is 2·4 in. high. This is merely the head of a female figure with fan-like head-dress and pannier ornament on the left side, in front of which is a band with a figure—of—8 brooch somewhat similar to the gold brooch in the jewellery hoard No. 8060 (Pl. CXXXVII, 15). Mound F, Trench V, Square L 12/5; Depth 14 ft. b.s.; Stratum IV.

Cylindrical seat with foot-board.

No. 25 (G183) is 1·5 in. high. It is a cylindrical seat with a rectangular foot-board in front on which is a pair of human feet. Area G, Trench II, Square AN 40/7; Depth 1 ft. 4 in. b.s.; Stratum I.

Figures seated on chairs.

No. 26 (11932), 4 in. high, is a female seated on a three-legged chair with legs hanging down in front. The arms are broken but parts of both hands adhere to the seat, the left one holding something like a biscuit. It has the usual fan-like head-dress, a riband to left with four conical bosses, a close-fitting necklace, and fairly well developed breasts. Mound AB, Trench at the Southern Edge, Square Q 27/20; Depth 14 ft. b.s.; Stratum V.

---

[1] For the significance of horns, *cf.* Sir John Marshall, *M. I. C.*, pp. 67-68.

[2] Sir John Marshall suggests that the so-called pannier ornaments were really distended ears which is undoubtedly the case with No. 49 in pl. LXXVII. He is of opinion that the ears could easily be distended into the shell-like shape. Or it may be, as he suggests in the alternative, that in some cases objects were worn in imitation of the older practice.

No. 27 (11819) is a male figure seated on a three-legged chair. Ht. 4·3 in. It has round eyes holed to represent pupils—an elaboration to which I have referred in describing figure 10. The hair is arranged in a single broad plait coiled over the head. Mound AB, Trench at the Southern Edge, Square R 27/5; Depth 13 ft. b.s.; Stratum V. **Pupils and coiled plait of hair.**

No. 28 (5590) is a mutilated figure of a pregnant female with prominent breasts. Ht. 3·8 in. The head-dress, arms, and legs are broken. A peculiarity of this figure is the indication of eyebrows. The head-dress is of the common type but the necklace is very elaborate and uncomfortably tight. There are traces also of another large necklace and a girdle, as well as of green paint. Mound AB, Extension of Pits I and II, Square P 24/6; Depth 7 ft. 6 in. b.s.; Stratum III. **Pregnant woman.** **Eyebrows.**

No. 29 (G222) is a plain figure of a pregnant woman which, unlike No. 28, is hollow. Ht. 3·5 in. Area G, Trench III, Square AM 35/12; Depth 4 ft. b.s.; Stratum II.

No. 30 (675) is a female figure carrying a loaf or some such object. Ht. 3·6 in. She wears a conical boss (*chauk*) on the head and a plain loin cloth. Mound F, Great Granary Area, Square I 9/7; Depth 2 ft. b.s.; Stratum I. **Woman carrying bread.**

No. 31 (213) is the standing figure of a mother suckling a baby. Ht. 2·8 in. She wears a fan-like head-dress, a conical boss (*chauk*) on the head from which hangs a riband of hair on the left side, conical pieces under the ears, a tight necklace around the throat and a longer one of three strings below with a discoid clasp at the centre. Mound F, Great Granary Area, Square J 9/21; Depth 5 ft. b.s.; Stratum II. **Mothers suckling babies.**

No. 32 (unmarked). Similar to preceding. Ht. 3·7 in. Arms and lower part missing.

No. 33 (5017). Similar. Ht. 2·9 in. Observe that the navel is indicated by a holed pellet of clay. Mound AB, Extension of Pits I and II, Square P 24/11; Depth 5 ft. b.s.; Stratum II. **Navel.**

No. 34 (7020) is the bust of a female figure wearing three flowers; which look like sun-flowers, in her head-dress. Ht. 3·1 in. Mound AB, Extension of Pits I and II, Square P 24/24; Depth 7 ft. b.s.; Stratum III. **Women with flowers in head-dress.**

Nos. 35, 37 (unmarked) and No. 38 (H76) are busts of female figures, each wearing three flowers in the head-dress, which was similar to that of Nos. 39 and 40. Each wears a tight necklace round the throat and a longer one hanging between the breasts. The latter has a clasp in front at the centre. No. 35 is 2·5 in. high, No. 37, 3·9 in. and No. 38 is 3·2 in. high. Cemetery H, Eastern Section, Square S 34/9; Stratum I.

No. 36 (4059). Similar. She is wearing the usual head-dress, but only one close-fitting necklace round the throat. The flowers in the head-dress are three-petalled. The cones under the pannier-like side ornaments are quite distinct. Mound F, Great Granary Area, Square K 8/5; Depth 3 ft. b.s.; Stratum I.

Nos. 39 and 40 (unmarked) are two female heads with fan-like head-dress and pannier ornaments at the sides. Each had three flowers in the head-dress, one of which is now missing from both.

No. 41 (196) is similar to No. 42. Mound F, Trench III, Square N 11/11; Depth 7 ft. 10 in. b.s.; Stratum IV.

Women with doubled plaits hanging down on either side.

No. 42 (7079) is the head of a highly decked female figure. Ht. 3·1 in. In front of the usual fan-like head-dress she wears a deep crown adorned between the upper and lower rim with a series of parallel bars which may represent tubes of metal or stone or faience. In two of the three examples (Nos. 41-43) the crown is joined to the fan-like head-dress, but in No. 42 it is carried round to the back of the head. Each of the heads has a thick plait of hair on either side falling on the shoulders and thence carried round to the back of the head. Mound F, Great Granary Area, Square I 9/1; Depth 10 ft. b.s.; Stratum V.

No. 43 (678). Similar to No. 42. Ht. 3·3 in. Mound F, Great Granary Area, Square I 18/17; Depth 5 ft. b.s.; Stratum III.

Prominent panniers.

No. 44 (3935) shows the fan-like head-dress with pannier ornamentation at the sides. On the left side hangs a braid of hair. Ht. 3·2 in. Area J, Trench I, Square Q 31/11; Depth 9 in. b.s.; Stratum I.

No. 45 (G221) is the bust of a female figure with exaggerated panniers and broken head-dress. Ht. 3·2 in. The face between the panniers is disproportionately small, and the neck disproportionately thick. The workmanship is very crude. Area G, Trench III, Square AM 35/12; Depth 4 ft. b.s.; Stratum II.

Pannier supported by a riband or braid of hair.

No. 46 (957). Similar type, but the pannier ornament on the left is supported by a band or braid of hair carried to the back of the head. Ht. 3·25 in. Mound F, Great Granary Area, Square J 9/18; Depth 2 ft. b.s.; Stratum II.

No. 47 (unmarked). Similar type but the riband or braid round the left pannier ornament is relieved with two bosses. Ht. 4·4 in.

Funerary female figure wearing bracelet.

No. 48 (3885a) is interesting by reason of the bracelet worn on her right arm. The head-dress, etc., are as usual. Ht. 6 in. The figure is painted with red colour. Coming, as it does, from the post-cremation burial urn No. 3885, it must be regarded as a funerary offering. In the same jar were found a terracotta animal figure, a horn of the same substance, a pottery goblet with pointed base, a cylindrical vase, sherds of a basin, two tiny lids, and two clay balls. Mound F, Great Granary Area, Square J 7/20; Depth 8 ft. 3 in. b.s.; Stratum III.

Distended ears.

No. 49 (Aa47) is a standing female figure with what appear to be distended ears pierced for the reception of rings. Ht. 5 in. Possibly the handiwork of a child. Mound F, Great Granary Area, Depth 4 ft. b.s.; Stratum II.

No. 50 (unmarked), though a female, is without any ornaments. She wears a plain, fan-like coif and loin cloth. Ht. 5·5 in.

Female figures carrying horned object on head.

No. 51 (8286) is similar to No. 53. Ht. 4·75 in. Mound F, Trench IV, Square I 13/10; Depth 3 ft. b.s.; Stratum II.

No. 52 (8535) is 5·2 in. high. This is also similar to No. 53, but like No. 50 wears no jewellery. Mound F, Trench IV, Square I 13/10; Depth 6 ft. b.s.; Stratum III.

No. 53 (8286) is 4·9 in. high. This wears conical ornaments on either side of the head, a close-fitting necklace and loin cloth with a triple girdle adorned with bosses. Mound F, Trench IV, Square I 13/10; Depth 3 ft. b.s.; Stratum I.

No. 54 (G37) is 2·6 in. high. This is the back view of the bust of a female figure similar to the preceding. From the back the object has almost the appearance of a legged stool. Area G, Trench II, Square AM 40/21 ; Depth 2 ft. b.s. ; Stratum I.

Figs. 51-54 are remarkable for the peculiar horned object carried on the head. Whatever this object was, the two hands are raised in every specimen to support it. Evidently, therefore, it was no ordinary head-dress, but what it was meant to represent must be left to conjecture. All that can be said is that it looks as though it was covered with some soft material. Sir John Marshall suggests that these figures may have been priestesses carrying some sacred or symbolical object.

No. 55 (A176) is 3·5 in. high. It is the right half of a female figure wearing the usual ornaments. The head-dress, if head-dress it is, is peculiar, having long curved ends hanging down to the shoulders. It retains traces of red paint. Mound F, Great Granary Area ; Depth 3 ft. 4 in. b.s. ; Stratum II.

Female carrying an offerings' stand.

No. 56 (12631) is 3 in. high. It is interesting for the object carried in the hollow of the left arm. A somewhat similar figure is illustrated in *M. I. C.*, Pl. XCIV, 13. The object in both cases appears to be an offerings' stand (*cf.* pp. 277 ff.) rather than a drum as suggested by Dr. Mackay[1]. A few other similar figures have been found at Harappā. Mound F, Trench IV, Square J 13/5 ; Depth 4 ft. b.s. ; Stratum II.

Eyebrows.

No. 57 (12475) is 3·9 in. high. This is the bust of a figure which, to judge by its necklace, broken fan-like head-dress, and the panniers which have completely broken off, is that of a female. The size is much larger than that of the ordinary pottery figures and can be matched only by that of the male figure No. 12 described above. Observe the long, arching eyebrows—a detail which is rarely represented. Mound F, Trench I, Square M 12/22 ; Depth 7 ft. 2 in. b.s. ; Stratum III.

No. 58 (unmarked) is merely the armless torso of a female figure. Besides the necklace round her throat, she wears a longer necklace of three strings ending in a central clasp which hangs down between the breasts as in Figs. 37 and 38.

Woman with loaves on her head.

No. 59 (G38) is the upper part of a female figure carrying some loaves of bread in a vessel on her head. Ht. 2·8 in. It may be compared with Fig. 12 in *M.I.C.*, Pl. XCV, which represents a woman holding a platter of loaves on her lap. Area G, Trench II, Square AM 40/21 ; Depth 2 ft. b.s. ; Stratum I.

Necklace of circular pendents.

No. 60 (unmarked) is the head of a female figure. Ht. 2·8 in. The hair or head-dress takes the form of a cone doubled over at the end and ornamented with three conical bosses. The necklace she wears consists of a series of circular holed pendents instead of the usual pointed ones. On the hair are traces of green point.

No. 61 (G268), 3·3 in. high, is similar to No. 62 but has no fillet to hold her doubled plait of hair. Area G, Trench II, Square AN 40/5 ; Depth 3 ft. b.s. ; Stratum I.

No. 62 (1248) is a standing female figure with lower legs and right arm missing. Ht. 3·1 in. Her hair is arranged in a single broad plait doubled up and bound with

[1] *M. I. C.*, p. 346.

a fillet over the head. The fillet is broken, but the brooch attached to it in front is still visible. On this, as well as on Fig. 33, 46 and 50-53, the navel is indicated by a hole. Mound F, Great Granary Area, Square J 9/18; Depth 1 ft. b.s.; Stratum I.

No. 63 (1458) is the bust of a female figure wearing a conical head-dress; it is probably the work of a child. Ht. 2·8 in. Mound F, Great Granary Area, Square J 8/11; Depth 8 ft. 9 in. b.s.; Stratum IV.

Criss-cross stool.

No. 64 (H557) is 4·6 in. high. This female figure is interesting in more ways than one. The hair hangs in tresses behind the head, and in addition to the close-fitting throat necklace, she wears a long necklace of three strings terminating in a triangular clasp of unusual shape. Below the clasp are the ends of the three strings. The stool on which she is sitting has a criss-cross surface in imitation of reed work. To hold the reeds in position there was a horizontal band across the middle made no doubt of leather or string. Cemetery H. Eastern Section, Square R 34/23; Depth 3 ft. 7 in. b.s.; Stratum II.

Bobbed hair.

No. 65 (7320) is a broken, standing female figure which is chiefly interesting on account of her bobbed and plaited hair.[1] Ht. 3·5 in. Mound AB, Extension of Pits I and II Square Q 23/10; Depth 6 ft. b.s.; Stratum III.

Figures with legs drawn out in front.

No. 66 (8258) is a nude male figure with legs stretched out in front and hands on knees. Ht. 2·4 in. He wears a necklace of the usual form. The figure was painted white. Mound F, Trench IV, Square J 12/10; Depth 3 ft. b.s.; Stratum I.

No. 67 (2384) is 2·8 in. high. The pose of this figure is somewhat exaggerated but appears to be similar to that of No. 66. From the head-dress it appears to represent a female. Mound AB, Extension of Pits I and II, Square R 24/6; Depth 14 ft. 2 in. b.s.; Stratum V.

Person on cot.

No. 68 (Ae190) is a figure lying on a cot of which only part is preserved. Ht. 2·3 in. Apparently the right hand was stretched along the edge of the bed. Mound F, Trench Ae; Depth 2 ft. b.s.; Stratum I.

Woman on board.

No. 69 (Ab1075) is 4·5 in. long. This is a thick, rectangular strip of baked clay apparently representing a long wooden board on which lies a pregnant woman. Her loin cloth is indicated. Mound F, Great Granary Area; Depth 2 ft. 6 in. b.s.; Stratum I.

Animal figurines in pottery, faience, stone, etc.

(See Pls. LXXVIII and LXXIX.)

Materials.

Animal figures, mostly in terracotta, have been found in very large numbers at Harappā. They are also fairly common in faience, specially the squirrels and rams,[2] both of which were used as amulets. More rarely, they were made of steatite, shell and bone. Only three examples of steatite have been found, and one of each of the other materials. Harappā offers a greater variety of animal figures than those yet published from Mohenjo-daro.

[1] Bobbed hair is still quite common among the male folk in the Rawalpindi and Multān Divisions of the Panjāb, and also fairly common among Muslim girls of these divisions up to the age of eight or ten.

[2] It is worthy of note that all the figures of rams in faience, of which a large number has been found at Harappā are pierced across the neck for suspension by means of a cord, whereas, none of the rams from Mohenjo-daro is so pierced. *Cf.* Mackay in *M. I. C.*, pp. 347-8.

Animals represented and the order of their frequency.

By far the largest number of these pottery toys are bulls, the humped variety preponderating over the humpless ones. On the seals, however, both varieties are about evenly represented. Next to the bull comes the rhinoceros, then the goat and ram. The tiger (and perhaps lion), the elephant and pig are also depicted, but the last one does not appear to have been popular. The dog, of which there are several varieties, is fairly common. The monkey and possibly the cat[1] are also known.

Rodents and reptiles.

Among the rodents and reptiles, squirrels, both in faience and pottery, were very popular, and the mongoose, snake, and armadillo are also found.

Aquatic animals and birds.

Among aquatic animals are the crocodile, which is commonly depicted on terracotta sealings and less frequently on those of faience, the turtle and fish, which are also represented on the seals. Among birds are the duck, peacock, hen, kite, pigeon, sparrow, dove which is almost invariably made in the form of a toy whistle (*ghugu*, lit. a toy dove)—parrot, owl, and grasshopper.

Technique.

Birds such as the goose, duck, etc., which were made with some care, were frequently holed on the underside for the separate insertion of the feet. In the case of the steatite bird No. 1 (J320) and faience parrot No. 2 (11259) the tail was separately inserted, a horizontal hole for the purpose being made under the wings. The fangs and head too in the faience snakes Nos. 23 (8157) and 24 (12358) were put in separately. Similarly, the bull's head No. 67 (2649) of faience and No. 68 (11566) of shell were provided with sockets for the eyes and ears. In the finer examples of birds in terracotta, faience, or stone the wings are shown in relief, and feathers are indicated by incised lines on the surface. The faience parrot No. 2 (11259) has depressions at the wings, presumably for inlay. Birds were also coloured white, yellow, green, or red to simulate their natural hues, and in No. 1 (J320) the wings were painted deep green, while the body was yellow.

Steatite bird.

No. 1 (J320) is a fragmentary, steatite bird carved in the round. It is 1·8 in. long and is split across the left side which, together with the head, is missing. It is exceedingly well modelled and has fine ribbing over the wings which cross each other above the tail. The tail and the legs were separately attached. A vertical hole under the wings suggests that it may have been suspended or fixed on a stand. The body was painted yellow and the wings green. Area J, Trench III, Square S 30/1; Depth 5 ft. b.s.; Stratum II.

Faience parrot.

No. 2 (11259) is a faience parrot ·8 in. long. It has a horizontal hole at the back for separate insertion of lower feathers which are missing. For the feet also there is a hole on the underside, and a through hole across the head for indicating eyes. At the wings there are two depressions, seemingly for inlay, as they showed traces of red colour when found. Mound F, Trench VI, Square O 9/18; Depth 5 ft. b.s.; Stratum II.

---

[1] No cat has been found at Mohenjo-daro. The only example of it at Harappā is not absolutely unmistakable. It is possible that after all figure No. 58 in Pl. LXXIX might represent only a hare and not cat, but the latter appears more likely. This identification is strengthened by the find of the skull of a cat at Harappā. Dr. Baini Prashad who has examined the Harappā collection of animal bones writes at p. 17 of *Mem. A. S. I.*, No. 51 " The Harappā cat appears to be the first representative of the Domestic Cat, the remains of which have so far been unearthed anywhere in India. I, therefore, following Hilzheimer and Pocock have adopted for it the name *Felis ocreata* Gmelin, race *domestica* Brisson ".

Pottery parrot. No. 3 (2395) is a pottery parrot 1·8 in. long. Its eyes are made of round pellets. The workmanship is rough. Mound AB, Extension of Pits I and II, Square Q 24/13; Depth 6 ft. b.s.; Stratum II.

Faience bird. No. 4 (J223) is a tiny bird of yellow faience ·5 in. long with a through hole across the forehead for eyes, and a crosswise incision to indicate wings. Retains traces of white glaze. Area J. Trench III, Square S 30/3; Depth 6 ft. 2 in. b.s.; Stratum III.

Steatite owl. No. 5 (5893) is a long eared or horned steatite owl 1·3 in. long. It has sockets at the eyes and ears for inlay and two holes on the underside for separate insertion of feet. Wings are indicated by crosswise incisions. This is the only example of an owl so far found. Mound F, Great Granary Area, Square I 9/2; Depth 2 ft. 8 in. b.s.; Stratum I.

Flying sparrow. No. 6 (211) is a flying sparrow of terracotta 1·4 in. long with eyes indicated by round pellets. Mound F, Great Granary Area, Square J 8/25; Depth 5 ft. 6 in. b.s.; Stratum II.

Seated bird. No. 7 (B315) is a well modelled bird of terracotta seated on the edge of a vessel or offerings' tank. Its wings are indicated by deep grooves, beak by lineal incisions, and eyes by small holes. Together with the existing edge of the tank or vessel it is 2·8 in. high. Mound AB, Trench B; Depth 3 ft. b.s.; Stratum II.

Pigeons. No. 8 (Ai133) is a pedestalled pigeon of terracotta. Mound F, Trench Ai; Depth 4 ft. b.s.; Stratum II.

No. 9 (1142) is another terracotta pigeon with two holes on the underside for the insertion of feet. Mound F, Great Granary Area, Square, J 8/16; Depth 7. ft. b.s.; Stratum II.

Flying kites? No. 10 (J385) is a flying kite(?) of terracotta with wings out-stretched and feathers realistically shown. It has two holes on the underside for the insertion of feet. L. 2·3 in. Area J, Trench I, Square Q 31/17; Depth 6 ft. b.s.; Stratum III.

No. 11 (1058) is another flying bird, probably a kite on a pedestal, but it is roughly modelled. L. 2·75 in. Terracotta. Mound F, Great Granary Area, Square I 9/12; Depth 6 ft. b.s.; Stratum II.

Cock. No. 12 (8300) is a well-modelled cock of terracotta, 2·6 in. long. Its crest, wings, and tail are indicated by incised lines, the eyes by slanting holes, but the feet were separately inserted in two deep holes on the underside. Mound F, Trench V, Square I 12/20; Depth 4 ft. 9 in. b.s.; Stratum II.

Hen. No. 13 (5092) is a pedestalled hen of terracotta, 3·1 in. high. This is quite roughly made, the eyes being indicated by round pellets, and the crest by horizontal cuts. Mound AB, Extension of Pits I and II, Square P 24/11; Depth 6 ft. b.s.; Stratum III.

Peacock. No. 14 (5040) is a roughly modelled peacock of terracotta with extended plumes. L. 2·7 in. Mound F, Great Granary Area, Square K 9/2; Depth 9 ft. 8 in. b.s.; Stratum III.

Flying peacock. No. 15 (A317) is a pedestalled peacock of terracotta in flight. L. 2 in. Mound F, Great Granary Area; Depth 2 ft. 6 in. b.s.; Stratum I.

Duck. No. 16 (621) is probably the figure of a duck but its neck is broken. The underside, which is flat, is pierced with two deep holes for the feet. L. 2·75 in. Terracotta. Mound AB, Extension of Pits I and II, Square P 24/17; Depth 2 ft. b.s.; Stratum I.

Goose. No. 17 (5573) looks like a goose. It has two deep holes on the underside for the feet. L. 1·9 in. Terracotta. Mound AB, Extension of Pits I and II, Square Q 25/1; Depth 4 ft. 3 in. b.s.; Stratum II.

Duck. No. 18 (11893) is a well-modelled duck in blue faience with head and tail broken. It must have required an elaborate mould for showing the details of neck, wings, tail, etc. Underneath are two holes for the insertion of feet. Retains clear traces of white glaze. Mound AB, Trench at the Southern Edge, Square Q 28/21; Depth 13 ft. b.s.; Stratum V.

Duck head. No. 19 (4997) is a duck-headed ivory rod, lower part broken. L. 1·5 in. Mound AB, Extension of Pits I and II, Square Q 25/9; Depth 7 ft. b.s.; Stratum III.

Fish. No. 20 (2391) is a faience fish with white glaze. L. 1·1 in. Mound F, Trench III, Square N 9/10; Depth 15 ft. 9 in. b.s.; Stratum VI. I may add that several tiny seals in faience and burnt steatite (Nos. 427, 428, 560 and 658), which are generally confined to the early strata, are made in the form of one or another kind of fish.

Tortoise. No. 21 (unmarked) is a tortoise of terracotta with its upper shell indicated by incised lines on either side of the spinal ridge. L. 2·2 in. From spoil-earth. Mound F. One tiny seal in steatite illustrated in Pl. LXXXIV, *ac* (No. 426) is fashioned like a tortoise.

Crocodile. No. 22 (H417) is the forepart of a fish-eating crocodile (*Gavialis gangeticus*) with its young evidently represented as basking on a river bank. L. 3·2 in. Cemetery H, Eastern Section, Square R 34/22; Depth 3 ft. 6 in. b.s.; Stratum II. There are several terracotta sealings on which the crocodile is represented (*e.g.*, Pl. XCIV, 333-340, Pl. XCVI, 430-436, etc.), often alone, but sometimes preying on fish in a river.

Faience snakes. No. 23 (8157) is a well-modelled faience snake-head of white colour, broken at the lower part. The eyes and ears, which are so peculiar in snakes,[1] are faithfully rendered and there is a socket hole in the mouth for the insertion of the fangs. The piece was evidently highly fired, as its surface has an unusual smoothness and gloss resembling porcelain. Like the faience monkey illustrated in *M. I. C.*, Pl. XCVI, 13 and described on page 350 thereof, this snake-head is of unusual composition. Figures of snakes are also found above the head of the kneeling devotees on the terracotta sealing Vs 210 illustrated in *M. I. C.*, Pl. CXVIII, 11. Ht. ·8 in. Mound F, Trench V, Square I 12/25; Depth 3 ft. 6 in. b.s.; Stratum II.

No. 24 (12358) is part of a faience snake with two deep holes for inserting the head. On the underside, the chain-like ribs are carefully indicated. Retains traces of white glaze. L. 1·35 in. Mound AB. Trench at the Southern Edge, Square R 27/5; Depth 16 ft. 5 in. b.s.; Stratum VI.

---

[1] It is noteworthy that in Sanskrit the snake is called *chakshuśravah*, i.e., he who hears with his eyes.

Stone mongoose. No. 25 (2086) is the forepart of a stone mongoose of which it is the only example at Harappā. L. 6·5 in. Mound F, Trench III, Square N 9/4; Depth 13 ft. 6 in. b.s.; Stratum V.

Armadillo. No. 26 (Ab923) is a fine representation in terracotta of an armadillo. Its head, eyes, long tail, and bony granulated skin are faithfully represented. The feet are broken. It was coated with a white slip of which clear traces have survived. L. 3·6 in. Mound F, Great Granary Area; Depth 8 ft. b.s.

Grasshopper. No. 27 (5460) is a tiny terracotta grasshopper of rough make, 1·4 in. in length. The eyes are indicated by round pellets. Mound F, Trench III, Square N 10/1; Depth 6 ft. 6 in. b.s.; Stratum III.

Faience squirrels. Nos. 28-30 (11908, 11457 and 3055) are exceptionally well-made faience squirrels with purple-black stripes down their back on a ground of blue, each posed sitting up with the tail upturned and eating a fruit held in its fore-paws. A large number of similar squirrels have been found at varying depths from all trenches sunk in the several mounds. In every specimen a hole is left between the mouth and fore-paws to take a string. There can be little doubt that they were worn as amulets. Similar squirrels have also been found in large numbers at Mohenjo-daro. No. 28: L. 1 in. Mound F, Trench IV, Square I 14/19; Depth 3 ft. 6 in. b.s.; Stratum II. No. 29: L. ·9 in. Mound AB, Extension of Pits I and II; from spoil earth. No. 30: L. ·8 in. Mound F, Great Granary Area, Square I 9/24; Depth 12 ft. b.s.; Stratum V.

No. 31 (B1560) is a small squirrel of terracotta with eyes indicated by round pellets as in Nos. 32 and 33. L. 1·4 in. Mound AB, Trench B; Depth 18 ft. b.s.; Stratum IV.

No. 32 (793), of terracotta, is the same animal climbing up the stump of a tree. L. 2·3 in. Mound AB, Extension of Pits I and II, Square Q 24/2; Depth 6 in. b.s.; Stratum I.

No. 33 (H21) represents two squirrels of terracotta, one going up and the other coming down the stump of a tree. L. 2·7 in. Cemetery H, Eastern Section, Square S 35/10; Depth 1 ft. 3 in. b.s.; Stratum I.

No. 34 (11598) is similar to No. 33. The head of the upper squirrel is broken. All the four terracotta squirrels Nos. 31-34 are very roughly made and can hardly be compared with the faience examples. L. 2·5 in. Mound F, Trench IV, Square I 13/21; Depth 6 ft. 7 in. b.s.; Stratum III.

Monkeys. No. 35 (11625) is an admirably modelled terracotta monkey posed climbing the branch of a tree which is firmly gripped with hands and feet. The end of the upraised tail is turned down. The hair[1] on the body and the spinal column are indicated by incised lines. Ht. 2·2 in. Mound AB, Trench at the Southern Edge, Square Q 27/22; Depth 8 ft. 8 in. b.s.; Stratum III.

No. 36 (PI-26) is a roughly made terracotta monkey with legs parted in front and hands on knees. The forepart of the left leg, the right leg and arm, as well as the tail, which appears to have been raised up, are broken. Ht. 2·8 in. Mound AB, Extension of Pits I and II; Depth 3 ft. 6 in. b.s.; Stratum I. The pose of this

[1] For a similar treatment of a terracotta monkey from Mohenjo-daro, *cf. M. I. C.*, Pl. XCVI, 11.

monkey may be compared with that of the male and female figures Nos. 66 and 67 in Pl. LXXVII.

Pigs. No. 37 (160) is the representation of a terracotta pig painted green. L. 2·4 in. Mound F, Great Granary Area, Square J 9/20; Depth 8 ft. 6 in. b.s.; Stratum III.

No. 38 (4758) is also a pig, painted green. Very roughly made. L. 2 in. Mound F, Great Granary Area, Square K 8/5; Depth 7 ft. 7 in. b.s.; Stratum III.

No. 39 (2390). What this roughly made terracotta animal represents must be left to conjecture. L 3·5 in. Mound AB, Extension of Pits I and II, Square Q 24/14; Depth 9 ft. 6 in. b.s.; Stratum IV.

Goat. No. 40 (Ah29) is the pedestalled head of a bearded goat. The twist of its horns was made by manipulating wet clay round a stick of which a clear trace is left behind the head.[1] The beard is shown by a series of incised vertical lines, the mouth by a pellet cut horizontally, the nostrils by holes, and the eyes by round pellets holed in the centre. The base is concave and holed for mounting. L. 2·1 in. Mound F, Trench Ah; Depth 7 ft. b.s.; Stratum III.

Ram. No. 41 (10383) is a realistic terracotta ram with three legs and one horn missing. The fleece is indicated by successive series of nail markings. L. 2·3 in. Mound F, Trench V; from spoil earth.

Faience rams. No. 42 (8766) is a faience ram in crouching position, holed across the neck for suspension as an amulet. L. 1 in. Mound F, Trench V, Square K 12/24; Depth 6 ft. 3 in. b.s.; Stratum III. In the Harappā faience rams the horns are invariably curved down. Their pose and expression is generally similar to the roughly carved limestone example No. Vs 116 found by me at Mohenjo-daro.[2] Compared with the faience ones figured in *M. I. C.*, Pl. XCVII, 1, 2, 3 and 5 they are distinctly inferior. Nos. 43-45 are similar to No. 42. No. 43: L. ·95 in. Mound AB, Extension of Pits I and II, Square R 24/7; Depth 6 ft. 2 in. b.s.; Stratum II. No. 44 (Ab616): L. ·9 in. Mound F, Great Granary Area; Depth 1 ft. 6 in. b.s.; Stratum I. No. 45 (11458): L. ·9 in. Mound AB. Trench at the Southern Edge; from spoil earth.

Hare. No. 46 (J587) is a running hare, roughly modelled. Its eyes are made of round pellets: the fore and hind legs are divided from one another only by a slight vertical depression. This and the following numbers up to 66 are all of terracotta. L. 2·2 in. Area J, Trench III, Square K 31/16; Depth 5 ft. 3 in. b.s.; Stratum II.

Mastiff. No. 47 (4067) appears to have been a mastiff. Three legs are missing and the mouth, ears and nose are damaged. The flowered patterns in shield-shaped perimeter on either side of the body executed in green on red ground appear to indicate that the animal wore a coat. Several tiny shield-shaped seals of burnt steatite were also recovered from the Intermediate strata in Trench I, Mound F, where this dog was found. L. 2·8 in. Square M 11/22; Depth 18 ft. b.s.; Stratum VII.

Hound carrying hare. No. 48 (4481) is a hound carrying a hare in his mouth. The victim is firmly held between the teeth of which the lower ones are conspicuously shown, though they are not visible in the photograph. The nostrils, eyes (indicated by thick

[1] For similar technique of twisting the horns compare terracotta bulls' heads Nos. 69 and 70 in Pl. LXXIX.

[2] This is not illustrated but is described in *M. I. C.*, p. 360.

circular pellets) and ears are holed. L. 3·15 in. Mound F, Great Granary Area, Square K 9/1; Depth 6 ft. b.s.; Stratum II.

Dog with collar and other trappings.

No. 49 (10682) is the roughly made figure of a dog with ears and hind legs broken. He wears a double collar from which rises on either side a pannier ornament which has not previously been found on animal figures. The head was covered with elaborate horned trappings which were presumably secured beneath the collar. L. 4 in. Mound F, Trench V, Square J 12/18; Depth 5 ft. b.s.; Stratum II.

Dogs with collars.

No. 50 (8567) is the highly conventionalised figure of a dog, 3·3 in. long, wearing a double collar with a holed clasp on one side, intended apparently for the chain. For a similar arrangement, *cf.* Fig. 18 in *M. I. C.*, Pl. XCVI, p. 352. Mound F, Trench IV, Square I 12/2; Depth 8 ft. 6 in. b.s.; Stratum IV.

No. 51 (2684) is the forepart of a dog similar to No. 50. L. 1·9 in. Mound F, Trench III, Square N 9/18; Depth 9 ft. b.s.; Stratum IV.

No. 52 (Aa24) is another dog with collar: shows traces of green paint on red ground. L. 3·4 in. Mound F, Great Granary Area; Depth 8 ft. b.s.; Stratum IV.

No. 53 (Af256). Similar with large erect ears and muzzle, carrying something in his mouth. L. 2·7 in. Mound F, Trench Af; Depth 4 ft. 3 in. b.s.; Stratum II.

No. 54 (1895). Dog with collar. L. 1·7 in. Mound F, Trench III, Square N 9/7; Depth 11 ft. b.s.; Stratum V.

No. 55 (7071). Similar, with broken ears. Of the collar round its neck only a trace is now left. L. 1·75 in. Mound F, Great Granary Area, Square I 9/5; Depth 3 ft. 2 in. b.s.; Stratum II.

No. 56 (H425). Similar. L. 1·7 in. Cemetery H, Eastern Section, Square S 34/17; Depth 3 ft. 8 in. b.s.; Stratum II.

No. 57 (1945). Similar. L. 1·65 in. Mound F, Great Granary Area, Square J 9/19; Depth 7 ft. b.s.; Stratum III.

Cat.

No. 58 (Ae317) appears to be the roughly made figure of a cat[1]. The face is made out of a single pellet of clay added on to the body—a feature not so far noticed on any other figure. Ht. 1·1 in. Mound F, Trench Ae; Depth 3 ft. 4 in. b.s.; Stratum II.

Humped bulls.

No. 59 (11510) is a humped bull larger in size than other terracotta figures from Harappā. Its legs, mouth, ears, and tail are broken. It was finished with a coating of red colour and then dipped in a whitewash. L. 7·3 in. Mound F, Trench IV, Square I 13/18; Depth 2 ft. 3 in. b.s.; Stratum I.

No. 60 (794) is a fairly well-made bull of terracotta with exaggerated hump. Like No. 59, it was finished first in red colour and then dipped in a whitewash. L. 3 in. Mound AB, Extension of Pits I and II, Square P 24/18; Depth 5 ft. b.s.; Stratum II.

No. 61 (J185) is a roughly made humped bull with legs treated in the same way as those of the hare No. 46. L. 2·7 in. Area J, Trench III, Square S 29/5; Depth 14 ft. 9 in. b.s.; Stratum V.

---

[1] See pp. 50 and 301 *supra*.

No. 62 (J188). Similar to No. 61. L. 3 in. Area J, Trench III, Square S 29/5; Depth 16 ft. b.s.; Stratum VI.

No. 63 (J172). Similar to No. 61. L. 2·8 in. Area J, Trench III, Square S 30/6; Depth 14 ft. 8 in. b.s.; Stratum V.

No. 64 (4738). Similar, but with each leg separately indicated. L. 2 in. Mound AB, Extension of Pits I and II, Square Q 24/1; Depth 1 ft. b.s.; Stratum I.

No. 65 (2863). Similar to No. 64. L. 1·75 in. Mound F, Trench III, Square N 9/4; Depth 9 in. b.s.; Stratum I.

No. 66 (739). Similar, with hole through mouth to take a cord. L. 2·1 in. Mound F, Trench I, Square M 11/20; Depth 7 ft. 10 in. b.s.; Stratum III.

No. 67 (2649) is the forepart of a well-modelled, humped bull in green faience. The folds of the dewlap are carefully defined by a series of incised lines but more stiffly than in the seal engravings of these animals. The eyes, centred with deep holes, were presumably intended to be inlaid; and so too were the ears and horns. Ht. 2·2 in. Mound F, Trench I; from spoil earth. **Bull's head in faience.**

No. 68 (11566) is a bull's head of *śaṅkh* with a garlanded and wrinkled neck. There are holes for the attachment of the horns, and it is possible that the eyes were inlaid with paste. This head may be compared with that of the terracotta bull figured in *M. I. C.*, Pl. XCVII, 23, and described on p. 354 thereof. As in the Mohenjo-daro example, the eyes of this figure are shown half closed. Mound AB, Trench at the Southern Edge, Square Q 28/22; Depth 6 ft. b.s.; Stratum II. **Bull's head in *śaṅkh*.**

Nos. 69 and 70 (10410) are two bulls' heads with twisted horns and socket holes beneath for fixing them to the bodies. In No. 69 the eye pellets are holed but not in No. 70. The impressions of the bits of straw round which the horns were twisted, are still visible on the clay. Ht. of each 1·6 in. Mound F, Trench IV, Square I 12/23; Depth 6 in. b.s.; Stratum I. **Twisting of horns round straw.**

No. 71 (11701). Similar, but rougher in appearance. Ht. 1·7 in. Mound AB, Trench at the Southern Edge, Square Q 28/22; Depth 10 ft. 4 in. b.s.; Stratum IV.

No. 72 (2111). Similar, but the base of the neck takes the form of a disc, concave on the underside, and grooved round the rim. Ht. 2·4 in. Mound F, Great Granary Area, Square J 7/5; Depth 4 ft. 3 in. b.s.; Stratum II.

No. 73 (11098) is a bull's head coated with deep red slip on which the decoration is executed in black. This is the only example of a painted animal figurine. The painting and fabric are typical of the Cemetery H pottery. L. 4·75 in. Mound F, Trench VI, Square Q 10/5; Depth 3 ft. b.s.; Stratum II. **Bull's head typical of Cemetery H wares.**

No. 74 (Af96) is an admirable little figure in burnt steatite of a sitting rhinoceros. It is executed with great fidelity, the prominent snout, short horns and rough hide being well brought out. There is a pin hole in the underside evidently for fixing it to a table or other flat surface. L. 1·15 in. Mound F, Trench Af; Depth 2 ft. 6 in. b.s.; Stratum I. **Rhinoceros of burnt steatite.**

No. 75 (11989) is a roughly modelled rhinoceros of terracotta. The rough and wrinkled hide is realistically depicted by incised lines and a pitted patch over the beast's hind quarters. Its eyes consist of two holed pellets. An interesting feature of this and of the two following figures is a collar of two bands suggesting domestication. In the representations of the rhinoceros on seals (No. 253 in Pl. XCI, also *M. I. C.*, Pl. CXI, 341-347) the animal is never shown with a collar, but has a feeding trough[1] before him, which, however, as shown by Sir John Marshall, cannot be regarded as a sign of domestication. L. 3 in. Mound F, Trench VI, Square P 9/1; Depth 5 ft. 6 in. b.s.; Stratum III.

No. 76 (1466). Similar, but in this case a second strip of clay with pittings is added above the beast's withers. Only a fragment of its collar survives under the neck. L. 3·6 in. Mound F, Great Granary Area, Square I 9/19; Depth 4 ft. 6 in. b.s.; Stratum II.

No. 77 (H269). Similar, with collar entire. L. 4 in. Cemetery H, Western Section, Square R 33/5; Depth 2 ft. 4 in. b.s.; Stratum I.

No. 78 (3300). Similar, but without collar. L. 3·7 in. Mound F, Great Granary Area, Square J 7/15; Depth 4 ft. b.s.; Stratum II.

No. 79 (12260). Similar but very roughly modelled and without pittings or incisions. The beast is standing on a strip of clay. L. 2·8 in. Mound F, Trench IV, Square I 13/25; Depth 3 ft. b.s.; Stratum I.

Elephants.

No. 80 (10070). This small terracotta figure of an elephant is hollow inside. The eyes consist of plain round pellets. The trunk is broken. Ht. 2 in. Mound F, Trench V, Square I 12/19; Depth 9 ft. b.s.; Stratum IV.

No. 81 (1924) is the forepart of an elephant of terracotta with broken ears. The eyes consist of pierced, round pellets. Ht. 2 in. Mound F, Trench I, Square M 10/20; Depth 12 ft. 6 in. b.s.; Stratum V.

No. 82 (1967) is merely the head with upraised trunk of a terracotta elephant with traces of green paint. L. 2·7 in. Mound F, Trench III, Square N 9/6; Depth 11 ft. b.s.; Stratum V.

Tigers.

No. 83 (J55) is a rough figure of a tiger in terracotta with fore and hind legs in single pieces. The ears are erect, tail short and curled up. There was a wash of white over the clay. L. 3 in. Area J, Trench III, Square S 29/15; Depth 3 ft. 4 in. b.s.; Stratum II.

No. 84 (3370) is a very grotesque figure of a tiger, recognizable only from the duff round its neck. The mouth might be that of a negro. L. 4·2 in. Mound F, Great Granary Area, Square I 9/16; Depth 7 ft. 8 in. b.s.; Stratum III.

No. 85 (1097). Similar, with traces of red and green paint. L. 3·4 in. Mound F, Great Granary Area, Square J 9/23; Depth 4 ft. b.s.; Stratum II.

No. 86 (5203). Similar, but very small. L. 1·5 in. Mound F, Great Granary Area, Square I 9/15; Depth 4 ft. b.s.; Stratum II.

No. 87 (12173). This little seated figure though roughly executed calls to mind the conventional tigers and lions of later times, so familiar among temple carvings. L. 3·6 in. Mound AB, Trench at the Southern Edge, Square Q 28/11; Depth 15 ft. b.s.; Stratum V.

Jugate chimaera-head.

No. 88 (A815) is a bi-jugate chimaera-head springing from a common neck. Each head has two holes on the top probably for fixing horns[2]. Representations

---

[1] *Cf. M. I. C.*, p. 70.

[2] These holes could also have been inlaid purely for ornamentation.

of bi-jugate and multi-jugate animal heads or figures are also found on seals illustrated in *M. I. C.*, Pl. CXII, 382, 383, 386 and 387. Possibly it was a cult object of worship, the duplication of heads being intended to increase at once the prowess and sacred character of the beast. Ht. 1·95 in. Mound F, North-West Extension of the Great Granary Area, Square H 8/7; Depth 2 ft. 6 in. b.s.; Stratum III.

CHAPTER XI.

Stone and Faience Vessels and Unguent Vases.

Stone vessels (Pl. LXXXIII, 1-7 and Pl. CXXXIX, 50 and 58).

Rarity of stone vessels.

Stone vessels at Harappā are rarer even than at Mohenjo-daro. Not more than sixteen examples, which with the exception of five smaller vessels are all very fragmentary, have been found. The majority of them are made of a rough kind of alabaster often badly cracked. Two broken dishes and one lid are made of a grey or dark grey stone, the fragment of a standard dish is of limestone, and two tiny vases are of burnt steatite. Of these vessels the roughest, and in some cases the most clumsy are those of alabaster.

Dishes.

Details.

Pl. LXXXIII, 2 (2496) is the fragment of an alabaster dish similar to the stone dishes illustrated in *M. I. C.*, Pl. CI, 20, 21, etc. Mound F, Trench I, Square M 11/19; Depth 9 ft. 8 in. b.s.; Stratum IV.

No. 11252 (unillustrated) are two fragments of an alabaster dish similar to No. 2496 above. Its restored diameter is 8 in. Mound F, Trench VI, Square O 10/16; Depth 7 ft. 4 in. b.s.; Stratum III.

No. PIV-119 (unillustrated) is the fragment of a flat-bottomed alabaster saucer with vertical sides. On the outside the rim is concave. Restored diameter 3·5 in. Mound AB, Pit IV; Depth 10 ft. 6 in. b.s.; Stratum IV.

No. 12366 (unillustrated) is part of a grey stone dish. Like the stone dishes illustrated in *M. I. C.*, Pl. CI, 21 and 32 the bottom increases in thickness towards the centre. Inside it are some irregular shallow pittings probably due to some of the conglomerate pebbles having fallen out. Restored diameter 6·5 in. Mound F, Trench IV, Square I 14/21; Depth 5 ft. 6 in. b.s.; Stratum II.

No. 3417 (unillustrated) is the fragment of a very shallow, dark grey limestone dish resembling the one illustrated in *M. I. C.*, Pl. CI, 26 though its convex underside was not so thick. Restored diameter 5·25 in. Mound F, Great Granary Area, Square J 7/4; Depth 2 ft. 6 in. b.s.; Stratum I.

Large offerings' dish.

Pl. LXXXIII, 7 (576) is a fragment of the base of a large limestone offerings' dish. Unfortunately, the photograph was taken on a very small scale. In shape, it resembles the bases of the standard dishes illustrated in Pl. LXX, 10-14, and in *M. I. C.*, Pl. LXXIX, No. 17 or 18, with this difference only that on the inside it has a projecting rim, ·8×·65 in. in section, at a distance of 1·8 in. from the edge. Like the pottery prototypes, it may be supposed to have been made in two parts, *i.e.*, the hollow pedestal and dish on the top of it. The pedestal, when complete, probably resembled the small faience pedestal illustrated in Pl. LXXXII, 32. Restored diameter 12 in. Mound F, Trench I, Square M 12/18; Depth 2 ft. 6 in. b.s.; Stratum I.

Vases.

Pl. LXXXIII, 3 (896) is a plain, alabaster cup with vertical sides. Diam. 1·5 in., ht. 1 in. Mound F, Trench I, Square M 12/6; Depth 11 ft. 10 in. b.s.; Stratum V.

No. 10308 (unillustrated) is the lower part of a flat-bottomed alabaster cup tapering upwards. Diameter at base 1·1 in. Mound F, Trench IV, Square I 12/2; Depth 6 ft. b.s.; Stratum III.

Pl. LXXXIII, 4 (1427) is an oval vase of alabaster badly cracked on the surface. It is the roughest of vessels and the interior is no larger than ·88 in. deep and ·7 in. in diameter. It appears to have been hollowed out by means of a tubular drill. Being pointed at the base it probably had a pedestal to rest on. Diam. ·9 in., ht. 2·4 in. Mound F, Trench I, Square M 12/12; Depth 18 ft. b.s.; Stratum VI.

Pl. CXXXIX, 50 (4219) is a very tiny vase of burnt steatite with flat projecting base. Diam ·4 in., ht. ·35 in. Mound AB, Extension of Pits I and II, Square Q 25/13; Depth 3 ft. b.s.; Stratum I.

Pl. CXXXIX, 58 (3825) is a tiny globular vase of burnt steatite with concave neck. In this also the interior of the vase is no more than a cylindrical hole ·35 in. deep, and ·15 in. in diameter. Of all the miniature vases, which are described here and under pottery and faience unguent vases, this is the smallest. It may have been merely a decorative object. Ht. ·48 in., diam. at mouth ·25 in. Mound AB, Extension of Pits I and II, Square Q 24/15; Depth 9 ft. b.s.; Stratum III.

Lids.

Pl. LXXXIII, 1 (12387g) is a conical alabaster lid with projecting flange—probably of an unguent vase. The hollow cavity at the top may well have been used for keeping a stoppered unguent stick. Diam. 1·6 in., ht. ·85 in. Mound AB, Trench at the Southern Edge, Square Q 29/11; Depth 2 ft. 6 in. to 4 ft. 6 in. b.s.; Stratum V.

Pl. LXXXIII, 5 (H240) is a knobbed alabaster lid also flanged. It has round, saucer-like cavity resembling the lid of the silver vase illustrated in *M. I. C.*, Pl. CXL, 1. Diam. 1·75 in., ht. 1·2 in. Cemetery H, Western Section, Square Q 33/21; Depth 3 in. b.s.; Stratum I.

No. Ab37 (unillustrated) is the fragment of a grey sandstone lid similar to the preceding but is a bit more shallow. On the surface it is incised with rows of double concentric circles. Restored diameter 3·2 in., ht. ·5 in. Mound F, Great Granary Area; Depth 9 ft. 6 in. b.s.; Stratum IV.

Faience vessels (Pl. LXXXII, 10, 12, 15-17, 19-28, 30 and 37).

Faience vessels have been recovered from all strata and in all parts of the site: they are more numerous than vessels of metal or stone. Their height ranges from ·9 to 2 in. and diameter at the mouth from ·55 to 1·9 in. They appear to have been used mostly for cosmetics of one kind or another, though some of them may have been meant for ornaments only. Inside the fragmentary beaker No. 16 (12124) in Pl. LXXXII was found a dirty white paste which proved on examination by the Archæological Chemist in India to be cerussite, a natural carbonate of lead mixed with earth. Pure cerussite is white and he thinks this substance was employed by women as paint for the face.

Shapes. The vessels are of various shapes, resembling vessels of pottery in common use such as the pointed based and oval goblets, bowls, globular, narrow, or pear-**Pedestals.** shaped vases and the like. Some have broad bases and could stand by themselves; others have pointed or narrow base and cannot stand without a support. For such vases separate pedestals were made of faience, for instance, No. 17 in Pl. LXXXII can be admirably fitted on to pedestal No. 32 in the same plate, the pointed base of the former fitting exactly into the top socket of the latter. Some of them, with finely finished interior, may have been made in piece moulds, but others were fashioned on cores of sand or clay in a piece of cloth which was tied round with thread. Traces of the latter can clearly be seen in several examples.

Colours. For the most part, the colour of these faience vessels ranges from light green and light blue to turquoise blue. Some of them are colourless and some white. Regarding their ingredients, glazing and the method of manufacture, which were **Glazing, etc.** identical with those in use at Mohenjo-daro, the reader is referred to pp. 576-7 of *M. I. C.* In a few cases a kind of bright frit is applied over the glaze, but its use is not general. On four vases, to which I shall refer in detail below, there are purple black bands added above the glazed surface precisely as in the vase illustrated in *M. I. C.*, Pl. CLIX, 4, and described on p. 577 thereof.

Description.

The following numbers, except those of objects not illustrated, refer to Pl. LXXXII.

Flat-bottomed vases. No. 25 (J11) is a flat-based goblet possibly made of powdered steatite as body material. Except for traces on the inside its glaze has disappeared and the colour is now pale yellow owing to the action of saltpetre. Ht. 1·4 in., diam. 1 in. Mound D, Trench III, Square S 29/21; Depth 1 ft. b.s.; Stratum I.

Toilet bottle. No. 30 (2564) is decorated with vertical flutings between horizontal bands. To judge from the slight traces of black colour inside, it appears to have contained collyrium or other eye paint. Such bottles made of silver, wood or ivory are still used in India for keeping eye paint. The mouth is broken. Ht. 1·5 in. Mound F, Trench I, Square M 11/21; Depth 9 ft. b.s.; Stratum IV.

Cerussite paint. No. 16 (12124) is a broken beaker of turquoise blue colour with traces of a bright frit applied over the glaze. It was found to contain cerussite paint for the face.[1] Diam. at base 1·35 in., ht. 1·6 in. Mound F, Great Granary Area, Square K 7/5; Depth 10 ft. b.s.; Stratum IV.

No. Ab709 (unillustrated) is a tiny beaker containing traces of a black paint. Ht. ·75 in., diam. at mouth ·45 in. A faience vessel of this shape is illustrated in *M. I. C.*, Pl. CI, 5. Mound F, Great Granary Area; Depth 10 ft. b.s.; Stratum IV.

---

[1] See para. 1 above.

No. 10 (7024) is a small, perforated, cylindrical bottle deeply scored at the neck and pierced through the bottom with a single hole ·35 in. in diameter. Owing to unequal firing its turquoise blue colour has changed into green over two-fifths of the body. Ht. 2·05 in., diam. at mouth ·65 in. Mound AB, Extension of Pits I and II, Square P 24/10; Depth 5 ft. b.s.; Stratum II. Even smaller than this is an earthenware specimen (No. 7429) which is only 1·4 in. high. **Perforated vase.**

No. 3183 (unillustrated) is the bottom of a flat-based goblet with traces of frit applied over the glaze by way of decoration. Diam. at base ·6 in. Mound F, Trench I, Square M 11/7; Depth 5 ft. 6 in. b.s.; Stratum II.

No. 23 (3629) is the lower part of a round vase with flat projecting base 1·05 in. in diameter. Mound AB, Extension of Pits I and II, Square Q 25/11; Depth 3 ft. b.s.; Stratum I. **Vases with flat projecting bases.**

Ab706 (unillustrated) is a broken squat vase with pedestalled base like the vases illustrated in *M.I.C.*, Pl. LXXX, 28-34. Ht. 2 in., restored diameter at mouth 1·9 in. Mound F, Great Granary Area; Depth 5 ft. b.s.; Stratum II. **Pedestalled vases.**

No. 24 (2591) is another fragment of a vase similar to the above. Ht. 1·5 in., restored diam. at mouth 1·7 in. Mound F, Great Granary Area, Square I 8/11; Depth 8 ft. b.s.; Stratum IV.

Nos. 20 (4801), 22 (220) and PII-19 (unillustrated) are three fragmentary bowls, each made of a rough paste of light green colour. In each case, the glaze, which has not penetrated deep, is adorned with bands which are purplish in No. 22, purplish black in No. 20 and almost black in No. PII-19. In No. PII-19 the bands being thicker have spread more than in the other two examples. They appear to consist of a frit coloured with manganese. These interesting vases may be compared with the Mohenjo-daro vase illustrated in *M.I.C.*, Pl. CLIX, 4, which, too, is of coarse texture and painted with similar bands of frit coloured with manganese.[1] No. 20: ht. 2 in. Mound AB, Extension of Pits I and II, Square Q 24/9; Depth 7 ft. 6 in. b.s.; Stratum III. No. 22: ht. 1·6 in. Mound F, Trench I, Square M 11/11; Depth 9 ft. b.s.; Stratum IV. No. PII-19: ht. 2·15 in. Mound AB, Extension of Pits I and II; Depth 3 ft. 6 in. b.s.; Stratum I. **Bands of coloured frit.**

No. 15 (8380) is one-half of a bowl of turquoise blue colour. Ht. 1·2 in. Mound F, Trench V, Square I 12/8; Depth 9 in. b.s.; Stratum I.

No. 37 (2705) is the smallest complete specimen of a bowl. It contained traces of a dirty white paste. Ht. and diam. ·65 in. Mound F, Great Granary Area, Square J 7/10; Depth 5 ft. 4 in. b.s.; Stratum II.

No. 21 (6054) is a fragment of the upper part of a round vase of biscuit-coloured faience with a broad band of purplish black colour on the upper half resembling that on Nos. 20, 22 and PII-19 described above. On account of excessive firing this band has spread unevenly, leaving numerous irregular depressions. Restored diameter at mouth 1 in. Mound AB, Extension of Pits I and II, Square Q 24/4; Depth 7 ft. b.s.; Stratum III. **Vase with coloured frit.**

---

[1] *M. I. C.*, p. 577.

Pear-shaped vase.

No. 19 (12226) is a pear-shaped vase with horizontal lip. The body is divided by a horizontal band into two registers ornamented with incised herring-bone patterns. It is of azure blue colour with darker tints here and there due to smoke in the kiln. Ht. 2·05 in. Mound F, Trench IV, Square I 13/19; Depth 1 ft. 6 in. b.s.; Stratum I.

Vases with pointed bases.

No. 12 (7762) is a spherical, well preserved, vase of light green colour with pointed base. It contained traces of a dirty white paste inside. Ht. and diam. 1 in. Mound AB, Extension of Pits I and II, Square P 23/15; Depth 9 ft. 6 in. b.s.; Stratum IV.

No. 28 (4784) is a miniature goblet of green colour with pointed base: it is scored round the body and is broken on one side. Ht. 1·5 in. Mound F, Great Granary Area, Square K 9/1; Depth 8 ft. 7 in. b.s.; Stratum IV.

No. 17 (5142). Similar to No. 28, of turquoise blue colour. Restored diameter 1·4 in. Mound AB, Extension of Pits I and II, Square Q 24/3; Depth 10 ft. b.s.; Stratum IV. There are a few more fragments of faience vases of this shape which need not be described. The pointed goblet was the most popular drinking vessel at Harappā and Mohenjo-daro, and is found in thousands at both sites.

Goblets.

No. 26 (7772) is coated with white glaze which has very nearly disappeared. It is damaged on one side of the mouth. The body material is powdered steatite. Ht. 1·9 in. Mound F, Great Granary Area, Square I 9/2; Depth 3 ft. 6 in. b.s.; Stratum II.

No. 27 (4764) is similar to No. 26 but of blue colour. Ht. 1·35 in. Mound AB, Extension of Pits I and II, Square Q 24/3; Depth 7 ft. b.s.; Stratum III.

No. 52 (11586) in Pl. CXXXIX is of dull white colour and has a grooved band round the body. The rim is missing, but the top has been smoothed. Ht. 1·8 in. Mound F, Trench IV, Square I 13/23; Depth 5 ft. 8 in. b.s.; Stratum II.

B1372 (unillustrated) is a tiny goblet of white colour. Ht. ·6 in. Mound AB, Trench B; Depth 26 ft. b.s.; Stratum VI.

Pedestals (Pl. LXXXII, 32-34).

No. 32 (3256) is a pedestal of green colour with broad, flat base and narrow splayed top, holed vertically. Ht. ·9 in. Mound F, Trench III, Square M 9/25; Depth 5 ft. 6 in. b.s.; Stratum III.

No. 4470 (unillustrated) of green colour is similar to No. 32 but its head is not splayed. Round the top is a spiral groove. Ht. ·7 in. Mound F, Trench III, Square N 9/14; Depth 9 ft. 4 in. b.s.; Stratum IV.

No. 33 (12036) of white colour is similar to No. 4470, but more squat and has only one groove round the top. Ht. ·45 in. Mound F, Trench IV, Square I 14/13; Depth 6 ft. 9 in. b.s.; Stratum III.

No. 34 (687) is almost wheel-shaped with a prominent hub. It is coated with white glaze on which are painted eleven equidistant bands of purplish black colour The hole through the hub is irregular. Its lower edge has been rubbed, and the glaze here destroyed. Ht. ·65 in. Mound F, Trench I, Square M 12/6; Depth 10 ft. b.s.; Stratum IV.

The above pedestals are likely to have been used to support vases with pointed or rounded bases such as have been described above. Vase No. 28, for instance, fits neatly on pedestal No. 4470.

Tiny pottery vases.

Miniature earthenware vases, which may have served equally well for cosmetics or as toys, are of several shapes, as shown in Pl. CXXXIX, 49, 53-57 and 59-64. Six of them (Pl. CXXXIX, 53-55 and 61-63) were found together in the vase No. A406 illustrated in Pl. LXXXII, 9. The latter is 2·2 in. high and was found in Mound F, Great Granary Area; Depth 2 ft. b.s.; Stratum III.

No. 36 (1329) in Pl. LXXXII is a knobbed faience lid. This shape is quite common in pottery and is found in silver also. Diam. 1·38 in. Mound AB, Extension of Pits I and II, Square P 24/13; Depth 9 ft. b.s.; Stratum IV. **Faience lid.**

CHAPTER XII.

Seals and Seal Impressions, with Tabulation.

(Pls. LXXXV-CI.)

Ubiquity of seals and sealings.

Thanks to their inscriptions the most interesting of all objects unearthed at Harappā are the seals and sealings. They have been found in large numbers in all parts of the site and at all levels. In this chapter my main object is to discuss the character and technique of the seals and sealings, not the inscriptions engraved upon them, but in order to facilitate the further study of the Indus script I give in Pls. CV-CXVI a Sign List of the pictograms found at Harappā except those[1] already included in Messrs. Smith and Gadd's List which was published in Sir John Marshall's work *Mohenjo-daro and the Indus Civilization.* A partial corrigendum to the Mohenjo-daro Sign List is given at the end of this chapter. As the arrangement of the two lists is the same the reader should have no difficulty in putting his fingers at once on any particulars required by him.

Sign List.

Its arrangement and limitation.

Number of seals.

In all, 974 seals and sealings have been recovered at Harappā, but as many of the smaller seals and some sealings bear identical inscriptions, all duplicates have been omitted from the illustrations. Fragments of seals also, unless of special interest, have been left out.

With but a few exceptions, the square stamp seals are engraved with the representation of an animal and a single line of pictograms in the upper field. Only four such seals are inscribed with two lines of pictograms. Of these, Nos. 75 and 123 in Pls. LXXXVIII and LXXXIX exhibit the figure of a unicorn. In the former, the line of pictograms in the upper field is again repeated on the upper edge of the seal; in the latter two lines of pictograms are inscribed on two of the edges, the field above the animal being left bare, though it should be added that this seal is not finished. Identical inscriptions also occur on both sides of sealings 304 and 306 (Pl. XCIII). In Nos. 251 and 256 (Pl. XCI) there are two lines of pictograms but both are without any animal figure. Among rectangular seals, No. 276 (Pl. XCII) has one line of letters on the obverse face and two letters, for which apparently there was no space on the face, on the edge.[2]

To enable the inscriptions to be read in the correct direction photographs of the stamp seals Nos. 1-302, 614-634 and 693-699 have been taken from plaster casts, and accordingly the illustrations are the reverse of the actual seals. In speaking about the direction of a particular animal or pictogram I shall therefore refer invariably to the impressions of the stamp seals and not to the originals. On the other hand, the sealings Nos. 303-400, 651-657 and 704 have been photographed direct from the originals and so also the tiny seals and sealings Nos. 401-598, 600-613, 635-650, 658-692, 700-703 and 705-707, as well as the only inscribed stone slab No. 599 (B951).

[1] *I.e.*, the inscriptions discovered up to the end of the year 1926-27.

[2] It is possible, however, that these are two separate inscriptions.

TYPES OF SEALS AND SEALINGS (Pl. LXXXIV).

The seals at Harappā may be conveniently classified as follows:—

I.—Large intaglio seals of steatite and terracotta engraved by hand and intended for making impressions. Classes 1-6.

(*a*) Square seals with perforated boss on reverse.

(*b-e*) Rectangular seals with plane face and with convex back perforated with one or two holes, or with plane back with or without a boss.

(*f*) Rhomboid seal with indented edges.

(*g*) T-shaped seal.

II.—Miniature seals or amulets of steatite, engraved by hand but not intended for making impressions. Classes 7-21.

(*h-k*) Oblong seals, sometimes with one or both ends rounded.

(*l*) Square seal.

(*m*) Triangular seals.

(*n*) Triangular prisms.

(*o-p*) Rectangular seals.

(*q-s*) Long or short cylinder seals with or without a hole.

(*t*) Plano-convex discs.

(*u*) Lanceolate seals with truncated ends.

(*v-w*) Heart-shaped seals.

(*x*) Shield-shaped seals.

(*y*) Leaf-shaped seals.

(*z-aa*) Seals shaped like a child's writing tablet.

(*ab*) Fish-shaped seals.

(*ac*) Tortoise-shaped seal.

(*ad*) Hare-shaped seals.

III.—Seals and sealings of terracotta or faience made from moulds with devices and inscriptions in relief. Probably not intended for making impressions. Classes 22-39.

(*ae*) Long cylindrical sealings.

(*af*) Oblong sealings, lenticular in section.

(*ag*) Oblong sealings, plano-convex in section.

(*ah*) Lenticular sealings.

(*ai*) Discoid tabular sealings.

(*aj*) Cuboid sealing.

(*ak*) Hexagonal sealings.

(*al*) Triangular sealings.

(*am*) Crescent-shaped sealing.

(*an*) Lanceolate sealing.

(*ao*) Leaf-shaped sealings.

(*ap*) Sealings shaped like a date seed.

(*aq*) Fish-shaped sealings.

I.—Large intaglio seals of steatite engraved by hand, etc.

Class 1.—Square seals with perforated boss on reverse. Type a.

Materials. Seals of this type largely preponderate over those of all other types and with the exception of four pottery examples, *viz.*, Nos. 44, 223, 257 and 258, are always made of steatite. Usually, they bear the representation of an animal with a line of pictograms in the upper field, and are almost invariably perfect squares. Their sizes vary considerably. The following list of 247 specimens, most of which are perfectly preserved, is arranged in the ascending order of sizes :—

In. sq.	Examples.	In. sq.	Examples.
0·45	1	1·55	5
0·5	1	1·6	6
0·55	2	1·65	4
0·6	6	1·7	5
0·65	8	1·75	1
0·7	13	1·8	6
0·75	10	1·85	1
0·8	20	1·9	..
0·85	11	1·95	..
0·9	19	2·0	1
0·95	12	2·05	1
1·0	23	2·1	2
1·05	12	2·15	..
1·1	18	2·2	1
1·15	8	2·25	..
1·2	11	2·3	..
1·25	11	2·35	..
1·3	8	2·4	..
1·35	2	2·45	..
1·4	7	2·5	..
1·45	6	2·55	..
1·5	4	2·6	1

From the above schedule it appears that the most favourite size of the seals of this type was 1·0 in. square followed fairly closely by 0·8 in. square, and 0·9 in. square. As at Mohenjo-daro, square seals of a very large size do not appear to have been popular at Harappā. After the above come 12 seals of 1·05 in. square and 11 of each of the sizes 0·8, 0·85, 0·95 and 1·25 in. square.

Favourite sizes at Harappā and Mohenjo-daro. At Mohenjo-daro, however, the first three favourite sizes of seals of this type were 1·1, 0·85 and 1·2 in. square,[1] while at Harappā they are the third, fifth and tenth sizes respectively in numerical order.

Rectangular seals with convex back, or with plane back with or without a boss. Types b-e.

These four types are analogous to the extent that they have a plane, rectangular face bearing one line of pictograms without any animal figure. On some of them the pictograms are deeply and clearly cut as will appear from Pl. XCII

[1] *M. I. C.*, p. 372.

Class 2.—Rectangular seals with convex back. Types b and c.

Of Type *b* there is only one specimen perforated with two parallel holes across the middle. It is one of the two longest seals with convex back.

Seals of Type *c* with only one hole across the middle were quite popular, altogether 57 examples of it having been found here. This type was also popular at Mohenjo-daro. One small seal of this type illustrated in No. 276 bears two pictograms on one of its sides. While at Harappā these seals are made exclusively of steatite, at Mohenjo-daro three pottery examples also occur.

Class 3.—Rectangular seals with plane back and perforated boss. Type d.

There are three seals of this type, *viz.*, Nos. 294, 298 (unfinished), and 262. Of these, the two finished ones have perforated bosses, similar to those at the back of the square seals. The other, when finished, would have been considerably thinner than the other two specimens. Their sizes vary from 0·9×0·6 to 1·4×0·7 in. Only one seal of this type (VS. 2846) has been recovered at Mohenjo-daro[1].

Class 4.—Rectangular seal, plane on both sides. Type e.

Unique type.

No. 1380 illustrated in No. 248 is part of a rectangular seal plane on both sides. Nearly half of it is missing. The device shows a man in an acacia tree apparently attacking a tiger below. There was a second tiger to the left, of which only the tail is preserved. No seal of this shape has been published from Mohenjo-daro.

Class 5.—Rhomboid seal with indented edges. Type f.

Seal with flying eagle and cross.

No. PIV-85 illustrated in No. 255 is another seal of an unusual type, being the only example known from Harappā or Mohenjo-daro. Two beads of similar shape,[2] but of much smaller size, were recovered from Trench IV, Mound F. Like this seal, they are perforated across the thickness of their longer axes. On the obverse the seal is engraved with the figure of a flying eagle; and on the reverse with a cross. This eagle motif is unique at Harappā and Mohenjo-daro. The cross, however, is fairly well known: for instance, on the faience sealings Nos. 390 and 391. A cross-shaped bead (Pl. CXXVIII, 27) and a button engraved with a cross (Pl. CXXVIII, 30), both of burnt steatite, have also been recovered at Harappā.

Class 6.—T-shaped seal. Type g.

Empanelled *svastikas*.

This is the only seal of this shape engraved in two rows with empanelled *svastikas*, the upper row containing three and the lower only one. Its back side is plain. At both ends it has a concave depression which is seen at the left end in the photograph. I surmise that this was meant for metal attachments whereby it could be used as a pendent.

---

[1] *M. I. C.*, p. 378.

[2] One of these is illustrated in Pl. CXXXII, fig. 4*d*. For objects of shell inlay with step design, see *M. I. C.*, Pl. CLV, 31-33. One such example from Ur is illustrated by Mr. H. C. Beck, see p. 397 *infra*, Pl. CXXXIV, fig. 4.

Some peculiar seals.

Seven square seals of Type *a*, which are peculiar for their inscriptions or certain features or show different stages of manufacture, may be noticed here. Three of them are of black and one of green steatite—all unfinished—two of burnt steatite, finished and glazed, and one of terracotta.

No. 617 (12002) is the only unicorn seal at Harappā in which no incense-burner is placed below the head of the animal[1] which in this case alone faces left instead of right. One such example[2] from Mohenjo-daro is illustrated in *M. I. C.*, Pl. CVIII, 167, where the object below the unicorn's neck, as pointed out by Sir John Marshall, appears to be "the third letter of the inscription, of which two letters are engraved above the animal".

Seal with incription and incense burner only.

No. 256 (10102) is peculiar in showing a two-line inscription to the right and an incense-burner alone—which is usually found placed under the neck of the unicorn—to the left. A two-line inscription also occurs on seal No. 251 and on several seals from Mohenjo-daro, while the incense-burner[3] without the unicorn is also seen on both sides of the terracotta sealing 309, on the reverse of sealings 320-322, and 665, and on one side of the miniature seals 440, 441 and 443.

Terracotta seal with diagonal cross.

No. 257 (725) is a rough terracotta seal with an equally rough boss at the back. Its face is divided into four triangles by a diagonal cross, and in each quadrant is a circle with a hole at the centre. This device is not found on any other seal.

Inscription engraved before fashioning of boss.

No. 254 (2789) is peculiar in that it is inscribed along three sides of the face and is not a perfect square being 1·45×1·3 in. The reverse side is unfinished but a boss was undoubtedly intended to be cut there, as its maximum thickness is between ·5 and ·8 in. This seal, like the three following and others which are not noticed here, shows that the inscription was engraved prior to the back knob being fashioned.[4]

No. 260 (2731) is broken across the lower right corner and unfinished on both sides, but is sufficiently thick to allow of a boss being made at the back. The face exhibits merely a line of pictograms along the upper edge, but it is obvious that an animal was intended to be carved in the field below. On the other hand, seal No. 123 shows only the unicorn above which the field was evidently meant for an inscription.

Grooved edge.

No. 60 (5551) is half of a unicorn seal of black steatite. It was 1 in. square ×0·55 in. thick; and its reverse side is flat and without a boss. A groove runs round the middle of the two existing edges and presumably ran round the other two also. This groove appears to be a substitute for the holed boss which could not possibly have been made in this case on account of the thickness of the seal being too small.

---

[1] The ground below is left blank.

[2] In *M. I. C.*, Pl. CVII, 112 also the unicorn faces left but there below the animal's head appears the usual incense-burner.

[3] For introduction of the incense-burner prior to the unicorn, see pp. 321-22 *infra*.

[4] The only exception to this rule is the terracotta seal No. 3130 (Pl. XCI, 258) which shows the boss on the reverse although the inscription (but not the animal) is seen on the obverse.

Unfinished seal.

No. 167 (12387h) is of black steatite: the unicorn and incense-burner and the three pictograms in upper field are all unfinished; the usual boss at the back is broken. This piece is not rectangular, being 0·65 in. along the upper length and 0·7 in. along the lower, while the width is 0·55 in. only. For bossed seals its thickness of 0·1 in. is unduly small. When the boss was broken, it was perforated with two holes, through which the cord could be passed—one between the forepart of the unicorn and the incense-burner and the other in the hind part of the animal.

Animals represented on the seals.

Noteworthy features of the unicorns.

The animal that most frequently recurs on the seals at Harappā or Mohenjo-daro is the unicorn seen on seals Nos. 1-221, 614-626 and 693-697. Its mythical nature has already been examined by Sir John Marshall in *M. I. C.*[1] Three features of these animals that have already been noticed in that publication, are (1) a kind of saddle or covering over its withers, (2) in many examples a number of bands or stripes over its neck and muzzle which may be intended for rings[2], and (3) a close fittings necklace observable on seals 5, 11, 29, 34, 50, 53, 54, 58, 71, 72, 82, 84, 103, 104, 106, 113, 121, etc. The last feature, too, has been noticed by Dr. Mackay on seals Nos. 2, 15, 22, 23 and 29 illustrated in *M. I. C.*, Pls. CIII and CIV. Two remarkable terracotta sealings (No. 314), both coming from the same mould,[3] exhibit an animal which, but for its two horns, is almost exactly like the unicorn. Its horns, however, do not appear to be quite so long. Below the neck of this, too, is the usual incense-burner. These two sealings point to the possibility—but to nothing more than the possibility—that the so-called unicorn may, after all, be no other than the Indian ox so posed that one horn is completely hidden behind the other.

Two-horned animal resembling the unicorn.

Incense-burner

The object which, at Harappā and Mohenjo-daro, is found almost invariably[4] placed beneath the head of the unicorn is an incense-burner. "This object", writes Sir John Marshall,[5] "which consists of two vessels fixed on to a short central staff, I take to have been an incense-burner, intended to be carried in the hands since there is nothing to suggest that it was fixed into the ground. That the lower bowl contained fire is, I think, indicated on some of the seals (*e.g.*, Pl. XIII, 22) by what seem to be small flames rising above the sides of the vessel. In the upper vessel, which appears to be of metal open-work possibly revolving on the stem, would be placed the incense consisting of fragrant wood, dried flowers, seeds, or gum resins, which would thus burn more slowly than if thrown direct on the fire". Flames in the lower bowl appear to be distinctly indicated rising above its sides in the Harappā seal illustrated in No. 3[6], while over its upper part of metal open-work, which appears to be

---

[1] Pp. 68 and 69.

[2] *M. I. C.*, p. 69.

[3] One of these is referred to by Sir John Marshall in *M. I. C.*, p. 69, and illustrated in Pl. XII, 24 thereof.

[4] No. 617 is the only exception at Harappā. See p. 320 *supra*.

[5] *M. I. C.*, p. 69.

[6] This seal has also been illustrated by Sir John Marshall in *M. I. C.*, Pl. XIII, 22.

threaded on to the upper end of the staff, is a ring in place of the knob seen in Nos. 2, 5 and 17. At Mohenjo-daro also a somewhat similar knob appears on the incense-burners of Nos. 3, 15 and 17 of *M. I. C.*, Pl. CIII. Again, in *M. I. C.*, Pl. CIV, 38 immediately below the fire bowl a horizontal pin is shown piercing the staff of the incense-burner, and a similar pin with its ends bent round can be seen in the same position on our Harappā seal No. 2.

Incense-burner itself an object of worship.

Sir John Marshall has pointed out on the strength of the Harappā seal No. 256 and sealings Nos. 309 and 322,[1] as well as of the Mohenjo-daro sealings illustrated in *M. I. C.*, Pl. CXVI, 5 and 8, that the incense-burner itself became an object of worship or veneration[2]. To the evidence cited by him may be added the two sealings 320 and 321, on the former of which the incense-burner is shown on a very large scale. While fully concurring with the above view, I myself would go further: for I am of opinion that the incense-burner was already being worshipped or venerated before ever it came to be associated with the cult of the unicorn. This, I think, is shown by the find in early strata of the three tiny rectangular seals Nos. 441, 443, and 440 bearing representations of incense-burners. No. 441 was found at a depth of 17 ft. in Stratum VI of the Deep Digging in Trench I, Mound F; No. 443 at a depth of 17 ft. 5 in. in Stratum VII to the west of the Great Granary in Mound F; while No. 440 was found in the spoil earth of Stratum VI in the Extension of Pits I and II in Mound AB. The special significance of these three seals lies in the fact that they appertain to a period anterior to that of the unicorn seals of Mohenjo-daro and Harappā, and that among the hundreds of miniature seals belonging to this early period not one has been found bearing the figure of a unicorn. It is this that leads me to infer that the worship of the incense-burner antedates that of the unicorn and in course of time came to be associated with it.

Elephant (Elephas maximus).

Short ears.

Only six seals (Nos. 226-231) engraved with the effigy of an elephant have been found at Harappā, and among pottery figurines there are only three examples (Pl. LXXIX, 80-82). On the seals the animal is shown with small ears and other features typical of the Indian elephant. In Nos. 226 and 227, however, there is a double finger-like process at the tip of the trunk similar to that observable on the Mohenjo-daro seals figured in *M. I. C.*, Pl. CXII, 367, 371, 372 and Pl. CXV, 534 and 535, which Lyddeker describes as a characteristic of the African elephant.[3]

Finger-like process at the tip of the trunk.

Brāhmanī bull or zebu (Bos indicus).

Of Brāhmanī bulls also there are six examples Nos. 232-234 and 236-237 and one unillustrated. With the exception of No. 233 they are all well delineated, especially No. 236, but none of them is comparable to the masterly relief on the Mohenjo-daro seal No. 337 (Pl. CXI). With the bulls on these

---

[1] These are illustrated in *M. I. C.*, Pl. XII, 23 and Pl. XIII, 18-20.

[2] *M. I. C.*, p. 69.

[3] *Ibid.*, p. 388 and Lyddeker, *Game Animals of India, Burma, Malaya and Tibet*, p. 10.

seals may be compared the fragments of the two fine heads in the round—one of faience and the other of shell—illustrated in Pl. LXXIX, 67 and 68.

Bison (Bos gaurus).

There are seven bison seals Nos. 235, 238 and 241-245. In each case the animal is shown bending over a trough before him, but is not actually feeding. Nos. 241-243 are particularly vigorous. Round the neck of No. 242 there seems to be a garland or necklace in front of the folds of skin which are indicated on the other animals also. In most cases, the feeding trough is fitted with a row of upright bars, but the one in No. 243 like those in Nos. 238 and 246, is without this feature.

Buffalo (Bos bubalis).

Of buffaloes there are only two examples (Pl. XCI, 239 and 240) depicted on the Harappā seals and both of them are fragmentary. In No. 239 little more than the horns of the animal is left, while in No. 240 the legs are missing. The animals are in the same attitude as those illustrated in *M. I. C.*, Pl. CX, 304-306 and No. 240 is a particularly effective bit of relief-work.

Rhinoceros (Rhinoceros unicornis).

Only two seals exhibiting this animal (Nos. 252 and 253) have been found at Harappā compared with seven found at Mohenjo-daro (*M. I. C.*, Pl. CXI, 341-347). In No. 252 only the hind quarters of the beast are left. No. 253 is perhaps the best representation of rhinoceros found at either site, the thick rough hide with its folds and excrescenses being quite well portrayed evidently by an engraver familiar with the animal. For pottery and steatite figures of the rhinoceros compare Pl. LXXIX, 75-79 and Pl. LXXIX, 74.

Tiger (Felis tigris).

The tiger is represented on seals 246 and 248. In the former, it is alone with a trough beneath its head; in No. 248 it is under an acacia tree, in which a hunter is seated. In both cases the portrayal is rough, the stripes on its body being shown by stiff, conventional lines in relief. Other representations of the tiger may be seen on the terracotta sealings Nos. 303, 306, and 308. On account of its ferocity the tiger was probably not so familiar to the engravers as were some of the other animals which they have portrayed more faithfully. It is noteworthy that the tigers engraved on the seals from Mohenjo-daro[1] are just as rough as those at Harappā.

Troughs. The troughs found in front of the tiger, rhinoceros, and bison, and in one case in front of an elephant (*M. I. C.*, Pl. CXII, 369), can hardly have been a sign of domestication. As suggested by Sir John Marshall[2] they probably symbolised nothing more than the offering of food to these animals, the implication being that the animals were objects of worship.

---

[1] *M. I. C.*, Pl. CXI, 349-53, 355 and 357.

[2] *Ibid.*, p. 70.

Composite monster.

The mythical, hybrid creature on seals 247, 249 and 250 from Harappā is found also on seals 377, 378, 380 and 381 from Mohenjo-daro. The first and last of the Harappā specimens are broken, but on No. 249, which is almost entire, the beast is seen to have the face of a man, the trunk of an elephant, the horns of a bull, the forepart of a ram, and the hind quarters of a tiger with tail erect.

Eagle (Aquila).

A unique rhomboid seal with undulating edges is illustrated in No. 255. On its obverse is a flying eagle with head turned left and on the reverse a cross. The wings and tail of the eagle and the arms of the cross are relieved with rows of deeply incised lines. Above the outstretched wings of the eagle are two snakes. Possibly it is a prehistoric prototype of Garuḍa, who as the vehicle of Vishṇu, is often represented flying with a snake in his beak.

Hare.

A running hare with long ears is represented on a small fragment of bossed seal (No. 568) which when entire was ·6 in. square.

II.—Miniature seals or amulets.

(Pl. LXXXIV, types *h-z* and *aa-ad.*)

Size and proportion of miniature seals in early strata.

Stamp seals of the types described above diminish both in size and numbers from the IVth stratum downwards in Mound F; and so also do the terracotta and faience sealings. Their place is taken by a class of very small seals and sealings[1] which are not represented at all at Mohenjo-daro presumably because the strata exposed on that site are posterior to the age to which these early seals belong. A few of the larger seals have, it is true, found their way into the earlier strata and a few of the miniature seals into the later, but such occasional finds can hardly cause surprise, when we bear in mind the extent to which this site has been dug into and despoiled in the past; nor do they invalidate the conclusion that the larger seals were preceded by the miniature ones. In the upper strata the size of the bossed square seals ranges mostly between 2·75 and 1·5 in.; in the fifth and earlier strata in Mound F it is reduced to about ·6 in. and at the same time the numbers of these square seals rapidly diminish. In the sixth stratum, only one rectangular and plano-convex seal has been found. On the other hand, from the fourth stratum downward there is an increasing abundance of miniature seals of burnt steatite measuring in length from ·7 to ·36 in., in width from ·6 to ·25 in. or slightly less, and in thickness from ·13 to ·05 in. In the fifth stratum these seals preponderate largely over the larger ones and in the sixth stratum they are found almost exclusively.

[1] Seals and sealings of this class are also quite common in Area J, which like Mound F, is low and belongs to an earlier period. They are found in small numbers in the earlier strata in Mound AB, and are scarce in Area G and the Cemetery H.

Besides being very small, the miniature seals are characterised by the absence of any knob or hole, and by the absence also of the unicorn and other animals found on the stamp seals. In the early strata in Mound F, they were everywhere abundant, especially in Trench I where a strikingly large number of them came from the Deep Digging. The small size and thinness of these seals make their handling difficult, and this coupled with the very superficial nature of the writing on them, which in some cases is little more than scratched on the surface, precludes the possibility of their having been used for stamping, which was undoubtedly the purpose of the larger[1] and later seals. There can be no doubt, therefore, that the miniature seals were meant to be read direct from their originals. Another significant fact about them is that the range of their inscriptions is very limited. Among them, the following are the commonest :—

1. Obverse  32 times.

   Reverse VIIII 6 times, VIII 19 times, VII twice.

2. Obverse  8 times.

   Reverse VIII 6 times, VIIII once.

3. Obverse  8 times.

   Reverse VIII 3 times,

   etc.

Their talismanic character.

Though the purport of these inscriptions is unknown to us, it can hardly be doubted that the seals served as amulets of some kind and were carried about the person. Had they been intended to be encased or capped with metal some evidence of that should have been apparent. The possibility of the inscriptions being no more than personal names of owners is, I think, ruled out by the frequent repetition of some of them; but it does not follow that none of them contained the owner's name.

Animals, inscriptions or other devices on them.

On a majority of these seals or sealings there is a line of pictograms on one side and a symbol resembling one of the signs VII, VIII, VIIII, IIV, IIIV, or IIIIV on the other, while in the case of three-sided prisms the third face is generally inscribed with a row of three dotted circles. But on eleven of them one face exhibits a crocodile (Pl. XCVI, 430-436 and Pl. XCVIII, 592), on six a fish (Pl. XCVI, 437, 438, Pl. XCVII, 576, and Pl. XCVIII, 588 and 590-591), on two a goat (Pl. XCVI, 429 and Pl. XCVIII, 601), on four an incense-burner (Pl. XCVI, 440, 441 and 443), on one a diagonal cross (Pl. XCVIII, 581) and on one a *pipal* leaf (Pl. XCVI, 439). Seals of the hare type are inscribed on one side only and usually have a cross-shaped groove on the underside (Pl. LXXXIV, *ad*), while the four-sided bars have in most cases a double parallel groove on the underside (Pl. LXXXIV, *p*). On two seals, however, there

---

[1] *Cf.* C. J. Gadd in *M. I. C.*, p. 410.

is a row of dotted circles on three sides (Pl. XCVII, 572) and inscriptions on the fourth. An interesting addition to bar-shaped seals found later is No. 13030 which shows inscriptions on three sides and a standing god with a tridental headdress on the fourth.

Class 7.—Oblong seals sometimes with one or both ends rounded.

Identical inscriptions.

Type h.—Among the miniature seals, the rectangular ones are the commonest. Of a total of 310, 191 belong to this type. Many of them are inscribed with identical inscriptions as shown below:—

1. Obverse  23 times, and 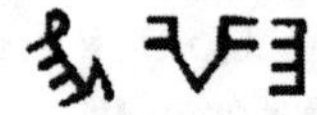 4 times.

   Reverse V||| 11 times, V|||| or V|| 9 times.

2. Obverse A| 8 times.

   Reverse V||| or V|||| 6 times.

3. Obverse  6 times, and  2 times.

   Reverse V||| 3 times.

Type i.—Rectangular seals rounded at one end.

There are only five seals of this type. In all respects they are essentially similar to those of type *h*.

Rectangular seals rounded at both ends.

Types j-k.—Nineteen seals of this type have been found. Of the type *j*, the curve at one end is rather narrow, while in *k* it is more or less even at both ends. Seals of the former shape predominate over the latter.

Class 8.—Square seal. Type l.

No. J581 (Pl. XCV, 406) is the only seal of this type.

Class 9.—Triangular seals. Type m.

Three examples of this type have been found.

Class 10.—Triangular prisms. Type n.

There are thirty-two seals of this type inscribed mostly with pictograms on two sides and a row of two or three dotted circles on the third (*e.g.*, Pl. XCVII, 573-575 and 580, and Pl. XCVIII, 587, 592 and 593). Three of them, however, are inscribed on one side with a fish (Pl. XCVII, 576, and Pl. XCVIII, 588 and 591), facing right in two cases and left in one. Of the remainder, No. 581 in Pl. XCVIII is inscribed with a diagonal cross on the third side, which is left blank in Nos. 577 and 579 in Pl. XCVII.

Class 11.—Rectangular bar seals. Types o and p.

There are five seals of type *o*, *viz.*, Nos. 450, 541, 572, 573 and 583. Of these, Nos. 450, 573 and 583 bear a line of pictograms on two faces, and a row of two dotted circles on each of the two sides. The remaining two seals of this type are inscribed with pictograms on one side only. Of these, No. 541 is uniformly inscribed with a row of three dotted circles on the three other sides, while No. 572 is inscribed with a row of two, three and four dotted circles respectively.

All the three seals, *viz.*, Nos. 401, 590 and 635 of type *p* are of smaller size, ranging in length from ·5 to ·37 in. Each has pictograms on one side and two parallel grooves on the other. On one of the remaining two sides two have a fish and the third has one pictogram, whereas the fourth side, except in No. 590 where it is blank, is inscribed with two dotted circles.

Class 12.—Cylinder seals. Types q, r and s. Type q. Long cylinder seal.

No. 561 is an impression of the only seal of this kind illustrated under type *q*. It is inscribed with two pictograms round its circumference and with a dotted circle at each end. It is ·6 in. long and ·17 in. in diameter.

Types r and s. Short cylinder seals.

No. 409 is a short, holed cylinder ·2 in. in height and ·35 in. in diameter, inscribed round the circumference. It is the only example of its kind so far found.

No. 409*a* is similar to the foregoing but is not holed. Its height is ·25 in. and diam. ·37 in. It is inscribed with pictograms round the circumference and top, and there is a dotted circle on the underside. This, too, is the only example of its kind.

Class 13.—Plano-convex discs. Type t.

Nos. 414 and 547 are the only two examples of this type—each inscribed with two identical pictograms on the plane face. Being cut into the shape of rough, facetted hemispheres, flat at bottom and bevelled along the edge, they were suitable for the bezels of rings or for other inlay.

Class 14.—Lanceolate seals with truncated ends. Type u.

There are five examples of this type, four numbered 1154c and one 12574 (Pl. XCVII, 553-555). In each case they have truncated ends and identical inscriptions on both faces. They are the thinnest of the miniature seals with a thickness ranging between ·05 and ·07 in. only.

Class 15.—Heart-shaped seals. Types v and w.

There is only one example of each of these types, *viz.*, Nos. 415 and 418. The difference between the two types is that the former is longer than the latter and somewhat rounded at the top, whereas the latter is pointed.

Class 16.—Shield-shaped seals. Type x.

There are three entire seals of this type, *viz.*, Nos. 407, 556 and 564, and two fragmentary ones, Nos. 557 and 558. They vary in size from ·75×·35 in. to ·6×·35 in. and are made by cutting semicircular segments from the centre of the longer sides of elliptical tablets. Shields of this shape are not figured

Minoan parallel. on the painted pottery or other objects at Harappā or Mohenjo-daro. In Minoan Crete, however, they are familiar cult objects[1].

Class 17.—Leaf-shaped seal. Type y.

Only one seal of this type, No. 417, has been found. It is inscribed on the obverse with 2 pictograms and bears incised circles on the reverse as well as on the sides. Another fragmentary seal which might be called leaf or dagger shaped is illustrated in Pl. XCVII, 559. Its shape is, however, different from the preceding.

Class 18.—Seals shaped like a child's writing tablet. Types z and aa.

Only two seals of these types have been recovered. Their shapes call to mind the modern writing boards of wood used by children in the primary vernacular schools and *pāṭhaśālās* of Northern India. No. 416 measures ·5×·35 in. and is inscribed on both faces. No. 408 is ·67×·4 in. and has an inscription of three pictograms on the obverse face and three dotted circles in triangular formation on the reverse.

Class 19.—Fish-shaped seals. Types ab and aq.

The fish-shaped seals are usually inscribed on both faces. Of the two examples illustrated No. 428 is ·6×·3 in.; No. 427 is ·56×·27 in.

Class 20.—Tortoise-shaped seal. Type ac.

No. 426 is the only example of a tortoise-shaped seal. It measures ·5×·3 in. and is inscribed with one pictogram on its plane underside. Its eyes and shell are depicted conventionally by means of a number of small inscribed circles.

Class 21.—Hare-shaped seals. Type ad.

There are nine seals in the form of hares either running or standing. Five of them are illustrated in Pl. XCV, 421-425 and one in Pl. XCVII, 565. Of the remaining three, one is blurred, one unfinished and one fragmentary. Except No. 12384 (unillustrated) all are inscribed on one side only, and except No. 4179 (Pl. XCV, 425), which has a lengthwise groove, all have a cross-shaped cut for attachment on the underside. They measure from ·5×·32 to ·55×·45 in. In all these specimens, the ears and eyes are incised, and in No. 1654 (Pl. XCV, 424) the mouth and nostrils are shown in the same way. Like the faience squirrels (p. 431 *supra*) they were evidently intended to be worn as amulets.

III.—Seals and sealings of terracotta or faience made from moulds, with devices and inscriptions in relief. Probably not intended for making impressions. Classes 22-39.

Owing to the relative coarseness of the material—clay or faience—of which these seals and sealings are made, the impressions inevitably lack some of the

---

[1] *Cf.* M. P. Nilsson, *The Minoan Mycenean Religion*, Chap. VI, pp. 162-200. A somewhat similar device with flowered patterns also appears on the coat of the animal figurine illustrated in Pl. LXXIX, 47.

sharpness of detail visible in the larger stone seals. A little detail, too, has been lost in the process of firing which has caused fine cracks, twisting and slight distortion of the paste.

Class 22.—Square seals or sealings (Type a) with linear designs.

Altogether 34 seals or sealings of this class have been found at Harappā. They are all square and provided with a perforated boss at the back, which with one exception is quite rough. Their sizes vary from ·7×·7×·1 in. to 1·2×1·2×·3 in. The largest example No. 11931 (Pl. XCV, 398) is provided with a boss bisected by a shallow groove (Pl. LXXXIV, type *a*) but this is exceptional; in others the bosses are plain. Only two[1] of them (Pl. XCV, 388 and 393) are made of steatite; the rest are of yellow or blue faience. The most common motif occurring on them is the *svastika* (*e.g.*, Pl. XCV, 392 and 396-399). Although the arms of the *svastika* are sometimes turned to the left, their prevailing direction at Harappā, as during the historic period in India, is to the right. At Mohenjo-daro[2] the arms are turned with equal frequency to right or left. The *svastika* has always been regarded in India as a peculiarly auspicious symbol. On all important occasions such as marriages, religious ceremonies, the starting of businesses, laying the foundations of houses, etc., it is customary among Hindus to invoke Gaṇeśa as the god of good luck by drawing him on the *vedi*[3] in the form of a *svastika*, which symbolizes him just as the *liṅga* symbolizes Śiva. **Svastika.**

The steatite seal illustrated in No. 388 is engraved with three rows of three concentric circles—a device which is not found on any other examples from Harappā or Mohenjo-daro, though the concentric circle motif is found enclosed in a square on seal No. 518 in *M. I. C.*, Pl. CXIX. **Rows of concentric circles.**

Three varieties of cross forms are represented on the seals 389-391. In No. 389, of green faience, the cross (if cross it can be called) is formed by 4 groups of parallel lines alternately vertical and horizontal. In No. 390 the cross is accentuated by small squares at the corners. In No. 391 the design is similar, but each of the corner squares encloses a circle. **Simple cross forms.**

No. 393 is a steatite seal incised diagonally with a cross-hatched pattern. **Cross-hatched pattern.**

No. 383 shows a double square enclosed in a border of lines (*cf. M. I. C.*, Pl. CXIV, No. 516). No. 394 survives only in the right half. The device consisted of four squares, with smaller squares inscribed in each. No. 395 exhibits three concentric squares with a chequer pattern in the smallest. No. 400 shows a square divided into two triangles with double borders.

Class 23.—Rectangular sealings plane on both sides (cf. *Types e and h*).

There are 74 sealings of this type, *viz.*, 55 of faience and 19 of terracotta. Of the larger faience sealings there are twenty examples which vary in size **Faience sealing.**

[1] Being seals of Type *a* with devices not in relief they might have been more appropriately transferred to Division I, but as evidently they are not meant for making impressions and bear only linear designs they may as well be dealt with here.

[2] *M. I. C.*, p. 374, and footnote 6.

[3] *Vedi* is an alter specially prepared for religious ceremonial worship.

2 Y

from 1·5×·5 to ·75×·4 in. Eleven of these bear pictograms on both sides, while No. Af22, illustrated in Pl. XCIII, 312 has a buffalo depicted on one side. This measures 1·1×·6 in. The remaining eight have pictograms on one side only, the other face being left blank. Some of the larger faience sealings of this type are illustrated in Pl. XCIV, 350-361 and 367*a*. In contrast with this all the miniature sealings with one exception are inscribed on both sides. Their size varies from ·7×·25 to ·5×·28 in.

Sealings with animal and other devices. Six of the miniature sealings with animal or other forms on them may be noticed in particular. No. 2276 (Pl. XCVIII, 601) has pictograms as well as a goat regardant on both faces. No. 11465 (Pl. XCIII, 313), half of which is missing, shows on one side a bison and on the other an acacia tree in front of which is a man kneeling. There are two other sealings (Nos. 4765=Pl. XCVIII, 595 and J409=Pl. C, 677) which are inscribed with pictograms on one side and a quadruped on the other, the former also bearing a pictogram in the upper field. Unfortunately, in both cases the neck of the animal is broken and its identity is not clear. No. 9041 (Pl. XCIV, 340) is inscribed with pictograms on one side and a crocodile (*Gavialis gangeticus*) with a fish on the other. Of No. 7156 (Pl. XCIX, 648) only one-half remains. It has pictograms on one side and a diagonal cross in a square panel on the other. Probably it had another square panel in the missing half.

Terracotta sealings. Of rectangular terracotta sealings there are only 19. Eleven of these are from three different moulds; two represented by Pl. XCIII, 314; three by Pl. XCIII, 322, and six by Pl. XCIV, 343. Of the others the following deserve notice.

Crocodile with fish. Sealing No. 2430 (Pl. XCIV, 337) shows a crocodile with fish on one side and five pictograms on the other.

Acacia tree and railing. Sealing No. 5617 (Pl. XCIII, 325) shows, on one side, a large acacia tree enclosed in a railing and a line of five pictograms on the other. The same motif of tree and railing also occurs on several faience sealings but on none of them it is so clear as here.

Three other sealings that are highly interesting by reason of the scenes depicted on them are Nos. 303, 304 and 306 which have already been described elsewhere.[1]

Of oblong sealings with one end rounded (Type *i*) there are only three examples, each ·6 in. long. Of these, No. 12562 is illustrated in Pl. XCVIII, 610; No. 2305 has the same inscription on the obverse face but on reverse it has IIV instead of VII; and No. 11417 is illustrated in Pl. XCVIII, 606.

Class 24.—Cylindrical sealings. Type ae.

There are a large number of cylindrical sealings, with many duplicates, both in terracotta and faience. A common feature of these, as well as of those of types *af* and *ah*, is that their moulds were made in two parts which on being pressed together formed a ridge at the point of juncture. (*Cf.* Pl. LXXXIV, *ae*, *af* and *ah*).

---

[1] See pp. 129-30, 42 and 146 *supra*.

Among these sealings are thirty-three duplicates from one and the same mould (No. 315). They are 1·33 in. long and ·6 in. in diameter with an inscription of four pictograms on one side and a unicorn on the other. Next in point of numbers come nine duplicates exhibiting a crocodile on one side and a line of eleven pictograms on the other (Nos. 334-336). These are 1·6 in. long and ·4 in. in diameter. In contrast with most of the other terracotta sealings, which are brick-red, their colour ranges from dark red to grey. Five other terracotta sealings also display a crocodile on one side and a line of four pictograms on the other, but they are smaller in size (Nos. 338 and 339). Another cylindrical terracotta sealing is 1·2 in. long and ·4 in. in diameter (Pl. XCIV, 333). It shows a snub-nosed crocodile (*magar*) in place of the more common, long-nosed gharial on one side and a line of blurred pictograms on the other. It is pierced with a blind hole at both ends—the only example of a terracotta cylinder provided with holes.

Unicorn.

Crocodile.

Six duplicates display an acacia tree on one side and a line of three pictograms on the other (Pl. XCIII, 323). They are 1·1 in. long and ·4 in. in diameter. Around the tree is a low platform.

Acacia trees.

Slightly larger than the foregoing are the two terracotta sealings from one mould illustrated in Pl. XCIII, 328. They are 1·2 in. long by ·5 in. in diameter. The acacia tree has a low platform round its base and is less conventional in form than on No. 327.

No. 319 shows on one side a two-horned figure, possibly a god walking towards the left, and on the other a line of seven pictograms.

Horned figure.

There are two cylindrical terracotta sealings from one mould which bear inscriptions on both sides. One of them is illustrated in Pl. XCIV, 362.

There is only one miniature cylindrical sealing of terracotta (No. J353) which has pictograms (much blurred) on both sides. It is ·85 in. long and ·2 in. in diameter. On the other hand, there are as many as sixteen of these sealings made of faience, six of which are from one and the same mould. These are inscribed with a row of four pictograms on one side and with one pictogram and a conventionalised acacia tree at right angles to it on the other (*e.g.*, Pl. XCIX, 646 and 650). The tree has six branches bifurcating symmetrically from the trunk. The sealings measure ·8 in. long and ·3 in. in diameter.

Three other miniature sealings, again from one mould, show a highly conventionalised branch on either side (Pl. CI, 705 and 706). They are ·6 in. long and ·3 in. in diameter.

Class 25.—Oblong sealings, lenticular or plano-convex in section. Types af and ag.

Type *af.*—There are nineteen sealings of this type, eight of terracotta and eleven of faience. Of these, No. 329 of terracotta and six of faience (two from one mould No. 326, and four from another No. 332) exhibit an acacia tree with a platform or railing round its base.

Acacia tree with platform or railing.

The terracotta sealing No. 307 has three pictograms on one side and a deity[1] (wearing a three-pointed or three-feathered head-dress and a number of

God under arch.

[1] As explained by Sir John Marshall in *M. I. C.*, p. 64 it is possible that the figure may, in the absence of clear indication of sex, be a female rather than a male deity.

armlets on the arms) beneath an arch made of the bent bough of a *pīpal* tree, a device which is also found on the faience sealings 316 and 317.

No. 318 is another terracotta sealing with three pictograms on one side and on the other a deity with three-feathered or three-pointed head-dress walking (perhaps with his back towards the reader) between two posts, each crowned by a *pīpal* leaf.

Incense-burners. No. 309 is also of terracotta. On both faces it shows a large incense-burner, but on one face there is a line of pictograms on either side of the supporting staff; on the other face there is a line of pictograms on one side only of the staff with the figure of a man on the other side. Incense-burners also appear on two sealings of faience—both from the same mould (No. 320) and with a line of five pictograms on the reverse; and this motif is repeated on five other sealings of faience from another mould (No. 321), but in these examples there are two pictograms on the side showing the incense-burner, and four on the reverse side.

Anchor. Sealing No. 341 of terracotta has four pictograms on one side and what looks like an anchor on the other. This motif is not known at Mohenjo-daro.

Two other terracotta sealings of this type bear inscriptions on both sides.

Type *ag.*—Altogether, there are fifteen oblong sealings, plano-convex in section, *viz.*, five of terracotta and ten of faience. Their section varies from a semicircle to a small segment. Two of them (Nos. 308 and 316) are particularly interesting owing to the subjects depicted on them (*cf.* pp. 59 and 195 *supra*). The former is of terracotta; the latter of faience. Of the other sealings, two of terracotta are inscribed on one side only; the remaining eleven (two of terracotta and nine of faience) have pictograms on both sides.

Class 26.—Lenticular sealings. Type ah.

There are only two sealings (Nos. 12060 and Ab707) of this type both in faience and from the same mould. They are inscribed with three pictograms on one side only (No. 380).

Class 27.—Discoid sealings, plane on both sides. Type ai.

There is only one large terracotta sealing of this type (No. 311) which displays a buffalo on one side and a pictogram in the upper field. It is 1·05 in. in diameter. Nineteen other sealings of this type, *i.e.*, two of terracotta and seventeen of faience are smaller. The terracotta ones are ·6 in. in diameter. No. 377 has pictograms on one side and a circumscribed four-pointed star on the other—a design commonly found in shell inlay and on painted pottery; the other (No. 5621) appears to be inscribed with pictograms on both sides, but is too blurred for reproduction.

The seventeen sealings of faience range in size from ·4 to ·7 in. in diameter. Of these, three are inscribed on one side only including two from one and the same mould (No. 379). All the remaining ones are either inscribed on both sides, or have on one side some other device with or without the inscription.

Four of the above sealings have circular inscriptions on the obverse face, but none of them is duplicated. They are illustrated in Pl. XCV, 371, 372, 375 and 381.

There are five other sealings of this type with pictograms on both sides but their inscriptions are in straight lines. Four of these are illustrated in Pl. XCV, 370, 373, 374 and 378.

No. 317 displays on one side a deity[1] under an arch made of the bent bough of a *pīpal* tree and on the other a small *svastika* enclosed in a square round which runs an inscription.

Pīpal rosette. No. 8650d (Pl. C, 664) exhibits a rosette of seven *pīpal* leaves on one side and three pictograms on the other. At Mohenjo-daro, seal No. 387[2] shows nine *pīpal* leaves issuing from between the jugate heads of unicorns. That the *pīpal* tree was held sacred by the Indus people is indicated by the above Mohenjo-daro seal and also by the *pīpal* leaves or branches in association with a deity on sealings 307 and 316-318.

Tortoise. No. 663 is a miniature sealing of faience inscribed with one pictogram on one side and a tortoise in relief on the other. This is the only example where the tortoise is depicted though the miniature steatite seal illustrated in Pl. LXXXIV, *ac* is itself shaped like a tortoise.

Incense-burner. No. 665 is inscribed with two pictograms on one side and one pictogram and an incense-burner on the other.

Class 28.—Cuboid sealing. Type *aj.*

No. H441e is an irregular cuboid sealing of yellow faience showing traces of white glaze. It measures ·5×·5×·4 to ·3 in. and is the only example of this shape found at Harappā. At Mohenjo-daro, however, five seals of this type have been recovered.[3] The Harappā sealing displays an acacia tree and two pictograms on opposite faces, and an incised circle with a hole at the centre (probably for inlay) in the middle of each side. It is much blurred.

Class 29.—Hexagonal sealings. Type ak.

Acacia tree. There are three irregular, hexagonal faience sealings Nos. H91, 9059 and 11358, all from the same mould (No. 324). They bear four pictograms on one face and one pictogram and an acacia tree by its side on the other.

Class 30.—Triangular prism sealings. Type n.

Of the twelve triangular prism sealings found at Harappā, three are of terracotta and nine of faience. Among the former, No. 305 is of large size[4] and shows on each face a composite figure, part human, part bovine, with a pictogram repeated at the bottom on each face. The sides of this prism taper upwards; in its base is a blind hole. No. 310 is of terracotta. The reliefs on its three faces are described on p. 129 *supra*. The third terracotta specimen

Composite figures.

---

[1] See footnote 1 on p. 331 *supra*.

[2] *Cf. M. I. C.*, Pl. CXII.

[3] *Ibid.*, p. 375.

[4] For fuller description, see p. 44 *supra*.

is No. 598. It is inscribed with a line of pictograms on one side, one pictogram and an acacia tree on the second, and a row of three dotted circles on the third.

Faience sealings.

All the faience sealings of this type are inscribed with pictograms on two sides, but on the third side Nos. 10010 and J219 (Pl. XCIX, 647 and 649) have a row of dotted circles; Nos. J358, J619 (Pl. XCIX, 642), 10177 (Pl. XCVIII, 600) and J359 (Pl. XCIX, 645) a fish; Nos. 12750 (Pl. XCIX, 641) and 10960 (Pl. XCVIII, 597) a crocodile; and No. 11511 (Pl. XCVIII, 596) an indistinct animal.

Class 31.—Tetrahedron-shaped sealing.

No. 5796 is a terracotta sealing of which the sides have partially flaked off. When entire, it took the form of a tetrahedron. The inscription on it is altogether blurred and it is not possible to state with certainty whether it was inscribed on all the four sides or not. This sealing is not illustrated.

Class 32.—Triangular sealing. Type al.

No. 3855 (Pl. XCV, 386) is of faience and the only specimen of a triangular sealing. It is roughly equilateral and shows two lines of pictograms on one face and one pictogram on the other.

Class 33.—Spherical.

Spherical sealing.

No. A233 (Pl. C, 657) is the only, example of a spherical sealing. It is of terracotta and impressed with a small seal at one point where it has become somewhat flattened. Diam. ·75 in.

Class 34.—Shield-shaped sealings. Type x.

There are only three sealings of this type, all of faience, *viz.*, Nos. 368, 369 and 376. They are all inscribed on both sides, but none is a duplicate.

Class 35.—Crescent-shaped sealing. Type am.

No. 387 is a lunette-shaped faience sealing inscribed with pictograms on both faces. This shape is unique at Harappā and is not represented at Mohenjo-daro.

Class 36.—Lanceolate sealing. Type an.

No. 11381 (Pl. C, 673) is the only lanceolate sealing. It is of faience and inscribed with pictograms on both sides. This shape is represented among miniature seals described under type *u*, but here the ends are not truncated.

Class 37.—Leaf-shaped sealing. Type ao.

Fish.

No. 644 is a leaf-shaped faience sealing exhibiting a line of pictograms on one side and a fish in relief (not a pictogram) on the other. The fish engraved on some of the miniature rectangular or triangular prism seals or sealings may also have been intended to represent living fish not pictograms.

Class 38.—Sealings shaped like a date seed. Type ap.

No. 385 and 385*a* are the only two examples of faience sealings shaped like a date seed.

Class 39.—Fish-shaped sealings. Types ab and aq.

Altogether there are four fish-shaped sealings of faience, two broken and two entire. Similar shapes are also found among the miniature seals (*e.g.*, No. 427). Two of these sealings, Nos. 3493 and 12380 (Pl. C, 658) with inscriptions on both sides, are from one mould; of the other two (Nos. J42 and 12329) only the head remains.

The following is a list of the animal, tree, plant and other forms which are found on the various types of seals and sealings from Harappā.

Large seals and sealings.

1. Unicorn.
2. Brāhmanī bull or Zebu (*Bos indicus*).
3. Bison (*Bos gaurus*).
4. Buffalo (*Bos bubalus*).
5. Elephant (*Elephas maximus*).
6. Rhinoceros (*Rhinoceros unicornis*).
7. Tiger (*Felis tigris*).
8. Eagle (*Equila*).
9. Goat.
10. Crocodile (*Gavialis gangeticus*).
11. Composite creatures.
12. Acacia tree with or without a railing or platform.
13. *Pīpal* (*Ficus religiosa*) or its boughs or leaves.
14. Model of a temple ?
15. Incense-burner.
16. *Svastika.*
17. Cross.
18. Anchor.
19. Linear patterns.

Miniature seals and sealings.

1. Bison (*Bos gaurus*).
2. Goat.
3. Hare.
4. Crocodile (*Gavialis gangeticus*).
5. Tortoise.
6. Fish.
7. Acacia tree.
8. *Pīpal* leaf or rosette of leaves.
9. Incense-burner.
10. *Svastika.*
11. Diagonal cross.

PARTIAL CORRIGENDUM TO MOHENJO-DARO SIGN MANUAL (*M.I.C.* PLS. CIII—CXXIX).

MISCOPIES.

SIGN No.	SIGN AS DRAWN	SIGN AS CORRECTED	PHOTO No.
XXI			21
XXX	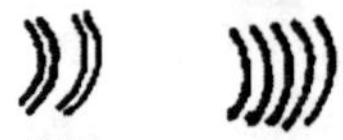		72
LII			60
CXXI			118
CXCIX			325
CCXC	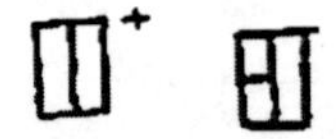 +		534
CCCLXXXII			427

IN THE FOLLOWING CASES VARIATIONS OF SIGNS SHOULD HAVE BEEN DRAWN EITHER WITH THE RELEVANT SIGNS OR NOTICED SEPARATELY.

SIGN No.	SIGN(S) AS DRAWN	SIMILAR SIGNS NOT NOTICED	PHOTO No.
XCV—XCVI			10
CLIV			466
			123
			22
CCXCVIII	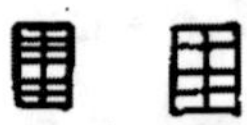		253
			159
		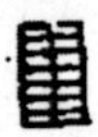	56
CCXCIX			121
			16
			4
			4
CCCLI	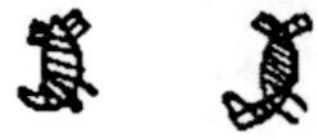		12
			87
			100
			194
			237
			262
			309
			370
CCCLII	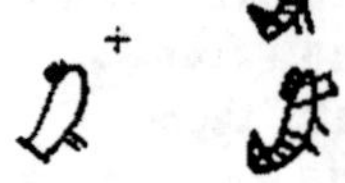 +		13
			21
			101
CCCLIII—CCCLIV			36

[*Continued in the next column.*]

+NOTE.—Had these signs been drawn correctly they would have merged in signs Nos. 292 and 351 respectively.

HARAPPĀ: TABULATION OF SEALS (PLS. LXXXV–CI).

Plate No.	Size in inches.	Level below surface.	Type.[1]	Materials and colour.			Mound or Area.	Find-No.
				Steatite.	Faience.	Pottery.		
1	2·6 × 2·6	5′ 6″	a	White	..	..	AB	3716
2	2·07 × 2·07	2′ 6″	a	Blue	..	..	F	1056
3	2·2 × 2·2	5′ 0″	a	White	..	..	AB	PI-40
4	2·05 × 2·05	5′ 0″	a	White	..	..	AB	PI-42
5	1·65 × 1·65	5′ 0″ to 5′ 8″	a	White	..	..	F	116
6	2·1 × 2·1	5′ 0″	a	White	..	..	AB	PI-39
7	1·8 × 1·8	3′ 9″	a	White	..	..	F	11476
8	1·8 × 1·8	5′ 0″	a	Blue	..	..	AB	PI-41
9	1·7 × 1·7	5′ 0″ to 5′ 8″	a	White	..	..	F	115
10	1·65 × 1·65	3′ 6″	a	White	..	..	F	Aa106
11	1·85 × 1·85	15′ 8″	a	White	..	..	F	2253
12	1·75 × 1·75	8′ 8″	a	White	..	..	F	5880
13	1·45 × 1·45	3′ 8″	a	White	..	..	F	3718
14	1·8 × 1·8	8′ 4″	a	White	..	..	AB	7411
15	1·2 × 1·2	3′ 0″	a	White	..	..	G	217
16	1·6 × 1·6	5′ 0″ to 5′ 8″	a	White	..	..	F	145
17	1·5 × 1·5	6′ 0″	a	White	..	..	F	3645
18	1·25 × 1·25	8′ 0″	a	White	..	..	AB	5068
19	1·6 × 1·6	5′ 0″	a	White	..	..	F	3170
20	1·8 × 1·8	11′ 0″	a	White	..	..	AB	PIV-114
21	1·45 × 1·45	8′ 2″	a	White	..	..	F	A263
22	1·35 × 1·35	5′ 9″	a	White	..	..	AB	3725
23	1·5 × 1·5	6′ 0″	a	White	..	..	F	150
24	1·65 × 1·65	..	a	White	..	..	AB	B101
25	1·55 × 1·55	5′ 0″	a	White	..	..	F	PII-21
26	1·3 × 1·3	7′ 6″	a	White	..	..	F	8921
27	1·7 × ?	..	a	White	..	..	F	Aa102
28	1·3 × 1·3	8′ 8″	a	White	..	..	F	12493
29	1·25 × 1·25	12′ 0″	a	Blue	..	..	F	1842
30	1·3 × 1·3	4′ 6″	a	White	..	..	F	368
31	1·25 × 1·25	12′ 7″	a	White	..	..	F	12561
32	1·25 × 1·25	15′ 8″	a	White	..	..	F	2892
33	1·15 × 1·15	7′ 8″	a	White	..	..	AB	4553
34	1·05 × 1·05	10′ 9″	a	White	..	..	AB	4991
35	1·1 × 1·1	4′ 0″	a	..	..	..	D	2975
36	1·1 × 1·1	2′ 1″	a	White	..	..	D	4079
37	1·1 × 1·1	9′ 2″	a	White	..	..	F	5258
38	1·65 × 1·65	7′ 8″	a	White	..	..	AB	8772
39	?	5′ 9″	a	White	..	..	F	5341
40	1·6 × 1·6	8′ 0″	a	Blue	..	..	F	10740
41	1·8 × 1·8	3′ 0″	a	White	..	..	F	3967
42	1·45 × 1·45	3′ 0″	a	White	..	..	AB	Bg7
43	1·5 × 1·5	6′ 9″	a	White	..	..	F	7683
44	1·55 × 1·55	5′ 0″	a	..	..	Grey	F	10625
45	1·45 × 1·45	3′ 0″	a	White	..	..	AB	2879
46	1·3 × 1·3	5′ 0″	a	White	..	..	F	483
47	1·3 × 1·3	6′ 5″	a	Blue	..	..	F	12414k
48	1·25 × 1·25	10′ 3″	a	White	..	..	F	2097
49	1·25 × 1·25	8′ 1″	a	White	..	..	F	11832
50	1·05 × 1·05	8′ 2″	a	White	..	..	F	12715
51	1·25 × 1·25	5′ 0″	a	White	..	..	F	3644

[1] For type on this and subsequent pages see Pl. LXXXIX.

HARAPPĀ: TABULATION OF SEALS (PLS. LXXXV-CI)—*contd.*

Plate No.	Size in inches.	Level below surface.	Type.	Materials and colour.			Mound or Area.	Find No.
				Steatite.	Faience.	Pottery.		
52	1·4 × 1·4	From surface	a	Blue	..	..	F	11869
53	1·35 × 1·35	11′ 0″	a	White	..	..	F	731
54	1·05 × 1·05	4′ 0″	a	White	..	..	AB	1514
55	1·05 × 1·05	9′ 0″	a	White	..	..	F	11879
56	1·25 × 1·25	..	a	White	..	..	..	....
57	1·14 × 1·14	2′ 0″	a	White	..	..	F	1240
58	1·35 × 1·35	9′ 0″	a	White	..	..	AB	PII-82
59	1·2 × 1·2	15′ 3″	a	White	..	..	F	2234
60	Extant side 1·3	0′ 9″	a	Black	..	..	F	5551
61	?	4′ 2″	a	White	..	..	F	12185
62	1·09 × 1·09	18′ 3″	a	White	..	..	F	2256
63	1·12 × 1·12	1′ 8″	a	Blue	..	..	D	J21
64	1·0 × 1·0	11′ 1″	a	White	..	..	F	1720
65	1·2 × 1·2	2′ 0″	a	White	..	..	F	11163
66	0·85 × 0·85	8′ 10″	a	Blue	..	..	F	12140
67	1·1 × 1·1	15′ 0″	a	White	..	..	F	2118
68	1·8 × 1·8	2′ 8″	a	White	..	..	F	4013
69	1·8 × 1·8	4′ 6″	a	White	..	..	AB	5383
70	1·3 × 1·3	9′ 0″	a	White	..	..	AB	5777
71	1·25 × 1·25	18′ 0″	a	White	..	..	F	10142
72	1·25 × 1·25	10′ 0″	a	White	..	..	F	10011
73	1·05 × 1·05	7′ 6″	a	White	..	..	AB	7008
74	1·05 × 1·05	9′ 6″	a	White	..	..	F	5810
75	1·0 × 1·0	12′ 0″	a	White	..	..	F	2340
76	1·15 × 1·15	4′ 10″	a	White	..	..	F	1097
77	1·2 × 1·2	7′ 9″	a	White	..	..	F	10927
78	1·2 × 1·2	5′ 0″ to 5′ 8″	a	White	..	..	F	117
79	1·1 × 1·1	3′ 5″	a	Blue	..	..	H	H220
80	1·15 × 1·15	8′ 0″	a	White	..	..	F	10779
81	1·55 × 1·55	4′ 0″	a	White	..	..	F	11942
82	1·05 × 1·05	8′ 6″	a	White	..	..	F	1055
83	1·05 × 1·05	6′ 9″	a	Blue	..	..	F	1591
84	1·1 × 1·1	7′ 3″	a	Blue	..	..	F	474
85	1·1 × 1·1	4′ 6″	a	Bluish	..	..	F	A214
86	0·95 × 0·95	1′ 6″	a	Blue	..	..	F	A19
87	1·1 × 1·1	5′ 10″	a	Bluish	..	..	F	11331
88	1·05 × 1·05	3′ 9″	a	White	..	..	F	945
89	1·05 × 1·05	8′ 4″	a	White	..	..	F	3459
90	0·95 × 0·95	15′ 6″	a	White	..	..	F	10185a
91	1·0 × 1·0	5′ 10″	a	White	..	..	AB	PII-53
92	0·95 × 0·95	4′ 6″	a	White	..	..	F	1190
93	1·0 × 1·0	20′ 0″	a	White	..	..	AB	B1341
94	0·9 × 0·9	6′ 0″	a	White	..	..	F	10061
95	1·05 × 1·05	10′ 0″	a	White	..	..	F	2930
96	1·05 × 1·05	9′ 0″	a	White	..	..	AB	PIV-99
97	0·9 × 0·85	5′ 10″	a	White	..	..	AB	5082
98	1·0 × 1·0	11′ 6″	a	Bluish	..	..	AB	11768
99	0·95 × 0·95	5′ 6″	a	White	..	..	AB	PII-23
100	1·05 × 1·05	10′ 11″	a	White	..	..	F	741
101	0·9 × 0·9	6′ 10″	a	White	..	..	F	11350

HARAPPĀ : TABULATION OF SEALS (PLS. LXXXV-CI)—*contd.*

Plate No.	Size in inches.	Level below surface.	Type.	Materials and colour.			Mound or Area.	Find No.
				Steatite.	Faience.	Pottery.		
102	0·95 × 0·95	6' 0"	a	Blue	..	..	F	1200
103	1·28 × 1·28	3' 2"	a	White	..	..	J	J46
104	1·25 × 1·25	4' 0"	a	White	..	..	J	J278
105	0·9 × 0·9	8' 0"	a	White	..	..	F	A236
106	1·3 × 1·3	6' 0"	a	White	..	..	J	J679
107	1·0 × 1·0	13' 7"	a	White	..	..	F	8767
108	1·0 × 1·0	3' 0"	a	White	..	..	F	2212
109	1·05 × 1·05	5' 4"	a	White	..	..	F	12139
110	1·0 × 1·0	16' 4"	a	White	..	..	F	3482
111	0·9 × 0·9	6' 6"	a	White	..	..	F	11368
112	0·85 × 0·85	3' 0"	a	Black	..	..	F	10635a
113	1·15 × 1·15	1' 3"	a	White	..	..	J	J500
114	1·1 × 1·1	10' 8"	a	White	..	..	AB	11706
115	0·85 × 0·85	15' 6"	a	White	..	..	F	1265
116	0·85 × 0·85	19' 8"	a	Blue	..	..	AB	2463
117	0·8 × 0·8	2' 6"	a	Blue	..	..	AB	PI-4
118	0·8 × 0·8	10' 3"	a	White	..	..	F	12637
119	0·8 × 0·8	8' 6"	a	White	..	..	F	2281
120	0·8 × 0·8	8' 5"	a	Blue	..	..	AB	II-71
121	1·0 × 1·0	4' 11"	a	White	..	..	F	11550
122	0·7 × 0·65	7' 0"	a	White	..	..	D	4015
123	0·9 × 0·9	14' 0"	a	Blue	..	..	F	2785
124	0·95 × 0·95	10' 4"	a	White	..	..	F	2531
125	0·85 × 0·85	9' 0"	a	White	..	..	F	1009
126	1·15 × 1·15	5' 7"	a	White	..	..	J	J451
127	0·8 × 0·8	15' 10"	a	White	..	..	F	2476
128	0·8 × 0·8	9' 2"	a	White	..	..	AB	1500
129	0·7 × 0·7	5' 8"	a	White	..	..	F	10815
130	0·9 × 0·9	5' 6"	a	Blue	..	..	F	517
131	1·05 × 1·05	4' 2"	a	White	..	..	D	J548
132	0·9 × 0·9	4' 4"	a	White	..	..	AB	17164
133	0·9 × 0·9	8' 2"	a	White	..	..	F	11630
134	0·9 × 0·9	7' 4"	a	White	..	..	F	12251
135	0·65 × 0·65	..	a	White	..	..	AB	B234
136	0·75 × 0·70	11' 4"	a	White	..	..	F	12180
137	0·65 × 0·65	5' 0"	a	White	..	..	F	272
138	0·9 × 0·9	14' 0"	a	White	..	..	F	12066
139	0·75 × 0·75	10' 0"	a	White	..	..	F	2266
140	0·8 × 0·8	18' 5"	a	White	..	..	F	2390
141	0·85 × 0·85	12' to 14'	a	White	..	..	F	11849
142	0·7 × 0·7	8' 0"	a	White	..	..	AB	2903
143	0·65 × 0·65	7' 6"	a	White	..	..	AB	5634
144	1·04 × 1·04	10' 3"	a	Blue	..	..	F	2347
145	0·9 × ?	12' 6"	a	White	..	..	F	11696
146	0·8 × 0·8	17' 6"	a	White	..	..	F	2532
147	0·7 × 0·7	12' 0"	a	White	..	..	F	2961
148	0·65 × 0·65	5' 8"	a	White	..	..	F	11204
149	0·8 × 0·8	12' 3"	a	White	..	..	F	2728
150	0·8 × 0·8	4' 0"	a	White	..	..	F	A1132
151	0·7 × 0·7	6' 5"	a	White	..	..	F	11812

HARAPPĀ : TABULATION OF SEALS (Pls. LXXXV-CI)—*contd.*

Plate No.	Size in inches.	Level below surface.	Type.	Materials and colour.			Mound or Area.	Find No.
				Steatite.	Faience.	Pottery.		
152	1·05 × 1·05	5' 2"	a	White	..	..	D	J38
153	?	13' 2"	a	White	..	..	F	2798
154	?	0' 7"	a	White	..	..	F	11961
155	0·7 × 0·7	5' 6"	a	Blue	..	..	F	10818
156	0·7 × 0·7	5' 2"	a	Bluish	..	..	AB	11884
157	0·65 × 0·65	11' 4"	a	White	..	..	F	12179
158	?	11' 4"	a	White	..	..	F	12181
159	0·77 × 0·77	15' 0"	a	White	..	..	F	2121
160	0·55 × 0·55	2' 4"	a	Blue	..	..	F	11716
161	0·55 × 0·55	13' 5"	a	White	..	..	F	2982
162	0·7 × 0·7	11' 8"	a	White	..	..	F	12066
163	0·65 × 0·65	1' 6"	a	White	..	..	D	J20
164	0·6 × 0·6	10' 3"	a	White	..	..	F	11796
165	0·7 × 0·65	13' to 14'	a	White	..	..	F	11850
166	0·8 × 0·8	5' 0"	a	White	..	..	F	12318
167	0·7 × 0·55	2' 6" to 4' 6"	a	Black	..	..	AB	12387h
168	1·45 × 1·45	8' 10"	a	White	..	..	F	7980
169	1·15 × 1·15	6' 4"	a	White	..	..	AB	7115
170	1·5 × 1·5	3' 6"	a	White	..	..	H	H845
171	1·15 × 1·15	2' 0"	a	White	..	..	F	A116
172	?	15' 6"	a	White	..	..	AB	12149
173	1·65 × 1·65	3' 5"	a	White	..	..	F	12442
174	?	11' 0"	a	White	..	..	F	11688
175	1·2 × 1·2	7' 6"	a	White	..	..	F	12283
176	?	From spoil earth.	a	White	..	..	F	2880
177	1·05 × 1·05	11' 0"	a	White	..	..	F	1062
178	1·1 × 1·1	13' 1"	a	White	..	..	AB	11837
179	1·2 × 1·2	8' 9"	a	White	..	..	F	2695
180	1·05 × 1·05	5' 0"	a	White	..	..	F	11035
181	?	4' 0"	a	White	..	..	G	G104
182	0·95 × 0·95	14' 4"	a	White	..	..	F	2811
183	0·9 × 0·9	5' 0"	a	White	..	..	F	11329
184	?	4' 0"	a	Blue	..	..	F	1884
185	?	1' 2"	a	White	..	..	H	H20
186	?	20' 3"	a	White	..	..	F	10170
187	?	9' 0"	a	White	..	..	F	11021
188	1·05 × 1·05	0' 9"	a	White	..	..	F	1244
189	1·0 × 1·0	11' 6"	a	Blue	..	..	F	2700
190	?	18' 0"	a	White	..	..	F	2120
191	?	8' 0"	a	White	..	..	F	11342
192	?	18' 5"	a	White	..	..	F	2250
193	?	4' 0"	a	White	..	..	F	A1130
194	0·1 × ?	2' 11"	a	White	..	..	F	8648
195	?	8' 9"	a	Blue	..	..	AB	7891
196	?	6' 6"	a	White	..	..	F	6834
197	0·8 × 0·8	10' 4"	a	White	..	..	F	2580
198	1·0 × 1·0	2' 10"	a	Blue	..	..	D	J41
199	?	8' 3"	a	Blue	..	..	F	11631
200	?	9' 0"	a	White	..	..	F	204
201	?	2' 0"	a	White	..	..	G	G201

HARAPPĀ : TABULATION OF SEALS (Pls. LXXXV-CI)—*contd.*

Plate No.	Size in inches.	Level below surface.	Type.	Materials and colour.			Mound or Area.	Find No.
				Steatite.	Faience.	Pottery.		
202	?	From spoil earth.	a	White	..	..	F	12381
203	?	5' 0"	a	White	..	..	AB	11558
204	1·45 × 1·45	4' 0"	a	White	..	..	F	1650
205	?	3' 10"	a	White	..	..	F	12702
206	0·8 × 0·8	4' 6"	a	White	..	..	F	11039
207	0·7 × ?	12' 8"	a	White	..	..	F	2726
208	?	15' 2"	a	White	..	..	F	2694
209	?	8' 0"	a	Blue	..	..	AB	2703
210	?	3' 0"	a	White	..	..	F	A1116
211	0·75 × 0·75	3' 0"	a	Bluish	..	..	F	11233
212	0·45 × ?	15' 0"	a	White	..	..	F	A125
213	1·45 × ?	3' 0"	a	White	..	..	F	1641
214	?	6' 6"	a	White	..	..	F	11940
215	0·8 × 0·8	7' 0"	a	White	..	..	F	12268
216	?	10' 0"	a	White	..	..	F	11797
217	?	6' 0"	a	Blue	..	..	F	5367
218	?	6' 0"	a	White	..	..	F	12332
219	?	11' 10"	a	White	..	..	F	898
220	0·9 × 0·9	8' 5"	a	White	..	..	F	10318
221	1·45 × 1·45	8' 0"	a	White	..	..	AB	PIII-54
222	1·7 × 1·2	8' 0"	..	Blue	..	..	F	1204
223	1·1 × 1·05	9' 0"	a	..	..	Brown	F	2125
224	0·95 × 0·95	3' 0"	a	Blue	..	..	F	10260
225	0·85 × 0·8	20' 1"	a	Bluish	..	..	F	2394
226	2·0 × 2·0	0' 4"	a	Bluish	..	..	F	4624
227	0·9 × 0·9	7' 6"	a	White	..	..	F	7726
228	0·95 × 0·95	7' 0"	a	White	..	..	F	1692
229	0·8 × 0·8	15' 8"	a	White	..	..	F	10185b
230	0·9 × 0·9	8' 0"	a	Blue	..	..	AB	3771
231	0·85 × 0·85	From spoil earth.	a	White	..	..	F	12747
232	0·95 × 0·95	From surface	a	White	..	..	AB	10310
233	0·7 × 0·7	17' 2"	a	White	..	..	F	9090
234	0·9 × 0·9	5' 6"	a	White	..	..	F	10995
235	0·65 × 0·65	10' 6"	a	White	..	..	F	2415
236	1·45 × 1·45	20' 0"	a	White	..	..	F	4299
237	1·2 × 1·2	15' 2"	a	White	..	..	AB	12132
238	0·7 × 0·7	11' 6"	a	White	..	..	F	4042
239	0·7 × ?	7' 9 to 11' 9"	a	White	..	..	F	3611
240	1·2 × 1·2	6' 3"	a	White	..	..	F	627
241	1·1 × 1·1	4' to 7'	a	Blue	..	..	F	8650a
242	?	6' 0"	a	Blue	..	..	F	2333
243	0·95 × 0·95	12' 0"	a	White	..	..	F	1276
244	0·9 × 0·9	From spoil earth.	a	White	..	..	F	1872
245	0·75 × 0·75	3' 4"	a	White	..	..	D	J261
246	0·95 × 0·95	7' 8"	a	White	..	..	F	11110
247	?	10' 6"	a	White	..	..	F	2453
248	0·9 × 0·55	14' 9"	a	Black	..	..	F	1280
249	1·1 × 1·1	10' 0"	a	White	..	..	F	6211
250	?	15' 2"	a	White	..	..	F	12131

HARAPPĀ: TABULATION OF SEALS (PLS. LXXXV-CI)—*contd.*

Plate No.	Size in inches.	Level below surface.	Type.	Materials and colour.			Mound or Area.	Find No.
				Steatite.	Faience.	Pottery.		
251	1·6 × ?	5′ 0″ to 5′ 2″	a	White	..	..	F	118
252	0·65 × ?	12′ 0″	a	White	..	..	D	J139
253	1·2 × 1·2	10′ 8″	a	White	..	..	F	5534
254	1·5 × 1·5	6′ 0″	a	Bluish	..	..	AB	2789
255	Diagonals 1·62 + 1·25	2′ 0″	f	White	..	..	AB	PIV-65
256	1·0 × 1·0	12′ 0″	a	White	..	..	F	10102
257	1·1 × 1·1	10′ 0″	a	..	..	Red burnt	F	725
258	1·05 × 1·0	5′ 6″	a	..	..	Brown	F	8130
259	1·05 × ?	6′ 0″	a	Bluish	..	..	F	11040
260	1·05 × ?	16′ 6″	a	Black	..	..	F	2731
..	1·3 × 1·3	9′ 6″	a	Yellowish	..	..	F	1578
..	1·0 × 1·0	9′ 0″	a	Bluish	..	..	F	11442
..	?	From spoil earth.	..	Bluish	..	..	AB	11455
..	0·6 × 0·4	3′ 0″	c	White	..	..	F	10485
..	0·85 × 0·4	3′ 0″	c	Yellowish	..	..	AB	5020
..	1·8 × 1·15	3′ 0″	c	White	..	..	F	15
..	1·05 × 0·5	3′ to 4′	c	Yellowish	..	..	F	10650a
..	1·05 × 0·4	3′ to 4′	c	Yellowish	..	..	F	10650a
..	0·85 × 0·4	3′ to 4′	c	Yellowish	..	..	F	10650a
..	0·55 × 0·4	3′ to 4′	c	Bluish	..	..	F	10650a
..	0·7 × 0·4	9′ 4″	c	Black	..	..	F	11626
..	?	15′ 0″	a	White	..	..	F	2122
..	?	5′ 2″	a	White	..	..	AB	3859
..	?	12′ 0″	a	White	..	..	F	2920
..	?	18′ 8″	a	White	..	..	F	1742
..	?	15′ 5″	a	Bluish	..	..	F	2401
..	?	16′ 1″	a	White	..	..	F	2529
..	?	14′ 4″	a	White	..	..	F	2812
..	?	12′ 6″	a	White	..	..	F	2732
..	?	17′ 3″	a	Bluish	..	..	F	2583
..	?	17′ 0″	a	White	..	..	F	3790
..	?	11′ 8″	a	White	..	..	AB	12363
..	?	8′ 0″	a	White	..	..	F	11894
..	?	9′ 0″	a	White	..	..	F	11377
..	?	4′ 2″	a	White	..	..	H	H449
..	0·75 × ?	6′ 0″	a	White	..	..	D	J452
..	?	2′ 6″	a	White	..	..	D	J440
..	?	2′ 3″	a	White	..	..	D	J382
..		From surface	a	White	..	..	G	G291
..	1·7 × 1·7	7′ 0″	a	White	..	..	F	Aa80
..	?	7′ 0″	a	White	..	..	AB	7384
..	?	5′ 0″	a	White	..	..	AB	5759
..	?	7′ 4″	a	White	..	..	F	4640
..	?	3′ 8″	a	White	..	..	F	3680
..	?	7′ 0″	a	White	..	..	F	Aa31
..	?	6′ 8″	a	White	..	..	F	12222
..	?	15′ 0″	a	White	..	..	F	3207
..	?	13′ 0″	a	Blue	..	..	F	2855
..	?	15′ 0″	a	Blue	..	..	F	2117
..	?	15′ 3″	a	White	..	..	F	2252
..	1·3 × ?	..	a	White	..	..	F	....

HARAPPĀ: TABULATION OF SEALS (PLS. LXXXV-CI)—*contd.*

Plate No.	Size in inches.	Level below surface.	Type.	Materials and colour.			Mound or Area.	Find No.
				Steatite.	Faience.	Pottery.		
..	?	2' 6"	a	White	..	..	F	2001
..	0·9 × ?	..	a	White	..	..	F	....
..	?	15' 2"	a	White	..	..	F	2835
..	1·3 × ?	7' 2"	a	White	..	..	F	3476
..	0·9 × ?	2' 6"	a	White	..	..	F	12749
..	1·4 × 0·6	7' 6"	c	White	..	..	H	H527
..	0·85 × 0·85	3' 3"	a	White	..	..	F	11500
..	? × 0·45	8' 8"	c	White	..	..	F	11370
..	0·7 × 0·45	3' 0"	c	White	..	..	F	A/28
..	0·8 × 0·5	3' 0"	c	..	Green	..	F	A241
..	0·5 × 0·45	1' 8"	c	White	..	..	AB	PIV-19
..	1·1 × 0·6	..	c	White	..	..	..	....
261	2·0 × 0·7	2' 0"	c	Blue	..	..	F	8360
262	1·4 × 0·7	7' 0"	d	White	..	..	F	4965
263	?	9' 2"	a	White	..	..	F	5634
264	1·6 × 0·7	5' 0"	c	White	..	..	F	5436
265	1·25 × 0·65	13' 8"	c	White	..	..	AB	7546
266	1·5 × 0·85	5' 0"	c	White	..	..	AB	PIII-7
267	1·2 × 0·6	8' 0"	c	White	..	..	AB	5542
268	1·15 × 0·55	3' 0"	c	White	..	..	F	4056
269	2·45 × 0·6	8' 0"	b	White	..	..	F	Ab130
270	1·65 × 0·65	5' 0" to 5' 8"	c	White	..	..	F	114
271	? × 0·75	6' 3"	c	White	..	..	AB	7354
272	1·4 × 0·55	1' 8"	c	White	..	..	AB	PI-2
273	1·45 × 0·7	4' 8"	c	Black	..	..	F	867
274	1·05 × 0·55	7' 0"	c	Black	..	..	F	Ab553
275	1·65 × 0·5	..	c	Blue	..	..	F	Ab022
276	0·85 × 0·4	11' 5"	c	White	..	..	F	2630
277	?	0' 5"	a	White	..	..	H	H604
278	1·2 × 0·95	9' 3"	f	Black	..	..	AB	11649
279	0·65 × 0·55	..	c	White	..	..	..	....
280	1·25 × 0·5	9' 0"	c	White	..	..	AB	2187
281	1·35 × 0·55	5' 5"	c	White	..	..	F	10698
282	0·95 × 0·4	5' 4"	c	White	..	..	F	6350
283	1·2 × 0·45	1' 9"	c	White	..	..	F	21
284	0·65 × 0·4	7' 0"	c	White	..	..	F	581
285	0·75 × 0·5	7' 9"	c	White	..	..	F	4396
286	0·6 × 0·55	5' 4"	c	Black	..	..	F	4276
287	1·7 × 0·55	3' 0"	c	White	..	..	F	396
288	2·3 × 0·65	8' 0"	c	White	..	..	AB	D88
289	0·65 × 0·4	6' 0"	c	White	..	..	AB	PI-44
290	0·9 × 0·9	9' 8"	c	White	..	..	F	11377
291	1·6 × 0·65	6' 10"	c	White	..	..	AB	PIII-36
292	1·2 × 0·5	9' 0"	c	White	..	..	AB	7409
293	? × 0·5	7' 6"	c	White	..	..	AB	4795
294	1·0 × 0·58	7' 2"	d	White	..	..	F	1259
295	? × 0·8	3' 0"	c	White	..	..	F	2893
296	1·25 × 0·6	20' 0"	c	Yellow	..	..	AB	B101
297	0·6 × 0·3	8' 6"	c	White	..	..	H	H80
298	1·05 × 0·6	6' 1"	d	Yellowish	..	..	AB	4432
299	1·4 × 0·75	4' 4"	c	White	..	..	AB	12173

HARAPPĀ: TABULATION OF SEALS (PLS. LXXXV–CI)—*contd.*

Plate No.	Size in inches.	Level below surface.	Type.	Materials and colour.			Mound or Area.	Find No.
				Steatite.	Faience.	Pottery.		
300	? × 0·6	6′ 0″	c	White	..	..	F	5389
301	1·6 × 0·6	12′ 0″	c	White	..	..	F	7787
302	?	4′ 0″	c	..	..	..	F	1239
..	0·55 × 0·4	8′ 0″	h	White	..	..	F	12494
..	0·65 × 0·55	4′ 5″	e	Yellowish	..	..	F	10502
303	1·9 × 0·58	7′ 5″	h	..	..	Red	F	11464
304	1·7 × 0·52	10′ 0″	h	..	..	Red	F	649
305	0·9 × 0·5	11′ 9″	n	..	..	Red	F	2409
306	?	1′ 3″	h	..	Red	..	AB	201
307	1·3 × 0·6	11′ 9″	af	..	..	Grey	F	2410
308	0·85 × 0·6	4′ to 7′	ag	..	..	Red	F	8850g
309	1·15 × 0·55	14′ 8″	af	..	Grey	..	F	2262
310	0·9 × 0·3	4′ 0″	n	..	Grey	..	F	11206
311	Diam. 1·0	7′ 9″	al	..	..	Red	F	1245
312	1·05 × 0·6	4′ 0″	b	..	Green	..	F	A122
313	0·7 × 0·5	6′ 6″	h	..	Yellow	..	F	11465
314	1·0 × 0·45	6′ 8″	h	..	..	Red	F	8801
315	L. 1·35 diam. 0·6	0′ to 4′	ae	..	..	Red	G	G254
316	1·0 × 0·5	3′ 6″	ag	..	Yellow	..	G	G107
317	Diam. 0·65	5′ 6″	al	..	Green	..	F	8716
318	0·9 × 0·4	5′ 1″	af	..	..	Red	F	7482
319	L. 0·9 diam. 0·35	2′ 5″	ae	..	..	Red	F	12721
320	1·35 × 0·48	9′ 0″	af	..	Green	..	F	4971
321	0·1 × 0·5	6′ 7″	af	..	Green	..	F	80
322	1·05 × 0·4	9′ 5″	ag	..	..	Red	F	2867
323	L. 1·1 diam. 0·4	3′ 0″	ae	..	..	Red	F	7098
324	1·0 × 0·45	18′ 0″	ak	..	Greenish	..	F	9069
325	1·15 × 0·55	7′ 2″	h	..	..	Red	F	5617
326	1·1 × 0·6	5′ 5″	af	..	Green	..	F	94
327	L. 1·3 diam. 0·5	2′ 0″	ae	..	..	..	F	12426a
328	L. 1·2 diam. 0·5	3′ 6″	ae	..	..	Red	F	4076
329	1·4 × 0·55	6′ 6″	af	..	Greenish	..	F	4129
330	L. 1·4 diam. 0·5	1′ 0″	ae	..	..	Grey	F	3333
331	0·9 × 0·1	5′ 6″	af	..	Green	..	F	11244
332	0·9 × 0·45	1′ 0″	af	..	Greenish	..	D	J10
333	L. 1·2 diam. 0·4	9′ 0″	ae	..	..	Red	D	J478
334	L. 1·7 diam. 0·4	6′ 9″	ae	..	..	Red	F	4582
335	L. 1·65 diam. 0·4	4′ 0″	ae	..	..	Red	F	1201
336	L. 1·55 diam. 0·35	6′ 9″	ae	..	..	Grey	F	4581
337	0·95 × 0·5	1′ 0″	h	..	..	Red	F	2490
338	L. 1·35 diam. 0·45	5′ 7″	ae	..	..	Red	F	4809
339	L. 1·2 diam. 0·4	5′ 0″	ae	..	..	Red	F	7591
340	0·65 × 0·3	8′ 0″	h	..	Yellow	..	F	9041
341	1·4 × 0·45	7′ 6″	af	..	..	Red	F	10102
342	0·7 × 0·4	12′ 0″	n	..	Yellowish	..	F	8800
343	1·5 × 0·6 to 1·2 × 0·5	9′ 0″	h	..	..	Red	F	1646
344	0·62 × 0·62	4′ 8″	a	.	..	..	F	59
345	0·65 × 0·4	6′ 2″	h	..	..	..	D	J462

HARAPPA: TABULATION OF SEALS (PLS. LXXXV-CI)—*contd.*

Plate No.	Size in inches.	Level below surface.	Type.	Materials and colour.			Mound or Area.	Find No.
				Steatite.	Faience.	Pottery.		
346	0·85 × 0·45	..	h	..	Brown	..	..	Presented by Mr. Price, former Superintendent of Police, Montgomery.
347	0·65 × 0·4	11' 9"	h	..	White	..	F	2891
348	0·7 × 0·43	12' 5"	ag	..	Green	..	F	10242
349	1·05 × 0·45	4' 0"	h	..	Grey	..	D	J456
350	0·8 × 0·37	4' 5"	h	..	Brown	..	D	J463
351	0·9 × 0·35	6' 8"	ag	..	Green	..	F	12377
352	1·1 × 0·25	6' 0"	ag	..	..	Red	F	10058
353	0·75 × 0·4	10' 2"	h	..	Grey	..	F	2177
354	0·65 × 0·45	16' 5"	h	..	White	..	F	2478
355	0·75 × 0·4	3' 8"	h	..	Green	..	D	J494
356	0·55 × 0·38	16' 2"	h	..	White	..	F	2270
357	0·55 × 0·38	2' 6"	h	..	Grey	..	F	8890
358	0·83 × 0·4	3' 6"	h	..	White	..	F	10997
359	0·65 × 0·45	From spoil earth.	h	..	Yellow	..	H	H715
360	0·75 × 0·33	13' 0"	h	..	White	..	F	8015
361	0·95 × 0·4	17' 6"	h	..	White	..	F	3780
362	L. 1·35 diam. 0·35	5' 5"	sc	..	..	Red	F	6489
363	0·5 × 0·45	16' 0"	a	..	White	..	F	647
364	0·6 × 0·4	11' 6"	ag	..	Yellowish	..	F	12060
365	Diam. 0·5	3' 1"	al	..	Dull white	..	F	10643
365a	1·15 × 0·5	11' 4"	h	..	..	Red	F	3565
366	1·05 × 0·4	11' 0"	h	..	..	Red	F	3047
366a	1·0 × 0·4	6' 7"	ag	..	..	Red	F	3750
367	1·05 × 0·6	6' 2"	ag	..	..	Red	F	6082
367a	1·05 × 0·4	11' 6"	h	..	Green	..	AB	1077
368	0·9 × 0·55	5' 2"	x	..	White	..	H	H550
369	0·6 × 0·45	12' 9"	x	..	White	..	F	3836
370	Diam. 0·5	2' 9"	al	..	Greenish	..	D	J364
371	Diam. 0·7	10' 3"	al	..	Greenish	..	F	12580
372	Diam. 0·6	9' 5"	al	..	Yellow	..	F	780
373	Diam. 0·6	From spoil earth.	al	..	Greenish	..	F	12440
374	Diam. 0·55	6' 0"	al	..	Green	..	F	11027
375	Diam. 0·45	10' 0"	al	..	Green	..	F	11383
376	0·7 × 0·4	8' 10"	x	..	Dull white	..	D	J449
377	Diam. 0·85	12' 5"	pl	..	..	Red	F	12514
378	Diam. 0·65	7' 9"	al	..	Greenish	..	D	J593
379	Diam. 0·7	4' 0"	al	..	White	..	F	2707
380	Diam. 0·7	3' 0"	ah	..	White	..	AB	12080
381	Diam. 0·55	4' 8"	al	..	Yellow	..	D	J276
382	0·6 × 0·6	6' 5"	a	..	Yellow	..	AB	5075
383	0·48 × ?	8' 0"	a	..	Greenish	..	D	J563
384	L. ? w. 0·55	5' 9"	aq	..	White	..	F	12929
385	L. 0·8 w. ?	10' 0"	ap	..	White	..	F	2701
385a	L. 0·7 w. 0·27	3' 6"	ap	..	White	..	F	12278
386	Side 0·7	5' 8"	al	..	White	..	F	3855
387	L. 1·65	11' 8"	am	..	Yellow	..	F	12544
Similar to 314	0·95 × 0·4	From spoil earth.	h	..	..	Red	F	10965
Similar to 315	L. 1·35 diam. 0·35	3' 0"	sc	..	..	Red	G	G290

HARAPPĀ: TABULATION OF SEALS (Pls. LXXXV-CI)—*contd.*

Plate No.	Size in inches.	Level below surface.	Type.	Materials and colour.			Mound or Area.	Find No.
				Steatite.	Faience.	Pottery.		
Similar to 320	1·5 × 0·45	4' 6"	af	..	Greenish	..	F	10645
Similar to 321	0·7 × 0·45	..	af	..	Greenish	..	..	....
Similar to 321	0·65 × 0·5	8' 0"	af	..	Greenish	..	G	G175
Similar to 321	1·0 × 0·5	11' 6"	af	..	Green	..	F	2993
Similar to 322	1·05 × 0·4	11' 3"	h	..	..	Red	F	1791 (two)
Similar to 322	1·0 × 0·4	7' 6"	h	..	..	Red	..	2075
Similar to 323	1·15 × 0·45	11' 3"	ag	..	..	Red	F	1791
Similar to 323	L. 1·05 diam. 0·4	10' 3"	ae	..	..	Red	F	3606
Similar to 323	L. 1·05 diam. 0·35	From spoil earth.	ae	..	..	Red	..	1661
Similar to 323	L. 1·05 diam. 0·38	3' 0"	ae	..	..	Red	..	2982
Similar to 323	L. 1·1 diam. 0·37	..	ae	..	..	Red	..	....
Similar to 323	L. 1·11 diam. 0·4	5' 2"	as	..	..	Red	F	5312
Similar to 324	1·0 × 0·45	5' 6"	..	..	Greenish	..	F	11356
Similar to 324	0·35 × 0·4	3' 0"	u	..	Green	..	H	H91
Similar to 328	0·9 × 0·5	5' 3"	h	..	White	..	F	Ab269
Similar to 332	0·9 × 0·4	5' 6"	af	..	Grey	..	D	J121
Similar to 332	0·7 × 0·43	2' 0"	af	..	Dull white	..	D	J29
Similar to 334	L. 1·65 diam. 0·4	7' 6"	ae	..	..	Red	F	1459
Similar to 334	L. 1·7 diam. 0·3	5' 8"	ae	..	..	Grey	F	4261
Similar to 334	L. 1·55 diam. 0·4	5' 6"	ae	..	..	Grey	F	1123
Similar to 335	L. 1·6 diam. 0·4	8' 0"	ae	..	..	Red	F	1236
Similar to 335	L. 1·6 diam. 0·4	3' 3"	ae	..	..	Grey	F	Af29
Similar to 335	L. 1·0 diam. 0·4	3' 0"	ae	..	..	Grey	F	Af166
Similar to 339	L. 1·25 diam. 0·4	10' 8"	ae	..	..	Grey	F	7055
Similar to 339	L. 1·3 diam. 0·35	9' 5"	ae	..	..	Grey	F	2366
Similar to 346	0·95 × 0·45	9' 0"	h	..	Yellow	..	AB	7537
Similar to 356	0·75 × 0·35	13' 0"	h	..	White	..	F	9015
Similar to 363	0·5 × 0·4	12' 3"	s	..	White	..	F	2900
Similar to 367a	1·0 × 0·45	4' 3"	h	..	Green	..	F	1338
Similar to 367a	0·96 × 0·43	5' 3"	h	..	Green	..	F	1399
Similar to 367a	1·0 × 0·45	5' 4"	h	..	Green	..	F	5388
Similar to 367a	0·95 × 0·45	2' 0"	h	..	Green	..	G	G113
Similar to 379	Diam. 0·75	From spoil earth.	af	..	Yellow	..	F	11452
Similar to 380	Diam. 0·7	5' 0"	af	..	White	..	F	Ab707
..	L. 1·25 diam. 0·4	5' 4"	ae	..	..	Red	F	7541
..	L. 1·1 diam. 0·5	5' 0"	ae	..	..	Red	F	4161
..	L. 0·9 diam. 0·25	4' 3"	ae	..	..	Red	D	J503
..	L. 0·5 diam. 0·25	..	ae	..	Greenish	..	..	....
..	1·3 × 0·5	11' 9"	af	..	..	Red	F	2411
..	1·1 × 0·5	..	af	..	White	..	..	....
Similar to 344	0·93 × 0·45	18' 6"	h	..	Grey	..	F	3561
..	0·65 × 0·35	4' 0"	h	..	Yellow	..	F	Af24
..	0·6 × 0·5	11' 0"	a	..	Green	..	AB	FII-86
..	0.4 × 0·5	8' 6" to 8' 0"	l	..	White	..	F	5630a
..	0·7 × 0·5	..	af	..	Green	..	F	....
..	0·5 × 0·35	..	h	..	White	..	F	....
..	0·9 × 0·8	..	h	..	White	..	..	....
..	0·5 × 0·45	..	h	..	White	..	..	....
..	0·5 × 0·4	11' 9"	h	..	Green	..	..	2891
..	Side 0·7	..	s	..	Blue	..	..	....
..	Side 0·65	2' 3"	..	..	..	White	F	5796

HARAPPĀ: TABULATION OF SEALS (PLS. LXXXV-CI)—*contd.*

Plate No.	Size in inches.	Level below surface.	Type.	Materials and colour.			Mound or Area.	Find No.
				Steatite.	Faience.	Pottery.		
388	0·6 × 0·6	1′ 0″	a	White	..	..	D	4156
389	0·75 × 0·75	5′ 3″	a	..	Green	..	AB	4546
390	?	4′ 5″	a	..	Green	..	F	12611
391	0·53 × 0·53	From spoil earth.	a	..	Grey	..	AB	11454
392	?	..	a	..	Yellow	..	F	?
393	0·63 × 0·6	8′ 6″	a	White	..	..	..	7562
394	0·65 × 0·65	..	a	..	Green	..	F	Ab44
395	0·65 × 0·65	17′ 0″	a	..	White	..	..	B1114
396	0·7 × ?	8′ 10″	a	..	Yellow	..	AB	2545
397	0·62 × 0·62	12′ 8″	a	..	White	..	F	5420
398	1·2 × 1·2	14′ 6″	a	..	Yellow	..	AB	11931
399	0·7 × 0·7	6′ 2″	a	..	Yellow	..	F	271
400	0·75 × 0·75	11′ 0″	a	..	Green	..	F	Ab43
Similar to 390	0·6 × 0·6	2′ 0″	a	..	White	..	F	5788
Similar to 390	0·7 × 0·7	..	a	..	Green	..	..	B12
Similar to 391	0·65 × 0·65	8′ 0″	a	..	Green	..	AB	5635
Similar to 396	0·6 × 0·6	18′ 0″	a	..	Yellow	..	AB	4603
Similar to 396	0·7 × 0·7	4′ 8″	a	..	Yellow	..	AB	5439
Similar to 396	0·65 × 0·65	15′ 10″	a	..	Yellow	..	AB	12064
Similar to 396	0·65 × 0·65	15′ 2″	a	..	Yellow	..	AB	12133
Similar to 396	0·65 × 0·65	15′ 6″	a	..	Yellow	..	AB	12065
Similar to 396	0·6 × 0·6	13′ 0″ to 15′ 6″	a	..	Yellow	..	AB	12098
Similar to 396	0·55 × 0·55	13′ 0″ to 15′ 6″	a	..	Yellow	..	AB	12096
Similar to 396	0·6 × 0·6	13′ 0″ to 15′ 6″	a	..	Yellow	..	AB	12098
Similar to 396	0·65 × 0·65	13′ 0″ to 15′ 6″	a	..	Yellow	..	AB	10298
Similar to 396	0·65 × 0·65	13′ 0″	a	..	Yellow	..	AB	12031
Similar to 396	0·6 × 0·6	13′ 0″ to 15′ 6″	a	..	Yellow	..	AB	12095
Similar to 397	0·65 × 0·65	2′ 6″	a	..	Yellow	..	F	A816
Similar to 397	?	4′ 6″	a	..	Yellow	..	F	5639
Similar to 399	0·6 × 0·6	7′ 9″	a	..	Yellow	..	AB	4762
Similar to 399	0·65 × 0·65	8′ 2″	a	..	Yellow	..	F	4226
401	0·45 × 0·25 × 0·22	7′ 0″	p	White	..	..	F	8148
402	0·5 × 0·22	15′ 0″	a	White	..	..	F	2256
403	0·55 × 0·3	5′ 2″	b	White	..	..	F	8102
404	0·65 × 0·3	18′ 3″	h	White	..	..	F	2257
405	0·6 × 0·3	15′ 2″	j	White	..	..	F	2355
406	0·45 × 0·45	6′ 4″	l	White	..	..	D	J581
407	0·75 × 0·35	16′ 6″	x	White	..	..	AB	1722
408	0·65 × 0·35	8′ 1″	aa	White	..	..	F	11334
409	L. 0·26, diam. 0·35	8′ 0″	s	White	..	..	F	12150
409a	L. 0·25, diam. 0·35	8′ 0″	s	White	..	..	AB	7121
410	Diam. 0·5	13′ 0″	al	White	..	..	F	9014
411	Diam. 0·5	17′ 0″	al	White	..	..	F	8171
412	Diam. 0·45	13′ 8″	al	White	..	..	F	11796
413	Diam. 0·5	8′ 7″	al	White	..	..	F	9086
414	Diam. 0·35	7′ 0″	t	White	..	..	F	1423
415	L. 0·6 w. 0·4	10′ 6″	v	Greenish	..	..	D	J321
416	0·5 × 0·35	11′ 9″	s	White	..	..	F	10861
417	L. 0·56 w. 0·35	18′ 2″	y	White	..	..	F	2534
418	L. 0·45 w. 0·45	14′ 0″	w	White	..	..	F	11793

HARAPPĀ : TABULATION OF SEALS (Pls. LXXXV-CI)—*contd.*

Plate No.	Size in inches.	Level below surface.	Type.	Materials and colour.			Mound or Area.	Find No.
				Steatite.	Faience.	Pottery.		
419	L. 0·7 and 0·6	1' 0"	m	White	..	..	D	4090
420	L. 0·65 and ?	4' 0"	m	White	..	..	F	10999
421	L. 0·55 ht. 0·45	6' 0"	ad	White	..	..	F	11268
422	L. 0·56 ht. 0·35	12' 0"	ad	White	..	..	F	1203
423	L. 0·5 ht. 0·32	0' 6"	ad	White	..	..	F	10409
424	L. 0·35 ht. ?	15' 0"	ad	White	..	..	F	1654
425	L. 0·5 ht. 0·4	12' 6"	ad	White	..	..	F	4179
426	L. 0·5 w. 0·3	13' to 14'	ae	White	..	..	F	11848
427	L. 0·6 w. 0·3	10' 9"	aq	White	..	..	D	J329
428	L. 0·6 w. 0·28	10' 3"	ab	White	..	..	F	8080
429	0·5 × 0·37	16' 6"	h	White	..	..	F	10359
430	0·6 × 0·32	19' 0"	h	White	..	..	F	1234
431	0·55 × 0·27	16' 8"	h	White	..	..	F	614
432	0·6 × 0·3	18' 0"	h	White	..	..	F	1623
433	0·55 × 0·3	4' to 7'	h	White	..	..	F	8650b
434	0·57 × 0·28	16' 0"	h	..	..	..	F	2542
435	0·55 × 0·28	11' 6"	h	White	..	..	F	2570
436	0·5 × 0·3	18' 7"	h	White	..	..	F	12575
437	0·55 × 0·3	10' 8"	h	White	..	..	D	J256
438	?	7' 3"	h	White	..	..	F	1282
439	0·7 × 0·35	4' to 7'	h	White	..	..	F	8650b
440	0·75 × 0·3	From spoil earth.	h	White	..	..	AB	11460
441	0·65 × 0·32	17' 0"	h	White	..	..	F	1498
442	0·7 × 0·3	5' 7"	h	White	..	..	F	10928a
443	0·88 × 0·36	17' 5"	h	White	..	..	F	10069
444	0·6 × 0·35	4' 2"	h	White	..	..	F	11291
445	0·7 × 0·4	8' 0"	h	White	..	..	D	J582
446	0·75 × 0·35	8' 6"	h	White	..	..	D	J690
447	0·65 × 0·3	5' 6"	h	White	..	..	F	10880
448	0·75 × 0·3	4' to 7'	h	Red	..	..	F	8650e
449	0·75 × 0·25	8' 8"	h	White	..	..	F	11077
450	0·65 × 0·3	18' 0"	o	White	..	..	F	3798
451	0·7 × 0·4	12' 0"	h	White	..	..	F	906
452	0·75 × 0·28	4' to 7'	h	Red	..	..	F	8650c
453	0·64 × 0·28	10' 8"	h	White	..	..	F	3484
454	0·7 × 0·3	12' 0"	h	White	..	..	F	2868
455	0·5 × 0·28	6' 0"	h	White	..	..	F	10989
456	0·6 × 0·3	14' 2"	h	White	..	..	F	12516
457	0·7 × 0·38	10' 0"	h	White	..	..	F	12584
458	0·55 × 0·3	4' to 7'	h	White	..	..	F	8650b
459	0·53 × 0·35	7' 4"	h	White	..	..	F	11095
460	0·4 × 0·3	18' 0"	h	White	..	..	F	11757
461	0·65 × 0·35	12' 0"	h	White	..	..	F	8668
462	0·6 × 0·35	15' 8"	h	White	..	..	F	2482
463	0·62 × 0·38	18' 4"	h	White	..	..	F	2431
464	0·55 × 0·28	14' 6"	h	White	..	..	F	2703
465	0·55 × 0·3	10' 0"	h	White	..	..	AB	5180
466	0·65 × 0·3	7' 2"	h	White	..	..	F	10224
467	0·62 × 0·3	12' 0"	h	White	..	..	F	2702
468	?	18' 3"	i	White	..	..	F	2832
469	0·45 × 0·35	..	h	White	..	..	..	6287

HARAPPA: TABULATION OF SEALS (Pls. LXXXV-CI)—*contd.*

Plate No.	Size in inches.	Level below surface.	Type.	Materials and colour.			Mound or Area.	Find No.
				Steatite.	Faience.	Pottery.		
470	0·56 × 0·3	5' 6"	h	White	..	..	F	10994
471	0·7 × 0·27	4' 5"	h	White	..	..	D	J276
472	0·65 × 0·3	6' 0"	h	White	..	..	F	12218
473	0·67 × 0·3	16' 8"	h	White	..	..	F	2481
474	0·5 × 0·3	18' 0"	h	White	..	..	F	3276
475	0·65 × 0·35	13' 0"	h	White	..	..	F	2730
476	0·4 × 0·3	..	h	White	..	..	..	....
477	0·65 × 0·28	2' 0"	h	White	..	..	D	J213
478	0·7 × 0·35	13' 0"	h	White	..	..	F	11758
479	0·7 × 0·3	8' 7"	h	White	..	..	D	J580
480	0·6 × 0·35	14' 4"	h	White	..	..	F	1497
481	0·7 × 0·3	13' 0"	h	White	..	..	F	11798
482	0·6 × 0·3	8' 6"	h	White	..	..	AB	7155
483	0·6 × 0·35	11' 8"	h	White	..	..	F	4043
484	0·55 × 0·3	13' to 14'	l	White	..	..	F	11851
485	0·6 × 0·32	15' 0"	h	White	..	..	F	2728
486	0·6 × 0·35 to 0·4 × 0·25	4' to 7'	h	White	..	..	F	8650b
487	0·65 × 0·3	17' 6"	h	White	..	..	F	1410
488	0·6 × 0·35	4' to 7'	h	White	..	..	F	8650b
489	0·6 × 0·3	4' to 7'	h	White	..	..	F	8650b
490	0·5 × 0·28	8' 0"	h	White	..	..	AB	5152
491	0·5 × 0·38	From spoil earth.	h	White	..	..	F	12101
492	0·5 × 0·28	3' 3"	h	White	..	..	D	J229
493	0·4 × 0·33	4' to 7'	h	White	..	..	F	8650b
494	0·33 × ?	4' 4"	h	White	..	..	F	10176
495	0·4 × 0·3	12' 0"	l	White	..	..	F	3025
496	0·25 × ?	7' 0"	h	White	..	..	D	J460
497	0·65 × 0·35	13' 0"	l	White	..	..	F	10186
498	0·55 × 0·3	10' 0"	h	White	..	..	F	9082
499	0·6 × 0·3	1' 0"	h	White	..	..	AB	PII-1
500	0·55 × 0·3	..	h	White	..	..	..	....
501	0·55 × 0·25	16' 0"	h	White	..	..	F	2544
502	0·57 × 0·3	12' 7"	h	White	..	..	F	1172
503	0·55 × 0·25	17' 0"	h	White	..	..	F	2636
504	0·5 × 0·25	6' 0"	h	White	..	..	F	10059
505	0·35 × 0·3	7' 2"	h	White	..	..	F	10826
506	0·43 × 0·3	15' 0"	h	White	..	..	F.	737
507	0·45 × 0·25	13' 7"	h	White	..	..	F	3179
508	0·45 × 0·28	19' 6"	h	White	..	..	F	2568
509	0·4 × 0·25	13' 0"	h	White	..	..	F	1280
510	0·5 × 0·3	5' 2"	h	White	..	..	D	J220
511	0·48 × 0·28	11' 6"	h	White	..	..	F	3696
512	0·55 × 0·3	12' 6"	h	White	..	..	F	3680
513	L. 0·53 and ?	19' 8"	m	White	..	—	F	4427
514	0·55 × 0·29	13' to 14'	h	White	..	..	F	11853
515	0·45 × 0·35	3' 6"	h	Black	..	..	F	10906
516	0·55 × 0·3	10' 0"	h	White	..	..	G	262
517	0·55 × 0·35	From spoil earth.	h	White	..	..	F	12099
518	0·45 × 0·28	From spoil earth.	h	White	..	..	F	13420

HARAPPĀ: TABULATION OF SEALS (PLS. LXXXV-CI)—*contd.*

Plate No.	Size in inches.	Level below surface.	Type.	Materials and colour.			Mound or Area.	Find No.
				Steatite.	Faience.	Pottery.		
519	0·6 × 0·4	5' 6"	h	White	..	..	F	12461
520	0·55 × 0·33	2' 0"	h	White	..	..	D	J30
521	0·4 × 0·25	14' 6"	h	White	..	..	F	12576
522	0·55 × 0·3	16' 9"	h	White	..	..	F	12581
523	0·55 × 0·3	5' 7"	h	White	..	..	F	10928a
524	0·35 × 0·32	1' 3"	h	White	..	..	D	J582
525	0·4 × 0·36	12' 0"	h	White	..	..	F	4044
526	?	3' 10"	h	White	..	..	F	12704
527	0·4 × 0·35	2' 0"	h	White	..	..	F	12684
528	? × 0·3	15' 8"	h	White	..	..	F	2477
529	0·27 × ?	11' 6"	h	White	..	..	F	4041
530	0·33 × ?	4' 9"	h	White	..	..	D	J238
531	?	8' 0"	h	White	..	..	D	4061
532	0·3 × 0·3	10' 0"	i	White	..	..	F	2807
533	0·4 × 0·25	14' 6"	h	White	..	..	F	3576
534	0·43 × ?	5' 6"	h	White	..	..	D	J322
535	0·4 × 0·3	9' 11"	h	White	..	..	D	J250
536	0·4 × 0·3	12' 0"	h	White	..	..	F	11767
537	0·35 × 0·3	11' 8"	h	White	..	..	F	12067
538	0·5 × 0·3	7' 0"	h	White	..	..	F	5154
539	?	7' 2"	h	White	..	..	F	10228
540	0·7 × 0·18	7' 0"	i	White	..	..	F	11440
541	0·75 × 0·18 × 0·18	15' 8"	p	White	..	..	F	2981
542	0·6 × 0·3	15' 3"	i	White	..	..	F	2365
543	0·4 × 0·3	11' 4"	i	White	..	..	F	1261
544	0·52 × 0·3	6' 0"	i	White	..	..	F	10060
545	0·4 × 0·35	4' 8"	i	White	..	..	D	J523
546	0·45 × 0·35	11' 0"	h	White	..	..	F	10067
547	Diam. 0·4	11' 0"	s	White	..	..	AB	3851
548	Diam. 0·3	16' 0"	al	White	..	..	F	2842
549	Diam. 0·5	5' 8"	al	White	..	..	F	Af113
550	Diam. 0·45	5' 0"	ai	White	..	..	F	4269
551	Diam. 0·4	9' 8"	al	White	..	..	F	3961
552	?	15' 0"	al	White	..	..	F	1154g
553	L. 0·65 w. 0·25	15' 0"	u	White	..	..	F	1154r
554	?	15' 0"	u	White	..	..	F	1154c
555	L. 0·65 w. ?	15' 0"	o	White	..	..	F	1154e
556	0·65 × 0·4	5' 3"	x	White	..	..	F	Af97
557	0·5 × ?	11' 6"	x	White	..	..	F	4041
558	?	12' 0"	x	White	..	..	F	3027
559	L. 0·7 w. 0·35	8' 0"	y	White	..	..	F	11306
560	?	12' 3"	ab	White	..	..	..	12515
561	0·6 × 0·15	13' 3"	q	White	..	..	F	11794
562	0·7 × 0·45	10' 5"	i	White	..	..	F	2307
563	0·63 × 0·37	1' 0"	i	Black	..	..	F	12104
564	0·6 × 0·4	12' 9"	x	White	..	..	F	1171
565	L. 0·45 ht. 0·35	9' 7"	ad	White	..	..	F	10940
566	0·39 × 0·3	14' 7"	h	White	..	..	F	6028
567	0·45 × 0·45	5' 2"	h	Black	..	..	F	11432
568	?	9' 0"	a	White	..	..	D	J337
569	Ht. 0·23 diam. 0·35	2' 6"	r	White	..	..	F	12150

HARAPPA: TABULATION OF SEALS (PLS. LXXXV-CI)—*contd.*

Plate No.	Size in inches.	Level below surface.	Type.	Materials and colour.			Mound or Area.	Find No.
				Steatite.	Faience.	Pottery.		
570	?	..	..	White	..	..	..	....
571	0·45 × 0·25	13' to 14'	..	White	..	..	F	11855
572	0·6 × 0·2 × 0·15	5' 5"	p	White	..	..	F	11696
573	0·9 × 0·8	13' to 14'	o	White	..	..	F	11854
574	0·55 × 0·25	11' 8"	n	White	..	..	F	2999
575	0·6 × 0·3	13' 0"	n	White	..	..	F	1278
576	0·7 × 0·35	10' 0"	n	White	..	..	F	3534
577	0·58 × 0·38	12' 3"	n	White	..	..	F	2895
578	0·5 × 0·22	15' 0"	n	White	..	..	F	1665
579	0·4 × 0·3	10' 0"	n	White	..	..	F	11390
580	0·6 × 0·2	14' 6"	n	White	..	..	F	12540
581	0·6 × 0·3	18' 5"	n	Black	..	..	F	2429
582	0·6 × 0·25	17' 10"	n	White	..	..	F	2528
583	0·65 × 0·25	11' 4"	o	White	..	..	F	11349
584	0·65 × 0·24	13' 6"	n	White	..	..	F	3608
585	0·65 × 0·25	13' 4"	n	White	..	..	F	2729
586	0·65 × 0·25	18' 3"	n	White	..	..	F	11715
587	0·7 × 0·2	15' 6"	n	White	..	..	F	550
588	0·4 × 0·3	From spoil earth.	n	White	..	..	F	12102
589	0·5 × ?	4' 6"	n	White	..	..	D	J212
590	0·4 × 0·2 × 0·2	4' to 7'	p	White	..	..	F	6650e
591	0·55 × 0·3	7' 9"	n	White	..	..	F	8480
592	0·35 × 0·16 × 0·14	6' 0"	p	White	..	..	F	10086
593	0·35 × 0·25	15' 0"	n	White	..	..	F	397
Similar to 414	Diam. 0·4	11' 0"	s	White	..	..	AB	3651
Similar to 414	Diam. 0·35	4' to 7'	s	White	..	..	F	6650f
Similar to 421	L. 0·33 ht. ?	8' 10"	sd	White	..	..	F	11912
Similar to 422	L. 0·5 ht. 0·35	From spoil earth.	sd	White	..	..	F	12334
Similar to 424	L. 0·4 ht. 0·2	13' to 14'	sd	White	..	..	F	11552
Similar to 431	0·5 × 0·26	19' 3"	h	White	..	..	F	1219
Similar to 433	0·31 × 0·25	17' 0"	h	White	..	..	F	1707
Similar to 433	?	15' 6"	h	White	..	..	F	3479
Similar to 433	?	17' 6"	h	White	..	..	F	2563
Similar to 433	?	11' 8"	h	White	..	..	F	2570
Similar to 439	0·65 × 0·35	10' 0"	h	White	..	..	F	11372
Similar to 448	0·75 × 0·25	4' to 7'	h	Red	..	..	F	6650e
Similar to 448	0·65 × 0·28	4' to 7'	h	Red	..	..	F	6450e
Similar to 449	0·48 × 0·3	..	h	White	..	..	..	....
Similar to 457	0·66 × 0·3	9' 0"	h	White	..	..	F	9057
Similar to 458	0·6 × 0·3	3' 4"	h	White	..	..	D	J402
Similar to 458	?	19' 3"	h	White	..	..	F	2631
Similar to 490	0·55 × 0·28	4' 0"	h	White	..	..	F	Ab24
Similar to 502	0·45 × 0·3	18' 4"	h	White	..	..	F	4253
Similar to 502	0·5 × 0·25	12' 6"	h	White	..	..	F	1963
Similar to 502	0·5 × 0·27	12' 3"	h	White	..	..	F	2907
Similar to 502	?	12' 6"	h	White	..	..	F	4105
Similar to 508	0·45 × 0·25	19' 0"	h	White	..	..	F	2360
Similar to 508	?	14' 0"	h	White	..	..	F	3535
Similar to 509	0·35 × 0·25	13' 0"	h	White	..	..	F	2036
Similar to 531	0·5 × 0·3	10' 6"	h	White	..	..	F	11391

HARAPPA: TABULATION OF SEALS (PLS. LXXXV-CI)—*contd.*

Plate No.	Size in inches.	Level below surface.	Type.	Material and colour.			Mound or Area.	Find No.
				Steatite.	Faience.	Pottery.		
Similar to 542	0·6 × 0·3	15′ 3″	i	White	..	..	F	2354
Similar to 542	0·52 × 0·3	15′ 3″	i	White	..	..	F	2357
Similar to 542	0·53 × 0·25	15′ 3″	i	White	..	..	F	2365
Similar to 542	0·57 × 0·28	15′ 3″	i	White	..	..	F	2409
Similar to 542	0·55 × 0·3	15′ 0″	i	White	..	..	F	2483
Similar to 542	0·45 × 0·23	12′ 0″	i	White	..	..	F	3825
Similar to 542	0·5 × 0·27	12′ 7″	i	White	..	..	F	3091
Similar to 542	0·5 × 0·25	13′ 2″	i	White	..	..	F	2124
Similar to 542	0·63 × 0·3	15′ 0″	i	White	..	..	F	3172
Similar to 543	0·3 × 0·28	15′ 0″	i	White	..	..	F	3260
Similar to 543	0·55 × 0·3	16′ 0″	i	White	..	..	F	2548
Similar to 544	0·53 × 0·3	12′ 0″	i	White	..	..	F	3173
Similar to 548	0·35 × 0·3	3′ to 5′	i	White	..	..	F	10185c
Similar to 553	?	12′ 0″	u	White	..	..	F	12576
Similar to 562	0·7 × 0·45	4′ 0″	i	White	..	..	D	J875
	Diam. 0·65 Th. 0·3	3′ 0″	ah	Yellow	..	..	D	J48
Similar to 575	0·45 × 0·25	12′ 0″	n	White	..	..	F	1280
Similar to 575	0·56 × 0·25	12′ 0″	n	Black	..	..	F	1260
Similar to 575	0·68 × 0·25	12′ 0″	n	Black	..	..	F	1264
Similar to 575	0·53 × 0·3	12′ 0″	n	White	..	..	F	1262
Similar to 575	0·6 × 0·25	13′ 0″	n	Black	..	..	F	1277
Similar to 575	0·6 × 0·25	13′ 0″	n	White	..	..	F	1279
Similar to 575	0·6 × 0·25	13′ 0″	n	Black	..	..	F	1345
Similar to 575	0·4 × 0·25	12′ 2″	n	White	..	..	F	2294
Similar to 575	0·47 × 0·38	12′ 0″	n	White	..	..	F	2917
Similar to 575	0·57 × 0·25	15′ 6″	n	Black	..	..	F	3509
Similar to 587	0·6 × 0·2	..	n	White	..	..	..	....
Similar to 593	0·5 × 0·2	16′ 6″	n	White	..	..	F	3341
..	0·5 × 0·25	9′ 0″	h	White	..	..	F	11280
..	0·55 × 0·3	10′ 0″	h	White	..	..	F	9082
..	0·65 × 0·4	5′ 6″	h	Black	..	..	F	11041
..	0·5 × 0·25	2′ 6″	h	Blue	..	..	F	10006
..	0·58 × 0·6	7′ 4″	h	White	..	..	D	J825
..	0·9 × 0·45	5′ 5″	h	White	..	..	D	J581
..	0·7 × 0·38	2′ 0″	h	Grey	..	..	F	11082
..	0·5 × 0·3	15′ 5″	i	White	..	..	F	1218
..	0·6 × 0·2	15′ 2″	n	White	..	..	F	2347
..	0·58 × 0·29	..	n	White	..	..	F	....
..	0·5 × 0·25	10′ 6″	n	White	..	..	..	11871
..	0·5 × 0·3	..	n	White	..	..	..	....
..	0·33 × ?	12′ 0″	h	White	..	..	F	2312
..	0·3 × 0·47	12′ 0″	h	White	..	..	F	2242
..	0·35 × 0·29	12′ 0″	h	White	..	..	F	1348
..	0·3 × ?	17′ 0″	h	White	..	..	F	2791
..	0·25 × ?	12′ 0″	h	White	..	..	F	3036
..	?	15′ 9″	h	White	..	..	F	1154
..	?	15′ 3″	h	White	..	..	F	3632
..	0·35 × 0·3	10′ 0″	h	White	..	..	AB	5181
..	?	2″	h	White	..	..	F	1282
..	0·45 × 0·25	0″	h	White	..	..	F	4970
..	?	7′ 2″	h	White	..	..	F	10223

HARAPPĀ: TABULATION OF SEALS (PLS. LXXXV-CI)—*contd.*

Plate No.	Size in inches.	Level below surface.	Type.	Materials and colour.			Mound or Area.	Find No.
				Steatite.	Faience.	Pottery.		
..	?	From spoil earth.	b	White	..	..	F	12100
..	0·25 × 0·3	15′ 6″	b	White	..	..	F	10160
..	?	13′ 0″	b	White	..	..	F	510
..	?	12′ 0″	b	White	..	..	F	1241
..	?	7′ 6″	b	White	..	..	F	1525
..	?	12′ 3″	b	White	..	..	F	2806
..	?	12′ 0″	b	White	..	..	F	3024
..	?	10′ 3″	b	White	..	..	F	3396
..	?	10′ 3″	b	White	..	..	F	3380
..	?	12′ 0″	b	White	..	..	F	4044
..	0·5 × 0·45	13′ 4″	b	White	..	..	F	4253
..	?	10′ 0″	b	White	..	..	F	12118
..	?	4′ 9″	b	White	..	..	D	J238
..	0·35 × 0·35	5′ 2″	l	White	..	..	D	J270
..	?	2′ 4″	b	White	..	..	D	J399
..	0·35 × 0·3	6′ 0″	b	White	..	..	D	J586
..	0·4 × 0·3	6′ 6″	b	White	..	..	F	11139
..	?	..	b	White	..	..	..	....
..	0·45 × 0·3	7′ 10″	b	White	..	..	AB	4552
..	?	..	b	White	..	..	..	....
..	?	15′ 0″	b	White	..	..	F	11540
..	0·4 × 0·35	16′ 8″	b	White	..	..	F	4428
..	?	10′ 5″	b	White	..	..	F	2794
..	0·45 × 0·4	19′ 3″	b	White	..	..	F	2631
..	0·4 × 0·37	7′ 5″	b	White	..	..	F	11717
..	0·55 × ?	16′ 0″	b	White	..	..	F	2843
..	?	12′ 6″	b	White	..	..	F	4180
..	?	12′ 0″	b	White	..	..	F	4044
..	?	14′ 7″	b	White	..	..	F	6026
..	?	10′ 0″	b	White	..	..	F	3290
..	?	12′ 6″	b	White	..	..	F	4195
..	0·45 × 0·33	9′ 10″	b	White	..	..	G	257
..	?	6′ 0″	b	White	..	..	F	11113
..	?	6′ 6″	b	White	..	..	F	11130
..	?	14′ 0″	b	White	..	..	F	11856
..	0·4 × 0·3	..	l	White	..	..	..	....
..	0·5 × 0·3	..	l	White	..	..	..	....
..	0·2 × 0·15	13′ 0″	a	White	..	..	F	1281
..	0·35 × 0·25	13′ 6″	a	White	..	..	F	1747
..	0·2 × ?	12′ 8″	a	White	..	..	F	11490
..	0·5 × 0·2	..	a	White	..	..	..	....
..	?	11′ 6″	al	White	..	..	F	4102
..	?	15′ 0″	al	White	..	..	F	11541
Similar to 490	0·35 × 0·25	..	b	White	..	..	F	Ab24
Similar to 499	0·7 × 0·4	10′ 0″	b	White	..	..	F	12534
Similar to 490	0·65 × 0·32	9′ 0″	b	White	..	..	F	9057
Similar to 509	0·35 × 0·28	12′ 0″	b	White	..	..	F	2058
Similar to 548	0·37 × 0·3	15′ 3″	l	White	..	..	F	2442
Similar to 582	0·65 × 0·4	10′ 5″	l	White	..	..	F	3397
604	?.. 0·7 diam. 0·35	16′ 3″	q	..	Yellow	..	F	2543
605	0·4 × 0·4	7′ 0″	b	..	Green	..	AB	4786

HARAPPĀ: TABULATION OF SEALS (PLS. LXXXV-CI)—*contd.*

Plate No.	Size in inches.	Level below surface.	Type.	Materials and colour.			Mound or Area.	Find No.
				Steatite.	Faience.	Pottery.		
596	0·95 × 0·3	4' 2"	n	..	White and grey.	..	F	11511
597	0·7 × 0·4	5' 0"	n	..	Yellowish	..	F	10960
598	0·7 × 0·25	From Spoil earth.	n	..	..	Grey	AB	11373
599	6·5 × 5·25 × 3·25	8' 0"	..	Red stone	..	..	..	B951
600	0·55 × 0·3	11' 9"	n	..	Yellow	..	..	10177
601	0·65 × 0·35	9' 6"	h	..	White	..	..	2276
602	0·3 × 0·3	2' 0" to 5' 0"	h	..	White	..	F	10014a
603	0·65 × 0·35	9' 4"	h	..	White	..	F	11022
604	0·65 × 0·35	14' 9"	h	..	White	..	..	12540
605	0·6 × 0·35	3' 9"	h	..	Greenish	..	F	12416
606	0·6 × 0·32	3' 0"	i	..	White	..	F	11417
607	0·6 × 0·3	12' 6"	h	..	White	..	F	10178
608	0·6 × 0·35	1' 6"	h	..	White	..	F	Af153
609	0·32 × ?	5' 5"	h	..	White	..	D	J294
610	0·6 × 0·3	12' 7"	..	..	White	..	F	12562
611	0·5 × 0·5	3' 0"	af	..	Greenish	..	F	Af115
612	0·6 × 0·28	8' 0"	h	..	Yellow	..	F	11848
613	L. 0·45 diam. 0·3	From spoil earth.	ae	..	White and grey.	..	F	4521
Similar to 594	L. 0·7 diam. 0·36	12' 10"	ae	..	White	..	F	4298
Similar to 597	0·65 × 0·28	20' 6"	n	..	Green	..	F	10140
614	1·15 × 1·15	5' 0"	a	White	..	..	F	5399
615	0·95 × 0·95	4' 7"	a	White	..	..	F	11266c
616	?	5' 0"	a	White	..	..	F	A441
617	0·85 × 0·85	14' 0"	a	White	..	..	AB	12002
618	0·7 × 0·7	..	a	White	..	..	F	E1214
619	1·75 × 1·75	From spoil earth.	a	White	..	..	AB	11453
620	0·9 × 0·9	12' 9"	a	White	..	..	F	2960
621	0·85 × 0·85	3' 3"	a	White	..	..	F	11600
622	?	12' 0"	a	Black	..	..	F	1379
623	?	4' 0"	a	White	..	..	AB	5633
624	0·9 × ?	..	a	White	..	..	..	....
625	?	20' 0"	a	White	..	..	AB	B1522
626	1·0 × 0·95	..	a	White	..	..	..	E290
627	0·95 × 0·48	5' 0"	c	White	..	..	F	12752
628	0·75 × 0·5	3' 3"	c	White	..	..	H	H637
629	0·85 × 0·5	7' 0"	c	..	Green	..	AB	4763
630	0·9 × 0·4	1' 6"	c	White	..	..	H	H405
631	1·05 × 0·4	..	c	White	..	..	AB	B-Summit
632	? × 0·35	8' 0"	e	White	..	..	F	4588
633	0·5 × 0·3	From spoil earth.	c	Grey	..	..	..	10420
634	0·9 × 0·38	2' 3"	c	White	..	..	F	10631
635	0·5 × 0·23 × 0·15	17' 9"	o	White	..	..	F	3897
636	0·4 × 0·32	0' 5"	h	White	..	..	..	3943
637	L. 0·35	15' 0"	..	..	White	..	F	2119
638	? × 0·4	5' 5"	h	..	White	..	D	J284
639	? × 0·35	2' 6"	h	..	White	..	F	2800
640	? × 0·4	..	h	..	Green	..	..	....
641	0·6 × 0·25	1' 6"	n	..	Green	..	..	12750

HARAPPĀ: TABULATION OF SEALS (PLS. LXXXV-CI)—*contd.*

Plate No.	Size in inches.	Level below surface.	Type.	Materials and colour.			Mound or Area.	Find No.
				Steatite.	Faience.	Pottery.		
642	0·63 × 0·4	4' 7"	n	..	White	..	D	J619
643	1·9 × 0·25	2' 0"	..	..	(Ivory rod)	..	F	Ab62
644	L. 0·65 w. 0·3	5' 10"	ao	..	White	..	..	11330
645	0·7 × 0·3	2' 10"	n	..	Yellow	..	D	J359
646	L. 0·8 diam. 0·3	3' 0"	ae	..	White	..	F	8640
Similar to 646	L. 0·8 diam. 0·27	2' 7"	ae	..	White	..	D	J383
Similar to 646	L. 0·8 diam. 0·3	13' 2"	ae	..	White	..	F	12343
647	0·65 × 0·25	10' 0"	n	..	White	..	F	10010
648	0·45 × 0·4	8' 8"	h	..	Green	..	AB	7156
649	0·5 × 0·3	7' 0"	n	..	Yellow	..	D	J219
650	L. 0·6 diam. 0·3	11' 6"	ae	..	White and grey.	..	F	2697
651	L. 1·3 diam. 0·35	6' 3"	ae	..	..	Red	F	Ae279
652	1·05 × 0·45	..	af	..	White	..	..	....
653	0·85 × 0·45	12' 0"	h	..	White	..	AB	B1829
654	1·5 × 0·5	10' 2"	h	..	White	..	F	4917
655	0·75 × 0·4	1' 10"	h	..	Yellow	..	F	5724
656	0·78 × 0·5	4' 5"	h	..	Green	..	F	11516
657	Diam. 0·75	8' 0"	..	..	..	Red	F	A233
658	L. 0·95 w. 0·3	8' 0"	aq	..	White	..	F	12380
Similar to 658	L. 0·9 w. 0·3	7' 4"	aq	..	Greenish	..	D	J493
659	0·69 × 0·4	12' 0"	h	..	White	..	F	11714
660	0·5 × 0·4	12' 0"	h	..	White	..	F	2910
661	0·6 × 0·25	5' 2"	h	..	White	..	F	11467
662	Diam. 0·6	6' 0"	al	..	..	Grey	F	5621
663	Diam. 0·45	7' 6"	al	..	Yellow	..	F	11341
664	Diam. 0·55	4' to 7'	al	..	Greenish	..	F	6650d
665	Diam. 0·5	From spoil earth.	al	..	Yellow	..	F	11449
666	Diam. 0·5	13' 3"	al	..	Yellow	..	F	4078
667	0·5 × 0·4	3' 0"	h	..	White	..	F	10137
668	0·6 × 0·45	From spoil earth.	h	..	White	..	F	11468
669	0·75 × 0·35	8' 10"	h	..	Green	..	AB	1976
670	0·7 × 0·4	..	h	..	Greenish	..	F	Af
671	L. 0·6 diam. 0·25	9' 0"	ae	..	White	..	F	10252a
672	0·75 × 0·35	4' 0"	h	..	Grey	..	F	Ab473
673	L. 0·9 w. 0·35	5' 7"	an	..	Green	..	F	11381
674	0·65 × 0·45	7' 6"	k	..	Yellow	..	AB	5074
675	?	7' 0"	..	..	..	..	D	J466
676	0·5 × 0·35	From spoil earth.	h	..	White	..	F	7060
677	0·45 × 0·3	9' 0"	h	..	White	..	D	J409
678	0·65 × 0·35	16' 6"	h	..	White	..	F	857
679	0·55 × 0·27	7' 7"	h	..	Green	..	F	4631
680	0·58 × 0·3	6' 9"	h	..	Yellow	..	D	J283
681	0·6 × 0·28	8' 0"	h	..	Yellow	..	F	11348
682	L. 0·6 w. 0·35	16' 9"	l	..	White	..	F	2325
683	0·3 × 0·3	15' 6"	h	..	Yellow	..	F	558
684	0·7 × 0·3	13' 0"	ag	..	Green	..	F	1032
685	0·5 × 0·35	2' 10"	h	..	Yellow	..	..	6053
686	0·65 × 0·3	4' 0"	h	..	White	..	..	?J403
687	L. 0·5 diam. 0·3	11' 3"	ae	..	..	White	F	1792

HARAPPĀ: TABULATION OF SEALS (Pls. LXXXV-CI)—*concld.*

Plate No.	Size in inches.	Level below surface.	Type.	Materials and colour.			Mound or Area.	Find No.
				Steatite.	Faience.	Pottery.		
Similar to 687	L. 0·5 diam. 0·25	6′ 5″	q	..	White	..	F	12160
688	L. 0·65 diam. 0·3	5′ 2″	q	..	White	..	F	11467
689	0·7 × 0·3	4′ 8″	ag	..	Yellow	..	D	3228
690	L. 0·5 diam. 0·3	13′ 9″	q	..	White and Yellow.	..	F	10162
691	0·48 × 0·27	13′ 4″	h	..	Grey and white.	..	F	2767
692	0·57 × 0·3	16′ 4″	h	..	White	..	F	3483
Similar to 646	L. 0·7 diam. 0·25	13′ 0″	q	..	Green	..	F	385
Similar to 654	1·6 × 0·55	6′ 6″	h	..	Yellow	..	F	1615
Similar to 669	0·4 × 0·35	6′ 0″	h	..	Green	..	..	1010
693	1·8 × 1·8	4′ 10″	a	White	..	..	F	12751
694	1·45 × 1·45	3′ 1″	a	White	..	..	H	H611
695	?	10′ 6″	a	Bluish	..	..	F	11392
696	?	13′ 4″	a	White	..	..	F	4252
697	0·95 × ?	8′ 1″	a	White	..	..	H	H540
698	1·8 × 0·6	2′ 0″	c	White	..	..	H	H160
699	0·9 × ?	4′ 6″	a(?)	Grey	..	..	F	5219
700	? × 0·4	6′ 7″	h	White	..	..	F	11507
701	0·55 × 0·45	6′ 5″	i	..	White	..	F	8150
702	Diam. 0·6	4′ 0″	ai	..	Green	..	H	H297
703	0·55 × 0·55 × 0·4	6′ 4″ to 6′ 8″	aj	..	Yellow	..	H	H441e
704	0·8 × 0·35	8′ 7″	af	..	..	Red	F	11064
705	L. 0·6 diam. 0·32	9′ 6″	ae	..	White	..	F	9040
706	L. 0·5 diam. 0·25	11′ 8″	ae	..	Grey	..	F	8965
Similar to 705-706	L. 0·35 diam. 0·25	11′ 3″	q	..	Grey	..	F.	9608
707	1·0 × 0·8	10′ 1″	..	..	..	Light red	F	11393

CHAPTER XIII.

Household Objects, Tools and Implements.

Querns.

Querns, which have been found in large numbers, are of two kinds: footed and saddle. They are made mostly of sandstone or grey granite but sometimes of basalt. The largest specimen (6018) is 23 in. long by 13·5 in. wide and 4 in. high. The smallest (8841) is 13 in. long by 6·5 in. wide and 2·75 in. high. **Footed and saddle-shaped querns. Material and size.**

The length of mullers ranges from 2·25 to 11 in. and their thickness or diameter from 1·25 to 4 in. The longer mullers are mostly cylindrical, but there are several examples which are four sided. The smaller mullers are usually four sided, but there are others which are triangular in shape and others which are irregular. An examination of the mullers shows that in a large majority of cases one or another side, and in some cases all the four sides are well worn. **Mullers.**

Footed querns (Pl. CXVII, 49 and 51).

No. 49 (6018) is of grey sandstone and almost exactly similar in shape and size to the quern illustrated in *M. I. C.*, Pl. CLVII, 54. It is the largest quern found at Harappā measuring 23 in. long by 13·5 in. wide by 4 in. high; the depression is 2·5 in. deep. Its short legs and part of the base may be presumed to have been embedded in the floor, otherwise it would have been liable to tilt under pressure. The surface of the depression, which is large enough to hold a fair quantity of grain, has been roughened with small pittings in order to make the grinding more effective. Mound F, Trench III, Square M 10/21; Depth 9 ft. 8 in. b.s.; Stratum IV. **Description.**

No. 51 (4713) is another four-legged grey sandstone quern 16·5 in. long by 12 in. wide and 3·5 in. high. Its centre is not much worn. The round muller placed upon it does not belong to it. Mound AB, Extension of Pits I and II, Square Q 24/9; Depth 6 ft. 4 in. b.s.; Stratum III.

No. 1941 (unillustrated) is a fragment of a four-legged grey sandstone quern rounded at the ends. Including the legs, which are quite short, its height is 3 in. and width 7·5 in. Mound F, Great Granary Area, Square I 9/9; Depth 1 ft. b.s.; Stratum I.

No. 4327 (unillustrated) is another fragment of a four-legged grey sandstone quern. Its ends are straight and the legs longer than those of No. 1941. Its height, including the legs, is 3·8 in. and width 6·5 in. It may be added that in these two examples the legs do not come at the corners as they do in No. 51 described above, but are more like the legs of a table with the edges of the quern projecting all round. Mound AB, Extension of Pits I and II, Square Q 24/6; Depth 8 ft. b.s.; Stratum IV.

Saddle querns.

These are too numerous to be described in detail. In shape they resemble the querns illustrated in *M. I. C.*, Pl. CXXX, 16 and 17.

Pestle (Pl. CXVII, 50).

Alabaster pestle. This is a cylindrical pestle of alabaster with tapered ends. It appears to have been used for grinding more valuable or finer objects. L. 7·5 in., diam. 1·9 in. No. 2412. Mound F, Great Granary Area, Square I 9/24; Depth 11 ft. 9 in. b.s.; Stratum. V.

There are several pestles of basalt and granite. They are four-sided rather than round and taper towards the upper end.

Palettes (Pl. CXVII, 52-55 and 61).

Several small slabs and discoid or oval tablets of stone—the latter ranging in diameter from 5·5 to 9 in., with slight depressions were probably used as palettes for rubbing pigments, glazes, etc. The palettes now-a-days used for rubbing sandalwood or saffron into paste are also round but not so thick as these.

Basalt. No. 12414h (unillustrated) is a rectangular slab of basalt measuring 7·5 by 2·8 by ·8 in. Its face is rubbed smooth. Mound F, Trench IV, Square I 14/16; Depth 6 ft. 5 in. b.s.; Stratum III.

Alabaster. Nos. 52-55 are four out of fifteen oval palettes of alabaster. Their sizes range between 2·1 by 2 by ·25 in. and 3·15 by 2·6 by ·25 in. They were found together along the southern edge of the north-western extension of the Great Granary Area at a depth of 4 ft. 5 in. below the surface in association with Stratum III.

Jaisalmer stone. No. 12084 (unillustrated) is rectangular and of yellow Jaisalmer lime stone broken in two parts. Its underside is rough, but the face remarkably smooth. Size 7·1×2·25×·43 in. Mound AB, Trench at the Southern Edge, Square Q 27/25; Depth 16 ft. 6 in. b.s.; Stratum V.

Sang-i-abri. No. 61 (11952) is a square block of *sang-i-abri* smoothed on the faces as well as sides which are slightly concave, but the top face is polished most. It is 7·25 in. square and 2·6 in. thick. Mound AB, Trench at the Southern Edge, Square Q 28/21; Depth 14 ft. b.s.; Stratum V.

Stone implements (Pl. CXVII, 56-58 and Pl. CXVIII, 37-63).

Chert flakes of two types. As at Mohenjo-daro, the stone implements found at Harappā are of the roughest description. The majority are made of a dull, often mottled, cream-coloured chert which when struck produces a metallic ring. Among them, flakes are found in very large numbers (cf. Pl. CXVIII, 37-48), and are of two kinds, (*a*) with a central ridge running down their whole length as in Nos. 37 and 42-45; and (*b*) with the ridge flaked off leaving a flat top, as in Nos. 39 and 40. Both varieties have sharp edges and could be effectively used for cutting meat, vegetables, etc. In most cases the edges have become serrated by use.

No. 45 (3727) is the largest flake, 5·4 in. long by 1·6 in. wide and 0·4 in. thick in the middle: its colour is partly light and partly dark grey. Mound AB, Extension of Pits I and II, Square Q 24/14; Depth 5 ft. b.s.; Stratum II. The smallest scraper is 2·65 in. long, 0·55 in. wide and 0·15 in. thick.

Cores. The cores from which the flakes were struck are flat at one end and wedge-shaped at the other. Some of them are illustrated in Pl. CXVIII, 49-62; their size ranges from 1·1 to 3·7 in. long, 0·4 to 1·6 in. wide, and 0·3 to 1·25 in. thick. In some cases their tips are rubbed smooth possibly because they were used as burnishers of some kind.

No. 56 (8650g) is 3·7 in. long, 1·6 in. wide and 1·25 in. thick. Mound F, Trench IV, Square H 12/21; Depth 7 ft. b.s.; Stratum IV.

No. 6093 (unillustrated) is sharply pointed at the tip; 1·1 in. long, 0·4 in. wide, and 0·3 in. thick. Mound F, Great Granary Area, Square K 9/4; Depth 11 ft. 10 in. b.s.; Stratum IV.

Celts (Pl. CXVII, 56-58).

Stone celts. The stone celts found at Harappā comprise three of chert, of which two are illustrated in Pl. CXVII, 56 and 57, one of slate (unillustrated), and one of basalt (Pl. CXVII, 58). Though varying in size they are generally similar in shape. In every case, the cutting edge is dented by use and the butt chipped in a way that shows that they were struck directly on the head.

Chert. No. 56 (3083) is of chert. Its lower edge, which is 5·3 in. wide, is sharp but not intact. It is 12·5 in. long, 3 in. broad at the butt and 2 in. thick in the middle. Mound F, Trench I, Square M 11/6; Depth 10 ft. b.s.; Stratum IV.

No. 57 (1034) is also of chert, but of smaller size. It is more handy, better preserved and finished. The lower edge is sharp and the faces almost convex giving it a lentoid section. It measures 9·4 in. long, 4·2 in. broad at the cutting edge, 2·9 in. at the butt end and 1·4 in. at the thickest part. Mound F, Trench I, Square M 12/6; Depth 13 ft. b.s.; Stratum VI.

No. Ab475 (unillustrated) is the lower part of another chert celt with unfinished cutting edge. It is 4·3 in. broad across the lower edge and its maximum thickness is 1·5 in. Mound F, Great Granary Area; Depth 8 ft. b.s.; Stratum IV.

Slate. No. 3998 (unillustrated) of slate is somewhat primitive in appearance; its width tapers more sharply towards the butt than that of any of the others either in stone or metal. The cutting edge is broken by use. It is 4·5 in. long, 3·2 in. wide at the edge, and only 1·5 in. at the butt, the maximum thickness being 0·85 in. only. Mound F, Great Granary Area, Square K 8/1; Depth 1 ft. 6 in. b.s.; Stratum I.

Basalt. No. 58 (12225) is the only example of basalt, and is the smallest and best finished specimen of its kind. At the same time it is also the earliest having been found in Stratum VII, at a depth of 16 ft. below the surface. Mound F, Deep Digging in Trench IV, Square J 13/23. Its cutting edge is sharp and polished up to a height of 1·5 in. only. The sides are rounded. It measures 3·3 in. long, 2·3 in. wide at the edge, 1·6 in. at the butt and 1 in. thick.

Arrow-head. No. 63 (4028) in Pl. CXVIII is the only example from Harappā of a chert arrow-head. It is leaf-shaped and of red colour. The edges, though a little rough, are sharp, but the tip and tang are slightly broken. It is 1·7 in. long, 0·75 in. wide and 0·2 in. thick. Mound AB, Extension of Pits I and II; from spoil earth.

Chert burnishers (Pl. CXVIII, 32-36).

Only five burnishers, all of chert, have been found at Harappā. Shaped like a shuttle, they are triangular in section, with slightly convex faces tapering to both ends. Thanks to the hardness of the material, they take a high polish and are well suited for burnishing metal objects, especially those of gold and silver. Such burnishers are still used by lapidaries in India.

No. 32 (10755) is of cream colour, mottled red—the only complete specimen found at Harappā. It is 6·6 in. long and 0·75 in. thick in the middle: somewhat shorter and thicker than the burnisher illustrated in *M. I. C.*, Pl. CXXX, 36. Mound F, Trench V, Square L 12/8; Depth 8 ft. b.s.; Stratum IV.

Nos. 33 (2469) and 34 (3143) are flesh-coloured with red and blue veins. Slightly less than half their original size they are 0·65 in. thick at the broken end, and 3·25 and 3·1 in. long respectively. Both of them were found in Mound AB, Extension of Pits I and II, the former in Square R 24/7; at a depth of 4 ft. 6 in. b.s., in Stratum II, and the latter in Square R 24/3, at a depth of 8 ft. b.s., in Stratum IV.

No. 35 (H33) is the smallest of the five. It is of a uniform buff colour so highly polished as to be almost translucent along the edges. More than half of it is missing. L. 1·8 in.; thickness in the middle 0·3 in. only. Cemetery H, Eastern Section, Square S 34/9; Depth 1 ft. 6 in. b.s.; Stratum I.

Grey. No. 36 (1849) is less than half the original size. Its original colour was grey mottled pale yellow, but the surface has been darkened, possibly by some artificial process such as heating in oil.[1] Mound F, Trench III, Square N 9/9; Depth 11 ft. 3 in. b.s.; Stratum. V.

Weights (Pl. CXVIII, 1-31, and Pl. CXVII, 47-48).

Material. Weights have been found in very large numbers in all parts of the site and in association with all the strata. Although in the table given below I have included only the finer class of weights made mostly of chert and granite, there can be little doubt but that larger weights of a rougher kind, made, perhaps, of natural pebbles were also in use. The small Harappā weights found up to the year 1927, have already been examined and weighed along with those of Mohenjo-daro by Mr. A. S. Hemmy, late Principal of the Government College, Lahore, who has summarised his results in Chapter XXIX of *M. I. C.* In preparing the table appended below I have followed Mr. Hemmy's designations and limits within which those designations apply.

[1] According to Sir Edwin Pascoe, the dark colour of hornblende pendents may be due to some process of artificial darkening, such as heating in oil. *cf. M. I. C.*, p. 520, footnote 2.

According to their shape the Harappā weights may be divided into the following types :— **Types.**

(*a*) Cuboid.

(*b*) Barrel-shaped.

(*c*) Cylindrical with flat base and top.

(*d*) Spherical with flattened base and top.

(*e*) Cone-shaped.

Type a : Cuboid weights (Pl. CXVIII, 1-28).

Most popular shape. Weights of this shape were most popular and easily predominate over those of all other types taken together. The smallest Harappā weight of this type (No. 10443) is of exactly the same dimensions as the Mohenjo-daro weight Dk. 140 which measures 0·3 by 0·3 by 0·25 in., but the largest weight (No. 635) here measures 4·3 by 4·3 by 3·2 in. as against that of Mohenjo-daro which measures 6·8 by 6·0 by 3·8 in. These weights are made mostly of chert. Among them there is not a single true cube, though it may be observed that in a very large majority of cases the top and bottom are perfect squares. As already pointed out by Dr. Mackay,[1] they were first roughly chipped into shape and then ground and polished. **Method of manufacture.** The first process of chipping into shape is illustrated by No. 12 (1095) in Pl. CXVIII which measures 4 by 4 by 2·6 in. Most of the chert weights are beautifully banded or mottled; those of granite are mottled grey and black.

Description. Nos. 4 and 13 (635) are two veiws[2] of the largest chert weight from Harappā. It is broken along the edges and corners and measures 4·3 by 4·3 by 3·2 in. Wt. 2652·8 gms. Mound F, Trench I, Square M 12/17; Depth 4 ft. b.s.; Stratum II.

No. 3 (7168) is chipped at the corners and is the second largest weight found at Harappā. It measures 4 by 4 by 3·7 in. Wt. 2703·9 gms. Mound AB, Extension of Pits I and II, Square Q 23/15; Depth 4 ft. b.s.; Stratum II.

No. 27 (902) is of grey granite mottled black: it measures 1·15 by 0·95 by 1 in. Wt. 49·75 gms. Mound F, Great Granary Area, Square J 9/23; Depth 2 ft. 3 in. b.s.; Stratum I.

No. 28 (4368) is similar to No. 27 and measures 0·9 by 0·9 by 0·65 in. Wt. 27·65 gms. Mound AB, Extension of Pits I and II, Square Q 24/21; Depth 3 ft. b.s.; Stratum I.

Type b : Barrel-shaped weights (Pl. CXVII, 47-48).

Eight complete and two fragmentary examples of this type have been found at Harappā. Their length varies between 1·75 and 4·15 in., diameter in the middle between 0·35 and 1 in., and diameter at the ends between 0·23 and 0·6 in. With the exception of three unfinished examples, two of grey stone and one of slate, they are quite symmetrically made and highly polished.

[1] *M. I. C.*, p. 462.

[2] The illustrations being cut-outs from different photographs bear no proportionate relation to the original size of objects.

No. 47 (1651) is of hornblende, as are also the four following examples. It is 3·1 in. long, 0·8 in. in diameter at the middle and 0·35 in. across the ends. Wt. 61·3 gms. Mound F, Great Granary Area, Square I 9/14; Depth 4 ft. b.s.; Stratum II.

No. 48 (1094) is 3·7 in. long, 1 in. in diameter at the middle and 0·6 in. at the ends. Wt. 130·2 gms. Mound F, Great Granary Area, Square J 9/23; Depth 4 ft. b.s.; Stratum II.

No. 7597 (unillustrated) is 4·15 in. long, 0·95 in. in diameter at the middle and 0·6 in. across the ends. Wt. 128·15 gms. Mound AB, Extension of Pits I and II, Square P 24/21; Depth 13 ft. b.s.; Stratum V.

No. B1480 (unillustrated) is the smallest and best finished weight of this type. It is 1·75 in. long, 0·35 in. in diameter at the middle and 0·23 in. at the ends. Wt. 7·65 gms. Mound AB, Trench B; Depth not recorded.

No. A333 (unillustrated). This is also of hornblende, slightly irregular and the least polished in that substance. Wt. 80·65 gms. It is 3·7 in. long, 0·85 in. in diameter at the middle and 0·55 in. across the ends.

Unmarked (unillustrated). This is of grey sandstone unfinished. It is 3·5 in. long, 0·95 in. in diameter at the middle and 0·6 in. across the ends.

No. 12063 (unillustrated) is also of grey sandstone measuring 2·3 in. long, 0·7 in. in diameter at the middle and 0·4 in. at the ends. Wt. 37·5 gms. Mound AB, Trench at the Southern Edge, Square Q 28/21; Depth 14 ft. 6 in. b.s.; Stratum V.

No. A347 (unillustrated) with oblique bands is the only example in slate. It is unfinished and slightly irregular in shape measuring 2·15 in. long, 0·7 in. in diameter at the middle and 0·4 in. across the ends. Wt. 25·5 gms. Mound F, Great Granary Area, Depth 3 ft. 2 in. b.s.; Stratum II.

Known in Egypt, Mesopotamia and Elam.

Dr. Mackay has pointed out that weights of this type were common enough in Egypt, early Mesopotamia and Elam, where they were made of various materials.[1]

Type c: Cylindrical weight with flat base and top.

No. 29[2] (4881) in Pl. CXVIII is made of finely banded dark grey chert and is the only example of this type. It is smaller than the similar example found at Mohenjo-daro being 0·43 in. in height and 0·6 in. in diameter at the top and base. Wt. 6·45 gms. Mound AB, Extension of Pits I and II, Square Q 24/9; Depth 8 ft. b.s.; Stratum IV.

Type d: Spherical weight with flattened base and top.

Carnelian.

No. 30 (J576) in Pl. CXVIII is the only example of this type. It is made of carnelian and coated with white paint which has partially disappeared. At Mohenjo-daro six examples of such weights have been found. This one is 0·8 in. high, 1·1 in. in diameter at the middle and 0·7 in. across the top and

---

[1] *M. I. C.*, pp. 463-64.

[2] But for the fact that its weighment fits within the limits of weights designated E in the table below it might have been described as an ear-plug.

base. Wt. 27·34 gms. Area J, Trench I, Square Q 31/18; Depth 4 ft. b.s.; Stratum III.

Type e: Cone-shaped weight.

No. 31 (11028) in Pl. CXVIII is the only cone-shaped weight found at Harappā. It is of grey granite and measures 1·2 in. high and 1·3 in. in diameter at the base. It is 53·6 gms. in weight and falls under the designation H according to Mr. Hemmy's nomenclature. Mound F, Trench VI, Square O 10/25; Depth 4 ft. 6 in. b.s.; Stratum II.

Large conical weights with a hole for suspension mentioned by Dr. Mackay in *M. I. C.*[1] under type *d* and those of a hemispherical shape described under type *g* are not found at Harappā. The following is a table of the weights:—

No.	Type.[2]	Weight[3] in grammes.	Substance.	Designation and limits of weights in grammes.	No.	Type.	Weight in grammes.	Substance.	Designation and limits of weights in grammes.
635[4]	a	2,652·8	Chert	2 N units. 2652·8—2708·9.	4993	a	54·0	Chert.	
7165[4]	a	2,703·9	Chert.		12106a	a	54·1	Chert.	
12218[4]	a	1,593·5	Sandstone	Uncommon.	3979	a	54·25	Chert.	
421	a	402·2	Cherty limestone.		771	a	54·35	Chert.	
8822	a	263·5	Chert		10953	a	54·6	Chert.	
11979	a	121·4	Chert	J 121·4—135·9	349	a	54·8	Chert.	
5730	a	124·25	Grey sandstone.		4540	a	56·0	Chert.	
1330	a	127·35	Chert.		1651	b	61·8	Hornblende.	
2480	a	127·45	Chert.		270	a	67·5	Chert.	
7597	b	128·15	Hornblende.		B1461	a	26·65	Grey stone	Uncommon.
1556	a	128·4	Chert.		3598	a	35·8	Chert	
A1161	a	129·0	Chert.		844	a	25·05	Grey stone	G 25·05—29·5
7099	a	129·3	Chert.		12440	a	25·2	Limestone.	
1094	b	130·2	Hornblende.		120	a	25·35	Grey stone.	
PtIV	a	130·8	Chert.		A347	b	25·5	Slate.	
11241	a	132·0	Chert.		8904a	a	25·72	Cherty limestone.	
..	a	132·5	Granite.		2942	a	25·87	Chert.	
2968	a	132·6	Chert.		4509	a	25·95	Motiled grey stone.	
PI-87	a	133·3	Limestone.		1156	a	26·1	Chert.	
1978	a	134·0	Chert.		8785	a	26·25	Chert.	
A616	a	134·8	Chert.		7070	b	26·3	Grey stone.	
11446b	a	135·45	Chert.		86501	a	26·3	Limestone.	
771	a	135·9	Chert.		8497	a	26·4	Limestone	G 25·05—29·5
903	a	49·75	Granite	H 49·75—67·5	5330	a	26·5	Chert.	
5056	a	52·2	Cherty limestone.		11421	a	26·5	Chert.	
10274	a	52·25	Granite.		8878	a	26·5	Chert.	
12500	a	52·3	Chert.		O248	a	26·6	Chert.	
As101	a	53·1	Chert.		8501	a	26·7	Chert.	
11072	a	53·6	Chert.		12856	a	26·75	Chert.	
11028	e	53·6	Granite.		525	a	26·8	Grey stone.	
H407	a	53·75	Chert.		12371	a	26·85	Agate.	
5448	e	53·9	Granite.						

[1] Pp. 463-64.

[2] For type, see p. 361 supra.

[3] Furnished by Pandit K. N. Sastri, Custodian, Archaeological Museum, Harappā.

[4] Khan Bahadur Mohammad Sana Ullah, Archaeological Chemist in India who has examined them, writes that "these weights are badly worn, the worst affected being No. 635. They are, therefore, not suitable at all for accurate work".

No.	Type.	Weight in grammes.	Substance.	Designation and limits of weights in grammes.
7416	a	26·95	Chert.	
Ae155	a	27·0	Chert.	
1252	a	27·0	Soapstone.	
..	a	27·0	Granite.	
A357	a	27·0	Granite.	
..	a	27·0	Chert.	
7640	a	27·0	Chert.	
10692	a	27·1	Banded agate.	
B1807	a	27·2	Chert.	
11512	a	27·2	Granite.	
854	a	27·25	Chert.	
1356	a	27·25	Chert.	
10051	a	27·3	Chert.	
5756	a	27·3	Chert.	
12106b	a	27·3	Chert.	
855	a	27·3	Chert.	
7664	a	27·3	Chert.	
2550	a	27·31	Chert.	
PII-38	a	27·32	Chert.	
4009	a	27·32	Chert.	
8197	a	27·35	Chert.	
7285	a	27·4	Granite.	
Af254	a	27·4	Chert.	
H666	a	27·45	Chert.	
1252	a	27·45	Chert	G 25·05—29·5
1308	a	27·45	Chert.	
3561	a	27·45	Granite.	
5531	a	27·65	Chert.	
4368	a	27·65	Granite.	
1356	a	27·7	Chert.	
5042	a	27·8	Chert.	
7110	a	27·8	Chert.	
4066	a	27·45	Chert.	
4198	a	28·0	Chert.	
3068	a	28·25	Chert.	
5755	a	28·37	Chert.	
645	a	28·6	Chert.	
Bg14	a	28·6	Chert.	
3995	a	29·5	Chert.	
..	c	19·0	Agate	Uncommon.
565	a	11·4	Limestone	F 11·4—15·0
J12	a	13·08	Chert.	
12248	a	13·2	Chert.	
11934	a	13·5	Cherty limestone.	
906	a	13·5	Chert.	
10742	a	13·55	Chert.	
Bg26	a	13·55	Chert.	
185	a	13·6	Chert.	
4836	a	13·6	Chert.	
J13	a	13·65	Chert.	
7567	a	13·67	Chert.	

No.	Type.	Weight in grammes.	Substance.	Designation and limits of weights in grammes.
120	a	13·7	Chert.	
120	a	13·7	Cherty limestone.	
120	a	13·7	Chert.	
10195	a	13·75	Chert.	
674	a	13·75	Chert.	
1575	a	13·75	Chert	F 11·4—15·0
1173	a	13·8	Chert.	
Af94	a	13·8	Granite.	
10651	a	13·8	Chert.	
8911	a	13·8	Chert.	
10942	a	13·8	Chert.	
1074	a	13·85	Chert.	
4054	a	13·9	Chert.	
H662	a	13·9	Limestone.	
8499	a	14·1	Chert.	
J102	a	14·25	Chert.	
278	a	15·0	Chert.	
120	a	6·31	Chert	E 6·31—7·9
12417	a	6·45	Banded greystone.	
4861	c	6·45	Agate.	
J513	a	6·55	Limestone.	
817	a	6·6	Chert.	
H70	a	6·6	Chert.	
5046	a	6·62	Chert.	
4783	a	6·65	Chert.	
4250	a	6·72	Chert.	
H606	a	6·75	Chert.	
Af306	a	6·75	Chert.	
11460	a	6·8	Chert.	
2556	a	6·82	Chert.	
J201	a	6·85	Chert.	
H539	a	6·85	Chert.	
7512	a	6·85	Limestone.	
6426	a	6·85	Chert.	
11517	a	6·9	Chert.	
Bg22	a	6·9	Chert.	
6829	a	6·9	Chert.	
12242	a	6·95	Chert	E 6·31—7·9
12352	a	6·95	Chert.	
2926	a	6·95	Limestone.	
4098	a	6·95	Granite.	
5451	a	7·0	Chert.	
10522	a	7·9	Chert.	
Af350	a	3·25	Limestone	D 3·25—4·3
5505	a	3·3	Limestone.	
4912	a	3·3	Chert.	
120	a	3·35	Chert.	
10738	a	3·4	Chert.	
6461	a	3·4	Chert.	
10073	a	3·4	Chert.	

No.	Type.	Weight in grammes.	Substance.	Designation and limits of weights in grammes.	No.	Type.	Weight in grammes.	Substance.	Designation and limits of weights in grammes.
4373	a	3·4	Chert.		10885B	a	1·15	Soapstone	B 1·15—1·92
A67	a	3·4	Chert.		Bg23	a	1·3	Chert.	
1959	a	3·4	Slate.		9046	a	1·65	Jade.	
5019	a	3·45	Chert.		J101	a	1·65	Chert.	
Ae155	a	3·45	Grey soapstone.		8400	a	1·65	Chert.	
J495	a	3·45	Chert.		J451	a	1·7	Chert.	
1706	a	3·5	Chert.		12711	a	1·7	Jade.	
5580	a	3·5	Chert.		A11	a	1·75	Chert.	
7569	a	3·55	Chert.		3831	a	1·75	Chert.	
4620	a	3·6	Chert.		8877	a	1·8	Chert.	
Ae159	a	3·65	Chert.		3093	a	1·85	Chert.	
1184	a	3·95	Chert.		11896	a	1·92	Chert.	
86501	a	4·3	Banded greystone.		10443	a	0·95	,,	A 0·95
J2	a	2·5	Chert	C 2·5—2·9	B82	b	9·6	Hornblende	Uncommon.
J88	a	2·5	Chert.		PIV-128	b	39·4	Greystone	
5012	a	2·75	Limestone.		A333	b	80·7	Hornblende	
J598	a	2·9	Limestone.		PIV-48	b	86·2	Greystone	
					A334	b	89·7	Hornblende	

Khan Bahadur Mohammed Sana Ullah, Archæological Chemist in India, has furnished the following interesting note on a bronze rod found at Harappā which he takes to be a linear measure used in the Indus Valley:—

Mohenjo-daro Measure.

"Dr. E. Mackay has discovered a linear measure at Mohenjo-daro, which now preserves nine definite divisions, the average length of one space being 0·264 in. It is neatly finished out of a piece of shell and bears the marks . and ⊕ five divisions apart, thus indicating a decimal scale of 1·32 ins. rising probably to a foot of 13·2 ins. Sir Flinders Petrie has identified this scale with the widespread standard which had been found hitherto, first in Egypt and subsequently, in Asia Minor, Greece, Lachish, Syria, etc. Therefore, the discovery of this scale at Mohenjo-daro at the earliest period, is of great significance. However, Dr. Mackay has remarked that there may possibly have been also a second system for few of the doorways are actual multiples of the unit marked on the scale that has been found.[1]"

13·2″ foot.

Harappā Measure.

Another fragmentary measure has been discovered at Harappā (Pl. CXXV, 39*a*). This is in the form of a bronze rod, 1·5 ins. long, broken at both ends, a little over ⅛″ in diameter, but bearing, unfortunately, only four complete divisions which are marked off by V-shaped indentations. The values of the divisions as determined with the aid of a travelling microscope, reading up to ·001 cm., were:—

0·3676″ Digit.

0·960; 0·905; 0·945; 0·925; average, 0·934 cm. = 0·3676 in. It is obvious that the value of a division of this scale, 0·3676 in. is half of the digit 0·737 (correct within ·3 per cent) or ⅛th of the palm (2·947 ins.) of an early Egyptian system which ran thus:—

Zebo, digit ·737.	4 = shep, palm 2·947.	7 = meh cubit 20·62.	100 = khet, reel 2060.	120 = ater or akhoinos 3·9 miles.

[1] Mackay's *Further Excavations at Mohenjo-daro*, p. 405.

20·6″ Cubit.

This ancient system is based on the standard cubit of 20·62 ins. which "was termed the 'Royal Cubit' throughout history" and occurs far and wide. It was used in Egypt from the time of the Predynastic royal tombs onwards; in Babylonia, as 20·89 of Gudea; in Asia Minor, as 20·55 to 20·94; in tombs at Jerusalem, as 20·57; in six English stone circles, as 20·55; and in New Mexico, as 20·68.[1] Therefore, the occurrence of this widespread standard in the Indus Valley also, is quite understandable, but the question cannot be settled definitely until complete measures are also found. However, evidence of the actual use of this system in the Indus Valley has been inferred as a result of over 150 checks which have been applied on the buildings at Harappā and Mohenjo-daro, comprising measurements of various well-planned houses, rooms, courtyards, streets and platforms. The value of the cubit seems to vary between 20·3 and 20·8 ins. while that of the foot, between 13·0 and 13·2 ins. For instance in the most important group of buildings, known as 'the Great Granary' at Harappā,

Checks on Buildings.

(a) length of main walls	51′-9″ = 621″ = 30 × 20·7
(b) width of main halls	17′-3″ = 207″ = 10 × 20·7
(c) width of corridors	5′-6″ = 66″ = 5 × 13·2
(d) width of central aisle	23′ = 276″ = 21 × 13·2

The diameter of the circular platforms at Harappā is 11 ft. = 132″ = 10×13·2. It is interesting that the width of the High Street, the principal highway of Mohenjo-daro, is 30′-9″ or 18 cubits of 20·5 ins. The well-planned house No. XIX (Vs. A, 3) measures 23×33 cubits of 20·5 ins. House No. XXIII (Hr. B, 5) measures 29×36 cubits of 20·7 ins. House No. LIV (Hr. B, 7) measures 17×19 cubits of 20·7 ins. The Great Bath is 36×21 ft. of 13·1 ins. The width of the doorways, referred to by Dr. Mackay,[2] include apparently ½, ¼, and ¾ fractions as at the present day, the value of the foot varying between 13·0 and 13·16 ins. The average width of the windows is 66 ins. or exactly five feet. These results indicate that several of these are simple multiples of either the cubit or the foot mentioned above.

It, therefore, appears very probable that both these systems, one based on the foot and the other on the cubit, were simultaneously in use in the Indus Valley. The value of the Harappā cubit, as determined from the well-planned 'Great Granary', is 20·7 ins., but in accordance with the bronze scale, it should be ·3676×8×7 = 20·58 ins. On the other hand if we take ten palms (·376×8×10 = 29·408) as the diagonal, then the length of the side of its square is equal to 20·79 ins.; but the value obtained from the measurements of the various buildings varies between 20·3 and 20·8. The standard of accuracy could not be expected to be better in the case of buildings anywhere.

---

[1] *Encyclopaedia Britannica*, 14th edition, Vol. XV, pp. 142-5, Article on Ancient Measures and Weights by Sir Flinders Petrie.

[2] *M. I. C.*, pp. 274-5.

Mace-heads (Pl. LXXXIII, 14-16, 19, 22 and 24, and Pl. CXXIII, 33 and 34).

Mace-heads are made of a very close-grained limestone, grey sandstone, alabaster, marble and copper. According to their shapes they fall into the following classes :—

(*a*) Round or pear-shaped.
(*b*) Lentoid.
(*c*) Spherical rings.

Type a : Round or pear-shaped (Pl. CXXIII, 33 and 34, and Pl. LXXXIII, 16).

No. 33 (277h) in Pl. CXXIII is also illustrated in Pl. CXXI, 9. It is the only example of a copper mace-head from Harappā or Mohenjo-daro. It was one of the numerous contents of the remarkable copper jar No. 277. It has beading round the base of the hole and retains many marks or cuts on its surface. Ht. and diam. 1·8 in. ; the central hole 0·85 in. across. Though small, it is heavy enough to have been used as a very effective weapon. Mound F, Trench I, Square M 11/15 ; Depth 5 ft. 9 in. b.s. ; Stratum III. **Copper.**

No. 34 (573) in Pl. CXXIII is similar to No. 33, and like it has beading round the base. It is the only example recovered of marble and is 2·8 in. high and 2·95 in. in diameter, but nearly half of it is missing. Mound F, Trench I, Square M 11/10 ; Depth 6 ft. 10 in. b.s. ; Stratum II.

No. 16 (3614) in. Pl. LXXXIII is of very close-grained, yellowish limestone drilled on the underside with a tapering blind hole 0·9 in. deep and 0·7 in. in diameter. This is holed like the mace-head No. 27 illustrated in *M. I. C.*, Pl. CXXXIV, but its shape is different and unlike that it has no beading round the base. It is the only mace-head at Harappā which is not holed through. Ht. 1·6 in. ; diam. 1·8 in. Mound F, Great Granary Area, Square I 8/14 ; Depth 1 ft. 9 in. b.s. ; Stratum V. Mace-heads of this type have been found in Elam, Mesopotamia and Egypt from the earliest times. **Yellow limestone.**

Type b : Lentoid (Pl. LXXXIII, 14, 15 and 24).

Mace-heads of this type were usually made of very hard limestone, or grey sandstone, and sometimes of alabaster. They are bored with a cylindrical or hour-glass type of hole. **Materials.**

No. 14 (B1728) of limestone is one of the best examples of this type. It is 3·3 in. in diameter, 0·9 in. thick and has a cylindrical hole 0·7 in. in diameter. Mound AB, Trench B ; Depth 2 ft. b.s. ; Stratum III. **Limestone.**

No. 1162 (unillustrated) is of grey sandstone. It is not perfectly circular, but the edge is quite sharp. It is 4·5 in. in diameter, 0·85 in. thick in the middle and has a double conical hole diminishing from 1·4 to 0·8 in. in diameter. Mound F, Trench I, Square M 12/20 ; Depth 15 ft. b.s. ; Stratum VI. **Grey sandstone.**

No. 285 (unillustrated) is the best and also the largest example in grey sandstone, being 4·8 in. in diameter and 1 in. thick in the middle. Its double conical hole is 1·4 to 0·9 in. in diameter. Mound F, Trench I, Square M 11/15 ; Depth 11 ft. 6 in. b.s. ; Stratum V.

No. 15 (1519) is of limestone; 3 in. in diameter; 1·15 in. thick; cylindrical hole ·7 in. in diameter. Mound F, Trench III, Square N 9/8; Depth 7 ft. 6 in. b.s.; Stratum IV.

Rectangular hole. No. 24 (644) of alabaster is now cracked. This is unique in being pierced with a rectangular hole which is 1·2 in. long, 0·7 in. wide and 2·4 in. deep. Being curvilinear, its greatest diameter is 2·6 in., at the base 2·4 in. and at the top 2·2 in. Mound F, Trench I, Square M 12/6; Depth 8 ft. 6 in. b.s.; Stratum IV.

Grey limestone. No. 732 (unillustrated) of grey limestone is pierced with a cylindrical hole: 3·5 in. in diameter; 0·75 in. thick; 1·2 in. across the hole. Fragmentary. Mound F, Great Granary Area, Square I 8/6; Depth 2 ft. b.s.; Stratum I.

Alabaster. No. 5553 (unillustrated) is of alabaster 3·75 in. in diameter; 0·9 in. thick; and its double conical hole is 1 to 0·65 in. in diameter. Mound F, Great Granary Area, Square H 9/22; from surface.

No. 6042 (unillustrated) is also of alabaster. It shows how the centre hole was drilled from opposite sides. This and the previous example of alabaster are badly cracked. 4·1 in. in diameter; 1·4 in. thick in the middle. Mound F, Great Granary Area, Square I 9/5; Depth 2 ft. b.s.; Stratum I.

Type c: Spherical rings (Pl. LXXXIII, 19 and 22).

Mace-heads of this type were common at Harappā. The hole is sometimes provided with two vertical grooves opposite for firmer hafting. Cf. Pl. LXXXIII, 22. The several examples of this type, so far recovered, are unfortunately all fragmentary. They are made of limestone or grey sandstone with height ranging between 2·2 and 4·8 in., diameter between 3·9 and 7·4 in., and diameter of the hole, which is always cylindrical, between 1·3 and 3·4 in. The size, shape and hole of the stone ring figured in *M. I. C.*, Pl. CLVII, 59,[1] suggest that that also is a mace-head. For description I shall select only the largest and the smallest examples of this type.

No. 19 (75) is of a soft but close-grained limestone and is the largest example. Over two-thirds of it is missing. Its height is 4·8 in., restored diameter 7·4 in. and diameter of the hole 3·4[2] in. Mound F, Trench I, Square M 12/11; Depth 5 ft. 4 in. b.s.; Stratum II.

No. 22 (7127) is of grey sandstone with two vertical grooves cut on opposite sides of the central hole. Restored height 2·2 in.; restored diameter 3·9 in.; hole 1·3 in across. Mound AB, Extension of Pits I and II, Square P 24/14; Depth 8 ft. 6 in. b.s.; Stratum IV.

Liṅgams, yonis and bætyllic stones.

Sir John Marshall has very ably dealt with the subject of phallic and bætyllic stones on pages 58-63 of *M. I. C.* giving several telling illustrations bearing on the subject in Pls. XIII and XIV. In further support of his views I would draw attention to the *liṅgams* and bætyls illustrated in Pl. CXVII.

[1] P. 473.
[2] Being of a large size it is likely to have been meant for ceremonial purposes.

Chessman-shaped liṅgams (Pl. CXVII, 28-32).

Chessman-shaped *liṅgams* are found in very large numbers and are made of various materials, *viz.*, chalcedony, carnelian, lapis lazuli, cherty limestone, grey sandstone with or without bands, yellow Jaisalmar stone, alabaster, imitation carnelian, faience, paste, shell, ivory and terracotta. Their height ranges between 0·5 in. to over 5 in. Of these, the faience, paste and pottery ones are frequently holed in the centre of the base.

Yellow sandstone. No. 28 (11537) is a well polished conventionalised *liṅgam* made of yellow Jaisalmer sandstone and adorned with a finely cut coil, which like the multiple necklaces or coils round the neck of the Mother goddess and Śiva (*M. I. C.*, Pl. XII, 8, 9 and 17) may be suspected of having some special religious significance. Its lower part, which may have taken the form of a broader base, as in No. 32, or possibly of a *yoni*, is broken away. 4·75 in. high; and 2·3 in. across the broken base. Mound F, Trench IV, Square I 13/11; Depth 3 ft. 6 in. b.s.; Stratum II.

Earthenware. No. 29 (Ad2) is a tall, broad-based example of earthenware pierced on the underside with a hole 1·75 in. deep and with another hole at the top. It is horizontally grooved round the upper edge and measures 4·4 in. high, and 2·2 in. in diameter at the base. Mound F, Great Granary Area; Depth 5 ft. b.s.; Stratum II.

Faience. No. 30 (8767) is of faience, 0·85 in. high, and provided with an unduly large hole at the base. Mound F, Trench V, Square K 12/24; Depth 6 ft. 3 in. b.s.; Stratum III.

No. 31 (7573) is of blue faience. This, too, is holed at the base and is 1·2 in. high. Mound AB, Extension of Pits I and II, Square O 23/20; Depth 6 ft. b.s.; Stratum II.

No. 32 (755) is squat, 3·2 in. high and 4·5 in. across the top. This is made of yellow Jaisalmer stone, but has a black band 1·2 in. wide round the body. Mound F, Great Granary Area, Square J 8/25; Depth 9 ft. b.s.; Stratum IV.

Large stone liṅgams and their miniatures (Pl. CXVII, 4, 5, 14, 15, 18-24, 27, 33-43).

Sandstone. No. 4 (12466) is the largest *liṅgam* found at Harappā. It is of grey sandstone, 17·5 in. high and 9 in. in diameter at the base. Mound F, Trench I, Square M 12/22; Depth 2 ft. 5 in. b.s.; Stratum I.

No. 5 (3463) is also of grey sandstone and slightly smaller than No. 4, being 16 in. high and 9 in. in diameter across the base. Mound F, Trench III, Square M 9/25; Depth 7 ft. 10 in. b.s.; Stratum IV.

No. Ai40 (unillustrated) is also of grey sandstone with some broad, yellow vertical bands. It is 11·5 in. high and 7·5 in. in diameter. Unlike Nos. 4 and 5, which are smooth dressed all over, the body of this is quite rough.

Limestone. No. 18 (10496) is a well finished and well proportioned *liṅgam* of white limestone, 6·3 in. high and 4·5 in. in diameter at the base. Mound F, Trench V, Square J 12/18; Depth 3 ft. 4 in. b.s.; Stratum II.

Several stone *liṅgams* from a jar.

In connection with *liṅgams* should be mentioned here a find made in an earthenware jar, No. 12414, recovered from Mound F, Trench IV, Square I 14/16 at a depth of 6 ft. 5 in. b.s. in Stratum III. In this jar, six *liṅgams* were found along with some tiny pieces of shell, a unicorn seal, an oblong grey sandstone block with polished surface, five stone pestles, a stone palette, and a block of chalcedony. Two of the six *liṅgams* are squat and made of limestone, three of grey sandstone ranging in height from 3·5 to 6·0 in., and one of red sandstone. This last is the best finished, 9·8 in. high and 5·4 in. across the base.

Terracotta *liṅgam*.

A fairly large-sized terracotta *liṅgam*, No. 11475 (unillustrated) was found in Mound F, Trench VI, Square P 9/15 at a depth of 6 ft. 4 in. b.s. in Stratum III. It is well finished, has a small depression at the top and is somewhat-squat being 4 in. high and 3·8 in. in diameter at the base.

Conical bætyls (Pl. CXVII, 14-15, 19-24, 27 and 33-43).

The miniature conical bætyls, some of which are illustrated in Pl. CXVII, are too numerous to be described in detail, but the following may be noticed n passing: No. 15 of chalcedony; No. 22 (J453) of ivory (which is rarely used for this purpose); No. 24 of grey sandstone mottled white; No. 27 (12292) of faience encircled like No. 28 with a spiral coil; an unillustrated and well-made pottery cone No. 12355 which also has a similar spiral coil; Nos. 33 and 34 (3717)—two different views of one and the same cone of yellow Jaisalmer stone with three equidistant vertical grooves meeting at the top; and lastly some other examples of cones with vertical or horizontal bands round the body like Nos. 35, 36 and 37-42.

Bætyls with indications of *yoni*.

No. 35 of imitation carnelian, No. 37 of yellow Jaisalmer stone, and Nos. 38-42 of terracotta have each some sort of ring round the body. No. 35 is 0·7 in. high and 0·45 in. across the base round which is an undulating ring of white with six oblique bands rising from the bends and meeting at the apex. This, too, is holed in the middle of the base. It was found in Mound F, Great Granary Area, Square I 9/1; Depth 2 ft. b.s.; Stratum I. In Nos. 37 (8920) and 38 (432) two grooves encircle the body, which were probably filled with a different coloured paste. Nos. 39-42 belong to a large find comprising 682 similar pottery cones all holed at the base. Round the body in every specimen is a broad band occupying about two-fifths of the whole. It is not, of course, to be assumed that all cones were necessarily bætyllic in character. The countless examples of earthenware with sharply pointed tops (*e.g.*, No. 44 in Pl. CXVII) may well have served some other purpose.

Paste.

Nos. 25 and 26 (4246) are two views of a tiny paste *liṅgam* with flat base, and circular incision at the top. It is 0·6 in. high and 0·35 in. in diameter at the base. Mound F, Great Granary Area, Square I 9/25; Depth 5 ft. 3 in. b.s.; Stratum III.

Pyramidal cones.

Nos. 45 and 46 in Pl. CXVII are two pyramidal cones with concave sides which were found along with 37 identical pieces and 682 cones with broad bands (Pl. CXVIII, 39-42) all made of under-burnt clay. They are square in section and flat at top and bottom where there is a hole for attachment. All are painted white, 1 in. high, 0·5 in. square at the base, and 0·2 in. square at the top. They were found together in a small pit in the northern slope of Area J in Squares Q 29/11, 12, 16 and 17 at a depth of 2 ft. 6 in. b.s. in Stratum V.

Yonis (Pl. CXVII, 2, 3, 6, 16 and 17, and Pl. LXXXIII, 20-21).

The large undulating *yoni* rings of stone Nos. 2, 6 and 16 and the round ring No. 3, have already been described in the account of Trench B.[1] To these may be added No. 17, which is a typical example of miniature rings of the same class. It is of imitation carnelian etched in white with a series of dotted within linear heart-shaped patterns. Restored diameter 1·5 in., ht. 0·9 in. Mound F, Trench IV, Square I 13/16; Depth 2 ft. 6 in. b.s.; Stratum I. **Imitation carnelian.**

Among other small undulating rings of the same kind, No. 96 (unillustrated) fits exactly on to the base of No. 42 (11806) in Pl. LXXXIII. This latter I take to be a *lingam*. Its shaft is holed through and etched round with trefoil patterns in white, and a quatrefoil rosette at the base. No. 96 was found in Mound F, Trench I, Square M 12/14 at a depth of 7 ft. 2 in. b.s. in Stratum III, and No. 11806 in Mound AB, Trench at the Southern Edge, Square Q 28/6 at a depth of 11 ft. 6 in. b.s. in Stratum IV.

Quatrefoil cones (Pl. LXXXIII, 20 and 21).

The two quatrefoil cones with flat bases illustrated in Pl. LXXXIII, 20 and 21 may also have been *yonis*[2]. Such cones are commonly made of alabaster and measure 2·35 to 3·2 in. in height, by 2·5 to 3 in. in diameter across the base, and are pierced through the centre with a cylindrical hole 0·9 to 1·1 in. in diameter. They also have in the centre of one of the foils a tubular drill hole 0·6 to 0·8 in. in diameter of which the purpose is not clear.

No. 20 is of alabaster and No. 21 (PII-20) of red sandstone. This latter is the best finished and best preserved example at Harappā. It measures 3·2 in. high by 3 in. across the base, 0·9 in. across the central hole and 0·6 in. across the side hole. Mound AB, Extension of Pits I and II; Depth 5 ft. b.s.; Stratum II.

Ring-bases and pedestals (Pl. LXXXIII, 8-10, 23 and 25, Pl. CXXIV, 33, and Pl. CXXII, 29).

Ring-bases and pedestals are of three kinds:—

(*a*) Rings with cavetto sides and flat base.

(*b*) Discs with convex body and flat base.

(*c*) Thick rings with flat top and base.

Bases of Type *a* are found in stone and copper. The only copper example is illustrated in Pls. CXXIV, 33 and CXXII, 29, and is described on p. 385 *infra*. The stone ones being all fragmentary are not illustrated, the following are typical.

---

[1] See p. 140 *supra*.

[2] *Cf. M. I. C.*, pp. 61-63.

No. 4570 is of grey sandstone mottled white and red. It is 8·4 in. in diameter, 3 in. across the hole, and 1·4 in. high. Mound AB, Extension of Pits I and II, Square P 24/23; Depth 4 ft. 9 in. b.s.; Stratum II.

No. B1396 is of buff-coloured limestone. It is 5·3 in. in diameter, 3 in. across the hole and 0·5 in. high. Mound AB, Trench B; Depth 17 ft. b.s.; Stratum IV.

No. 3583 is of grey limestone and measures 1·3 in. high and 5·5 and 2·5 in., respectively, in diameter and across the hole. Mound F, Trench I; from spoil earth.

The above bases would be suitable for the support of stone dishes like those illustrated in *M. I. C.*, Pl. CI, 20, 21, 24-26, etc. The Mohenjo-daro ring-stands Nos. 33 and 36 illustrated in the same plate would be more appropriate for large vessels with pointed bottoms.

Type b (Pl. LXXXIII, 8-10). Pedestals of this type are exclusively of alabaster; one of the same substance is illustrated in *M. I. C.*, Pl. CXXXIII, 18. [1]

Description. No. 8 (PIII-74) has a shallow socket on top, 1·3 in. in diameter, and 0·2 in. deep, and three equidistant holes, 0·4 in. deep in the underside for attachment (*cf.* Pl. LXXXIII, 9). It measures 3·5 in. across the base and 1·2 in. high. Mound AB, Pit III; Depth 9 ft. b.s.; Stratum IV.

Nos. 9 (PIII-56) and PIII-95 (unillustrated) are similar and almost exactly of the same size as No. 8. The former was found in Mound AB, Pit III at a depth of 8 ft. 3 in. b.s. in Stratum IV; the latter was found near No. 8.

No. 10 (5228) is also of alabaster, and differs from Nos. 8 and 9 in having a hollowed projection on top instead of a round depression. It measures 1 in. high and 2·7 in. across the base. Mound AB, Extension of Pits I and II, Square Q 24/1; Depth 7 ft. b.s.; Stratum III.

Type c (Pl. LXXXIII, 23 and 25). Rings of this type are of alabaster and of common occurrence.

No. 23 (3340) is 2 in. in diameter and 1·05 in. thick. The photograph shows its underside where the diameter of the hole is only 0·5 in.; on the other side the hole widens out to 0·9 in. It may have been used as a pedestal for a vase with pointed base. Mound F, Great Granary Area, Square I 9/23; Depth 16 ft. 6 in. b.s.; Stratum VII.

No. 25 (540) is 2 in. in diameter; the diameter of its hole as well as its thickness are both 0·9 in. Mound F, Trench I, Square M 12/18; Depth 1 ft. b.s.; Stratum I.

Caps (Pl. LXXXII, 11, and LXXXIII, 13).

Shell caps, often hemispherical, with a circular hole through the apex are as common at Harappā as at Mohenjo-daro. Their purpose, however, is not clear. At Harappā, there are a few examples which are a quarter of a hemisphere. From Mohenjo-daro Dr. Mackay[2] has described one example in which the hemisphere is made up of three pieces.

---

[1] For description *see* p. 479.

[2] *Ibid.*, Pl. CLVI, 13.

No. 11 (2160) in Pl. LXXXII is half of a hemisphere similar to Nos. 16-18 in *M. I. C.*, Pl. CLVI. It is 2·4 in. across the base. Mound F, Great Granary Area, Square I 8/10; Depth 4 ft. b.s.; Stratum II.

No. 13 (2438) in Pl. LXXXIII is of polished yellow Jaisalmer limestone. It is 7 in. across the base and pierced through the centre with a hole 1·05 in. square. At the base, where the core narrows from 1·1 in. to 0·7 in., it is smoothly dressed and pierced with three equidistant tubular drill holes each 0·4 in. deep. The central hole was probably meant for a square shaft intended to support a cap or finial; the small holes in the smooth base suggest that it was fitted to another member with equally smooth surface. Mound F, Great Granary Area, Square I 7/10; Depth 5 ft. b.s.; Stratum II. **Tubular drill sockets.**

Ladles and cups (Pl. LXXXII, 3 and 4; 2, 5 and 6).

Numerous ladles of shell and a few of pottery modelled in imitation have been found at Harappā. Their length, including the handles, varies from 2·0 to 7·2 in. The largest example from Harappā No. Ae14 is illustrated in *A. S. R.*, 1924, Pl. XXVII, *e*. **Ladles of shell.**

No. 3 (5805) is one of the smallest examples, 2 in. long. Mound F, Trench III, Square N 10/1; Depth 8 ft. 8 in. b.s.; Stratum IV.

No. 4 (156) is 2·4 in. long. Mound F, Great Granary Area, Square J 8/25; Depth 8 ft. b.s.; Stratum IV.

No. 4879 (unillustrated) is similar to the pottery example illustrated in *M. I. C.*, Pl. CXXXIII, 12. It is 5·2 in. long. Mound AB, Extension of Pits I and II, Square P 24/18; Depth 10 ft. 3 in. b.s.; Stratum IV. Pottery dippers of this shape are occasionally given a flat base. **Pottery.**

No. 6 (2714) is a plain, oval cup of shell and the only example of its kind from Harappā. Its outer conical processes have been rubbed smooth and the whole thing is neatly cut and finished. It is 5·3 in. long by 3·75 in. broad. Mound AB, Extension of Pits I and II, Square R 24/11; Depth 9 ft. b.s.; Stratum IV. **Cups.**

No. 2 (1640) is a large flattish cup with thick, undulating edge from which it thins down on the inside. It is the largest piece of shell found at Harappā. On its underside are numerous holes which almost hide the radial ribs. It is 7 in. long and 5·3 in. broad. Mound F, Trench I, Square M 10/10; Depth 9 ft. b.s.; Stratum IV. **Scallop shell.**

No. 5 (2973) is a mussel shell with prominent radial ribs. It is 2·8 in. long, 2·5 in. broad and 1·2 in. high. Mound F, Trench III, Square M 9/25; Depth 2 ft. 6 in. b.s.; Stratum I. **Mussel shells.**

No. H393 (unillustrated) is another mussel shell with much finer radial ribs. Its outer surface is divided into three portions by two latitudinal joints. It measures 2·2 in. long, 2·4 in. wide and is 1·3 in. high. Its shell is much thinner than that of No. 5 and in spite, therefore, of its being a little smaller its capacity is slightly larger. Cemetery H, Eastern Section, Square S 34/5; Depth 6 ft. 4 in. b.s.; Stratum II.

Bivalve example. No. E25 (unillustrated) is a small, fossilised bivalve mussel shell. It is 1·1 in. long and 1 in. both in width and height. Mound AB, Ravine near Trench B; Depth 3 ft. b.s.; Stratum I.

Earthenware flesh-rubbers.

Shape and fabric. Nos. 3 and 11-13 in Pl. LXXI appear to have been earthenware flesh-rubbers. Of these, Nos. 11-13 are hollow and roughly barrel-shaped; No. 11 is flat at both ends, whereas Nos. 12 and 13 are flat only at the base. The upper end is holed in all cases. Some of them, *e.g.*, No. 11, are very coarse, the clay of which they are made being mixed with a disproportionately large quantity of sand; others are made of finer clay to which a rough surface was given by dipping them in a gummy solution of earth and sand. This is clearly seen in the worn surfaces of Nos. 12 and 13 the core of which is quite soft. In the upper part of No. 12 finger striations are seen along the edge of the photograph. Some of the unillustrated examples are shaped like long barrels, but with the exception of Nos. 11 and 819 (unillustrated) which are flat at both ends and handmade, all others are wheel-turned, hollow and light. Similar examples are illustrated in *M. I. C.*, Pl. CXXXIII, 13 and 14.

Examples. No. 11 (930) has been used so much that it has become almost four-sided. It is 5·8 in. long, 3·25 in. in diameter at the middle and 1·3 in. across the ends. Mound F, Great Granary Area, Square J 9/22; Depth 5 ft. b.s.; Stratum II.

Nos. 12 and 13 (3818) were found together. In both, the outer sandy coating has been rubbed down by friction over a part of the surface and the softer core exposed. They are 6·4 and 6·8 in. long, 3·5 in. each in diameter at the middle, and 1·4 and 1·9 in. across the flat base. Mound AB, Extension of Pits I and II, Square Q 23/10; Depth 6 ft. b.s.; Stratum II.

Rasp. No. 3 (3844) is a flat, handled rasp with notched depressions. Its surface is much rubbed and it was fast becoming unfit for use. This is the only example of a rasp from Harappā. L. 7 in., w. 2·4 in. Mound AB, Extension of Pits I and II, Square P 24/23; Depth 1 ft. b.s.; Stratum I.

Lamps (Pl. LXXI, 81-88).

High-backed lamps. Nos. 81 and 82 appear, from the marks of burning, to have been lamps. They are of rectangular shape with high backs and, as far as I am aware, unique of their kind. No. 81 (560) is 4·5 in. long, 4 in. high and 2 in. wide. Mound F, Trench I, Square M 12/16; Depth 6 ft. 7 in. b.s.; Stratum III. No. 82 (7304) is 4·75 in. long, 3·3 in. high and 2·1 in. wide. Mound AB, Extension of Pits I and II, Square P 23/15; Depth 4 ft. b.s.; Stratum II.

Four-pointed lamp. No. 83 (Bg4) is a four-pointed, pedestalled lamp rising from the centre of a saucer-shaped container. In shape it anticipated the modern *patīl-soz* or *shamādān* which is usually made of brass and rises from the centre of a broad dish-like pedestal. It is 2·3 in. high and 2·6 in. long from point to point, the diameter of its cup-like container being 4 in. Mound AB, Trench B; Depth 2 ft. b.s.; Stratum IV.

No. 84 (G6) is also a pedestalled lamp but the wick-channel is broken. It was pierced below the edge with three holes of which only one has survived. It is 2·75 in. high, 3 in. in diameter and 2·5 in. across the base. Area G, Trench II, Square AM 41/24; Depth 1 ft. b.s.; Stratum I. **Pedestalled lamp.**

Nos. 85 (12651), 86 (12650) and 12701 (unillustrated) are identical in shape and the only examples of long-stemmed lamps. In each case, the shaft is fluted horizontally and the oil cup is quite small; the lower part is broken. The cup of No. 86 is 3 in. in diameter; the diameter of the shaft in each case is 1·8 in. Nos. 85 and 86 were found together in Mound F, Trench IV, Square J 13/1 at a depth of 4 ft. 2 in. b.s. in Stratum II. **Lamps with fluted stems.**

No. 87 (12387f) is an unusual cylindrical lamp with closed top and oval spout for the wick. It is underburnt, and of greyish colour; 2·8 in. high and 2·25 in. in diameter. It was part of a large find from Mound AB, Trench at the Southern Edge, Squares Q 29/11, 12, 16 and 17; Depth 2 ft. 6 in. to 4 ft. 6 in. b.s.; Stratum V. **Spouted example.**

No. 88 (A419) is a pedestalled lamp with four equidistant, holed lugs; 1·7 in. high and 3·75 in. across. Mound F, Trench A; Depth 3 ft. b.s.; Stratum I. **Lug-handled lamp.**

Ordinary *chiraghs* have also been found in large numbers; they are too well known to require notice. **Ordinary chiraghs.**

Feeding cups (Pl. LXXI, 89-90).

No. 89 (12387e) is of unique shape with pear-shaped bowl and a very narrow spout, 0·15 in. in diameter. It is ill-burnt and of smoky colour; 4·75 in. long and 3·1 in. high. The spout is broken at the end. It was found along with No. 87 described above.

No. 90 (4127) has a long, curved spout attached at the base. It is particularly interesting in that it was recovered at a depth of 21 ft. in association with the VIIIth or earliest stratum in Mound F. A precisely similar vessel has been described as a neo-Babylonian lamp by Professor S. Langdon,[1] but that is of a much later date. Similar feeding cups of metal with oblique spout are still being extensively used in Northern India. Ht. 1·9 in.; L. 4·6 in. Mound F, Trench I, Square M 11/23.

Screens (Pl. LXXII, 27-29).

No stone screens have been recovered at Harappā; the examples described below are of earthenware.

The broken screen No. 27 (12609) comprises a rectangular sunk panel at one side with probably a corresponding panel at the other and between them two rows of open bars, divided horizontally by a narrow sunk panel. 7·75 in. wide and 1 in. thick. Mound F, Trench IV, Square J 13/2; Depth 1 ft. b.s.; Stratum I. **Perforated screens.**

No. 28 (J58) is the fragment of a rectangular frame painted green on the outside; its inner edge is thinner than the main border. 1·5 in. wide and

[1] *Excavations at Kish*, Pl. XXV, 2.

0·65 in. thick. Area J, Trench III, Square S 30/6; Depth 5 ft. 9 in. b.s.; Stratum II.

No. 29 (12390) is a rectangular screen broken diagonally. It is pierced with an irregular pattern based on the familiar scheme of intersecting circles. 7·4 in. long; 5·75 in. wide and 0·7 in. thick. Mound AB, Trench at the Southern Edge, Square Q 29/17; Depth 3 ft. b.s.; Stratum I.

Tile. No. 26 (8100) in Pl. LXXII is a well-baked, rectangular tile incised somewhat irregularly with a series of straight and oblique lines. It shows no signs of wear. 10 in. long by 8·75 in. wide and 1·25 in. thick. Mound F, Trench IV, Square I 12/2; Depth 5 ft. 10 in. b.s.; Stratum II.

Chakalās(?).

Two large earthenware discs, each with three equidistant, short feet near the edge have been found at Harappā. Probably, they were meant for rounding *chapātīs* like the similar discs of stone or wood now used for that purpose. Both specimens are handmade and of coarse clay with choppings of straw freely mixed. They were first dried in the sun and then lightly baked. In both, the feet were added afterwards. No such discs have yet been found at Mohenjo-daro.

No. 12691 (unillustrated) is 12·75 in. in diameter, 1·9 in. high and 0·9 in. thick. Mound F, Trench IV, Square J 13/7; Depth 2 ft. 10 in. b.s.; Stratum I.

No. 4 in Pl. CII is broken into three pieces and is slightly larger than the preceding, being 13·75 in. in diameter, 1·8 in. high and 1 in. thick. A pictogram is inscribed near one of its legs.

Door pivots (Pl. LXXII, 39-43).

Brick pivots. Door pivots were frequently made of brick, but sometimes also of fairly large sized stones or of discoid pebbles. The brick examples illustrated in Pl. LXXII, 39-43 are rectangular, hemispherical or rectangular with one end rounded. Their size ranges between 9·7 by 5 by 2·5 in. and 10·6 by 5·5 by 2·6 in., and they have evidently been chiselled from bricks of the usual size, *viz.*, 11 by 5·5 by 2·5 to 3 in. The diameter of their sockets varies from 1·5 to 3·5 in. and the depth from 0·65 to 1·5 in.

No. 39 (1479)—the best dressed example—is rounded at the pivot end. It measures 9·7 in. long. Mound F, Trench III, Square N 9/9; Depth 7 ft. 3 in. b.s.; Stratum III.

No. 40 (3222) is 10·3 in. long. Mound F, Great Granary Area, Square I 9/4; Depth 3 ft. b.s.; Stratum I.

Nos. 41 (881) and 42 (5927) are both broken but their pivot holes are intact. No. 41 measures 5·75 in. square by 2·5 in. thick. Mound F, Trench I, Square M 11/17; Depth 6 ft. 10 in. b.s.; Stratum III. No. 42 is 5 in. wide and 2 in. thick. Mound AB, Extension of Pits I and II, Square P 24/8; Depth 8 ft. b.s.; Stratum IV.

Hemispherical. No. 43 (unmarked) is the only example of hemispherical shape. It is 5·2 in. in diameter and 2·7 in. high.

Drain channels (Pl. LXXII, 48 and 49).

The few drain channels that have been found are rectangular in section and either made of coarse earthenware (with straw profusely mixed with the clay) or carved out of brick.

No. 48 (1462) is of coarse earthenware. It is heavily fired and coated with a white slip. Being broken, the exact width or length of this channel cannot be given; its height is 2·4 in. and th. 0·7 in. Mound F, Great Granary Area, Square I 9/24; Depth 4 ft. 6 in. b.s.; Stratum II.

No. 49 (Af160) is carved from a brick measuring 10·5 by 5·4 by 2 in. Its channel section is 3 by 0·9 in. Mound F, Trench Af; Depth 4 ft. 10 in. b.s.; Stratum II. It was found projecting from a paved bath; beneath it was a jar for receiving the water.

No. 2627 (unillustrated) is only one half of a carefully moulded pottery channel. Its thickness varies from 1 to 0·9 in., one side being 3·5 in. Mound F, Great Granary Area, Square J 7/10; Depth 7 ft. 10 in. b.s.; Stratum III.

Miscellaneous objects.

Ballista(?) balls of roughly rounded chert (Pl. CXVII, 59 and 60) or pottery, sling balls of pottery, exclusively of the round type, and spindle whorls—mostly of pottery though sometimes also of shell and faience have been recovered in fairly large numbers at Harappā. They are in all respects similar to those described by Dr. Mackay in *M. I. C.*, Chapter XXIV, and need not be described again.

CHAPTER XIV.

PART I

The Sources, Composition, and Technique of Copper and its Alloys, *by Khan Bahadur Mohammad Sana Ullah, M.Sc., F.C.S., Archæological Chemist in India.*

Further Investigations.

The remarks regarding the composition, sources and technique of metals, which have appeared already in *M. I. C.*,[1] apply also to similar finds which have been made at Harappā. Further light, however, has since been thrown on these problems as a result of additional investigations and analyses of objects from the latter site. The most important discovery of metallic antiquities that has so far been made at this site, is that of lot No. 277,[2] comprising a large hoard of copper and bronze implements and other objects of daily use, all in an exceptionally fine state of preservation. These were contained in a copper pot, securely covered with an inverted dish which has prevented the infiltration of saline earth and water into the vessel throughout the long period of its inhumation. Consequently, the objects found inside have suffered only superficially from oxidation and the original marks of tools or of wear and tear have been faithfully preserved on them. For this reason these specimens lend themselves specially well for the study of composition and microscopic structure, as well as of the technique employed by the craftsmen of the Indus Valley.

Chemical Analyses.

The chemical composition of a number of typical specimens of copper and bronze from Harappā, which include seven from this lot, are given in the following table :—

Chemical Analyses of Copper and its Alloys found at Harappā.

(By Khan Bahadur Mohammad Sana Ullah, M.Sc., F.C.S.)

Serial No.	Description of specimen.	Copper.	Tin.	Antimony.	Arsenic.	Lead.	Nickel.	Iron.	Zinc.	Total.	Remarks.
1	Spear-head No. J125 .	97·66	0·33	..	0·06	0·70	0·14	1·11	..	100·00	C. O.
2	Saw Lot No. 277g/2 . .	98·12	0·33	..	0·65	0·10	0·39	0·41	..	100·00	U. M.
3	Fragment Lot No. 277 .	98·50	0·07	..	0·66	tr.	0·26	0·41	..	100·00	U. M.
4	Lance-head Lot No. 277e/2	98·69	0·10	..	0·68	tr.	0·40	0·13	..	100·00	U. M.
5	Folded sheet Lot No. 277 .	97·69	0·16	tr.	1·19	0·85	0·05	0·07	..	100·00	U. M.
6	Celt Lot No. 277a/19 .	98·37	0·00	..	1·40	0·11	0·10	0·02	..	100·00	U. M.
7	Needle No. 11659 . .	92·35	0·29	..	2·96	3·72	0·21	0·20	0·07	100·00	U. M.
8	Dagger	90·05	0·00	..	6·58	2·80	0·18	0·39	..	100·00	U. M.
9	Rectangular Rod No. 5133	97·20	0·84	0·19	0·70	0·00	0·09	0·98	..	100·00	C. O.
10	Chisel Lot No. 277b/3 .	94·92	3·60	..	0·60	0·20	0·29	0·39	..	100·00	U. M.
11	Chisel No. B1754 . .	92·61	6·43	0·31	0·36	tr.	0·20	0·09	..	100·00	P. O.
12	Dagger No. 4255 . .	91·87	6·42	..	0·26	0·98	tr.	0·47	..	100·00	C. O.
13	Dagger No. 1206 . .	91·00	6·76	0·44	0·04	0·88	0·14	0·74	..	100·00	C. O.
14	Celt Lot No. 277a/21 .	91·10	7·85	tr.	0·42	tr.	0·22	0·41	..	100·00	U. M.
15	Awl No. Af150 . .	88·38	9·16	0·42	0·40	0·10	0·17	1·37	..	100·00	C. O.
16	Chisel X	87·42	10·45	..	1·10	0·52	0·17	0·34	..	100·00	U. M.

(NOTE.—U. M.—Unaltered Metal. C. O.—Completely oxidized. P. O.—Partly oxidized. Sulphur is frequently present in minute quantities.)

[1] pp. 481-8.

[2] See pp. 85ff. *supra*, also Pl. CXXIII, excepting No. 34, and Pl. CXXIV, Nos. 1-21 and 23-25.

Characteristics of Indus Valley Copper.

The study of impurities which may be present in ancient metals has assumed special importance recently, as some of these are characteristic of the ores themselves and therefore serve as clues in determining their different sources.[1] It is to be noted, therefore, that these objects contain generally an appreciable and sometimes considerable proportions of arsenic, besides a small amount of nickel. Lead is either absent or much below 1 per cent.; but specimens with higher proportions are met with occasionally. In the 48 Indus Valley specimens which have been analysed so far, in our laboratory, these elements are distributed as follows:—

	Per cent.	Per cent.
Arsenic	0— ·3 in 19;	·3—·5 in 5:
	·5—1·0 in 10;	1—2 in 7;
	2—7 in 7.	
Nickel	0— ·2 in 22;	·2—·5 in 18;
	·5—1·0 in 6;	1·0—1·5 in 2.
Lead	*nil* in 15;	0— ·5 in 14;
	·5—1 in 12:	1—3 in 4;
	3—5 in 2:	32 in 1.

From the above it will be seen that nickel is generally below ·5 per cent. and seldom exceeds 1 per cent., but the proportion of arsenic is relatively higher and sometimes excessive. The Sumerian copper also contains similar proportions of nickel but it can be distinguished from the Indus Valley metal by its practical freedom from arsenic.[2]

Sources of copper.

In *M. I. C.*[3] mention has been made of the more important copper mines in India and the neighbouring countries, which, there is reason to believe, were being worked in ancient times. Through the kindness of the Geological Survey of India, ores from some of these sources have been made available for examination, and it has been found that the samples from Khetri, Alwar, Singhbhūm and Afghānistān contain both nickel and arsenic, while those from Bilaspur and Nellore are entirely free from nickel. These specimens may be regarded as representing the various groups of copper mines distributed over Rājputāna Bihār, Central Provinces, the Deccan and Afghānistān. The Rājputāna mines are not only the nearest of all to Harappā and Mohenjo-daro, but also fulfil the test for the key elements, *i.e.*, nickel and arsenic. It is very likely, therefore, that these mines supplied the bulk of the metal for the Indus Valley.

The extensive remains of ancient workings and heaps of slag in some of these mines[4] indicate the existence of a flourishing copper industry in early India and the discovery of numerous prehistoric implements and other objects of copper at many places (notably at Bālāghāt) beides Mohenjo-daro and Harappā, points to the same conclusion. Indeed there is abundant evidence, as we shall see, that the early Indians made notable advance not only in the metallurgy of pure copper but also in that of its alloys with tin and arsenic. Remains of ancient workings also occur in Balūchistān, Afghānistān and Irān,[5] and Frankfort has

[1] Harold Peake, *The Copper Mountains of Magan*; *Antiquity*, Dec. 1928, pp. 452-7.

[2] Desch, *Report of the British Association for the Advancement of Science*, 1928, pp. 437-41; *Ibid.*, 1929, pp. 264-65; *Ibid.*, 1930, pp. 267-68; *Ibid.*, 1931, pp. 269-72.

[3] Pp. 483 and 676.

[4] T. H. D. La Touche, *A Bibliography of Indian Geology and Physical Geography*, Part II, pp. 113-37.

[5] Curzon, *Persia*, p. 519.

pointed out that there must have been an important centre of metal working somewhere south of the Caucasus, with which the Sumerians were in close touch.[1]

Sources of Tin. As to the source of tin, I have to repeat what has been said in the volume on Mohenjo-daro that there were ancient tin mines in Khorāsān and Kārādāgh district in Northern Irān and that it is very probable that India drew her main supply of tin from those regions.[2] However, it has been suggested recently that the earliest supplies of tin may have been derived from the alluvial deposits of Cassiterite which were used up without leaving any evidence of the operations behind.[3] It is quite conceivable that such alluvial deposits may have existed once in certain parts of India where only traces of the ore occur now and which were consumed by the ancients. In particular, the tin mines of Hazāribāgh, though poor at present, may have been quite rich and formed an important source of the metal in the earliest times. In support of this view, it is noteworthy that several objects of bronze have been discovered in the 'Asur' graves which are scattered all over this part of the country and within measurable distances from these mines.[4]

Copper Implements. Small amounts of tin, arsenic, antimony, lead, nickel and iron which have been found in specimens of copper from Harappā, imply impurities derived from the ores and not intentional additions for any specific purpose. However, all these foreign elements influence the working properties of copper in varying degrees and add to its hardness or strength; but the effect produced by tin is very marked. If copper containing even such small amounts as 1 to 3 per cent. of tin is hammered in the cold, its hardness and strength are considerably increased, as compared with pure copper.[5] This property was turned to account by the ancients for improving the cutting edges of their implements, and it explains the serviceable qualities of celts, knives, spear-heads, etc., fashioned out of unalloyed copper or poor grade bronze, which have been found abundantly at these sites. Most of the objects in the find (Harappā No. 277) bear distinct evidence of hammering along their cutting edges which was undoubtedly done to harden and improve their durability.

Bronze and Bronze Forging. It is generally accepted that 'bronzes containing 8-11 per cent. of tin are the most suitable when a combination of strength, elasticity, toughness, and ability to withstand shock are required.[6]' It is, therefore, interesting to find that among the Harappā specimens the proportion of tin in the celts or chisels does not exceed 11 per cent., the only apparent exception noted so far being a completely oxidized specimen with 12·38 per cent. tin. The celts and certain other objects were probably cast, as they do not seem to have been subjected to much hammering except along their cutting edges. Seeing that bronze containing 4-8 per cent. tin can be forged only by frequent annealing, and that higher grades (with over 8 per cent. tin), owing to their brittleness, have to be worked at dull red

---

[1] Frankfort, *Sumerians, Semites, and the Origin of Copper-working*; *Antiquaries Journal*, Apr. 1928, VIII, pp. 217-35.

[2] *M. I. C.*, p. 483.

[3] Rickard, *Man and Metals*, p. 344.

[4] Sarat Chander Roy, *Distribution and Nature of Asur Sites in Chota Nagpur*, *J. B. & O. R. S.*, Sept. 1920, pp. 393-423.

[5] Rickard, *op. cit.*, p. 131.

[6] E. F. Law, *Alloys*, p. 153.

heat, it is clear that the ancient craftsmen of the Indus Valley must have been fully conversant with the art of casting and forging bronze whether for implements or for the more elaborate objects of daily use. This conclusion has been fully confirmed by the evidence derived from metallographic examination of the bronzes, for which we are specially indebted to Mr. E. A. Wraight, Metallurgical Inspector, Indian Stores Department, Tatanagar.[1]

The extent to which tin was mixed with copper in the various grades of bronze in use at Harappā and Mohenjo-daro is apparent from the analyses of 48 specimens, in which the percentage of tin was found to be as follows:—

	Per cent.	Per cent.
Tin	0—1 in 28;	1—4 in 3;
	4—8 in 7;	8—11 in 6;
	11—14 in 4.	

Bornze Casting. Bronze casting was undoubtedly practised, but the art does not appear to have made any great advance at Harappā. It is very probable that this was due primarily to the high cost of tin (*vide infra*) which must be added in liberal proportions to produce good casting bronze. Moreover, the advantages of the addition of lead to bronze for casting purposes had evidently not been realised, since none of the bronze objects which have been examined so far, contain appreciable proportion of lead. *Cire perdue* process was probably unknown.

Soldering. No direct proof of the use of solder for joining copper is yet available as all the utensils are in an advanced state of oxidation; but there is little doubt that soldering was well known to the Indus people, and it is very likely that a simple tin solder or its alloy with lead, was employed for this purpose. We possess definite evidence that soldering of both gold and silver, which is a more difficult process, was commonly practised by them.

Copper-Arsenic Alloys. A small amount of arsenic occurs frequently in ancient copper as a natural impurity derived from the ores employed. However, the arsenic content of the copper objects found in the Indus Valley is often considerable, as noted above, so that specimens over 1 per cent. of this element are not uncommon. The maximum amount, found so far, is 6·58 per cent., as revealed by the analysis of a dagger from Harappā. These arsenic-rich alloys are comparable with low grade bronze in hardness and strength, but can be worked either in the cold or hot state.[2] It is, therefore, not surprising that these were also employed sometimes for tools and weapons. Similar copper-arsenic alloys were in use in China Egypt, Turkestan and Cyprus in very early times.

Scarcity of Tin. The employment of virtually pure copper or of copper containing only a small proportion of tin for most of the tools and weapons, is striking enough to indicate the difficulty of obtaining tin in the Indus Valley in the 4th and 3rd Millenia B. C. Scraps of bronze carefully stored in copper vessels which have been discovered at Harappā and Mohenjo-daro along with valuable implements also point to the precious nature of this commodity. Dr. Plenderleith has come to the conclusion that this scarcity also affected Sumer and that bronze manufacture

[1] Appendix, pp. 382-83 *infra*.

[2] Gregg, *Arsenical and Argentiferous Copper*, pp. 94 and 154.

died out there about c. 2700 B. C.[1] This was the reason evidently why bronze did not come into regular use in Egypt before the 18th Dynasty (c. 1600 B. C.). Whether the deposits of tin known at that time ran out or the supply was cut off owing to some political or other causes, is a question that we have no means of answering.

APPENDIX.

Report of the Metallography of two Ancient Bronze Specimens found at Harappā, by Mr. E. A. Wraight, A.R.S.M., M.I.M.M., F.I.C., Metallurgical Inspector, Indian Stores Department, Tatanagar.

Two specimens of Ancient Bronze. The Superintendent, Government Test House, Alipore, forwarded to this office for investigation two samples of "ancient bronze" which he received from the Archæological Chemist, Dehra Dun.

Composition of the Specimens. The Archæological Chemist supplied the following results of chemical analyses on the two bronze specimens:—

	Specimen No. 'X' (chisel).	Specimen No. 277*a*/21 (celt).
Copper per cent.	87·42	91·10
Tin per cent.	10·45	7·85
Arsenic per cent.	1·10	0·42
Lead per cent.	0·52	trace
Nickel per cent.	0·17	0·22
Iron per cent.	0·34	0·41

Photo-Micrographic Examination. The two specimens were polished on one of their edges and when examined under a microscope showed a number of cracks. The specimens were then lightly etched by acid ferric chloride solution, and again examined. Specimen 'X' showed a number of small bluish white areas slightly elongated in one direction in a ground mass of dark colour, while No. 277*a*/21 also showed similar areas, but less in number and not elongated. Polishing scratches on the specimens left no mark on these bluish white areas, showing thereby the presence in them of some harder constituent than the surrounding mass. See photos Nos. 1 and 2 (Pls. CXXVI-CXXVII).

The specimens were then lightly polished after etching and the process repeated several times, until a definite structure of the metal appeared. Photo-micrographs Nos. 3 and 4 (Pls. CXXVI-CXXVII) were obtained on the two samples under a magnification of 10 dia. It will be noticed that the structure of specimen No. 277*a*/21 is dendritic, whereas that of 'X' is very ill-defined at this magnification (10 d.).

The specimens were further etched and polished until the internal grain structure was revealed, which may be seen in photo-micrographs Nos. 5 and 6 (Pls. CXXVI-CXXVII) under a magnification of ×100 dia.

It will be seen that the structures are somewhat different—specimen 'X' showing a regular polygonal structure, but that of 277*a*/21 being less pronouncedly polygonal. A number of striations inside the crystals are apparent in both photo-micrographs.

---

[1] Woolley, *Ur Excavations*, Vol. II, p. 286.

The same specimens were again examined under a magnification of ×500 dia. and photo-micrographs Nos. 7 and 8 (Pls. CXXVI-CXXVII) taken.

It appears from the micro-examination of the two specimens that— **Conclusions.**

(1) 277a/21 is a sample of bronze in the "cast" condition, and it is improbable that it has received any form of heat-treatment. It is possible that a certain amount of cold work may have been effected on this specimen.

(2) 'X' is a sample of bronze in the annealed condition. From the appearance of the specimen under the microscope it is probable that after casting, the metal was subsequently heated and hammered until it reached a low temperature.

PART II.

Copper, Bronze and Silver Utensils and other Metal objects.[1]

Relative scarcity of metal objects.

Despite the fact that copper and bronze objects are found from the earliest strata upwards, they have not been recovered in such large numbers as might have been expected. Outstanding, however, among them is the remarkable group found in the copper jar No. 277 (Pl. CXXIV, 27 and 28) which comprised a hundred examples not only of a very varied character but in a wonderfully good state of preservation. These objects are figured in Pl. CXXIII, 1-33, and 35-67, and in Pl. CXXIV, 1-21 and 23-25. Usually, the copper and bronze utensils unearthed at Harappā are so thoroughly corroded that they are hardly able to withstand chemical treatment. The weapons and implements, too, are also badly corroded, while most of the thinner objects, such as antimony rods, pins, arrow-tips, finger, ear, and nose-rings, etc., are frequently in small bits. Most of these objects have been found in Mounds F and AB, but a fair proportion also, commensurate with the extent of the digging, in Area J. From the Cemetery H there came the single fragmentary spear-head No. H410, and from Area G only one bit of copper and another rectangular piece. Perhaps the fact that these areas are saturated with saltpetre to a greater degree than the higher mounds explains the rarity of metal objects now left in them.

See Pls. CXXIII and CXXIV.

Variety of tools, implements, etc.

That there was a large variety of copper and bronze tools, implements, weapons and utensils in use at Harappā, is revealed by the contents of the copper jar No. 277. Those illustrated in Pl. CXXIII comprise thirteen blade-axes with or without shoulders (Nos. 1-13), eight long and narrow axes (Nos. 14-21), two double-axes (Nos. 22 and 23), eleven daggers with tapering sides and with or without curved tips (Nos. 24-32, and 64-65), one mace-head (No. 33), thirteen spear-heads and flaying knives (Nos. 35-47), one lance-head (No. 66), one arrow-head (No. 63), one chopper (No. 67), two saws (Nos. 61 and 62), ten chisels with or without shanks (Nos. 49-58), two cast bars for making chisels (Nos. 59 and 60), and a flat strip (No. 48). Other objects forming part of the same group are

---

[1] This part has been written by the author.

illustrated in Pl. CXXIV. These are a stilus (No. 19), a beam of a weighing scale (No. 14), a semi-oval, hollow terminal (No. 20), five solid bangles (Nos. 1, 2, 3, 5 and 7), a rod intended to be fashioned into a solid bangle (No. 4), three hollow bangles (Nos. 11-13), two flattened leaves broader at the centre than at the ends and destined to be made into hollow bangles (Nos. 8 and 9), and two more flattened but thicker strips (Nos. 6 and 10) showing still earlier stages in the process of manufacturing these hollow bangles. In addition to these there were recovered from the same jar, four thick rectangular copper pieces (Nos. 15-18), a thin bowl with tapering sides (No. 23), two large folded sheets of copper (Nos. 24 and 25), two thick broken pieces bearing prominent hammer marks (No. 21), several thick pieces (not illustrated), and a small lump of löllingite.[1] The presence of löllingite is particularly interesting as arsenic may have been extracted from it and used for hardening the cutting edges of tools instead of the tin alloy. A detailed description of the above hoard will be found on pp. 86—90, Chapter II *supra.*

Description of copper, bronze and silver utensils other than those from the copper jar No. 277.

See Pl. CXXIV.

Vessels.

Copper jar PII-13. No. 26 (PII-13). See also Pl. CXXII, 24. Carinated copper jar broken through the bottom and originally covered with a shallow inverted dish (Pl. CXXII, 32) similar to Nos. 30 and 31 in Pl. CXXIV. Its height without the cover is 7·8 in., diameter at mouth 7·7 in., and across the body 11·5 in. Its rim is straight, not concave like that of No. 27 in Pl. CXXIV. It is made in two parts, the upper being lapped on to the lower part by hammering the two together. The joint, owing to lathing, is imperceptible now. The jar contained nothing but pieces of its own cover, and two or three teeth of a wild beast. Mound AB, Pit II; Depth 3 ft. 6 in. b.s.; Stratum II.

Copper vase. Pl. CXXII, 26 (No. 8250) is a round copper vase 6 in. in diameter, and 2·75 in. across the mouth. It has a long straight neck, and shallow projecting bottom. Mound F, Trench V, Square L 12/5; Depth 5 ft. 6 in. b. s.; Stratum II.

Cup. No. 22 (12392C). See also Pl. CXXII, 30. Deep cup with flared mouth and tapering sides raised from sheet metal ·13 in. thick.[2] It is 2·4 in. high and 5·7 in. across the mouth. Mound AB, Trench at the Southern Edge, Square Q 27/24; Depth 11 ft. 6 in. b. s.; Stratum IV.

Dishes. No. 30[3] (7018) is a plain, fragmentary dish pieced together from several much corroded fragments. It has short, straight and tapering sides like the dishes illustrated in *M. I. C.*, Pl. XCL, 9-11. Diameter 8 in., ht. 1·3 in. Mound AB, Extension of Pits I and II, Square Q 24/3; Depth 6 to 8 ft. b. s.; Stratum III.

---

[1] For properties of löllingite, *cf. M. I. C.*, p. 485, and for its sources, *Ibid.*, pp. 684-85.

[2] It is possible that the thickness has been increased by corrosion.

[3] Two very substantial dishes No. 13303 d & e with tapering ends were found in 1936 in the eastward extention of Trench I, Area J, Stratum II. Their diametres are 9·5 & 10·5 in. and ht. 1·5 & 2 in.

No. 31 (7282) is similar to No. 30 but its rim is shorter. It is about a quarter of the original dish, the restored diameter being 8·9 in., and height 1 in. Mound F, Great Granary Area, Western Extension, Square H 9/22; Depth 3 ft. 6 in. b. s.; Stratum II.

No. 34 (11266*a*). See also Pl. CXXII, 31. Saucer with rim slightly incurved. Diam. 4 in. Mound F, Trench VI, Square O 9/20; Depth 4 ft. 6 in. to 5 ft. b. s.; Stratum II. **Saucer.**

No. 32 (10129*a*). See also Pl. CXXII, 27. Copper imitation of a river shell pierced with two holes in the raised rim. A similar object with one hole is illustrated in *M. I. C.*, Pl. CXLI, 7. From a post-cremation urn at a depth of 7 ft. 6 in. below the surface. Mound F, Trench I, Square M 10/15; Stratum III. **Imitation of river shell.**

No. 33 (10824). See also Pl. CXXII, 29. Ring-stand for jar with cavetto moulding. Diam. 3·9 in.; ht. 0·9 in. Mound F, Trench VI, Square P 9/3; Depth 8 in., b. s.; Stratum I. **Jar-stand.**

Implements and weapons.

No. 36 (Ae 342). See also Pl. CXXII, 13. Adze. A similar implement is published in *M. I. C.*, Pl. CXXXIX, 8,[1] and other examples are also known from prehistoric Egypt.[2] It is 8·7 in. long, 2·5 in. broad at the lower edge, and 1·7 in. across the butt end. Its maximum thickness is ·25 in. which tapers down to ·04 in. at the cutting edge and to ·05 in. at the butt end. Probably bronze. Mound F, Trench Ae; Depth 4 ft. 2 in. b. s.; Stratum II. **Adze.**

No. 37 (PII-2) is a tapering blade-axe with rounded edge similar to axes 1-4 in Pl. CXXIII. It is 6·8 in. long, 3·25 in. broad at the cutting edge, and 2·25 in. at the butt end. Its thickness tapers from ·25 to ·05 in. at the edge and to ·15 in. at the butt. Mound AB, Extension of Pits I and II; Depth 1 ft. 3 in. b. s.; Stratum I. **Blade-axe.**

No. 38 (10185*j*). See also Pl. CXXII, 19. Adze inscribed with three faint pictograms on one side. It is 5·15 in. long, 2·15 in. broad at the cutting edge, and 1·4 in. across the upper end. Its thickness tapers from ·2 to ·03 in. at both ends. It was found at a depth of 15 ft. 6 in. below the surface in association with Stratum VI, and is one of the earliest tools from Harappā. Mound F, Trench I, Square M 12/7.

No. 39 (11154) is similar in shape to No. 12 in Pl. CXXIII but has a much burred butt, and seems to have served as a chisel. It is 4·8 in. across the butt end. Its thickness of ·15 in. tapers down to ·04 in. at the cutting edge and to ·07 in. at the butt end. Mound F, Trench IV, Square P 10/1; Depth 8 ft. 4 in. b. s.; Stratum IV. **Chisel.**

No. 40 (12393). See also Pl. CXXII, 18. Lower part of a broken axe possibly socketted as shown in the restoration. The broad edge, though dented, is still very sharp. Width at the cutting edge 3·75 in.; existing length 2·7 in.; and maximum thickness ·23 in. The metal appears to be bronze. Mound AB, Trench at the Southern Edge, Square Q 28/11; Depth 17 ft. 2 in. b. s. Stratum VI. **Socketted (?) axe.**

---

[1] It is described there as a long and narrow axe, see p. 495.

[2] *Cf.* Petrie, *Tools and Weapons*, p. 15, Pl. XVI, 63-64.

Dagger-knives.

Comparative rarity.

Daggers or knives are less numerous than blade-axes, only five examples having been found at Harappā in addition to those which came from the copper jar No. 277. They are all tanged.

No. 45 (12115) has a long convex cutting edge and concave back edge. Part of the cutting edge and tip, which is rejoined, are broken, and the whole is highly corroded. L. 10 in. Mound AB, Trench at the Southern Edge, Square Q 28/12; Depth 15 ft. 6 in. b. s.; Stratum V.

No. 46 (J483) tapers evenly along both edges; its tang is broken. The cutting edge appears to have been resharpened many times. L. 8·15 in. Area J, Trench I, Square Q 30/14; Depth 5 ft. 7 in. b. s.; Stratum IV.

No. 47 (10012) has a long, narrow, and curved tip with double edge and incipient, vertical mid-rib down the centre. It is pierced with two rivet holes. This shape is unique at Harappā and Mohenjo-daro. L. 10·75 in. Mound F, Trench IV, Square I 12/10; Depth 10 ft. b. s.; Stratum IV.

No. 3291 (not illustrated) tapers along both edges and has a long tang. L. 8·55 in. Mound F, Great Granary Area, Western Extension, Square I 9/8; Depth 3 ft. b. s.; Stratum II.

No. 48 (10916) also tapers along both edges and has a short tang. It is highly corroded. L. 11·3 in. Mound F, Trench VI, Square O 10/21; Depth 2 ft. 6 in. b. s.; Stratum I.

Spear-heads.

Spear-heads are relatively common at Harappā. They are of various shapes (see Pl. CXXIII, 36-47 and Pl. CXXV, 65-77), often with long tangs which are sometimes holed for rivets. Generally the tips are pointed; less frequently rounded.

No. 49 (3291) in Pl. CXXIV is unique in having a strengthening mid-rib. There are two holes at the base of the head and a third one at the far end of the tang. L. 8·5 in. Mound F, Great Granary Area, Western Extension, Square I 9/8; Depth 3 ft. b. s.; Stratum II.

See *Pl. CXXV, 65-77.*[1]

No. 65 (J125) is leaf-shaped with symmetrically tapered edges and long tang. It is one of the longest and finest examples from Harappā. L. 10·9 in. Area J, Trench III, Square S 29/15; Depth 8 ft. 10 in. b. s.; Stratum IV.

No. 66 (J220) is broad at the base with thin tip and long tang which is holed at the lower end. Its cutting edge is concave owing to resharpening. L. 7·4 in. Area J, Trench II, Square S 30/8; Depth 5 ft. 6 in. b. s.; Stratum II.

No. 67 (J38) has broad base, sharply tapering to the point, concave edges and long tang. L. 6·4 in. Area J, Trench II, Square S 30/11; Depth 2 ft. b. s.; Stratum I.

---

[1] Some, if not most of the very thin examples, may have been used as flaying knives which were a common necessity for the Indus people who depended so much on animal food. See also p. 87 *supra*.

No. 68 (12001). Similar to the foregoing but smaller and tapering more sharply to the point. The tang, also, which is a little bent, is proportionately longer and thinner for its size. L. 5·87 in. Mound AB, Trench at the Southern Edge, Square Q 28/8; Depth 13 ft. 10 in. b. s.; Stratum IV.

No. 69 (J484). Similar to No. 67 but with sharper point and shorter and broader tang. L. 6·5 in. Area J, Trench I, Square Q 30/14; Depth 5 ft. 7 in. b. s.; Stratum III.

No. 70 (12001). Leaf-shaped and symmetrical like No. 65 with which it was found. L. 6 in.

No. 71 (11858). Similar to foregoing but rounded at base. The tip is broken and the right edge damaged. L. 4·3 in. Mound F, Trench IV, Deep Digging, Square I 13/17 and 18; Depth 13 to 14 ft. b. s.; Stratum V.

No. 72 (J485). Similar to No. 70, but broader at base and with bigger tang. It has three rivet holes, two in the head and one at the lower end of the tang. The former are clumsily punched and unsymmetrically placed. When hafted, little more than the tip would have remained clear of the wood. L. 6·4 in. Area J, Trench I, Square Q 30/14; Depth 5 ft. 7 in. b. s.; Stratum III.

No. 73 (11858). Leaf-shaped with long, broad tang. This is one of the least corroded specimens. A slight concavity at the tip is due to resharpening. The metal appears to be bronze. L. 6·58 in. It was found close to No. 66 and at the same depth.

No. 74 (12177) is of dagger-like form but of thin sheet metal, the middle being hardly thicker than the edges. Base and tang damaged. L. 7·35 in. Mound AB, Trench at the Southern Edge, Square Q 28/12; Depth 15 ft. 6 in. b. s.; Stratum V.

No. 75 (11289) originally tapered evenly on both edges, but one edge is now concave owing to resharpening. This specimen is badly corroded and damaged on both sides. L. 10·4 in. Mound F, Trench VI, Square O 10/17; Depth 7 ft. b. s.; Stratum III.

No. 76 (10008) shows much resharpening in the irregularity of its edges. The tip and tang are broken. On both sides, it retains clear impressions of what appears to have been a bamboo handle. L. 6·5 in. Mound F, Trench V, Square J 12/25; Stratum V. It was found at a depth of 9 to 10 ft. below the surface along with two bovine leg bones and two foreparts of horned skulls underneath a wall of Stratum IV.[1]

No. 77 (10104) is similar in form to No. 66, with a rivet hole at the lower end of its tang. It was pieced together from several fragments, and is badly corroded. L. 9 in. Mound F, Trench I, Square M 10/25; Depth 5 ft. b. s.; Stratum II.

Chisels.

The chisels from Harappā are of three kinds: (*a*) with long flattened shanks, (*b*) small and strong chisels with burred butts used for cutting metals or dressing stone, and (*c*) tanged chisels. Of these, the first two varieties are quite common **Three varieties.**

[1] See p. 78 *supra*.

both at Harappā and Mohenjo-daro.[1] At Harappā, these types are well represented among the contents of the copper jar No. 277[2], but the tanged chisels are rare as only two such examples[3] have been recovered so far, and none is yet published from Mohenjo-daro.

See Pl. CXXV, 15-18 and 22-24.

Type *a*. No. 15 (4384) is a long narrow chisel with flattened shank and splayed edge; its butt is not burred. L. 5·95 in. Mound AB, Extension of Pits I and II, Square Q 24/21; Depth 4 ft. b. s.; Stratum II.

No. 16 (8301) is a thick, flat and short chisel with slightly burred butt. L. 3·45 in. Mound F, Great Granary Area, Eastern Extension, Square J 9/2; Depth 12 ft. b. s.; Stratum IV.

No. 17 (11086) is a flat strip tapering towards the edge and probably intended for a small chisel. L. 3·15 in. Mound F, Trench VI, Square O 10/24; Depth 4 ft. 6 in. b. s.; Straum III.

Type *b*. No. 22 (7830) is a short, thick and strong chisel of Type *b* with splayed edge and burred butt, made from a bar rectangular in section. L. 2·5 in. Mound F, Great Granary Area, Square I 8/20; Depth 9 ft. 8 in. b. s.; Stratum IV.

No. 23 (7016) is similar to No. 22 but is of smaller size. L. 1·85 in. Mound AB, Extension of Pits I and II, Square P 24/24; Depth 7 ft. b. s.; Stratum III.

Type *c*. No. 18 (10719) has a round tang and straight cutting edge. Rare. L. 2·7 in. Mound F, Trench V, Square J 12/23; Depth 5 ft. 6 in. b. s.; Stratum III.

No. 24 (12486) is similar to No. 18. Its tang is shorter. L. 3·75 in. Mound F, Trench I, Square M 12/21; Depth 7 ft. 2 in. b. s.; Stratum III.

Knives and sickles. Pl. CXXV, 28-31, and 52 and 62-64.

Straight edged knives. No. 28 (8960) is a short, broad and straight edged knife with broad tang in which there is a rivet depression but not a hole. L. 2·5 in.; w. ·7 in. Mound F, Trench V, Square L 12/9; Depth 10 ft. 11 in. b. s.; Stratum IV.

No. 30 (10225) is a perfectly straight edged knife with short tang on one side and rounded head. It is well preserved but the edge is corroded. L. 3·3 in. Mound F, Trench IV, Square H 11/25; Depth 7 ft. 2 in. b. s.; Stratum IV.

Curved knives. No. 29 (12113) is the upper part of a curved knife. L. 1·8 in. Mound AB, Trench at the Southern Edge, Square Q 28/11; Depth 15 ft. 6 in. b. s.; Stratum V.

No. 31 (11116*g*) is another curved knife in four pieces. Its tip is not so pointed as that of No. 29. Mound F, Trench VI, Square O 9/23 and P 9/3; Depth 1 to 4 ft. 4 in. b. s.; Strata I and II.

Sickles. No. 52 (4025) looks like a sickle with narrow pointed tip curved back. L. 1·55 in. Area J, Trench I, Square Q 31/17; Depth 5 ft. 10 in. b. s.; Stratum IV.

No. 62 (H661) is also recurved but its tip and lower part are broken. L. 2·45 in. Cemetery H, Eastern Section, Square R 31/14; Depth 3 ft. 3 in. b. s.; Stratum I.

---

[1] *Cf. M. I. C.*, pp. 501-2 and Pl. CXXXVII, 3A, and 8-10.

[2] *Cf.* Pl. CXXIII, 48-58, and Pl. CXXI, 10, 11 and 15-19.

[3] Pl. CXXV, 18 and 24.

No. 63 (J537) is a thin and extremely narrow curved sickle broken at the base. It may have been used for cutting grass or vegetables or for frying grains in the heated sand of a pan on the oven as is still done in India. L. 2·05 in. Mound D, Trench I, Square Q 31/18; Depth 3 ft. 7 in. b. s.; Stratum III.

No. 64 (J551) is the upper part of a sickle with tip curved back. L. 2·15 in.; greatest width ·95 in. Area J, Trench I, Square Q 30/21; Depth 5 ft. b. s.; Stratum IV.

Scrapers. Pl. CXXV, 38 and 58.

No. 38 (11292). See also Pl. CXXII, 16. Flattened scraper with sharp, round edge, upper part broken. L. 3·35 in. Mound F, Trench VI, Square O 9/20; Depth 5 ft. 4 in. b. s.; Stratum III.

No. 58 (2078) is another scraper made of a long, narrow and thin strip with rounded edge. Bent into L shape, upper part broken, but much does not appear to have been lost. L. 4 in. Mound F, Trench III, Square N 9/7; Depth 12 ft. 2 in. b. s.; Stratum V.

Razors. Pl. CXXV, 46 and 47.

No. 46 (12391) is a fine, well-rounded bronze razor similar to the one illustrated in *M. I. C.*, Pl. CXXXVIII, 12. It is much corroded, and its round tang is broken at the lower end. L. 2·5 in.; length across the blade 3 in. Mound AB, Trench at the Southern Edge, Square Q 27/24; Depth 13 ft. 3 in. b. s.; Stratum IV.

No. 47 (2892). See also Pl. CXXII, 17. This is another similar razor, but its form is not fully brought out in the photograph which was taken before treatment. Its tang is 3 in. long and rectangular in section. L. 3·9 in.; length across the blade 2·05 in. Mound F, Great Granary Area, Southern Extension, Square I 9/23; Depth 12 ft. b. s.; Stratum V.

Gouges. Pl. CXXV, 40-42 and 44.

Gouges were used for hollowing out, grooving or ribbing wood, bone, ivory and stone. All of them are of bronze, their cutting edges being either semicircular or approximately so.

No. 40 (12392*a*) is a thin flat strip rounded at the cutting edge into less than a semicircle. L. 4 in. It was found with No. 41 described below.

No. 41 (12392*b*). See also Pl. CXXII, 23. Gouge fitted with an alabaster handle. Its upper part is tubular and the cutting edge three-fourths of a circle. Length together with the handle 5·5 in. Mound AB, Trench at the Southern Edge, Square Q 27/14; Depth 11 ft. 6 in. b. s.; Stratum IV.

Nos. 42 and 43 (8801) are two out of three tools which were found together. Of these, No. 42 is a small gouge, much corroded, while No. 43 is a pointed rod, and the third object (Pl. CXXV, 16) is an equally small chisel.[1] Length of gouge and pointed rod 2·8 in. each. Mound F, Great Granary Area, Eastern Extension, Square I 9/2; Depth 12 ft. b. s.; Stratum IV.

No. 44 (8802) is another gouge similar to No. 42 and was found close to it. Its cutting edge is semicircular. L. 2·8 in.

[1] For its description see p. 388 *supra*.

Nail-parer.

No. 39 (A608) in Pl. CXXV. See also Pl. CXXII, 14. Probably a nail-parer, as it is exactly similar to those now in use in the Panjāb. Square in section. L. 5·05 in. Mound F, Great Granary Area; Depth 11 ft. b. s.; Stratum IV.

Surgical or toilet set.

No. 1 (E3) in Pl. CXXV is a bunch of three bronze instruments[1] held together by their looped and interlaced ends. Of these, the right hand instrument is a double-edged knife damaged by corrosion, the middle one a pair of pincers and the left hand one a piercing rod. Length of knife 4·4 in.;[2] of pincers 5·2 in.; and of piercing rod 5·3 in. Mound AB, Trench in the ravine to south of *Naugazā* tomb; Depth 3 ft. b. s.

Cobbler's awl (?).

No. 32 (825) in Pl. CXXV. See also Pl. CXXII, 21. This looks like a cobbler's awl made of a bar rectangular in section. Near the point is a slight inward cut, perhaps for putting the thread through the leather. The butt end appears to have been let into a handle. L. 4·3 in. Mound F, Great Granary Area, Eastern Extension, Square J 8/24; Depth 10 ft. 6 in b. s.; Stratum IV.

Needles. Pl. CXXV, 37 and 45.

No. 37 (2551) is made of a rectangular bar, but its pointed end, which retains a vestige of the needle's eye, is round in section. The eye being at the point, the stitching was presumably done with two threads. The shaft, which is ·17 by ·13 in. in section, is too thick to have been drawn through the material. L. 3·4 in. Mound AB, Extension of Pits I and II, Square Q 24/14; Depth 9 ft. 9 in. b. s.; Stratum IV.

No. 45 (5678) is made of a round bar, and shows more of the eye than No. 37. Like the latter it has the eye near the point, and was not intended to be drawn bodily through the material. L. 2·2 in. Mound AB, Extension of Pits I and II, Square P 24/25; Depth 5 ft. b. s.; Stratum II.

Pins. Pl. CXXV, 25-27.

Nos. 25-27 (8103, 1879 and 1992) are pins, pointed at both ends and measuring 4, 3·93 and 3·85 in. long, respectively. Nos. 25 and 27 were found in Mound F, in association with Strata II and IV respectively, and No. 26 in Stratum V, Mound AB.

Antimony rods. Pl. CXXV, 33, 34 and 36.

No. 33 (J50) is a plain antimony rod tapering both ways from the centre. L. 4·2 in. Area J, Trench III, Square S 29/14; Depth 4 ft. 1 in. b. s.; Stratum II.

Nos. 34 and 36 (J19) are photographs of the same antimony stopper-rod before and after treatment. Crowning it is a dog biting the ear of a goat. The lower end is broken. L. 4·4 in.; diameter of rod ·2 in. Area J, Trench III, Square S 30/16; Depth 1 ft. b. s.; Stratum I.

---

[1] For similar sets of instruments, *cf.* Petrie, *op. cit.*, p. 52, Pl. LXIV, figs. 48 and 50-53.

[2] Its length appears to have been reduced by corrosion.

Mirror.

No. 29 (12748) in Pl. CXXIV is an oval copper mirror,[1] with long tang. Length including tang 9·75 in.; diams. 6·25 and 7 in. Mound F, Trench V, Square J 13/22; Depth 2 ft. 6 in.; Stratum II.

Fish-hook.

No. 8 (1057) in Pl. CXXV is a fish-hook similar to the examples illustrated in *M. I. C.*, Pl. CXLIII, 24 and 25, but in this specimen the inside barb has disappeared through corrosion. L. 1·75 in.; width across the hook ·9 in. Mound F, Great Granary Area, Eastern Extension, Square J 9/24; Depth 4 ft. 6 in. b. s.; Stratum II.

Arrow-heads. Pl. CXXV, 13 and 14.

No. 13 (J496) is a V-shaped arrow-head of copper without tang or socket. Both ends are broken. L. ·8 in., w. ·55 in. Mound D, Trench I, Square Q 30/15; Depth 7 ft. 4 in. b. s.; Stratum IV.

No. 14 (11488) is similar to No. 13. One barb is entire; the other broken. 1·25 in. long, and 1 in. across. From surface of Square Q 27/18, Mound AB. Another entire arrow-head, which is not illustrated, is 1·15 in. long and 1 in. broad. A similar example is illustrated in *M. I. C.*, Pl. CXLIII, 12.[2] It may be remarked here that the only stone arrow-head from Harappâ is of chert. It is leaf-shaped and illustrated in Pl. CXVIII, 63. For its description see p. 360 *supra.*

Silver vase. Pl. CXXV, 53.

No. 53 (J339). See also Pl. CXXII, 25. Small, open-mouthed silver vase with well-defined base, and thick rim. Shows clear hammer marks both inside and out, the former being more distinct. Ht. 1·13 in.; diam. 1·1 in. Area J, Trench II, Square S 30/8; Depth 9 ft. 9 in. b. s.; Stratum IV. Silver vase.

Hasp.

No. 57 (12024) in Pl. CXXV is a hasp (typical Indian *kuṇḍi*) made of a round copper bar. L. 2·25 in. Mound AB, Trench at the Southern Edge, Square Q 28/17; Depth 13 ft. 5 in. b. s.; Stratum V.

Hook.

No. 44 (504) in Pl. CXXIV is a strong copper hook 1·95 in. across the loop and 2 in. long. It is made of a round bar, ·35 in. in diameter which tapers down to ·1 in. at the thinner end. Mound F, Great Granary Area, Eastern Extension, Square J 9/22; Depth 7 ft. b. s.; Stratum III.

Latches (?).

Nos. 42 and 43 (12359) in Pl. CXXIV. See also Pl. CXXII, 28 and 33. Two strong objects of cast bronze identical in shape. No. 42 is 3·75 in. long and 1·37 in. broad, while No. 43 is 2·37 in. long and 1 in. broad. They may be latches[3] of some sort, but their purpose is uncertain.

[1] A similar mirror (No. 13303a) but of a smaller size (length including tang 7·7 in.) was found in 1936 in square R 30/9 in the eastward extension of Trench I, Area J, Stratum II.

[2] For similar examples from Greece and Caucasus see Petrie, *op. cit.*, p. 35, Pl. XLI, 85-89.

[3] For their conjectural restoration and detailed description see p. 56 *supra.*

CHAPTER XV.

PART I.

Report on Selected Beads from Harappā, *by Mr. H. C. Beck, F.S.A.*

At the request of Mr. Madho Sarup Vats, Deputy Director General of Archæology in India, I have undertaken to write a chapter on selected beads from Harappā. The fact that I cannot see the whole collection has made it very difficult to weigh the probabilities of such a subject as importation from foreign countries, but Mr. Vats has greatly assisted me by sending particulars as to whether each specimen is unique, rare or common, and also as to which layer they were found in.[1] The information, together with an examination of the beads, has shown some interesting results as to the possibility of their being connected with other civilizations, particularly with the Sumerian civilization in Mesopotamia.

As there does not seem to be a great difference between the beads from different layers, many kinds of beads being found in several layers, I have thought it best to arrange the beads into groups according to the materials of which they are made.

In explanation of the text there are several plates.[2] The first two, which are diagrammatic, show the beads arranged according to their shape in the Beck Method of classification.[3] Pl. CXXIX shows the beads in group I, *i.e.*, those with circular transverse sections, and Pl. CXXX shows those belonging to other groups and of which the transverse sections are not circular. In this plate the transverse section is shown as well as the longitudinal. Pls. CXXXI to CXXXIV show photographs of the beads, natural size, beads of similar materials being grouped together, whilst Pls. CXXXV and CXXXVI consist of microphotographs showing the internal structure.

Steatite beads. One very interesting fact about the Harappā beads is the great number that are made of steatite. In no other country have such a large proportion of the beads found been of this material. In addition to the number found, the variety of treatment that they have received is quite exceptional. Some specimens are in the natural stone, but the great majority have had some sort of treatment with heat, which has whitened the surface. Such beads have been called "Burnt" steatite beads and although I am not certain that in all cases great heat has been applied I am using the same term.

The hardness is about 3 in most cases, but there are a few exceptions, and in one case it is nearly 6. These are all harder than untreated steatite which has a hardness of 1½, but are quite different from the Egyptian glazed steatite beads which have a hardness varying from 5½ to 7.[4]

The exact process by which the whitening has been done is not clear, and the same methods may not have been applied in all cases, but the effect is very

---

[1] See Appendix A.—List of selected beads from Harappā, pp. 412-17 *infra*.

[2] For their detailed description see Appendix B, pp. 418-30.

[3] Classification and Nomenclature of beads and pendents, *Archæologia*, Vol. LXXVII.

[4] The hardness numbers refer to the mineralogical scale, thus: 1 Talc, 2 Gypsum, 3 Calcite, 4 Fluorspar, 5 Apatite, 6 Felspar, 7 Quartz, 8 Topaz, 9 Sapphire, 10 Diamond.

similar to the white bands produced on the etched carnelians (referred to later). In that case it is caused by the penetration of small opaque white particles of alkali which are arranged in layers of greater and lesser density. In the case of the burnt steatite also, the whitened portion is not uniform, and the layer near the surface is not so white as layers further in. The concentration goes in layers of alternately greater and lesser density, the maximum density being a considerable distance from the surface. These layers when examined in a microscopic section with transmitted light appear as dark semi-opaque bands. The opacity varies greatly in different specimens. It is clearly shown in the section of the small white steatite bead seen in Pl. CXXXV, 3, *a*. In this specimen, which is from the small beads No. 117,[1] and is magnified 40 diameters, several layers of varying intensity are visible. Two very dark bands, one having come from the outside and the other from the perforation, divide the bead into three almost equal parts.

When viewed from above with reflected light the particles show as white. This can be seen in Pl. CXXXV, 3, *b* which is the same view as in 3, *a* but lighted from above by the Beck ring illuminator. Figs. 4, *a* and 4, *b* are corresponding views of a minute steatite bead from grave 55 in the old Cemetery at Ur. This grave had unfortunately been plundered. It was originally very rich and may have been royal. It is dated by Sir Leonard Woolley to the 4th millenium. This shows great similarity of structure, whilst the similarity of external appearance can be seen in Pl. CXXXIV, 8-11.

A large number of experiments made on steatite specimens of all periods from Egypt and Mesopotamia and on modern steatite show that to get any results similar to the Harappā and Mohenjo-daro seals and beads, something in addition to heat is necessary.

It has been suggested that the Mohenjo-daro seals were finished with a steatite paste. This, however, can be definitely disproved by a microscopic examination. All specimens which have been heated with a glaze or alkali show a distinct layer of altered material near the surface. This layer, which is very white and opaque, frequently flakes off and gives the impression that it has been put on as a paste. A section cut from a typical Mohenjo-daro seal is shown in Pl. CXXXV, 1. This shows the dark semi-opaque affected layer adjoining the surface. It also shows a similarly affected part extending up a crack in the stone, which could not happen if the layer had been put on as a paste. Also the crystalline structure of the stone goes through the layer to the surface of the specimen.

The seals have a hardness of 3 and a very beautiful surface, generally quite white. It is difficult to say how this result has been produced, as if steatite is heated sufficiently to get the surface really white, it is generally much harder, in fact, over 5. I think that some alkali was probably used but not in very large quantities, otherwise the surface would have become unstable.

The Egyptian glazed steatite beads have had a vitreous glaze, and even when the glaze has flaked away, it leaves a very hard surface, sometimes

[1] This and other similar numbers are referable to Appendix A.

considerably over 6 and rarely, if ever, under 5½. Until I saw the beads from Harappā, I thought that the Indus specimens were treated with an alkali, but no silicate glaze. Amongst the Harappā steatite beads, however, are a number which show the remains of a blue or green glaze. A much larger number have a brown material which appears to be the same sort of glaze in a broken down condition.

The most probable reason why all the Indian beads are soft and the Egyptian are hard, is that a different kind of glaze was used, and that the Egyptians used a much greater heat. An analogy is found in the quartz beads of Mesopotamia and Egypt, where the glazed quartz beads of Egypt and one series from Mesopotamia have a brilliant surface remaining, whilst another series from Mesopotamia, have a completely frosted appearance. The difference in this case appears to be due to the temperature used to melt the glaze.

Steatite is not always a pure material, and there is no doubt that different specimens of steatite react in a different way to heat treatment, in the same way that different carnelians vary greatly in their reaction to soda and heat.

Two hundred numbered beads or sets of beads were sent to me for examination.[1] Of these, 77 are steatite beads; but very large numbers of small steatite beads have been in some cases included under one number, so that the actual number of steatite beads is over 450. A careful examination of these shows that a considerable number of the larger beads, *viz.*, those in 38 of the numbers, have traces of broken down glaze or some similar material over portions of the surface. In 12 cases this glaze shows a light green colour. A small fragment examined under the microscope shows, with the ring illuminator, an extremely vivid bluish green vitreous material, with numerous spots of iridescence apparently formed from bubbles in a flowing glaze. The layer of steatite beneath the glaze is affected and whitened, but is not hardened nearly so much as in the Egyptian specimens.

Most of the beads have evidently received a different treatment from the seals, as the former in many cases, have a white powdery surface, whilst the original surface of the seals remains. I think it probable that most of the beads had a coloured blue glaze, whilst the seals did not.

A few steatite beads have an outside coating which appears to be flexible. In one bead, No. 176 (Pl. CXXXII, 5, *s*) this is curling up round the edge and seems to be more of a paint than a glaze. It is dissolved by pyridine. No. 52 (Pl. CXXXII, 5, *d*) is a similar specimen.

Painted steatite beads.

Among the steatite beads those that show the most striking novelty as far as decoration is concerned are the painted steatite beads. The method by which these were made is not yet clear, but both the red and the brown colours are due to iron. The red colour can be produced by painting the pattern on the stone with ferric nitrate solution and then heating it to red heat in a crucible which is packed with magnesium oxide. The nearest approach to the Indian specimens that I have been able to produce was done by stopping out the white portions by means of a grease before putting on the ferric nitrate solution, as, unless that is done the colour spreads out over the unpainted part whilst the

[1] *Vide* Appendix A, pp. 412 ff.

specimen is being fired. A dark brown very similar to No. 56 (Pl. CXXXIII, 2, *b*) can be produced by a mixture of ferruginous clay and caustic soda painted on and fired in the same way. In all the Harappā specimens of painted steatite it is the white band that is the original colour of the bead, and the red and brown colour that is added. Owing to the sharpness and shape of the white bands it looks at first sight as if they are painted on a brown background.

The different painted beads vary greatly in hardness. This may be due to some extent to the paint used, but is probably chiefly due to the different temperature to which it has been heated. The usual rule is the greater the heat used, the harder and whiter the surface of the finished stone. This is probably only a partial explanation. It is also possible that originally, when first made these beads had a much higher degree of hardness, and have become softer owing to the prolonged period during which they have been buried, but I think this improbable. The hardest specimen is No. 11 (Pl. CXXXIII, 2, *h*) which has a hardness of nearly 5¼, but none of the other painted beads has a hardness much over 3. No. 11 is a very dark brown, but there is no explanation for its great hardness. The specimen of which a section was cut (Pl. CXXXV, 7) has a hardness of rather less than 3.

Another remarkable fact about the painted steatite beads is that, although the surface is whitened and the hardness increased from 1½ to about 3, there is scarcely any sign of an affected layer adjoining the surface. This is shown in the figure.

There is no evidence of any attempt to put a blue glaze on to any of the "painted" beads. This is of interest because the surface of some of the "painted" beads resembles the surface of the seals more nearly than the surface of most of the unpainted steatite beads does.

Whilst testing the painted steatite beads I discovered that in some cases the colour could be dissolved to a certain extent by means of pyridine. Testing a small fragment of red coloured bead I got a large amount of colour which dissolved into the pyridine and then deposited out again when the pyridine evaporated. Further tests with a portion of the same bead showed that heating the fragment red hot did not make any difference to its colour, but made it much less, if at all, soluble in pyridine.

The result of these experiments and various other observations has made me wonder whether these beads and many of the so called "burnt" steatite beads may not have been made by some method which does not require great heat. In certain experiments that I tried I found that prolonged heat at the temperature of boiling water applied to a steatite specimen coated with alkali had a considerable effect.

Small steatite beads.

The steatite beads vary greatly in size. The smallest of those sent are about 1/40 in. in diameter (·0025 in.); they vary in shape from disc to long cylinders and are very well made. Photographs of these, both enlarged and natural size, are shown on Pl. CXXXIV, 8-11. A number of beads identical to them have been found in grave P. G. 55 in the old cemetery at Ur. The effect of the treatment has been very similar. Pl. CXXXV, 3 shows a section through one

3 G 2

of the beads from Harappā, whilst fig. 4 shows a section through one from grave P. G. 55 at Ur. The similarity in their external appearance is clearly seen in Pl. CXXXIV, 8-11, where specimens from the two sites are shown side by side.

These are the smallest beads made from stone that I have seen, although equally small ones are said to have been made in Egypt from faience. The occurrence of these small beads at Ur is very surprising, as they are almost the only specimens from there until the Persian period, and very few specimens of early date are found in other sites in Mesopotamia.

Steatite disc beads.

The steatite disc beads, both large and small, appear to be typical of the Indus Valley as large numbers have been sent over. Some are illustrated in Pl. CXXXIII, 1. The same idea has been carried out in Egypt, but there the thin disc beads are generally made of faience. A few disc beads, said to be of horn, have been found at Abydos dated to about the XXth Dynasty.

Large steatite beads.

The largest bead sent over is the zone bead No. 1 (Pl. CXXXII, 2, *a*). This is a new type. It has along the profile a series of raised and sunk zones. It has been suggested that the sunk zones were originally filled with some other material. I do not think that this was so, as in that case the zones at the ends would be raised to hold the filling material, instead of being sunk[1]. The beads 125b and 123 (Pl. CXXXII, 2, *b*, *c*) appear to be variants of the same motif, also the ivory bead No. 158 (Pl. CXXXIV, 3).

Painted steatite beads.

The painted beads Nos. 55, 56, 57, 58 (Pl. CXXXIII, 2, *a*, *b*, *c*, *e*) are decorated with trefoils. This design although occasionally met with elsewhere evidently belonged to the Indus Civilization. No. 55 (Pl. CXXXIII, 2, *e*) is carved and painted, whilst Nos. 56, 57, and 58 (Pl. CXXXIII, 2, *b*, *a*, *c*) are only painted.

The other painted beads have all either zone or spiral designs (Pl. CXXXIII, 2, *d*, *f*, *g*, *h*, *i*, *j*, *k*). Very similar beads were made in faience (Pl. CXXXIII, 8).

The fact that many of these beads have very flat elliptical cross sections is a point in which they closely resemble the beads of Mesopotamia. Representative beads of this shape are shown on Pl. CXXX. In some cases, however, the beads merge gradually into a very definite double convex shape with fairly sharp edges. These belong to Group IV, beads with lenticular cross sections. As it is difficult to draw the line between the two groups, they are classified together on Pl. CXXX and numbered 1 to 16.

The beads of Group I, those with circular cross sections, are shown in outline on Pl. CXXIX, whilst photographs of many of them are shown on Pl. CXXXII. Comparatively few of the steatite beads are circular barrels but a number are cylinders. A few of these are large, but the majority are small. Specimens of the long cylinders are Nos. 91 and 93 (Pl. CXXXII, 1, *c*, and 5, *i*). The majority of the steatite beads sent are disc cylinders, 180 being on one string. Of short beads there are very few.[2]

Steatite beads with unusual technique.

Nos. 134 and 168 (Pl. CXXXII, 5, *l*, *k*) are interesting as they seem to have had a rather different technique. They have a heavy patination which is very

---

[1] See, however, No. 19 on p. 436 *infra* M. S. V.

[2] Technically short beads are those which are longer than disc beads, and shorter than standard beads. The former have a length less than a third their diameter, whilst the latter have a length approximately equal to their diameter.

thin and opaque but do not seem to have lost the soapy feeling of the stone. One of the fragments sent for microscopic examination was similar. A section cut from this is shown on Pl. CXXXV, 6. The two views *a* and *b* are taken with transmitted light and reflected light, respectively. They show how opaque and narrow the affected part is. In order to prevent the affected layer from breaking away the specimen was embedded in a reinforcing material. This shows very clearly in the photograph, where it is marked R to distinguish it from the base of the stone, which is marked B. The affected layer is marked A.

Among the other steatite beads of Group I the most interesting are the long cones Nos. 175 and 94 (Pl. CXXXII, 5, *g*, *h*) and the concave cone No. 120 (Pl. CXXXII, 5, *cc*). The large short very steep angle cones Nos. 104 and 106 (Pl. CXXIX, 54, 53) are also unusual. Of the other groups of regular beads, the disc rectangular cylinder No. 82 (Pl. CXXX, 22), which is quite new to me, and the plano convex circular bead No. 109 (Pl. CXXX, 17) should be noted; the latter is a form found both in Mesopotamia and Egypt. **Cone beads.**

Steatite spacing beads are not very common, although several shapes occur. They are generally elliptical or rectangular cylinders or barrels, and have only two perforations. See Nos. 79, 80, 84, 85, and 159 (Pl. CXXXII, 3, *a*, *b*, *e*, *f*, *d*). A very unusual type is the oblate bead No. 115 (Pl. CXXXII, 3, *c*). **Steatite spacing beads.**

Gadrooned beads (Group XXII) are not common. There are three of steatite. One small oblate one with five gadroons, No. 124 (Pl. CXXXII, 5, *ee*) is a type found elsewhere, but it is unusual to have so few gadroons, whilst the conical specimens Nos. 89, 90 (Pl. CXXXII, 5, *t*, *u*) are, so far as I know, only found in the Indus Civilization. **Gadrooned beads.**

Amongst the emblems (Group XXIX), the cross has two variations. One, No. 126 (Pl. CXXXII, 4, *a*) is cut in the shape of a cross. I have not seen a similar steatite specimen from any other site, but a similar one in agate was found at Taxila. The second cross bead is a lenticular circular bead with different designs on each side, both representing a form of cross. No. 118 (Pl. CXXXII, 4, *b*, *c*) is a very well-cut specimen, which both in quality of workmanship and condition of surface resembles more closely the seals than do any of the other beads. **Cross beads.**

Another bead, No. 127 (Pl. CXXXII, 4, *d*), seems to be a variant of the step design found at Mohenjo-daro and in other countries. At Mohenjo-daro it is generally used for inlay as in specimens Nos. 31, 32, 33 on Pl. CLV in *M.I.C.* A similar design is also shown on a fragment of an etched carnelian bead from Kish.[1] A plaque for inlay, from Ur is figured on Pl. CXXXIV, 4. **Step beads.**

A small annular bead of steatite, No. 128 (Pl. CXXXII, 5, *ii*) is pierced sideways. This is very unusual at an early period but one specimen in hard blue frit has been found at Ur, and bronze beads pierced in the same manner are frequently found in the Irish Bronze Age.

One cylinder bead, No. 185 (Pl. CXXXII, 5, *j*), has had the portion adjoining the ends slightly reduced in diameter, probably for fitting gold caps on.

A unique bead with four points, possibly representing a tooth, No. 119 (Pl. CXXXII, 4, *e*) also of steatite, is very suggestive of the chain beads which fit **Tooth bead.**

[1] See H. C. Beck, *Etched Carnelian Beads*, *Antiquaries Journal*, Vol. XIII, No. 4, LXXI, A. 18.

together so as to make a flexible chain. The latter, however, always have three or more points to fit together. Moreover, as this is a unique specimen, it is very improbable that long strings of similar beads were worn.

Natural steatite beads.

The steatite beads with the natural surface still remaining and with no signs of patination are shown in Pl. CXXXII, 1. The specimens *a* to *d* are well finished but those from *e* to *h* are such rough specimens that they may be only partly made. No. *d* has curious marks cut into the end of it. The position of these marks is difficult to understand, as when strung they would be invisible. Similar marks are found on some of the other beads; particularly interesting are those on beads shown on Pl. CXXXII, 5, *k* and *l*. In the former, seven holes have been drilled for a short distance into the stone. This was done before the surface of the stone was whitened.

Copper tube in bead.

One bead, No. 8 (Pl. CXXXII, 5, *x*), has a metal tube in the perforation. This looks like copper. Copper cores have been found in glass beads at a much later date, but in those cases it may have been used to prevent the glass from sticking on to the mandrel on which it was made. This, however, would not happen with steatite unless the glaze ran in. One possible but improbable explanation is that it formed part of an ornamental drinking tube such as have been found at Ur. If this was the case one would expect the bead to be cylindrical instead of the slight barrel shape that it is.

Amongst the small beads, No. 117 already referred to was an extremely small dark bead. Externally it had some resemblance to lapis, but I could not see a trace of the blue colour when examined under the microscope. I think that it may be natural steatite. Its diameter is ·025 in. and its length ·023 in.

Beads made of silicate stones.

Next to steatite the greatest number of stone beads are made from the silicate stones which are all more or less pure varieties of quartz. There are two main divisions of silicate stones. The first includes the transparent varieties of quartz of which the chief are colourless quartz or rock crystal, amethyst, yellow quartz or cairngorm, and smoky quartz. The second division includes the pellucid and opaque varieties such as agate, carnelian, chalcedony, chert, etc.

A very curious feature of these beads from Harappā is that there are none made from the transparent varieties of quartz included in the first division. This is impossible to explain as clear rock crystal beads are fairly common in Mesopotamia and Egypt, and are very common from later sites in India, both amongst the beads from Taxila, and amongst those from the megalithic tombs of South India. Again amethyst beads, also absent from Harappā, are found in reasonable number in Mesopotamia, but much more frequently at Taxila and in Egypt. In the latter country many of them date to the same period as the Harappā beads, although most of the Egyptian beads were made about 2000 B.C. Cairngorm beads have not been found much in Mesopotamia, but great numbers have been discovered in later Indian sites such as Taxila and Sabaur[1] in the Bhagalpur District of Bihar.

---

[1] No ancient site as such has yet been located at Sabour, but beads of the type mentioned were found about 30 years ago by Mr. C. E. A. W. Oldham, I.C.S., while digging for the foundations of the building of the Agricultural Research Institute. M. S. V.

The second divisions of silicate stone, the pellucid and opaque varieties all contain a certain amount of water. The amount varies greatly in apparently identical stones. They have a very wide range of colour, due to small quantities of colouring matter being mixed with the silica, and in a great many specimens the colouring matter is in bands or belts.

The stones of different colours have different names, but there is no very definite line between them, and many specimens can be called by several different names. Amongst the beads from Harappā are 48[1] made from these materials, which I divide as follows, but many of the stones which I have placed in one division might equally well be put into another:—

Agate 19	Chalcedony 3
Carnelian 11	Milky quartz 1
Jasper 6	Lydian stone, or Black Chert 3
Chalcedonic Agate Breccia 3	Chert 2

Agate beads. The agate beads are chiefly of interest on account of the beauty of many of the stones used. The shapes, except Nos. 69 and 70 (Pl. CXXXI, 1, *p*, *o*), are almost all of types well known elsewhere but some are unusually large. Eight of the agate beads belong to Group I with circular section, and 8 to Groups II and IV with elliptical or lenticular sections. One has a circle and flat section (Pl. CXXXI, 1, *a*). It is an unusually large bead, not very well made, but it is a shape which is found here in various materials and is well known in Mesopotamia.

Agate is evidently a favourite material for beads at Harappā, and is also particularly noticeable in Mesopotamia, where agate beads with both circular and elliptical sections are common, and many are beautifully made. Comparatively few of the specimens from Harappā show specially good workmanship, but No. 60 (Pl. CXXXI, 1, *g*) is a striking exception.

Unfinished beads. Amongst the circular long barrels are several which are not perforated. These are very much the shape of Mesopotamian weights. In some cases they are comparatively well finished off, whilst in others they have a definitely unfinished appearance. These have been weighed to see if they fitted into a series. The results are as follows, assuming one gramme to be the unit.

Number.	Weight.	Suggested number of units.	Error.
	Grammes.		
No. 5 . . .	20·780	21	—·220
No. 19 . . .	7·015	7	·015
No. 32 . . .	6·708	7	—·292
No. 39 . . .	5·990	6	—·010
No. 61 . . .	5·599	6	—·401
No. 20 . . .	4·762	4½	·262
No. 34 . . .	4·220	4½	—·308
No, 15	3·061	3	·061

The results do not look sufficiently regular for these specimens to be weights, moreover one of them has a perforation started at one end. It is probable that this specimen at least, and possibly all of them are unfinished beads. In Mesopotamia, the weights, although of this shape, were very beautifully finished.

[1] This number refers only to the beads sent to him for examination, *vide* p. 394 *supra*. M. S. V.

If these are really partly made beads it shows that, at any rate in many cases, the bead was finished, or nearly finished, externally before the perforation was made. The specimen which is partially perforated shows that it has been drilled by a hollow drill and some abrasive. This method of drilling was also in vogue in Mesopotamia, but differs from the method used by many primitive tribes, where the hole is jumped through by a series of small cold chisels, whilst the piece of material used is much larger than the finished bead.

Owing to the water contained in the stones of the second division, they have the power of absorbing some materials to a small degree, especially when heated. In this way, by treating first with sugar and then with sulphuric acid, the more absorbent layers become black. Bead No. 19 (Pl. CXXXI, 1, *i*) has, I think, been treated in some such manner. It is also an interesting bead because the material is exactly like that used for making a number of agate beads found in Europe. The European ones, however, have not had the colour artificially heightened. The writer has seen similar beads from very different sites, including Ur.[1] The late Prof. Gregory was of opinion that the European specimens were very like an Indian stone and that they probably came from there.

Bead No. 65 (Pl. CXXXI, 1, *e*) is very skilfully cut from coloured stone so as to get almost exactly the same design at each end[2]. At first sight it looked as though the colouring was partly artificial, but closer examination shows that it is natural. Dr. Thomas, of the Geological Survey, confirms this and suggests that some of the colour is due to manganese. Beads of this shape are found at Ur. The cutting of these is so arranged as to get the colour at the two ends different to that of the centre; but I have not seen any bead from Mesopotamia which is as elaborate as this specimen from Harappā.

Chalcedonic agate breccia.

The beads Nos. 25, 71, and 129 (Pl. CXXXI, 1, *s*, *q*, *r*) are made of a chalcedonic agate breccia. To form this material a number of broken pieces of agate have been cemented together in a chalcedony matrix. This is a rare material. The only other beads made from it that have been found up to now are from Mohenjo-daro; probably the material for both the Harappā and Mohenjo-daro beads comes from the same place.

Carnelian beads.

Two very interesting beads of carnelian, Nos. 49 and 129 (Pl. CXXXI, 2, *b*, *a*), are exceptionally long barrel beads. These beads are exactly similar in shape to some from Mesopotamia; but the latter are shorter, rarely exceeding two inches in length, whilst No. 129 from Harappā must have been over 3¼ in. long and some from Mohenjo-daro are over five in. long. Sir Leonard Woolley, however, states that a very few similar beads from Ur are nearly four inches long.

Bicone No. 41 (Pl. CXXXI, 2, *f*) and barrel No. 42 are types of bead frequently found at Ur. The carnelian short barrel on string 128 (pl. CXXXI, 2, *e*) is also of interest. The perforation which is of the double cone or hour-glass variety, looks distinctly primitive. Similar beads have been found in Mesopotamia, where they are supposed to be very early, though this is not quite certain.

---

[1] See H. C. Beck, *Note on Certain Agate Beads*, *Antiquaries Journal*, 1930, Vol. 10, No. 2.

[2] See also No. 1 on p. 440 *infra*.

Etched carnelian beads.

The most interesting carnelian specimens are Nos. 78 and 88 (Pl. CXXXI, 4, *a*, *c*) which have a design etched upon them in white lines on the natural colour of the stone. This effect is produced by drawing the pattern on the stone with carbonate of soda and heating till red hot. A chemical change is made in the material and the soda enters in as a great number of minute opaque white spots. The coefficient of expansion of the material is so altered that the white layer sometimes flakes off owing to the strain caused by continual change in temperature, which accounts for beads of this type being originally described as inlaid.

A curious feature of this process is that the extreme surface of the stone does not seem to be affected by the soda, which extends in layers of alternate greater and lesser density for some distance into the stone. The unaltered outside surface is not nearly so clearly shown in the specimens from Harappā as in more recent specimens. It seems as though a slow chemical change continued after burial.

A cut through an etched carnelian from Harappā, is shown in Pl. CXXXVI, 1. It is a bead of the usual type, that is it has the design in white lines on the natural colour of the stone. It is illuminated by light from above so that the affected layer shows as a white band (A) the base is on the left (B). The bubbles on the right hand are in the cement which holds the specimen. The magnification is 40.

Fig. 2 on the same plate shows a section through an irregular white line on another bead from Harappā. In fig. 2, *a* it is seen with transmitted light, whilst in fig. 2, *b* the light is from above. The affected layer shows a series of alternate dark and light concentric bands radiating from nuclei. The second fig. 2, *b* shows how intensely bright a thin section of this affected part is, whilst the first fig. 2, *a* shows its great opacity. The alternating effect of the white layers is very clearly seen.

This process has only been used in certain countries and at this early date, so far as is at present known, was only used in Mesopotamia and in India. This in itself would show an almost certain connection between these countries, but the link is greatly strengthened by the fact that identical elaborate patterns made by this method have been found on beads at Ur. and at Mohenjo-daro.[1] Bead No. 78 (Pl. CXXXI, 4, *a*) is an elaborate eye bead. It is elliptical in section and when complete was very similar to a bead from Ur. The latter, however, has one less ring round the eye and is circular in section.[2] No. 88 (Pl. CXXXI, 4, *c*) is a diamond oblate bead with a white line etched round it. This is a very common form of etched bead in Mesopotamia, but usually the white line crosses over in the centre so as to make a spectacle pattern.

A second variety of etched bead is sometimes met with, in which the whole surface of the bead is whitened over to a considerable depth by the usual method, and then a design in black is etched on the top by means of a metal salt. The exact method by which this was done is not known, but, if the stone is first treated with carbonate of soda, the black lines can be produced by painting it

[1] H. C. Beck, *Etched Carnelians*, Antiquaries Journal, Vol. 13, Pl. LXVII, figs. 1a and 2a.

[2] Beck, *op. cit.*, Pl. LXVII, fig. 1*b*.

with a nitrate of one of the metals and then firing the stone again. Iron, copper, lead, and manganese, were tried, but the results most resembling the early specimen were obtained by copper and iron.

A modification of this process has been met with at Taxila, in which the black line appears to have been put directly on the carnelian. In this case the lines of the design were exceptionally black. The bead fragment (Pl. CXXXI, 4, *d*) seems to have been of the same technique, but the carnelian is turned to rather a pink colour with many white spots. As, however, this patination extends over the broken surface and does not go under the black line, it is probable that it is also a change due to some chemical action whilst the bead has been buried in the earth. A microphotograph (Pl. CXXXVI, 3) shows that the black line goes into the stone for a depth of ·005 in. The white corrosion spots at the ends of the black line go more deeply into the surface but do not extend appreciably under the black line, showing that they are a later addition and that the black line was put direct on to the natural stone.

The long bead No. 49 (Pl. CXXXI, 2, *b*), already referred to, has also considerable patination on the surface. Due to the absorbing powers of different layers, the patination has the effect of emphasizing the natural pattern of the stone. This patination may have been put on by some special treatment at the time of manufacture, but it is more probable that it has been formed after burial. The fact that one or two spots are on the broken surface suggests that it has been caused by the stone being in contact with damp earth containing soda, either carbonate or chloride, and that the great time it has been buried may have had the same effect at normal temperature as that caused by great heat for a few minutes. This, however, is not certain, as one chip, which looks old, goes right through a very heavy patch of patination, while, on the other hand, many specimens show no signs of patination. If it is intentional, it has probably been done to enhance the eye effect.

Chalcedony. A few of the other beads, from silicate stones, are very well made, especially those of chalcedony. The green chalcedony specimen No. 67 (Pl. CXXXI, 3, *l*) is very curious. It has natural veins running across it which are nearly colourless except near the surface where they may have been stained with iron, evidently after the bead was ground to shape, as they are coloured for approximately the same depth all round.

Chert jasper. The flattened shape of the beads made of Lydian stone (Pl. CXXXI, 3), which is really black chert, is reminiscent of beads from Mesopotamia. The jasper beads are good specimens. No. 188 (Pl. CXXXI, 3, *a*) with the dark band along the axis is attractive, whilst No. 29 (Pl. CXXXI, 3, *e*) is of interest, as a large inclusion has been dissolved away or fallen out evidently after the bead was made. Another variety of chert, brown with bands, was used to make bead No. 86 (Pl. CXXXI, 3, *g*).

Sundry hard stones. In addition to the silicate stones, several other hard stones have been used. Nos. 43 and 63 (Pl. CXXXI, 7, *l*, *k*) are made of a true jadeite, but are unusually transparent. Five specimens are of felspar (Pl. CXXXI, 5, *a-e*). The green monocline variety is called either "mother of emerald" or plasma, and when rather more blue it is called amazonite. Although not particularly common in any country, beads made from it are found in Mesopotamia and in Egypt at all periods from Predynastic to Roman.

The bead No. 39 (Pl. CXXXI, 7, *d*) is a hornblende granitic breccia, and No. 18 (Pl. CXXXI, 7, *h*) is a diorite. The latter material was frequently used in Egypt at an early date.

Lapis. Only three specimens of lapis beads have been sent over. They are all elliptical barrels. This is very surprising, as enormous numbers of lapis beads have been found in Mesopotamia, especially at the period of the Royal Graves at Ur. In addition to their great quantity, too, the shapes of the lapis beads at Ur are of much interest. The small bicone is common, in both the circular and elliptical form. This shape is not found among the Harappā beads; nor is one of the most elaborate forms—the octagonal long barrel, made in lapis and carnelian. Although rare, these are a very distinct Mesopotamian type.

Limestone stalagmite. The steatite specimens are not the only ones made of soft stone. There are several others, most of which are made of varieties of limestone or stalagmite. The majority belong to Group I, but there are a few elliptical ones. Two fine large yellow specimens, Nos. 135 and 136 (Pl. CXXXI, 6, *a*, *b*), are made of "Jaisalmer" stone a form of muddy limestone. Bead No. 45 (Pl. CXXXI, 6, *e*) is a barrel bead made out of a limestone with a well defined structure. No. 46 (Pl. CXXXI, 6, *g*), also a barrel bead, is made of stalagmite with markings like an agate, and No. 35 (Pl. CXXXI, 6, *h*) is made from a stratified form of stalagmite.

Serpentine. There are three beads of serpentine. Nos. 16 and 48 (Pl. CXXXI, 7, *g*, *e*) are beautifully made beads, whilst No. 44 (Pl. CXXXI, 7, *f*) is a barrel bead which appears to have had a coating of some sort of paint or enamel covering almost all the surface. Two large beads, Nos. 132 and 133 (Pl. CXXXI, 7, *a*, *b*), are made of a fine grained statuary marble. They have corroded very extensively.

Faience. Faience is a term that was originally applied to a material made in the town of Faenza, but is now used to describe a large variety of ceramic products. In archæology it generally refers to a material consisting chiefly of quartz grains covered with a glaze. This is best known as an Egyptian product as so much is found there, but it is also found in several other countries, particularly Crete, Mesopotamia, and India, whilst a rather similar material is found in China.

Egyptian faience consists of fine powdered quartz which has been mixed with a small quantity of some other material to act as a flux and then has been fired. Its appearance when examined in thin sections under the microscope is very similar to that of a quartz brick made by fusing fine grains of quartz with 2 per cent. of lime, added in the form of milk of lime before fusing. Analyses of Egyptian faience,[1] show that in four different specimens lime was present and in three of them the quantity was between 1·6 per cent. and 2 per cent. In two cases there was also a little alkali. A small amount of alkali such as soda would enable the quartz grains to fuse together at a lower temperature.

[1] A. Lucas, *Ancient Egyptian Materials*, p. 231.

Faience varies greatly in the way it is affected by age, some early specimens can be crushed between finger and thumb whilst others are extremely hard, almost as hard as quartz.

There are several varieties of faience sent from Harappā but all those examined consisted of fine quartz grains in an isotropic medium, with in some cases the addition of a colouring material. Most, if not all, of the beads were coloured, the original colours seem to have been blue, yellow and black, but some have corroded to a different colour from what they originally were.

Hard blue faience.

There are at least two varieties of blue faience, one has the colour going right through the bead, whilst the other has the colour put on the surface of the bead after it has been moulded and probably after it has been fired.

In the former type the colouring matter must have been mixed with the quartz grains in the original material before it was moulded to shape. A particularly hard form of this, made from very fine grains, is similar to samples from Mohenjo-daro where they are called vitreous paste. This material has been fused until the air bubbles have become circular. The great majority of the quartz grains are extremely small. A typical example of this material is No. 161 (Pl. CXXXIII, 3, *a*) and a section of this magnified 40 diameters is reproduced on Pl. CXXXVI, 7. This shows that, except for slight corrosion on the surface, the structure and colour are uniform throughout. Nos. 95 and 177 (blue) (Pl. CXXXIII, 9, *c*, *b*) are probably similar materials. There is a considerable difference in the specific gravities. No. 161 has sp. g. 2·48, No. 177 has 2·39, and No. 95 has 2·21. The reason for these variations is probably that some have more bubbles that are completely enclosed than others and that the difference is not due to alteration in the material.

By completely enclosed, I mean bubbles containing air that cannot be exhausted in an airpump. All these have been tested after being for five or more hours in water in an airpump where the pressure was reduced to about an inch of mercury. Even with the hardest faience beads, a quantity of air escaped when under the airpump.

Under certain circumstances this faience completely loses its blue colour and becomes white, or slightly yellow or reddish and has a rougher outer surface. A spherical bead of this sort looked a slightly reddish-white colour, but when cut in half showed the remains of the typical blue colour. A microscopic section shows such a similarity of depth of yellow material all round that it may have had a yellow colour originally.

The second type of blue glazed bead has the colour put on as an outside layer. Nos. 166 and 167 (Pl. CXXXIII, 9, *d*, *e*) are beads of this type. A fragment of a similar bead was also sent and from this a microscopic section has been made. A great part of the glaze has either soaked in or corroded away, but a vitreous glaze still shows in some of the indentations of the surface (Pl. CXXXVI, 5). The grains of quartz are very much bigger than in the fine-grained variety. In the fracture of this specimen there is a slight suggestion of blue.

No. 166 has a bright green glaze, whilst No. 167 has a dull surface with a number of red spots on it which are the residue of a broken down glaze. It is not possible to say with certainty what colour this glaze was originally.

Small pale blue bead. Amongst the 117 minute beads sent over is one which has a pale blue tint with white corrosion. It is very translucent and looks like a glass, but is I think a faience. It is quite different from any of the other beads sent. It has some resemblance to XIIth dynasty Egyptian beads but I have not seen such a small specimen previously. It is shown on Pl. CXXXIV, 8 and is numbered 1.

Hard yellow faience. Hard yellow faience is a material in which the yellow colouring is produced by a glaze that is put on after the bead has been moulded to shape. In this section the difference of the layer through which the glaze had percolated was quite clear whilst the section was thick, but when it was ground down to a thin section, say ·002 to ·003 in. thick the difference in transparency of the outer layer becomes very difficult to detect, but it does seem to have fewer quartz crystals. Nos. 157 and 174 (Pl. CXXXIII, 7, *b*, *c*) are typical specimens of this type. The former has sp. g. 2·56 and the latter 2·43.

Hard white faience. There are several specimens of hard white faience. They have a beautiful smooth surface, but are not quite so hard as some found in Mesopotamia. Most of them are quite colourless now, but a small segmented bead of two segments on string No. 177 (Pl. CXXXIII, 6, *c*) has blue glaze adhering to the whole surface of one of the ends. A very fine specimen No. 33 (Pl. CXXXIII, 6, *a*) to say for certain whether all these beads were originally glazed, but if so, the beads must first have been fired and then covered with a glaze which melted at a low temperature and never stuck very well to the base.

Black faience. Most of the black faience beads have the colour applied after the bead has been moulded to shape so that it remains quite a thin layer on the surface. The specimens of this technique are on string No. 180 (Pl. CXXXIII, 5, *b*). The glaze on some specimens is arranged so that parts of the white base show through giving very much the same effect as some of the crumb beads from Egypt. It is difficult to be certain of the colouring matter of this glaze. I feel sure from testing it that it is not all iron, although there is some iron in it. It has a great external resemblance to the manganese glazes of the VIth dynasty of Egypt, but microscopic examination does not show the typical purple colour of manganese. I think that it may be copper, as one of the black glazes of early Mesopotamia, which has a similar colour, has been proved to be copper.

There is one black faience bead, No. 177 (Pl. CXXXIII, 5, *a*), in which the colouring matter goes right through the base. In this case a microscope shows that it consists of a mixture of quartz grain and grains of some intensely black material. This shows opaque even in small particles when viewed by direct light, but the ring illuminator gives the black pieces an appearance of ruby red round their edges. I think that the colouring matter is very probably the same as that used in No. 180.

Variegated faience. There are a number of zone and spiral beads which are made of two varieties of faience, either white and red or white and brown, the brown in some cases being almost black. The zone beads are made of alternate layers which go transversely right through the bead. A section cut through a red and white layer is shown in Pl. CXXXVI, 6, *a*, *b*. In Fig. *a* the section is shown by transmitted light, whilst in Fig. *b* it is shown with polarized light in which the isotropic material does not show and only the quartz grains come out white. The material is very finely ground and both red and white seem to be of the same nature, except that the red portion includes a great number of small particles which show as black in transmitted light and bright red when seen illuminated from above. This is the finest grained faience sent. There are scarcely any grains which are as much as ·001 in. in any direction—a great contrast to the specimen in Pl. CXXXVI, 5, where some of the quartz grains are as much as ·015 in. long.

A very remarkable feat has been to produce the bead No. 74 (Pl. CXXXIII, 8, *h*) which is a copy of an elaborate agate. The colour of the outside zones is dark brown, the two next zones are greyish white, and the central zone is red. I have not seen a similar specimen elsewhere. Another unusual variety is a white barrel with black spots (No. 159, pl. CXXXIII, 8, *i*). This is in a very corroded condition and it is difficult to say if the white portion was originally coloured, but after prolonged saturation in water it seemed to have a definitely blue tint.

Median ribbed beads.

There are several interesting shapes among the faience beads. One of the most important series comprises the beads with median ribs, Nos. 161, 164a, 171, 172 (Pl. CXXXIII, 3, *a*, *d*, *c*, *b*). These beads are the same shape as beads found in Mesopotamia both at Tell Asmar and at Ur, although in the latter site they are usually made of gold or lapis.

Gadrooned beads.

The gadrooned bead No. 162 (Pl. CXXXIII, 9, *o*) is a well made melon bead with 13 gadroons. Similar specimens have been found in Mesopotamia at Ur and in the cemetery at Diqdiqqeh, but those I have seen are not so well made. Beads of the same shape cut in lapis come from the royal graves at Ur.

Segmented beads.

On string No. 177 are two segmented beads, one with two (Pl. CXXXIII, 6, *c*), and the other with five segments (Pl. CXXXIII, 6, *b*). The larger one has a hard, polished white surface all over; the smaller is the same except that, as already stated, it is still covered with a blue glaze over the greater part of one end. Evidently these were originally blue. This is of great interest, as small segmented beads of blue faience have been discovered in Egypt, Crete, and England. In Egypt, a very small variety of them appears to have started in the VIth Dynasty, about 2800 B.C. but beads of the size of those from Harappâ seem to have begun in the XVIIIth dynasty and continued to at least the XXth. In England, they are generally supposed to date to about 1200 B.C. but this is not quite certain. In Crete they date to between 1400 and 1200 B.C. Beads exactly like these have not been found in Mesopotamia, but a rather larger variety made out of a faience that is now very corroded and black, but which was originally coloured, has been found in Nineveh in great numbers, in Dr. Campbell Thompson's excavation.[1] These cannot be accurately dated, but there seems little doubt that they are as early as, if not earlier than, the Royal graves at Ur.

[1] See H. C. Beck, *Beads from Nineveh*, *Antiquity*, Dec., 1931.

Amongst the beads sent over are two decorated short barrel beads Nos. 166, 167 (Pl. CXXXIII, 9, *d*, *e*). These are said to be very common and are found in all layers. A section of one of these (Pl. CXXXVI, 5) has already been referred to. They are unlike any beads that I have seen from other sites, and, if only a few had been found, I should have thought that they might have been later inclusions (see also terracotta bead No. 146, Pl. CXXXIV, 1, *g*, p. 408 *infra*). At the same time there is a certain resemblance between the rough criss-cross pattern that is suggestive of early beads from Tell-al-'Ubaid and Ur. **Decorated short barrel beads.**

Four specimens of faience spacing beads have been sent over. One is a lenticular barrel with two perforations (No. 163=Pl. CXXXIII, 4, *b*); another is a cylindrical one with four perforations on string 171= Pl. CXXXIII, 4, *c*). On the same string is a semicircular bead like a terminal spacing bead but the three perforations are almost parallel (Pl. CXXXIII, 4, *d*). The most interesting one, however, is No. 160 (Pl. CXXXIII, 4, *a*). This is moulded so that the surface looks like a multiple spacing bead with about fifteen parallel tubes, it has, however, only two perforations. The general effect is very similar to certain carved lapis and gold beads from Mesopotamia, but it is not nearly so tapered and the Mesopotamian specimens usually have at least three perforations.

There are a few other faience beads which should be mentioned No. 9 (Pl. CXXXIII, 8, *c*) is a brown and white wave bead, the preservation of which is most surprising. It looks as though it had only recently been made. No. 157 (Pl. CXXXIII, 7, *b*), a yellow square long bicone, is not a very common shape, but copper and carnelian specimens have been found at Ur and carnelian specimens have been found in Egypt which are late Roman. Similar shaped beads in jet, also of the Roman period, have been found in England. No. 164 (Pl. CXXXIII, 9, *m*) is an elliptical barrel, it has a circular eye design consisting of two concentric circles, in the centre of which there is a dot. The other side is plain. I have not seen a bead like this previously. No. 165 (Pl. CXXXIII, 9, 1), a hemispherical bead, is an unusual shape. No. 170 (Pl. CXXXIII, 7, *a*) is a yellow bicone, which, although very well preserved, is roughly made, the perforation being a very long way from the centre. No. 181 (Pl. CXXXIII 9, *f*) comprises a number of spherical faience beads. They are very roughly made and the glaze has bubbled extensively on the surface. **Sundry faience beads.**

A general investigation shows that many, if not all, of the faience specimens have been fired at a very considerable heat and probably for a long time, as whether the quartz grains are as coarse as those in Pl. CXXXVI, 5 or as fine as those in Pl. CXXXVI, 6 the faience is thoroughly well cemented together. The dissolved quartz and lime or alkali have flowed extensively so as to envelop the larger pieces completely. Moreover, several of the specimens examined show that the enclosed air has been able to form into spherical bubbles.

The material of which the terracotta beads are made contains a large amount of mica. It is a form of lateritic clay consisting of broken down granite. The particles of mica, although so numerous, are very small. **Pottery and terracotta.**

With the exception of two (Nos. 142 and 146=Pl. CXXXIV, 1, *c*, *g*) all the beads are unusually fine red, the colour of which is probably due to iron.

No. 139 (Pl. CXXXIV, 1, *b*) is a large segmented or pulley bead. It is an unusual shape, but a very similar article, not pierced, has been found in a Bronze Age burial in England. Nos. 141 and 142 (Pl. CXXXIV, 1, *k*, *c*) are convex bicones, an uncommon shape in pottery. The pear-shaped bead with one concave end, No. 146 (Pl. CXXXIV, *d*, *g*, also Pl. CXXIX, 58) is identical with beads which have been found extensively in the mounds round some of the megalithic tombs in Hyderabad. So far as I know, such beads have not been found in any of the tombs, and I suppose them to be of the same date as the coins found on the mounds, *i.e.*, from the second century B.C. to the sixth century A.D. A section has been cut from one of the Hyderabad specimens which shows that they were made of a very coarse pottery and that they have been fused at a great heat. A comparatively large number of these pear-shaped beads have been found in the Hyderabad District, I have seen two strings of them, and, as I have not seen any other beads from that district which resemble those of the Indus Civilization, I cannot help thinking that this bead is an inclusion. Apparently only a few of them have been found, all associated with the top layer. Probably they have no connection with the early Indus Civilization, but belong to a later settlement, perhaps of the Gupta period. Nos. 149 and 150 (Pl. CXXXIV, 1, *n*, *o*) are very roughly made. The spiral bead on string No. 148 (Pl. CXXXIV, 1, *p*) is interesting as an early specimen. Some of the large bicone beads are almost the same size and shape as Aegean specimens.

Shell beads. Only one complete shell, No. 190 (Pl. CXXXIV, 2, *g*) a natural dentalium shell, has been sent, the other shell beads being cut from large shells. I am surprised that the pusiostoma shells are not represented, as they are common in Mesopotamia and come from the Indo-Pacific ocean.

The beads cut from shell are mostly very roughly made, but there are two or three exceptions. The concave bead No. 158 (Pl. CXXXIV, 2, *d*) is an unusual shape. The annular ring No. 155 (Pl. CXXXIV, 2, *c*) suggests that it was used for inlay. The segmented bead No. 153 (Pl. CXXXIV, 2, *f*) is interesting in connection with the segmented faience beads already referred to.

Beads cut from shell are not as a whole common in Mesopotamia or in Egypt, but a large number of complete shell and copies of complete shell carved in stone are found in Egypt.

Ivory bead. Apart from the metals the only other material represented among the specimens sent to me is ivory. One bead of this material, No. 158 (Pl. CXXXIV, 3), a large short barrel zone bead, is in a fairly good state of preservation. The sunk zones appear to have been roughened, as though some inlay had originally been added, but this is very doubtful.

Copper beads. The copper beads Nos. 130 and 131 (Pl. CXXXIV, 5, *a*, *b*) are relatively unimportant. The long barrel smaller bead appears to be copper, and the corrosion is not excessive considering the age. The large bead is a short barrel. Large cavities on the outside show where special corrosion has taken place, whilst in the perforation are some patches of yellow coloured material which looks like a mixture of red and yellow cuprous oxide.

In damp climates silver beads almost always corrode very badly, and this is especially so in Mesopotamia. A few small silver beads (No. 198=Pl. CXXXIV, 6) sent over from Harappā are almost equally corroded. The triangular portion may be separate beads corroded together, but it is very like the wedge-shaped beads from Ur, made of numbers of small spherical beads soldered together. **Silver beads.**

If the amount of gold beads sent over is proportional to the number found, they are a very small number compared to the great quantities in Queen Shub Ad's grave but, although not numerous, they are of considerable interest. No. 194 (Pl. CXXXIV, 7, *b*) is a long barrel bead with the ends of the profile concave. This shape is rare, and I have not seen it among Mesopotamian specimens. From the thickness of the metal this bead seems to have been hammered to shape and there is no sign of a join. No. 195 (Pl. CXXXIV, 7, *a*) consists of heavy gold spherical beads, three of which are soldered together. Similar beads soldered so as to make wedge-shaped spacing beads were found in large number in Queen Shub Ad's grave, and a similar bead has been found at Tell Asmar. These beads from Harappā show that the use of gold solder was understood; from the colour it appears to have been made of gold with the addition of a little copper. **Gold beads.**

The two beads No. 196 (Pl. CXXXIV, 7, *d*) are long forms of the twisted square. The shape is as though a square bicone were cut in half and one half rotated forty-five degrees, after which they were joined together again. It is a very favourite design in Europe. Like No. 194, these beads show no sign of having been soldered.

No. 197 represents two gold caps to fit on beads (Pl. CXXXIV, 7, *c*). The habit of filling gold beads with various materials is frequently met with in Mesopotamia and Egypt. Bitumen is sometimes used, and at other times soft stones such as steatite. Some of those from Mesopotamia are made on a copper base. In this case the whole bead is covered. In many cases at Ur the gold caps fit on to the ends of an agate bead showing a broad band of agate between the gold.

There are several varieties of perforation. In some cases they have been carefully ground out with a hollow-ended drill, whilst others are very roughly made hour-glass holes. Some of the steatite beads have large square or rectangular perforations which suggest that such beads must have been mounted on wooden or metal bars. **Perforations.**

The steatite specimen No. 116, sent over with the beads, is the lower portion of a female torso. The carving is extremely crude but the modelling of the stomach and the indication of hair are quite clear.

A general survey of the beads sent from Harappā shows several very interesting anomalies. A number of points seem to point with absolute certainty to contact between the Indus and Mesopotamian civilizations. On the other hand, there are several facts which make this contact seem very improbable. If there were only one or two points suggesting definite contact, it might be thought that there was no close contact, and that the individual cases were due to some haphazard trade, but they are too frequent. The Indus seal discovered at Kish, if alone could have been explained in this way, but how can one explain the closely allied but different seals from Ur? **Conclusions. Points of similarity between Indus and Sumerian civilizations.**

Perhaps the most striking connection are the etched carnelians. This rare and difficult process is not likely to have originated in more than one country. Then the two plaque beads from Mohenjo-daro and Ur are so identical in design that it cannot be accidental, and at least two of this design come from each place. The lenticular circular beads with the white line round the edge (Pl. CXXXI, 4, *b*, *c*) is very similar to beads from Ur. The same remark applies to the broken eye bead (Pl. CXXXI, 4, *a*). Although etched beads are very rare at Mohenjo-daro, I understand that a fair number are found at Harappā.

Then the tabular beads with central rib, both circular (Pl. CXXXIII, 3, *a*, *b*, *d*) and bicone (Pl. CXXXIII, 3, *c*), are types found in considerable numbers in Mesopotamia, made especially of gold or lapis.

Again, the peculiar long carnelian beads from the Indus are identical with specimens from Mesopotamia. The Indus beads are sometimes longer than the Mesopotamian, but the latter are as much as three or even four inches long, whilst a somewhat similar shape in shell is found in Mesopotamia up to six inches long. These large shell beads belong to the Jemdet Nasr period.

The very flat lenticular and elliptical barrels are shapes that are numerous on the Indus, and also well known in Mesopotamia, but are practically unknown in Egypt.

Then the small steatite beads from Harappā (Pl. CXXXIV, 8-11) are practically the same as the beads from grave P. G. 55 in the early cemetery at Ur. The great number of these small beads in this grave is very extraordinary, since the use of burnt or treated steatite is very rare in Mesopotamia at that period. These beads were associated with an approximately equal number of lapis and carnelian beads. It is suggested that they formed a girdle. To suggest that such a girdle was imported complete is not a satisfactory explanation as lapis beads are apparently very rare on the Indus, and I have not seen any carnelian beads from Harappā which are at all like those from Grave 55 at Ur. Sections of steatite beads from both these sites are shown in Pl. CXXXV, 3-4.

Another interesting point of resemblance is the use of the trefoil ornament. This design which is painted on the beads and engraved on the steatite statue from Mohenjo-daro[1] has evidently a special significance. The motif, as pointed out by Mr. Sidney Smith (*op. cit.*), has been found on a bull discovered at Ur by Sir Leonard Woolley. The same design is carved in the centre of the forehead of a stone ram's head pendent from Persia, almost certainly from the Kirmanshah District, and now in the British Museum (No. 122131); and a trefoil shaped piece of inlay cut out of ostrich egg shell has also been found at Ur.

Another design found in India and Mesopotamia is the stepped design. A specimen from Harappā (Pl. CXXXII, 4, *d*) has already been described, while from Mohenjo-daro come two pieces of shell inlay practically identical with specimens from Ur (Pl. CXXXIV, 4). At Kish the same design is found on a fragmentary etched carnelian bead.

---

[1] *M. I. C.*, Pl. XCVIII.

On the other hand, the following facts point to there having been no very close connection between the two countries.

Points of dissimilarity between Indus and Sumerian civilizations.

Firstly, the Indus civilization, as far as beads are concerned, is primarily a steatite civilization. More beads were made of this material than of all the other materials put together, whilst in Mesopotamia, with the exception of the small beads from Grave 55, very few beads of steatite have been found. In Egypt, although glazed steatite beads were commoner, they were generally small until a much later date, and never reached the size of the larger Indian specimens.

Secondly, the technique of painting steatite. which appears to have been frequently practised at Harappā, is not known elsewhere, either in Mesopotamia, Egypt, or Crete.

Thirdly, there is the rareness of lapis in the Indus civilization. The fact that this material is so rare at Harappā and Mohenjo-daro, and is so extremely common at Ur, is difficult to account for. It seems certain that it came to Ur from North East Afghanistan and that the Trade route must have been fairly close to the Indus Valley; also, the distance from Afghanistan to Mesopotamia being so much greater than the distance to the Indus Valley, one would expect to find more lapis at Harappā than at Ur.

Fourthly, from the representative collection sent to me it appears that no beads of crystalline quartz, amethyst, garnet, or obsidian occur at Harappā, though beads of the first three materials are fairly common in Mesopotamia, and beads of obsidian are not very rare; and they are all found in considerable numbers in Egypt.

Fifthly, one of the favourite shapes for lapis beads at Ur was the bicone about standard length and often elliptical. This shape I have not seen amongst the beads from Harappā.

Sixthly, flattened leach beads have not been reported from Harappā. This is strange, as quite a number made of faience, agate, and other stones have been found in Mesopotamia, and also large numbers have been found at Taxila.

Seventhly, objects called plumb-bobs[1] have been found in some numbers at Ur, but they have not been found at Harappā. They consist of a drop-shape or spherical pendent which is perforated vertically for a short way and then in a transverse direction until the perforations meet. The suggestion is that a string with a knot on it could be pulled into the transverse perforation so that the pendent would then hang true at the end of the string.

Eighthly, in Egypt and Mesopotamia a number of beads are made of blue frit. This material is not faience but is a chemical compound. It is a double silicate of lime and copper. There are two varieties, hard and soft. Most of the Mesopotamian beads are made of the soft frit. Neither variety occurs amongst the beads sent from Harappā.

Summary.

To summarise, we have eight facts which point very strongly to extensive intercourse between the Indus and Mesopotamian civilizations. One, the seal from Kish. Two, similar etched carnelians. Three, the tabular beads with median ridge. Four, flat elliptical and lenticular barrels. Five, the long carnelian

[1] For ear-drops shaped like a plumb-bob or drop see Pl. CXXXIX, 31 & 33—35, p. 447 *infra*. M. S. V.

barrels. Six, the small "burnt" steatite beads like those from Ur. Seven, the trefoil design. Eight, the step design.

As against this, we have the following eight facts which suggest that the connection between the two civilizations was not very close. One, great quantities of steatite at Harappā. Two, "painted" steatite only known in the Indus Valley. Three, rareness of lapis at Harappā. Four, no beads of quartz, garnet, or obsidian. Five, no standard elliptical bicones. Six, no leach beads. Seven, no plumb-bobs. Eight, no blue frit.

The only solution that I can suggest to account for these anomalous facts is that the two civilizations met in a third one, not at present discovered, and that this acted like a filter, handing on some articles and detaining others.

APPENDIX A.

List of selected Beads from Harappā supplied by the author.

Serial No.	Field Reg. No.	Material.	Shape.	Size.	Depth b. s.	Stratum.	Square.	Mound.	Peculiarities (frequency of occurrence).	Remarks.
1	2	3	4	5	6	7	8	9	10	11
1	10700	Steatite	Barrel-shaped	L. 2-3/16"; diam. at centre 1-1/16".	7' 6"	III	L 12/9	F	Unique	It has 4 circular bands in relief cut over it.
2	H892	Agate	Do.	L. 1-1/2"; diam. at centre 7/8".	10'	IV	S 34/12	Area H	Rare.	
3	202	Do.	Do.	L. 1-1/4"; diam. 7-8".	8' 3"	III	M 12/12	F	Unique.	
4	8490	Quartzite	Do.	L. 1-1/2"; diam. 11/16".	4' 9"	II	I 14/8	F	Rare.	
5	7438	Burnt steatite	Do.	L. 15/16"; diam. 3/4".	9' 0"	IV	Q 24/3	AB	Only a few.	
6	4783	Steatite paste	Do.	L. 1"; diam. 1/2".	8' 7"	III	K 9/1	F	Ditto.	
7	5641	Burnt steatite	Do.	E. L. 1-1/8"; diam. 1/2".	6' 0"	II	P 24/6	AB	A considerable number (extends into other strata).	Fragmentary. Painted in white with bands over brown surface.
8	778	Do	Cylindrical	L. 9/16"; diam. 5/16".	10' 0"	IV	M 12/16	F	Ditto.	
9	G203 (2 beads).	Do.	Barrel-shaped	L. 1/2" and 5/8"; diam. 1/4".	4' 0"	II	AM 35/22	Area G	Ditto	Painted with sets of white bands, the steatite one on red ground and the other on chocolate ground.
10	Ae281	Do.	Do.	L. 11/16"; diam. 1/4".	4' 8"	II	..	F	Ditto	Painted with sets of white bands.
11	A	Do.	Do.	L. 5/16"; diam. 3/16".	..	..	..	..	Quite common (extends into other strata).	Ditto.
12	10567	Faience	Do.	L. 3/4"; diam. 3/8".	3' 0"	II	P 10/4	F	A few.	
13	3028	Stalagmite	Do.	L. 3/4"; diam. 3/8".	18' 0"	VI	M 11/10	F	Do.	
14	5915	Jasper	Do.	L. 5/8"; diam. 3/8".	6' 6"	III	P 24/9	AB	Rare.	
15	3422	Ferruginous argillaceous limestone.	Do.	L. 11/16"; diam. 3/8".	5' 10"	II	N 10/1	F	Unique.	
16	A307	Serpentine	Do.	L. 9/16"; diam. 3/8".	4' 6"	II	..	F	Rare.	
17	11074	Agate	Do.	L. 5/8"; diam. 5/16".	8' 0"	III	J 12/3	F	Do.	
18	PII-28	Obsidian or pitchstone.	Do.	L. 5/8"; diam. 3/8".	..	..	..	AB	Do.	
19	5670	Agate	Do.	L. 7/8"; diam. 9/16".	10' 0"	IV	M 10/21	F	Common enough (extends into other strata).	Unperforated.
20	B1182	Do.	Do.	L. 7/8"; diam. 7/16".	24' 0"	..	..	AB	Ditto	Ditto.
21	PIV-105	Chrysoprase and sard.	Do.	L. 5/8"; diam. 7/16".	10' 0"	IV	..	AB	Rare.	
22	7452	Limestone	Do.	L. 3/4"; diam. 7/16".	3' 6"	II	P 25/1	AB	Do.	
23	B1180	Carnelian or sard.	Do.	L. 1/2"; diam. 3/8".	24' 0"	IV	..	AB	Common (extends into other strata).	
24	10803	Limestone	Do.	L. 9/16"; diam. 5/16".	4' 5"	II	P 0/3	F	A few (extends into other strata).	

APPENDIX A—*contd.*

Serial No.	Field Reg. No.	Material.	Shape.	Size.	Depth b. s.	Stratum.	Square.	Mound.	Peculiarities (frequency of occurrence).	REMARKS.
1	2	3	4	5	6	7	8	9	10	11
25	PH-28	Amphibolite .	Barrel-shaped	L. 3/4"; diam. 5/16".	5' 0"	II	.	AB	Unique	
26	2567	Green stone .	Do. .	L. 9/16"; diam. 5/16".	11' 6"	V	M 11/21	F	Rare.	
27	G111	Jasper . .	Do .	L. 7/16"; diam. 1/4".	1' 0"	I	AM 35/23	Area G	A few.	
28	5003	Steatite .	Do. .	L. 3/4"; diam. 5/16".	8' 10"	III	P 24/8	AB	Rare	
29	12495	Jasper . .	Do. .	L. 11/16"; diam. 1/2".	8' 8"	III	M 11/25	F.	Unique.	
30	3058	Carnelian .	Do. .	L. 13/16"; diam. 7/16".	13' 0"	V	I 9/14	F	Rare.	
31	4740	Lapis lazuli .	Do. .	L. 11/16"; diam. 3/8".	8' 0"	III	Q 23/25	AB	A few.	
32	10650K	Steatite .	Do. .	L. 1"; diam. 1/2".	3' to 4'	II	J 12/23	F	Common enough (extends into other strata).	Unperforated.
33	11869	White faience	Do. .	L. 1"; diam. 7/16".	13' 0"	V	Q 28/21	AB	Rare.	
34	11583	Jadeite .	Do. .	L. 3/4"; diam. 7/16".	5' 8"	II	I 13/17	F	A few (extends into other strata).	Unperforated.
35	2522	Stalagmite .	Do. .	L. 13/16"; diam. 3/8".	16' 0"	VI	N 9/9	F	Rare.	
36	Ac281	Jadeite .	Do. .	L. 1/2"; diam. 3/8".	4' 8"	II	..	F	Do.	
37	H475	Chalcedony .	Do. .	L. 7/8"; diam. 9/16".	7' 5"	III	R 33/13	Area H	Common (extends into other strata).	
38	2064	Do. . .	Do. .	L. 11/16"; diam. 3/8".	14' 0"	V	N 9/7	F	Common.	
39	B	Hornblende breccia.	Do. .	L. 13/16"; diam. 3/8".	..	..	..	..	Considerable number found (extends into other strata).	
40	7850	Sard . .	Do. .	L. 5/8"; diam. 5/16".	10' 6"	IV	I 9/14	F	Common (extends into other strata).	
41	3104	Carnelian .	Do. .	L. 7/16"; diam. 1/4".	0' 4"	I	I 13/3	F	Ditto.	
42	5318	Do. .	Do. .	L. 3/8"; diam. 1/4".	5' 2"	II	N 10/8	F	Ditto.	
43	1608	Jadeite .	Do. .	L. 5/8"; diam. 3/8".	2' 0"	I	I 9/14	F	Ditto.	
44	B313	Serpentine .	Do. .	L. 1/8"; diam. 7/16".	0' to 4'	II	..	AB	Unique.	
45	145a	Limestone .	Long barrel-shaped.	L. 2-5/8"; diam. 3/4".	5' to 5' 6"	II	M 11/15	F	Considerable number found (extends into other strata).	
46	G50	Banded limestone.	Do. .	L. 2-3/8"; diam. 1/2".	3' 4"	II	AO 36/5	Area G	Rare.	
47	8606	Agate . .	Do. .	L. 1-7/8"; diam. 9/16".	3' 0"	I	M 13/25	F	Common (extends into other strata).	
47a	Ac281	Do. . .	Do. .	L. 1-7/16"; diam. 1/2".	4' 8"	II	..	F	Rare.	
48	513	Jadeite .	Do. .	L. 1-3/16"; diam. 1/2".	16' 0"	VI	M 11/25	F	Unique.	
49	10566	Carnelian .	Do. .	B. L. 2-3/4"; diam. 3/8".	2' 0"	I	P 10/5	F	Common enough (extends into other strata).	Broken at one end.
50	Ab167	Steatite .	Elliptical double convex.	L. 1-5/8"; W. 1-1/8".	7' 0"	III	..	F	Considerable number (extends into other strata).	Fragmentary.
51	1910	Steatite paste	Do. .	L. 1-3/16"; W. 7/8".	11' 0"	IV	N 9/7	F	Ditto . .	Ditto.
52	8650o	Burnt steatite	Do. .	L. 7/8"; W. 3/4".	4' to 7'	III & IV.	H 12/21 & I 12/1.	F	Ditto . .	Ditto.
53	11062 (2 beads).	Do. .	Do. .	L. 3/4"; W. 1/2".	5' 0"	II	O 9/9	F	Ditto . .	2nd bead is discular and of greenish stone (diam. [illegible]).
54	Ac281	Limestone .	Do. .	L. 11/16"; W. 1/2".	4' 8"	II	..	F	A few.	
55	8650N	Burnt steatite	Do. .	L. 3/4"; W. 1/2".	4' to 7'	III	H 12/21 & I 12/1.	F	Rare	It is drilled with trefoil designs for inlay.
56	J120	Do. .	Do. .	E. L. 1-5/8"; W. 1-1/4".	4' 5"	II	R 30/16	D	Common (extends into other strata).	It is fragmentary and painted in white with trefoil designs over brownish surface.
57	12445	Do. .	Do. .	L. 1-3/16"; W. 1-1/16".	4' 6"	II	M 12/23	F	Rare	It is painted with trefoil design over chocolate surface.
58	6848	Do. .	Do. .	L. 7/8"; W. 11/16".	7' 8"	III	J 12/8	F	Do.	It is painted in white and red with trefoil designs over red ground.
59	487	Agate . .	Do. .	L. 13/16"; W. 3/4".	11' 0"	IV	Q 24/22	AB	Do.	
60	10830	Onyx . .	Do. .	L. 1"; W. 11/16".	1' 0"	I	O 10/21	F	Unique.	
61	11860	Milky quartz.	Do. .	L. 13/16"; W. 5/8".	13' 4"	V	Q 28/21	AB	A few.	
62	10671	Lapis lazuli .	Do. .	L. 13/16"; W. 1/2".	3' 6"	II	P 10/3	F	A few (extends into other strata).	

APPENDIX A—*contd.*

Serial No.	Field Reg. No.	Material.	Shape.	Size.	Depth b. s.	Stratum.	Square.	Mound.	Peculiarities (frequency of occurrence).	REMARKS.
1	2	3	4	5	6	7	8	9	10	11
63	J31	Jadeite	Elliptical double convex.	L. 11/16"; W. 1/2".	1' 6"	I	S 60/11	D	Common (extends into other strata).	
64	4063	Andesite (?)	Do.	L. 11/16"; W. 7/16".	3' 0"	I	K 8/4	F	Rare.	
65	3857	Banded agate	Rectangular double convex.	1-3/16" × 5/8"	5' 3"	III	I 8/5	F	Do.	
66	1734	Limestone	Do.	3/4" × 3/8"	14' 6"	V	R 24/6	AB	A few (extends into other strata).	
67	5172	Chalcedony	Do.	3/4" × 3/5"	10' 0"	III	K 9/2	F	Ditto.	
68	A426	Andesite	Do.	11/16" × 3/8"	4' 0"	II	..	F	Rare.	
69	8417	Jasper	Do.	3/4" × 3/8"	4' 6"	II	I 14/7	F	A few (extends into other strata).	
70	B363	Do.	Rectangular plano-convex.	3/4" × 3/8"	0' to 4'	II	..	AB	A few.	
71	H232	Agate	Do.	11/16" × 5/16"	3' 10"	II	S 34/1	Area H	Considerable number (extends into other strata).	
72	3377	Variegated faience.	Do.	13/16" × 3/8"	6' 6"	II	Q 24/24	AB	Rare.	
73	C	Limestone	Barrel-shaped double convex.	7/16" × 5/16"	..	..	..	..	Common (extends into other strata).	
74	4376	Banded stone	Do.	9/16" × 5/16"	5' 0"	II	Q 24/16	AB	A few (extends into other strata).	
75	d	Black stone	Do.	7/16" × 5/16"	..	..	..	..	Ditto.	
76	9085	Banded stone	Elliptical double convex.	9/16" × 3/8"	8' 7"	III	I 12/2	F	Rare.	
77	9062	Agate	Barrel-shaped double convex.	9/16" × 5/16"	13' 0"	V	J 9/3	F	Do.	
78	E	Carnelian	Do.	L. 1/2"; W. broken	..	..	..	..	Unique	It is painted in white with a set of concentric circles, fragmentary.
79	7468	Burnt steatite	Rectangular plane on both sides.	1-9/16" × 1-1/6"	6' 6"	II	M 12/9	F	Common enough (extends into other strata).	
80	715	Do.	Do.	1" × 5/8"	11' 0"	V	M 12/6	F	Ditto.	
81	5716	Do.	Rectangular plano-convex.	1-3/16" × 1"	7' 0"	III	M 10/21	F	Rare	It has only one hole.
82	8523	Do.	Rectangular plane on both sides.	1-1/16" × 13/16"	6' 0"	III	I 14/6	F	Unique	Holed through centre.
83	7674	Agate	Rectangular double convex.	L. 13/16"	18' 6"	V	P 24/21	AB	Rare	Fragmentary.
84	2251	Burnt steatite	Do.	9/16" × 7/16"	17' 7"	VI	N 9/7	F	A few	Rounded at both ends.
85	10470	Do.	Do.	1/2" × 7/16"	3' 2"	II	I 12/23	F	Do.	Double holed.
86	11051	Steatite	Do. (4 beads).	7/16" × 3/5"	4' 0"	II	O 9/25	F	Common	Unfinished.
87	10432	Do.	Rectangular (4 sided).	5/16" × 1/4"	1' 9"	I	J 12/18	F	Do.	
88	3223	Carnelian	Oval double-convex.	1/2" × 3/5"	10' 0"	V	I 7/25	F	Rare.	
89	5407	Burnt steatite	Cylindrical ribbed.	L. 1-7/16"; diam. 13/16".	5' 0"	II	I 9/10	F	Very few (extends into other strata).	Fragmentary, tapers upwards.
90	1977	Do.	Do.	L. 13/16"; diam. 7/16".	4' 0"	I	M 10/25	F	Ditto.	
91	7292	Do.	Cylindrical	L. 1"; diam. 5/16".	10' 0"	IV	Q 24/4	AB	Considerable number (extends into other strata).	
92	7628	Do.	Do.	L. 1/2"; diam. 5/16".	8' 4"	III	P 24/14	F	Ditto.	
93	10634	Steatite	Do.	L. 7/8"; diam. 5/16".	2' 0"	I	P 10/5	F	Rare.	
94	10872	Burnt steatite	Do.	L. 1-3/16"; diam. 5/16".	7' 4"	III	I 12/19	F	A few	Broken at one end.
95	11636	Faience	Tubular	L. 7/8"; diam. 3/16".	7' 9"	III	Q 20/21	AB	Do.	
96	G42	Burnt steatite	Do.	L. 7/16"; diam. 1/16".	0' 9"	I	Am 48/25	Area G	Considerable number (extends into other strata).	
97	2668(6)	Do.	Discular plane on both sides.	Diam. 15/16"	..	..	..	..	Rare	From spoil earth.

APPENDIX A—*contd.*

Serial No.	Field Reg. No.	Material.	Shape.	Size.	Depth b. s.	Stratum.	Square.	Mound.	Peculiarities (frequency of occurrence).	REMARKS.
1	2	3	4	5	6	7	8	9	10	11
98	5586	Burnt steatite	Discular plane on both sides.	Diam. 1-1/8" . .	5' 0"	II	P 24/9	AB	A few (extends into other strata).	
99	f	Do. .	Do. .	Diam. 11/16" .	..	..	..	..	Rare.	
100	4155	Do. .	Do. .	..	1' 0"	I	Q 30/20	AB	Considerable number (extends into other strata).	A string consisting of 58 beads of which 48 are large thin (diam. ⅛"), 5 small thin (diam. ¼") and 5 thick (diam. ⅛").
101	10981	Do. .	Discular .	Diam. 5/8" to 3/8".	4' 0"	II	O 9/23	F	Common enough (extends into other strata).	A string of 4 thick beads.
102	H449	Do. .	Do. .	Diam. 3/16" to 5/8".	4' 2"	II	S 34/18	Area H	Ditto.	A string of 35 beds. 2 being other than discular in shape.
103	10983	Do. .	Do. .	Diam. 3/16" .	5' 0"	IV	J 12/19	F	Large number (extends into other strata).	A string of 133 tiny thin beads.
104	904	Do. .	Discular plano-convex.	Diam. 13/16" .	3' 6"	I	J 9/29	F	Common (extends into other strata).	
105	B1454	Do. .	Do. .	Diam. 11/16" .	16' 0"	..	..	AB	Ditto.	
106	3004	Do. .	Do. .	Diam. 3/4" . .	2' 6"	I	K 9/2	F	Ditto.	
107	4783	Do. .	Do. .	Diam. 5/8" . .	8' 0"	III	J 9/25	F	Ditto.	
108	4392	Do. .	Do. .	Diam. 11/16" .	6' 0"	III	Q 23/22	AB	Ditto.	
109	G	Do. .	Do. .	Diam. 9/16" .	..	..	..	..	Unique	Holed across the thickness.
110	H471	Do. .	Discular double-convex.	Diam. 1-1/16" .	4' 2"	II	R 34/21	Area H	A few.	
111	7030	Carnelian .	Do. .	Diam. 3/4" . .	8' 5"	IV	P 24/9	AB	Rare	Cut flat at top and bottom.
112	883	Milky quartz	Do. .	Diam. 1/2" . .	4' 0"	II	J 8/22	F	Do.	
113	H	Steatite .	Discular, plane on both sides.	Diam. 7/8" . .	..	..	..	..	A few.	
114	11446c	Do. .	Do. .	Diam. 3/8" . .	11' 2"	V	K 12/22	F	Do.	
115	12290	Burnt steatite	Do. .	Diam. 11/16" .	15' 6"	V	Q 28/21	AB	Rare	Double holed.
116	625	Steatite .	Rectangular oval in section.	L. 1-1/8"; W. 1-3/8".	3' 4"	II	M 12/7	F	Unique	It is pierced with a rectangular hole.
117	I	Burnt steatite	Discular 1/48" to ¼", cylindrical 1/16" to ⅛".	..	7' 4"	III	I 14/15	F	Rare	150 tiny beads, the tiniest of them measures about 1/48" diam.
118	4584	Do. .	Discular double convex.	Diam. 1/2" . .	9' to 12'	V	N 9/15 & 20.	F	Unique	On one face it is relieved by a cross and on the other by a 4-petalled flower.
119	2250	Do. .	Tooth-shaped	L. 9/16" . .	7' 8"	IV	N 0/13	F	Do.	
120	656	Do. .	Bugle-shaped	Ht. 7/8" . .	7' 0"	III	M 12/18	F	Do.	It is more like a pendent
121	11629	Do. .	Conical .	Ht. 9/16" . .	8' 5"	III	Q 27/4	AB	Rare.	
122	10726	Do. .	Do. .	Ht. 3/8" . .	5' 0"	II	K 13/18	F	Do.	
123	7097	Do. .	Round . .	Diam. 11/16" .	8' 0"	III	Q 24/3	AB	Unique	It has a broad band in relief carved on it.
124	1758	Do. .	Round ribbed	Diam. 1/4" .	5' 0"	II	M 11/24	F	Do.	
125	760	Do. .	1. Hemispherical. 2. Tubular.	Diam. 1", L. 3/4" .	9' 0"	IV	M 12/17	F	Rare.	
126	12086	Do. .	Cross-shaped	11/16" × 5/8" .	14' 0"	V	Q 28/6	AB	Unique.	
127	5877	Do. .	Rhomboidal with fluted edges.	7/16" × 3/8" . .	4' 3"	II	M 10/21	F	Rare	Fragmentary.
128	12197	Stone and faience.	Varying shapes	Smallest diam. 3/16"; largest 1-1/2".	11' 0"	IV	R 28/2	AB	Common (extends into other strata).	A string of 14 beads.
129	A8205	Carnelian, sard and faience.	Tubular .	L. 5/16" to 1-7/8".	3' 6"	II	..	F	Ditto . .	A string of 4 beads, 2 of carnelian and 2 of other stones.
130	10868	Copper .	Cylindrical .	L. 3/8" . .	10' 0"	IV	K 12/23	F	Rare.	
131	6853	Do. . .	Discular thick	Diam. 1/2" . .	9' 8"	IV	P 24/6	AB	Do.	
132	7225	Alabaster .	Discular .	Diam. 1-1/4" .	6' 6"	IV	P 24/14	AB	Common (extends into other strata).	
133	G154	Do. .	Do. .	Diam. 1" . .	4' 3"	II	AM 35/17	Area G	Ditto.	

APPENDIX A—*contd.*

Serial No.	Field Reg. No.	Material.	Shape.	Size.	Depth b. s.	Stratum.	Square.	Mound.	Peculiarities (frequency of occurrence).	REMARKS.
1	2	3	4	5	6	7	8	9	10	11
134	10418	Steatite with white glaze.	Discular	Diam. 1"	3' 10"	I	M 12/20	F	Unique.	
135	11820	Jaisalmer yellow lime-stone.	Discular, double-convex.	Diam. 1-1/4"	13' 0"	V	R 27/28	AB	A few (extends into other strata).	Cut flat on both sides.
136	5183	Do.	Do.	Diam. 1"	5' 6"	II	Q 24/1	AB	Ditto	Ditto.
137	J	Terracotta	Barrel-shaped	L. 13/16"	..	..	..	..	A few.	
138	4797	Do.	Discular	Diam. 1-3/4"	7' 0"	III	Q 24/9	AB	Very common (extends into other strata).	
139	2587	Do.	Do.	Diam. 1-3/8"	11' 5"	V	I 2/16	F	Common (extends into other strata).	It has grooved rim.
140	5502	Do.	Do.	Diam. 1-1/2"	5' 0"	II	P 24/6	AB	Common enough (extends into other strata).	
141	7144	Do.	Discular, double-convex.	Diam. 7/8"	4' 6"	II	P 23/25	AB	A few (extends into other strata).	
142	5215	Do.	Discular	Diam. 1-5/16"	10' 3"	III	K 9/2	F	Ditto.	
143	10545	Do.	Do.	Diam. 7/8" to 1-1/8".	3' 0"	I	K 12/13	F	Very common (extends into other strata).	3 beads.
144	K	Do.	Biconical	Diam. 1"	..	..	..	..	A few.	
145	E29	Do.	Do.	Diam. 1-1/8"	3' 0"	I	..	AB	Common enough (extends into other strata).	
146	B23	Do.	Conical	Diam. 1"; ht. 3/4".	..	..	..	AB	A few	Generally connected with upper strata.
147	12401d	Do.	Round	Diam. 9/16	13' 0"	..	Q 27/25	AB	Do.	
148	10730	Do.	3 tubular and 1 discular.	L. 7/8" to 1"; diam. 3/4".	9' 0"	IV	L 12/9	F	Considerable number (extends into other strata).	String of 4 beads.
149	12401c/1	Do.	Biconical	L. 3/16" to 7/16"	13' 0"	V	Q 27/25	AB	Common	String of 10 beads.
150	12401c/2	Do.	Discular, double-convex.	Diam. 1/4" to 3/8".	13' 0"	V	Q 27/25	AB	Do.	Ditto.
151	L	Shell	Barrel-shaped	L. 1-3/8"; diam. 3/4".	..	..	..	..	Considerable number (extends into other strata).	Unperforated.
152	12431	Do.	Cylindrical	L. 13/16"; diam. 13/16".	15' 9"	V	R 27/5	AB	Ditto.	
153	12270	Do.	Do.	L. 11/16"; diam. 9/16".	7' 0"	III	P 11/1	F	Ditto.	
154	6704	Do.	Discular convex.	Diam. 1-1/2"	5' 0"	II	L 12/4	F	Common (extends into other strata).	
155	127	Do.	Do.	Diam. 15/16"	5'-5' 8"	III	M 11/16	F	Ditto.	
156	1979	Do.	Discular wheel-shaped.	Diam. 15/16"	4' 0"	I	M 10/25	F	A few	Fragmentary.
157	1773	Faience	4 sided biconical.	L. 5/8"	9' 0"	IV	N 9/8	F	Unique.	
158	2923	Ivory	Discular thick	Diam. 1"	13' 0"	VI	R 24/7	AB	Do.	
159	10885d	Faience, steatite, lapis lazuli.	4 barrel-shaped and 3 of other shapes	L. 3/16" to 3/4"	15' 8"	VI	M 12/7	F	Rare	String of 7 beads.
160	2638	Faience	Flat rectangular tapering.	13/16" × 5/8"	11' 4"	V	N 9/18	F	Unique	Double holed and ribbed on one side.
161	12506	Do.	Discular	Diam. 2-1/4"	10' 0"	IV	M 12/22	F	Rare	It has a tubular hole across centre. Fragmentary.
162	8508	Do.	Gadrooned	Diam. 7/16"	5' 6"	II	I 13/10	F	Do.	
163	3082	Do.	Elliptical double-convex.	L. 11/16"	3' 0"	II	Q 31/11	D	Do.	Double holed.
164	7035	Do.	Elliptical	L. 9/16"	2' 0"	I	P 23/23	AB	A few	It is incised with concentric circle on one side.
164a	4227	Do.	Oval	9/16" × 7/16"	8' 3"	IV	N 9/15	F	Rare.	
165	PIII-50	Do.	Hemispherical	Diam. 11/16"	7' 6"	III	..	AB	Unique.	
166	PIII-70	Do.	Discular	Diam. 1-1/16"	9' 0"	IV	..	AB	Very common (extends into other strata).	
167	BG30	Do.	Do.	Diam. 7/8"	..	..	..	AB	Ditto.	
168	4423	Steatite	Round	Diam. 3/4"	8' 3"	III	K 8/3	F	Rare.	
169	Ab809	Faience	Discular	Diam. 5/8"	5' 0"	II	..	F	A few.	

APPENDIX A—*concld.*

Serial No.	Field Reg. No.	Material.	Shape.	Size.	Depth b. s.	Stratum.	Square.	Mound.	Peculiarities (frequency of occurrence).	REMARKS.
1	2	3	4	5	6	7	8	9	10	11
170	3721	Faience .	1 discular and the other cylindrical.	Diam. 5/8" and L. 3/6" respectively.	6' 0"	III	Q 25/11	AB	A few	2 beads.
171	1612	Do. .	..	L. 3/32" to 13/16".	7' 0"	III	K 12/6	F	Common (extends into other strata).	String comprising 2 beads, 1 spacer and 1 and piece.
172	1486	Do.	4 being thin discular 1 tubular and 1 oval.	Diam. 3/16"; L. 5/8" to 9/16".	3' 6"	I	N 9/18	F	Common	String of 6 beads.
173	391	Do. .	Long barrel .	L. 2-3/16"; diam. 1/4".	3' 0"	I	M 11/10	F	A few (extends into other strata).	
174	G89	Do. .	Cylindrical .	L. 1-3/4"; diam. 3/8".	4' 6"	II	AO 36/15	Area G	Rare.	
175	368	Steatite	Tubular .	L. 3"; diam. 3/8".	..	..	..	..	Unique	Broken into two pieces.
176	9060	Do. .	Do .	L. 1-7/8"; diam. 5/8"	6' 9"	III	I 12/7	F	Do.	
177	11984	Faience .	4 tubular and one discular.	L. 1/4" to 1-11/16"; diam. 3/8", respectively.	19' 8"	VII	I 12/20	F	Common	String of 5 beads.
178	10185E	Do. .	Cylindrical .	L. 1/6" to 3/8" .	15' 8"	VI	M 12/7	F	Common (extends into other strata).	String of 84 beads.
179	8592D	Do. .	Round . .	Diam. 1/8" to 3/16"	6' 9" to 7'	III	I 14/10	F	Ditto . .	String of 20 beads including one double segmented bead.
180	8592E	Do. .	Cylindrical .	L. 1/4" to 3/8" .	6' 9" to 7'	III	I 14/10	F	Ditto . .	String of 23 beads.
181	7311	Do. and shell.	3 round, 2 barrel-shaped and 1 discular.	Diam. 3/8" to 1/2"; L. 5/16" to 1/2".	7' 0"	III	Q 23/25	AB	Ditto . .	String of 6 beads.
182	12174	Do. and jasper.	2 discular, 1 elliptical.	Diam. 5/16" to 1/2"; L. 1/2".	15' 6"	V	Q 28/6	AB	Ditto . .	String of 3 beads.
183	B1373	Lapis lazuli steatite and faience.	1 discular, 1 barrel-shaped and 1 oval.	Diam. 1/2"; L. 5/16" to 1/2".	20' 0"	IV	..	AB	Ditto . .	Ditto.
184	Ab745	Faience and terracotta.	2 discular, 2 round and 2 barrel-shaped	Diam. 3/8"; L. 1/4" to 7/16".	8' 0"	IV	..	F	Ditto . .	String of 6 beads
185	12588	Burnt steatite	Cylindrical .	L. 1-5/16"; diam. 5/16".	2' 0"	I	J 14/1	F	Unique	It has a broad belt in the centre.
186	12484	Do. and faience.	1 discular, and the other cylindrical.	Diam. 7/8"; L. 5/16".	5' 4"	II	M 12/25	F	Discular bead rare . .	2
187	J414	Faience .	Barrel-shaped	L. 1-3/8" . .	4' 3"	II	Q 30/9	D	A few	
188	10486	Jasper .	1 elliptical plano-convex 1 cylindrical.	L. 5/8" and 7/16".	3' 6"	II	I 12/23	F	Elliptical bead rare . .	2
189	A7	Agate . .	Ovoid, lentoid in section.	3/8" × 2/3" . .	..	..	..	F	Rare.	
190	J87	Shell . .	Tubular tapering. ;	L. 11/16"; diam. 5/32".	8' 0"	IV	S 30/6	D	Unique	Fluted.
191	12572	Burnt steatite, etc.	1 round, 1 discular and 1 elliptical.	Diam. 1/2" and 5/16"; L. 7/16", respectively.	6' 2"	II	M 12/21	F	Common (extends into other strata).	
192	1880	Sard . .	Tubular .	L. 1/8"; diam. 1/8".	11' 4"	V	M 10/11	F	Rare	
193	J 129	Felspar .	Do. . .	L. 13/16"; diam. 3/16".	9' 0"	IV	S 30/11	D	Do.	
194	4247	Gold . .	Barley-shaped	L. 11/16"; diam. at centre 3/16".	6' 6"	III	N 9/16	F	....	Wt. 2 gms.
195	8060	Do. . .	String of 5 round beads.	Diam. 3/32" .	7' 8" to 8' 4".	III	I 14/1	F	....	Wt. ½ gm.
196	8060	Do. . .	2 biconical facetted beads.	Each measuring 9/16" in length and 1/4" in diameter.	7' 8" to 8' 4"	III	I 14/1	F	....	Wt. 1·5 gms.
197	8060	Do. . .	2 cylindrical beads.	Each measuring 1/2" in length and 3/16" in diameter.	7' 8" to 8' 4"	III	I 14/1	F	....	Wt. 1·2 gms including that of the encased cylindrical steatite beads.
198	8060	Silver . .	10 decayed beads.	Each measuring about 1/8" in diameter.	7' 8" to 8' 4"	III	I 14/1	F	....	

APPENDIX B.

Beads from Harappā : Description of plates.

No. on	No. on List of selected beads.[1]	Harappā Reference No.	No. on Pls. CXXXI-CXXXIV.	Material.
Plate CXXIX—1 .	178	10185E	....	Faience.
„ 2 .	192	1860	CXXXI, 2, *g* .	Carnelian.
„ 3 .	95	11636	CXXXIII, 9, *c* .	Faience.
„ 4 .	93	10634	CXXXII, 1, *c* .	Steatite.
„ 5 .	91	7292	CXXXII, 5, *i* .	Steatite.
„ 6 .	174	G89	CXXXIII, 7, *c* .	Yellow faience.
„ 7 .	152	12431	CXXXIV, 2, *c* .	Shell.
„ 8 .	155	127	CXXXIV, 2, *e* .	Shell.
„ 9 .	97	2668	CXXXII, 5, *o* .	Steatite.
„ 10 .	101	10981	CXXXIII, 1, *b* .	Steatite.
„ 11 .	102	H449	CXXXIII, 1, *d* .	Steatite.
„ 12 .	100	4155	CXXXIII, 1, *c* .	Steatite.
„ 13 .	102	H449	CXXXIII, 1, *d* .	Steatite.
„ 14 .	100	4155	CXXXIII, 1, *c* .	Steatite.
„ 15 .	103	10983	CXXXIII, 1, *a* .	Steatite.
„ 16 .	37	H475	CXXXI, 3, *n* .	Chalcedony.
„ 17 .	3	202	CXXXI, 1, *c* .	Agate.
„ 18 .	5	7438	CXXXII, 5, *c* .	Steatite.
„ 19 .	4	8490	CXXXI, 1, *b* .	Agate.
„ 20 .	187	J414	CXXXIII, 9, *h* .	Faience.
„ 21 .	173	391	CXXXIII, 9, *a* .	Faience.
„ 22 .	46	G50	CXXXI, 6, *g* .	Stalagmite.
„ 23 .	45	145*a*	CXXXI, 6, *e* .	Limestone.
„ 24 .	48	518	CXXXI, 7, *e* .	Serpentine.
„ 25 .	49	10566	CXXXI, 2, *b* .	Carnelian.
„ 26 .	42	5318	CXXXI, 2, *h* .	Carnelian.

[1] See Appendix A, pp. 412ff.

APPENDIX B—*contd.*

No. on	No. on List of selected beads.	Harappā Reference No.	No. on Pls. CXXXI-CXXXIV.	Material.
Plate CXXIX—27 .	128	12197	CXXXI, 2, *e* .	Carnelian.
„ 28 .	114	11446c	CXXXII, 1, *d* .	Steatite.
„ 29 .	168	4423	CXXXII, 5, *k* .	Steatite.
„ 30 .	167	BG50	CXXXIII, 9, *e* .	Faience.
„ 31 .	134	10418	CXXXII, 5, *l* .	Steatite.
„ 32 .	166	PIII-70	CXXXIII, 9, *d* .	Faience.
„ 33 .	132	7225	CXXXI, 7, *a* .	Marble.
„ 34 .	181	7511	CXXXIII, 9, *f* .	Faience.
„ 35 .	184	Ab745	CXXXIII, 9, *n* .	Faience.
„ 36 .	143	10546	CXXXIV, 1, *d* .	Terracotta.
„ 37 .	145	E29	CXXXIV, 1, *f* .	Terracotta.
„ 38 .	143	10545	CXXXIV, 1, *h* .	Terracotta.
„ 39 .	143	10545	CXXXIV, 1. *h* .	Terracotta.
„ 40 .	135	11820	CXXXI, 6, *a* .	Limestone.
„ 41 .	136	5183	CXXXI, 6, *b* .	Limestone.
„ 42 .	113	H	CXXXII, 1, *a* .	Steatite.
„ 43 .	111	7039	CXXXI, 2, *c* .	Carnelian.
„ 44 .	141	7144	CXXXIV, 1, *l* .	Terracotta.
„ 45 .	142	5215	CXXXIV, 1, *c* .	Terracotta.
„ 46 .	111	7039	CXXXI, 2, *c* .	Carnelian.
„ 47 .	170	3721	CXXXIII, 7, *a* .	Yellow faience.
„ 48 .	181	7511	CXXXIII, 9, *f* .	Faience.
„ 49 .	149	12401c/1	CXXXIV, 1, *n* .	Terracotta.
„ 50 .	150	12401c/2	CXXXIV, 1, *o* .	Terracotta.
„ 51 .	175	658	CXXXII, 5, *g* .	Steatite.
„ 52 .	169	Ab309	CXXXIII, 9, *k* .	Faience.
„ 53 .	106	3994	CXXXIII, 9, *k* .	Faience.

APPENDIX B—*contd.*

No. on	No. on List of selected beads.	Harappā Reference No.	No. on Pls. CXXXI-CXXXIV.	Material.
Plate CXXIX—54	104	904	CXXXII, 5, *p*	Steatite.
,, 55	121	11629	CXXXII, 5, *dd*	Steatite.
,, 56	94	10872	CXXXII, 5, *h*	Steatite.
,, 57	120	656	CXXXII, 5, *cc*	Steatite.
,, 58	146	B23	CXXXIV, 1, *g*	Steatite.
CXXX—1	56	J120	CXXXIII, 2, *b*	Steatite.
,, 2	50	Ab167	CXXXII, 5, *a*	Steatite.
,, 3	57	12445	CXXXIII, 2, *a*	Steatite.
,, 4	58	8843	CXXXIII, 2, *c*	Steatite.
,, 5	51	1910	CXXXII, 5, *b*	Steatite.
,, 6	65	3857	CXXXI, 1, *r*	Steatite.
,, 7	60	10820	CXXXI, 1, *g*	Agate.
,, 8	52	8650*a*	CXXXII, 5, *d*	Steatite.
,, 9	59	487	CXXXI, 1, *h*	Agate.
,, 10	63	11062	CXXXII, 5, *w*	Steatite.
,, 11	72	3377	CXXXIII, 8, *a*	Faience.
,, 12	76	9085	CXXXI, 6, *j*	Stalagmite.
,, 13	189	A7	CXXXI, 1, *k*	Agate.
,, 14	67	5172	CXXXI, 3, *l*	Chalcedony.
,, 15	68	A426	CXXXI, 3, *k*	Lydian stone.
,, 16	122	10726	CXXXII, 5, *ff*	Steatite.
,, 17	109	G	CXXXII, 5, *z*	Steatite.
,, 18	81	5716	CXXXII, 5, *e*	Steatite.
,, 19	105	B1454	CXXXII, 5, *e*	Steatite.
,, 20	157	1773	CXXXIII, 7, *b*	Faience.
,, 21	87	10432	CXXXII, 1, *i*	Steatite.
,, 22	82	8523	CXXXII, 5, *f*	Steatite.

APPENDIX B—*contd.*

No. on	No. on List of selected beads.	Harappā Reference No.	No. on Pls. CXXXI-CXXXIV.	Material.
Plate CXXX—23 .	88	3223	CXXXI, 4, *c* .	Carnelian.
„ 24 .	79	7468	CXXXII, 3, *a* .	Steatite.
„ 25 .	160	2638	CXXXIII, 4, *a* .	Faience.
„ 26 .	80	715	CXXXII, 3, *b* .	Steatite.
„ 27 .	85	10470	CXXXII, 3, *f* .	Steatite.
„ 28 .	171	1613	CXXXIII, 4, *c* .	Faience.
„ 29 .	177	11984	CXXXIII, 6, *c* .	Faience.
„ 30 .	177	11984	CXXXIII, 6, *b* .	Faience.
„ 31 .	163	3982	CXXXIII, 4, *b* .	Faience.
„ 32 .	115	12290	CXXXII, 3, *c* .	Steatite.
„ 33 .	171	1613	CXXXIII, 4, *d* .	Faience.
„ 34 .	159	10885*d*	CXXXII, 3, *d* .	Steatite.
„ 35 .	195	8060	CXXXIV, 7, *a* .	Gold.
„ 36 .	148	10750	CXXXIV, 1, *p* .	Pottery.
„ 37 .	90	1977	CXXXII, 5, *u* .	Steatite.
„ 38 .	162	8508	CXXXIII, 9, *o* .	Faience.
„ 39 .	124	1758	CXXXII, 5, *ee* .	Steatite.
„ 40 .	126	12086	CXXXII, 4, *a* .	Steatite.
„ 41 .	127	5377	CXXXII, 4, *d* .	Steatite.
„ 42 .	164	7035	CXXXIII, 9, *m* .	Faience.
„ 43 .	78	E	CXXXI, 4, *a* .	Carnelian.
„ 44 .	129	Af205	CXXXIII, 8, *e* .	Faience.
„ 45 .	89	5497	CXXXII, 5, *t* .	Steatite.
„ 46 .	118	4584	CXXXII, 4, *b*, *c* .	Steatite.
„ 47 .	119	2250	CXXXII, 4, *e* .	Steatite.
„ 48 .	99	F	CXXXII, 5, *r* .	Steatite.
„ 49 .	159	10885*d*	CXXXIII, 8, *i*, *j*, *k*	Faience.

APPENDIX B—*contd.*

No. on	No. on List of selected beads.	Harappā Reference No.	No. on Pls. CXXXI-CXXXIV.	Material.
Plate CXXX—50 .	1	10700	CXXXII, 2, *a* .	Steatite.
„ 51 .	125	769	CXXXII, 2, *b* .	Steatite.
„ 52 .	123	7097	CXXXII, 2, *c* .	Steatite.
„ 53 .	128	12197	CXXXIII, 2, *i* .	Steatite.
„ 54 .	161	12508	CXXXIII, 3, *a* .	Faience.
„ 55 .	164*a*	4227	CXXXIII, 3, *d* .	Faience.
„ 56 .	171	1613	CXXXIII, 3, *c* .	Faience.
Plate CXXXI—				
Figure, 1, *a* . .	2	H692	....	Agate.
„ *b* . .	4	8490	CXXIX, 19 . .	Agate.
„ *c* . .	3	202	CXXIX, 17 . .	Agate.
„ *d* . .	47	8605	....	Agate.
„ *e* . .	65	3857	CXXX, 6 . .	Agate.
„ *f* . .	47*a*	Ae281	....	Agate.
„ *g* . .	60	10820	CXXX, 7 . .	Agate.
„ *h* . .	59	487	CXXX, 9 . .	Agate.
„ *i* . .	19	5670	....	Agate.
„ *j* . .	20	B1182	....	Agate.
„ *k* . .	189	A7	CXXX, 13 . .	Agate.
„ *l* . .	191	12572	....	Agate.
„ *m* . .	77	9022	....	Agate.
„ *n* . .	17	11074	....	Agate.
„ *o* . .	70	B363	....	Agate.
„ *p* . .	69	8417	....	Agate.
„ *q* . .	71	H232	....	Agate.
„ *r* . .	129	Af205	....	Agate.
„ *s* . .	25	PII-28	....	Agate.

APPENDIX B—*contd.*

No. on	No. on List of selected beads.	Harappā Reference No.	No. on Pls. CXXIX or CXXX.	Material.
Plate CXXXI—*contd.*				
Figure 2, *a* . .	129	Af205	....	Carnelian.
„ *b* . .	49	10566	CXXIX, 25 . .	Carnelian.
„ *c* . .	111	7039	CXXIX, 46 .	Carnelian.
„ *d* . .	30	3058	....	Carnelian.
„ *e* . .	128	12197	CXXIX, 27 . .	Carnelian.
„ *f* . .	41	8104	....	Carnelian.
„ *g* . .	192	1860	CXXIX, 2 . .	Carnelian.
„ *h* . .	42	5318	CXXIX, 26 . .	Carnelian.
Figure 3, *a* . .	188	10486	....	Jasper.
„ *b* . .	14	5915	....	Jasper.
„ *c* . .	182	12174	....	Jasper.
„ *d* . .	15	5422	....	Jasper.
„ *e* . .	29	12495	....	Jasper.
„ *f* . .	128	12197	....	Jasper.
„ *g* . .	66	1754	....	Chert.
„ *h* . .	112	883	....	Chert.
„ *i* . .	64	4063	....	Lydian stone.
„ *j* . .	75	*d*	....	Lydian stone.
„ *k* . .	68	A426	CXXX, 15 . .	Lydian stone.
„ *l* . .	67	5172	CXXX, 14 . .	Chalcedony.
„ *m* . .	38	2084	....	Chalcedony.
„ *n* . .	37	H475	CXXIX, 16 . .	Chalcedony.
„ *o* . .	61	11869	....	Milky quartz.
Figure 4, *a* . .	78	E	CXXX, 43 . .	Etched carnelian.
„ *b* . .	8 of List B	..	.... .	Etched carnelian.
„ *c* . .	88	3223	CXXX, 23 . .	Etched carnelian.

APPENDIX B—*contd.*

No. on	No. on List of selected beads.	Harappā Reference No.	No. on Pls. CXXIX or CXXX.	Material.
Plate CXXXI—*contd.*				
Figure 4, *d* . .	17 of List B	..	....	Etched carnelian.
Figure 5, *a* . .	53	11062	....	Felspar.
„ *b* . .	21	PIV-105	....	Felspar.
„ *c* . .	34	11583	....	Felspar.
„ *d* . .	36	Ae281	....	Felspar.
„ *e* . .	193	J129	....	Felspar.
Figure 6, *a* . .	135	11820	CXXIX, 40 . .	Limestone.
„ *b* . .	136	5183	CXXIX, 41 . .	Limestone.
„ *c* . .	22	7452	....	Limestone.
„ *d* . .	73	c	....	Limestone.
„ *e* . .	45	145*a*	CXXIX, 23 . .	Limestone.
„ *f* . .	24	10803	....	Stalagmite.
„ *g* . .	46	G50	CXXIX, 22 . .	Stalagmite.
„ *h* . .	35	2522	....	Stalagmite.
„ *i* . .	13	3028	....	Stalagmite.
„ *j* . . .	76	9085	CXXX, 12 . .	Stalagmite.
Figure 7, *a* . .	132	7225	CXXIX, 34 . .	Marble.
„ *b* . .	133	G154	....	Marble.
„ *c* . .	27	G111	....	Calcite.
„ *d* . .	39	B	....	Hornblende breccia.
„ *e* . .	48	518	CXXIX, 24 . .	Serpentine.
„ *f* . .	44	B313	....	Serpentine.
„ *g* . .	16	A307	....	Serpentine.
„ *h* .	18	PII-28	....	Diorite.
„ *i* .	31	4740	....	Lapis-lazuli.
„ *j* . .	62	10671	....	Lapis-lazuli.

APPENDIX B—*contd.*

No. on	No. on List of selected beads.	Harappā Reference No.	No. on Pls. CXXIX or CXXX.	Material.
Plate CXXXI—*contd.*				
Figure 7, *k* . .	63	J31	....	Jadeite.
„ *l* . .	43	1608	....	Jadeite.
Plate CXXXII—				
Figure 1, *a* . .	113	H	CXXIX, 42 . .	Steatite.
„ *b* . .	32	10650H	....	Steatite.
„ *c* . .	93	10634	CXXIX, 4 . .	Steatite.
„ *d* . .	114	11446c	CXXIX, 28 . .	Steatite.
„ *e-h* . .	86	11051	....	Steatite.
„ *i* . .	87	10432	CXXX, 21 . .	Steatite.
Figure 2, *a* . .	1	10700	CXXX, 50 . .	Steatite.
„ *b* . .	125	769	CXXX, 51 . .	Steatite.
„ *c* . .	123	7097	CXXX, 52 . .	Steatite.
Figure 3, *a* . .	79	7468	CXXX, 24 . .	Steatite.
„ *b* . .	80	715	CXXX, 26 . .	Steatite.
„ *c* . .	115	12290	CXXX, 32 . .	Steatite.
„ *d* . .	159	10885*d*	CXXX, 32 . .	Steatite.
„ *e* . .	84	2251	....	Steatite.
„ *f* . .	85	10470	CXXX, 27 . .	Steatite.
Figure 4, *a* . .	126	12086	CXXX, 40 . .	Steatite.
„ *b* and *c* .	118	4584	CXXX, 46 . .	Steatite.
„ *d* . .	127	5377	CXXX, 41 . .	Steatite.
„ *e* . .	129	Af205	CXXX, 47 . .	Steatite.
Figure 5, *a* . .	50	Ab167	CXXX, 2 . .	Steatite.
„ *b* . .	51	1910	CXXX, 5 . .	Steatite.
„ *c* . .	5	7438	CXXIX, 18 . .	Steatite.
„ *d* . .	52	8650*a*	CXXX, 8 . .	Steatite.

APPENDIX B—*contd.*

No. on	No. on List of selected beads.	Harappā Reference No.	No. on Pls. CXXIX or CXXX.	Material.
Plate CXXXII—*contd.*				
Figure 5, *e* . .	81	.5716	CXXX, 18 . .	Steatite.
„ *f* . .	82	8523	CXXX, 22 . .	Steatite.
„ *g* . .	175	368	CXXIX, 51 . .	Steatite.
„ *h* . .	94	10872	CXXIX, 55 . .	Steatite.
„ *i* . .	91	7292	CXXIX, 5 . .	Steatite.
„ *j* . .	185	12588	....	Steatite.
„ *k* . .	168	4423	CXXIX, 29 . .	Steatite.
„ *l* . .	134	10418	CXXIX, 31 . .	Steatite.
„ *m* . .	98	5586	....	Steatite.
„ *n* . .	186	12454	....	Steatite.
„ *o* . .	97	2668	CXXIX, 9 . .	Steatite.
„ *p* . .	104	904	CXXIX, 54 . .	Steatite.
„ *q* . .	116	625	....	Steatite.
„ *r* . .	99	F	CXXX, 48 . .	Steatite.
„ *s* . .	176	9060	....	Steatite.
„ *t* . .	89	5497	CXXX, 45 . .	Steatite.
„ *u* . .	90	1977	CXXX, 37 . .	Steatite.
„ *v* . .	6	4785	....	Steatite.
„ *w* . .	53	11062	CXXX, 10 . .	
„ *x* . .	8	778	....	Steatite.
„ *y* . .	92	7626	....	Steatite.
„ *z* . .	109	G	CXXX, 17 . .	Steatite.
„ *aa* . .	191	12572	....	Steatite.
„ *bb* . .	191	12572	....	Steatite.
„ *cc* . .	120	656	CXXIX, 57 . .	Steatite.
„ *dd* .	121	11629	CXXIX, 55 . .	Steatite.

APPENDIX B—*contd.*

No. on	No. on List of selected beads.	Harappā Reference No.	No. on Pls. CXXIX or CXXX.	Material.
Plate CXXXII—*concld.*				
Figure 5, *ee* . .	124	1758	CXXX, 39 . .	Steatite.
„ *ff* . .	122	10726	CXXX, 16 . .	Steatite.
„ *gg* . .	159	10885*d*	....	Steatite.
„ *hh* . .	96	G42	....	Steatite.
„ *ii* . .	128*a*	12197	....	Steatite.
„ *jj* . .	128*b*	12197	....	Steatite.
Plate CXXXIII—				
Figure 1, *a* . .	103	10983	CXXIX, 15 . .	Steatite.
„ *b* . .	101	10981	CXXIX, 10 and 13	Steatite.
„ *c* . .	100	4155	CXXIX, 12 and 14	Steatite.
„ *d* . .	102	H449	CXXIX, 11 . .	Steatite.
Figure 2, *a* . .	57	12445	CXXX, 3 . .	Painted steatite.
„ *b* . .	56	J120	CXXX, 1 . .	Painted steatite.
„ *c* . .	58	8843	CXXX, 4 . .	Painted steatite.
„ *d* . .	7	5641	....	Painted steatite.
„ *e* . .	55	8650N	....	Painted steatite.
„ *f* . .	9	G203	....	Painted steatite.
„ *g* . .	125	769	....	Painted steatite.
„ *h* . .	11	A	....	Painted steatite.
„ *i* . .	123	12197	CXXX, 53 . .	Painted steatite.
„ *j* . .	28	5003	....	Painted steatite.
„ *k* . .	10	Ae281	....	Painted steatite.
Figure 3, *a* . .	161	12508	CXXX, 54 . .	Faience.
„ *b* . .	172	1486	....	Faience.
„ *c* . .	171*b*	1613	CXXX, 56 . .	Faience.

APPENDIX B—*contd.*

No. on	No. on List of selected beads.	Harappā Reference No.	No. on Pls. CXXIX or CXXX.	Material.
Plate CXXXIII—*contd.*				
Figure 3, *d* . .	164*a*	4227	CXXX, 55 . .	Faience.
Figure 4, *a* . .	160	2638	CXXX, 25 . .	Faience.
„ *b* . .	163	3982	CXXX, 31 . .	Faience.
„ *c* . .	171*c*	1613	CXXX, 28 . .	Faience.
„ *d* . .	171*a*	1613	CXXX, 33 . .	Faience.
Figure 5, *a* . .	177	11984	....	Black faience.
„ *b* . .	180	8592E	....	Black faience.
„ *c* . .	..	..	....	....
Figure 6, *a* . .	33	11869	....	White faience.
„ *b* . .	177	11984	CXXX, 30 . .	White faience.
„ *c* . .	177	11984	CXXX, 29 . .	White faience.
Figure 7, *a* . .	170	3721	CXXIX, 47 . .	Yellow faience.
„ *b* . .	157	1773	CXXX, 20 . .	Yellow faience.
„ *c* . .	174	G89	CXXIX, 6 . .	Yellow faience.
Figure 8, *a* . .	72	3377	CXXX, 11 .	Variegated faience.
„ *b* . .	181	7511	....	Variegated faience.
„ *c* . .	9	G203	....	Variegated faience.
„ *d* . .	184	Ab745	....	Variegated faience.
„ *e* . .	129	Af205	CXXX, 44 . .	Variegated faience.
„ *f* . .	159	10885*d*	....	Variegated faience.
„ *g* . .	182	12174	....	Variegated faience.
„ *h* . .	74	4376	....	Variegated faience.
„ *i, j, k* .	159	10885*d*	CXXX, 49 . .	Variegated faience.
Figure 9, *a* . .	173	391	CXXIX, 21 . .	Faience.
„ *b* . .	177	11984	....	Faience.
„ *c* . .	95	11636	CXXIX, 3 . .	Faience.

APPENDIX B—*contd.*

No. on	No. on List of selected beads.	Harappā Reference No.	No. on Pls. CXXXI or CXXX.	Material.
Plate CXXXIII —*concld.*				
Figure 9, *d* . .	166	PIII-70	CXXIX, 32 . .	Faience.
,, *e* . .	167	Bg50	CXXIX, 30 . .	Faience.
,, *f* . .	181	7511	CXXIX, 48 . .	Faience.
,, *g* . .	179	8592D	....	Faience.
,, *h* . .	187	J414	CXXIX, 20 . .	Faience.
,, *i* . .	12	10567	....	Faience.
,, *j* . .	128	12197	....	Faience.
,, *k* . .	169	Ab309	CXXIX, 52 . .	Faience.
,, *l* . .	165	PIII-50	....	Faience.
,, *m* . .	164	7035	CXXX, 42 . .	Faience.
,, *n* . .	184	Ab745	....	Faience.
,, *o* . .	162	8508	CXXX, 38 . .	....
Plate CXXXIV—				
Figure 1, *a* . .	140	5502	....	Terracotta.
,, *b* . .	139	2587	....	Terracotta.
,, *c* . .	142	5215	CXXIX, 45 . .	Pottery.
,, *d* . .	143*b*	10545	CXXIX, 36 . .	Terracotta.
,, *e* . .	143*a*	10545	....	Terracotta.
,, *f* . .	145	E29	CXXIX, 37 . .	Terracotta.
,, *g* . .	146	B23	CXXIX, 58 . .	Pottery.
,, *h* . .	143*c*	10545	CXXIX, 38 . .	Terracotta.
,, *i* . .	144	K	....	Terracotta.
,, *j* . .	137	J	....	Terracotta.
,, *k* . .	184	Ab745	....	Terracotta.
,, *l* . .	141	7144	CXXIX, 44 . .	Terracotta.

APPENDIX B—*concld.*

No. on	No. on List of selected beads.	Harappā Reference No.	No. on Pls. CXXIX or CXXX.	Material.
Plate CXXXIV—*contd.*				
Figure 1, *m* . .	147	12401*d*	....	Terracotta.
„ *n* . .	149	12401*c*/1	CXXIX, 49 . .	Terracotta.
„ *o* . .	150	12401*c*/2	CXXIX, 50 . .	Terracotta.
„ *p* . .	148	10750	CXXX, 36 . .	Terracotta.
„ *q*, *r* . .	148	10750	....	Terracotta.
Figure 2, *a* . .	154	8704	....	Shell.
„ *b* . .	151	L	....	Shell.
„ *c* . .	152	12431	CXXIX, 5 . .	Shell.
„ *d* . .	156	1979	....	Shell.
„ *e* . .	155	127	CXXIX, 8 . .	Shell.
„ *f* . .	153	12270	....	Shell.
„ *g* . .	190	J87	....	Shell.
„ *h* . .	181	7511	....	Shell.
Figure 3 . . .	158	2928	....	Ivory.
Figure 4 . . .		Shell inlay from Ur.		
Figure 5, *a* . .	131	5853	....	Copper.
„ *b* . .	130	10866	....	Copper.
Figure 6 . . .	198	8060	....	Silver.
Figure 7, *a* . .	195	8060	CXXX, 35 . .	Gold.
„ *b* . .	194	4247	....	Gold.
„ *c* . .	197	8060	....	Gold.
„ *d* . .	196	8060	....	Gold.
Figure 8 . . .	Steatite beads from No. 117 Harappā and from Ur ×4			
Figure 9 . . .		Ditto	ditto	×1
Figure 10 . . .		Ditto	ditto	×4
Figure 11 . . .		Ditto	ditto	×1

Method of illumination for Microphotographs.

The microphotographs are taken by three different methods of illumination called ordinary transmitted light, polarized light, and light reflected from above.

In the first method an apochromatic 16 mm. objective and a compensating eyepiece ×6 were used together with an achromatic condenser slightly out of focus.

In the second method, the same optical system was used, and in addition a nicol prism was added below the condenser and a tourmaline over the eyepiece.

In the third method the same object glass and eyepiece were used but the condenser was removed and a Beck ring illuminator was used to throw the light down on the specimen. A Bracey colour corrector was inserted in the substage.

In all cases a low voltage electric light, run from batteries, was used.

Plate CXXXV—

Fig. 1. Microscopic section of "burnt" steatite seal from Mohenjo-daro, transmitted light, showing crack . . . . ×50

Fig. 2, *a*. Microscopic section of "burnt" steatite seal from Harappā, transmitted light . ×40

„ *b*. Microscopic section of "burnt" steatite seal from Harappā, light reflected from above.

Fig. 3, *a*. Microscopic section of "burnt" steatite bead from Harappā No. 117. Transmitted light . . . . ×40

„ *b*. Microscopic section of "burnt" steatite bead from Harappā, No. 117 Light reflected from above . . . . ×40

Fig. 4. Similar bead from Ur . . . . ×40

Fig. 5. Section through edge of a "burnt" steatite disc bead from Harappā. The base is affected right through this specimen . . . . ×40

Fig. 6. Section through a "burnt" steatite bead of unusual type from Harappā . . ×40

„ *a* Section through a "burnt" steatite bead of unusual type from Harappā. Transmitted light.

„ *b*. Section through a "burnt" steatite bead of unusual type from Harappā. Light reflected from above.

Fig. 7, *a*. Section of painted steatite bead. Transmitted light . . . . . . ×40

„ *b*. Section of painted steatite bead. Light reflected from above.

Plate CXXXVI—

Fig. 1. Microphotograph of a section of an etched carnelian Type I. Light reflected from above . . . . ×40

Fig. 2, *a*. Section through an irregular band on an etched carnelian. Tramsmitted light . ×40

„ *b*. Section through an irregular band on an etched carnelian. Light reflected from above.

Fig. 3. Section through an etched carnelian of unusual type. Illuminated by light from above . . . . ×40

Fig. 4, *a*. Section of faience of ordinary type. Transmitted light . . . . ×40

„ *b*. Section of faience of ordinary type. Polarized light.

Fig. 5, *a*. Section of very coarse faience. Ordinary transmitted light . . . . ×40

„ *b*. Section of very coarse faience. Polarized light.

Fig. 6, *a*. Section of very fine variegated faience. Ordinary transmitted light . . . ×40

„ *b*. Section of very fine variegated faience. Polarized light.

Fig. 7, *a*. Section of very hard faience sometimes called "Vitreous Paste". Transmitted light . . . . ×40

„ *b*. Section of very hard faience sometimes called "Vitreous Paste". Polarized light.

PART II.

Personal Ornaments.[1]

Beads of gold, silver and copper, of stones of various descriptions and of other materials such as faience, shell and pottery[2] are as common at Harappā as they are at Mohenjo-daro. To judge from the numerous female figurines of pottery which are found loaded with torques, necklaces and girdles, beads must have been exceedingly popular. Male figures also wore jewellery but not frequently; for instance figure No. 20 in Pl. LXXVI wears a torque of the same pattern as do the female figures, and another one No. 12 in the same plate wears a necklace of four strings and a loin-cloth bejewelled with conical bosses.

Metal jewellery. The only hoard (No. 8060) comprising gold, silver, and other jewellery was recovered from Trench IV, Mound F, in the courtyard of House 2 of Stratum IV, in square I 14/1, at a depth of 7 ft. 8 in. to 8 ft. 4 in. below the surface. A detailed account of this has already been given on pp. 63-65 *supra*. The hoard is illustrated in Pl. CXXXVII, but item No. 22 figured therein, *viz.*, a gold fillet, 5·2 in. long, was found in Trench B of Mound AB. A few bracelets and finger-rings of copper (including a ring with silver bezel, No. 49 in Pl. CXXV), one finger-ring of gold (No. 55) in the same plate, a nose-disc and a conical temple ornament inlaid at the top with a cylindrical piece of shell, which are illustrated in Pl. CXXV, 48 and 51, have also been described on pp. 444 and 443 *infra*. Gold and silver, though occurring in the early strata, were not very freely used for personal ornaments. Side by side with beads must also be mentioned spacers and terminals which are made of gold, bronze and copper, as well as of faience and pottery.

The personal ornaments recovered at Harappā consist mostly of a large variety of beads the majority of which are of stone. In Part I of this Chapter Mr. H. C. Beck has given an illustrated and illuminating account of some 200 selected beads or sets of beads from Harappā. Hence, in the following remarks I shall confine myself to the beads illustrated in Pl. CXXVIII which represent most of the common shapes, though I shall also refer in passing to certain metal beads seen in Pl. CXXXVII. The Harappā beads being generally similar to those of Mohenjo-daro, which have already been classified into types and fully dealt with by Dr. Mackay in *M. I. C.*, Chapter XXVI, Pls. CXLV, CXLVI, etc., there is no necessity to go over the same ground again. In describing these beads I shall make use of Dr. Mackay's nomenclature so that there may be no risk of confusion.

Metal beads. See Pl. CXXXVII.

Shapes in gold. At Harappā, the most common variety of gold beads are the tiny round ones seen in the wristlets ? and necklace Nos. 3 and 7. Besides these, there are the tiny gold cylinders which were used for capping the ends of burnt steatite beads, *e.g.* those inlaid in the gold brooch No. 15. Again, at the ends of

[1] This part has been written by the author.

[2] Beads of ivory are also occasionally found, *e.g.*, Pl. CXXVIII, 31, and Pl. CXXXIV, 3.

necklaces Nos. 9-12 there are larger gold cylinders and in string No. 18 some smaller ones. In addition to the latter, there are, in necklace No. 18, some irregular, short-barrel beads. In necklace No. 17 may be seen alternating with jade beads a number of double convex, hollow discoid beads which were made by soldering the edges of two convex discs. Still another variety is afforded by some facetted, hexagonal barrel-shaped beads, four of which are strung horizontally at the centre of necklace No. 9. There are also some tiny gold discs strung between the tips and pendents of necklaces Nos. 9-13, caps, spacers, and terminals in necklace No. 7 and in the mixed lots Nos. 23, 26 and 28.

Beads of silver and copper are usually of small size: the former are globular in shape, but the latter are cylindrical as well (Pl. CXXV, 11). Of the silver beads, a number of which were found corroded together in the jewellery hoard illustrated in Pl. CXXXVII, some are seen detached and placed in the broken bangles 26 and 29. **Silver and copper.**

Next to those of stone, beads of faience were very popular. Their shapes in the order of frequency are: globular; short-barrel with round section; tubular (ranging from thin tubes to fairly large ones); short-barrel with oval section; segmented (as in the necklace No. 2 in Pl. CXXVIII); rectangular, with rectangular, oval or half round section. Among the rarer types are discs which are plane on both sides; or plane on one side and convex on the other; discs with a median tube hole raised either equally on both faces or entirely on one face; tapered cylinders (*e.g.* No. 17 in Pl. CXXVIII) with or without flutes; gadrooned beads; and long barrel cylinders. **Faience.**

Beads of shell are not frequent. With the exception of 155 beads which were unearthed in one lot and have been strung in the necklace 25 in Pl. CXXXVII, they have turned up only occasionally in different parts of the site. This necklace comprises thick discs, discs round or oval in section, small to fair-sized cylinders, and short-barrel beads, generally oval but occasionally round in section. **Shell.**

Pottery beads seem to have been less popular than those of stone and faience, but compared with shell ones they are far more numerous. Apart from the short-barrels with round section, of the kind illustrated in *M. I. C.*, Pl. CXLVII, 37-40, and the long-barrel cylinders such as Nos. 45 and 46 in Pl. CXXVIII, the pottery beads are rarely well finished. The remaining shapes are; discs with oval section; globular; short-barrel, round in section; segmented and a few medium-sized-barrel cylinders with spiral groves on the outside. **Pottery.**

I shall now proceed to describe the beads and other objects illustrated in Pl. CXXVIII, to which the numbers given below are referable.

Rings.

Nos. 1, 20, 22 and 24 are alabaster finger-rings and will be described later. **Alabaster.**

Ivory bead.

No. 31 (see also Pl. CXXXIV, 3) is a short-barrel, zone bead of ivory. **Ivory.**

Segmented beads.

Faience.

No. 2 is a string of 23 segmented faience beads found at different places and in association with various strata. These beads consist of two, three, four or five segments and their colours are white, blue, green, buff and grey.

Hexagonal (?) bead.

No. 3 is the end fragment of a hexagonal faience bead pierced transversely through two raised parallel tubes.

Pottery beads.

No. 4 is a string of 42 miscellaneous pottery beads mostly discoid with oval section and of rough make.

Barrel-shaped beads.

No. 5 (J120) is a broad, barrel-shaped bead of burnt steatite, oval in section. It was first painted red to simulate carnelian and then decorated in white with trefoil patterns. It is broken across one side and is 1·65 in. long and 1·25 in. broad. Area J, Trench I, Square R 30/16; Depth 4 ft. 5 in. b.s.; Stratum II.

No. 11 (8843) is similar to No. 5, but is smaller in size. L. ·88 in.; w. ·68 in. Mound F, Trench V, Square J 12/8; Depth 7 ft. 8 in. b.s.; Stratum III.

Beads of imitation carnelian have also been found at Mohenjo-daro.[1]

Etched carnelian.

Of etched carnelian beads decorated with white bands, there are four examples. One of these No. E29 (Pl. CXXXI, 4, *a*) is a barrel-shaped eye bead oval in section. Though half of it is broken along the hole, it retains traces of a series of fine concentric rings in white etched on it. L. ·5 in. Mound AB, Trench E; Depth 3 ft. b.s.

Another bead, No. 3223, is heart-shaped oblate and convex on both sides. This is etched[2] on either side with a white band along the periphery (Pl. CXXXI, 4, *c*). Size ·5×·37 in. Mound F, Great Granary Area, Square I 7/25; Depth 10 ft. b.s.; Stratum V.

Etched carnelian beads are rare both at Harappā and Mohenjo-daro. At the latter site also no more than four examples have been found.[3]

Barrel beads, round in section.

Bead threaded on copper wire.

No. 6 is a barrel bead of serpentine round in section, and No. 16 of similar shape is of carnelian threaded on a piece of copper wire with a copper disc bead sticking at its upper end suggesting that it formed part of a necklace of pendent beads like those illustrated in Pl. CXXXVII, 9-13. It is ·5 in. long and ·3 in. in diameter. This shape was extremely popular in various stones, faience and other materials. Mound F, Trench III, Square M 11/6; Depth 10 ft. 11 in. b.s.; Stratum IV.

---

[1] *M. I. C.*, p. 517.

[2] For the technique of etching see Beck, pp. 401-02 *supra*.

[3] *M. I. C.*, p. 515.

No. 8 (3377) is also similar. It is made of dark grey faience with three irregular bands in white.

No. 9 is of white faience with rough and powdery surface. It is painted at the ends with black bands between which there are four horizontal rows of three dots each. The dots and bands have spread irregularly in the course of firing. **Decorated steatite.**

Trapezoidal pendent bead.

No. 7 is a plano-convex, trapezoidal pendent bead of agate-jasper with deep red conical band in the centre. This is exactly similar to the three central pendent beads in necklace No. 9 in Pl. CXXXVII. Such beads are rare, but their shapes and colours are very effective. **Rare shape.**

Gadrooned bead.

No. 10 (8508) is a round gadrooned[1] bead of blue faience, ·45 in. in diameter. This shape is unique at Harappā and Mohenjo-daro. Mound F, Trench IV, Square I 13/10; Depth 5 ft. 6 in. b.s.; Stratum II. **Unique shape.**

Miscellaneous strings.

No. 12 (8650*g*) is a string of 12 miscellaneous stone beads found together. Counting from the top right hand side, the first bead is globular oblate made of milky quartz, the second is tubular and made of obsidian or pitchstone, the third and fourth are barrel-shaped, with oval section and made of jasper and limestone respectively. Nos. 5, 6 and 7 are long-barrels, round in section and made of limestone, nummulitic limestone and jasper respectively. Nos. 8, 9, 10 and 11 again are barrel-shaped; they are of limestone, nummulitic limestone, agate with veins of calcite and limestone respectively. No. 12 is a disc bead of microline felspar.[2] Mound F, Trench IV, Square H 12/21, and I 12/1; Depth 4 to 7 ft. b.s.; Stratum III.

Hexagonal bead with tubular hole.

No. 13 (5706) is a beautiful hexagonal bead of blue faience in which material a few other similar examples have been found, but this shape is not known in stone or metal. It has a raised median tubular hole[3] as in bead No. Hr. 2211 illustrated in *M. I. C.*, Pl. CXLVI, 38. L. ·8 in.; w. at centre ·55 in.; w. at the ends ·3 in. Mound AB, Extension of Pits I and II, Square P 24/11; Depth 8 ft. 4 in. b.s.; Stratum III. **Tube hole confined to faience.**

Convex bicone beads with truncated ends.

No. 14 (8650*n*) is a convex bicone bead of burnt steatite engraved on the surface with trefoil circles which are ·05 in. deep. In the centre of each foil is a key-hole ·05 in. deep for holding coloured inlay. L. ·75 in.; w. ·5 in. It was found at the same place as necklace No. 12 described above. **Trefoil decoration.**

---

[1] See also pp. 397 and 406 *supra* where Mr. Beck refers to gadrooned beads found at Harappā, Ur and in the cemetery at Diqdiqqeh.

[2] I am indebted for the determination of these beads to Mr. A. L. Coulson of the Geological Survey of India.

[3] For other beads with median tube hole from Harappā and their Mesopotamian parallels, see Beck, p. 406 *supra*, Pl. CXXXIII, 3, *a-d*.

Traces of red and black paste.

No. 15 (4774) is similar to No. 14 but its trefoil patterning is not so regular. There are traces of red and black pastes in two adjoining foils which suggest that patterns were inlaid with pastes of different colour to a certain scheme. Altogether, four such beads have been discovered at Harappā. Beads with similar patterning are also known from Mohenjo-daro.[1] The robe of the statuette illustrated in *M. I. C.*, Pl. XCVIII is throughout covered with trefoil patterning. L. ·8 in.; w. ·6 in. Mound AB, Extension of Pits I and II, Square Q 24/3; Depth 7 ft. b.s.; Stratum III.

Tapered fluted bead.

Faience.

No. 17 (1977) is a tapered fluted bead of faience of the kind illustrated in *M. I. C.*, Pl. CXLV, 21-23. Beads of this type are rare and always made of faience. They may have been used as central pendents. L. ·8 in.; diam. ·44 in. Mound F, Trench I, Square M 10/25; Depth 4 ft. b.s.; Stratum I.

Chalcedonic agate. breccia.

No. 18 (PII-28) is a bead of chalcedonic agate breccia.[2] This shape was popular in stone, faience and even in shell. L. ·75 in.; diam. ·3 in. Mound AB, Extension of Pits I and II; Depth 5 ft. b.s.; Stratum II.

Long-barrel bead, round in section.

Capping and inlay.

No. 19 (10070) is a long-barrel bead of burnt steatite round in section. It is one of the largest beads and the type is rare. Its surface is divided into five zones by four equidistant bands in relief which run along the profile. The ends were no doubt intended to be capped with metal, possibly gold, and the sunk zones between, which have a rough surface, to be inlaid with coloured pastes. L. 2·2 in.; diam. 1·06 in. Mound F, Trench V, Square L 12/9; Depth 7 ft. 6 in. b.s.; Stratum III.

Miscellaneous strings.

Faience.

No. 21 is a string of 33 assorted faience beads recovered from different places. It consists of 31 round, 1 cylindrical and 1 barrel-shaped beads. Their colours are white, green, blue and pale yellow.

Steatite and faience.

No. 23 consists of 21 tubular beads of which five are of faience, *viz.*, 3 green, 1 grey and 1 colourless, and the remaining sixteen of burnt steatite. They were found separately and at varying levels.

Steatite discs.

No. 25 is a string of 455 extremely thin miscellaneous disc beads of burnt steatite. Their average thickness is as little as ·02 in. and diam. ·23 in. Neatly finished, they were always found in large numbers lying in a row, so that the fact of their having been strung together may be taken as certain. It is conceivable,

Their probable use.

however, that they were intended to be stitched on cloth precisely as sequins of almost the same size and thickness are now stitched on children's caps, and ladies' garments and shoes.

Faience and steatite.

No. 32 is a string of 25 short-barrel beads, round in section, comprising 20 of faience and 5 of burnt steatite. Of the latter material one is nearly tubular.

---

[1] *M. I. C.*, pp. 516-17, Pl. CXLVI, 40, 49 and 53.

[2] For the formation of this rare material, see Beck, p. 400 *supra* and Pl. CXXXI, 1, *s*.

The steatite beads show traces of some colour which has all but disappeared; it may have been red or yellow. Faience beads are of green, blue and pale yellow colours. The beads in this string were recovered from different findspots.

Buttons.

No. 26 (3837) is a plano-convex, discoid faience button ·62 in. in diameter. **Faience.** It is provided on the underside with a short cylindrical projection which is pierced with a segmental hole, and decorated on the face with a scheme of incised circles within a beaded edge. This is the only example of its kind in faience. Buttons of burnt steatite are also similar but of smaller size. Two of them, Nos. 5477 and 5585, are illustrated in Pl. CXXXIX, 30 and 44. The former is ·4 in. in diameter and the latter ·3 in. only. Nos. 5477 and 5585 were both found in Mound AB, Extension of Pits I and II, Squares P 23/10 and P 24/14; at a depth of 5 ft. 3 in. b.s.; in association with Stratum II. No. 26 was also found in the same trench, Square Q 24/15; Depth 9 ft. b.s.; Stratum IV.

Cross-shaped bead.

No. 27 (12086) is a unique cross-shaped bead of burnt steatite. Its vertical **Steatite.** arm is convex on both sides, and the other, which is holed for threading, square in section. Size ·67×·63 in. Mound AB, Extension of Pits I and II, Square Q 28/6; Depth 14 ft. b.s.; Stratum V.

Brooches.

No. 28 (H412) is a six-petalled faience brooch holed through the centre. **Faience.** Its circular nucleus and dentate petals are relieved on the face with their own outline. The brooch is 2·25 in. in diameter, and being concave its petals rise ·5 in. above the centre. Only the darker portion at the centre is original, the petals being all restored on the model of several detached ones of similar shape recovered from different parts of the site. Cemetery H, Eastern Section, Square S 34/18; Depth 3 ft. 8 in. b.s; Stratum II.

Another faience brooch (12394) is illustrated in Pl. CXXXIX, 41. It is a plano-convex disc relieved with a four-pointed star enclosed in a border with linear decoration. At each point of the star is a pair of fine stitch-holes for attachment. It may be observed that the resulting depressions along the border and the lozenge-shaped depression at the centre were probably intended to be inlaid with shell or coloured pastes or with both as such inlays are quite common both at Harappā and Mohenjo-daro. Mound F; from spoil earth.

An 8-shaped gold brooch illustrated in the jewellery Pl. CXXXVII, 15 has **Gold.** already been described on p. 64 *supra*.

Tooth-shaped bead.

No. 29 (2250) is a tooth-shaped bead of burnt steatite bifurcating at both **Steatite.** ends in opposite directions.[1] This shape is unique. L. ·56 in. Mound F, Trench III, Square N 9/13; Depth 7 ft. 6 in. b.s.; Stratum IV.

[1] A somewhat similar shape with another variant from Mohenjo-daro has just been published by Dr. Mackay in *Further Excavations at Mohenjo-daro*, Pl. CXXXVI, 55, 56, 64 and 65.

Lenticular bead.

Cross-shaped pattern.

No. 30 (4584). See also Pl. CXXXII, 4, *b* and *c*. Lenticular bead, holed horizontally across the thickness. It is decorated on both sides with a cross motif which occurs in its simple form on No. 27 described above. Diam. ·5 in. Mound F, Trench III, Square N 9/15; Depth 9 to 12 ft. b.s.; Stratum V.

Biconical bead.

Agate.

No. 33 (202) is a beautiful biconical bead of agate not yet polished. Such sharp bicones were not popular. L. 1·5 in.; diam. ·87 in. Mound F, Trench I, Square M 12/12; Depth 8 ft. 3 in. b.s.; Stratum III.

Short-barrel beads.

Different stones.

Nos. 34-36 are short-barrel beads round in section. They are made of sard, agate-chalcedony and banded jasper[1] respectively. This shape was very popular.

Nos. 37 (3857), 38 (3311) and 39 (3800) are barrel-shaped beads, oval in section. No. 37 is of banded agate, 38 of burnt steatite, and 39 of limestone.

Long-barrel beads.

Carnelian and pottery.

Nos. 40-44 are long barrel-cylinder beads of carnelian and 45-46 of pottery. They were probably worn in the form of necklaces (?) or girdles as shown in *M. I. C.*, Pl. CLI, *b*, 10. Found in different parts of the site and at varying levels.

No. 48 (G50) is a long-barrel bead of banded limestone 2·38 in. long and ·5 in. in diameter at the middle. It is not quite well graded. Area G, Trench I, Square AO 36/5; Depth 3 ft. 4 in. b.s.; Stratum II.

No. 49 (145*a*) is a long-barrel bead of agate 2·62 in. long and ·75 in. in diameter. Mound F, Trench I, Square M 11/15; Depth 5 to 8 ft. 6 in. b.s.; Stratum II. This and Nos. 19 and 48 are among the heaviest beads from Harappā. Such a large size was not popular.

Globular bead.

Faience.

No. 47 (4423) is a globular oblate bead of white faience. At one end, half of its thickness is incised with shallow pittings of which the purpose is not clear. Diam. ·7 in., and across ends ·54 in. Mound F, Great Granary Area, Square K 8/3; Depth 6 ft. 3 in. b.s.; Stratum III.

Rectangular bead with oval section.

Banded agate.

No. 50 (7574) is a rectangular bead of banded agate with oval section. It is broken across the left end. Size ·64 by 1 in. Mound AB, Extension of Pits I and II, Square P 24/21; Depth 13 ft. 6 in. b.s.; Stratum V.

Globular bead.

Crystal.

Before finishing with beads I may state that only one globular bead (3958) of crystal, ·4 in. in diameter, has been recovered at Harappā. Mound F, Trench

[1] The determination of the stones is due to Mr. A. L. Coulson.

III, Square N 9/14; Depth 4 ft. b.s.; Stratum II. Crystal beads are also rare at Mohenjo-daro,[1] where their shape is short-barrel and round in section.

Spacers.

Spacers are of two kinds: firstly, flat strips, straight or segmented and pierced with the required number of holes; and secondly, those shaped like beads. At Harappā, spacers of the former kind are found in gold, copper, bronze, faience and pottery, while those of the latter class are made only of faience or burnt steatite, their shapes being round with round or oval section, or rectangular, with rectangular, semi-oval or oval section Pl. CXXXII, 3. Spacers of the latter class generally have two parallel holes. Spacers of the types illustrated in *M. I. C.*, Pl. CXLVII, 6 and 10 are not found at Harappā. With the further exception of No. 14 in the above Mohenjo-daro plate, which by the way may not be a spacer at all, the other types are all represented at Harappā.

Bead-like spacers. Pl. CXXXVIII, 41.

Bead-like spacers were equally common in faience and burnt steatite, but the rectangular variety, semi-oval in section is found in burnt steatite only.

No. 41 (2924) is rectangular with oval section. It is made of faience. L. ·65 in. Mound AB, Extension of Pits I and II, Square R 24/2; Depth 3 ft. b.s.; Stratum I.

The rectangular type, semi-oval in section is not illustrated.

Strip-shaped spacers. Pl. CXXXVIII, 46-48.

Strip-shaped spacers are of two kinds: firstly, rectangular, which is the commonest variety and found in the several materials enumerated above; secondly, rectangular with semi-oval section. Spacers of the first variety have three to six holes (Pl. CXXXVIII, 46-48), but such examples in faience are generally rounded at the ends, while the pottery examples, which are equally common, are rough all over and their ends are never rounded.

No. 46 (7908) of copper has four holes and is rounded at the ends. **Description.**

No. 47 (4812) is of faience with three holes. A peculiarity, not found in any other spacer, is that this is also bored vertically through the length, and for that reason its ends are not rounded. L. ·7 in. Mound AB, Extension of Pits I and II, Square Q 24/8; Depth 8 ft. b.s.; Stratum IV.

No. 48 (7828) is one of numerous pottery spacers with six holes. These are usually much larger than those of faience or metal. **Pottery.**

Segmented spacer.

No. 4653 (unillustrated) of faience is a segmented rectangular bar broken at one end. Probably, it had three holes of which only two have survived. For a very similar example, *cf. M. I. C.*, Pl. CXLVII. 19. This type is rare. **Rare shape.**

[1] *M. I. C.*, p. 512.

L. ·9 in. Mound AB, Extension of Pits I and II, Square Q 25/6; Depth 5 ft. b.s.; Stratum II.

Unique. 8652 (unillustrated) is a rectangular faience spacer, semi-oval in section. Both on the plane and convex sides its surface is uneven. This is the only example of its kind from Harappā or Mohenjo-daro, all other bar-shaped spacers of faience being perfectly rectangular in section. L. ·9 in. Mound F, Trench V, Square J 12/4; Depth 3 ft. b.s.; Stratum I.

Terminals.

At Harappā, all terminals are semi-circular in shape; the types illustrated in *M. I. C.*, Pl. CXLVII, 22, 23, 25 and 27 are not represented. The semi-circular type is, however, found in gold, copper, bronze,[1] faience and pottery. The gold examples are illustrated in Pl. CXXXVII, 3 and 7, the copper example in Pl. CXXIV, 20, and the faience one in Pl. CXXXVIII, 49. The gold ones are described with the jewellery group No. 8060[2] from Trench IV, Mound F, and the largest copper example with the contents of copper jar No. 277[3] from Trench I.

Combined terminal and spacer.

No. 49 in Pl. CXXXVIII is of faience, semi-oval in shape with lentoid section. It is unique in that the three holes in the face converge and terminate in a common hole at the apex.[4] L. ·95 in. Mound F, Trench V, Square L, 12/9; Depth 9 ft. 6 in. b.s.; Stratum IV.

Pendents for necklaces.

Pendents for necklaces were made of gold, stone, faience and pottery. They were, however, most popular in stone and faience of which some excellent examples have been recovered.

Gold. Pl. CXXXVII, 8 is a heart-shaped pendent in gold repoussé with two hooks on the underside for suspension. It is inlaid with ribbed bands of blue faience and has already been described on p. 64 *supra* with the group of jewellery from Trench IV, Mound F.

See Pl. CXXXIX, 1-7, 32, 36-39 and 42.

Crescent-shaped. No. 1 (949) is a crescent-shaped pendent of banded agate symmetrically tapered at both ends, but not quite finished or polished. At the centre, it shows a broad red band resembling a pointed lozenge followed on either side by three alternating, well balanced bands in red and white. Broader bands at the ends were probably intended to be partially covered with gold caps. Seen in sun-light, the bands are very attractive. L. 2·5 in. Mound F, Trench I, Square M 11/19; Depth 9 ft. b.s.; Stratum IV.

---

[1] The metal terminals are made like those of Mohenjo-daro. *Cf. M. I. C.*, p. 518.

[2] P. 64 *supra*.

[3] P. 89 *supra*.

[4] For two examples in steatite and one in vitreous paste from Mohenjo-daro showing a somewhat similar disposition of holes see Dr. Mackay, *op. cit.*, pp. 520-21 and Pl. CXXXVIII, 35-37.

No. 2 (3537) is a semicircular, fan-shaped pendent of faience holed at the apex.[1] It is of light biscuit colour and relieved at the centre by six parallel V-shaped bands with hatched border around. L. 1·55 in.; th. ·5 in. Mound F, Great Granary Area, Square J 7/25; Depth 9 ft. 7 in. b.s.; Stratum IV. **Fan-shaped.**

No. 3 (B955), of blue faience, is leaf-shaped, with rows of incised lines on either side of the mid-rib. The stalk was evidently intended to be capped with metal. L. 1·7 in.; w. ·65 in. Mound AB, Trench B; Depth 17 ft. b.s.; Stratum IV. **Leaf-shaped.**

No. 4 (5679), of burnt steatite, is shaped like a lemon leaf. It is chamfered at the base where there is a key-hole ·25 in. deep presumably for a metal attachment. L. 1·75 in.; w. ·5 in. Mound AB, Extension of Pits I and II, Square P 25/21; Depth 4 ft. 8 in. b.s.; Stratum II.

No. 5 (1682), of faience, is heart-shaped, tapered towards the edges and holed for attachment at the base. Its tip is sharply pointed. The fine cracks now seen on its surface are likely to have been covered with some kind of glaze which is no longer preserved. Size ·95×·9 in. Mound F, Trench III, Square M 9/23; Depth 8 ft. b.s.; Stratum IV. **Heart-shaped.**

No. 5784 (unillustrated) is also of steatite and similar to No. 5. It is broken at the tip where there is a small hole for some attachment. Size ·7×·6 in. Mound AB, Extension of Pits I and II, Square P 24/11; Depth 8 ft. b.s.; Stratum IV.

No. 6[2] (3251), of burnt steatite,[3] is flower-shaped with six petals carved in relief, and a conical projection on the underside meant, perhaps, for a metal cap. The petals and the small sunk hole at the centre were evidently intended for shell or paste inlay. Mound F, Trench III, Square N 9/5; Depth 5 ft. 8 in. b.s.; Stratum III. **Flower-shaped.**

No. 7 (H500), again, is a flower pendent with eight petals which were inlaid alternately with lapis lazuli and red stone. The lapis inlay survives intact in three petals and the red one in half a petal only. The centre also was, no doubt, inlaid. The convex back, decorated with incised circlets, has a small cylindrical projection transversely holed for suspension. Diam. ·75 in. Cemetery H, Western Section, Square R 34/22; Depth 5 ft. b.s.; Stratum II. **Inlaid flower.**

No. PI-58 (unillustrated) is also a 6-petalled flower, holed through the centre for suspension. Three of its petals are broken. Diam. 1 in. Mound AB, Extension of Pits I and II; Depth 5 ft. 3 in. b.s.; Stratum II.

No. 32 (9084) is *triratna*-shaped pierced with three holes. This shape is unique. I have classed this among the pendents but it may equally well have been a necklace bead or terminal. L. ·6 in.; w. ·3 in. Mound F, Trench IV, Square I 12/9; Depth 9 ft. 6 in. b.s.; Stratum IV. ***Triratna*-shaped pendent.**

Nos. 37-39 are cylindrical tapering pendents of hornblende. No. 36 may have been a similar pendent with its cap cemented on.[4] **Amphibolite.**

No. 42 (H469), of burnt steatite, is a rectangular pendent holed near the centre of its upper end which, like the bottom, is broken. It is relieved on the **Inlaid crescentic pendent.**

[1] For a similar faience ornament from Mohenjo-daro, *cf.* Dr. Mackay, *op. cit.*, p. 545, Pl. CXL. 40.

[2] It is possible that Nos. 6 and 7 ought really to go with ear-buttons Nos. 8-14 in this plate.

[3] The following three pendents are also of burnt steatite.

[4] For plano-convex tops cemented on to frustums, see p. 124 *supra*.

face by a series of five crescentic bands the sunk spaces between which were inlaid with some coloured paste of which traces are still discernible. L. 1 in.; w. 1 in. Cemetery H, Eastern Section, Square S 34/1; Depth 4 ft. 10 in. b.s.; Stratum II.

To the above are probably to be added a number of pottery discs with one or two rows of tiny pittings around the border or, in some cases, pitted all over. They are provided with a pair of holes near the edge and sometimes a strip of clay with two holes evidently representing a kind of clasp. These are what Dr. Mackay describes as "roundels" (*M. I. C.*, Pl. CXXXIII, 3) but I think they probably served as pendents. Their diameter varies between 1·3 and 1·9 in. One such example is illustrated in Pl. CXXXVIII, 32.

Chauks or conical ornaments for the head.

Conical ornaments for the head, called *chauks* at the present day in Northern India, are found in gold, faience, ivory and pottery. Now-a-days, *chauks* of silver are worn by the poor and of gold by the rich. By Hindus in Northern India *chauks* are regarded among the essential ornaments which every man, rich or poor, has to give at the wedding of his daughter-in-law. This ornament is now worn chiefly on religious and important domestic ceremonies only. That the *chauks* were popular among the Indus people, is evident from the figurines illustrated in Pl. LXXVI, 23, 26 and 30, and Pl. LXXVII, 31, 47, 53 and 60.

Gold. Pl. CXXXVII, 2 (8060c) is a conical *chauk* of thin gold sheet turned over at the rim. It is provided with a loop inside below the conical top and is described on pp. 63-64 *supra*, with the hoard of jewellery from Trench IV, Mound F.

See Pl. CXXXVIII, 24-29.

Ivory. Nos. 24 and 25 are identical ivory *chauks* with flat, projecting rim. They are holed across the thickness as shown by a piece of stick in No. 24. In each case, this hole is intersected at right angles by a slit cut in the centre of the base and measuring 1·15 by ·25 in. by 1·15 in. deep. No. 24—ht. 1·63 in.; No. 25—ht. 1·75 in. Diameter of each 2·45 in. Mound F, Trench I, Square M 10/21; Depth 7 ft. 1 in. b.s.; Stratum III.

Pottery. Nos. 26 (12699) and 27 (12618) are plain, cup-like pottery cones relieved inside with three concentric grooves on the flat projecting rim. Through the apex each has a hole splayed outwards. They are perhaps too heavy for use as *chauks*. No. 26—diam. 3·65 in Mound F, Trench IV, Square J 13/7; Depth 2 ft. 8 in. b.s.; Stratum I. No. 27—diam. 2·45 in. Mound F, Trench IV, Square J 13/2; Depth 3 ft. 6 in. b.s.; Stratum II.

Faience. No. 28 (PIV-100) is a hollow hemispherical *chauk* of faience with rolled and cabled rim. It is relieved on the outside with three wavy bands of cable pattern. Unfortunately, more than half is missing. At the edge on one side is the vestige of a hole; the corresponding hole on the other side is destroyed. At the apex is another hole, ·4 in. in diameter. Diam. 2·9 in.; ht. 1·1 in. Mound AB, Pit IV; Depth 10 ft. b.s.; Stratum IV.

No. 29 (7082) is a small, conical faience *chauk* with flat projecting rim. Inside, below the apex, it is provided with a hook for attachment, and is similar in shape and size to the gold *chauk* illustrated in Pl. CXXXVII, 2, or the one illustrated in *M. I. C.*, Pl. CXLVIII, A, 2. Diam. 1 in.; ht. ·85 in. Mound AB, Extension of Pits I and II, Square P 24/24; Depth 8 ft. b.s.; Stratum IV.

Temple ornaments. Pl. CXXXVIII, 30-39.

Temple ornaments were equally popular in burnt steatite, faience, shell and pottery and there is one example in silver also. They take the form of plano-convex discs with or without a projecting knob at the top or sometimes of flattish cones, and are usually provided with an arc-shaped hole or loop for attachment, but the larger convex discs (*e.g.*, 36-39) which were made of shell or faience, are holed through the apex.

(a) *Temple ornaments with a loop or arc-shaped hole.*

No. 30 (8595) is a flattish faience cone coated with white glaze. It was provided inside with a loop (now missing) below the apex. Diam. ·75 in. Mound F, Trench V, Square K 12/10; Depth 2 ft. b.s.; Stratum I.

No. 3311 (unillustrated) is a tiny conical faience boss ·65 in. in diameter and ·2 in. in height. It has two small holes at opposite points of the rim. Mound F, Great Granary Area, Square J 7/15; Depth 6 ft. b.s.; Stratum II.

No. 51 (11793) in Pl. CXXV is a tiny conical boss of silver inlaid at the top with a cylindrical piece of shell. It looks like a temple ornament but the inside hook has disappeared. The boss itself is thin like paper. Diam. ·65 in. Mound F. Deep Digging in Trench IV, Square I 13/21; Depth 14 ft. b.s.; Stratum VI.

No. 31 (H569) is a plano-convex disc with an arc-shaped hole on the plane side. This type, though fairly common in other materials, is rare in burnt steatite. Diam. 1·15 in. Cemetery H, Western Section, Square Q 34/23; Depth 6 ft. b.s.; Stratum II.

Nos. 4183 and 6028 (unillustrated) are pottery bosses each provided on the inside with a loop for attachment. The former is 2·3 in. in diameter and the latter 2 in. Both of them were found in Mound F—No. 4183 in Trench III, Square N 9/23, at a depth of 10 ft. 11 in. b.s., in Stratum V; No. 6028 in Great Granary Area, Square I 9/25, at a depth of 14 ft. b.s., in Stratum VI.

No. 33 (8760), of faience, is a plano-convex disc with a knob at the centre round which it is roughly decorated with pitted and incised circles and cabled border. On the underside, it has an arc-shaped hole and retains the impression of woven cloth on which it was moulded. Diam. 1·6 in. Mound F, Trench V, Square L. 12/4; Depth 6 ft. b.s.; Stratum III.

No. 34 (Af12) is a plano-convex disc of burnt steatite decorated with six incised concentric circles and a cabled border. On the underside also it has an incised circle almost touching the inner edge of the border and at the centre a semi-oval hole ·2 in. in diameter, presumably intended for inserting a metal attachment. Simple in design, this is the most effective temple ornament found at Harappā. Diam. 1·2 in. Mound F, Trench Af; Depth 1 ft. b.s.; Stratum I.

No. 35 (11514) is an ordinary, plano-convex disc of shell with raised middle to take arc-shaped hole such as that in No. 31 described above. Diam. 1·4 in. Mound F. Trench IV, Square I 13/16; Depth 2 ft. 6 in. b.s.; Stratum I.

(b) *Temple ornaments holed through the apex.*

Nos. 36 (3651, diam. 2 in.), 37 (1283, diam. 1·9 in.) and 39 (2554, diam. 2 in.) are hollow convex discs of shell holed through the apex. No. 36 came from Mound F, Great Granary Area, Square K 9/4; Depth 3 ft. 6 in. b.s.; Stratum II; No. 37 from Mound F, Trench I, Square M 10/15; Depth 2 ft. 6 in. b.s.; Stratum I; and No. 39 from Mound AB, Extension of Pits I and II, Square Q 24/13; Depth 9 ft. 9 in. b.s.; Stratum IV.

No. 38 (1669) is of blue faience and similar to the shell specimen No. 39 which has a flat projecting rim. Diam. 2·2 in. Mound F, Trench III, Square N 9/10; Depth 10 ft. 6 in. b.s.; Stratum V.

No. 526 (unillustrated) is the only example in ivory. It is plane, not hollow, on the underside. Diam. 2·18 in. Mound F, Trench I, Square M 12/16; Depth 5 ft. 3 in. b.s.; Stratum II.

Nose discs. Pl. CXXXIX, 15-20 and 29.

The discs illustrated in *M. I. C.*, Pl. CXLV, 13-20, have been described by Dr. Mackay as cog-wheel type of beads.[1] But these, specially the thinner ones with long projecting cogs, would, as he himself has pointed out, be inherently weak and therefore unsuitable as beads. Most of the specimens from Harappā, provided as they are with a circular groove on one side only, are similar to No. 15 of the above Mohenjo-daro Plate; those without the groove, like No. 19 in the same plate, are much less frequent. In a string of beads this groove, which is on the obverse face and in several cases retains traces of coloured inlay, would be altogether hidden from view. In my opinion these discs were intended as ornaments for the nose like the gold *tīlīs* or discoid nose-pins so commonly worn in India to-day. All that they require to complete them is an L-shaped knob-headed metal pin fixed in the central hole. The types of discs illustrated in *M. I. C.*, Pl. CXLV, 16 and 18, which are not represented at Harappā, may also be included among the nose-discs, but No. 20 in the same Plate looks like a bead.

Materials and size. The nose-discs found at Harappā are made of steatite and faience only. Their diameter ranges from ·35 in. in No. 10334 (unillustrated) to 1 in. in No. H450 (Pl. CXXXIX, 15). In shape, they are either plane on both sides, plano-convex, convexo-concave, or squat and tapered. The tapered discs such as No. 48 in Pl. CXXV are in effect similar to the gold studs illustrated in *M. I. C.*, Pl. CLI, *b*, 7, 8 and 11. Nose-discs of shell are unknown at Harappā but one example is mentioned from Mohenjo-daro.[2]

---

[1] *M. I. C.*, pp. 510-11.
[2] *Ibid.* p. 511.

No. 15 (H450) is of steatite paste and the largest example from Harappā. It has an unusually large hole at the centre with a small key hole on either side. Diam. 1 in.[1] Cemetery H, Eastern Section, Square S 34/17; Depth 4 ft. 5 in. b.s.; Stratum II. **Description.**

No. 16 (1547) is a plane disc of faience ·75 in. in diameter. Its cogs are perfectly preserved. Mound AB, Extension of Pits I and II, Square P 24/19; Depth 9 ft. 6 in. b.s.; Stratum IV.

No. 17 (6027), of steatite paste, has a circular groove on the face. Diam. ·85 in. Mound F, Great Granary Area, Square J 9/25; Depth 14 ft. 6 in. b.s.; Stratum VI.

No. 18 (Pl-124), of blue faience, is similar to No. 17, but is convex on the underside. Diam. ·7 in. Mound AB, Extension of Pits I and II; Diam. 8 ft. b.s.; Stratum IV.

No. 19 (12117) is similar to No. 17. Its groove shows traces of coloured inlay. Diam. ·65 in. Mound F, Trench IV, Square I 14/23; Depth 10 ft. b.s.; Stratum IV.

No. 20 (1483) is of faience and similar to No. 18. Diam. ·7 in. Mound F, Trench III, Square N 9/7; Depth 6 ft. b.s.; Stratum III.

No. 48 (2188) in Pl. CXXV is a tapering nose-disc of burnt steatite finely fluted on the outside. It is holed through the top, which is flat, apparently for threading on a bossed metal attachment. This type is rare, only a few examples of it having been found. Mound AB, Extension of Pits I and II, Square Q 24/14; Depth 3 ft. b.s.; Stratum I.

No. 29 (12027) is similar to the preceding. Diam. ·5 in. Mound AB, Trench at the Southern Edge, Square Q 28/17; Depth 13 ft. 5 in. b.s.; Stratum V.

Ear ornaments.

The ear ornaments found at Harappā may be divided into several classes, *viz.*, discoid buttons, usually made of faience though sometime also of burnt steatite; studs; long pendents of faience presumably depending from metal rings; plum-shaped ear-drops of burnt or unburnt steatite; and ear-rings of copper or bronze. Of these, ear-buttons were more common than ear-drops, but ornaments of the other three kinds are comparatively scarce.

Ear-buttons. Pl. CXXXIX, 8-14, and 21-23.

Ear-buttons are knob-headed discs, sometimes quite flat, sometimes slightly convex on the face. They are invariably provided with a stud-shaped knob in the centre of the back side as shown in Nos. 21-23, their thickness varying between 0·65 and 1 in. Only the face, which is occasionally plain but more often relieved by a four-pointed, circumscribed star and enclosed by a plain, cabled, petalled, or foliate border. was intended to be seen, the back knob[2]

[1] This size would not be considered too large in modern Mārwar.

[2] Similar ear-buttons are in vogue at present in Kāthiāwād, Deccan and South India, but in the two latter parts the knob at the back is made separately and screwed on, whereas in Kāthiāwād it is undetachable.

being required merely as a stopper to prevent the ornament from slipping down the ear. Except No. 12, which is of burnt steatite, all other buttons described below are of faience.

No. 8 (8794) is ornamented with a four-pointed, circumscribed star and cabled border. Diam. 0·85 in. Mound F, Trench V, Square L 12/9; Depth 5 ft. b.s.; Stratum II.

No. 9 (5785) is similar to No. 8 but is broken along the edge at one point. Diam. 0·95 in. Mound AB, Extension of Pits I and II, Square P 23/10; Depth 7 ft. b.s.; Stratum III.

Petalled border. No. 10 (2935) has a petalled border (somewhat damaged) but is otherwise similar to No. 8. Diam. 1 in. Mound F, Trench I, Square M 10/10; Depth 4 ft. b.s.; Stratum II.

Circular ornament. No. 11 (336) has a shallow pit in the centre round which is first a plain and then a cabled circle. Its border is deeply indented—perhaps to simulate petals. Diam. 0·85 in. Mound AB, Extension of Pits I and II, Square R 24/2; Depth 4 ft. 3 in. b.s.; Stratum II.

Foliate border. No. 12 (10269) is easily the best ear-ornament from Harappā. It is of burnt steatite and similar to No. 10 except that it has a delicate, foliate border resembling the twig of a date-palm. Its surface is convex and the ornament, besides being in higher relief than in any other example, is also much nicer and chaste. In its centre is a deep hole which is intersected at right angles by a pin-hole across the stem of the back knob. This, as well as the shallow pit in No. 11, were probably intended to be inlaid. Diam. 0·85 in. Mound F, Trench IV, Square I 14/13; Depth 3 ft. b.s.; Stratum I.

No. 13 (3081) is similar to No. 8, but has a plain border. Diam. 0·8 in. Mound F, Trench III, Square M 9/24; Depth 4 ft. 6 in. b.s.; Stratum II.

No. 14 (3259) has sunk, plain face and raised cable border. It was probably inlaid with a four-pointed star or some other design in shell or coloured paste. Diam. 0·9 in. Mound F, Trench III, Square M 9/25; Depth 5 ft. 7 in. b.s.; Stratum II.

Ear-studs. Pl. CXXXIX, 26-28.

Only three ear-studs, all of faience, have been found at Harappā. Their shape roughly resembles a reel with convex ends, but none of them is quite regular. Their length varies between 0·35 and 0·4 in.

No. 26 (H663) is 0·4 in. long and 0·35 in. in diameter at the ends. Cemetery H, Eastern Section, Square R 32/24; Depth 3 ft. b.s.; Stratum I.

No. 27 (11413) is 0·4 in. long and 0·3 in. in diameter at the ends. Mound F, Trench VI, Square P 11/6; Depth 3 ft. b.s.; Stratum I.

No. 28 (5566) is 0·35 in. long and 0·45 in. in diameter at one end and 0·4 in. at the other. Mound F, Trench III, Square N 10/6; Depth 7 ft. b.s.; Stratum III.

Ear-pendents. Pl. CXXXIX, 25 and 40.

There are only two ear-pendents, both of faience. No. 25 (5030) is a disc bevelled at the edge and inlaid at the centre with a thick piece of copper, 0·3 in.

in diameter, which may have been covered with thin gold leaf. At its back is a cylindrical projection with transverse hole probably for suspension from an ear-ring of metal wire like those illustrated in Pl. CXXV, 3-7. Ht. with projection 0·8 in.; diam. 0·9 in. Mound F, Trench III, Square N 10/1; Depth 3 ft. b.s.; Stratum I.

No. 40 (5207) is a tapering cylinder with holed conical head for suspension. Ht. 1·7 in. Mound F, Great Granary Area, Square I 9/20; Depth 4 ft. 3 in. b.s.; Stratum II.

Ear-drops. Pl. CXXXIX, 31 and 33-35.

The ear-drops so far recovered are made of burnt and unburnt steatite only and look like a plumb or plum. The latter shape was found in fairly large numbers, mainly in unburnt steatite. The drop is always holed at the upper end for a metal attachment.

No. 31 (8382a), of burnt steatite, is plumb-shaped and holed across the projecting upper end. Ht. 0·45 in. Mound F, Trench V, Square J 12/25; Depth 7 ft. 4 in. b.s.; Stratum III.

No. H317 (unillustrated), also of burnt steatite, is the only other example similar to No. 31; its upper end is broken. Diam. 0·25 in. Cemetery H, Western Section, Square Q 34/4; Depth 3 ft. 10 in. b.s.; Stratum II.

Nos. 33 and 35, of unburnt green steatite, are plum-shaped and almost identical in size. No. 35 (191) is 0·6 in. high. Mound F, Trench I, Square M 11/15; Depth 8 ft. 10 in. b.s.; Stratum IV.

No. 34 (6001) is a similar but rare example in burnt steatite and better shaped. Ht. 0·55 in. Mound AB, Extension of Pits I and II, Square P 24/19; Depth 6 ft. 6 in. b.s.; Stratum III.

Copper ear-rings. Pl. CXXV, 3-7, and 54.

Nos. 3-7 are ear-rings of thin wire; their diameter varies between 1·2 and 1·65 in.

No. 54 (8370) is a small ear-ring of fairly thick wire. Diam. ·75 in. only. Mound F, Trench IV, Square I 13/6; Depth 1 ft. 6 in. b.s.; Stratum I.

Ear-rings of the above types in gold and silver are still commonly used in India.

Finger-rings.

Finger-rings, besides those of copper and gold, are common in faience, but rare in alabaster, burnt steatite and pottery.

Pl. CXXV, 55, 49, 12 and 56.

No. 55 (J260) is a plain finger-ring of gold rectangular in section. Diam. ·67 in. Area J, Trench II, Square S 30/8; Depth 9 ft. 3 in. b.s.; Stratum IV. **Gold.**

No. 49 (J47) is of copper and oval in shape. It has a plano-convex, discoid silver bezel soldered on the joint. Greatest diam. ·85 in. Area J, Trench III Square S 29/20; Depth 2 ft. b.s.; Stratum I. **Copper.**

No. 12 (12190) is also of copper, and flattened at the joint for bezel which may have been of silver like that of No. 49. Diam. ·64 in. Mound AB, Trench at the Southern Edge, Square Q 28/8; Depth 12 ft. b.s.; Stratum IV.

No. 56 (3627) consists of three overlapping coils of thin copper wire. Diam. ·7 in. Mound AB; from spoil earth of Pits I and II.

Nos. 9 and 10 in this plate are two small, distorted rings of copper made of flat strip.

Faience. No. 43 (4766) in Pl. CXXXIX is of faience with cable moulding on the outside. Diam. 0·9 in. Mound AB, Extension of Pits I and II, Square Q 24/3; Depth 7 ft. 6 in. b.s.; Stratum III.

Steatite. No. 24 (unmarked) in Pl. CXXXIX is of burnt steatite and the only keeled example. It is very well made and has four equidistant transverse holes—perhaps for inlay or suspension. It might as well have been an ear-ring. Outer diam. 1·2 in.

Alabaster. Two other finger-rings of alabaster are illustrated in Pl. CXXVIII, 1 and 20.

No. 1 (602) is oval and measures 1·1 by 0·9 in. across the major and minor axes. Mound F, Trench I, Square M 12/10; Depth 7 ft. 2 in. b.s.; Stratum III.

No. 20 (G154) is but slightly oval, measuring 1·15 by 1 in. across the two axes. Area G, Trench II, Square AM 35/23; Depth 2 ft. b.s.; Stratum I.

Bracelets.

Bracelets are found in various materials but not in stone or ivory. Those of gold and silver are illustrated in Pl. CXXXVII, 1, 4 and 14,[1] and of copper in Pl. CXXV, 2, 59, 60 and 61. The latter are described below.

No. 2 (2147) is made of a round bar ·13 in. in diameter. Diam. of bracelet, 1·7 in. Mound F, Great Granary Area, Square J 9/19; Depth 11 ft. 6 in. b.s.; Stratum IV.

No. 60 (7947) consisting of two overlapping coils is of a slightly oval shape and made from a rectangular bar ·25 by ·15 in. in section. Diams. 2·1 and 1·8 in. Mound F, Trench IV, Square I 14/1; Depth 4 ft. b.s.; Stratum II.

Nos. 59 and 61 are also solid bracelets but of a smaller size.

See Pl. CXXXVIII, 1-23.

Bracelets of faience, pottery and shell were equally popular. Most of the faience examples are ornamented with cog-wheel edges or incised linear patterns (*e.g.*, Nos. 5, 6, 10-16 and 18-22), but some are plain, *e.g.*, Nos. 17 and 23. Pottery bracelets of superior make are keeled on the outer edge (*e.g.*, Nos. 4 and 7), round (*e.g.* Nos. 1 and 8), or rectangular in section. They are usually plain, but the keeled bangle No. 7 is painted with a series of heart-shaped designs in white on red ground, while some fragments are also found coated with a green slip. Let

[1] For their description, see pp. 63-65 *supra*.

me add in passing that there are countless pottery bangles of rough make which it is not necessary to describe.

No. 1 (8986) is a superior pottery bracelet round in section. It is so heavily fired as to give a metallic ring and stone-like fracture. Its colour is grey mottled with darker shades. The material of similar bracelets from Mohenjo-daro, which he prefers to call "stoneware", has been analysed[1] by Khan Bahadur Mohammad Sana Ullah, Archæological Chemist in India. According to him the dark colour is due to ferrous oxide. Diam. 3·25 in.; ht. 0·55 in. Mound F, Trench V, Square L 12/9; Depth 9 ft. 6 in. b.s.; Stratum IV. One complete bracelet like this is illustrated in *M. I. C.*, Pl. CLII, 1.

No. 8 (7366) is similar to No. 1. Diam. 3·25 in. Mound AB, Extension of Pits I and II. Square P 23/15; Depth 7 ft. 6 in. b.s.; Stratum III.

No. 4 (4101) is keeled at the outer edge and flat inside. It is made of the same material as No. 1, but its colour is bright red which indicates an oxidizing atmosphere in the kiln. Diam. 3·6 in.; ht. 0·55 in. Mound F, Great Granary Area, Square K 8/11; Depth 4 ft. b.s.; Stratum II.

No. 7 (7129) is half of a terracotta bangle with keeled rim. It is painted with a row of heart-shaped designs in white on red ground. Diam. 3·75 in. Mound AB, Extension of Pits I and II, Square P 24/19; Depth 8 ft. 6 in. b.s.; Stratum IV.

No. 1573 (unillustrated) is similar to No. 4, but its appearance is greyish to dark grey. Diam. 4·1 in. Mound F, Trench III, Square N 9/6; Depth 7 ft. 6 in. b.s.; Stratum III.

No. 3114 (unillustrated) is also similar to No. 4, but its colour is brick-red. Diam. 3·7 in. Mound F, Great Granary Area, Square I 9/5; Depth 1 ft. b.s.; Stratum I.

No. 11538 (unillustrated) is the only fragment rectangular in section. It is not so hard and shows some air bubbles. Diam. 2·9 in.; Section ·6×·45 in. Mound F, Trench IV, Square I 13/23; Depth 3 ft. 6 in. b.s.; Stratum II.

Nos. 2 and 3 (A182) are excellent, heart-shaped bangles of faience with **Faience.**
deeply cogged surface. They are more heavily fired than most of the other faience examples. Greatest diam. 3·7 in. Mound F, Great Granary Area; Depth 3 ft. 4 in. b.s.; Stratum II.

No. 9 (2851) is a plain faience bracelet tapered at the ends which are left apart as in the gold bracelet illustrated in Pl. CXXXVII, 1. It was coated with white glaze which has nearly disappeared. Diams. 2·7 and 2·25 in. Mound AB, Extension of Pits I and II, Square R 24/7; Depth 5 in. b.s.; Stratum I.

No. H448 (unillustrated) is the best example in shell. It is perfectly cir- **Shell.**
cular, and L-shaped in section. There is a break between its ends probably due to fracture. Diam. 2 in. Cemetery H, Eastern Section, Square S 34/11; Depth 4 ft. 3 in. b.s.; Stratum II.

Rough bangles of shell are found in fairly large numbers, and are seldom finished.

---

[1] *M. I. C.*, p. 530.

Amulets ? Pl. CXXXVIII, 40 and 42-45.

Certain objects which I take to have been charms or amulets are figured in Pl. CXXXVIII, 40 and 42-45. They are made of burnt steatite, faience and shell.

No. 40 (5968) is of burnt steatite and not thick like other examples in the same material and has only one hole drilled through the raised rib on the reverse. Size 0·95 by 0·55 in. Mound F, Great Granary Area, Square H 9/12; Depth 3 ft. b.s.; Stratum II.

Nos. 42-44 are of faience. Of these, No. 42 (2638) is trapezoidal in shape and fluted on the face. It has two holes as shown in Pl. CXXX, 25. Size 0·8 by 0·63 in. Mound F, Trench III, Square N 9/18; Depth 11 ft. 4 in. b.s.; Stratum V.

No. 43 (3847) is similar to No. 42. On reverse, it has narrow projections along the shorter ends for taking two parallel holes across the second and third flutes counting from below. Size 1·2 by 0·88 in. Mound F, Great Granary Area, Square I 8/10; Depth 4 ft. 9 in. b.s.; Stratum II.

No. 44 (G193) is rectangular with a holed projection at the head. It is incised on both sides with a cross-hatched pattern. Size 0·88 by 0·65 in. Area G, Trench III, Square AM 35/20; Depth 3 ft. 6 in. b.s.; Stratum II.

No. B1465 (unillustrated) is similar to No. 44 but of smaller size. Size 0·58 by 0·55 in. Mound AB; from surface of Trench B.

No. 45 (7468) is a double holed, flat rectangle of burnt steatite with traces of a green glaze. Objects of this type and material were popular. Size 1·56 by 1·14 by ·25 in. Mound F, Trench I, Square M 12/9; Depth 5 ft. 6 in. b.s.; Stratum II.

No. 7538 (unillustrated), of shell, is trapezoidal in shape. It is relieved on the face by a series of seven overlapping crescentic ribs and is holed at the ends. Its broader end, though broken, leaves a vestige of the second hole. L. 1·4 in.; w. at broader end 0·8 in.; at shorter end 0·6 in. Mound F, Trench I, Square M 12/12; Depth 6 ft. 2 in. b.s.; Stratum II.

CHAPTER XVI.

Playthings and Games.

Toys, mostly of terracotta, have been found universally at Harappā. Of these, the human and animal figures, already dealt with in Chapter X, have not been dealt with again under playthings as it is not possible to distinguish those which are mere toys from those which are *ex voto* or funerary offerings. **Distinction between playthings and other toys.**

Toy carts (Pl. CXX, 1-9).

Clay carts, as well as wheels, have been found in numbers at Harappā where there is a greater variety of the former than at Mohenjo-daro. Wheels from these sites have the hub only on the outside as at Anau[1] and not on both sides, as at Kish.[2] Some of the Harappā wheels are painted round the hub with thick black lines in triangular formation. On the inner side, which is comparatively rough, the wheel is often flat, but in some instances, as at Mohenjo-daro,[3] the reverse side is slightly concave.

No. 1 (2081) is slightly concave and measures 3·7 by 2·5 by ·9 in. It is provided with four vertical holes around the edge for attaching a superstructure or covering, with a pair of through holes in the centre of each of the longer sides for the axle, and with another hole in the front for the pole. It is not much different from the modern Sindh cart and is the only example of this type so far recovered. Mound F, Trench III, Square N 9/9; Depth 14 ft. b.s.; Stratum V.

No. 2 (2932) is a cart frame essentially similar to the Mohenjo-daro examples described by Dr. Mackay,[4] with this difference only that in this case the front and back instead of being straight have a V-shaped projection. Mound AB, Extension of Pits I and II, Square R 24/3; Depth 3 ft. 6 in. b.s.; Stratum II. This type of cart frames, as well as the Mohenjo-daro type, is fairly common at Harappā; still more common is the type represented by numbers 3 and 7.

Nos. 3 and 7 are approximately square, with concave body, low side walls and a vertical, flattened projection at each corner, evidently intended for the occupants to hold on to. They resemble the modern *bahlis* (bullock vehicles) of Northern India. **Square carts.**

No. 4 (4867) measures 4 in. long, 3 in. broad, and 3·3 in. high. With its side walls rising 1·5 in. above the seat it looks like a modern tipping truck. It is red-washed and better finished than other examples from Harappā. No other specimen of this type has been found. Mound AB, Extension of Pits I and II, Square P 24/16; Depth 2 ft. b.s.; Stratum I. **Truck-shaped cart.**

Nos. 5 and 6 represent a different type of small cart with slanting struts at the corners which, on being reversed, look like a pack-saddle, as shown in figure 8. This type was fairly popular. **Carts resembling an inverted pack-saddle.**

---

[1] R. Pumpelly, *Explorations in Turkestan*, Vol. I. Pl. 47, fig. 9.

[2-4] *M. I. C.*, p. 554 and Pl. CLIV. 7 and 10.

No. 9 (1795) is another type of a rough and ready hand-made cart shaped like a canoe. Only a few examples of this type have been recovered.

Bird and animal chariots (Pl. CXX, 10-15).

Two and four-wheeled examples.

Bird and animal chariots are common at Harappā. They are hollow inside and often pierced with a transverse hole across the body for wheels, and provided with a second hole in the neck or head for the attachment of a cord by which they could be pulled along. Some specimens have four instead of two wheels, but such examples are scarce. Now-a-days, too, four-wheeled bird and animal chariots of terracotta are made in India, but the more usual kind are made of wood for which Hoshiarpur in the Panjāb is well known. Similar wood chariots of the Roman Age are illustrated by Sir Flinders Petrie in his *Objects of Daily Use.*[1] Of the four wheeled examples, No. 13 (J180), with a bull's head, was found in Area J, Trench III, at a depth of 14 ft. 9 in. below the surface, and No. 14 (D33), with a cock's head, in Mound AB, Trench B, at a depth of 4 ft. below the surface. These two are holed across the shoulders and, although, their back part is broken, the position of the hole leaves hardly any doubt that there was a corresponding one across the back part also. In No. 13 the hole for the string is driven obliquely from below the muzzle to a point above the neck, while in No. 14 the beak is pierced horizontally for this purpose.

Theriomorphic vessel-chariot.

No. 15 (3702) was a curious chariot with a long animal neck, of which the head is broken. It takes the form of a flat-topped, oval vessel with small, cylindrical neck. The string hole was pierced through the length of the vessel a little above the bottom. The chariot is painted with flying kites and chevrons, the former of which are a motif commonly associated with the Cemetery wares. Mound AB, Extension of Pits I and II; Depth 4 ft. b.s.; Stratum II.

Harappā copper chariot and foreign examples.

In connection with the carts and chariots attention may also be invited to the Harappā copper chariot No. 355[2] (Pl. CXXV, 35), and to the foreign instances of chariots mentioned by Dr. Mackay on pages 554 and 555 of *M. I. C.*

Toy animals (Pl. CXX, 16-18).

Toy bulls with moveable heads.

No. 16 (5029) is the body of a quadruped (l. 3·5 in.) to which a moveable bull's head, No. 3568, has been fitted.[3] This was found at a depth of 2 ft. 8 in. below the surface in square N 10/1, Trench III, Mound F. Several examples of this kind have been recovered from different parts of the site.

No. 17 also consists of two separate finds, *viz.*, a headless quadruped No. 8929 and a bull's head No. 10410, the two together measuring 3·5 in. high. They are held together by a piece of pivotal stick whereby the head can revolve on the neck. This makes a very likely restoration. A few more examples of this kind have been found at Harappā but none has yet been published from Mohenjo-daro. The head was found at a depth of 6 in. below the surface in square I 12/23, Trench IV, Mound F, and the body at a depth of 6 ft. 4 in. below the surface in square J 12/5, Trench V, Mound F.

---

[1] Pl. LV, 590 and 602.

[2] For its description see pp. 99-100 *supra*.

[3] For a similar restoration from Mohenjo-daro, *cf. M. I. C.*, p. 550, Pl. CLIII. 39.

No. 18 (8636) is a strange animal with bulging body and upturned tail; its forelegs are not portrayed. Holed across the muzzle for a cord. L. 3·3 in. Mound F, Trench V, Square L 12/5; Depth 3 ft. b.s.

Bird whistles (Pl. CXX, 19-21).

Bird whistles, which have a wide vogue even to this day, are numerous at Harappā. Their generic Panjābī name '*ghuggu*' literally means a whistle in the form of a dove, and it is therefore not a little surprising to find that most of the bird whistles should frequently have taken the same form in prehistoric times also. As at present, they are sometimes with, sometimes without a pedestal. In order to produce a whistling sound they are hollow within and provided with a hole at the tail end. At best, they are rough and ready toys for children, and, to my mind, were never intended to be so well fashioned as to be capable of producing various modulations or the calls of different birds as suggested by Dr. Mackay.[1]

Bird cages (Pl. CXX, 22-26).

Five pottery toy cages have been recovered at Harappā, four from Mound F and one from Area G. They are of two shapes, *viz.*, pear-shaped and oval. No cage has yet been reported from Mohenjo-daro.

Of the pear-shaped cages, No. 22 (Ab554) is the best preserved. It shows two birds, one coming out of an opening and the other perched on the outside wall. The cage is pierced with three vertical openings, alternating with sets of three horizontal slits. Ht. 3·9 in. Mound F, Great Granary Area; Depth 4 ft. 6 in. b.s.; Stratum II.

Nos. 23 and 24 (5043 and G144), each with a bird seated on top, are merely the upper parts of cages, apparently similar to No. 22. Of these, the former was found in Mound F, Great Granary Area, Square K 9/5; Depth 9 ft. 3 in. b.s.; in association with Stratum III; and the latter in Area G, Trench II, Square AM 40/24, at a depth of 7 ft. below the surface in Stratum III.

No. 25 (4173) is rather more squat than the preceding examples. Though complete, it is without any bird, and is an ill-baked example with a smoky appearance. Ht. 2·5 in. Mound F, Trench III, Square N 9/20; Depth 8 ft. b.s.; Stratum IV.

No. 26 (3826) is an oval cage, 2·9 in. high, and 3·1 and 2·2 in. along the two axes. It is larger than the others described above, and is pierced by five vertical openings ranging in width from ·5 to 1 in. Behind the broad opening in front it has a rectangular opening in the roof which shows a circular break at the back indicative perhaps of a bird no longer there. It was found in an utterly crushed, post-cremation urn which lay at a depth of 9 ft. 10 in. below the surface in square I 7/10, Great Granary Area, Mound F, and was probably a funerary offering, like some of the human and animal figurines described in Chapter X, pp. 293 and 298. **Probably a funerary offering.**

[1] *M. I. C.*, p. 551.

Mould, sieve and basket (Pl. CXX, 27-29).

No. 27 (9020) is half of a spiraliform mould (?) 4 in. in diameter and ·4 in. deep. Two similar objects illustrated in *M. I. C.*, Pl. CXXXIII, 7 and 8 have been described by Dr. Mackay as cake moulds for fancy bread or for shaping sweetmeats.[1] Mound F, Trench V, Square J 12; Depth 3-6 ft. b.s.; Stratum II.

No. 28 (1557) is a toy sieve of sorts (?) with a rough bull's head for handle. It is pierced with four holes through the bottom and four at equal intervals in the sides. It is 2·4 in. in diameter and 1·2 in. deep. Mound F, Great Granary Area, Square I 9/24; Depth 4 ft. b.s.; Stratum II.

No. 29 (5800) is a toy basket made of long rolls of clay. It is 2·4 in. in diameter and 1·1 in. high, and the only example of its kind known from Harappā. Mound F, Eastern Extension of the Great Granary, Square J 9/22; Depth 12 ft. b.s.; Stratum IV.

Rattles (Pl. CXX, 30-34).

Pottery rattles, which are as common at Harappā as at Mohenjo-daro, are usually simple, round spheres but at Harappā there is one round example with a handle, and two others are shaped like a turnip. Their size ranges between 1·4 and 2 in. in diameter. In the hollow core are baked pellets of clay. In some examples there are a few perforations on one side to increase the sound (*e.g.*, No. 31); in a few others the pittings are superficial only.

The ordinary plain ball rattles are not illustrated. No. 30 (1517), which is inscribed, is 2 in. in diameter and was found at a depth of 8 ft. 1 in. below the surface in Square N 9/9, Trench III, Mound F; of the perforated ones, No. 31 (J338) is 1·95 in. in diameter and was found at a depth of 12 ft. below the surface in Square S 30/4 in the Deep Digging in Trench III, Area J.

No. 32 (11605) is a handled ball rattle 2·9 in. long. It was found at a depth of 6 ft. 6 in. below the surface in Square Q 27/9 in the Trench at the Southern Edge of Mound AB.

Nos. 33 and 34 (955 and 5200) are shaped like turnips. Both of them were found in the Great Granary Area, Mound F. No. 955 is 1·5 in. high and was found at a depth of 2 ft. below the surface in Square J 9/18; while No. 5200 is 1·9 in. high and was found at a depth of 3 ft. 9 in. below the surface in Square I 9/15.

Games.

Objects used for games are not many. Those that may be said to be unmistakable are balls and marbles in stone, shell, faience and pottery; dice of the same materials except shell; and some gamesmen of tetrahedral[2] or chessman shape,[3] the latter hardly distinguishable from bætyls. It is also possible that certain small tapering cylinders, usually made of hornblende, but sometimes of steatite and occasionally of lapis lazuli, which are grooved near the head[4]

---

[1] P. 473.

[2] Tetrahedral forms at Harappā are found in clay, faience and stone.

[3] Chessman-shaped forms are found in stone, faience, shell and terracotta.

[4] For similar cylinders from Mohenjo-daro, *cf. M. I. C.*, pp. 526-27

(Pl. CXXXIX, 36-39), and similar cylinders with plano-convex bead-like tops threaded and cemented on to them, may also have been gamesmen rather than pendents. Now-a-days, in the Panjāb, many of the most popular games are played with objects of wood which is of course a perishable material. Such are *gulli-daṇḍā*, *ḍanḍ-palām*, *gaiṇḍi*, and turning tops (*lāṭū*), on the other hand, *samundar-ṭāpū* or *kīḍī-kāḍā* and *bārah-gāṭī*, which are equally popular, are often played with potsherds or pebbles. But even the latter would hardly leave any recognizable traces.

Balls and marbles (Pl. CXX, 35-45).

Balls in terracotta, stone, shell, and faience have been found universally at Harappā, those in terracotta being recovered in specially large numbers. The smaller ones of earthenware, with a diameter of ·8 to ·9 in., may well have served as sling balls which were required for the protection of crops, etc.; and the larger ones, ranging from 1 to 1·9 in. in diameter must have been used for other purposes than playing marbles, for which they would have been too heavy.

Some of the balls are decorated, but the marbles are usually plain, though wonderfully smooth and wrought in a charming variety of stones. Several of the terracotta balls are decorated either with superficial perforations or with pellets of clay affixed to their surfaces; those of shell are almost invariably decorated with a series of four double concentric circles round the circumference with a similar pair in each of the resultant spaces at the opposite ends; while the faience ones are decorated either like those of shell or with incised hatching.

In the order of frequency the materials of which the balls are made are terracotta, flint, sandstone (chiefly of a buff colour), yellow Jaisalmer stone, alabaster, limestone of several colours, hornblende, shell, and faience. **Order of frequency.**

No. 35 (3469) of terracotta is 1·3 in. in diameter. It is decorated with pricked pellets of clay sunk into depressions in the body of the ball[1] and painted with two cross bands. Mound F, Great Granary Area, Eastern Extension, Square J 7/25; Depth 7 ft. 4 in. b.s.; Stratum IV. **Balls of terracotta.**

No. 36 (6050), also of terracotta, is 1·8 in. in diameter. It is pitted with holes all over. Mound AB, Extension of Pits I and II, Square P 24/9; Depth 7 ft. b.s.; Stratum III.

No. 37 (760) is of limestone, 1·25 in. in diameter. Retains traces of white paint. Mound F, Great Granary Area, Eastern Extension, Square J 9/21; Depth 9 ft. b.s.; Stratum III. **Stone.**

No. 38 (929) is of chert, 1·1 in. in diameter. It is highly polished. Mound F, Great Granary Area, Eastern Extension, Square J 9/22; Depth 5 ft. b.s.; Stratum I.

No. 39 (5649) of alabaster is cracked, 1·25 in. in diameter. Mound AB, Extension of Pits I and II, Square P 24/6; Depth 7 ft. b.s.; Stratum III.

No. 40 (1323) is of shell, 1·25 in. in diameter. It is decorated with six double concentric circles round the circumference. Mound AB, Extension of Pits I and II, Square P 24/17; Depth 12 ft. 5 in. b.s.; Stratum V.

---

[1] For a similarly decorated ball from Mohenjo-daro, *cf. M. I. C.*, Pl. CLIII, 6.

No. 41 (H665) is of faience, 1·2 in. in diameter. It is decorated like the previous shell ball.[1] Cemetery H, Western Section, Square R 32/14; Depth 4 ft. 2 in. b.s.; Stratum I.

No. 42 (53) is of faience, 1·3 in. in diameter. It is divided by bands into four quadrants which are decorated with incised hatching running alternately in different directions. Mound F, Great Granary Area, Eastern Extension, Square J 9/21; Depth 2 ft. b.s.; Stratum I.

No. 43 (12048) is of carnelian, ·95 in. in diameter. Mound AB, Trench at the Southern Edge, Square R 28/2; Depth 10 ft. b.s.; Stratum IV.

No. 44 (11867) is of hornblende, ·95 in. in diameter. Mound AB, Trench at the Southern Edge, Square Q 28/11; Depth 13 ft. 4 in. b.s.; Stratum V. It is worth remarking that most of the stone balls, except those of alabaster, are exquisitely polished, and in several cases the selection of their colours is remarkably good. The polish on the alabaster ones may have perished with age.

No. 45 (12283) is of shell and decorated like No. 40. This ball is not perfectly round as its diameter varies between 1 and ·95 in. Mound AB, Trench at the Southern Edge, Square Q 29/21: Depth 2 ft. b.s.; Stratum IV.

Dice (Pl. CXX, 46-48 and 51-54).

The game of dice was played both at Harappā and Mohenjo-daro. In all, seven pieces have been recovered at the former site, *viz.*, two of stone, four of terracotta, and one of faience, whereas at Mohenjo-daro the dice are all made of terracotta.[2] Mostly, they are perfect cubes, those from Harappā ranging from 0·65 in. to 1·85 in. cube. No. 48 of terracotta, however, measures 1·2 by 1·2 by 1·05 in[3].

Marking on the dice.

The marking of the numbers is not always alike. Four of the seven Harappā dice bear marks like those of Mohenjo-daro, *viz.*, 1 opposite 2, 3 opposite 4, and 5 opposite 6;[4] two are marked with 1 opposite 2, 3 opposite 5 and 4 opposite 6;[5] while No. 54 (G72), which is of terracotta, is marked like the modern dice, that is to say, with 1 opposite 6, 2 opposite 5, and 3 opposite 4. The last scheme of marking is similar to that on the cubical dice found at Brāhmanābād in 1854 by Mr. Bellasis[6] who pointed out that their marking was similar to that of modern dice. Bone dice from Egypt with size ranging from 0·26 to 0·75 in. cube, are in some cases also found marked like the modern dice.[7]

Vedic dice.

Dicing was also known to Vedic India and its ruinous effect resulting from heavy wager-laying is graphically depicted in the famous Gambler's lament in the Ṛigveda.[8] The Vedic dice was, however, made of *Vibhītaka* wood (*Terminalia bellerica*), known as *bahēḍā* in the Panjāb.

[1] For similar decoration, see also *M. I. C.*, Pl. CLIII, 3-5.
[2] *Ibid.*, p. 551.
[3] At Mohenjo-daro also one die is not a perfect cube: it measures 1·6 by 1·4 by 1·1 in. *cf. ibid.*, p. 551.
[4] *Ibid.*, p. 552.
[5] This marking does not appear to be similar to any known examples from elsewhere.
[6] *A. S. R.* for 1908-9, p. 85.
[7] Flinders Petrie, *Objects of Daily Use*, p. 57, Pl. XLIX, 234-58.
[8] R. T. H. Griffith, *Hymns of the Ṛigveda*. third edition, Xth Maṇḍala, XXXIV, p. 429. footnte, 1.

It is apparent from the above remarks that the Harappā dice were marked in at least three different ways, and it is possible that, like the dice in Egypt,[1] their marking may have been still more diverse. Unlike Mohenjo-daro dice, the Harappā examples, including those of stone, are all worn by use at the edges. Dr. Mackay has pointed out that two dice found in the Dk. Area at Mohenjo-daro, not far from each other, are of exactly the same size, but whether they were used in pairs or not is doubtful. Three of the dice from Harappā (two of terracotta and one of stone) are of the same size, *viz.*, 1·25 in. cube, but one of them was found in Mound F, Trench I, the second one in Mound AB in the Trench at the Southern Edge, and the third one in Area G, which are situated far apart from each other. **Method of marking and play.**

No. 46 (8670) is of red sandstone. It is 1·85 in. cube and is marked with 1 opposite 2, 3 opposite 4, and 5 opposite 6. Mound F, Trench V, Square K 12/24; Depth 4 ft. 6 in. b.s.; Stratum I.

No. 47 (unmarked) of terracotta is a 1·5 in. cube. The marking on this and the following two examples is similar to that of No.46.

No. 48 (10697) is also of terracotta and measures 1·2 by 1·2 by 1·05 in. Mound F, Trench V, Square K 12/23; Depth 7 ft. 3 in. b.s.; Stratum II.

No. 51 (H413) is of yellow faience, coated with white glaze. It is ·65 in. cube. It is worth remarking that on the side with 5 marks the pitting is arranged in two rows of 2 and 3 each, whereas in other cases the number 5 is obtained by four pittings at the corners and one at the centre. Cemetery H, Eastern Section, Square S 34/17; Depth 3 ft. 8 in. b.s.; Stratum I.

No. 52 (11201) is of red stone. It is a 1·5 in. cube, and marked with 1 opposite 2, 3 opposite 5, and 4 opposite 6. Mound F, Trench VI, Square O 9/18; Depth 2 ft. 3 in. b.s.; Stratum I.

No. 53 (12423), of terracotta, is a 1·25 in. cube. It is marked like No. 52, but is broken on one side. Mound AB, Trench at the Southern Edge, Square R 27/5; Depth 15 ft. 8 in. b.s.; Stratum V.

No. 54 (G72) is of flesh-coloured terracotta from which the usual light red glaze has mostly flaked off. It is 1·25 in. cube and is one of the finest specimens in terracotta. Area G, Trench I, Square AO 36/5; Depth 3 ft. 2 in. b.s.; Stratum II.

Tetrahedral gamesmen (?) (Pl. CXX, 55-57).

Numerous tetrahedrons, probably used as gamesmen, have been recovered at Harappā. With one notable exception, which I shall specify below, they are made of faience. Two such examples, one in faience and the other in white limestone, have been published from Mohenjo-daro.[2] The Harappā examples, of which only three are reproduced (Pl. CXX, 55-57), are usually glazed either white or blue, but, in one instance (No. 57) where the piece has been highly fired the colour is chocolate with three white parallel bands on it. There is only one example which is without any glaze. These tetrahedrons are either plain, or

[1] *Cf.* Petrie, *op. cit.*, p. 57, Pl. XLIX, 234-58.
[2] *M. I. C.*, p. 559.

inscribed with a dotted circle on each face, and in one case, with a hole in place of the dotted circle.

Their size ranges from 0·55 to 0·8 in. Usually each triangular face is equilateral and equal to one another, but occasionally one face is a little smaller than the other three, and in some slightly irregular specimens the other faces also vary.

Jar No. 5630a half full of clay tetrahedrons.

In connection with these small tetrahedrons, it should be mentioned that hundreds of similar objects of unbaked clay were found in a medium-sized, oval *ghaṛā* (No. 5630a), in Square N 10/1, Trench III, Mound F, Stratum III. All of them are rounded and pierced with a hole at each corner, and their size ranges from 0·7 to 0·9 in. The Kish and Ur examples, which are of Pre-Sargonic period, also have rounded corners frequently decorated with a small spot of inlay.[1] Possibly the holes at the corners of the Harappā examples were for the same purpose.

Details of faience tetrahedrons.

No. 55 (38) is covered with white glaze and shows an incised circle on each side. It is 0·75 in. on each side. Mound F, Great Granary Area, Square J 8/23; Depth 9 in. b.s.; Stratum I.

No. 56 (1059) is severely plain but covered with blue glaze. It is 0·8 in. on each side except one which is 0·75 in. only. Mound AB, Extension of Pits I and II, Square R 24/2; Depth 18 ft. b.s.; Stratum V.

No. 57 (3932) is very highly fired. It is of chocolate colour and has three white bands. Originally, these bands were laid on parallel to each other but as the result of firing they have spread somewhat irregularly. One side measures 0·67 in., and the remaining ones 0·65 in. each. From the surface of Mound AB.

Miscellaneous. See Pl. CXX, 58-60.

Carnelian spheroid.

No. 58 (J576) is a carnelian spheroid coated with white paint. It is rubbed flat at the top and bottom and is 1·1 in. in diameter, the facets being 0·65 in. in diameter and the height 0·8 in. It is likely to have been a weight,[2] but has been mentioned here again as it could also have been used for some other purpose. Area J, Trench I, Square Q 31/18; Depth 4 ft. b.s.; Stratum II.

Granite discs.

No. 59 (276) is a well-made granite disc, 1·45 in. in diameter and 0·35 in. thick. Mound F, Trench I, Square M 12/11; Depth 11 ft. b.s.; Stratum IV.

No. 60 (4292) is also of granite, but not quite regular as its thickness varies between 0·35 and 0·43 in. It is 1·35 in. in diameter and was found in Mound F, Trench III, Square N 9/15; Depth 9 ft. 6 in. b.s.; Stratum IV.

---

[1] *M. I. C.*, p. 559.

[2] See pp. 362-63 *supra*.

CHAPTER XVII.

Ivory, Shell, Faience and other objects of Technical Interest.

Ivory (Pl. CXIX, 1-57).

Bone or ivory objects are not so few at Harappā as they are reported to be at Mohenjo-daro, nor are they, on the other hand, so frequent as those of shell and faience. They comprise combs, *chauks*,[1] a cup, handles, kohl-sticks, pins, awls, a gamesman (Pl. CXIX, 55), a spatula (Pl. CXIX, 57), and some small balusters. There is nothing among these pieces which could have been used for inlay.

No. 2 (1652) is part of an unguent (?) cup with flat horizontal rim. It has been restored in plaster of Paris. Diam. 2·5 in. Mound F, Great Granary Area, Square I 9/14; Depth 4 ft. b.s.; Stratum II. **Unguent cup.**

No. 6 (7038) is a fragmentary comb, with only one preserved tooth. Like the Mohenjo-daro combs illustrated in *M. I. C.*, Pl. CXXXII, 13 and 21, its body, and that of No. 1, is ornamented with double incised circles. Length, including tooth and handle, 3·8 in. Th. 0·2 in. Length of tooth 0·7 in. Mound AB, Extension of Pits I and II, Square Q 23/15; Depth 2·6 in. b.s.; Stratum I. **Combs.**

No. 1 (4530) is another comb fragment similar to No. 6. It is 1·75 in. wide and 0·2 in. thick. Mound F, Great Granary Area, Square J 9/25; Depth 7 ft. b.s.; Stratum III.

No. 7 (5449) is a goblet-shaped terminal, flat at the top which is pierced at the centre with a hole 0·3 in. in diameter and 0·85 in. deep. Ht. 1·5 in. Mound F, Trench III, Square N 10/6; Depth 5 ft. b.s.; Stratum II.

No. 8 (12061) is another fragmentary terminal knobbed at the end which is 0·65 in. in diameter. Ht. 1·65 in. Mound AB, Trench at the Southern Edge, Square Q 28/16; Depth 15 ft. 10 in. b.s.; Stratum V.

No. 9 (PIII-9) is a concave pillar-shaped piece with flat ends. Round the shaft are two wavy patterns separated from each other by horizontal bands. Similar decoration also occurs on the ivory pieces illustrated in *M. I. C.*, Pl. CXXXII, 15 and 17. At both ends, the piece is pierced with lathe holes, 0·4 in. in depth as well as in diameter. Ht. 1·8 in. Mound AB, Pit III; Depth 5 ft. 6 in. b.s.; Stratum II.

No. 10 (9099) is the end of a lathe-turned shaft with flat base. The shaft is relieved with reel and bead motifs. It may be the handle of a copper mirror such as that illustrated in Pl. CXXIV, 29. Its present height is 1·9 in. and maximum diameter 1 in. Mound F, Trench V, Square K 12/14; Depth 1 ft. 6 in. b.s.; Stratum I.

No. 11 (11648) is a long-necked, oval-shaped handle, flat on the underside (not seen in the photograph) but otherwise rounded. In the top is a hole 0·2 in. in diameter which tapers down to 0·15 in. at the lower end. L. 1·9 in. Mound

[1] See Pl. CXXXVIII, 24 and 25 and p. 442 *supra*.

AB, Trench at the Southern Edge, Square Q 28/17; Depth 8 ft. 6 in. b.s.; Stratum III.

Kohl sticks. Kohl sticks (Pl. CXIX, 13 and 15-16) are generally cylindrical but No. 13 (1308) is rectangular in section. Usually, they taper a little at both ends, which are fairly thick and rounded, but sometimes only one end is finished, the other being left rough. No. 13 (3808) is of unusual shape and the only one of its kind. It is 2·8 in. long and somewhat rounded at the ends, one end being considerably thicker than the other. Mound AB, Extension of Pits I and II, Square 24/15; Depth 8 ft. b.s.; Stratum IV.

Duck-headed example. No. 19 in Pl. LXXVIII (4997) is probably the handle of a duck-headed kohl-stick, of which the lower part is broken, the existing length being 1·45 in. Mound AB, Extension of Pits I and II, Square Q 24/9; Depth 7 ft. b.s.; Stratum III.

Metal example. Kohl sticks were also made of copper and bronze, but in those materials they have mostly perished by corrosion. One well preserved example is, however, illustrated in Pl. CXXV, 34 and 36.[1]

Hair pins, needles and awls. Besides those of metal, hair pins,[2] needles and awls were made of ivory and bone also. They are sharply pointed at one end, and vary in length from 1·9 to 5 in. and in diameter from 0·25 to 0·35 in. (Pl. CXIX, 12 and 17-29). Only five of these—Nos. 12, 21 and 25 of ivory and Nos. 26 and 28 of bone—, representing different shapes, are described below.

No. 12 (4956), the smallest, is unusually more pointed at one end and unfinished at the other. L. 1·9 in. Mound AB, Extension of Pits I and II, Square P 24/11; Depth 4 ft. b.s.; Stratum II.

No. 21 (4896), the longest example, is broken at one end. L. 5 in. Mound AB, Extension of Pits I and II, Square Q 24/9; Depth 10 ft. b.s.; Stratum IV.

No. 25 (2052) is sharply pointed at the upper end and less so at the lower. Sir John Marshall is of the opinion that this shape closely resembles arrow-points of the historic period from Taxila and elsewhere. L. 3·4 in.; diam. 0·4 in. Mound F, Trench I, Square M 11/20; Depth 12 ft. b.s.; Stratum V.

Bone. No. 26 (unmarked), made of a tubular bone, is very sharply pointed. Except the channelled portion it is polished all over. Fragmentary. L. 2·8 in.

No. 28 (3431) is a flattish, curved piece of bone very sharply pointed at one end. Retains traces of spongy core. L. 3·4 in. Mound AB, Extension of Pits I and II, Square Q 24/24; Depth 7 ft. 6 in. b.s.; Stratum III.

Balusters. The balusters etc., illustrated in Pl. CXIX, 3-5, 30-41, 43 and 45-54 probably belonged to small caskets or miniature furniture. The uniformity of their ornaments on all sides is against their having been used as dice or for casting in any game of chance.

No. 43 (3788) is a flat strip, 1·8 in. long, and 0·52 by 0·2 in. in section. The longest specimen of this shape (7701) is 2·85 in. long and 0·45 by 0·2 in. in section.

There are a few balusters triangular in section, *e.g.*, Nos. 5 and 40. Their length varies from 0·95 to 2·1 in.; the width of their sides is 0·4 in.

---

[1] For its description see p. 390 *supra*.
[2] *Ibid.* and Pl. CXXV, 25-27 and 33.

The four-sided specimens, square in section, are both plane and decorated with bands. The former are similar to No. 38 which is 0·3 in. square in section; but their length varies from 1·35 to 2·25 in. Nos. 3, 4 and 36 are segmented, each being divided into three sections by four bands. In No. 4 (10111c), there are three holes pierced through two sides: in No. 3 there is one hole only (in the middle); the third one being without holes. Their length varies between 2·4 and 2·38 in. Another example, rectangular in section, is No. 54. This is the smallest specimen being only 1·1 in. long.

Nos. 47 (3894) and 48 (5059), have two flat and two convex sides, the latter decorated with a series of horizontal lines, and the former with double concentric circles. No. 47 is 1·45 in. long; No. 48, 1·75 in. long.

Nos. 30 and 32-34 are cylindrical. Their length varies between 1·34 and 2 in.

No. 31 and a few others like it are obliquely fluted and have cross-hatched bands at the ends. Their length is only 2 in. In No. 53 (4389) the shaft of the baluster tapers from the middle towards both ends. It measures 1·4 in. long.

Nos. 45 and 46 are curious club-shaped objects. The former is 2·3 in. long.

Spatula.

No. 57 (4164) is a spatula of sorts with pointed ends, its upper part being cut flat on one side for a length of three inches. L. 6·2 in. Area J, Trench I, Square Q 30/20; Depth 1 ft. 6 in. b.s.; Stratum I.

Gamesman.

No. 55 (10800) is a cylindrical gamesman, like one of the pieces used in the present day game of draughts. It is ornamented on both faces with seven double concentric circlets incised round one at the centre, and with a series of single circlets round the circumference. Diam. 1 in. Mound F, Trench V, Square J 13/23; Depth 6 ft. b.s.; Stratum II.

Flat strip with barbed edges.

No. 42 (7045) is a flat strip, 2·1 in. long by 0·45 in. wide. On either face it has a row of incised circles and 3 barbs or notches on each side at the base. Mound AB, Extension of Pits I and II, Square Q 23/15; Depth 2 ft. 6 in. b.s.; Stratum I.

No. 44 (3934) is a tanged, flat ivory strip decorated on each face with a series of shallow incisions in imitation, perhaps, of a feather. It is 2·3 in. long, 0·7 in. wide and 0·15 in. thick in the middle. Cemetery H, Eastern Section, Square S 34/7; from pot-burial No. 3934b; Stratum I.

No. 56 (7083) is nearly half of a tanged, oval object with pointed tip. split vertically. It tapers gradually towards the edge. L. 2·8 in.; thickness at centre 0·1 in. Mound AB, Extension of Pits I and II, Square Q 24/4; Depth 7 ft. 6 in. b.s.; Stratum III.

Shell inlay (Pl. CXXXIX, 77-81 and 84-89 and Pl. LXXXII, 42).

At Harappā as at Mohenjo-daro inlay objects have been found in very large numbers, mostly in shell, less frequently in faience, burnt steatite, red sandstone, yellow Jaisalmer stone and alabaster. As the working and various forms of shell inlay have already been fully dealt with by Dr. Mackay in *M. I. C.*, Vol. II, pp. 563-70, I shall refer only to a few examples of particular interest.

Probable mode of their inlay.

A glance at the illustration of inlay objects will show that some of the shapes were specifically designed, such as Nos. 84 and 85 in Pl. CXXXIX, while other forms, *e.g.*, Nos. 79, 80 and 88 in the same plate, result from the fretting out of the designs. For instance, by cutting out the core of the heart-shaped design No. 84 the form No. 79 is produced, and similarly by cutting out the central core of No. 85 the lozenge shape No. 88 results. A similar pattern to No. 85 occurs, it may be noticed, in the centre of the faience ear-buttons Nos. 8-10, 12 and 13 in Pl. CXXXIX. No. 14 in the same plate has a sunk face and cable border, but it seems highly probable that in conformity with the decoration of other ear-buttons it was also inlaid with a piece of the same design as No. 85. Similarly, the heart-shaped pieces Nos. 79 and 84 in the same plate find an exact counterpart in the gold pendent No. 8 in Pl. CXXXVII which is inlaid with blue ribbed faience in the centre and outer depressions. Ordinarily, the shell would probably be inlaid in the wooden surface of furniture, boxes, etc., just as ivory is inlaid to-day in many parts of India, but in some cases the effect of the inlay was also enhanced by the use of coloured pastes or stones to fill the cloisons. Thus, as we have seen, the petals of pendent No. 7 in Pl. CXXXIX were inlaid alternately with lapis lazuli and deep red stone with possibly another kind of stone or shell at the centre; and the petals of pendent No. 6 in Pl. CXXXIX were almost certainly inlaid in the same way. Coloured pastes must also have been used to fill the circular groove in the nose discs illustrated in Pl. CXXXIX, 17-20 two of which still retain traces of colour.

The flower petals illustrated in Pl. CXXXIX, 89 and LXXXII, 42 may be assumed to have been arranged round a central circle in the manner of the faience flower No. 28 in Pl. CXXVIII. Precisely similar petals have been recovered at Mohenjo-daro also. The largest petal of this kind is 1·75 in. long and 1·8 in. across the base.

Shell was worked with great skill, and every part of it was turned to account in the manufacture of dippers, cups, bangles,[1] balls, cylinders, wavy rings,[2] beads, discs, temple ornaments, inlays etc., etc.

An interesting group of inlay objects made of burnt steatite and faience was found sticking to some broken copper objects recovered from a well in Trench IV, Mound F. The pieces comprised in this group are illustrated in Pl. CXXXIX, 65-76, 82 and 83. All the pieces are fluted, presumably with a gouge, like those illustrated in Pl. CXXV, 40-42 and 44. This group has already been described in the account of Trench IV,[3] but it may be added that, so far as faience inlay is concerned, only two shapes are usually met with, the crescentic (Pl. CXXXIX, 73 and 76) and almond, the colour of the latter being always light or deep green.

Inlay pieces of stone are cut from alabaster as well as from red and yellow Jaisalmer stones. One and all are lozenges with incurved sides like Nos. 39 and 40 in Pl. LXXXII. This form, as elsewhere pointed out, results from five intersecting circles.

---

[1] In connection with Dr. Mackay's remark in *M. I. C.*, p. 339, that shell bracelets are „so profusely worn by females in India at the present day as to cover the whole of the forearm, it may be pointed out that the sets of bracelets (*chūḍā*) in Northern India are made of ivory and not of shell.

[2] For example Nos. 10-12 in Pl. CXVII are rings of shell with five to eight undulations, and height ranging between 0·2 to 1·15 in.

[3] See p. 61 *supra*.

See Pl. CXXVIII, 5, 11, 14, 15 and 19.

As already noticed stone beads were sometimes inlaid. Of the examples illustrated in Pl. CXXVIII, 14, 15 and 19,[1] the two first have trefoil grooves, each foil being holed at the centre for keying the inlay, which may have taken the form of tiny disc beads such as those illustrated in Pl. CXXVIII, 25. Bead No. 19, however, was presumably intended to be finished off with coloured inlay and perhaps with metal caps at each end. Trefoil patterning is also found etched in white on beads of imitation carnelian (Pl. CXXVIII, 5 and 11) the body of which is burnt steatite. Precisely similar decoration also occurs on the imitation carnelian cylinder illustrated in Pl. LXXXIII, 42.

See Pls. LXXXIII, 43, 44 and CXVII, 17.

No. 43 (12375) is a wheel-like disc of imitation carnelian[2] with flat, holed hub. On the outside, it is etched in white with a dotted scaly pattern which has spread somewhat irregularly. Inside, round the hole is a dotted circle in white followed first by a plain band and then by a similar circle. Diam. 1·8 in.; th. at hub 0·35 in. Mound AB, Extension of Pits I and II, Square R 27/5; Depth 13 ft. 6 in. b.s.; Stratum V.

No. 44 (5467) is the fragment of a hollow cylinder etched with white bands and undulating patterns. Ht. 1·45 in.; diam. 1 in. Mound AB, Extension of Pits I and II, Square 24/24; Depth 3 ft. 6 in. b.s.; Stratum II.

Similar cylinders of large size are also found but none is fully preserved.

No. 17 in Pl. CXVII is a small, fragmentary undulating ring etched with heart-shaped designs in white within which recur dotted outlines of the same shape. This has already been described in connection with *liṅgams* and *yonis*.[3]

Glazed decoration (Pl. LXXXII, 13 and 14).

No. 13 (5472) is a small fragment of a faience vase covered with white glaze. Over this are painted cross-hatched bands in black coloured frit which stand out perceptibly above the surface. L. 0·9 in. Mound AB, Extension of Pits I and II, Square P 24/24; Depth 3 ft. 6 in. b.s.; Stratum II.

No. 14 (4746) is a small cylinder of faience 0·85 in. long and 0·33 in. in diameter. It was first glazed green and then painted with dots of white frit standing out slightly above the surface. L. ¾ in. Mound AB, Extension of Pits I and II, Square Q 24/8; Depth 6 ft. 6 in. b.s.; Stratum II.

Tube drilling.

Nos. 28, 30-32, 36, 45, 46, etc., in Pl. LXXXIII illustrate the use of the tubular drill, which was also employed in Egypt as far back as the beginning of the First Dynasty where its existence is proved by a core of black and white porphyry.[4]

---

[1] See p. 396 *supra*.

[2] The two following objects are also of imitation carnelian.

[3] See p. 371 *supra*.

[4] Petrie, *Tools and Weapons*, pp. 44-45, Pl. LII, 68; for tubular drilling also compare cores 59, 62, 69-71 and cylinders, vases, etc., Nos. 61 and 63-66 in the same plate.

The drills used were doubtless of bronze. The width of the groove left between the core and the wall varies between 0·05 and 0·2 in. Whereas the cores were perfectly cylindrical, the hole itself tapered slightly towards the bottom from which it follows that the thickness of the tube drills increased only on the outside, the inside hollow remaining perfectly vertical. Allowing, at least, a fourth of the width of the groove for an abrasive and for the free movement of the drill, the net thickness of the drills would seem to have varied between 0·0375 and 0·15 in.

Size of dowel holes. Stones drilled in this way are of varying hardness. They include chert, very close grained yellow Jaisalmer stone, basalt, dark grey and red sandstones, as well as alabaster which was the softest of all and used most frequently. The tube-drill holes were presumably meant for the insertion of dowels of some sort in order to fix the stones together. The diameter of these holes ranges from 0·25 to 2·8 in. and their depth from 0·2 to 1·1 in.

Pointed drill. Dowel holes are also to be seen in the objects illustrated in Pl. LXXXIII, 29 and 41, but these are made by the ordinary pointed drill. In the former, the maximum diameter of the hole is 0·35 in. and depth 1·7 in. In No. 41, which is part of a channelled object with rectangular groove, the hole is 0·1 in. in diameter and 0·3 in. deep. Again, allowing a fourth of the diameter of these holes for an abrasive and movement of the drill it may be presumed that the actual thickness of the pointed drills used on Nos. 29 and 41 would be about 0·2625 in. and 1·275 in. in diameter.

Description. No. 28 (B815) is a rectangular block of yellow Jaisalmer limestone with five tube-drill holes in the thickness of its sides. It measures 8·5 in. long, 5·5 in. wide and 2·3 in. thick, and was found with a number of other architectural stones in Trench B near *Naugazā* in association with the IVth stratum.

No. 30 (2847) is a very well dressed and polished slab of red sandstone, 2·5 in. thick. Originally, it appears to have been triangular in shape, but being broken at the corners it now looks like an irregular pentagon. By restoration its sides would come to 2 ft. 10 in., 2 ft. 7 in., and 1 ft. 5 in. Besides four dowel holes (0·8 to 1 in. in diameter) drilled in the thickness of its sides, it has two sector-shaped cuts in the longest side which is partly broken along with the corners. Mound AB, Extension of Pits I and II, Square R 24/7; Depth 7 ft. b.s.; Stratum IV.

No. 31 (B17) is a fragment of a dark red stone broken on three sides. To judge from the position of dowel holes it was intended to be placed on edge like No. 28. It is 3·5 in. thick. This was also found in Trench B near *Naugazā* in association with the IVth stratum.

No. 32 (3404) is a rectangular slab of yellow Jaisalmer stone which was probably laid flat as one of its longer sides is finished smooth. To obtain an imperceptible joint its top edge was also made smooth for a width of 2·25 in. only. It measures 12·75 by 5·75 by 2·75 in., and has three small and two large dowel holes, each of the latter being 2·3 in. in diameter. Mound F, Trench I, Square M 10/15; Depth 7 ft. b.s.; Stratum III.

No. 36 (B815), of grey sandstone, is broken on all sides except the top face and shows fine tube-drill holes. It was found with No. 31 above.

No. 45 is the end fragment of a curved tube of yellow Jaisalmer stone. Its hole is irregular and not exactly in the centre. The diameter of the tube is 2 in. and the hole, which is slightly oval, is 1 in. and 1·15 in. along the minor and major axes. Several tubes of the same shape, with more or less regular holes, have been found in alabaster (*e.g.*, No. 46). The finished examples indicate that they were not much longer than 3 in.

Channelling (Pl. LXXXIII, 33-35 and 41).

No. 33 (B1) is fragment of a circular piece of red sandstone with 2 bands (0·95 by 0·25 in. in section) raised in relief. Size 5 by 3·25 in. In this, as well as in No. 35, the curvature of the raised bands is not absolutely regular, as it was obtained only by gradual sawing and adjustment. In this case, as in other examples which are not illustrated, the grooves between the bands were made by chiselling away sawn-out portions which might have been finished with some kind of plaster.

No. 35 (unmarked), of yellow Jaisalmer stone, is of the same shape as No. 33, but of smaller size. Size 2·9 by 2·4 in.

No. 34 (B22) is the fragment of a rectangular channel of grey stone. Size 4·75 by 3·75 in. This and No. 33 were found along with other stones in Trench B near *Naugazā* in association with Stratum IV.

Specimens of fluted faience and stone (Pl. LXXXIII, 47-49, 51 and 52).

No. 48 is of faience and the rest of stone. They are all vertically fluted, and so are the pieces of inlay illustrated in Pl. CXXXIX, 65-76, 78, 82 and 83, which are made of faience, burnt steatite and shell. Among stones, alabaster, being soft, was more commonly fluted, but No. 47 is of red sandstone, 49 of yellow Jaisalmer stone, and No. 51 of *sang-i-abri*.

No. 47 (unmarked) is a rectangular piece fluted in opposite directions on its two faces. Its ribbing, as compared with that of Nos. 51 and 52, is rather flat and shallow. Looks like a false screen.

No. 48 (10078) is a fragment of a hollow, faience cylinder 0·25 in. thick and 1·6 in. in diameter. Mound F, Trench I, Square M 12/8; Depth 10 ft. 6 in. b.s.; Stratum IV.

Piece of drapery on Egyptian parallel.

No. 49 (1012) is a round and tapered fragment of yellow Jaisalmer stone with fine close fluting possibly representing folds of drapery, like those on the loin cloth of the Egyptian statue of King Khafra (IVth dynasty) and of Ranofer.[1] For closeness the original fluting had to be sub-divided several times and this explains why the fluting of this piece is not uniform. Mound F, Great Granary Area, Square J 9/24; Depth 3 ft. b.s.; Stratum II.

No. 51 (11994) is of *sang-i-abri* of dark red colour. Its flutes are deeper and wider, the distance between them being 0·25 in. and depth of flutes 0·15 in.

[1] Petrie, *Arts and Crafts of Ancient Egypt*, Figs. 27 and 31.

Mound AB, Trench at the Southern Edge, Square Q 27/23; Depth 14 ft. 4 in. b.s.; Stratum V.

No. 52 (unmarked) is one of the several fluted fragments of alabaster. Being photographed on a large scale its flutes, though actually smaller, appear larger than those of No. 51.

Textiles.

No remnants of textiles have been recovered at Harappā, though clear evidence regarding the use of cotton cloth in the Indus Valley was obtained from Mohenjo-daro.[1] At Harappā, however, there are several unmistakable traces of the woven materials and threads—presumably of cotton—with which cores of sand were secured for moulding on them faience objects such as unguent vases, temple ornaments, etc. Some of the faience vases, which bear clear traces of woven materials on the inside, are illustrated in Pl. LXXXII, 15, 17, 19,[2] 28, etc. A temple ornament of the same substance illustrated in Pl. CXXXVIII, 33, bears an impression of cloth on its underside, while imprints of woven material are also found on two bricks (Pl. LXXII, 50 and 51) which also show foot-prints of a man and a dog.

Cereals and fruits.

Wheat. Carbonized remains of wheat, partly lumped together and partly scattered, were recovered from two places at Harappā. Of these, lump No. 5346A was found in Mound F, Great Granary Area in Square I 9/15, at a depth of 5 ft. 1 in. in association with the IIIrd stratum. Rai Sahib Jai Chand Luthra, Associate Professor of Botany at the Panjāb Agricultural College, Lyallpur, reports that "These are grains of wheat. Resemble closely the grains of *Triticum Compactum* (dwarf wheats)". This variety of wheat is still cultivated in the Panjāb and precisely the same variety was found at Mohenjo-daro also.[3] A part of the same lump was examined by Mr. B. C. Burt, Agricultural Expert of the Imperial Council of Agricultural Research, New Delhi, who reports that "The grains while unlike those of most wheat species, strongly resemble those of *Triticum sphærococcum* Percival. They differ slightly in that the furrow is usually extremely shallow and in that grain size and shape is rather more variable than in the variety of *T. sphærococcum* available at Pusa. *T. sphærococcum* is believed to be cultivated only in India though specimens of it have also been recovered from Persia."

The other specimen of wheat, No. 12387V, was found in the Trench at the Southern Edge of Mound AB in association with Stratum II. This was submitted for examination to the Director, Royal Botanic Gardens, Kew, Surrey, England, who writes that "This specimen, owing to being so completely carbonized, cannot be identified with certainty, but it appears to be a species of *Triticum* (wheat)".

Barley. A small quantity of charred barley No. 3429 was recovered from the Extension of Pits I and II in Mound AB at a depth of 6 ft. below the surface in associa-

[1] *Cf. M. I. C.*, pp. 585-86.

[2] On this impressions of thread decoration are apparent, but the inside of vases is not illustrated.

[3] *Cf. M. I. C.*, p. 586.

tion with Stratum III. This was also examined by Rai Sahib Jai Chand Luthra and, according to him, proved to be grains of common husked barley. According to Mr. Burt these probably belong to a small-seeded variety of *Hordeum vulgare* L. var. *hexastichon* (6-rowed barley). The samples resemble the variety locally known as *Chutjawa* of which Pusa Type 17 is an example.

Mr. Burt also kindly examined some charred peas No. 8366 recovered in association with Stratum III from the hollow of circular Platform P8 in Trench V. He reports that they are in all probability field peas (*Pisum arvensu L.*). **Peas.**

A lump of charred sesamum (No. 8827) was found at the eastern end of Trench V, Mound F, at a depth of 6 ft. below the surface in association with the IInd stratum. The identification was made at the Panjāb Agricultural College, Lyallpur. **Sesamum.**

No actual date seeds have been found at Harappā, but familiarity with this fruit is proved by two tiny faience sealings from Mound F which are shaped like a date seed. Of these, No. 2701 (Pl. LXXXIV,—ap) was found in the Great Granary Area at a depth of 10 ft. below the surface in association with the IVth stratum, and No. 12278 in Trench IV in the same mound at a depth of 3 ft. 6 in. b.s. in association with Stratum III. Let me also add that the border of the ear-button No. 12 in Pl. CXXXIX simulates a twig of the date palm. **Date palm.**

In the Extension of Pits I and II in Mound AB was found an interesting earthenware jar No. 7765 in square P 24/5 at a depth of 9 ft. 5 in. below the surface in association with the IVth stratum. Besides other contents[1] it had porous earth which contained a few vestiges of seeds of the melon species which unfortunately were too brittle to be successfully lifted up. **Melon seeds.**

A well-made pendent in the form of a lemon leaf made of burnt steatite is illustrated in Pl. CXXXIX, 4. The faithfulness with which it is made leaves no doubt that the lemon tree was well known to the people of Harappā. **Lemon leaf.**

While speaking of fruits, attention may also be drawn to two polychrome earthenware vases Nos. 21 and 22[2] illustrated in Pl. LXXI. The former is shaped like a pomegranate and the latter like a cocoanut fruit. Both of them were recovered from Trench III, Mound F, in association with Stratum III. A representation of lotus fruit in faience was found in Pit III, Mound AB.[3] **Pomegranate, cocoanut and lotus fruit.**

Varieties of charcoal.

In the Extension of Pits I and II in Mound AB in and around Square Q 24/9 was found in Stratum IV an appreciable quantity of charcoal from the burnt down reed-and-bamboo huts of poor people. Samples were sent for examination to the Director, Royal Botanic Gardens, Sibpur, Calcutta, who has furnished the following report of their examination by Mr. V. Narayanaswami :—

"I have examined these and find that :—(1) is the charcoal of a *Bambusa* from the nature of the closed and scattered vascular bundles seen in the cross-section and the hollow internodes ; (2) is the charcoal of *Saccharum arundinaceum*, **Bamboo.** **Reed.**

[1] See p. 165 *supra*.
[2] For their description, see p. 288 *supra*.
[3] See p. 169 *supra*.

compared with a cross-section of the same from a herbarium specimen and found to agree, and (3) is the charcoal of a pine-wood, confirmed by the presence of resin ducts in the numerous annular rings."

Pine-wood.

Shīsham leaf.

An interesting representation of a round *Shīsham* (*Dalbergia latifolia*) leaf is found in pottery. It is illustrated in Pl. LXXI, 72 and shows that this tree was also familiar to the Indus people.

Conglomerate of chalcedony and calcite.

No. 37 (12722) in Pl. LXXXIII is a curiously curved stone object of an unusual stone. The Director, Geological Survey of India, to whom it was sent for examination writes that "It is made up mostly of light bluish green chalcedony. The cavities and brownish patches contain calcite. The specific gravity of the specimen is 2·51. It resembles material which fills up amygdaloidal cavities in basic igneous rocks. It may have been obtained from one of the Deccan trap exposures in north Bombay, Kathiawar or Cutch or from near Pishin. It is not known whether similar material is found in the Panjal traps in Kashmir". I believe no such stone has been found at Mohenjo-daro.

Minerals.

Orpiment.

No. 10046 is a small lump of decomposed orpiment, a mineral, trisulphide of arsenic, used as yellow dye. It was found in Mound F, Trench V, Square K 12/18; at a depth of 10 ft. 6 in. b.s.; in Stratum IV.

Haematite.

A lump of rose coloured grains was found in Trench V. It was examined along with a faience vase No. 12124 by the Archæological Chemist in India who writes that "The black crystalline substance is hæmatite, ferric oxide, mixed with quartz. It yields a deep red powder when ground and it was meant evidently for use as red ochre. The second specimen was a dirty white paste found sticking inside a faience vase No. 12124.[1] On analysis it has turned out to be cerussite, a natural carbonate of lead, mixed with earth. Pure cerussite is white and I think this substance was employed as a paint for the face by the women".

Pigments.

Red ochre.

Two cakes of red ochre were found from the Great Granary Area in Mound F. Of these, No. Ab104 measures 1·8 by 0·8 by 0·35 in. and No. 1233, 1·75 by 0·85 by 0·4 in. The former was found in Stratum II and the latter in Stratum IV.

Painted glaze.

Manganese and iron mixed in varying proportions in the natural ore are also found used on the glazed colour bands applied to the surface of faience vases illustrated in Pl. LXXXII, 20-22. The presence of these colours may thus be inferred but no direct specimen of this ore has been found.[2]

For the following analyses of blue and green earth, white faience and mortars found at Harappâ I am indebted to Khan Bahadur Mohammad Sana Ullah, Archæological Chemist in India :—

Blue earth.

Blue Earth (No. 2764) :—silica, 57·89 per cent.; alumina, 18·70 per cent.; titanium dioxide, 0·88 per cent.; ferric oxide, 4·38 per cent.; lime, 0·35 per cent.;

[1] This vase is illustrated in Pl. LXXXII, 16. For its description, see p. 312 *supra*.

[2] For the examination of a painted glaze on a piece of faience from Mohenjo-daro, see Dr. M. A. Hamid's note in *M. I. C.*, p. 577. See also p. 313 *supra*.

magnesia, 2·93 per cent.; potassium oxide, 9·80 per cent.; combined water, 4·32 per cent.; moisture, 1·97 per cent.

Green earth. Green Earth[1] (No. 7443) :—silica, 49·59 per cent.; alumina, 15·27 per cent.; ferric oxide, 7·95 per cent.; magnesia, 4·31 per cent.; combined water, 10·05 per cent.; moisture, 2·82 per cent.

White faience. White faience ribbed bangle,[2] with >—shaped incision :—silica, 87·45 per cent.; alumina, 6·57 per cent.; lime, 0·10 per cent.; magnesia, 1·09 per cent.; water, 0·73 per cent.; alkalies, 4·56 per cent.

Analysis of mortars[3] from Harappā.

(By Khan Bahadur Mohammad Sana Ullah, M.Sc., F.C.S.)

Serial No.	Specimen and locality.	Gypsum %	Calcium carbonate %	Magnesium carbonate %	Clay, sand, etc. %	Moisture %	REMARKS.
1	Pointing of Circular Platform P6, Trench V, Mound F.	56·90	0·94	*nil*	42·16	*nil*	
2	Concrete Floor . . .	tr.	37·63	2·18	59·29	0·90	Mortar freed from brick fragments.
3	Brick Floor, Trench I, Mound F.	*nil*	26·50	8·46	61·60	3·44	
4	Lump, Mound F .	*nil*	56·01	4·81	34·85	4·33	Loose lumps.
5	Brick Platform, Trench VI, Mound F.	tr.	35·02	10·62	51·37	2·97	
6	Concretionary Lime or '*Kankar*' (Harappā).	*nil*	43·80	4·56	51·64	..	Picked up at Harappā from the soil.
7	Ditto . .	*nil*	45·55	0·44	54·01	..	Ditto.

Shells.

Besides ***Turbinella pyrum Linn*** and ***Fasciolaria trapezium Linn*** shells, which are quite common both at Harappā and Mohenjo-daro, the following varieties deserve mention. One of them is the mussel shell with two single[4] and one fossilized bivalve example, the other is a dentalium[5] shell, and lastly three specimens of the marine gastropod,[6] Galeodes (*Hemifusus*) *pugilinus* (Born) and a coral, *Favia fabus* (Förskal).

---

[1] *Vide M. I. C.*, p. 685.

[2] See Pl. CXXXVIII, 18.

[3] It will be seen that No. 1 represents a gypsum mortar and Nos. 2-4 are examples of lime mortar. It is noteworthy that the lime mortar contains appreciable and sometimes considerable proportion of magnesium carbonate. Although limestones associated with magnesium carbonate are quite common, yet I am very much inclined to believe that the local concretionary nodules or *kankar*, which were found handy, were burnt for the mortar. Two analyses of such nodules picked up at Harappā are given here for comparison. It is obvious that the proportion of magnesium carbonate in '*kankar*' may be quite appreciable, as in the mortars in question.

[4] One of these is illustrated in Pl. LXXXII, 5. For their description see p. 373 *supra*.

[5] See p. 406 *supra*.

[6] Baini Prashad, *Mem. A. S. I.*, No. 51, p. 3.

CHAPTER XVIII.

Furnaces in Trench IV, Mound F.

Findspot. Sixteen furnaces, all situated in Trench IV, Mound F, have been discovered at Harappā (Pl. XI). Starting from the southern edge of the trench, they are confined to an area about 200 ft. square and are associated with Strata I to IV. Ten of these lie in or over the Workmen's Quarters (Blocks I and II), which seem to extend still further east, while six occur to the north of Lane I scattered among bits of walls which may have supported thatched huts. None of them, however, is complete, but in some cases sufficient has survived to enable an idea of their shape to be formed with a fair degree of accuracy.

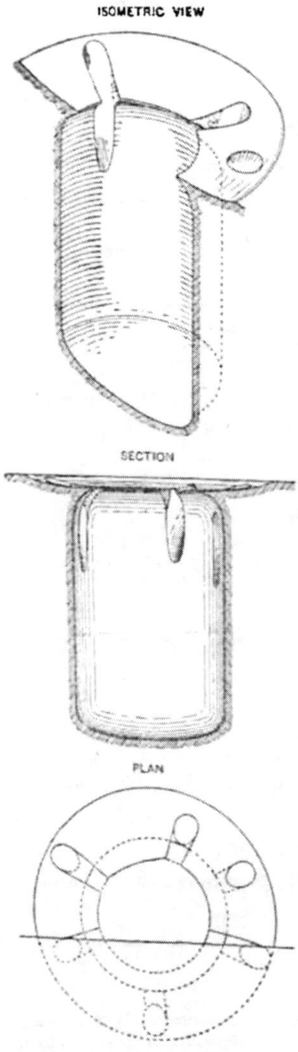

FIG. *d.* Furnace Fa

Shapes. They are of three kinds :—

(*a*) Part of round pottery jar.

(*b*) Cylindrical pits dug in the ground with or without brick lining.

(*c*) Pear-shaped pits dug in the ground with or without brick lining.

Jar-furnace. There was only one jar-furnace, *viz.*, No. Fb in square I 14/9, associated with Stratum II. It consisted of three-fourths of a round pottery jar with its lower part bedded in earth. It contained ashes, and on the inside showed marks of frequent contact with fire. The fuel used seems to have been, at least partly, cowdung cakes of which calcined lumps containing burnt pieces of straw were recovered in the ashes. This kind of furnace, with charcoal as fuel, is still used by gold and silversmiths in India.

Cylindrical furnaces. Furnace Fm situated in square I 13/21 is one of the two examples of cylindrical shape. It lies in a corner and belongs to the 1st stratum. The other furnace Fa of this kind (Fig. *d.*) belongs to Stratum II. This shape, being the latest, may be due either to gradual development, or to its being required for a purpose different from that of the pyriform ones, of which no less than thirteen examples have been found. Furnace Fm is paved and lined exclusively with courses of brick-on-edge. Its diameter is 3 ft. 5 in. and existing depth 1 ft. 10 in. only. The walls are mud plastered and along with ashes a lot of highly vitrified slag was found in it. This indicates fairly intense firing, but no object was recovered in or around it.

Furnace Fa is also cylindrical and lies in square H 14/25 along the western edge of the trench (Fig. *d*). It consists of a pit 3 ft. 4 in. in diameter and really survives to a depth of 3 ft. 8 in. only as below that level there is no trace of fire. It was, however, excavated to a depth of 5 ft. 3 in. This appears to have been subjected to most intense firing as may be inferred from the fact that its mud walls have actually run down in pencil-like formations of slag (Pl. XVII, *a* and *b*). Being split vertically, only half of it has survived, but there is no doubt that it had vaulted roof, the springing of which is clearly seen in the above photographs. In Pl. XVII, *a*, a part of its broken and vaulted roof is seen lying in the furnace, and in Pl. XVII, *b*, its interior and flues are seen after the removal of fallen stuff. Among the latter, but at a lower level, is also seen faintly at the right hand side the section of a slanting flue which forms an obtuse angle with the body of the furnace.[1] Since its vitrified walls do not go much lower than the

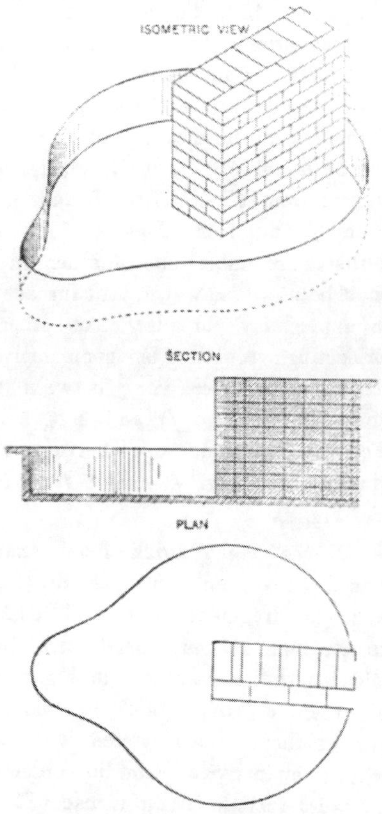

Fig. *e*. Furnace Fa

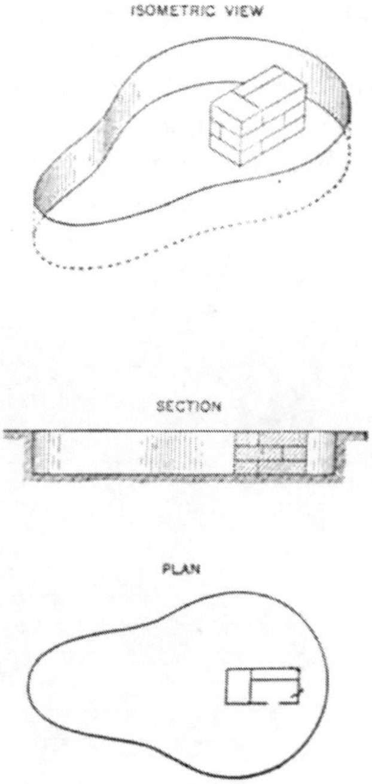

Fig. *f*. Furnace Fn.

point of inlet of this flue, the latter seems likely to have been used as an air channel worked by bellows from above. It is possible that there was another air

[1] Twenty feet south of this furnace has since been recovered a fragmentary earthenware crucible whose contents show that it was used for melting bronze.

channel in the remaining half which has disappeared. The flues in the vault were seemingly intended as outlets for smoke, but whenever needed in course of operation, they could also be used for putting in more fuel or closing with mud or earthenware covers to conserve the heat. Now-a-days, when making a furnace, some village smiths in the Panjāb dig a cylindrical or rounded pit in the ground, raise its mud walls a little higher, and then gradually add the roof vault which takes four or five days to make and dry. From inside, the walls are plastered with mud in which straw is added as an adhesive. A window is left at a convenient point whereby the fuel, the metal to be melted together with the crucible are put inside, and the window closed by a cover kept at hand.

The remaining 13 furnaces are all pear-shaped in plan. Eight of them, *viz.*, Fe in square J 13/5, Fh in square I 13/20, Fi in square I 13/15, Fj in square I 13/13, Fk in square I 13/3, Fl in square J 13/2, Fo in square J 13/10 and Fp in square J 13/16, are lined with burnt brick; while the remaining five, *viz.*, Fc in square I 14/17, Fd in square I 14/16, Ff in square I 13/24, Fg in square I 13/19 and Fn in square J 13/10, are mere pits dug in the ground. None of them has survived to a height greater than that of furnace Fj, of which the present height is only 2 ft. 6 in. (Fig. *g*). As will appear from Pl. XVII, *c*, *d*, and *f*, Pl. XVIII, *e* and *f*, and from Figs. *e*, *f* and *g* all these furnaces resemble one another in shape. It may be noted, however, that furnace Fc (Fig. *e*) is appreciably broader than others, but its projecting tongue is comparatively small. Their major axes vary between 6 ft. 2 in. (furnace Fn, Fig. *f*) and 8 ft. 3 in. (furnace Fo), and the minor ones between 3 ft. 4 in. (furnace Fn, Fig. *f*) and 5 ft. 6 in. (furnace Fc, Fig. *e*).

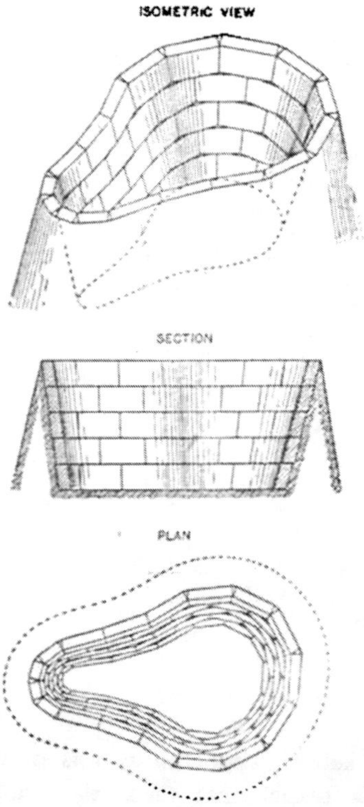

Fig. *g*. Furnace Fj.

Construction of brick-lined furnaces.

Of the eight brick lined examples mentioned above, only furnace Fj (Pl. XVII, *c*) and the fragmentary one Fl, both belonging to Stratum III, are lined with brick-on-edge laid lengthwise as shown in Fig. *g*. The lining of others is half a brick in thickness. Every one of them was plastered with mud mixed with a quantity of sand in order the better to resist fusibility.

Small pillar in centre.

In furnace Fk there is a small rectangular pillar set at the back but with an air passage for the circulation of heat between itself and the back wall. This pillar, like that of furnace Fn (Fig. *f*), which is not brick-lined, is also plastered with mud-and-sand all over. No doubt it was used to support the articles to be fired, which may have been contained in a large earthenware vessel. In furnace Fc (Fig. *e*) the pillar is replaced by a dividing wall[1] which extends from the centre of the minor axis up to the back wall. It is noteworthy that at many places owing to intense vitrification the surface of this brick wall has run down. The furnace was found filled with ashes of light weight, in which some slag was also found. **Dividing wall.**

Firing not uniform. In the above furnaces it appears that varying degrees of heat was employed. Thus, furnaces Fa, Fc, Fj, and Fm afford evidence of more intense firing than most of the others, while furnace Fi, which is slightly irregular in construction, indicates firing with cowdung cakes or other light fuel such as is now used in the Panjāb for baking bread in native ovens. To judge from the light weight of the ashes and the intensity of the fire, charcoal seems to have been used in most cases. That these furnaces were repeatedly used is clear from the fact that in several instances the original mud-and-sand plaster, which was generally turned into slag, had to be covered afresh with about half an inch thick layer of similar plaster. The second layer, however, does not appear to have undergone many firings.

Parallel from Mohenjo-daro. An almost exact parallel of the pear-shaped furnaces from Harappā is furnished by the smaller brick kiln found by Dr. Mackay at Mohenjo-daro, in the Dk. Area (G. Section), Block 9, Court 21.[2] This, too, is intensely fired and contains a detached pillar[3] in the centre. I quote its description by Dr. Mackay. "Traces of another kiln of a smaller size lie just to the west of the one described (Pl. XXVI, *d*). It is situated at a slightly higher level and is of different construction. It measures 4 ft. 8 in. in diameter and has a rough column in the centre which probably supported a roof.[4] An aperture on one side of it is 12 inches wide. Unlike the first kiln, which seems to have been used only once as it shows very little evidence of burning, this second kiln is much vitrified inside; the surface of the bricks of which it was constructed has run in several places. Such a heat can hardly have been necessary for making pottery and possibly this kiln was used for firing the articles of vitreous paste which are so common at Mohenjo-daro, though no traces of these articles, either broken or whole, have actually been found in the vicinity of this kiln."

At Khairpur Mirs in Sindh a furnace for making glazed pottery with an astonishingly similar plan is still in use. I give a sketch plan and sectional elevation of it in Fig. *h*.

Probable nature of objects fired. Since nothing was recoverd inside these furnaces we can only guess as to the nature of the articles fired in them. For pottery they are hardly likely to have been used, since pottery does not require such intense heat as is evidenced by the vitrification in some of these furnaces, and moreover the furnaces themselves would be inconveniently small for the firing of pottery. More probably they were designed for the casting of metal objects, which there is abundant

---

[1] It is possible that this wall supported the roof.

[2] *A. S. R.* for 1927-8, p. 75, plan in Pl. XXIII, and photograph in Pl. XXVI, *d*.

[3] *Cf.* Furnaces Fk and Fn, p. 472 *supra*.

[4] Since pillars in furnaces Fk and Fn described above are finished all over, it is unlikely that the column referred to was intended to support a roof.

evidence to show were manufactured locally,[1] or for the firing of faience objects such as small vessels, squirrels, rams, beads, sundries for inlay, jewellery of

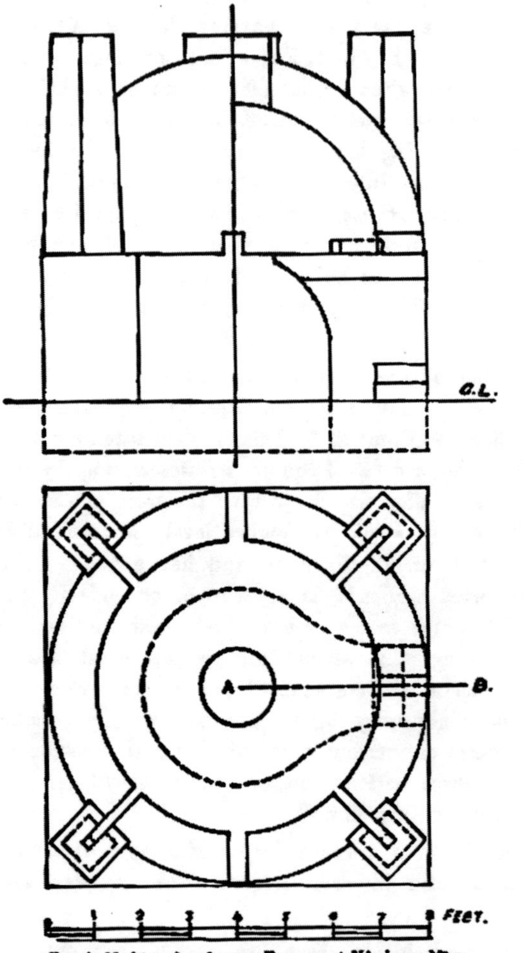

FIG. A. Modern glazed ware Furnace at Khairpur Mirs.

this material and stoneware bangles; as well as for glazing steatite seals, faience sealings, vessels, etc.; for putting on bands of coloured frit on some faience vases; for etching carnelian beads—processes which imply efficient arrangements for quickly reaching a very high degree of heat and equally rapid cooling arrangements in order to keep the colours bright.[2]

---

[1] The copper jar No. 277 recovered from Stratum III in Trench I, Mound F contained one hundred weapons, implements, and utensils both finished and unfinished (Pl. CXXIII, 1-33 and 35-67; and Pl. CXXIV, 1-21, and 23-25); among the latter are cast bars, a lance-head, several solid and hollow bangles and a thick sheet of copper with prominent hammer marks. Indeed, it is more than likely that most, if not all, the metal objects illustrated in Pls. CXXIII-CXXV were manufactured locally.

[2] For painting dyes on modern porcelain ware a heat of 700-800 degrees centigrade is required in an enamelling furnace. Cf. *Encyclopadia Britannica*, fourteenth edition, Vol. XVIII, *Potteries and Porcelains*, p. 365.

CHAPTER XIX.

Chak Pūrbāne Syāl and Koṭla Nihang Khān.

Discovery of two more prehistoric sites.

In concluding this account of my excavations at Harappā, I propose to add a few words about two other prehistoric sites which have been discovered by me in the Panjāb.[1] One of them is in Chak Pūrbāne Syāl across the great Dhāyā ridge on the right bank of the old deserted bed of the Beās[2] about 13 miles south-east of Harappā and 11 miles south-west of Montgomery. The other is at Koṭla Nihang Khān,[3] near Rupar, on the Sutlej, in the Ambala District below the Simla hills and some 220 miles due east of Harappā.

Mound in Chak Pūrbāne Syāl.

Situation, Size and external features of the mound.

This mound, which lies at the southern end of Bahlolwālā minor,[4] is of irregular shape and rises to a maximum height of 15 to 20 ft. towards the north, though most of it is not more than a few feet high. On the west and north, it slopes down gradually to the level of cultivated fields, while on the south and greater part of the east it is bounded by the Vyāh, which winds round it in the form of an arc. Covering an area of about five acres, it is excessively charged with saltpetre and profusely littered with potsherds and shattered brick-bats of blackened hue. On its surface I picked up the following objects which are typical of the Indus Valley culture.

(*a*) *Pottery objects* (Pl. LXXIV, *c*, 1-34).

Surface finds.

1. Goblet with pointed base, scored round the body. Broken on one side. Ht. 6 in.; diam. 4·5 in.

2-4. Bottom fragments similar to No. 1.

5. Bottom of a cylindrical tumbler.

6. Fragment of a ringstand with low wall, plano-convex in section. Red washed. Diam. 10 in.

7. Dish-on-stand, stem broken. Restored ht. 5·5 in.; diam. 6 in.

8. Fragmentary bowl with tapering sides. Ht. 2·5 in.; diam. 8·5 in.

9-10. Bottom portions of thickware long oval vases.

11. Tiny lid with projecting top, damaged. Ht. 1·25 in.

12-13. Fragments of rough circular cakes. Th. ·75 and 1 in. respectively.

14-15. Fragments of two flanged, blackware vessels, No. 14 being deeply grooved above the flange.

16. Fragment with irregular, shallow depressions over the surface. Reminds of finger-tip[5] patterning.

---

[1] Since writing this I have discovered another prehistoric site at Rangpur in the Limbdi State of Kāṭhiāwāḍ. An account of my trial trenches there is published in *A. S. R.*, for 1934-35, pp. 34-38, Pls. XII-XV.

[2] Also called *sukh* (dry) Beās or Vyāh to the southward receding of which the destruction of this site is probably due. See p. 7 *supra*.

[3] *M. I. C.*, p. 93.

[4] For the meaning of the term see p. 7 *supra*, footnote 4.

[5] See p. 204 *supra*.

17-20. Neck fragments of goblets with pointed bases resembling No. 1 above.
21-28. Fragments of rings and bangles.
29. Fragmentary horned bull. L. 1·7 in.
30. Rough squirrel or monkey. L. 1·5 in.
31. Peacock with eyes made of round pellets and collar of a long dab of clay. Ht. 2·2 in.; L. 2 in.
32. Female head with pannier ornament at the ears, crescentic protuberance at the back of the head and pinched out nose—features common to female figurines from Harappā and Mohenjo-daro.
33-34. Female torsos. In both, breasts were added by affixing conical dabs of clay; the left breast of No. 33 is still preserved.

(b) *Miscellaneous objects* (Pl. LXXIV, b, 1-16).

1 & 3. Fragments of cream-coloured faience bangles, triangular in section.
6. Fragment of a blue faience bangle, round in section.
2, 4 & 9. Fragments of blue faience bangles with lineal hatching.
5. Oblong carnelian bead oval in section, broken along the hole.
7-8. Extremely thin, disc beads of burnt steatite. Diam. ·23 and ·09 in.
11. Short-barrel bead of banded agate, plano-convex in section. L. ·4 in.
10 & 12. Pieces of alabaster.
13-16. Irregular chert fragments.

Two small and shallow pits sunk in the mound yielded typical Indus potsherds and the core of a burnt brick wall. The bricks measured—

13 by $6\frac{1}{2}$ by $2\frac{3}{4}$ in.;
$11\frac{1}{2}$ by $6\frac{1}{2}$ by 3 in.;
Broken by 6 by $2\frac{1}{2}$ in.

Essential similarity with the Indus sites.

The resemblance of the above finds with those from Harappā and Mohenjo-daro will strike any one at a glance. The mound is situated on a dried up river bed, though it does not appear to have been an extensive and prosperous site.

Koṭla Nihang.

Location.

The second mound is situated about a mile to the east of Rupar, a terminus of the Sirhind-Rupar Section of the North-Western Railway. The mound extends irregularly from west to east: its western part is occupied by the village of Koṭla Nihang Khān and the east end by a small hamlet or *tapri* of the same village. On the north, it is bounded by a mountain torrent which flows only when it rains, on the south by a mango garden and on the other two sides by cultivated fields.

Composition and general appearance of the mound.

Situated at the foot of the Sivalik Range, the mound is a natural hillock of gravelly formation highest at the west and gradually falling eastward, till, close to the *tapri*, it is only a few feet high but rises again to about 12 ft. at the eastern end. Throughout its length along the southern half, the mound gradually falls from about 30 to 12 ft., while in the northern half the fall is noticeable only near the centre, where there are two basin-like depressions forming village tanks.

Extent. Besides the portion occupied by the village and *tapri*, a part of the mound is occupied by cultivated fields and several patches have been cleaned and levelled for winnowing corn. Even so, however, the ancient remains are visible over some 12 acres. Four trial trenches, each running north and south and measuring 30 by 8 ft. were sunk between the village and the hamlet. Starting from the former, they were named I, II, III and IV and excavated to 7 ft., 5 ft., 6 ft. and 4 ft. respectively. None of them revealed any structure. Potsherds were abundant in Trench III, less in II, scarce in I and absent in IV, while natural **Finds from trenches.** pebbles were plentiful in Trench II, comparatively few in III and practically non-existent in I and IV. The antiquities found in them include a tiny chert weight (Pl. LXXIII, 38), three goblets with pointed bases (Pl. LXXIII, 12 and 14), one pear-shaped (Pl. LXXIII, 16), and a tumbler-shaped vase (Pl. LXXIII, 19), stem of a standard dish (Pl. LXXIII, 13), a broken jar-stand, a wheel (Pl. LXXIII, 32), handle of a cup (Pl. LXXIII, 20), a miniature handled lid (Pl. LXXIII, 35), two triangular terracotta cakes (Pl. LXXIII, 30) and fragments of similar and circular ones, a number of terracotta nodules (Pl. LXXIII, 31), fragment of a ribbed faience ring (Pl. LXXIII, 36), and part of an incised faience bangle (Pl. LXXIII, 34). Besides these, I also recovered numbers of sherds belonging to vessels similar to those enumerated above as well as to dishes of several types and a trough, the neck of a *hāṇḍi*-shaped vessel with incised chevron at the shoulder, the bottom of a large napiform jar, and some thick wares painted with black bands. A few more vases and cups, as well as four stone beads were acquired locally. With a few exceptions the finds are all fragmentary.

Only one small bit of an ancient wall, not more than three courses high, was brought to light outside the trenches; for the little that had survived of brick remains on this site had already been utilised in building the present village. From the trenches only four complete bricks were recovered. They measured $12\frac{1}{2}$ by 6 by 3 in., 12 by $5\frac{1}{2}$ by $2\frac{1}{2}$ in., $10\frac{3}{4}$ by $5\frac{1}{2}$ by $2\frac{1}{4}$ in. and 10 by 5 by $2\frac{3}{4}$ in.

Finds typical of Indus Valley sites. To demonstrate the identity of these Koṭla Nihang antiquities with those of Harappā I have illustrated the former in the second and fourth rows, and the latter in the first and third rows of Pl. LXXIII, selecting for comparison only such entire and broken specimens from Harappā as are approximately similar to those from Koṭla Nihang. Although certain things typical of Indus culture, such as seals, chert knives, pottery figurines, metal and finer stone objects have not been found at Koṭla Nihang, their absence can hardly surprise us in view of the extremely limited nature of the operations carried out and of the fact that nothing more than the barest traces of the ancient civilization have survived. The value of this discovery, however, lies in its extending the zone of the prehistoric civilization, hitherto restricted to the Valley of the Indus and its tributaries, to the Doāb between the Sutlej and the Jumna. A survey of this region and of the Gangetic plain seems called for if the true eastern limits of this civilization are to be ascertained.

INDEX.

E

F

G

R

S

V

W

Y